ISBN 978-0-260-62331-7
PIBN 10960231

SUBJECT HEADING LIST

PRELIMINARY EDITION

VOLUME 4
REC-Z

NATIONAL AGRICULTURAL LIBRARY

UNITED STATES DEPARTMENT OF AGRICULTURE

WASHINGTON, D. C.   JULY 1963

United States
Department of
Agriculture

NATIONAL
AGRICULTURAL
LIBRARY

Advancing Access to
Global Information for
Agriculture

Receipts.
Under this heading are entered
receipt-books of a general
character, including receipts
useful to machinists and other
artisans. If it contains only
cooking receipts it is entered
under Cookery. If medical in
character it is entered under
Medicine. Formulae, receipts,
prescriptions. If chemical in
character it is entered under
Chemistry. Technology. Formulae,
receipts, prescriptions.
x Recipes.
xx Handbooks, vade-mecums, etc.

Receipts and shipments. See Fruit trade.
Statistics; Produce trade. Statistics.

Receivers. (DIRECT)

Receptors. See Immunity. Mechanism and
theories.

Recherche (Corvette)

Recife disease.
xx Mango. Diseases.

Recipes. See Receipts.

Reciprocal trade agreements. See Commercial treaties; Reciprocity.

Reciprocal trade agreements act.

Reciprocals.
xx Mathematics. Tables, etc.

Reciprocating motion.

Reciprocity.
x Reciprocal trade agreements.
--Bibliography.

Reciprocleaners. See Cotton cleaners.

Reclaimed fibers. See Fibers, Reclaimed.

Reclaimed rubber. See Rubber, Reclaimed.

Reclaimed wool. See Wool, Reclaimed.

Reclamation of land. (INDIRECT)
When used with a geographic subdivision, indicate a see also
ref. from name of place with
subdivision Agriculture.
sa Moors and heaths.
Sand flora.
Marshes.
Rathdrum prairie project.
Clearing of land.
Drainage.
Irrigation.
Waste lands.
Shore-protection.
x Land reclamation.
Land. Reclamation.
xx Agriculture.
--Abstracts.
sa Reclamation of land ₍geographic
subdivision₎ Abstracts,
e.g., Reclamation of land.
Japan. Abstracts.
--Bibliography.
sa Reclamation of land ₍geo-
graphic subdivision₎ Bib-
liography, e.g., Reclama-
tion of land. U.S. Bib-
liography.
-- --Periodicals.
sa Subdivision Bibliography.
Periodicals under Reclama-
tion of land ₍geographic
subdivision₎ e.g., Reclamation of land. Japan. Bib-
liography. Periodicals.
--Congresses.
--History.
xx Agriculture. History.
--Implements and machinery.
sa Machine-melioration stations.
x Land reclamation machinery.
xx Agriculture. Implements and
machinery.
--Law.
--Periodicals.
--Research.
--Societies.

Reclamation projects.
sa North Platte reclamation
project.
Baker irrigation project.
Wehatchee reclamation dis-
trict//
--Directories.

Reclassification of government employees.
See U.S. Government salaries.

Recoaro, Italy.
--Water-supply.

Recombined milk.   See Milk, Remade.

Reconstituted milk.   See Milk, Remade.

Reconstruction.
This subject used for reconstruction in the United States after the Civil War. Subdivide by State.

Reconstruction (1914-1939)   (INDIRECT)
sa Veterans. Employment.
x European war, 1914-1918. Reconstruction.
Reconstruction (1914-1939)
Agriculture.
xx International organization.
--Agriculture.   See Reconstruction (1914-1939); Rehabilitation, Rural.
--Bibliography.
--Food relief.
sa Subdivision Food relief under Reconstruction (1939-   ) and country subdivisions, i.e., Reconstruction (1914-1939) U.S.S.R. Food relief.
x Food relief (1914-1939)
xx Food supply.

Reconstruction (1939-   )   (INDIRECT)
sa World War, 1939-1945. Peace.
World War, 1939-1945, Civilian relief.
Public works, International.
Demobilization.
Veterans. Employment.
International organizations.
Economic assistance.
x Reconstruction (1939-   ) Agriculture.
Post-war reconstruction (1939-   )
Planned economy.
Post defense planning.
Planning, Postwar (1939-   )
Postwar planning (1939-   )
World War, 1939-1945. Reconstruction.

Reconstruction (1939-   )   (Continued)
xx International cooperation.
World War, 1939-1945. Peace.
War. Economic aspects.
International organization.
Economic assistance.
--Agriculture.   See Reconstruction (1939-   ); Rehabilitation, Rural.
--Bibliography.
sa Subdivision Bibliography under:
Reconstruction (1939-   )
East (Far East)//
--Congresses.
--Food relief.
sa Subdivision Food relief under Reconstruction (1914-1939) and country subdivisions, i.e., Reconstruction (1939-   ) France. Food relief.
x Food relief (1939-   )
xx Food supply.
--Industrial aspects.   See Industrial reconversion.
--Jews.
xx Jews.
--Medical relief.
sa Subdivision Medical relief under Reconstruction (1939-   ) ⌜country subdivision⌝ i.e., Reconstruction (1939-   ) Europe. Medical relief.
x Medical relief (1939-   )
--Periodicals.

Reconstruction, Rural.   See Rehabilitation, Rural.

Reconstruction finance corporation.   See U.S. Reconstruction Finance Corporation.

Reconstruction finance corporation act.
sa U.S. Reconstruction Finance Corporation.
xx U.S. Reconstruction Finance Corporation.

Reconversion, Industrial.   See Industrial reconversion.

Reconversion of industries.   See Industrial reconversion.

Record of performance (Cattle)   See
Cattle, Dairy. Performance records and
registration.

Record of performance (Poultry)   See
National poultry improvement plan.
Record of performance; Poultry. Per-
formance records and registration.

Record of performance (Swine)   See Swine.
Performance records and registration.

Recording systems (Data storage)
    x Magnetic recorders and record-
        ing.
    Magnetic recordings (Data stor-
        age)
    Magnetic tape recordings.
    Tape recordings (Data storage)
    xx Automatic data processing.
    Files and filing (Documents)
    Information storage and re-
        trieval systems.
    Programming (Electronic com-
        puters)
    --Bibliography.

Records, Business.   See Business records.

Records, Domestic animals.   See Live
stock records.

Records, Farm.   See Farm records.

Records, Forest.   See Forest records.

Records, Public.   See Archives.

Records and correspondence.
    sa Subdivision Record and corres-
        pondence files under:
        Railroads.
        U.S. War Dept.
        U.S. Bureau of Animal In-
            dustry//
        Subdivision Records and corres-
            pondence under various sub-
            jects, e.g., U.S. Office of
            Marketing Services. Records
            and correspondence.

Recovered wool.   See Wool, Reclaimed.

Recovery act.   See Nationa industrial
recovery act, 1933.

Recreation.   (INDIRECT)
    sa Vacations.
    Forest recreation.
    Amusements.
    Community centers.
    Hobbies.
    Leisure.
    Community organization.
    Subdivision Recreational ac-
        tivities under names of
        cities, government depart-
        ments, etc.
    xx Community centers.
    Leisure.
    Play.
    Amusements.
    --Bibliography.
        sa Subdivision Bibliography under:
            Forest recreation.
            Hobbies.
    --Congresses.
    --Directories.
    --History.
    --Law.

Recreational, Rural.
    sa Recreation extension work.
    x Rural recreation.

Recreation.
    --Societies.
    --Statistics.

Recreation areas.   See Forest reserva-
    tions; National parks and reserves;
    Parks.

Recreation centers.   See Community cen-
    ters.

Recreation extension work.
    x Extension work in recreation.
    xx Recreation, Rural.
    --Directories.

Recreation leaders.
    x Recreation personnel.
    Recreation workers.
    --Education.
    xx Education.

Recreation personnel.   See Recreation
    leaders.

Recreation workers.   See Recreation
leaders.

Recreational camps.   See Camps (Recreational)

Recreational forestry.   See Forest recreation.

Recreational use of forests.   See Forest
recreation.

Recreational use of land.   See Land
utilization.

Recreations, Mathematical.   See Mathematical recreations.

Recruiting and enlistment.
     sa Bounties, Military.
        Military service, Compulsory.
        Subdivisions Army. Recruiting,
           enlistment, etc., and Navy.
        Recruiting, enlistment, etc.,
           under names of countries,
           e.g., U.S. Army. Recruiting,
           enlistment, etc.
        Subdivision Recruiting, en-
           listment, etc. under:
        U.S. Officials and employees.
        U.S. Dept. of Agriculture.
           Officials and employees.

Rectidon.
     xx Narcotics.

Rectification of spirits.   See Distillation.

Rectum.
     sa Cloaca (Zoology)

Recurvaria milleri.
     x Evagora milleri.
        Lodge-pole pine needle-miner.
     xx Pine. Pests.

Recurvaria nanella.

Recurvaria piceaella.

Recurvirostridae.

Red alder.   See Alnus rubra.

Red-banded leaf-roller.   See Eulia velu-
tinana.

Red-banded thrips.   See Heliothrips
rubrocinctus.

Red bread-mold fungus.   See Monilia
sitophila.

Red brush.   See Quercus ilicifolia.

Red bugs.   See Trombidiidae.

Red cedar.   See Juniperus virginiana.

Red cedar, Western.   See Thuya plicata.

Red Cliffs irrigation district, Victoria,
Australia.
     --Soils.
        xx Victoria, Australia. Soils.

Red clover.   See Clover.

Red copper oxide.   See Copper oxide, Red.

Red Cross.
     --Japan.
     --U.S.S.R.
     --U.S.
     -- --American National Red Cross.
        x European war, 1914-1918. War
           work. Red Cross.
        World War, 1939-1945. War work.
           Red Cross.
     -- -- --Bibliography.

Red cypress.   See Bald cypress.

Red Danish cattle.
     xx Cattle.

Red date scale.   See Phoenicoccus
marlatti.

Red deer.

Red fescue.
     x Creeping red fescue.
        Festuca rubra.

Red fir.   See Abies magnifica.

Red fox.
     xx Foxes.

Red German cattle.
    x Ukrainian Red cattle.
    xx Cattle.

Red gram.   See Cajanus indicus.

Red-gum.   See Liquidambar styraciflua;
   Eucalyptus resinifera; Eucalyptus
   camaldulensis.

Red-gum wood.   See Eucalyptus camaldulensis (Wood)

Red harvester ant.   See Pogonomyrmex
   barbatus.

Red-headed flea beetle.   See Systena
   frontalis.

Red-headed pine sawfly.   See Neodiprion
   lecontei.

Redheaded pine sawfly.   See Neodiprion
   lecontei.

Red heart stain of lodgepole pine.
    xx Pinus contorta. Diseases.

Red-necked raspberry cane-borer.   See
   Agrilus ruficollis.

Red Lake River, Minn.
    sa Flood control. Red Lake River.

Red lead.
    xx Pigments.

Red locusts.   See Nomadacris septem-
   fasciata.

Red maple.   See Acer rubrum.

Red oak.
    sa Quercus falcata.
    Quercus borealis.

Red oak wood.
    sa Quercus falcata (Wood)

Red oxide of iron.   See Iron oxides.

Red pepper.
   Here are entered publications on
   the pepper as a crop, both
   the mature red peppers and the
   immature (green) peppers. Here
   also are entered publications
   on red pepper as a condiment.
   For botanical studies of the
   pepper, see Capsicum.
   sa Pepper.
   x Capsicum annuum.
   Capsicum frutescens.
   Bush redpeppers.
   Pimiento.
   Chillies.
   Paprika.
   Spanish paprika.
   Bell pepper.
   Pepper, Green.
   Pepper, Bell.
   Green pepper.
--Breeding.

Red pepper, Canned.
--Statistics.

Red pepper.
--Diseases.
   sa Root-rot of red pepper.
   xx Vegetable pathology.
--Estimating of crop.
--Genetics.
--Germination.
   xx Germination.
--Grading and standardization.
   xx Vegetables. Grading and
   standardization.
--Inspection.
--Marketing.   (DIRECT)
--Pests.
--Physiology and morphology.
   xx Vegetables. Physiology and
   morphology.
--Storage.
   xx Storage of farm produce.

Red pied Holstein cattle.
    x Schleswig-Holsteiner Rot-
   buntes.
   Rotbuntes Holsteiner.
   Rotbuntes Schleswig-Holsteiner.
   Holstein marsh cattle.
   Holstein red pied cattle.

Red pied Holstein cattle (Continued)
    x Red pied Schleswig-Holstein
        cattle.
    Red-White Schleswig-Holstein
        cattle.
    Holstein cattle (Germany)

Red pied lowland cattle.

Red pied Schleswig-Holstein cattle.   See
    Red pied Holstein cattle.

Red pine.   See Pinus resinosa.

Red pine scale.   See Matsucoccus resin-
osae.

Red poll cattle.
    The breed originating in England
    is correctly called Red poll
    cattle; in Norway, Red polled
    Østland cattle; in Sweden,
    Swedish red polled cattle. For
    publications on each breed see
    under the appropriate heading.

Red-polled cattle.
    x Norfolk polled cattle.
    Norfolk and Suffolk red polled
        cattle.
    xx Cattle.
--Periodicals.

Red polled Østland cattle.
    x Norwegian red polled cattle.
    Østland cattle.

Red pumpkin beetle.   See Aulacophora ab-
dominalis.

Red-ray rot.   See Red rot.

Red ring disease of coconuts.
    xx Coconut. Diseases.
    Nematode diseases.

Red River of Louisiana.
    Red River of Louisiana flows
    through Arkansas, Oklahoma,
    Texas and Louisiana.
    sa Subdivision Red River under:
        Flood control.

Red River of the North.
    sa Red River Valley (Red River of
        the North)

Red River Parish, La.
--Social conditions.
    sa Subdivision Louisiana. Red
        River Parish under:
        Community life.

Red River Valley, Tex.
    sa Arkansas-White-Red River
        Valleys.
--Botany.
    xx Texas. Botany.
--Forestry.
--Geology.
    xx Texas. Geology.
--Industries.
--Soils.
    xx Texas. Soils.
--Water-supply.

Red River Valley (Red River of the North)
    xx Red River of the North.
--Agriculture.
    sa Wheat. Red River Valley (Red
        River of the North)
    xx Canada. Agriculture.
    U.S. Agriculture.
--Dairying.
--History.
    xx U.S. History.
    Canada. History.

Red rot.
    Used for red rot of Western
    yellow pine (Pinus ponderosa)
    x Western red rot.
    Red-ray rot.

Red rot of sorghum.   See Anthracnose of
    sorghum.

Red rot of sugar-cane.
    xx Sugar-cane. Diseases.

Red sanders. See Pterocarpus santa-
    linus.

Red scale.   See Aonidiella aurantii.

Red Sea.
--Botany.
   sa Subdivision Red Sea under:
      Algae.
   xx Africa. Botany.
      Asia. Botany.
--Zoology.
   sa Subdivision Red Sea under:
      Marine fauna.

Red Sindhi cattle.
   x Sindhi cattle.

Red slug. See Heterusia.

Red soil. See Soil, Red.

Red spider. See Tetranychus telarius.

Red spider, Fruit tree. See Para-
tetranychus pilosus.

Red spider, Two-spotted. See Tetranychus
bimaculatus.

Red spotted highland cattle. See
Simmental cattle.

Red spruce. See Picea rubens.

Red squill. See Urginea maritima.

Red Steppe cattle.
   xx Cattle. Breeds.

Red tulip oak wood. See Tarrietia
argyrodendron var. peralata (Wood)

Red turnip beetle. See Entomoscelis
adonidis.

Red turpentine beetle. See Dendroctonus
valens.

Red water disease.
   x Bacillary hemoglobinuria.
     Hemoglobinuria, Bacilliary.

Red weevil. See Rhynchophorus ferrugineus.

Red White Russian cattle.
   xx Cattle.

Red-White Schleswig-Holstein cattle. See
Red pied Holstein cattle.

Redbacked mouse. See Evotomys.

Redberry juniper. See Juniperus pin-
choti.

Redgram. See Cajanus indicus.

Redon, France.

Redonda. W.I
--Census.

Redox. See Reduction Electrolytic;
Oxidation, Electrolytic.

Redpoll, Mealy. See Acanthis linaria.

Redtop grass.
   x Fiorin.
     Agrostis alba.
     Agrostis stolonifera.
   xx Grasses and forage plants.
--Seed.
-- --Statistics.

Redtop grass seed. See Redtop grass.
Seed.

Reduction, Catalytic. See Catalysis.

Reduction, Chemical.
   sa Dehydrogenation.
     Clemmensen reduction.

Reduction, Electrolytic.
   sa Oxidation, Electrolytic.
   x Redox.
     Chemical reduction.
     Electrolytic reduction.
   xx Electrochemistry.

Reduviidae.
   sa Sinea.
     Ploiariinae.
     Spiniger.
     Reduvius.
     Triatoma.
     Pirates.
   x Triatominae.

Reduvius.
   xx Reduviidae.

Redwater.   See Texas fever.

Redwood.
    This subject is used for works on
    the physical properties, tech-
    nology, lumbering, diseases and
    pests of redwood. For works on
    the botany, description and
    conservation of redwood see
    Sequoia.
    sa Sequoia.
    x Sierra redwood.
       Coast redwood.
    --Diseases.
    --Periodicals.
    --Pests.
    --Research.
    --Societies.
    --Statistics.

Redwood Co., Minn.
    xx Minnesota.
    --Social conditions.

Redwood mealy bug.   See Dactylopius
    sequoiae.

Redwood Park, Calif.   See California
    Redwood Park.

Reed.
    sa Phragmites communis.
       Arundo donax.

Reed as building material.
    xx Building materials.

Reed warblers.   See Acrocephalus.

Reeves Co., Tex.
    --Geology.
    --Water-supply.
       sa Subdivision Texas. Reeves Co.
          under: Water, Underground.

Reference books.
    --Bibliography.

Reference work.   See Libraries. Reference
    dept.

References.
    sa Bibliographical references.

Refining of sugar.   See Sugar. Manu-
    facture and refining.

Reflection (Optics)
    xx Optics.

Reflectors, Solar.   See Solar reflectors.

Reflex bleeding.

Reflexes.

Reforestation.   See Afforestation and
    reforestation.

Reform schools.

Reformatories.   See Reform schools.

Refraction.
    xx Light.
       Optics.

Refractometer.

Refractory materials.

Refreshment stands.

Refrigerants.
    sa Ammonia refrigerant.
    xx Refrigeration and refrigera-
       ting machinery.
    --Bibliography.
    xx Refrigeration and refrigera-
       ting machinery. Bibliog-
       raphy.

Refrigerated food lockers.   See Cold
    storage lockers.

Refrigerated lockers for food.   See Cold
    storage lockers.

Refrigerated motor trucks.   See Motor
    trucks in freight service, Refrigerated.

Refrigerated self-service stores.   See
    Self-service stores, Refrigerated.

Refrigerating machinery.   See Refrig-
    eration and refrigerating machinery.

Refrigeration.   See Refrigeration and
    refrigerating machinery.

Refrigeration (Continued)
--Effect on insects. See Cold. Effect
  on insects.

Refrigeration, Household. See Refrigeration and refrigerating machinery,
  Household.

Refrigeration and refrigerating machinery.
  sa Ice.
    Milk. Cooling.
    Refrigerator-cars.
    Pre-cooling.
    Refrigerator-barges.
    Cold storage.
    Food, Frozen.
    Freon.
    Cold storage on shipboard.
    Refrigerators, Electric.
    Refrigerators, Gas.
    Beer. Cooling.
    Carbon dioxide in refrigera-
      tion.
    Cold storage lockers.
    Refrigerants.
    Self-service stores, Refrig-
      erated.
    Motor trucks in freight service,
      Refrigerated.
    Refrigerator-trailers.
    Subdivision Preservation under:
      Poultry.
      Meat.
      Farm produce//
  x Refrigerating machinery.
    Storage of food.
    Refrigeration.
  xx Food. Storage.
    Cold storage.
--Abstracts.
--Bibliography.
  sa Subdivision Bibliography under:
    Refrigerants.
-- --Periodicals.
--Congresses.
--Costs.
    xx Cost.
--Directories.
--Exhibitions.
--Grading and standardization.
    xx Standardization.
--History.

Refrigeration and refrigerating machinery,
  Household.
    sa Freezer-storage chests, House-
      hold.
    Evaporator cooler.
  x Frozen food cabinets.
    Cabinets, Frozen food.
    Refrigeration, Household.
    Household refrigeration.
    Electric household refrigera-
      tion.

Refrigeration and refrigerating machinery.
--Law.
--Periodicals.
--Research.
--Safety appliances.
--Societies.
--Statistics.
--Tables, calculations, etc.

Refrigeration locker plants. See Cold
  storage lockers.

Refrigeration on ships. See Cold storage on shipboard.

Refrigerator-barges.

Refrigerator-cars.
    x Railroads. Refrigerator-cars.
    xx Refrigeration and refrig-
      erating machinery.
--Statistics.

Refrigerator doors.

Refrigerator-trailers.
    xx Motor trucks in freight
      service, Refrigerated.
    Motor trucks. Trailers.
    Refrigeration and refrig-
      erating machinery.

Refrigerators.

Refrigerators, Electric.
    x Electric refrigeration.
    xx Refrigeration and refrigera-
      ting machinery.

Refrigerators, Gas.
    xx Refrigeration and refrigera-
      ting machinery.

Refrigerators.
--Statistics.

Refugee beans.   See Beans, Refugee.

Refugees, Political.
    sa Subdivision Refugees under:
        World War, 1939-1945.
    x Political refugees.
    xx International law.
        International relations.
        International relief.
--Colonization.
    x Colonization of political
        refugees.
    xx Colonies and colonization.

Refuse and refuse disposal.   (DIRECT)
    sa Garbage as feeding stuff.
        Refuse as fertilizer.
    x Garbage grinders.
    xx Sewage disposal.
        Sewerage.
--Bibliography.
--Disinfection.

Refuse as fertilizer.
    sa Sewage sludge as fertilizer.
    xx Waste products.
        Refuse and refuse disposal.

Regal lily.
    x Lilium regale.
    xx Lily.

Regelia.

Regeneration (Biology)
    sa Transplantation (Biology)
        Plant regeneration.

Regeneration (Botany)   See Plant re-
    generation.

Regeneration of forests.   See Forest
    reproduction.

Regensburg, Ger.
--Botany.
    sa Subdivision Germany. Regensburg
        under: Mushrooms.
--Entomology.

Reggio Emilia, Italy (Province)
--Agriculture.
    sa Subdivision Italy. Reggio
        Emilia under: Irrigation.
        Subdivision Italy. Reggio
        Emilia (Province) under:
        Reclamation of lahd.
        Agriculture. Cooperative.
--Commerce.
-- --Periodicals.
--Economic conditions.
-- --Periodicals.

Regional 4-H club camp.
    x Four-H club camp.

Regional libraries.   See Libraries,
    Regional.

Regional markets.   See Markets, Regional.

Regional planning.   See Planning, Re-
    gional.

Regionalism.   (DIRECT)
    sa Sectionalism (U.S.)

Registers of birth, etc.   (DIRECT)
    x Birth, Registers of.

Registration of ships.   See Ships.
    Registers.

Registration of title.   See Land titles.
    Registration and transfer.

Re-grassing.   See Revegetation.

Regulation of commerce.   See Government
    regulation of commerce.

Regulation of supply.   See Production.
    Control of.

Regulations, Administrative.   See Sub-
    division Legislation under the names
    of specific government agencies, e.g.,
    U.S. Dept. of Agriculture. Legisla-
    tion.

Regulators, Voltage.   See Voltage regu-
    lators.

Regulatory law.
　　For general works, See Admini-
　　strative law. For regulatory
　　laws administered by specific
　　government agencies, See sub-
　　division Legislation under the
　　name of the agency, e.g., U.S.
　　Dept. of Agriculture. Legis-
　　lation.

Reh.

Rehabilitation.

Rehabilitation, Rural.　(INDIRECT)
　　x Rural restoration.
　　Agricultural reconstruction.
　　Agricultural rehabilitation.
　　Agriculture. Reconstruction.
　　Agriculture. Rehabilitation.
　　Rural reconstruction.
　　Reconstruction, Rural.
　　Reconstruction (1914-1939)
　　　　Agriculture.
　　Reconstruction (1939-　　)
　　　　Agriculture.
　　Rehabilitation of agriculture.
　　xx Sociology, Rural.
　--Congresses.
　　xx Agriculture. Congresses.
　--Statistics.

Rehabilitation of agriculture.　See
　　Rehabilitation, Rural.

Rehabilitation of war disabled.　See
　　Disabled. Rehabilitation, etc.

Rehoboth, Mass.

Reibel.

Reichenau (Island)
　--Entomology.

Reichsbank, Berlin.

Reichstadt, Austria. Höhere forstlehr-
　　anstalt.

Reigate, Eng.
　--Botany.
　--Zoology.

Reims, France.
　--Entomology.

Reindeer.
　　sa Caribou.
　--Anatomy and physiology.
　--Bibliography.
　--Cookery.　See Cookery (Reindeer)
　--Diseases.
　　xx Veterinary medicine.
　--Legislation.
　--Parasites.
　--Periodicals.
　--Research.

Reindeer farms.

Reindeer meat.

Reindeer-moss.

Reinforced concrete construction.　See
　　Concrete construction; Concrete,
　　Reinforced.

Reinforced lumber.　See Lumber,
　　Reinforced.

Reithrodontomys.

Reithrodontomys halicoetes.

Rejuvenation.
　　xx Organotherapy.

Rejuvenescence (Botany)

Relapsing fever.

Relative humidity.　See Humidity.

Relativity (Physics)
　　xx Space and time.

Release cuttings.　See Thinning.

Relict plants.

Relief, International.　See Inter-
　　national relief.

Relief work. (DIRECT)
This subject is used for relief of
unemployment and other peace-
time ills. For relief work due
to war see World War, 1939-1945.
Civilian relief; Reconstruction
(1914-1939); Reconstruction
(1939-)
sa Drought relief.
Gardens, Employees'.
Work camps.
Public works as relief measure.
Disaster relief.
x Unemployment relief.
xx Charities.
--Bibliography.
-- --Periodicals.
xx Economics. Bibliography. Peri-
odicals.
--Congresses.
--Directories.
--Legislation.
--Research.
xx Research.
--Statistics.

Religion.
sa Monism.
Rural churches.
Sociology, Christian.
Spiritual life.
Subdivision Religion under:
McHenry Co., Ill.
Appalachian Mountains.
Swedes in the U.S.//
xx Religions.
--Bibliography.

Religion and agriculture. See Church
and agriculture.

Religion and science.
sa Natural theology.
xx Natural theology.

Religion and social problems. See Church
and social problems.

Religions.
sa Gods.
Religion.

Religions (Proposed, universal, etc.)

Religious denominations.
sa Church of the brethren.

Religious education.
x Christian education.
Education, Christian.
--Bibliography.

Religious history. See Church history.

Relishes. See Cookery (Relishes)

Remade cream. See Cream, Remade.

Remade milk. See Milk, Remade.

Remodeling of buildings. See Building.
Repair and reconstruction.

Ren policysticus.

Renal system.

Rendering (Fats and oils) See Fats and
oils. Processing.

Renegotiation of war contracts. See War
contracts. Renegotiation.

Renfrewshire, Scot.
--Agriculture.
--Roads.

Renguera.

Renmark irrigation district, South
Australia.
--Soils.
sa Subdivision South Australia.
Renmark irrigation district
under: Soil-surveys.

Rennes.
--Antiquities.
--Botany.

Rennes. L'école nationale d'agriculture.

Rennes.
--Milk supply.

Rennet.

Reno, Nev.
--Climate.

Renovated butter.   See Butter, Renovated.

Rensselaer, N.Y.
--Maps.

Rensselaer Co., N.Y.
--Soils.
    sa Subdivision New York (State)
        Rensselaer Co. under:
        Soil-surveys.
--Water-supply.
    xx New York (State) Water supply.

Rent.   (DIRECT)
    sa Landlord and tenant.
        Real estate business.
        Leases.
    x Agricultural rent.
        Farm rent.
        Rents.
--Abstracts.
--Bibliography.

Rents.   See Rent.

Renville Co., Minn.
    xx Minnesota.

Renville Co., N.D.
--Agriculture.
    xx North Dakota. Agriculture.

Reorganization act of 1945.

Reorganization of executive departments.
    See U.S. Executive departments. Re-
    organization.

Reorganization of government departments.
    See U.S. Executive departments. Re-
    organization.

Reorganization of state government.   See
    State governments. Reorganization.

Repairing.
    sa Farm repairs.
        Subdivision Maintenance and
        repair under: Agriculture.
            Implements and machinery.
        Electric apparatus and ap-
            pliances, Domestic.
        Roads.
        Diesel engines.

Repairing (Continued)
    sa Subdivision Repairing under:
        Automobiles.
        Carpets.
        Pottery.
        Rugs.
        Clothing and dress.
        Textile machinery.
        Shoes.
        Home economics. Equipment
            and supplies.
        Subdivision Repair and re-
            construction under:
        Building.
        Dwellings.
    x Mending.

Reparations.   See European war, 1914-
    1918. Reparations; World War, 1939-
    1945. Reparations.

Repatriation.
    sa World War, 1939-1945. Dis-
        placed persons.
    xx International law.

Repellents.
    sa Insect baits and repellents.
--Toxicity.
    xx Toxicology.

Replacement crops.
    xx Agriculture.

Report preparation.   See Reports. Pre-
    paration.

Report writing.   See Reports. Prepara-
    tion.

Reporters and reporting.
    sa Journalism.
    xx Journalism.
        Newspapers.

Reports.

Reports, Industrial.   See Corporations.
    Reports and year-books.

Reports.
--Preparation.
    Here are entered works on the
    preparation of technical and
    scientific reports and papers.
    For guides on the technical
    problems of writing, and works
    on the preparation of manu-
    scripts preliminary to printing
    and publications, See Author-
    ship. Handbooks, manuals, etc.
  sa Scientific papers.
    English language. Technical
      English.
    Technology. Language.
  x Report writing.
    Report preparation.
    Engineering papers.
    Technical writing.
    Medical writing.
    Scientific writing.
    Technology. Authorship.
    Science. Authorship.

Repository libraries. See Libraries,
  Storage.

Representation, Proportional. See
  Proportional representation.

Representative government and representation.
  sa Proportional representation.

Reproduction.
  sa Asexual reproduction.
    Parthenogenesis.
    Fertilization of plants.
    Pedogenesis.
    P lant reproduction.
    Spermatogenesis.
    Homogenesis.
    Impregnation, Artificial.
    Fetus.

Reproduction, Asexual. See Asexual
  reproduction.

Reproduction.
--Dietary requirements.
--Effect of climate.
  x Climate. Effect on reproduction.

Reproduction (Continued)
--Insects.
  sa Generative organs. Insects.
  x Reproduction of insects.
  xx Generative organs. Insects.
--Mammals.
-- --Congresses.
-- --Text-books.
--Periodicals.

Reproduction in plants. See Plant
  reproduction.

Reproduction of forests. See Forest
  reproduction.

Reproduction of insects. See Reproduction. Insects.

Reptilia. (INDIRECT)
  sa Pelycosauria.
    Rhynchocephalia.
    Chelonia.
    Crocodiles.
    Lacertilia.
    Sphenodontidae.
    Lampropeltis.
    Lizards.
    Amphiuma.
    Alligators.
    Serpents.
    Subdivision Reptiles under:
      Embryology.
--Bibliography.

Reptilia, Fossil.
  sa Dinosaurus.
    Pterodactyl.
    Pleiosauria.
    Dimetrodon gigas.
  xx Dinosauria.

Reptilia.
--Metabolism. See Metabolism in
  reptiles.
--Parasites.
  sa Nematoda. Parasitic in
    reptiles.

Republica Argentina. See Argentine
  Republic.

Republican Party.
  xx Political parties.

Republican River.
    sa Subdivision Republican River
       under: Flood control.

Requisitioning of food.   See Food.
   Requisitioning.

Requisitions.   (DIRECT)
    x Property, Requisition of.
    xx Industry and state.

Requisitions, Military.   (DIRECT)

Requisitions of service.   See Military
   service,.Compulsory; Service, Compulsory non-military.

Resale price fixing.   See Price maintenance.

Resale price maintenance.   See Price
   maintenance.

Resazurin.
    sa Milk. Resazurin test.

Rescue-grass.

Research.
    sa Subdivision Research under:
      Africa, South.
      Australia.
      Belgium//
      Chemistry.
      Forestry.
      Roads//
      Municipal research.
      Government research.
      Photography. Scientific ap-
       plications.
      Operations research.
      Communication in science.
    x Science. Research.
      Applied research.
    xx Learning and scholarship.
  --Abstracts.
  --Addresses, essays, lectures.

Research, Agricultural.   See Agriculture.
   Research.

Research.
  --Bibliography.
    sa Subdivision Bibliography un-
      der: Government research.
      Home economics. Research.
      Economics. Research//
  -- --Periodicals.
  --Congresses.
    sa Subdivision Congresses under:
      Agriculture. Research.
      Research, Industrial.
      Rural population. Research//
  --Costs.
    sa Subdivision Costs under: U.S.
      Research.
  -- --Bibliography.
  --Directories.   See Research. Socie-
    ties. Directories.

Research, Endowment of.   See Endowment
  of research.

Research.
  --Government aid.
    x Science. Government aid.
      Federal aid for research.
    xx Government aid.
  --History.

Research, Industrial.
    sa Subdivision Research under:
      Business.
      Marketing.
      Operations.
    xx Business. Research.
      Operations research.
  --Abstracts.
  --Bibliography.
  --Congresses.
  --Periodicals.
  --Societies.

Research.
  --Methodology.
    sa Agriculture. Statistical
      methods.
    x Experimental design.
      Design, Experimental.
    xx Methodology.

Research, Military.
    x Military research.

Research. Naval.
    x Naval research.

Research.
--Periodicals.
    sa Subdivision Research. Periodi-
    cals under names of coun-
    tries, e.g., Africa, West.
    Research. Periodicals.
--Policies and programs.
    x Research policies and programs.
--Societies.
    sa Learned institutions and socie-
    ties.
    xx Learned institutions and socie-
    ties.
-- --Directories.
    sa Subdivision Directories under:
    Learned institutions and
      societies.
    Laboratories.
    Forest genetics.
    Subdivision Research. Direc-
    tories under: Chemistry.
    Medicine.
    Pharmacy.
    Veterinary medicine.
--Study and teaching.
    xx Study and teaching.
--Year-books.

Research and marketing act of 1946. See
  Agricultural marketing act (U.S.) of
  1946.

Research as an occupation.
    xx Occupations.

Research libraries. See Libraries,
  Scientific.

Research policies and programs. See Research. Policies and programs.

Resedaxeae.

Reseeding. See Revegetation.

Reserpine.
--Research.

Reservations, Indian. See Indians, North
  American. Reservations.

Reservoirs.
    sa Flood dams and reservoirs.
    Irrigation.
    Water-storage//

Reservoirs (Continued)
--Protection from birds.
    xx Ornithology.

Resettlement. See Colonization, Agricultural.

Residences. See Dwellings.

Residues from spraying and dusting. See
  Spraying and dusting residues.

Resin. See Gums and resins.

Resin acids. See Rosin acids.

Resin impregnated Wood. See Impreg
  (resin impregnated wood)

Resin-oil. See Rosin-oil.

Resinous products. See Gums and resins,
  Artificial.

Resins. See Gums and resins.

Resistance.
    sa Conduction resistance.

Resistance in plants. See Disease resistant plants; Pest resistant plants;
  Drought resistant plants.

Resistance of materials. See Strength
  of materials.

Resistance to fungicides. See Fungi,
  Pathogenic. Resistance to fungicides.

Resistance to insecticides. See Insect
  resistance to insecticides.

Resistance to plant diseases. See
  Disease resistant plants.

Resistance to plant pests. See Pest
  resistant plants.

Resistant insects. See Insect resistance to insecticides.

Resistant vines.
    x Phylloxera resistant stock.
    Grapes. Pest resistant varie-
        ties.
    Grapes. Disease resistant
        varieties.

Resonance (Chemistry)   See Mesomerism.

Resorption.   See Absorption.

Resource-use.   See Conservation of natural resources.

Resources, Natural.   See Natural resources.

Respiration.
    sa Subdivision Respiration under:
        Seeds.
        Cereals.
        Insects.
        Araneida.
        Vegetables.
        Invertebrates.
        Domestic animals.
        Mammalia.
        Intramolecular respiration.
        Fruit respiration.
        Plant respiration.
    xx Altitudes.

Respiration, Artificial.
    sa Respirators.

Respiration.
--Bibliography.

Respiration, Effect of fattening on.   See
    Fattening. Effect on respiration.

Respiration calorimeter.
    sa Respirometer.

Respiration of insects.   See Insects.
    Respiration.

Respiration of plants.   See Plant res-
    piration.

Respirators.
    x Respiratory apparatus.
        Oxygen breathing apparatus.
    xx Respiration, Artificial.

Respiratory apparatus.   See Respirators.

Respiratory disease.   See Respiratory
    organs. Diseases.

Respiratory organs.
    sa Inhalation.
--Diseases.
    x Respiratory disease.
    xx Pathology.
--Worms.

Respirometer.
    sa Respiration calorimeter.

Response.

Rest period of plants.
    sa Germination, Delayed.
    x Plants. Dormancy.
        Quiescence.
        Dormancy.
    xx Germination, Delayed.
        Botany. Physiology.

Rest period of trees.
    xx Trees. Physiology and mor-
        phology.

Rest rooms for women.

Restaurant sanitation.   See Restaurants,
    lunch rooms, etc. Sanitation.

Restaurants, lunch rooms, etc.   (DI-
    RECT)
        sa Hotels, taverns, etc.
            Community kitchens.
            Canteens (War-time, emergency,
                etc.)
            School lunchrooms.
            Food for institutions.
        x Employee lunch rooms.
            Employees' lunch rooms.
            Industrial lunch rooms.
--Accounting.
--Bibliography.
--Congresses.
--Directories.
--Equipment.
--Legislation.
--Periodicals.

Restaurants, lunch rooms, etc. (Continued)
--Sanitation.
    x Caterers and catering. Sanita-
        tion.
      Restaurant sanitation.
    xx Sanitation.
--Statistics.

Restiaceae.
    sa Restio.

Restio.

Restionaceae.

Restoration of buildings. See Architecture. Conservation and restoration.

Restraint of animals.

Restraint of trade.
    sa Price maintenance.
      Prices. Fixing.
      Price discrimination.

Restriction of ribbon development act.
1935.

Resuscitation.
    x Anabiosis.

Retail buying associations, Cooperative.
    See Cooperative retail buying associa-
    tions.

Retail trade.   (DIRECT)
    When used with a geographic sub-
    division, indicate see also
    ref. from name of place with
    subdivision Commerce.
    sa Department stores.
      Stores (Retail trade)
      Trade relations.
      Chain stores.
      Display of merchandise.
    x Food distribution.
      Food. Distribution.
--Accounting.
    xx Accounting.
      Bookkeeping.
--Advertising.
    sa Subdivision Advertising under:
      Chain stores.
--Bibliography.

Retail trade (Continued)
--Directories.
    sa Retail trade. U.S. Directories
--Legislation.
    xx Commercial law.
--Periodicals.
--Societies.
    sa Names of individual societies;
      i.e., American retail fed-
      eration.
--Statistics.
    xx Commerce. Statistics.
--Taxation.
    xx Taxation.

Retaining walls.

Retentio secundinarum. See Afterbirth.

Reticular-endothelial system.

Reticulitermes.
    xx Termites.

Reticulitermes hesperus.

Reticulitermes lucifugus.

Reticulocytes. See Blood. Corpuscles
and platelets.

Retina.
--Bibliography.

Retinitis.

Retinodiplosis inopsis.
    x Gouty pitch midge.
    xx Pine. Pests.

Retirement.
    xx Leisure.
      Old age.
--Bibliography.
--Periodicals.

Retouching (Photography) See Photography. Retouching.

Retrievers.
    sa Chesapeake bay retriever.
      Labrador dogs.
    x Golden retrievers.

Retronecine.

Retting.
    sa Subdivision Retting under:
        Fibers.
        Flax.

Réunion, Ile de la.
--Agriculture.
--Botanic garden.
--Botany.
    xx Africa. Botany.
--Commerce.
    sa Subdivision Réunion, Ile de la
        under: Sugar trade.
--Commercial policy.
    sa Subdivision Réunion, Ile de la
        under: Import quotas.
--Entomology.
--Industries and resources.

Reuss, Thuringia.
--Botany.

Reuss Valley, Switzerland.
--Botany.

Revegetation.
    x Ranges. Seeding.
        Ranges. Reseeding.
        Grasses. Seeding.
        Grasses. Reseeding.
        Reseeding.
        Re-grassing.
--Congresses.
--Implements and machinery.
--Research.

Revegetation of overgrazed range areas.
    x Range revegetation.
    xx Ranges. Management.

Revenue.
    sa Subdivision Revenue under: U.S.
        India.
        Brazil//
        Government monopolies.
        Public domain.
        Taxation.

Revenue, Internal.   See Internal revenue.

Revenue laws.
    sa Taxation.

Reverse lend-lease.   See Lend-lease
    operations (1941-   )

Reversion.
    xx Heredity.

Revilla Gigedo Islands, Mexico.
--Botany.
--Natural history.

Revolution, American.   See U.S. History.
    Revolution.

Revolution, Chinese.   See China. History.
    Revolution.

Revolution, Russian.   See U.S.S.R. His-
    tory. Revolution.

Rewards (Prizes, etc.)
    sa Subdivision Prizes under:
        Agriculture. Fairs and ex-
            positions.
        Floriculture. Exhibitions.
        Domestic animals. Exhibi-
            tions.
        Agriculture.
        Gardening. Exhibitions.
        Pomology. Exhibitions.
    Suggestion systems.
    Stalin prizes.
    Subdivision Rewards (Prizes,
        etc.) under: U.S. Dept. of
        Agriculture. Officials
            and employees.
        Poultry. Research.
        Agricultural laborers.
        U.S. Officials and em-
            ployees.
        Science. Societies.
        Technology. Societies.
    Subdivision Competitions under
        various subjects, e.g.,
        Architecture, Domestic.
        Competitions.
    x Awards.
        Premiums (Prizes, rewards)
        Premium lists.
        Prizes (Rewards)
        Competitions.
        Awards.
    xx Suggestion systems.
--Directories.

Rex rabbits.
    x Rabbits, Rex.
    xx Rabbits.

Reynolds Co., Mo.
 xx Missouri.
--Agriculture.
 sa Subdivision Missouri. Reynolds
  Co. under: Farm management
  surveys.
 xx Missouri. Agriculture.
--Forestry.
 sa Subdivision Missouri. Reynolds
  Co. under: Forest surveys.
 xx Missouri. Forestry.

Rhabditis lambdiensis.

Rhabditis oxyuris.

Rhabdoblatta brunneonigra.

Rhabdocnemis obscura.
 xx Calandridae.

Rhabdocoela.

Rhabdoides cellus.

Rhabdonema strongyloides.

Rhabdopterus picipes.

Rhaboides.
 x Hesperiidae.

Rhacodineura antiqua.

Rhagionidae.
 x Worm-lions.

Rhagium lineatum.
 x Ribbed pine-borer.
 xx Pine. Pests.
  Cerambycidae.

Rhagoletis cerasi.

Rhagoletis cingulata.

Rhagoletis completa.

Rhagoletis fausta.

Rhagoletis pomonella.
 x Apple maggot.

Rhagoletis suavis.

Rhagophthalmidae.
 x Coleoptera.

Rhagovelia.
 xx Veliidae.

Rhamnaceae.
 sa Sageretia.
 Phylica.
 Rhamnus.
 Karwinskia.

Rhamneae.
 sa Rhamnus.

Rhamnose.

Rhamnus.

Rhamnus cathartica.
 x European buckthorn.
 Buckthorn, European.

Rhamnus eradication.

Rhamnus frangula.

Rhamnus purshiana.
 x Cascara.

Rhaphidia. See Raphidia.

Rhaphidopherinae.

Rhaphiomidas.
 xx Apioceridae.

Rhaptopetalum.

Rhea. See Ramie.

Rhea Americana.

Rhea (Bird)
--Parasites.
 xx Birds. Parasites.

Rhea Co., Tenn.
--Soils.
 sa Subdivision Tennessee. Rhea
  Co. under: Soil-surveys.

Rheae.

Rheingau.
--Viticulture.

Rheinland-Pfalz.　See Rhineland-
Palatinate.

Rheinländer (Poultry)

Rhenania phosphate.　See Phosphates,
Rhenania.

Rhenaniaphosphat.
xx Fertilizers.
Phosphoric acid.

Rhenium.

Rheola Forest, Wales.
xx Wales. Forest reservations.

Rheology.
sa Viscosity.
Deformations (Mechanics)
Colloids.
Elasticity.
Plasticity.
xx Colloids.
Deformations (Mechanics)
Elasticity.
Plasticity.
Viscosity.
--Abstracts.
--Congresses.
--Periodicals.
--Societies.

Rheosporangium aphanidermatus.

Rheotaxis.

Rheotropism.

Rhetian Alps.　See Alps, Swiss.

Rhetoric.
sa Subdivisions Composition and
exercises and Rhetoric under
names of languages, e.g.,
English language. Composition and exercises; English
language. Rhetoric.
Debates and debating.
Letter-writing.
Oratory.

Rhetoric (Continued)
sa Punctuation.
Persuasion (Rhetoric)
x Composition (Rhetoric)

Rheum.
sa Rhubarb.

Rheumatism.
xx Pathology.

Rheumatobates.

Rheumatoid arthritis.　See Arthritis.

Rhigopsidius tucumanus.

Rhinanthus.
x Alectorolophus.

Rhine, The.　See Rhine River and Valley.

Rhine Province.
--Agriculture.
sa Subdivision Rhine Province　.
under: Agriculture. Economic
aspects.
Agriculture, Cooperative.
-- --Education.
-- --Statistics.
--Botany.
sa Subdivision Botany under:
Elberfeld.
Subdivision Rhine Province
under: Vegetable pathology.
--Entomology.
sa Subdivision Rhine Province
under: Coleoptera.
xx Germany. Entomology.
--Forestry.
--Horse.
--Land.
sa Subdivision Rhine Province
under: Land tenure.
xx Germany. Land.
--Milk supply.
xx Germany. Milk supply.
--Natural history.

Rhine River and Valley.
sa Floods. Rhine River.
Flood dams and reservoirs.
Rhine River and Valley.

Rhine River and Valley (Continued)
--Agriculture.
　　sa Subdivision Rhine River and
　　　　Valley under: Agricultural
　　　　industries.
--Botany.
　　sa Subdivision Rhine River and
　　　　Valley under: Fungi.
--Description and travel.
　　xx Germany. Description and travel.
--Economic conditions.
　　sa Subdivision Rhine River and
　　　　Valley under: Geography,
　　　　Economic.
-- --Periodicals.
--Geography.
　　sa Subdivision Rhine River and
　　　　Valley under: Geography,
　　　　Economic.
--Industries.
　　sa Subdivision Rhine River and
　　　　Valley under: Agricultural
　　　　industries.
--Pomology.
--Transportation.
--Viticulture.
--Zoology.
　　sa Subdivision Germany. Rhine
　　　　River and Valley under:
　　　　Batrachia.
　　　　Reptilia.

Rhineland-Palatinate.
　　x Rheinland-Pfalz.
--Agriculture.
-- --History.
--Forestry.
-- --Bibliography.
--Soils.
　　sa Subdivision Rhineland-
　　　　Palatinate under: Soil con-
　　　　servation.
--Viticulture.

Rhinitis, Atrophic.　See Rhinitis (Swine)

Rhinitis (Swine)
　　x Atrophic rhinitis.
　　　　Rhinitis, Atrophic.
　　xx Swine. Diseases.

Rhinobatidae.

Rhinoceros.
--Parasites.
　　xx Parasites.

Rhinoceros beetle.　See Dynastes tityus;
　　Oryctes.

Rhinocerotidae.

Rhinocola.

Rhinocyllus conicus.

Rhinocypha.
--Larvae.
　　xx Larvae.

Rhinolophus.

Rhinolophus ferrum-equinum.

Rhinoscapha thomsoni.

Rhinosia pometella.　See Dichomeris
　　ligulella.

Rhinosporidium seeberi.

Rhinotermitidae.
　　sa Prorhinotermes.
　　xx Isoptera.
　　　　Termites.

Rhinotragine beetles.　See Cerambycidae.

Rhipicephalus appendiculatus.

Rhipicephalus phthirioides.

Rhipicephalus pulchellus.

Rhipicephalus sanguineus.
　　x Dog-tick.
　　　　Brown dog tick.

Rhipiceridae.
　　x Coleoptera.

Rhipidandri.

Rhipidius.

Rhipiphoridae.
　　sa Macrosiagon.
　　xx Coleoptera.

Rhipiphoridae.
    sa Macrosiagon.
    xx Coleoptera.

Rhipophoridae.

Rhipsalis.

Rhizina inflata.

Rhizobium.

Rhizobium japonicum.

Rhizobium leguminosarum.

Rhizobium meliloti.
    xx Soil bacteria.

Rhizobium radicicola.
    x Bacterium radicicola.
    xx Nitrifying bacteria.

Rhizobium trifolii.

Rhizocarpeae.

Rhizocephala.

Rhizoctonia.

Rhizoctonia napi.   See Sclerotinia
   sclerotiorum.

Rhizoctonia solani.

Rhizoctonia subepigea.

Rhizoctonia tuliparum.
    x Sclerotium tuliparum.

Rhizoctonia violacea.

Rhizoctonus.
    Aphididae.

Rhizoctonus ampelinus.

Rhizoecus lendea.

Rhizoid.

Rhizome.
    xx Botany, Physiological and
      structural.

Rhizomorpha.   See Agaricus.

Rhizomyzides.

Rhizopertha dominica.

Rhizophagidae.

Rhizophaginini.

Rhizophora.
    xx Rhizophoraceae.

Rhizophora mangle.
    x Mangrove, Red.

Rhizophoraceae.
    sa Anisophyllea.
      Anopyxis ealaensis.
      Rhizophora.

Rhizophyllidaceae.

Rhizopoda.
    sa Actinosphaerium.
      Foraminifera.
      Cyphoderia.

Rhizopogon.
    xx Hymenogastraceae.

Rhizopus.

Rhizopus nigricans.

Rhizopus oryzae.

Rhizopus rot of maize.
    x Scutellum rot.
    xx Maize. Diseases.

Rhizopus tritici.

Rhizostomata.
   --Parasites.
    xx Medusae. Parasites.

Rhodamines.
    xx Dyes and dyeing.

Rhodanates.   See Thiocyanates.

Rhode Island.
--Agriculture.
    sa Subdivision Rhode Island under:
      Agricultural policies and
        programs.
      Farms.
      Agriculture. Economic
        aspects.
      Agricultural extension.
-- --Education.
    sa Subdivision Rhode Island under:
      Agricultural extension.
--Bibliography.
--Botany.
    sa Subdivision Botany under:
      Roger Williams Park,
        Providence, R.I.
      Subdivision Rhode Island under:
        Vegetable pathology.
        Algae.
--Boundaries.
    xx Boundaries, State.
--Census.
--Commerce.
    sa Subdivision Rhode Island under:
      Cotton trade.
      Wholesale trade.
--Description and travel.
--Economic conditions.
    sa Subdivision Economic conditions
      under: Providence.
-- --Bibliography.
--Education.
    sa Rhode Island. Dept. of Public
      Instruction.
--Entomology.
    sa Subdivision Rhode Island under:
      Entomology, Economic.
      Coleoptera.
--Forestry.
    sa Subdivision Rhode Island under:
      Forest fires.
      Wood-lots.
    xx U.S. Forestry.
--Gazetteers.
--Geology.
--Government publications.
-- --Bibliography.
--History.
--Industries and resources.
--Land.
    sa Subdivision Rhode Island under:
      Land utilization.
    xx U.S. Land.
--Legislative manuals.

Rhode Island (Continued)
--Maps.
    sa Subdivision Maps under:
      Providence, R.I.
--Marketing.
    sa Subdivision Rhode Island under:
      Farm produce. Marketing.
--Markets.
--Milk supply.
    sa Subdivision Milk supply under:
      Providence, R.I.
    xx Milk supply.
--Milk trade.
    sa Subdivision Milk trade under:
      Providence, R.I.
    xx U.S. Milk trade.
--Ornithology.
    sa Washington Co., R.I. Orni-
      thology.
--Paleontology.
--Parks.
    sa Subdivision Parks under:
      Providence.
    xx U.S. Parks.
--Politics and government.
    xx U.S. Politics and government.
--Population.
    xx U.S. Population.
--Public works.
    xx U.S. Public works.
--Roads.
--Soils.
    sa Subdivision Rhode Island under:
      Soil-surveys.
      Soil conservation.
      Subdivision Soils under names
        of counties, etc.
    xx U.S. Soils.
--Statistics.
    sa Rhode Island. Census.
--Water-supply.
    sa Subdivision Water-supply under:
      Newport.
--Zoology.

Rhode Island reds.
--Periodicals.

Rhodea japonica.

Rhodes grass.
--Bibliography.

Rhodes grass scale.   See Antonina
    graminis.

Rhodesgrass scale.   See Antonina graminis.

Rhodesia.
--Agriculture.
      sa Rhodesia, Northern. Agri-
         culture.
      Subdivision Rhodesia under:
         Agriculture, Cooperative.
--Biography.
--Botany.
      xx Africa. Botany.
--Cattle.
      xx Africa. Cattle.
--Census.
      sa Rhodesia, Southern. Census.
--Cattle trade.
      xx Africa, South. Cattle trade.
--Commerce.
-- --Statistics.
--Description and travel.
      sa Subdivision Rhodesia under:
         Hunting.
      xx Africa, South. Description and
         travel.
--Domestic animals.
--Entomology.
      sa Subdivision Rhodesia under:
         Entomology, Economic.
      Subdivision Entomology under:
         Zazungula, Rhodesia.
      xx Africa. Entomology.
--Forestry.
      xx Africa. Forestry.
--Industries and resources.
      sa Rhodesia, Southern. Industries
         and resources.
--Natural history.
      xx Africa. Natural history.
--Ornithology.
      xx Africa, South. Ornithology.
--Statistics.
      sa Subdivision Statistics under:
         Rhodesia, Southern.
--Zoology.
      sa Rhodesia, Southern. Zoology.
      Subdivision Rhodesia under:
         Arachnida.

Rhodesia, Northern.
--Agriculture.
      sa Subdivision Rhodesia, Northern
         under: Peanuts.
      Agriculture. Economic
         aspects.
      Maize.
      Colonization, Agricultural.
      Agricultural surveys.
      Agricultural policies and
         programs.
--Botany.
      sa Subdivision Rhodesia, Northern
         under: Trees.
--Cattle trade.
--Civilization.
--Commerce.
-- --Statistics.
--Description and travel.
--Economic conditions.
-- --Periodicals.
--Forestry.
      sa Subdivision Rhodesia, Northern
         under: Trees.
         Tree planting.
--Industries.
--Land.
      sa Subdivision Rhodesia, Northern
         under: Land tenure.
      Land. Classification.
      Land utilization.
--Maps.
--Social conditions.
--Soils.
      xx Africa, Central. Soils.
--Statistics.
--Surveys.
--Water-supply.

Rhodesia, Southern.
--Agriculture.
      sa Subdivision Rhodesia, Southern
         under: Maize.
      Colonization, Agricultural.
      Agricultural policies and
         programs.
      Agricultural surveys.
-- --Education.
 - --History.
-- --Periodicals.
-- --Statistics.
--Apiculture.

Rhodesia, Southern (Continued)
--Botany.
    sa Subdivision Rhodesia, Southern
       under: Trees.
       Shrubs.
       Vegetable pathology.
--Census.
--Dairying.
--Domestic animals.
-- --Statistics.
--Economic conditions.
--Entomology.
--Forestry.
    sa Subdivision Rhodesia, Southern
       under: Trees.
       Forest products.
       Lumber trade.
       War and forestry (1939-1945)
--Geology.
--Industries.
-- --Statistics.
--Land.
    sa Subdivision Rhodesia, Southern
       under: Land utilization.
--Maps.
--Meteorology.
    sa Subdivision Rhodesia, Southern
       under: Precipitation (Mete-
       orology)
--Native races.
--Population.
--Public lands.
--Soils.
    sa Subdivision Rhodesia, Southern
       under: Soil conservation.
       Soil erosion.
--Statistics.
    sa Subdivision Statistics under:
       Rhodesia, Southern. Agri-
       culture.
       Rhodesia, Southern. Domestic
       animals.
       Rhodesia, Southern. Census.
--Zoology.

Rhodesia and Nyasaland (Federation)
--Agriculture.
    sa Subdivision Rhodesia and
       Nyasaland (Federation)
       under: Agriculture. Economic
       aspects.
       Agricultural policies and
       programs.
-- --Congresses.
-- --Periodicals.

Rhodesia and Nyasaland (Federation).(Con.)
--Biography.
--Commerce.
-- --Statistics.
--Economic conditions.
--Industries.
-- --Statistics.

Rhodeus amarus.   See Bitterling.

Rhodites.

Rhodochaetaceae.

Rhodochorton.

Rhododendron.
--Bibliography.
    xx Floriculture. Bibliography.
--Diseases.
--Leaves.   See Rhododendron leaves.
--Periodicals.
--Pests.
    sa Dialeurodes chittendeni.
--Propagation.
    xx Plant propagation.
--Societies.

Rhododendron catawbiense.

Rhododendron leaves.
    x Rhododendron. Leaves.
    xx Leaves.

Rhododendron mariesii.

Rhododendron-Park, Bremen. See Bremen.
    Rhododendron-Park.

Rhododendron whitefly. See Dialeurodes
    chittendeni.

Rhodolphyceae.
    sa Erythrophyllum.

Rhodomelaceae.
    sa Laurencia.
    Spirocladia.

Rhodopeltis.
    xx Algae.

Rhodophyceae.

Rhodophyllidaceae.

Rhodotorula.
  xx Saccharomycetaceae.

Rhodoxanthin.

Rhodymenia palmata.

Rhodymeniaceae.
  sa Rhodymeniales.

Rhodymeniales.
  xx Rhodymeniaceae.

Rhoeo discolor.

Rhogas.   See Rogas.

Rhön Mountains.
  --Sheep.

Rhone River and Valley.
  --Agriculture.
  -- --Periodicals.
  --Botany.
  --Entomology.
  --Paleobotany.
  --Soils.
      xx France. Soils.
          Soil.
  --Viticulture.

Rhopalocera.   See Butterflies.

Rhopalomelus angusticollis.

Rhopalomeridae.
  sa Willistoniella.

Rhopalosiphum prunifoliae.

Rhopalosiphum ribis.

Rhopalosiphum rubiphila.

Rhopobota naevana.

Rhothane.
      x DDD.

Rhubarb.
  sa Cookery (Rhubarb)
  --Analysis.
  --Diseases and pests.

Rhubarb, Frozen.
  --Grading and standardization.
      xx Rhubarb. Grading and stand-
          ardization.
          Fruit, Frozen. Grading and
          standardization.

Rhubarb.
  --Grading and standardization.
      sa Subdivision Grading and
          standardization under:
          Rhubarb, Frozen.
      xx Vegetables. Grading and
          standardization.
  --Marketing.
      xx Vegetables. Marketing.
  --Pests.
      xx Entomology, Economic.

Rhus.
      xx Anacardiaceae.

Rhus coriaria.

Rhus cotinus.

Rhus glabra.
  --Composition.

Rhus radicans.   See Rhus toxicodendron.

Rhus succedanea.

Rhus toxicodendron.
      x Rhus radicans.
  --Eradication.
      xx Weeds. Eradication.

Rhus venenata.

Rhus vernicifera.

Rhyacionia buoliana.
      x European pine shoot moth.

Rhyacionia frustrana.
      x Pine tip moth.
          Nantucket pine moth.
          Nantucket pine tip moth.
  --Parasites.
      xx Parasites.

Rhyephenes.
    xx Curculionidae.

Rhynchites.

Rhynchites betulae.
    sa Leaf-rollers.
    xx Leaf-rollers.

Rhynchobolus dibranchiatus.

Rhynchocephalia.

Rhynchocephalus sackenii.

Rhynchonella.

Rhynchophora.
    sa Balaninus.
       Curculionidae.
       Attelabidae.
       Brachyrhinidae.
       Polydrusus.
       Snout-beetle.
       Dyslobius.
       Brachyrhinus.
    x Weevils.
       Snout-beetle.

Rhynchophorus cruentatus.

Rhynchophorus ferrugineus.

Rhynchophorus palmarum.

Rhyncogonus.

Rhyncoprion penetrans.

Rhynchospermum.

Rhynchosporium graminicola.

Rhynchosporium orthosporum.

Rhynchota.   See Hemiptera.

Rhyncophorus.   See Rhynchophorus.

Rhyngodea.

Rhyngota.   See Hemiptera.

Rhynocyllus.   See Rhinocyllus.

Rhynophorus ferrugineus.

Rhysodidae.

Rhyssemus.

Rhythm in plant development.

Rhytina.

Rhytirhinini.
    sa Rhigopsidius.

Ribbed cocoon maker.   See Bucculatrix
    pomifoliella.

Ribbed pine-borer.   See Rhagium
    lineatum.

Ribbon.
    xx Textile industry and fabrics.

Ribe amt, Denmark.
    --Agriculture.

Ribes.
    sa Gooseberries.
       Currants.

Ribes eradication.

Ribes nigrum.   See Currants, Black.

Ribesieae.

Riboflavin.   See Vitamins (G)

Ribonucleic acids.   See Nucleic acids.

Ribs.
    xx Anatomy, Comparative.

Ricardia montagnei.

Riccardia.

Riccia.

Ricciocarpus natans.

Rice.   (INDIRECT)
    sa Brewing.
       Agriculture, Tropical.
       Oryza glutinosa.

Rice (Continued)
    sa Indian rice.
      Cipher and telegraph codes.
      Rice trade.
      Cookery (Rice)
      Cooking quality (Rice)
    x Water rice.
      Rice, Water.
--Federated Malay States. See Rice.
    Malay States, Federated.
--Abstracts.
--Acreage adjustments.
--Bacteriology.
--Bibliography.
    sa Subdivision Bibliography
      under: Wild rice.
      Rice. Breeding.
      Rice. Cost of production.
    xx Cereals. Bibliography.
--Breeding.
-- --Bibliography.
-- --Congresses.
--Bulk handling.
    xx Cereals. Bulk handling.
--By-products.
-- --Bibliography.
--Color.
--Composition.
    sa Vitamins in rice.
-- --Bibliography.
--Congresses.
--Control of production. See Rice.
    Acreage adjustments.
--Cooling quality. See Cooking quality
    (Rice)
--Cost of production.
    xx Farm produce. Cost of produc-
      tion.
-- --Bibliography.
    xx Rice. Bibliography.
    Cereals. Cost of production.
      Bibliography.
--Crop insurance.
    xx Crop insurance.
--Cytology.
    xx Plant cells and tissues.
--Disease resistant varieties.
--Diseases.
    sa Fusarium diseases of rice.
      Rice blast.
      Virus diseases of rice.
-- --Bibliography.

Rice (Continued)
--Drying.
    sa Rice driers.
    xx Cereals. Drying.
--Economic aspects.

Rice, Effect of cold on. See Cold.
    Effect on rice.

Rice.
--Effect of fertilizers. See Ferti-
    lizers. Effect on rice.

Rice, Effect of heat on. See Heat.
    Effect on rice.

Rice, Effect of light on. See Light.
    Effect on rice.

Rice Effect of nitrogen on. See
    Nitrogen. Effect on rice.

Rice, Enriched.
    xx Food, Enriched.

Rice.
--Estimating of crop.
--Fertilization.
--Fertilizers. See Fertilizers for
    rice.
--Financing.
--Genetics.
--Germination.
    xx Germination.
--Grading and standardization.
    sa Smith shelling device.
--Growth.
--Hail injury.
    xx Hail injury.
--Harvesting.
--History.
--Hybrids.
    xx Hybridization.
--Implements and machinery.
    sa Rice driers.
--Inspection.
    xx Grain inspection.
--Irrigation.
--Juvenile literature.
    xx Cereals. Juvenile literature.
--Laws and legislation.
    sa Agricultural adjustment act,
      1933. Licenses (Rice)

Rice (Continued)
--Loading and unloading equipment.
    xx Loading and unloading equip-
        ment.
--Marketing.
-- --Control.
    xx Farm produce. Marketing.
        Control.
--Marketing, Cooperative.
-- --Societies.
--Marketing.
-- --Costs.
    xx Cereals. Marketing. Costs.
--Marketing agreements.
    xx Cereals. Marketing agreements.
--Marketing quotas.
    xx Marketing quotas.
--Milling.
    x Rice mills.
    xx Flour-mills.
-- --Costs.
--Milling and baking qualities.
    xx Milling and baking qualities
        (of cereals)
--Milling tests.
    xx Milling tests.
-- --Congresses.
--Moisture content.
    xx Cereals. Moisture content.
--Packaging.
    xx Packaging.
--Parboiling.
--Periodicals.
    sa Rice. Statistics. Periodicals.
    Rice ₍geographic subdivision₎
        Periodicals, e.g., Rice.
        Colombia. Periodicals.
--Pests.
    sa Leptocorisa varicornis.
    Lissorhoptrus simplex.
    Schoenobius incertellus.
    Laphygma exempta.
    Proceras auricilia.
--Physiology and morphology.
    xx Cereals. Physiology and
        morphology.
--Pictorial works.
--Prices.
    sa Subdivision Prices under:
        Rice bran.
- --Fixing.
    xx Prices. Fixing.
-- --Periodicals.
-- --Subsidies.

Rice (Continued)
--Processing.
-- --Congresses.
--Processing tax.
    xx Processing tax.
--Research.
    sa Rice ₍geographic subdivision₎
        Research, e.g., Rice.
        Japan. Research.
--Seed.
-- --Disinfection.
    xx Seeds. Disinfection.
--Seedlings.
    x Rice seedlings.
--Shelling.
    xx Rice. Milling.
--Societies.
-- --Directories.
--Standards. See Rice. Grading and
    standardization.
--Statistics.
    sa Rice ₍geographic subdivision₎
        Statistics, e.g., Rice.
        Japan. Okayama-ken. Sta-
        tistics.
    xx Rice supply.
- --Maps.
-- --Periodicals.
--Storage.
    xx Cereals. Storage.
    Uniform grain storage agree-
        ment.
-- --Congresses.
--Tariff.
--Terminology.
    x Rice terminology.
--Toxicity.
--Transplanting.
--Transportation.
    sa Railroads. Rates. Rice.
    xx Grain transportation.
--Varieties.
-- --Research.

Rice, Water. See Rice.

Rice.
--Water requirements.
    xx Water requirements of plants.
--Weather influences.
--Weed control.
--Weights and measures.
    xx Cereals. **Weights** and measures.

Rice and rice culture. See Rice.

Rice as feeding stuff.

Rice as food.

Rice beer.
    sa Sake.
    xx Alcoholic liquors.

Rice blast.
    x Blast of rice.
    xx Rice. Diseases.

Rice bran.
    xx Bran.
--Digestibility.
--Prices.
    xx Rice. Prices.

Rice bug. See Leptocorisa varicornis.

Rice caterpillar. See Laphygma frugi-
perda.

Rice consumption.

Rice Co., Kan.
--Land.
    sa Subdivision Kansas. Rice Co.
        under: Land utilization.
--Soils.
    sa Subdivision Kansas. Rice Co.
        under: Soil conservation
        surveys.

Rice Co., Minn.
    xx Minnesota.

Rice culture. See Rice.

Rice curls.

Rice driers.
    xx Grain driers.
    Rice. Drying.
    Rice. Implements and machinery.

Rice Expedition to Brazil, 1916.

Rice flour.

Rice futures. See Rice trade. Futures.

Rice grass.

Rice grasshopper. See Heiroglyphus banian.

Rice hull grits.

Rice hulls.
--Bibliography.
--Industrial uses.
    xx Chemurgy.

Rice industry and trade. See Rice trade.

Rice-juice sapper. See Leptocorisa
acuta.

Rice leaf miner. See Agromyza. oryzella.

Rice meal.

Rice mills. See Rice. Milling.

Rice moth. See Corcyra cephalonica.

Rice policies and programs. (INDIRECT)
    xx Agricultural policies and
        programs.

Rice, rats.
    sa Oryzomys.

Rice-scouring.

Rice seedlings. See Rice. Seedlings.

Rice soils.
    xx Cereal soils.
        Soil, Waterlogged.
--Bibliography.

Rice stinkbug. See Solubea pugnax.

Rice straw.
--Bibliography.
--Digestibility.

Rice supply.
    sa Subdivision Statistics under:
        Rice.

Rice trade.   (DIRECT)
    sa Subdivision Rice under:
        National industrial re-
        covery. act, 1933. Codes.
    x Rice industry. and trade.
--Directories.
--Futures.
-- --Statistics.
--Periodicals.

Rice trade (Continued)
--Statistics.
    sa Rice trade ₍geographic subdi-
       vision₎ Statistics, e.g.,
       Rice trade. U.S. Statistics.
--Tables and ready-reckoners.
    xx Tables (Systematic lists)
--Terminology.

Rice water-weevil.   See Lisorhoptrus
   simplex.

Rice weevil.   See Sitophilus oryza.

Rice yields.
    xx Crop yields.
--Maps.

Richfield area, Utah.
--Soils.
    sa Subdivision Utah under: Soil-
       surveys.

Richland Co., S.C.
    sa Subdivision South Carolina.
       Richland Co. under: County
          surveys.
--Economic conditions.
--Social conditions.
    sa Subdivision South Carolina.
       Richland Co. under: Social
          surveys.

Richland Co., Wis.
--Soils.
    sa Subdivision Wisconsin. Richland
       Co. under: Soil-surveys.

Richland Parish, La.
--Geology.

Richmond, N.H.
    xx New Hampshire.

Richmond, Va.
--Botany.
--Commerce.
    sa Subdivision Richmond, Va. under:
       Produce trade.
--Economic conditions.
    xx Virginia. Economic conditions.
--Harbor.
    xx Harbors. Virginia.
--Markets.

Richmond Co., N.Y.
--Botany.

Richthofen-Boguslawitz (estate) Ger.

Ricin.

Ricinin.

Ricinin in feeding stuffs.

Ricinulei.   See Cryptosstemmatoidae.

Ricinus.   See Castor-oil plant.

Ricinus communis.   See Castor-oil plant.

Rickets.
    x Rachitis.
    xx Deficiency diseases.

Rickets, Fetal.   See Achondroplasia.

Rickett's organism.

Rickettsia.
    x Heart water (in domestic ani-
       mals)
    Rickettsial diseases.
--Catalogs and collections.

Rickettsia tsutsugamushi.

Rickettsial diseases.   See Rickettsia.

Rictularia.

Rictularia splendida.

Ricturia.

Riddelliine.
    xx Senecio riddellii.

Riddles.
    xx Folk-lore.

Rideal-Walker test.

Ridge culture.

Riding.   See Horsemanship.

Riding Mountain National Park.

Rieti (Province)
--Agriculture.
    sa Subdivision Italy. Rieti
        (Province) under: Agri-
        culture. Economic as-
        pects.

Rifles.

Riga, N.Y.
--Statistics.
    xx Monroe Co., N.Y. Statistics.

Right of assembly. See Assembly, Right
    of.

Right of pasture. See Pasture, Right of.

Right of way. (DIRECT)
    x Rights of way.
    xx Servitudes.

Right to labor.
    sa Unemployed.
        Discrimination in employment.

Rights of way. See Right of way.

Rights, Civil. See Civil rights.

Rigid frame bridges. See Bridges, Rigid
    frame.

Rimpau's dike cultivation of moors.

Rimu. See Dacrydium cupressinum.

Rinderpest.
    sa Cattle. Diseases.
--Congresses.
--Preventive inoculation.

Rindge, N.H.
    sa Subdivision Rindge, N.H. under:
        Cities and towns. Planning.

Ringbarking. See Girdling.

Ringbone.

Ringer's solution.

Ringkjøbing amt, Denmark.
--Agriculture.

Ringspot of crucifers.
    xx Cruciferae. Diseases.

Ringspot of sugar-cane.
    xx Sugar-cane. Diseases.

Ringspot of tobacco.
    xx Tobacco. Diseases.

Ringsted, Denmark. Ungskue.

Ringworm.
    sa Tinea imbricata.
       Tinea tonsurans.
    xx Mycosis.

Rinorea.
    xx Violaceae.

Rio Arriba Co., N.M.
--Geology.
--Water-supply.
    sa Subdivision New Mexico. Rio
        Arriba Co. under: Water,
        Underground.

Rio Blanco Co., Colo.
--Geology.

Rio de Janeiro.
--Botanic garden. See Rio de Janeiro.
    Jardim botanico.
--Botany.
--Sanitary affairs.

Rio de Janeiro (Federal District)
--Agriculture.
    sa Subdivision Brazil. Rio de
        Janeiro (Federal District)
        under: Agriculture, Eco-
        nomic aspects.
--Economic conditions.
--Statistics.
    xx Brazil. Statistics.

Rio de Janeiro (State)
--Agriculture.
    sa Subdivision Brazil. Rio de
        Janeiro (State) under:
        Sugar-cane.
--Census.
--Economic conditions.

Rio de Janeiro (State) (Continued)
--Entomology.
    sa Subdivision Rio de Janeiro
        (State) under: Hemiptera.

Río de Oro.
    xx Africa, Spanish West.

Rio Grande.
    sa Subdivision Rio Grande under:
        Flood control.
        Floods.
--Power utilization.

Rio Grande do Norte, Brazil (State)
--Agriculture.
--Industries and resources.

Rio Grande do Sul, Brazil (State)
--Agriculture.
    sa Subdivision Brazil. Rio Grande
        do Sul (State) under: Rice.
        Agriculture, Cooperative.
        Flax.
        Agriculture. Economic
            aspects.
-- --Statistics.
--Botany.
    sa Subdivision Brazil. Rio Grande
        do Sul (State) under:
        Vegetable pathology.
-- --Research.
--Climate.
--Commerce.
    sa Subdivision Rio Grande do Sul
        (State) under: Rice trade.
-- --Statistics.
--Dairying.
--Description and travel.
--Domestic animals.
    sa Rio Grande do Sul, Brazil
        (State) Horse.
-- --Statistics.
--Economic conditions.
-- --Periodicals.
--Entomology.
    sa Subdivision Brazil. Rio Grande
        do Sul (State) under:
        Entomology, Economic.
        Culicidae.
--History.
--Horse.
    xx Rio Grande do Sul, Brazil
        (State) Domestic animals.
--Industries and resources.

Rio Grande do Sul, Brazil (State) (Con.)
--Population.
--Public lands.
--Statistics.
--Viticulture.
--Water-supply.
--Zoology.

Rio Grande federal reclamation project,
    New Mexico-Texas.
    sa Middle Rio Grande conservancy
        district, New Mexico.
    xx Irrigation projects.

Rio Grande irrigation project.

Rio Grande National Forest.
    sa Wagon Wheel Gap Experiment
        Station, Colo.

Rio Grande Valley.
    sa Subdivision Rio Grande Valley
        under: Drainage.
--Agriculture.
    sa Subdivision Rio Grande Valley
        under: Agricultural la-
        borers.
--Botany.
--Entomology.
    sa Subdivision Rio Grande Valley
        under: Coleoptera.
--Industries and resources.
    sa Subdivision Rio Grande Valley
        under: Conservation of
        natural resources.
--Pomology.
    sa Subdivision Rio Grande Valley
        under: Citrus.
--Social conditions.
--Soils.
    sa Subdivision Rio Grande Valley
        under: Soil erosion.
        Soil conservation.
    xx New Mexico. Soils.
        Soil.
--Water-supply.
    sa Subdivision Rio Grande Valley
        under: Water. Conservation.

Río Hondo.
    x Hondo, Río.

Rio Jamary, Brazil.

Rio Juquiriquerê.

Río Lempa.   See Lempa River.

Río Mayo Valley, Mexico.
    x Mayo River Valley, Mexico.
  --Botany.

Rio Medellin, Colombia.

Rio Negro, Argentine Republic.
  --Agriculture.
      sa Colonization, Agricultural.
          Argentine Republic. Rio
          Negro.
  --Botany.
  --Land.
  --Pomology.
      xx Argentine Republic. Pomology.

Rio Negro, Patagonia.
      xx Argentine Republic.

Rio Primero.   See Primero River.

Rio Puerco Valley, N.M.

Río Salado irrigation project.

Río São Francisco, Brazil.
    x São Francisco River, Brazil.
      San Francisco River, Brazil.

Riodinidae.
      sa Nemeobiinae.

Rioja, Spain.
  --Pomology.

Rios, Ecuador (Province)
      xx Ecuador.

Riparian rights.   (DIRECT)

Ripening.
      sa Subdivision Ripening under:
          Banana.
          Fruit.
          Grape//

Ripersia radicicola.
      x Mealy-bug.
      xx Sugar cane. Pests.

Ripersiella.

Ripley Co., Ind.
  --Agriculture.
  -- --Periodicals.

Ripley Co., Mo.
      xx Missouri.
  --Agriculture.
      sa Subdivision Missouri. Ripley
          Co. under: Agriculture.
          Economic aspects.

Ripon College, Ripon, Wis.

Ripple-marks.

Risk.

Risk in agriculture.
      x Agricultural risks.
        Farm risks.
      xx Agriculture. Economic aspects.
  --Bibliography.

Rissoina.

Ritchie Co., W.Va.
      xx West Virginia.

Ritnitz, Ger.
  --Agriculture.

Rittergut Krzyzanki.
      xx Farms.

Riu Kiu Islands.   See Ryukyu Islands.

Rivea.
      xx Convolvulacea.

Rivea corymbosa.
      x Ololiuqui.

River and stream improvement.   See
    Stream regulation.

River discharge.   See Rivers.

River-dolphins.

River gages.

River gagings.   See Stream measurements.

River management.   See Stream regulation.

River pollution.   See Water. Pollution.

River purification.   See Water. Purification.

River red gum.   See Eucalyptus camaldulensis.

River regulation.   See Stream regulation.

River service.

River stages.   (DIRECT)
    x Flood elevations.
      Flood heights.

River traffic.

Rivers.   (INDIRECT)
      Works on a river or its valley are
      put under two separate headings
      for North American countries,
      i.e., St. Lawrence River or St.
      Lawrence\Valley. But most of
      the foreign rivers and valleys
      are entered jointly, i.e., Duero
      River and Valley.
    sa Stream measurements.
       Stream regulation.
       River traffic.
       Names of rivers.
    x River discharge.
      Stream discharge.
--History.
    sa Subdivision History under:
       Mississippi River.
--Pollution.   See Water. Pollution.
--Purification.   See Water. Purification.
--Regulation.   See Stream regulation.
--Temperature.
    xx Temperature.
       Meteorology.

Riverside, Calif.
    sa Subdivision Riverside, Calif.
       under: Planning, Regional.
--Botany.
    sa Subdivision California. Riverside under: Trees.
       Shrubs.
--Forestry.
    sa Subdivision California. Riverside under: Trees.
--History.

Riverside Co., Calif.
--Soils.
--Water-supply.
      sa Subdivision California, Riverside Co. under: Water,
         Underground.
      xx California. Water-supply.

Riverton Area, Wyo.
--Water-supply.

Riverton irrigation project, Wyo.

Riverton reclamation project, Wyo.   See
    Riverton irrigation project, Wyo.

Rivets.

Riviera.
--Botany.
--Description and travel.
--Natural history.
--Ornithology.

Rivoli, Italy.
--Botanic garden.

Rivoli, Italy. Hortus ripulensis.   See
    Rivoli, Italy. Botanic garden.

Rivulariaceae.

Roach.   See Blattidae.

Road guides.
    x Road maps.

Road machinery.   See Roads. Implements
    and machinery.

Road maintenance.   See Roads. Maintenance and repair.

Road maps.   See Road guides.

Road markers and signs.   See Road
    marking.

Road marking.
    sa Traffic lines.
       Zero milestone.
    xx Signs and sign-boards.
       Signs.

Road materials.
    sa Bituminous road materials.
       Tarmac.
       Tar as a road material.
       Stone as a road material.
       Slag as a road material.
       Cotton fabric as a road
          material.
       Asphalt.
       Concrete.
       Gravel as a road material.
       Soil cement.
    --Bibliography.
    --Directories.
    --Specifications.
    --Testing.

Road-runners.

Road signs.   See Road marking.

Roads.
    sa Subdivision Roads under:
       Arizona.
       Arkansas.
       Connecticut//
       Forest roads.
       Pavements.
       Military roads.
       Roads, Tarred.
       Transportation, Highway.
       Road marking.
       Explosives in road building.
       Agriculture and roads.
       Highway barriers.
       Driveways.
       Unemployment and roads.
       Mileages.
       Roadside improvement.
       Names of specific roads and
          highways, e.g., Inter-
          American Highway.
     x Highway engineering.
       Highway construction.
    --Accounting.

Roads, Asphalt.   See Pavements, Asphalt.

Roads.
    --Bibliography.
       sa Subdivision Roads. Bibliography
          under: Great Britain.
          U.S.
          France.

Roads (Continued)
    --Bibliography.
       sa Subdivision Bibliography
          under: Roads. Maintenance
          and repair.
          Road materials.
          Roads. Finance.
          Roads. Maintenance.
          Traffic regulations.
          Accidents. Prevention.
          Roads. Legislation.
          Roads. Safety measures.
          Roadside improvement.

Roads, Bitumen.   See Pavements, Bitu-
    minous.

Roads, Brick.   See Pavements, Brick.

Roads, Clay.

Roads, Concrete.   See Pavements, Con-
    crete.

Roads.
    --Congresses.
       sa Subdivision Congresses under:
          Traffic regulations.
          Tar as a road material.
          Bituminous road materials.
    --Contracts and specifications.
       sa Road materials. Specifica-
          tions.
    --Conventions.   See Roads. Congresses.
    --Cost.
    --Dictionaries.
    --Drainage.
       x Highway drainage.

Roads, Earth.

Roads.
    --Economics.
       sa Roads. Finance.
          Roads. Cost.
       x Highway economics.
    --Exhibitions.

Roads, Experimental.

Roads.
    --Finance.
       sa Roads. Economics.
          Roads. Cost.
          Roads. Government aid.

Roads (Continued)
--Finance.
-- --Bibliography.

Roads, Forest.   See Forest roads.

Roads.
--Freezing and frost injury.
        xx Frost.
--Government aid.
        xx Roads. Finance.
--Grades.

Roads, Gravel.

Roads.
--Handbooks, manuals, etc.
--History.
        sa Subdivision Roads. History
            under: Gt. Brit.
            France.
            New England//
        Subdivision History under:
            Transportation.
            Communication and traffic.
--Implements and machinery,
        sa Steam-shovels.
            Trails.
-- --Directories.
--Legislation.
        sa Subdivision Legislation under:
            Cattleways.
        Subdivision Roads. Law under:
            Argentine Republic.
            Austria.
            Australia//
--Lighting.
        sa Street-lighting.
        xx Lighting.
            Street-lighting.
-- --Bibliography.

Roads, Macadamized.

Roads.
--Machinery.   See Roads. Implements and
    machinery.
--Maintenance and repair.
        x Highway repairing.
            Roads. Repairing.
-- --Bibliography.
-- --Cost.
--Maps.   See Road guides.

Roads, Military.   See Military roads.

Roads, Mountain.

Roads, Oiled.

Roads.
--Periodicals.
-- --Bibliography.

Roads, Plank.

Roads.
--Planning.
        x Highway planning.
-- --Zone system.
        x Zoning.
            Highway zoning.
        xx Roadside improvement.
--Preservation.   See Roads. Maintenance
    and repair.
--Repairing.   See Roads. Maintenance
    and repair.
--Research.

Roads, Roman.
        sa Appian Way.
            Dean Road.

Roads, Rubber.   See Pavements, Rubber.

Roads.
--Safety measures.
        sa Automobiles. Accidents.
            Traffic lines.

Roads, Shell.

Roads.
--Societies.

Roads, Soil-cement.
        x Soil-cement roads.
        xx Pavements, Concrete.
            Soil (Engineering)

Roads.
--Specifications.   See Roads. Contracts
    and specifications.
--Statistics.
        sa Subdivision Statistics under:
            U.S. Roads.
            Gt. Brit. Roads.

Roads, Steel-track.

Roads.
--Study and teaching.
--Superhighways.
x Controlled-access highways.

Roads, Tarred.

Roads.
--Taxation. See Roads. Finance.
--Testing.
sa Subdivision Testing under:
Pavements, Concrete.
Road materials.

Roadside improvement.
sa Roadside planting.
Roads. Planning. Zone system.
x Roadside protection.
Protection of roadsides.
xx Roads.
--Bibliography.

Roadside markets.
x Markets, Roadside.
Markets, Farmers'.
xx Markets.
--Bibliography.

Roadside planting.
sa Roadside improvement.
Trees. Wire clearance.
--Law.
xx Law.
--Societies.

Roadside protection. See Roadside improvement.

Roane Co., Tenn.
sa Subdivision Roane Co., Tenn.
under: Planning, County.
Subdivision Tennessee. Roane
Co. under: County surveys.
Agricultural policies and
programs.
Landlord and tenant.
Rural rehabilitation.
--Agriculture.
sa Subdivision Roane Co. under:
Agricultural policies
and programs. Tennessee.
Farm management surveys.
Tennessee.
--Economic conditions.

Roane Co., Tenn. (Continued)
--Land.
sa Land utilization. Tennessee.
Roane Co.
--Soils.
sa Subdivision Tennessee. Roane
Co. under: Soil-surveys.

Roane Co., W.Va.
xx West Virginia.

Roanoke, Va.
--Commerce.
sa Subdivision Roanoke, Va. under:
Farm produce. Marketing.
--Markets.

Roanoke Co., Va.
sa Subdivision Roanoke Co. under:
County surveys. Virginia.
xx Virginia.
--Economic conditions.
sa Subdivision Roanoke Co. under:
Economic. surveys. Virginia.
xx Virginia. Economic conditions.
--Industries and resources.
sa Industrial surveys. Virginia.
Roanoke Co.
--Social conditions.
sa Subdivision Virginia, Roanoke
Co. under: Social surveys.

Roanoke River.
sa Subdivision Roanoke River
under: Flood control.

Roaring.

Roaring Fork Valley, Colo.
--Agriculture.
sa Subdivision Colorado. Roaring
Fork Valley under:
Irrigation.

Roasters, Electric.
x Electric roasters.
xx Electric cookery.

Robber-flies. See Asilidae.

Robert Strickland agricultural memorial
award.

Robertson Co., Tex.
xx Texas.

Roberts's anti-abortion serum.
    xx Abortion.

Robeson Co., N.C.
    sa Drainage. North Carolina.
        Robeson Co.

Robinia.
    sa Locust (Tree)

Robinia pseudacacia.   See Robinia pseudo-
    acacia.

Robinia pseudo-acacia.
    x Robinia pseudacacia.
        Black locust.
--Bibliography.
--Decay resistance.
    xx Wood. Decay resistance.
--Diseases.
    xx Trees. Diseases.
        Locust (Tree) Diseases.
--Fertilizers.   See Fertilizers for
    black locusts.
--Growth.
    xx Trees. Growth.
--Pests.
--Seed.
    xx Trees. Seed.
-- --Germination.

Robins.
    xx Ornithology.

Robinson-Patman act, 1936.
--Bibliography.

Roby, Tex.

Roccellei.

Rochdale system.

Rochebaucourt, Quebec.

Rochefort, France.
--Botany.

Rochester, N.Y.
    sa Subdivision New York (State)
        Rochester under: Flood
            control.

Rochester, N.Y. (Continued)
--Commerce.
    sa Subdivision Rochester, N.Y.
        under: Farm produce. Mar-
            keting.
        Produce trade.
        Wholesale trade.
--Markets.
--Milk supply.
    xx New York. Milk supply.
--Officials and employees.
--Parks.

Rock-badger.   See Hyrax.

Rock bee.   See Apis dorsata.

Rock chestnut oak.   See Quercus prinus.

Rock Co., Minn.
    xx Minnesota.
--Soils.
    sa Subdivision Minnesota. Rock
        Co. under: Soil-surveys.

Rock Co., Neb.
--Soils.
    sa Subdivision Nebraska. Rock Co.
        under: Soil-surveys.

Rock Co., Wis.
--Soils.
    sa Subdivision Wisconsin. Rock
        Co. under: Soil-surveys.

Rock Creek, Washington, D.C.
    xx Washington, D.C.

Rock Creek Lake Basin.
--Botany.
    xx Inyo Co., Calif. Botany.

Rock Creek Park, Washington, D.C.   See
    Washington, D.C. Rock Creek Park.

Rock cress.   See Arabis.

Rock disintegration.
    xx Petrology.

Rock-drills.
    x Jackhammers.
    xx Drilling and boring machinery.

Rock flora.   See Alpine flora.

Rock-forming plants.

Rock gardens.
    sa Alpine gardens.
--Bibliography.
--Societies.

Rock Island Co., Ill.
    xx Illinois.
--Soils.
    sa Subdivision Illinois. Rock
        Island Co. under: Soil-
        surveys.

Rock maple. See Acer saccharum.

Rock melon. See Muskmelon.

Rock phosphates.
    x Phosphate rock.
--Transportation.
    sa Subdivision Rock phosphates
        under: Railroads. Rates.

Rock powders.

Rock-rabbit. See Hyrax.

Rock River.

Rock River Basin.
--Water-supply.
    xx U.S. Water-supply.

Rock-rose. See Cistaceae.

Rock salt.
    sa Guano, Rock salt in.

Rock weathering. See Rock disintegra-
    tion.

Rock wool. See Mineral wool.

Rockanje Lake.

Rockbridge Co., Va.
--Agriculture.
    sa Subdivision Virginia. Rock-
        bridge Co. under: Agri-
        cultural policies and
        programs.
--History.
    xx Virginia. History.
--Sanitary affairs.

Rockbridge Co., Va. (Continued)
--Soils.
    sa Subdivision Virginia. Rock-
        bridge Co. under: Soil-
        surveys.

Rocket flight. See Space flight.

Rockford, Ill.
    sa Subdivision Rockford, Ill.
        under: Relief work.

Rockingham Co., N.H.
--Soils.
    sa Subdivision New Hampshire.
        Rockingham Co. under:
        Soil-surveys.

Rockingham Co., N.C.
--Soils.
    sa Subdivision North Carolina.
        Rockingham Co. under:
        Soil-surveys.

Rockingham Co., Va.
    sa County surveys. Virginia.
        Rockingham Co.
    xx Virginia.
--Economic conditions.
--Social conditions.
    sa Subdivision Virginia. Rocking-
        ham Co. under: Social
        surveys.

Rockland Co., N.Y.
    sa Subdivision Rockland Co., N.Y.
        under: Planning, Regional.
--Ornithology.

Rocks.
    sa Rocks, Igneous.
        Pegmatites.
        Olivin-diabase.
        Stone.
        Petrology.
--Analysis.
--Classification and nomenclature.
    x Rocks. Nomenclature.
    xx Classification.
        Nomenclature.
--Cleavage.

Rocks, Gases in. See Gases in rocks.

Rocks.
--Handbooks, manuals, etc.

Rocks, Igneous.
    sa Volcanic ash, tuff, etc.

Rocks.
--Nomenclature. See Rocks. Classifica-
    tion and nomenclature.
--Periodicals.

Rocks, Sedimentary.
    x Sedimentary rocks.
    xx Petrology.
    . Sedimentation and deposition.
--Bibliography.
    xx Petrology. Bibliography.
--Periodicals.
    xx Petrology. Periodicals.

Rocks used as road material. See Stone
    as a road material.

Rockville, Va.
--Social conditions.
    xx Hanover Co., Va. Social condi-
    tions.

Rockwall Co., Tex.
    xx Texas.
--Soils.
    sa Subdivision Texas. Rockwall Co.
    under: Soil-surveys.

Rockweeds. See Fucaceae.

Rockwell, Iowa.
--Agriculture.
    sa Agriculture, Cooperative. Iowa.
    Rockwell.

Rocky Mountain Forest Experiment Station.
    See U.S. Forest Experiment Station,
    Rocky Mountain, Fort Collins, Colo.

Rocky Mountain goat.

Rocky Mountain locust. See Melanoplus
    spretus.

Rocky Mountain National Park.
--Botany.
--Geology.
    xx Colorado. Geology.
--Ornithology.

Rocky Mountain National Park (Continued) 'ʼ
--Zoology.
    xx Colorado. Zoology.   ʼ ' 'ᴏ

Rocky Mountain region.   See Rocky '.. --
    Mountains.

Rocky Mountain sheep. ¯See ʹBighorn ¯ ꞌ,ꞌ
    sheep.

Rocky Mountain spotted fever.
    x Spotted fever of the Rocky
    Mountains.
    xx Tick fever.

Rocky Mountain spotted-fever tick.   See
    Dermacentor venustus'.

Rocky Mountains.
--Agriculture.
    sa Subdivision Rocky Mountains ·
    •   under: Agricultural la-
    borers.
    Sugar-beet.
--Botany.
    sa Bitter Root Mountains. Botany.
    Subdivision Rocky Mountains.
    under: Trees.
    Shrubs.
    Forage plants.
--Description and travel.   ·
--Economic conditions.
    xx U.S. Economic conditions.
--Entomology.
    sa Subdivision Rocky Mountains ¯¯
    under: Trees. Pests.
    Alphididae.
--Forest reservations.
--Forestry.
    sa Subdivision Rocky Mountains ..
    under: Afforestation and
    reforestation.
    Lumbering.
    Trees.
    Forest fires.
    Forest surveys.
    Forest industries. ·
    Wood-using industries.
--Geology.
    sa Subdivision Rocky Mountains
    under: Mines and mineral
    resources.
--Industries.
--Maps.

Rocky Mountains (Continued)
--Meteorology.
   sa Precipitation (Meteorology)
     Rocky Mountains.
--Natural history.
--Ornithology.
   xx Colorado. Ornithology.
--Paleobotany.
   xx U.S. Paleobotany.
--Paleontology.
--Social conditions.
   sa Subdivision Rocky Mountains
     under: Cost and standard of
     living.
--Soils.
--Water-supply.
   xx U.S. Water-supply.
--Zoology.
   sa Subdivision Rocky Mountains
     under: Game.

Rocky Mountains, Canada.
   sa Selkirk- Range.
     Rocky Mountains Park.
--Botany.
   sa Subdivision Rocky Mountains,
     Canada under: Wild flowers.
--Description and travel.
--Geology.
   sa Subdivision Rocky Mountains,
     Canada under: Mines and
     mineral resources.
--Zoology.
   xx Canada. Zoology.

Rocky Mountains Forest Reserve, Canada.

Rocky Mountains Park.
   sa Rocky Mountains, Canada.

Rocky Mountains Park Museum, Banff.

Rodent control.   See Rodentia. Control.

Rodentia.
   sa Castoridae.
     Sciuridae.
     Muridae.
     Saccomyidae.
     Zapodidae.
     Lophiomys.
     Georychus.
     Dipodomys.
     Notiomys.
     Plagiodontia.

Rodentia (Continued)
   sa Leporidae.
     Ochotonidae.
     Cricetidae.
--Anatomy and physiology.
--Control.
   sa Rodenticides.
     Bacteriological control of
     rodents.
     Subdivision Control under:
     Arvicola.
     Rabbits.
   x Rodent control.
     Control of rodents.
-- --Abstracts.
-- --Bibliography.
-- -- --Periodicals.
--Damage to forests.
   xx Forest reproduction.
     Trees. Pests.
--Diseases.
--Extermination.

Rodentia, Fossil.
   sa Beaver,. Fossil.
     Aplodontia.
     Castoridae, Fossil.

Rodentia.
--Parasites.
--Pests.
   sa Subdivision Pests under:
     Ochotona.
     Rabbits.
     Moles (Animals)
     Soricidae.
     Mice.
     Ground-squirrels.
   xx Pests.

Rodentia as carriers of contagion.
   sa Rats as carriers of contagion.
   x Rodents and disease.
--Bibliography.

Rodenticidal plants.   See Rodenticide
   plants.

Rodenticide plants.
   x Rodenticidal plants.
     Plants, Rodenticidal proper-
     ties.
     Plants for rodenticides.
   xx Rodenticides.
     Botany, Economic.

Rodenticides.
    sa Rodenticide plants.
    Names of specific rodenticides,
      e.g., Warfarin.
    x Raticides.
    xx Pesticides.
    Rodentia. Control.
    Chemicals, Agricultural.
--Legislation.
    sa Federal insecticide, fungicide
      and rodenticide act.
--Research.

Rodents.   See Rodentia.

Rodents and disease.   See Rodentia as
  carriers of contagion.

Rodolia cardinalis.

Rodriguez (Island)
--Agriculture.
    sa Subdivision Rodriguez (Island)
      under: Grasses.
    xx Mauritius. Agriculture.
--Entomology.
    sa Subdivision Rodriguez Island
      under: Coleoptera.
    xx Mauritius. Entomology.

Rodriguez reservoir irrigation project.

Roe, Fish.   See Fish roe.

Roe-deer.
    xx Deer.

Roentgen rays.   See X-rays.

Roentgenology.   See X-rays.

Roesleria.

Roesleria hypogaea.

Rogaland, Norway.
--Agriculture.
    sa Subdivision Norway. Rogaland
      under: Farm buildings.

Rogas terminalis.

Rogas unicolor.

Roger Williams Park, Providence, R.I.
--Botany.
    xx Rhode Island. Botany.

Roggenkeime.
    xx Feeding stuffs.

Roggow, Ger. (Estate)

Rogue River, Or.

Rogue River Bridge.

Rogue River National Forest.
    xx Oregon. Forest reservations.
    California. Forest reserva-
      tions.

Rogue River Valley.
--Pomology.

Roller bearings.
    sa Ball bearings.
    xx Ball bearings.
    Bearings (Machinery)

Roller cotton gins.   See Cotton gins.

Roller-towels.

Rollers (Tillage)
    xx Tillage machinery.

Rollinia.

Rolliniopsis.

Rolnik.

Romagna, Italy.
--Botany.

Romagna cattle.

Romaine.
--Grading and standardization.
    xx Vegetables. Grading and
      standardization.

Romalea.

Roman architecture.   See Architecture,
  Roman.

Roman campagna.   See Campagna di Roma.

Roman empire.   See Rome.

Romanoff sheep.
    xx Sheep.

Rome.
    Works about Rome as Kingdom, Re-
        public, Empire. For works about
        the city see Rome (City) For
        works about the province see
        Rome (Province)
    --Agriculture.
        sa Subdivision Rome under:
            Farm management.
            Cereals.
            Agriculture. Economic
                aspects.
    - --History.
    -- --Periodicals.
    --Antiquities.
        xx Archaeology.
    --Architecture.   See Architecture,
        Roman.
    --Domestic animals.
    --Economic conditions.
        sa History, Economic. Rome.
    --History.
        sa History, Economic. Rome.
    --Politics and government.
    --Roads.   See Roads, Roman.
    --Social life and customs.
        xx Italy. Social life and customs.
    --Viticulture.

Rome (City)
    sa Farnese Gardens, Rome.
    --Agriculture.
        sa Subdivision Agriculture under:
            Agro romano.
        xx Italy. Agriculture.
    --Botany.
        xx Italy. Botany.
    --Description.
    --Markets.
        xx Markets.
    --Milk trade.

Rome (Province)
    --Agriculture.
        sa Subdivision Italy. Rome
            (Province) under: Agri-
            culture. Economic as-
            pects.
    - --History.
    -- --Periodicals.

Rome (Province) (Continued)
    --Agriculture.
    -- --Statistics.
    --Economic conditions.

Romerkessel (Farm)
    xx Farms.

Romney Marsh, Kent, Eng.
    --Agriculture.
        xx Kent, Eng. Agriculture.
    --Sheep.
        xx England. Sheep.

Romney Marsh sheep.
    --Breeding.
        xx Sheep. Breeding.

Romorantin, France.
    --Botany.

Romsdals amt, Norway.
    --Forestry.

Roncet.   See Court-noué.

Rondane Mountain.
    --Botany.
        xx Norway. Botany.

Ronne Antarctic Research Expedition, 1947-
    1948.

Ronneby, Sweden.
    --Botany.
    --Zoology.

Röntgen rays.   See X-rays.

Roof gardening.
    xx Floriculture.
        Gardening.

Roof rats.   See Rats.

Roof-trusses.   See Trusses.

Roofing.
    sa Tiles. Roofing.
        Shingles.
    xx Building.

Roofing, Asphalt.
    x Asphalt roofing.

Roofing.
--Periodicals.

Roofing, Steel.
x Steel roofing.

Roofing, Wooden.
sa Gutters.
x Wooden roofing.
xx Wood as building material.

Roofs.
sa Trusses.

Roofs, Thatched.
--Bibliography.

Rooks.
xx Corvidae.
Crows.

Rooks Co., Kan.
--Land.
sa Subdivision Kansas. Rooks Co.
under: Land utilization.
--Soils.
sa Subdivision Kansas. Rooks Co.
under: Soil conservation
surveys.

Room gardening. See House plants.

Roosevelt-Churchill eight point declaration. See Atlantic declaration,
Aug. 14, 1941.

Roosevelt Co., N.M.
--Soils.
sa Subdivision New Mexico.
Roosevelt Co. under: Soil
conservation.
Wind erosion.
--Water supply.
sa Subdivision New Mexico.
Roosevelt Co. under: Water,
Underground.

Roosevelt elk.
x Olympic elk.
Cervus canadensis Roosevelt.
xx Elk.

Roosevelt National Forest, Colo.
x Colorado National Forest.
xx Colorado. Forest reservations.
Forest reservations.

Roosevelt-Sequoia National Park.

Rooseveltia.
xx Palmae.
Phoenicaceae.

Rooseveltia frankliniana.

Root cancer. See Roots. Diseases.

Root-collar disease of cinchona. See
Collar-rot of cinchona.

Root-crops.
x Root vegetables.
--Breeding.
xx Vegetables. Breeding.
--Cost of production.
xx Farm produce. Cost of production.
--Diseases.
sa Sclerotinia libertiana.
--Fertilizers. See Fertilizers for
root crops.
--Pests.
--Seed.
xx Seeds.
--Sprout prevention.
xx Sprout prevention.

Root-crops as feeding stuff.
xx Feeding stuffs.

Root-crops as food.
xx Vegetables as food.

Root-disease of sugar-cane. See Root-
rot of sugar-cane.

Root diseases. See Roots. Diseases.

Root excretions.

Root forming substances. See Growth
substances for plants.

Root hairs.
sa Heterotrophy.

Root-knot.
    sa Heterodera marioni.
    xx Nematode diseases of plants.

Root louse of grape vines.   See Phyll-
  oxera vitifoliae.

Root-maggot.

Root nodule bacteria.   See Nitrifying
  bacteria.

Root parasites.
    sa Root tubercles.
       Nitrogen assimilation.
       Sanninoidea opalescens.

Root-pressure.

Root River Valley.

Root-rot.

Root-rot of alfalfa.
    xx Alfalfa. Diseases.

Root-rot of apple.

Root-rot of beans.
    xx Beans. Diseases.

Root-rot of camellias.
    x Camellia root-rot.
    xx Camellia. Diseases.

Root-rot of cauliflower.
    xx Califlower. Diseases.

Root-rot of cereals.
    sa Root-rot of maize.
       Root-rot of wheat.
       Root-rot of oats.
    xx Cereals. Diseases.

Root-rot of cinchona.   See Collar-rot of
  cinchona.

Root-rot of coffee.
    xx Coffee. Diseases.

Root-rot of corn.   See Root-rot of maize.

Root-rot of cotton.
    sa Phymatotrichum omnivorum.
    xx Cotton. Diseases.

Root-rot of.Douglas fir.   See Poria
  weirii.

Root-rot of flax.

Root-rot of grapes.
    xx Vine. Diseases.

Root-rot of legumes.
    xx Legumes. Diseases.

Root-rot of maize.

Root-rot of milo.
    xx Milo. Diseases.

Root-rot of oats.
    xx Root-rot of cereals.

Root-rot of orange.
    xx Orange. Diseases.

Root-rot of peas.
    xx Peas. Diseases.

Root-rot of pepper.

Root-rot of red pepper.
    xx Red pepper. Diseases.

Root-rot of pumpkin.
    xx Pumpkin. Diseases.

Root-rot of radish.

Root-rot of soy-bean.
    xx Soy-bean. Diseases.

Root-rot of sugar-beet.

Root-rot of sugar-cane.
    x Root disease of sugar-cane.
    xx Sugar-cane. Diseases.

Root-rot of sweet potatoes.
    xx Sweet potatoes. Diseases.

Root-rot of tobacco.
    xx Tobacco. Diseases.

Root-rot of vanilla.
    xx Vanilla. Diseases.

Root-rot of wheat.
    sa Browning root-rot of wheat.

Root tubercle bacteria.   See Nitrifying
   bacteria.

Root tubercle bacteria, Pure cultures of.

Root-tubercles.
   sa Nitrogens assimilation.
      Nitrification.
      Nitrifying bacteria.
   x Nodules on plants.
   xx Bacteriology.
      Bacteroids.

Root tumor.   See Roots. Diseases.

Root vegetables.   See Root-crops.

Roots.
   sa Rhizoid.
      Aerial roots.
   x Trees. Roots.
      Fruit trees. Roots.
--Bibliography.
--Collection and preservation.
      xx Plants. Collection and pre-
         servation.
--Diseases.
      x Root tumor.
         Root diseases.
         Root cancer.
      xx Vegetable pathology.
-- --Effect of burning on.
      x Burning. Effect on root
         diseases.
--Effect of defoliation on.
      x Defoliation. Effect on roots.
--Effect on soils.   See Soil. Effect of
   roots.

Rope.
   sa Cordage.
      Wire rope.
      Knots and splices.

Rope (in bread)   See Bread, Ropiness in.

Ropeways.   See Cableways.

Ropiness.   See Bread, Ropiness in.

Roque, Mexico. National Agricultural
   School.
      xx Mexico. Agriculture. Education.

Roquefort, France.
--Sheep.
      xx France. Sheep.

Rorippa nasturtium-aquaticum.
   x Nasturtium officinale.

Rosa.
   sa Roses.

Rosa candolleana.

Rosa damascena.
   x Oil rose.
   xx Oleaginous plants.

Rosa damascena trigintipetala.
   x Kazanlik rose.

Rosa multiflora.
   x Multiflora rose.

Rosa odorata.

Rosaceae.
   sa Potentilla.
      Kerria.
      Spiraea.
      Hulthemia.
      Alchemilla.
      Acaena.
      Brayera.
      Geum.
      Rosa.
      Licania.
      Filipendula.
--Bibliography.
--Diseases.
      sa Crown-gall of Rosaceae.

Rosario, Argentine Republic.
      xx Argentine Republic.
--Census.
--Commerce.
--Statistics.
      sa Rosario, Argentine Republic.
         Census.

Rosario region. Argentine Republic.
--Agriculture.

Roscommon Co., Mich.
--Soils.
      sa Subdivision Michigan. Roscommon
         Co. under: Soil-surveys.

Roscommon sheep.
   xx Sheep.

Roseau Co., Minn.
--Soils.
      sa Subdivision Minnesota. Roseau
         Co. under: Soil-surveys.

Rose-aphis.

Rose-beetle.   See Aramigus fulleri.

Rose-chafer.   See Macrodactylus sub-
   spinosus.

Rose gardens.
   xx Gardens.
--Directories.
      xx Gardens. Directories.

Rose-geranium oil.

Rose hips.
   xx Roses.

Rose jar.   See Rose pot-pourri.

Rose leaf-beetle.   See Nodonota puncticollis.

Rose leaf-hopper.   See Typhlocyba rosae.

Rose mallow.   See Hibiscus.

Rose oil.   See Attar of roses.

Rose pot-pourri.
   x Rose jar.
      Pot-pourri, Rose.
   xx Roses.

Rose slug-caterpillar.   See Euclea in-
   determina.

Roseate spoonbills.
   x Ajaia ajaja.
   xx Spoonbills.

Rosebud Co., Mont.
--Geology.
      xx Montana. Geology.
--Water, Underground.

Roselle.
   x Hibiscus sabdariffa.

Roselle (Continued)
   xx Fiber plants and vegetable
      fibers.

Rosellinia.
   xx Sphaeriaceae.

Rosemary.

Roses.
   sa Rosaceae.
      Wild roses.
      Rose hips.
      Attar of roses.
      Rose pot-pourri.
--Bibliography.
--Diseases.
      sa Anthracnose of roses.
         Streak disease of roses.
         Mosaic disease of roses.
--Exhibitions.
      xx Floriculture. Exhibitions.
--Fertilizers.   See Fertilizers for
   roses.
--Grafting.
--History.
--Marketing.
      xx Marketing.
--Packaging.
--Periodicals.
--Pests.
      sa Aphis rosae.
         Nodonota puncticollis.
         Macrodactylus subspinosus.
         Euclea indetermina.
         Macrosiphum rosae.
--Pictorial works.
      xx Flowers. Pictorial works.
--Propagation.
      xx Plant propagation.
--Pruning.
      xx Pruning.
--Societies.
--Storage.
--Spraying.   See Spraying. Roses.
--Varieties.

Roses, Wild.   See Wild roses.

Roses.
--Year-books.

Rosette disease of wheat.   See Mosaic
   disease of wheat.

Rosewood, Brazilian.   See Dicypellium
   caryophyllatum.

Rosewood, East Indian.   See Dalbergia
   latifolia.

Rosewood oil.
   xx Essences and essential oils.

Roseworth Agricultural College, Roseworthy
   South Australia.

Rosin.   See Gums and resins.
--Statistics.

Rosin acids.
      x Acids, Rosin.
         Resin acids.

Rosin-oil.
      x Resin-oil.

Ross and Cromarty, Scot.
--Agriculture.

Ross Co., Ohio.
      sa Subdivision Ohio. Ross Co.
         under: County surveys.
      xx Ohio.
--Population.
      sa Subdivision Ohio. Ross Co.
         under: Rural population.

Ross, Eng.

Rossendale Forest.

Rossitten, Germany.

Rossland, B.C.
--Maps.

Rostherne Mere, Eng.
--Entomology.
      sa Subdivision England. Rostherne
         Mere under: Lepidoptera.
--Zoology.
      sa Subdivision England. Rostherne
         Mere under: Vertebrates.

Rostov-on-Don.

Rostov Region.
--Agriculture.
--Apiculture.

Rostov Region (Continued)
--Cattle.
--Domestic animals.
-- --Bibliography.
--Forestry.
      sa Subdivision Rostov Region
         under: Afforestation and
         reforestation.
--Sheep.
--Soils.
--Swine.
--Viticulture.

Rostrella coffeae.

Rosy apple aphis.   See Anuraphis roseus.

Rot (Disease)
      xx Sheep. Diseases.

Rot of tomato.   See Tomato rots.

Rotary tillers.   See Rototillers.

Rotation.

Rotation of crops.
      sa Cropping systems.
         Travopol'naia sistema zemle-
         deliia.
      xx Soil conservation.
         Cropping systems.
--Bibliography.
--Cereals.
      x Grain rotation.
      xx Cereals.
--Cotton.
      xx Cotton.
--Flax.
      xx Flax.
--Forage plants.
      xx Forage plants.
--Fruit.
      xx Pomology.
--Grasses.
      xx Grasses.
--Legumes.
--Research.
--Rice.
--Sugar-beet.
      xx Sugar-beet.
--Tobacco.
      xx Tobacco.
--Vegetables.
      xx Vegetables.

Rotation of crops (Continued)
--Wheat.
    xx Wheat.

Rotatoria. See Rotifera.

Rotbuntes Holsteiner. See Red pied
    Holstein cattle.

Rotbuntes Schleswig-Holsteiner. See Red
    pied Holstein cattle.

Rote Vorwerk (Farm)

Rotenone.
--Prices.
--Statistics.

Rotenone as an insecticide.
    xx Insecticides.

Rothamsted Experimental Station, Harpenden,
    Eng.
    xx Fertilizers. Experiments.

Rothamstead experiments.

Rothaugezd, Bohemia.
--Agriculture.
    sa Subdivision Bohemia. Rothaugezd
        under: Agriculture. Economic
        aspects.

Rothschildia.
    xx Lepidoptera.

Rotifera.
    sa Apsilus vorax.
        Philodinidae.
        Dimophilus.
        Gastrotricha.
        Hydatina.
        Lepadella.
        Lophocharis.

Rototillers.
    x Rotary tillers.
    xx Agriculture. Implements and
        machinery.

Rots of tomato. See Tomato rots.

Rotterdam.
--Commerce.
    sa Subdivision Rotterdam under:
        Grain trade.
        Cotton trade.
-- --Statistics.
--Population.
--Statistics.

Rotting. See Decomposition.

Rottweiler dogs.

Rouen-Jardin des plantes.

Rouen.
--Milk supply.
    xx France. Milk supply.

Rough-bark disease.

Roulers, Belgium. Laboratoire provincial
    de chimie agricole.

Roumanian language. See Rumanian lan-
    guage.

Roundheaded apple-tree borer. See
    Saperda candida.

Roundworm. See Nematoidea.

Roup. See Fowl diphtheria.

Roussillon, France (Province)
--Pomology.
--Viticulture.

Routt Co., Colo.
--Water-supply.

Routt National Forest, Colorado.
    xx Colorado. Forest reservations.

Rovigo, Italy (Province)
--Agriculture.
-- --Statistics.
--Economic conditions.
-- --Periodicals.

Roving. See Cotton roving.

Rowan tree. See Sorbus aucuparia.

Royal jelly.
    x Bee jelly.
    xx Apis mellifera. Anatomy and
        physiology.

Royal palm.
    x Roystonea rigia.
    Oreodoxa rigia.
    xx Palmae.

Royan, France.
--Description and travel.

Roye, France.
--Agriculture.

Roystonea rigia.   See Royal palm.

Ruanda.
    Formerly a district of German East
    Africa; now part of Ruanda-
    Urundi Trust Territory of Bel-
    gium. All entries in this cata-
    log are under Ruanda-Urundi.

Ruanda-Urundi.
    Belgian Trust Territory, Central
    Africa. Formerly part of German
    East Africa; ceded to Belgium
    1919 as mandatary of the League
    of Nations; made a trust terri-
    tory Dec. 1946.
--Agriculture.
    sa Subdivision Ruanda-Urundi under:
        Agriculture. Economic
        aspects.
--Apiculture.
--Bibliography.
--Biography.
-- --Dictionaries.
--Botany.
--Commerce.
-- --Statistics.
--Economic conditions.
    sa Subdivision Ruanda-Urundi
        under: Geography, Economic.
--Geography.
    sa Subdivision Ruanda-Urundi under:
        Geography, Economic.
--Social conditions.
--Soils.
    sa Subdivision Ruanda-Urundi under:
        Soil-surveys.
--Statistics.
--Water-supply.

Rubber.   (DIRECT)
    sa Apocynaceae.
    Ficus elastica.
    Castilla elastica.
    Funtumia elastica.
    Hevea.
    Guayule.
    Landolphia.
    Sapium.
    Rubber producing plants, Mis-
        cellaneous.
    Mascarenhasia.
    Euphorbia intisy.
    Taraxacum kok-sagyz.
    Cryptostegia.
    Elastomers.
    Balata.
    Latex.
    Rubber goods.
    Castilla rubber.
    Goldenrod rubber.
    Guayule rubber.
    Acrylic rubber.
    Subdivision Rubber under:
        Rationing.
        Classification of books.
    x Caoutchouc.
    India-rubber.
    xx Elastomers.
--Abstracts.
--Analysis.

Rubber, Artificial.
    sa Elastomers.
    x Hycar.
    Lactoprene.
    Buna.
    Rubber, Synthetic.
    Thiokol.
    Neoprene.
    xx Elastomers.
    Synthetic products.
--Abstracts.
--Bibliography.
--Control of production.
--Patents.
-- --Bibliography.
--Periodicals.   See Rubber. Periodicals.
--Research.
--Statistics.

Rubber.
--Bibliography.
    sa Subdivision Bibliography under:
      Guayule.
      Rubber producing plants,
      Miscellaneous.
-- --Periodicals.
    xx Rubber. Periodicals.

Rubber, Castilla.   See Castilla rubber.

Rubber, Chlorinated.
    x Chlorinated rubber.
      Chloride of caoutchouc.

Rubber.
--Congresses.
    sa Subdivision Congresses under:
      Rubber industry. ·
    xx Rubber industry. Congresses.
--Control of production.
    x Rubber control.
      Rubber regulation.
    xx Commercial products. Control
      of production.
--Cost of production.
    xx Cost of production.
--Dictionaries.
    sa Subdivision Dictionaries under:
      Rubber industry.
--Diseases.   See Hevea brasiliensis.
    Diseases.
--Exhibitions.
--Fertilizers.   See Fertilizers for
    rubber.

Rubber, Goldenrod.   See Goldenrod rubber.

Rubber.
--History.
    sa Rubber industry. History.
--Marketing.
    xx Marketing.
· --Control.
    x Rubber control.
      Rubber regulation.
    xx Marketing of commercial prod-
      ucts. Control.
--Marketing, Cooperative.
--Periodicals.
    sa Subdivision Periodicals under:
    · Rubber. Bibliography.
    x Rubber, Artificial. Periodicals.
-- --Bibliography.

Rubber (Continued)
--Prices.
    sa Subdivision Prices under:
      Tires, Rubber.
--Rationing.   See Rationing. Rubber.

Rubber, Reclaimed.
    sa Rubber, Scrap.
    x Reclaimed rubber.
      Rubber reclamation.
      Rubber salvage.
    xx Rubber, Scrap.
      Salvage (Waste, etc.)
--Bibliography.
--Statistics.

Rubber.
--Research.
-- --Abstracts.
-- --Bibliography.
-- --Periodicals.
-- --Societies.

Rubber, Scrap.
    sa Rubber, Reclaimed.
    x Scrap rubber.
      Rubber waste.
      Waste rubber.
    xx Rubber Reclaimed.
      Waste products.
--Bibliography.

Rubber.
--Societies.
--Standards.
--Statistics.
    sa Rubber industry. Statistics.
-- --Bibliography.
    sa Rubber industry. Statistics.
      Bibliography.
--Substitutes.   See Rubber substitutes.

Rubber, Synthetic.   See Rubber, Arti-
    ficial.

Rubber.
--Terminology.
--Transportation.

Rubber as building material.
    xx Building materials.
      Rubber industry.

Rubber-bearing plants, Miscellaneous.
See Rubber producing plants, Miscellaneous.

Rubber cement.
    x Latex cement.
    xx Cement.

Rubber control.   See Rubber. Control of
production; Rubber. Marketing. Control.

Rubber derivatives.

Rubber goods.
    sa Gloves, Rubber.
    x Rubber products.
    xx Rubber.
        Rubber industry.
--Statistics.

Rubber industry.   (DIRECT)
    sa Rubber goods.
        Rubber as building material.
--Abstracts.
--Bibliography.
-- --Periodicals.
--Biography.
--Congresses.
    sa Rubber. Congresses.
    xx Rubber. Congresses.
--Dictionaries.
    xx Rubber. Dictionaries.
--Directories.
--Diseases and hygiene.
--Exchanges.
    xx Commodity exchanges.
--Finance.
--History.
    sa Rubber. History.
--Juvenile literature.
    xx Juvenile literature.
--Patents.
--Periodicals.   See Rubber. Periodicals.
--Safety measures.
    xx Accidents. Prevention.
--Societies.
-- --Directories.
--Statistics.
    sa Rubber. Statistics.
        Subdivision Statistics under
        Rubber industry ₍geographic
        subdivision₎ e.g., Rubber
        industry. India. Statistics.
-- --Bibliography.

Rubber latex.   See Latex.

Rubber pavements.   See Pavements, Rubber.

Rubber producing plants, Miscellaneous.
    sa Cryptostegia.
        Taraxacum kok-saghyz.
        Actinea.
    x Eucommia ulmoides.
        Carpodinus gracilis.
        Tabernaemontana.
        Rubber-bearing plants Miscel-
        laneous.
    xx Rubber.
        Asclepias.
--Bibliography.
    xx Rubber. Bibliography.
--Physiology and morphology.
--Research.

Rubber products.   See Rubber goods.

Rubber rationing.   See Rationing. Rubber.

Rubber reclamation.   See Rubber Re-
    claimed.

Rubber regulation.   See Rubber. Control
    of production; Rubber. Marketing. Con-
    trol.

Rubber roads.   See Pavements, Rubber.

Rubber salvage.   See Rubber, Reclaimed.

Rubber substitutes.
    x Rubber. Substitutes.
    xx Substitute products.

Rubber tapping.

Rubber technology.
    xx Technology.

Rubber tires.   See Tires, Rubber.

Rubber trade.   See Rubber industry.

Rubber tree Hevea.   See Hevea brasi-
    liensis.

Rubber waste.   See Rubber, Scrap.

Rubberweed.   See Actinea.

Rubiaceae.
    sa Cinchona.
       Houstonia.
       Cascarilla.
       Galium.
       Sabicea.
       Spermacoce.
       Cremaspora.
       Mitragyna.
       Adina cordifolia.
       Coprosma.
       Mussaendopsis.
       Anthocephalus.
       Sarcocephalus.

Rubidium.

Rubus.
  --Diseases.
    sa Phytomonas rubi.

Rubus macropetalus.   See Logan blackberry.

Ruddy duck.   See Erismatura jamaicensis.

Rüdersdorf, Ger.
  --Maps.

Rue-anemone.   See Syndesmon thalistroides.

Rugby, Eng.
  --Botany.
  --Natural history.

Rugby, Tenn.
  --Agriculture.
     xx Tennessee. Agriculture.

Rugs.
    x Rugs, Braided.
      Braided rugs.
    xx Arts and crafts movement.
  --Bibliography.

Rugs, Braided.   See Rugs.

Rugs, Oriental.

Rugs.
  --Repairing.
     xx Repairing.

Ruhr area.   See Ruhr River and Valley.

Ruhr occupation.   See Germany. History.
    Allied occupation.

Ruhr River and Valley.
    x Ruhr area.
  --Economic conditions.
  -- --Periodicals.
  --Industries.
  --Maps.
  --Milk supply.
     xx Germany. Milk supply.
  --Social conditions.
     xx Germany. Social conditions.

Rules of order.   See Parliamentary prac-
    tice.

Rum.
     xx Alcoholic liquors.
  --Periodicals.

Rumania.
  --Agricultural experiment stations.
    sa Bucharest. Statiunea agro-
      nomica.
      Tara. Statiunea agronomica.
  --Agriculture.
    sa Subdivision Agriculture under:
      Transylvania.
    Subdivision Rumania under:Flax.
      Wheat.
      Maize.
      Agricultural laborers.
      Agriculture. Economic
        aspects.
      Farm produce.
      Farm management.
      Agricultural policies and
        programs.
      Agriculture and business.
      Poultry.
      Farm produce. Cost of pro-
        duction.
      War and agriculture (1939-
        1945)
      Field crops.
      Farm organization.
      Agriculture, Cooperative.
      Mechanized farming.
      Irrigation farming.
     xx Europe Agriculture.
  -- --Bibliography.
     xx Europe. Agriculture. Bibliog-
      raphy.

Rumania (Continued)
--Agriculture.
-- --Education.
 sa Bucharest. Scoalei centrale de
  agricultura.
 Bucharest. Scoala superioara
  de agricultura dela hera-
  strau.
· --History.
 xx Agriculture. History.
-- --Periodicals.
-- --Statistics.
 sa Rumania. Domestic animals. Sta-
  tistics.
-- -- --Bibliography.
--Apiculture.
 sa Banat. Apiculture.
-- --Periodicals.
--Bibliography.
--Botany.
 sa Subdivision Botany under:
  Soroca, Rumania.
 Subdivision Rumania under:
  Algae.
    Vegetable pathology.
  Botany, Medical.
-- --Bibliography.
-- --Research.
--Cattle.
 xx Cattle.
--Census.
--Commerce.
 sa Subdivision Rumania under:
  Wheat trade.
-- --Periodicals.
 xx Commerce. Periodicals.
-- --Statistics.
--Commercial treaties.
--Description and travel.
--Domestic animals.
 sa Subdivision Domestic animals
  under names of regions, etc.
 Rumania. Sheep.
 xx Europe. Domestic animals.
-- --Research.
-- --Statistics.
--Economic conditions.
 sa Subdivision Economic conditions
  under: Bessarabia.
 Subdivision Rumania under:
  Geography, Economic.
-- --Periodicals.
 xx Economic conditions. Periodi-
  cals.
--Economic policy.

Rumania (Continued)
--Education.
 sa Subdivision Rumania under:
  Technical education.
--Entomology.
 sa Subdivision Entomology under:
  Transylvania.
 · Subdivision Rumania under:
  Entomology, Economic.
  Coleoptera.
  Lepidoptera.
  Locusts.
--Forestry.
-- --Research.
.--Geography.
 sa Subdivision Rumania under:
  Geography, Economic.
--Geology.
--History.
--Horse.
--Ichthyology.
--Industries.
--Land.
 sa Subdivision Rumania under:
  Land reform.
  Farm valuation.
  Land utilization.
--Language. See Rumanian language.
--Monopolies.
--Natural history.
-- --Research.
--Ornithology.
 sa Subdivision Ornithology under:
  Dobrudja, Rumania.
--Physical geography.
--Politics and government.
--Pomology.
-- --Statistics.
 xx Pomology. Statistics.
--Population.
 sa Subdivision Population under:
  Bucharest.
 xx Europe. Population.
-- --Bibliography.
--Roads.
-- --Law.
 xx Roads. Legislation.
--Sheep.
 sa Subdivision Sheep under names
  of regions, etc.
 xx Europe. Sheep.
 Rumania. Domestic animals.
--Social life and customs.
 xx Europe. Social life and
  customs.

Rumania (Continued)
--Soils.
    sa Subdivision Rumania under:
      Soil conservation.
--Statistics.
    sa Subdivision Statistics under:
      Dobrudja, Rumania.
      Moldavia.
      Rumania. Agriculture.
      Rumania. Commerce.
      Rumania. Census.
      Rumania. Monopolies.
--Viticulture.
-- --Periodicals.
--Zoology.
-- --Research.

Rumanian language.
    x Rumania. Language.
    Roumanian language.
--Dictionaries.
--Glossaries, vocabularies, etc.

Rumanian literature.
--Bibliography.

Rumanian periodicals.
--Bibliography.

Rumen.
    xx Stomach.
    Ruminantia. Anatomy and
      physiology.

Rumenotomy.
    xx Veterinary surgery.

Rumex.

Rumex acetosella.

Rumex crispus.

Rumex hymenosepalus. See Canaigre.

Rumex magellanicus.
    x Rumex patientia.

Rumex patientia. See Rumex magellanicus.

Ruminantia.
    sa Antelopes.
    Musk-ox.
    Bison.
    Buffaloes.

Ruminantia (Continued)
    sa Camels.
    Cattle.
    Deer.
    Giraffes.
    Goats.
    Llamas.
    Sheep.
    xx Mammalia.
    Artiodactyla.
--Anatomy and physiology.
    sa Rumen.
--Diseases.
    sa Bloat in ruminants.
--Feeding.
--Nutrition.
--Parasites.
    xx Parasites.

Rumination.

Run-off.
    x Runoff.
    xx Hydrology.
    Stream measurements.
    Drainage.

Rundøy, Norway.
--Botany.
    xx Norway. Botany.

Runnels Co., Tex.
--Geology.

Runner ducks. See Indian runner ducks.

Runoff. See Run-off.

Runsten, Sweden.
--Botany.

Rupela.
    xx Pyralididae.

Ruphyllin.

Rupicapra tragus. See Chamois.

Ruppia Maritima.
    x Paspalum scrobiculatum.

Ruptures. See Hernia.

Rural architecture. See Farm buildings.

Rural arts.   See Art, Rural.

Rural charities.   See Social service,
    Rural.

Rural churches.   (INDIRECT)
    sa Missions, Agricultural.
       Rural clergy.
       Federated churches.
    xx Missions, Agricultural.
--Bibliography.
--Congresses.
--Finance.
    xx Church finance.
--Periodicals.

Rural clergy.
    x Rural pastors.
    xx Clergy.
       Rural churches.
--Salaries, pensions, etc.
    xx Salaries.

Rural community organization.   See Rural
    organization.

Rural credit.   See Agricultural credit.

Rural dental service.   See Dental service,
    Rural.

Rural development program.
    xx Agricultural policies and
       programs.
--Congresses.

Rural education.   See Education, Rural.

Rural electric cooperative associations.
    See Electric cooperative associations,
    Rural.

Rural electrification.   (DIRECT)
    Beginning March 5, 1946 this sub-
    ject will be used for publica-
    tions on the extension of elec-
    tric service to both farms and
    rural communities. Before March
    5, 1946 such publications were
    covered by the subjects Elec-
    tricity in agriculture and Elec-
    tricity in rural communities.
    sa Electricity in rural communities.
       Electricity in agriculture.
    x Electrification, Rural.

Rural electrification (Continued)
    xx Electricity in agriculture.
       Electric power distribution.
       Electric utilities.
--Abstracts.
-- --Periodicals.
--Accounting.
--Bibliography.
-- --Periodicals.
--Congresses.
--Finance.
    sa Subdivision Finance under:
       Electric cooperative-asso-
       ciations, Rural.
    xx Electric industries. Finance.
--Indexes.
--Legislation.
    xx Law.
--Periodicals.
--Policies and programs.
    xx Agricultural policies and
       programs.
--Research.
--Societies.
    sa Electric cooperative associa-
       tions, Rural.
--Statistics.
    sa Rural electrification [country
       subdivision] Statistics,
       e.g., Rural electrification.
       U.S. Statistics.
--Study and teaching.

Rural electrification act.
    x R.E.A. act.

Rural engineering.   See Agricultural en-
    gineering.

Rural exodus.   (INDIRECT)
    sa Rural population.
    x Farm abandonment.
       Migration from farms.
       Rural migration.
--Addresses, essays, lectures.
--Bibliography.

Rural fiction.   See Fiction, Agricul-
    tural.

Rural fraternal organizations.   See
    Fraternal organizations, Rural.

Rural free delivery.

Rural government.   See County government;
    Local government.

Rural health.   See Hygiene, Rural.

Rural health service.   See Medical
    service, Rural.

Rural hospitals.   See Hospitals, Rural.

Rural housing.   See Housing, Rural.

Rural hygiene.   See Hygiene, Rural.

Rural indebtedness.   See Agricultural
    indebtedness.

Rural industries.   (INDIRECT)
    sa Handicraft.
    x Industry, Rural.
      Industries, Rural.
    xx Industry.
--Bibliography.

Rural league.

Rural libraries.
    sa Libraries, County.
    x Libraries, Rural.
    xx Libraries.
      Libraries, County.
--Bibliography.
    xx Libraries. Bibliography.

Rural life.   See Country life; Farm life.

Rural medical care.   See Medical service,
    Rural.

Rural medicine.   See Medical service,
    Rural.

Rural migration.   See Rural exodus.

Rural organization.
    sa Rural organization extension
      work.
    x Rural community organization.
    xx Community life.
--Bibliography.
--History.
    xx History.

Rural organization extension work.
    x Extension work in rural
      organization.
    xx Rural organization.

Rural pastors.   See Rural clergy.

Rural poetry.   See Agriculture. Poetry.

Rural population.   (INDIRECT)
    sa Rural exodus.
      Migrant labor.
    x Farm population.
    xx Population.
--Bibliography.
    sa Rural population [country
      subdivision] Bibliography,
      e.g., Rural population.
      U.S. Bibliography.
    xx Population. Bibliography.
--Research.
-- --Congresses.
    xx Research. Congresses.
      Population. Congresses.
--Statistics.
    sa Subdivision Statistics under
      Rural population [geo-
      graphic subdivision] e.g.,
      Rural population. Formosa.
      Statistics.
    xx Population. Statistics.

Rural psychology.   See Psychology,
    Rural.

Rural public welfare.   See Social
    service, Rural.

Rural reconstruction.   See Rehabilita-
    tion, Rural.

Rural recreation.   See Recreation,
    Rural.

Rural rehabilitation.   See Rehabilita-
    tion, Rural.

Rural restoration.   See Rehabilitation,
    Rural.

Rural school fairs.
    xx Agriculture. Fairs and
      expositions.

Rural schools.   (INDIRECT)
    sa Education, Rural.
    School management and organi-
        zation.
    x Schools, Rural.
    xx Schools.
        Education, Rural.
--Bibliography.
--Congresses.
--Curricula.
    xx Education. Curricula.
--Periodicals.
--Sanitary affairs.

Rural sewerage.   See Sewerage, Rural.

Rural social programs.   See Social
    service, Rural.

Rural social service.   See Social service,
    Rural.

Rural sociology.   See Sociology, Rural.

Rural sociology extension work.
    sa Family life extension work.
    x Extension work in rural
        sociology.
    xx Sociology, Rural.
--Directories.

Rural surveys.   (DIRECT)
    When subdivided by place, indicate
        see also ref. from name of
        place with subdivisions: Agri-
        culture; Economic conditions;
        Social conditions.
    xx Economic surveys.
--Periodicals.

Rural teachers.   (INDIRECT)
    xx Teachers.

Rural telephone.   See Telephone, Rural.

Rural telephone cooperatives.
    xx Electric cooperative associa-
        tions, Rural.
        Telephone, Rural.

Rural-urban relationships.   (DIRECT)
    x Urban-rural relationships.
    xx Agriculture. Economic aspects.
        Agriculture and business.
        Community life.

Rural water-supply.   See Water-supply,
    Rural.

Rural young folk.   See Youth in rural
    communities.

Rural youth.   See Youth in rural com-
    munities.

Rural youth act.   See 4-H club and
    rural youth act.

Rural zoning.   See Planning County.
    Zone system.

Ruralidae.

Rurick (Ship)

Ruscus.

Rusguniella.

Rush (Botany)   See Juncaceae.

Rush, Flowering.   See Butomus umbellatus

Rush Co., Ind.
--Agriculture.
-- --Periodicals.
--Soils.
        sa Subdivision Indiana. Rush Co.
            under: Soil-surveys.

Rush nut.   See Chufa.

Rushes (Botany)   See Juncaceae.

Rushmore, Minn.
        sa Subdivision Minnesota.
            Rushmore under: World
                War, 1939-1945.
--Social conditions.
        sa Subdivision Minnesota.
            Rushmore under: Social
                surveys.

Rusk (Bread)
        xx Dried bread.

Rusk Co., Wis.
        xx Wisconsin.

Russ (Pony)   See Gotland pony.

Russell Co., Va.
    sa Subdivision Russell Co. under:
        County surveys. Virginia.
--Agriculture.
    sa Subdivision Russell Co., Va.
        under: Farm management.
    Subdivision Virginia. Russell
        Co. under: Types of farming.
    Agriculture. Economic as-
        pects.
    xx Virginia. Agriculture.
--Cattle.
    xx Virginia. Cattle.
--Economic conditions.
    sa Subdivision Russell Co. under:
        Economic surveys. Virginia.
        Farm management.
        County surveys. Virginia.
    xx Virginia.
        Virginia. Agriculture.
        Virginia. Economic conditions.
--Forestry.
--Geology.
--Industries and resources.
    sa Industrial surveys. Virginia.
        Russell Co.
--Social conditions.
    sa Subdivision Virginia. Russell
        Co. under: Social surveys.
--Soils.
    sa Subdivision Virginia. Russell
        Co. under: Soil-surveys.

Russell hybrids.   See Lupinus polyphyllus.

Russell Sage Foundation.
--Bibliography.

Russia.
    Used for subjects concerning the
    Russian Empire (to Mar. 1917);
    the provisional governments
    (Mar. 1917-1922) and the Russian
    Socialist Federated Soviet Re-
    public (RSFSR) For subjects
    concerning Soviet Russia (1923-
) use U.S.S.R.
--Agricultural experiment stations.
    sa Plotianskaia sel'skokhoziaist-
        vennaia stantsïia.
    Riga. Landwirthschaftlich
        chemische versuchs-und samen-
        control station.
    Verkhosunkaia ferma//

Russia (Continued)
--Agricultural schools.   See Russia.
    Agriculture. Education; Petrograd.
    Agronomicheskii institut; Saratov.
    Sel'skokhoziaistvennyi institut.
--Agriculture.
    sa Subdivision Agriculture under:
        Kursk, Russia.
        Transcaspian District.
        Don, Russia//
    Russia. Soils.
    Russia. Domestic animals.
    Khourorok-Tereshchenko es-
        tates.
    Subdivision Russia under:
        Cotton.
        Wheat.
        Agricultural laborers.
        Agriculture. Economic as-
        pects.
        Colonization, Agricultural.
        Reclamation of land.
        Flax.
        Maize.
        Farm buildings.
        Poultry.
        Sugar-beet.
        Farm produce.
        Agricultural policies and
        programs.
        Cropping systems.
        Potatoes.
        Cereals.
        Drug plants.
        Farms.
        Farm management.
        Field crops.
-- --Bibliography.
    sa Subdivision Agriculture. Bib-
        liography under: Ukraine.
-- --Education.
    sa Moscow. Sel'skokhoziaistvennyi
        institut.
    Petrovsk. Sel'skokhoziaist-
        vennaia akademiia.
    Caucasus. Agricultural
        schools//
-- --History.
    sa Subdivision Agriculture. His-
        tory under: Union of So-
        cialist Soviet Republics.
    Ukraine. Agriculture. His-
        tory.

Russia (Continued)
--Agriculture.
-- --History.
-- -- --Bibliography.
    xx Europe. Agriculture. History.
      Bibliography.
-- --Periodicals.
-- --Statistics.
    sa Subdivision Agriculture. Sta-
      tistics under: Kharkov.
      Transcaucasia.
      Ufa//
    xx Agriculture. Statistics.
-- --Study and teaching.
--Apiculture.
    sa Subdivision Apiculture under:
      Caucasus.
    xx Europe. Apiculture.
--Bibliography.
--Botanic gardens.
    sa Gorenki. Botanic garden.
--Botany.
    sa Subdivision Botany under:
      Balkan Provinces.
      Caucasus.
      Crimea//
      Subdivision Russia under:
      Fungi.
      Trees.
      Shrubs.
      Vegetable pathology.
      Weeds.
      Botany, Medical.
-- --Bibliography.
-- --History.
--Cattle.
    sa Subdivision Cattle under:
      Aginsk Steppe.
    xx Cattle.
-- --Periodicals.
--Cattle trade.
--Census.
    sa Subdivision Census under:
      White Russia.
--Climate.
    sa Subdivision Climate under:
      Poltava district, Russia.
      Nizhnii-Novogord (Govern-
        ment)//
--Colonies.
    sa Siberia.
-- --Agriculture.
--Commerce.
    sa Subdivision Commerce under:
      Kherson.

Russia (Continued)
--Commerce.
-- --Periodicals.
-- --Statistics.
    sa Subdivision Commerce. Sta-
      tistics under: U.S.S.R.
--Commercial treaties.
--Cyclopedias.
--Dairying.
    sa Subdivision Dairying under:
      Vologda.
--Description and travel.
    sa Subdivision Description and
      travel under: Caucasus.
      Daghestan.
      Crimea//
      Hunting. Russia.
--Domestic animals.
    sa Russia. Cattle.
      Russia. Sheep.
      Russia. Swine.
      Subdivision Domestic animals
        under: Caucasus.
-- --Research.
-- --Statistics.
    sa Subdivision Domestic animals.
      Statistics under: Minsk
        (Government)
--Economic conditions.
    sa Subdivision Economic condi-
      tions under: Siberia.
      U.S.S.R.
      Ozero//
-- --Periodicals.
--Economic policy.
    sa Subdivision Economic policy
      under: U.S.S.R.
-- --Five-year plan (1928-1932) See
    U.S.S.R. Economic policy. Five-
    year plan (1928-1932)
--Education.
    sa Russia. Agriculture. Educa-
      tion.
--Entomology.
    sa Subdivision Entomology under:
      Tula, Russia.
      Baltic Provinces.
      Ingermanland//

Russia (Continued)
--Entomology.
    sa Subdivision Russia under:
      Entomology, Economic.
      Pseudoneuroptera.
      Coleoptera.
      Lepidoptera.
      Orthoptera.
      Diptera.
      Heteroptera.
      Hemiptera.
      Trees. Pests.
-- --Bibliography.
    sa Subdivision Entomology. Bib-
      liography under: U.S.S.R.
--Famines.
--Fisheries.
--Foreign relations. See U.S.S.R.
    Foreign relations.
-- --Treaties.
    sa Brest-Litovsk, Treaty of,
      March 3, 1918.
--Forestry.
    sa Russia. Liesnoi departement.
      U.S.S.R. Forestry.
      Subdivision Russia under:
      Afforestation and re-
        forestation.
      Trees.
-- --Bibliography.
-- --History.
-- --Research.
-- --Statistics.
--Geodesy.
--Geology.
--History.
    sa History, Economic. Russia.
      U.S.S.R. History.
      History, Economic. U.S.S.R.
--Horse.
    sa Subdivision Russia under:
      Horses. Breeding.
--Ichthyology.
--Industries and resources.
--Land.
    sa Subdivision Russia under:
      Land laws.
      Land reform.
      Farm valuation.
      Land utilization.
    xx Europe. Land.
--Language. See Russian language.
--Manufactures.

Russia (Continued)
--Maps.
    sa Subdivision Maps under:
      U.S.S.R.
      Siberia.
--Maritime Province. See Primorskaia
    (Province)
--Meteorology.
    sa Subdivision Meteorology under:
      Caucasus//
--Natural history.
    sa Subdivision Natural history
      under: Viatka.
      Voronezh.
      Don Valley//
    xx Europe. Natural history.
--Ornithology.
    sa Subdivision Ornithology under:
      Kazan, Russia.
      Crimea.
      U.S.S.R.
      Subdivision Russia under:
      Game-birds.

Russia. Osoboe sovieshchanie o nuzhdakh
    sel'skokhoziaistvennoi promyshlennosti,
    1902-1905.

Russia.
--Paleobotany.
--Paleontology.
    sa Subdivision Paleontology under:
      Baltic Provinces.
--Parks.
--Politics and government.
    sa Subdivision Russia under:
      Administrative and political
        divisions.
--Pomology.
    sa Subdivision Pomology under:
      Kazan, Russia.
      Chernomorsk.
      Kuban.
      U.S.S.R.
 --History.
    xx Pomology. History.
--Railroads.
--Roads.
    sa Subdivision Roads under:
      U.S.S.R.

Russia (Continued)
--Roads.
-- --Law.
    xx Roads. Legislation.
--Sericulture.
--Sheep.
    sa Subdivision Sheep under:
        U.S.S.R.
--Social conditions.
    sa Social conditions under:
        U.S.S.R.
--Soils.
    sa Subdivision Soils under:
        Peterhof.
        Mugan Steppe.
        Don Valley//
        Chernozem soils.
        Subdivision Russia under: Peat.
        Soil conservation.
--Statistics.
    sa Subdivision Statistics under:
        Russia. Agriculture.
        Russia. Census.
        Russia. Commerce.
        U.S.S.R.
        Ukraine.
        White Russia.
        Irkutsk.
        Siberia.
-- --Bibliography.
--Swine.
    xx Russia. Domestic animals.
-- --Periodicals.
--Viticulture.
    sa Subdivision Viticulture under:
        Caucasus//
--Water-supply.
    sa Subdivision Water-supply under:
        Caucasus.
        Don Valley.
--Zoology.
    sa Subdivision Zoology under:
        Petrograd, Russia (Govern-
          ment)
        U.S.S.R.
        Kola Bay.
        Volga Region.
        Saratov (Government)
        Orlov (Government)
        Severo-Dvinskoe (Govern-
          ment)
        Ural Mountains.

Russia (Continued)
--Zoology.
    sa Subdivision Russia under:
        Arachnida.
        Mammalia.
        Batrachia.
        Reptilia.

Russia, Asiatic. See U.S.S.R., Asiatic.

Russia, Northwest.
--Agriculture.
-- --Periodicals.

Russia, Tropical.
--Agriculture.

Russia, White. See White Russia.

Russia in Asia. See U.S.S.R., Asiatic.

Russian comfrey. See Comfrey.

Russian dandelion. See Taraxacum kok-
    saghyz.

Russian dictionaries. See Russia. Lan-
    guage. Dictionaries.

Russian fiction.
    sa Short stories, Russian.

Russian knapweed. See Centaurea repens.

Russian language.
    x Russia. Language.
--Chrestomathies and readers.
--Dictionaries.
    x Russian dictionaries.
-- --Bibliography.
--Glossaries, vocabularies, etc.
    xx Vocabulary.
--Grammar.
--Transliteration. See Slavic lan-
    guages. Transliteration.

Russian literature.
--Bibliography.
-- --Periodicals.
--Information services.

Russian newspapers.
--Bibliography.

Russian occupation of Poland. See
    Poland. History. Occupation, 1939-1945.

Russian olive. See Elaeagnus angusti-
    folia.

Russian periodicals.
    x U.S.S.R. Periodicals.
    --Bibliography.
    -- --Union lists.
    --Indexes.

Russian propaganda. See Propaganda.
    Russian.

Russian satellites. See U.S.S.R. bloc.

Russian thistle.
    x Salsola kali var. tenuifolia.

Russian thistle as feeding stuff.

Russian wild-rye. See Elymus junceus.

Russians in Central Asia.

Russians in the United States.

Russula.

Rust. See Corrosion and anti-corrosives.

Rust (Botany) See Uredineae.

Rust fungi. See Uredineae.

Rust in barley. See Barley rust.

Rust in beans. See Bean rust.

Rust in cereals. See Cereal rust.

Rust in flax. See Flax rust.

Rust in pine. See Pine rust.

Rust in wheat. See Wheat rust.

Rust-mites. See Phyllocoptes.

Rusts. See Uredineae.

Rusty blotch of barley.
    xx Barley. Diseases.

Rusty plum aphid. See Hysteroneura
    setariae.

Rusty tussock moth. See Notolophus
    antiqua.

Rut. See Estrus.

Ruta.

Rutabaga.
    sa Brassica.
        Cookery (Rutabaga)
        x Swedes (Vegetable)
    --Breeding.
        xx Vegetables. Breeding.
    --Composition.
        xx Vegetables. Composition.
    --Diseases.

Rutabaga, Dried. See Dried rutabaga.

Rutabaga,
    --Drying.
        xx Drying of fruits and vege-
            tables.
    --Fertilizers. See Fertilizers for
        rutabagas.
    --Grading and standardization.
        sa Subdivision Grading and
            standardization under:
            Dried rutabaga.
        xx Vegetables. Grading and
            standardization.
    --Storage.

Rutaceae.
    sa Ruta.
        Casimiroa.
        Esenbeckia.
        Poncirus.
        Feronia.
        Microcitrus.
        Merope.
        Pilocarpus.
        Diosma.
        Galipea.
        Citrus.
        Flindersia.
        x Aurantiaceae.
    --Pests.
        xx Entomology, Economic.

Rutaceous plants.
--Disease resistance.
    xx Disease resistant plants.

Rutelidae.   See Scarabaeidae.

Ruthenian language.   See Ukrainian language.

Rutherford Co., N.C.
--Soils.
    sa Subdivision North Carolina.
       Rutherford Co. under:
       Soil-surveys.

Rutherford Co., Tenn.
    xx Tennessee.
--Hygiene.
--Soils.

Rutherglen bug.   See Nysius vinitor.

Rutin.   See Vitamins (P)

Rutland, Eng.
--Zoology.

Rutlandshire, Eng.
--Agriculture.

Ruurlo.
--Economic conditions.
--Social conditions.

Ruwenzori Mountains.
--Botany.
--Entomology.
    xx Africa, East. Entomology.

Ruysselede. École agricole de réforme des
    garçons.
    xx Belgium. Agriculture. Education.

Ryania as an insecticide.

Ryder, N.D.

Rye.   (INDIRECT)
    sa Bran.
--Acreage adjustments.
    x Rye. Control of production.
    xx Acreage adjustments.

Rye (Continued)
--Bibliography.
    sa Subdivision Bibliography under:
       Rye. Cost of production.
       Rye. Breeding.
--Breeding.
-- --Bibliography.
    xx Rye. Bibliography.
       Cereals. Breeding. Bibliography.
--Cleaning.
--Control of production.   See Rye.
    Acreage adjustments.
--Cost of production.
-- --Bibliography.
--Disease resistant varieties.
    xx Disease resistant plants.
--Diseases.
    sa Mosaic disease of rye.
       Powdery mildew of rye.
       Rye rust.
       Fusarium diseases of rye.
--Dockage.
    xx Dockage.
--Estimating of crop.
    xx Cereals. Estimating of crop.
--Fertilizers.   See Fertilizers for
    rye.
--Financing.
--Grading and standardization.

Rye, Green.
--Effect on milk.   See Milk. Effect of
    green rye.

Rye.
--Growth.
--Hardiness.
--Hybrids.
    sa Wheat-rye hybrids.
       Rye.
       Haynaldia hybrids.
--Laws and legislation.
--Marketing.
    xx Cereals. Marketing.
--Milling and baking qualities.
--Morphology.   See Rye. Physiology and
    morphology.
--Nutritive value.   See Rye as feeding
    stuff.
--Pests.
    sa Cecidomyia secalina.
--Physiology and morphology.
    x Rye. Morphology.

Rye (Continued)
--Prices.
-- --Subsidies.

Rye, Proteins in.

Rye.
--Seed.
--Statistics.
--Steaming.

Rye, Stearic acid in.

Rye.
--Teratology.
    xx Abnormalities (Plants)
--Transportation.
    xx Grain transportation.
--Varieties.
    xx Cereals. Varieties.
--Weather influences.
    x Weather. Effect on rye.
--Weights and measures.

Rye as culture media.
    xx Bacteriology. Cultures and
        culture media.

Rye as feeding stuff.
    x Rye. Nutritive value.
    xx Feeding stuffs.

Rye bran.

Rye flour.

Rye gall-gnat.   See Cecidomyia secalina.

Rye germ.

Rye grass.   See Lolium perenne.

Rye-Haynaldia hybrids.

Rye meal.
    xx Meal.

Rye products.
--Statistics.

Rye rust.
    x Leaf rust of rye.
    xx Rye. Diseases.

Rye seed.

Rye seedlings.
--Effect of nitrogen compounds.   See
    Nitrogen compounds. Effect on rye
    seedlings.

Rye trade.   (DIRECT)
--Futures.
    xx Grain trade. Futures.

Rye yields.
    xx Crop yields.

Ryegrass.   See Lolium.

Rygja sheep.

Ryukyu Islands.
    x Riu Kiu Islands.
      Liu Kiu Islands.
--Agriculture.
    sa Subdivision Ryukyu Islands
        under: Agricultural poli-
            cies and programs.
            Crops and climate.
-- --Statistics.
--Botany.
--Census.
--Climate.
    sa Subdivision Ryukyu Islands
        under: Crops and climate.
--Economic conditions.
--Forestry.
--Geology.
--Ichthyology.
--Industries.
--Ornithology.
--Physical geography.
--Population.
--Statistics.

SALTE plan.

SPM.   See Serum of pregnant mares.

SRB (Sweden)   See Swedish red and white
    cattle.

STS.   See Machine-tractor stations
    (Czechoslovak Republic)

S-W radio.   See Radio, Short wave.

SZHK.   See Serum of pregnant mares.

Saanen goats.   See Goats, Saanen.

Saar.
--Agriculture.
    sa Subdivision Saar under:
        Agriculture. Economic as-
        pects.
--Census.
    xx Germany. Census.
--Economic conditions.
--Maps.

Saar Basin Territory.
--Dairying.
    xx Europe. Dairying.
--Economic conditions.

Saaz, Bohemia.

Sabacide.
    xx Sabadilla as an insecticide.

Sabadilla as an insecticide.
    sa Sabacide.

Sabal causiarum.
--Diseases.
    xx Palmae. Diseases.

Sabal serrulata.
    sa Saw palmetto.

Sabal uresana.   See Palmetto.

Sabellariidae.
    xx Annelida.

Sabi Game Reserve, Transvaal.   See Kruger
    National Park, Transvaal.

Sabiaceae.

Sabicea.

Sabina herba.   See Juniperus sabina.

Sabine Co., Tex.
    xx Texas.

Sabine herb.   See Juniperus sabina.

Sabine-Neches Canal.
    xx Canals.

Sable.
    xx Fur-bearing animals.

Sablefish.

Sabotage.   (DIRECT)
    x Subversive activities.
      World War, 1939-1945. Sabotage.
--Bibliography.

Sabots.

Sac Co., Iowa.
--Soils.
    sa Subdivision Iowa. Sac Co. un-
        der: Soil-surveys.

Sacadodes pyralis.
    xx Cotton. Pests.

Sacaline.

Sacaton, Ariz. Cooperative Testing Sta-
    tion.   See Sacaton Field Station,
    Sacaton, Ariz.

Sacaton Field Station, Sacaton, Ariz.
    x Sacaton, Ariz. Cooperative
      Testing Station.
    xx U.S. Dept. of Agriculture.
      Bureau of Plant Industry.

Sacbrood.

Saccharic acid.

Saccharides.

Saccharification.
    sa Wood saccharification.

Saccharimeter.

Saccharin.
    xx Sweeteners, Synthetic.
--Bibliography.

Saccharine products.
    xx Sweeteners, Synthetic.

Saccharinic acids.

Saccharomyces.
    sa Yeast.
    xx Saccharomycetaceae.

Saccharomyces cerevisiae.   See Yeast.

Saccharomyces ellipsoideus.

Saccharomycetaceae.
    sa Zygosaccharomyces.
       Nadsonia.
       Schizosaccharomyces.
       Saccharomyces.
       Rhodotorula.

Saccharose.
--Determination.

Saccharum.
    xx Gramineae.
--Cytology.
--Physiology and morphology.

Saccharum barberi.

Saccharum officinarum.   See Sugar-cane.

Saccharum sinense.

Saccharum spontaneum.

Saccogynaceae.
    sa Plagiochila.

Saccomyidae.
    sa Perognathus.

Sacculmic acid.
    xx Acids.

Sachalin.   See Saghalin (Island)

Sachaline.   See Sacaline.

Sachsen.   See Saxony.

Sachsse-Kormann method.

Sackenia gibbosa.

Sacks.   See Bags.

Sacramento, Calif.
--Botany.
    sa Subdivision California. Sacra-
       mento under: Trees.
         Shrubs.
--Forestry.
    sa Subdivision California. Sacra-
       mento under: Trees.
         Shrubs.

Sacramento, Calif. (Continued)
--Geology.
    sa Subdivision California. Sacra-
       mento under: Water, Under-
         ground.
--Parks.

Sacramento Co., Calif.
--Domestic animals.

Sacramento River.
    sa Subdivision Sacramento River
       under: Flood control.
       Floods.

Sacramento Valley, Calif.
    xx Central Valley, Calif.
--Agriculture.
    sa Subdivision California. Sacra-
       mento Valley under: Rice.
        Irrigation.
-- --Periodicals.
--Geology.
--Water-supply.
    sa Subdivision California. Sacra-
       mento Valley under: Water,
        Underground.
       Subdivision Water-supply under:
        Putah Creek area, Calif.

Sacred mushroom of the Aztecs.   See
    Lophophora williamsii.

Saddle horses.
    sa American saddle horse.
    xx Horses.
--History.
    xx Horses. History.
--Periodicals.

Saddleback pig.   See Wessex saddleback
    pig.

Saddles.
    xx Leather industry and trade.

Safes.

Safety.   See Accidents. Prevention.

Safety appliances.
    sa Subdivision Safety appliances
        under: Electric power-plants.
        Refrigeration and refrig-
          erating machinery.
        Factories.
        Chemical industries.
    x Safety equipment.
--Directories.
--Statistics.

Safety clothing. See Clothing, Protec-
    tive.

Safety education.
    sa Accidents. Prevention.
    xx Education.
--Bibliography.
    xx Accidents. Prevention. Bibliog-
        raphy.
--Periodicals.

Safety engineering. See Accidents. Pre-
    vention.

Safety equipment. See Safety appliances.

Safety films. See Moving-pictures in
    safety education.

Safety measures. See Accidents. Preven-
    tion (for general works); Subdivision
    Safety measures under specific subjects,
    e.g., Forestry. Safety measures.

Safety zones. See Roads. Safety measures.

Safflower.
    x Carthamus tinctorius.
    xx Oleaginous plants.
--Bibliography.
--Diseases.
    xx Vegetable pathology.
--Seed.

Safflower oil.

Saffordia.

Saffron.
--Diseases.
--Varieties.

Safole.

Sag channel.

Saga-ken, Japan.
--Agriculture.
    sa Subdivision Saga-ken, Japan
        under: Farm management.
        Subdivision Japan. Saga-ken
        under: Rice.
--Soils.
    sa Subdivision Japan. Saga-ken
        under: Soil-surveys.

Sage. See Salvia.

Sagebrush. See Artemisia.

Sagenopteris.

Sageretia.

Saghalien. See Saghalin (Island)

Saghalin (Island)
    x Saghalien.
      Sachalin.
      Sakhalin.
--Agriculture.
--Botany.
--Entomology.
    xx Asia. Entomology.
--Forestry.
--Ornithology.

Saginaw Co., Mich.
--Agriculture.
    sa Subdivision Michigan. Saginaw
        Co. under: Agricultural la-
        borers.
    xx Michigan. Agriculture.
--Soils.
    sa Subdivision Michigan. Saginaw
        Co. under: Soil-surveys.

Saginaw Forest, Mich.
    xx Demonstration forests.
      Michigan. University. School
        of Forestry and Conserva-
        tion.

Saginaw silo.

Saginaw Valley, Mich.
    sa Subdivision Michigan. Saginaw
        Valley under: Flood control.

Saginaw Valley, Mich. (Continued).
--Agriculture.
        sa Subdivision Michigan. Saginaw
            Valley under: Colonization,
            Agricultural.
--Antiquities.

Sagitta bipunctata.

Sagittaria.
        x Arrow head.
        xx Alismataceae.

Sagittaria eatoni.

Sagittaria variabilis.

Sago.
        xx Starch.
--Tariff.
--Taxation.

Saguaro.   See Cereus giganteus.

Sahara.
        sa Libyan Desert.
            Mzab.
            Laghouat.
        x Algerian Sahara.
--Agriculture.
        sa Subdivision Sahara under:
            Wheat.
--Botany.
--Forestry.
--Geology.
        xx Africa. Geology.
--Maps.
--Ornithology.
        xx Ornithology.
            Africa. Ornithology.
--Physical geography.
--Soils.
--Water-supply.
--Zoology.

Saharanpur, India.
--Botanical garden.

Sahlbergella singularis.

Sahune sheep.   See Préalpes du Sud sheep.

Saidapet Experiment Farm, Madras, India.

Sain.   See Terminalia tomentosa.

Sainfoin.
        xx Onobrychis.
--Varieties.

St. Augustine grass.   See Stenotaphrum
    secundatum.

St. Bartholomew.
--Botany.

St. Bernard dogs.
--Periodicals.

Saint Bernard, Great.
--Botany.

St. Charles Co., Mo.
        sa Subdivision St. Charles Co.
            under: Agricultural la-
            borers. Missouri.
            Subdivision St. Charles Co.,
            Mo. under: Labor and la-
            boring classes.
--Soils.
        sa Subdivision Missouri. St.
            Charles Co. under: Soil-
            surveys.

St. Christopher.   See St. Kitts.

St. Clair Co., Ala.
--Economic conditions.
--Industries and resources.
        sa Industrial surveys. Alabama.
            St. Clair Co.

St. Clair Co., Ill.
        xx Illinois.
--Agriculture.
        sa Subdivision St. Clair Co. un-
            der: Agriculture. Economic
            aspects. Illinois.
        xx Illinois. Agriculture.

St. Clair Co., Mich.
--Soils.
        sa Subdivision Michigan. St.
            Clair Co. under: Soil-
            surveys.

St. Clair River.

Saint Croix.   See Santa Cruz.

St. Croix Co., Wis.
    xx Wisconsin.

St. David's, Wales.
--Botany.

St. Denis, Quebec. (Kamouraska Co.)
--Social life and customs.
    xx Quebec (Province) Social life
        and customs.

Saint-Domingue.   See Dominican Republic.

St. Francis Dam, Calif.
    xx California. Water-supply.

St. Francis River.
    sa Subdivision St. Francis River
        under: Flood control.

St. Gall (Canton) Switzerland.
--Agriculture.
    sa Subdivision St. Gall (Canton)
        under: Grasses. Switzerland.
--Botany.
--Climate.
--Forestry.
--Statistics.
--Antiquities.
    xx Missouri. Antiquities.

St. George, Kan.
    sa Subdivision Kansas. St. George
        under: Social surveys.

Saint-Georges-d'Orques, Près Montpellier.

Saint-Gironnaise cattle.

St. Gotthard Tunnel.

St. Helena.
--Census.
--Entomology.
    sa Subdivision St. Helena under:
        Coleoptera.

Saint Helena Island, S.C.
    sa Subdivision Saint Helena Is-
        land, S.C. under: Negroes.
    xx South Carolina.

St. Helen's Island, Quebec.
--Paleontology.

St. Hilaire-sur-Helpe, France.

St. Joe, Ark.
--Paleontology.

St. Joe National Forest, Idaho.
    xx Idaho. Forest reservations.

St. John, Lake.   See Lake St. John,
    Quebec.

St. John River, N.B.
--Botany.

St. John's River, Fla.

St. Johnswort.   See Hypericum.

St. Joseph, Mo.
--Statistics.

St. Joseph Co., Ind.
    xx Indiana.
--Agriculture.
--Milk trade.
--Soils.
    sa Subdivision Indiana. St.
        Joseph Co. under: Soil-
        surveys.

St. Josephs Bay, Fla.
    xx Florida.

St. Kitts.
--Agriculture.
    sa Subdivision St. Kitts under:
        Sugar-cane.
    xx West Indies (Brit.) Agri-
        culture.

Saint-Laurent Chabreuges, France.
--Agriculture.
    sa Subdivision France. Saint-
) Laurent Chabreuges under:
        Agriculture. Economic
        aspects.
  --History.

St. Lawrence Co., N.Y.
--Agriculture.
    xx New York (State) Agriculture.
--Dairying.
    xx New York (State) Dairying.

St. Lawrence Co., N.Y. (Continued)
--Soils.
    sa Subdivision New York (State)
      St. Lawrence Co. under:
      Soil-surveys.

St. Lawrence Island, Alaska.
--Botany.
    xx Alaska. Botany.
--Ornithology.

St. Lawrence navigation and power project.
    See St. Lawrence Waterway.

St. Lawrence project.   See St. Lawrence
    Waterway.

St. Lawrence Reservation, N.Y.

St. Lawrence River.
--Bibliography.
--Bridges.
    sa Quebec Bridge.
--Commerce.
    xx Canada. Commerce.
--History.
--Navigation.
    sa St. Lawrence Waterway.
    xx Navigation.
--Power utilization.
    sa St. Lawrence Waterway.
    xx Power (Mechanics)
      Power utilization.
      Water-power.

St. Lawrence Seaway project.   See St.
    Lawrence Waterway.

St. Lawrence Valley.
--Botany.
--Water-supply.
--Zoology.

St. Lawrence Waterway.
    x Great Lakes-Saint Lawrence
      Waterway project.
      St. Lawrence navigation and
      power project.
      St. Lawrence Seaway project.
      St. Lawrence project.
    xx St. Lawrence River. Navigation.
      St. Lawrence River. Power
      utilization.

St. Lawrence Waterway (Continued)
--Bibliography.
    x St. Lawrence River. Bibliog-
      raphy.
    xx Inland navigation. Bibliog-
      raphy.

St. Louis.
--Botany.
    sa Subdivision Missouri. St.
      Louis under: Fungi.
      Trees.
--Bridges.
    sa Municipal Bridge, St. Louis.
--Commerce.
    sa Subdivision St. Louis, Mo.
      under: Wholesale trade.
--Directories.
--Forestry.
    sa Subdivision Missouri. St.
      Louis under: Trees.
    xx Missouri. Forestry.

St. Louis. Louisiana Purchase Exposi-
    tion, 1904.
--Brazil.
-- --Amazonas.
--Connecticut.
--Cuba.
--Germany.
--Indiana.
--Louisiana.
--Mexico.
--Minnesota.
--New York (State)
--Prussia.
--Tennessee.
--U.S.

St. Louis.
--Maps.
    xx Missouri. Maps.
--Markets.
--Milk supply.
    xx Missouri. Milk supply.
--Milk trade.
--Parks.
    sa St. Louis. Tower Grove Park.
--Streets.
    xx Streets.
--Tower Grove Park.
--Transportation.
--Zoology.
    sa Subdivision Missouri. St.
      Louis under: Reptilia.

St. Louis Co., Minn.
--Politics and government.
xx County government. Minnesota.

St. Louis Co., Mo.
--Roads.

St. Lucia.
--Agriculture.
sa Subdivision St. Lucia under:
Cotton.
Sugar-cane.
xx West Indies (British) Agri-
culture.
--Census.
--Commerce.
-- --Statistics.
--Domestic animals.
xx West Indies (British) Domestic
animals.
--Entomology.
--Forestry.
--Ornithology.
xx West Indies. Ornithology.
--Pomology.
sa Subdivision St. Lucia under:
Citrus.
--Soils.

St. Mary Parish, La.
--Soils.
sa Subdivision Louisiana. St. Mary
Parish under: Soil-surveys.

St. Mary River, Mont.

St. Mary's Co., Md.
--Geology.
--Soils.
sa Subdivision Maryland. St.
Mary's Co. under: Soil-
surveys.

St. Marys River, Mich.
--Power utilization.
xx Power utilization.

St. Moritz, Lake.   See Lake St. Moritz.

St. Nazaire sheep.   See Préalpes du Sud
sheep.

St. Paul.
--Commerce.
sa Subdivision St. Paul under:
Farm produce. Marketing.
Fruit trade.
--Maps.
--Markets.
xx Markets.
--Milk supply.
xx Minnesota. Milk supply.
--Parks.
--Public works.
xx Minnesota. Public works.
--Social conditions.
sa Subdivision St. Paul under:
Cost and standard of living.
xx Minnesota. Social conditions.
--Statistics.

St. Petersburg.   See Leningrad.

St. Petersburg (Government)   See Leningrad (Government)

St. Pierre lez-Maastricht.
--Botany.

Saint-Pons, France.
--Geology.

Saint Roque Cape.
--Viticulture.
xx Brazil. Viticulture.

St. Thomas (Island) West Africa.
x Sao Thome (Island) West Africa.
San Tomé (Island) West Africa.
--Botany.
--Entomology.

Saint Tropez.
--Botany.

Saint-Vaast-La-Hougue.
--Botany.
sa Subdivision France. Saint-
Vaast-La-Hougue under:
Marine flora.

St. Vincent.
--Agriculture.
sa Subdivision St. Vincent under:
Agricultural credit.
--Census.

St. Vincent (Continued)
--Commerce.
-- --Statistics.
--Entomology.
    sa Subdivision St. Vincent under:
        Hymenoptera.
    xx West Indies (British) Entom-
        ology.
--Ornithology.
--Statistics.

St. Wendel-Baumholder, Ger.
--Soils.
    xx Germany. Soils.

Sainte Anne de la Pocatière, Quebec.
    École d'agriculture.

Ste-Anne-de-Roquemaure, Quebec.

Sainte-Baume.
--Botany.

Sainte-Suzanne Estate.

Sainte Victoire Mountains.

Saintpaulia.
        x Violet, African.
            African violet.
--Nomenclature.
        xx Botany. Nomenclature.
--Periodicals.
--Societies.
--Varieties.

Saintpaulia ionantha.

Saipan.
--Geology.
--Physical geography.

Sais.
    xx Nymphalidae.

Saisan region.
--Zoology.

Saissetia oleae.
        xx Olive. Pests.
--Parasites.

Saitama-ken, Japan.
--Agriculture.
-- --Maps.

Saitama-ken, Japan (Continued)
--Forestry.
--Maps.
--Pomology.
--Soils.
    sa Subdivision Japan. Saitama-ken
        under: Soil-surveys.

Saj. See Terminalia tomentosa.

Sajodin.

Sake.
    xx Rice beer.

Sakhalin. See Saghalin (Island)

Saksaul.

Sakura-jima, Japan.
--Agriculture.

Sâl. See Shorea robusta.

Sal bark-borer. See Sphaerotrypes
    siwalikensis.

Salad dressing.
        sa Mayonnaise.
--Grading and standardization.
        sa Subdivision Grading and stand-
            ardization under: Mayon-
            naise.
        xx Food standards.

Salad plants.
--Breeding.
        xx Vegetables. Breeding.

Salads.

Salamanders.
        sa Desmognathus.
        Eumicrerpeton.

Salaries.
        sa Subdivision Salaries, pensions,
            etc. under: Engineers.
        Railroads.
        Teachers//
        U.S. Government salaries.

Salaries (Continued)
sa Subdivision Officials and
employees. Salaries, allowances, etc. under names of
countries, e.g., Brazil.
Officials and employees.
Salaries, Allowances, etc.
x Pay.
xx Wages.
--Statistics.

Salaries of Government employees. See
U.S. Government salaries.

Salididae.
xx Heteroptera.

Salem, Mass.

Salem, Mass. City Plans Commission. See
Salem, Mass. Planning Board.

Salem, Mass. Horticultural exhibition,
1850.

Salem, Or.
--Industries and resources.

Salem Co., N.J.
sa Subdivision New Jersey. Salem
Co. under: County surveys.
xx New Jersey.
--Social conditions.
sa Subdivision New Jersey. Salem
Co. under: Social surveys.

Salerno (Province)
--Commerce.
-- --Periodicals.
--Economic conditions.
-- --Periodicals.
--Pomology.
sa Subdivision Salerno (Province)
under: Citrus. Italy.

Sales.
--Cases.

Sales, Conditional.

Sales.
--Law.
sa Commercial law.

Sales management.
sa Salesmen and salesmanship.
x Management, Sales.
xx Industrial management.
Marketing.

Sales of government owned foodstuffs.
x Government sales of foodstuffs.
Selling government owned
foodstuffs.
Government owned foodstuffs.
Sales.
Food sales (Government owned
stocks)
xx Marketing.
--Law.

Sales of government owned non-foodstuffs.
x Government owned non-foodstuffs. Sales.
--Law.

Sales tax.   (DIRECT)
xx Taxation.
--Bibliography.

Salesmen and salesmanship.
xx Sales management.
--Bibliography.
--Periodicals.

Saléve.
--Botany.

Salicaceae.

Salicariaceae.
sa Cuphea.

Salices.   See Salix.

Salicin.

Salicornieae.

Salicyl.
sa Mesotan.
Spirosal.

Salicylates.
--Bibliography.

Salicylic acid.
    sa Ester-dermasan.
       Salol.
    xx Acids.
       Adulterations.

Salientia. See Anura.

Salina Canyon, Utah.
--Soils.
    sa Subdivision Utah. Salina
       Canyon under: Soil erosion.
       Prevention and control.

Salinan Indians.
    xx Indians, North American.

Salinas River, Calif.
    xx California.

Salinas River Watershed, Calif.

Salinas Valley, Calif.
--Water-supply.
    xx California. Water-supply.

Saline Co., Ill.
    xx Illinois.

Saline Co., Kan.
--Land.
    sa Subdivision Kansas. Saline Co.
       under: Land utilization.
--Soils.
    sa Subdivision Kansas. Saline Co.
       under: Soil conservation
         surveys.
       Soil-surveys.

Saline Co., Miss.
--Education.
    sa Subdivision Mississippi. Saline
       Co. under: Rural schools.

Saline Co., Neb.
--Soils.
    sa Subdivision Nebraska. Saline
       Co. under: Soil-surveys.

Saline irrigation.

Saline soil. See Soil, Salts in.

Saline waters.
    sa Mineral waters.
       Sea-water.
    x Waters, Saline.
      Water, Saline.
    xx Mineral waters.
--Demineralization.
    x Demineralization of saline
       waters.
-- --Bibliography.
-- --Congresses.

Salines.

Salinity.
    sa Irrigation water. Salt content.
       Soil, Salts in.
--Bibliography.

Salipyrine.

Salisbury treatment.

Salishan languages.

Saliva.
--Abstracts.
--Bibliography.

Salivary glands.

Salix.
    sa Basket-willow.
--Bibliography.
--Diseases.
    xx Trees. Diseases.
--Pests.
    sa Phryneta spinator.

Salix alba.

Salix caerulea.
--Diseases.

Salix laurina.

Salmon.

Salmon, Canned.
    x Canned salmon.
    xx Fishery products, Canned.
--By-products.
    xx Waste products.
--Directories.
--Statistics.

Salmon.
--Parasites.

Salmon as food.
xx Fish as food.

Salmon canneries.
--Accounting.
xx Cost. Accounting.
--Waste.
xx Canneries. Waste.

Salmon-fisheries.   (DIRECT)
xx Fisheries.

Salmon-fishing.   (INDIRECT)
xx Fishing.

Salmon National Forest, Idaho.

Salmonella abortus ovis.

Salmonella cholerae suis.

Salmonella enteritidis.   See Bacillus
enteritidis.

Salmonella gallinarum.   See Salmonella
pullorum.

Salmonella group.
--Culture media.
xx Bacteriology. Cultures and
culture media.

Salmonella pullorum.
sa Pullorum disease.
x Salmonella gallinarum.
Bacterium pullorum.
xx Pullorum disease.

Salmonella schottmuelleri.

Salmonella typhimurium.

Salmonella typhosa.

Salol.

Salomonia.
sa Epirrhizanthes.

Salonika, Greece.
--Commerce.
-- --Statistics.

Salop.   See Shropshire, Eng.

Salpa.

Salpidae.
xx Ascidia.

Salpinx.   See Eustachian tube; Oviduct.

Salsify.
--Diseases.

Salsk District.
--Agriculture.

Salsk sheep.

Salsola kali tragus.   See Russian
thistle.

Salsola kali var. tenuifolia.   See
Russian thistle.

Salsola nodulosa.
xx Halophyte.

Salsola palezkiana.

Salsola richteri.

Salsolaceae.

Salt.
sa Rock-salt.
Cotton fibre. Salt content.
--Abstracts.
--Bacteriology.
xx Bacteriology.
--Bibliography.
--Determination.
--Effect on germination.   See Germina-
tion. Effect of salt.
--Effect on metabolism.   See Metabo-
lism. Effect of salt.
--Effect on plants.

Salt, Iodized.
x Iodine in Salt.
Iodized Salt.
xx Iodine.
Salt. Therapeutic use.

Salt. Physiological effect of.
sa Salt-free diet.

Salt.
--Prices.
--Research.
--Therapeutic use.
     xx Materia medica and therapeutics.

Salt as a cause of disease.

Salt as a fertilizer.

Salt as an aid to digestion.

Salt as culture media.
     xx Bacteriology. Cultures and
          culture media.

Salt as feeding stuff.
     xx Feeding stuffs.

Salt-bush.
     sa Atriplex.

Salt-bush as food.

Salt cedar.   See Tamarix gallica.

Salt deposits.

Salt-free diet.
     x Cookery (Saltless)
     Saltless cookery.
     Low sodium diet.
     Diet, Salt-free.
     xx Cookery for the sick.
     Diet in disease.
     Salt, Physiological effect of.

Salt in feeding stuffs.   See Salt,
     Physiological effect of.

Salt industry and trade.   (DIRECT)

Salt Lake Area, Utah.
--Soils.
     sa Subdivision Utah. Salt Lake
          Area under: Soil-surveys.

Salt Lake City.
--Water-supply.
     xx Water-supply.

Salt Lake Co., Utah.
     sa Subdivision Utah. Salt Lake Co.
          under: Irrigation.

Salt Lake Valley, Utah.
--Soils.

Salt-marsh caterpillar.   See Estigmene
     acraea.

Salt-marsh lands.   See Marshes, Tide.

Salt peter.   See Saltpeter.

Salt River.

Salt River irrigation project.

Salt River Valley, Ariz.
          sa Subdivision Arizona. Salt
               River Valley under:
               Irrigation.
               Drainage.
--Agriculture.
          sa Subdivision Arizona. Salt
               River Valley under:
               Poultry.
               Irrigation.
--Geology.
--Maps.
          xx Arizona. Maps.
--Soils.
          sa Subdivision Salt River Valley,
               Ariz. under: Soil erosion.
--Water-supply.
          sa Subdivision Arizona. Salt
               River Valley under: Water,
               Underground.

Salt solution.

Salt springs.   See Mineral springs.

Salt-Wahoo Creeks Watershed, Neb.

Salt-water fishing.
          Here are entered works on sea or
               coast fishing as a sport.
               Works on ocean fishing for
               commercial purposes are en-
               tered under heading Fisheries.
          x Sea angling.
          Sea fishing.
          Surf fishing.
          xx Fishing.

Salta, Argentine Republic (Province)
--Botany.
--Cattle.

Salta, Argentine Republic (Province)
(Continued)
--Domestic animals.
-- --Legislation.
--Entomology.
--Forestry.
--Roads.
-- --Law.
    xx Argentine Republic. Roads. Law.
--Statistics.
    xx Argentine Republic. Statistics.
--Zoology.

Saltatoria.

Saltatoriae.

Saltbush.   See Salt-bush.

Saltcake.   See Sodium sulphate.

Saltless cookery.   See Salt-free diet.

Salton Basin, Calif.
    sa Salton Sea, Calif.
--Botany.
--Soils.

Salton Sea, Calif.
    sa Salton Basin, Calif.

Saltpeter.
    sa Sodium nitrate.

Saltpeter, Chile.   See Sodium nitrate.

Saltpeter.
--Effect on meat.
--Effect on plants.

Saltpeter, Physiological effect of.
    sa Sodium nitrate, Physiological
        effect of.
    xx Physiology.

Salts.
    sa Ammonium salts.
    Potassium salts.
    Soil, Salts in.
    Alkali salts.
    Mineral salts.
    Potash salts.
    Sodium salts.
    Copper salts.
    Manganese salts.

Salts (Continued)
--Binary theory.

Salts, Double.

Salts.
--Effect on plants.
    sa Salts in plant nutrition.
    Salts in plants.
    Subdivision Effect on plants
        under: Mineral salts.
        Germination.
--Effect on soils.   See Soil. Effect
    of salts.
--Physiological effect.
    sa Mineral salts. Physiological
        effect.
--Saturated solutions.

Salts, Soluble.

Salts, Stassfurt.   See Stassfurt salts.

Salts, Toxic.
    sa Toxic substances.

Salts in plants nutrition.
    sa Salts in plants.
    Subdivision Effect on plants
        under: Salts.
        Mineral salts.

Salts in plants.
    sa Subdivision Effect on plants
        under: Mineral salts.
        Salts.
        Salts in plant nutrition.

Saltusaphis.
    xx Aphididae.

Saltwort.   See Halophyte.

Saluda Co., S.C.
    xx South Carolina.
--Soils.
    sa Subdivision South Carolina.
        Saluda Co. under: Soil-
        surveys.

Salvador.
--Agriculture.
  sa Subdivision Salvador under:
    Coffee.
    Agriculture. Economic as-
      pects.
    Forage plants.
    Soy-bean.
    Agricultural extension.
-- --Education.
  sa Subdivision Salvador under:
    Agricultural extension.
-- --Periodicals.
-- --Statistics.
  xx Central America. Agriculture.
    Statistics.
--Botany.
  sa Subdivision Salvador under:
    Botany, Economic.
    Trees.
--Cattle.
  xx Central America. Cattle.
-- --Periodicals.
--Census.
-- --Statistics.
--Commerce.
  sa Salvador. Coffee trade.
    Salvador. Commercial treaties.
-- --Statistics.
--Commercial policy.
--Commercial treaties.
  xx Commercial treaties.
    Salvador. Commerce.
--Dairying.
  sa Subdivision Salvador under:
    Dairy industry and trade.
  xx Central America. Dairying.
--Domestic animals.
--Economic conditions.
  sa Subdivision Salvador under:
    History, Economic.
-- --Bibliography.
-- --Periodicals.
  xx Central America. Economic con-
    ditions. Periodicals.
--Economic policy.
--Fisheries.
--Foreign relations.
-- --Treaties.
--Forestry.
  sa Subdivision Salvador under:
    Trees.
    Afforestation and reforesta-
      tion.
  xx Central America. Forestry.

Salvador (Continued)
--Geographic names.
--History.
  sa Subdivision Salvador under:
    History, Economic.
--Horses.
--Ichthyology.
--Industries.
-- --Statistics.
--Land.
  sa Subdivision Salvador under:
    Land utilization.
--Manufactures.
--Maps.
--Meteorology.
--Population.
  xx Central America. Population.
--Public works.
  xx Public works.
--Railroads.
--Research.
--Roads.
--Soils.
  sa Subdivision Salvador under:
    Soil erosion.
--Statistics.
  sa Subdivision Commerce. Sta-
    tistics under: Salvador.
--Statistics, Vital.

Salvador, Brazil.   See Bahia, Brazil
  (City)

Salvadora.

Salvadoraceae.
  sa Salvadora.

Salvadorian literature.
--Bibliography.

Salvadorian periodicals.

Salvage (Waste, etc.)
  sa Railroads. Scrap material.
    Rubber, Reclaimed.
    Fat salvage.

Salvages Islands.
--Botany.
--Entomology.
  sa Subdivision Salvages Islands
    under: Coleoptera.
--Hydrographic survey.

Salvarsan.
    sa Neo-arsphenamin.
       Neosalvarsan.

Salvation Army.
--Farm colonies.

Salves. See Ointments.

Salvia.
    sa Oiticica oil.
    x Sage.

Salvia argentea.

Salvia glutinosa.

Salvia officinalis.
--Bibliography.
    xx Drug plants. Bibliography.

Salvia sclarea.

Salvia splendens.

Salvinia natans.

Salviniaceae.
    sa Salvinia.

Salwatty (Island)
--Entomology.
    sa Subdivision Salwatty (Island)
       under: Diptera.

Salzburg (Province)
--Agriculture.
    sa Subdivision Salzburg (Province)
       under: Colonization, Agri-
         cultural.
-- --Education.
--Apiculture.
--Botany.
    xx Austria. Botany.
--Cattle.
--Entomology.
    sa Subdivision Austria. Salzburg
       under: Lepidoptera.
--Geography.
    sa Anthropo-geography. Austria.
       Salzburg.
--Land.
    sa Subdivision Salzburg (Province)
       under: Land tenure.

Salzburg (Province) (Continued)
--Ornithology.
-- --Bibliography.
--Soils.
    sa Subdivision Austria. Salzburg
       under: Peat.

Samai. See Millet, Proso.

Samara (Government)
--Soils.

Samarang (Ship)

Samarium.

Samarkand.
--Agriculture.
    sa Subdivision Uzbekistan. Samar-
       kand under: Colonization,
         Agricultural.
--Pomology.
--Viticulture.

Sambucus.
--Pests.

Samia.
    xx Attacus.

Samia cecropia.
    x Cecropia moth.

Samia columbia.

Samia gloveri.

Samoa. See Samoan Islands.

Samoa, American. See American Samoa.

Samoa, Western. See Western Samoa
  (New Zealand)

Samoan Islands.
    sa American Samoa.
--Agriculture.
    sa Subdivision Agriculture under:
       American Samoa.
--Bibliography.
--Botany.
--Climate.
--Commerce.

Samoan Islands (Continued)
--Entomology.
    sa Subdivision Samoan Islands
        under: Coleoptera.
--Land.
    sa Subdivision Land under:
        American Samoa.
--Natural history.
    sa Subdivision Natural history
        under: Tutuila.
--Population.
    sa Subdivision Population under:
        American Samoa.
    xx Population.
--Zoology.
    sa Subdivision Samoan Islands
        under: Arthropoda.

Samos.

Samoyeds (Dogs)
    xx Dogs.

Sample plots.
    x Permanent sample plots.

Sampler, Cotton.   See Cotton sampler.

Sampling (Statistics)
--Bibliography.

Sampling apparatus.
    xx Chemistry. Apparatus.

Sampling of food.   See Food. Flavor.
    Testing.

Sampling of soil.   See Soil sampling.

Sampson Co., N.C.
--Economic conditions.
    xx North Carolina. Economic con-
        ditions.
--Social conditions.
    sa Subdivision North Carolina.
        Sampson Co. under: Social
        surveys.
--Soils.
    sa Subdivision North Carolina.
        Sampson Co. under: Soil-
        surveys.

Samydaceae.

San Angelo, Tex.
--Water-supply.

San Antonio, Tex.
--Botany.
    sa Subdivision Texas. San Antonio
        under: Trees.
        Shrubs.
--Commerce.
    sa Subdivision San Antonio, Tex.
        under: Markets.
--Forestry.
    sa Subdivision Texas. San Antonio
        under: Trees.
--Markets.
    xx San Antonio, Tex. Commerce.

San Antonio area.
--Water-supply.
    sa Subdivision San Antonio area
        under: Water, Underground.
        Texas.

San Antonio Experiment Farm.

San Antonio joint stock land bank.

San Benito Co., Calif.
--Agriculture.
-- --Periodicals.
--Water-supply.
    xx California. Water-supply.

San Benito Island.
--Botany.

San Bernardino Co., Calif.
--Agriculture.

San Bernardino Forest Reserve, Calif.

San Bernardino Mountains.
--Botany.
--Forestry.
    sa Subdivision San Bernardino
        Mountains under: Afforesta-
        tion and reforestation.
--Geology.
--Zoology.

San Bernardino National Forest, Calif.
    xx Forest reservations.
        California. Forest reserva-
        tions.

San Bernardino Valley, Calif.
--Geology.
    sa Subdivision California. San
       Bernardino Valley under:
       Water, Underground.
--History.
--Water-supply.
    sa Subdivision California. San
       Bernardino Valley under:
       Water, Underground.

San Blas (Harbor)
--Botany.
    sa Subdivision San Blas (Harbor)
       under: Algae.

San Carlos irrigation project.

San Cataldo, Italy.
--Agriculture.
    sa Subdivision Italy. San Cataldo
       under: Reclamation of land.

San Cesareo, Italy.

San Diego, Calif.
--Balboa Park.
    xx San Diego, Calif. Parks.
--Botany.
    xx California. Botany.
--Climate.
--Entomology.
--Markets.
--Milk supply.
    xx California. Milk supply.
--Natural history.
--Parks.
    sa San Diego, Calif. Balboa Park.
    xx California. Parks.
--Water-supply.
    xx Water-supply.

San Diego Co., Calif.
    sa Subdivision San Diego Co.
       under: County surveys.
       California.
--Agriculture.
    sa Subdivision San Diego Co.,
       Calif. under: Ranges.
       Agricultural surveys.
       Forage plants.
--Botany.

San Diego Co., Calif. (Continued)
--Entomology.
    sa Subdivision San Diego Co.
       under: Coleoptera. Cali-
       fornia.
    xx California. Entomology.
--Geology.
--Ornithology.
    xx California. Ornithology.
--Roads.
    xx California. Roads.
--Soils.
    sa Subdivision California. San
       Diego Co. under: Soil-
       surveys.
       Soil erosion.
--Water-supply.

San Diego region.
--Economic conditions.
    sa Subdivision San Diego region
       under: Economic surveys.
       California.
--Industries and resources.
    sa Subdivision San Diego region
       under: Industrial surveys.
       California.

San Dimas Experimental Forest, Calif.
    xx Experimental forests.
--Zoology.
    sa Subdivision California. San
       Dimas Experimental Forest
       under: Vertebrates.

San Domingo. See Dominican Republic.

San Fernando Valley, Calif.
--Agriculture.
    xx California. Agriculture.
--Economic conditions.
    xx California. Economic conditions.
--Soils.
    sa Subdivision California. San
       Fernando Valley under:
       Soil erosion.

San Francisco.
--Botany.
--Bridges.
    sa Golden Gate Bridge.
       San Francisco-Oakland Bay
       Bridge.
       San Francisco Bay Bridge.
--Climate.

San Francisco (Continued)
--Commerce.
       sa Subdivision San Francisco under:
         Meat industry and trade.
         Produce trade.
-- --Directories.
       xx California. Commerce. Direc-
         tories.
-- --Statistics.
       xx California. Commerce. Sta-
         tistics.
--Description.

San Francisco. Earthquake and fire, 1906.

San Francisco.
--Forestry.
       sa Subdivision California. San
         Francisco under: Tree
         planting.

San Francisco. Golden Gate International
  Exposition.
       x Golden Gate International Ex-
         position.

San Francisco.
--Harbor.
       xx Harbors.
--History.
--Maps.
--Markets.
       xx California. Markets.
--Milk trade.
--Ornithology.
--Sewerage.
--Water-supply.

San Francisco Bay Bridge.

San Francisco Bay region.
       xx California. Transportation.
--Economic conditions.
       sa Subdivision San Francisco Bay
         region under: Economic
         surveys. California.
--Industries and resources.
       sa Subdivision San Francisco Bay
         region under: Industrial
         surveys. California.
--Land.
       sa Subdivision California. San
         Francisco Bay region under:
         Land utilization.

San Francisco Co., Calif.

San Francisco Mountains, Ariz.
--Zoology.

San Francisco Mountains Forest Reserve.

San Francisco Peninsula, Calif.
--Geology.

San Francisco-Oakland Bay Bridge.
       xx Oakland, Calif. Bridges.
         San Francisco. Bridges.
         Bridges.

San Francisco River, Brazil. See Río
      São Francisco, Brazil.

San Gabriel Forest Reserve, Calif.

San Gabriel Mountains, Calif.
       xx California.
--Geology.
--Water-supply.

San Gabriel River.
       xx California.

San Gabriel River watershed, Calif.

San Isabel National Forest, Colo.
       xx Forest reservations.
         Colorado. Forest reservations.

San Jacinto Experimental Forest, Tex.

San Jacinto Forest Reserve, Calif.

San Jacinto Mountain.
--Botany.

San Joaquin Co., Calif.
--Agriculture.
       sa Subdivision California. San
         Joaquin Co. under: War and
         agriculture (1939-1945)
--Defenses.
--Irrigation.
--Population.
       sa Subdivision California. San
         Joaquin Co. under: Rural
         population.

San Joaquin Experimental Range, Calif.
    x Ranges.
    xx Ranges, Experimental.

San Joaquin River.
    sa Subdivision San Joaquin River
        under: Flood control.

San Joaquin Valley, Calif.
    xx Central Valley, Calif.
--Agriculture.
    sa Subdivision California. San
        Joaquin Valley under:
        Sugar-beet.
        Agriculture. Economic as-
          pects.
        Farm ownership.
        Types of farming.
        Agricultural surveys.
        Irrigation.
--Botany.
--Dairying.
-- --Statistics.
    xx California. Dairying. Sta-
        tistics.
--Geology.
--Land.
    sa Subdivision San Joaquin Valley
        under: Land tenure.
--Pomology.
--Soils.
--Water-supply.
    sa Subdivision California. San
        Joaquin Valley under: Water,
        Underground.

San José, Calif.
--Social conditions.
    sa Subdivision California. San
        José under: Social surveys.
    xx California. Social conditions.

San Jose, Uruguay.
--Roads.

San Jose Co., Calif.

San José scale.

San Juan, Argentine Republic (Province)
--Agriculture.
-- --Statistics.
--Statistics.

San Juan, Majorca.
--Agriculture.
    xx Majorca. Agriculture.

San Juan, P.R.
--Commerce.
    sa Subdivision San Juan, P.R.
        under: Produce trade.
--Markets.
--Social conditions.
    sa Subdivision San Juan, P.R.
        under: Cost and standard of
        living.

San Juan Canyon, Utah.

San Juan-Chama project.

San Juan Co., N.M.
--Water-supply.

San Juan Co., Utah.
--Geology.
    xx Utah. Geology.

San Juan Exploring Expedition.

San Juan (Farm)
    xx Farms.

San Juan region, Colo.
--Geology.
    xx Colorado. Geology.

San Juan region, N.M.
--Geology.

San Juan National Forest, Colo.
    xx Forest reservations.
        Colorado. Forest reservations.

San Juan National Monument, P.R.
    xx National parks and reserves.

San Justo, Argentine Republic.
--Maps.

San Luis, Argentine Republic (Province)
--Agriculture.
    xx Argentine Republic. Agri-
        culture.
--Climate.

San Luis. Argentine Republic (Province)
(Continued)
--Entomology.
    sa Subdivision Argentine Republic.
    San Luis (Province) under:
    Hymenoptera.

San Luis Obispo Co., Calif.

San Luis Obispo Forest Reserve, Calif.

San Luis Potosí, Mexico (State)
--Botany.
--Domestic animals.
-- --Legislation.

San Luis Valley, Colo.
    sa Flood dams and reservoirs.
        Colorado. San Luis Valley.
--Agriculture.
    sa Subdivision Colorado. San Luis
        Valley under: Agricultural
        policies and programs.
        Irrigation.
        Potatoes.
--Demonstration Farm.
    xx Demonstration farms.
--Domestic animals.
--Geology.
--Soils.
--Water-supply.

San Marino.
--Botany.

San Martín, Argentine Republic.
--Maps.

San Martin, Peru (Dept.)
--Social conditions.

San Mateo Atenco.
--Economic conditions.
--Social life and customs.

San Mateo Co., Calif.
    sa Subdivision San Mateo Co.,
        Calif. under: Planning,
        County.
    xx California.
--Description and travel.
--Education.

San Mateo Co., Calif. (Continued)
--Land.
    sa Subdivision California. San
        Mateo Co. under: Land
        utilization.
--Maps.
--Politics and government.
--Soils.
    sa Subdivision California. San
        Mateo Co. under: Soil con-
        servation surveys.
        Soil-surveys.

San Miguel Co., Colo.
    xx Colorado.

San Miguel Co., N.M.

San Remo.
--Botany.

San Simon River, Ariz.

San Tomé (Island) West Africa. See St.
    Thomas (Island) West Africa.

Sanatalum album. See Sandal tree.

Sanatol. See Creolin.

Sanatoriums.

Sanchezia.
    xx Acanthaceae.

Sanchezia nobilis.

Sanctions (International law)
    xx Economic policy.

Sand.
    sa Soil, Sandy.
        Phylloxera immune soils.
        Oil sands.
    x Sands.

Sand, Musical. See Singing sands.

Sand.
--Periodicals.

Sand, Singing. See Singing sands.

Sand.
--Transportation.
    xx Transportation.

Sand-binding plants.

Sand blowing.   See Sand-dunes; Soil
    drifting.

Sand brick.

Sand culture.
    x Plants. Sand culture.

Sand drifting.   See Sand-dunes; Soil
    drifting; Wind erosion.

Sand-drown.
    xx Tobacco. Diseases.

Sand-dunes.
    sa Sand Hill region, Neb.
       Indiana Dunes State Park.
       Soil drifting.
       Wind erosion.
    x Sand shifting.
       Shifting sands.
       Sand drifting.
       Sand blowing.
    xx Afforestation and reforesta-
       tion.

Sand fauna.
    xx Zoology.

Sand flea.   See Talorchestia longicornis.

Sand flora.
    x Arid regions. Botany.
       Psammaphites.
    xx Botany.

Sand Hill region, Neb.

Sand Hill region, Southeastern States.
    x Sandhill region, Southeastern
       States.

Sand-lime brick.

Sand pine.   See Pinus clausa.

Sand shifting.   See Sand-dunes; Soil
    drifting.

Sand wireworm.   See Horistonotus uhlerii.

Sandal tree.   See Sandal-wood.

Sandal-wood.
--Diseases.
       sa Spike-disease of sandal.
--Pests.

Sandalwood Island.
       x Sumba.
          Soemba.
--Horse.
       sa Subdivision Sandalwood Island
          under: Horses. Breeding.

Sandal-wood oil.

Sándan.   See Oudeinia dalbergioides.

Sandarac.

Sandhill region, Neb.   See Sand Hill
    region, Neb.

Sandhill region, Southeastern States.
    See Sand Hill region, Southeastern
    States.

Sanding-machines.
    xx Machine-tools.
       Woodworking machinery.

Sandomir wheat.   See Wheat, Sandomir.

Sandoval Co., N.M.
    xx New Mexico.
--Geology.
    xx New Mexico. Geology.

Sands.   See Sand.

Sandstone.

Sandusky, Ohio.
--Entomology.

Sandwich construction.
       x Sandwich panels.
       xx Panels.
--Core materials.
       x Core materials.
          Honeycomb core materials.
          Core stock.
--Testing.

Sandwich Islands.   See Hawaii.

Sandwich panels.   See Sandwich construc-
    tion.

Sandwiches.
--Bibliography.

Sandy Lake area, Newfoundland.
--Soils.
        sa Subdivision Newfoundland. Sandy
            Lake area under: Soil-
            surveys.

Sandy River, Or.

Sandford, Fla.

Sangamon Co., Ill.
        xx Illinois.
--Geology.
--Soils.

Sangamon River.

Sangamon River Basin.
        xx Illinois.

Sangir Islands.
--Ornithology.

Sanguinaria canadensis.

Sanguisorba.   See Burnet.

Sanhedrin, Mount.   See Mount Sanhedrin.

Sanilac Co., Mich.
--Soils.
        sa Subdivision Michigan. Sanilac
            Co. under: Soil-surveys.

Sanitariums.   See Sanatoriums.

Sanitary affairs.   See. Sanitary engi-
    neering; Sanitation; Subdivision Sani-
    tary affairs under names of countries,
    cities, etc., e.g., Egypt. Sanitary
    affairs.

Sanitary boards.

Sanitary chemistry.
--Bibliography.
        x Chemistry. Bibliography.

Sanitary engineering.
        sa Plumbing.
        Garbage.
        Sewerage.
        Water-supply.
        Plants as sanitary agents.
        Sanitation, Household.
        Filters and filtration.
        Dust. Removal.
        Municipal engineering.
        Public comfort stations.
        Refuse and refuse disposal.
        Street-cleaning.
        Subdivision Sanitary affairs
            under names of countries,
            cities, etc., e.g., Egypt.
            Sanitary affairs.
        x Sanitary affairs.
--Congresses.
--Dictionaries.
--Periodicals.
--Study and teaching.
--Terminology.

Sanitary food handling.   See Food han-
    dling.

Sanitary reports.   See Hygiene, Public.

Sanitation.
        sa Subdivision Sanitation under:
            Railroads.
            Ships.
            Camping//
        Air. Purification.
        Cemeteries.
        Disinfection and disinfectants.
        Factory. sanitation.
        Hygiene.
        Hygiene, Public.
        Military hygiene.
        Naval hygiene.
        Plants as sanitary agents.
        Refuse and refuse disposal.
        Sanitary chemistry.
        Sanitary engineering.
        School hygiene.
        Smoke prevention.
        Ventilation.
        Water. Purification.
        Water-supply.
        Poultry sanitation.
        Agricultural sanitation.
    Bibliography.

Sanitation, Household.
    sa Food handling.

Sanitation.
--Periodicals.

Sanitoriums. See Sanatoriums.

Sann.
    x Crotalaria juncea.
      Indian hemp.
      Hemp, Indian.
      Sunn hemp.
--Marketing.
    xx Fiber plants and vegetable
      fibers. Marketing.

Sannina exitiosa. See Sanninoidea
  exitiosa.

Sanninoidea exitiosa.
    x Peach-tree borer.
      Aegeria exitiosa.
      Conopia exitiosa.
      Sannina exitiosa.
    xx Peach. Pests.

Sanninoidea opalescens.
    x Conopia opalescens.
      Peach borer, Western.
      Western peach borer.
      Aegeria opalescens.
    xx Root parasites.
      Prune. Pests.

Sanninoidea pictipes.
    x Conopia pictipes.
      Peach tree borer, Lesser.
      Aegeria pictipes.
      Lesser peach borer.
      Lesser peach tree borer.
    xx Peach. Pests.

Sanocrysin.

Sansan, France.
--Paleontology.

Sansevieria.
--Planting machinery.
    xx Planting machinery.

Sanskrit language.

Santa Ana Mountains.

Santa Ana River.
    sa Subdivision Santa Ana River
      under: Flood control.

Santa Ana River watershed, Calif.

Santa Barbara, Calif.
--Botany.
    sa Subdivision California. Santa
      Barbara under: Algae.
      Trees.
    xx California. Botany.
--Forestry.
    sa Subdivision Santa Barbara un-
      der: Trees.
    xx California. Forestry.
--Water-supply.

Santa Barbara Co., Calif.
--Economic conditions.
--Forestry.
--Geology.
--Parks.

Santa Barbara Islands.
--Ornithology.
    xx California. Ornithology.

Santa Catalina Island, Calif.
    x Catalina Island, Calif.
--Botany.
--Entomology.
    sa Subdivision California. Santa
      Catalina Island under:
      Hymenoptera.

Santa Catharina. Brazil (State)
--Agriculture.
    sa Subdivision Brazil. Santa
      Catharina (State) under:
      Agriculture. Economic as-
      pects.
-- --Statistics.
    xx Brazil. Agriculture. Sta-
      tistics.
--Botany.
--Commerce.
--Economic conditions.
    xx Brazil. Economic conditions.
-- --Periodicals.
    xx Brazil. Economic conditions.
      Periodicals.
--Statistics.
    xx Brazil. Statistics.

Santa Clara, Cuba (Province)
--Agriculture.

Santa Clara Co., Calif.
 sa Subdivision Santa Clara Co.,
  Calif. under: Planning,
  County.
--Agriculture.
-- --Periodicals.
--Soils.
 sa Subdivision California. Santa
  Clara Co. under: Soil-
  surveys.

Santa Clara River watershed, Calif.

Santa Clara Valley, Calif.
--Agriculture.
--Economic conditions.
 sa Subdivision California. Santa
  Clara Valley under: Geog-
  raphy, Economic.
--Geology.
 sa Subdivision California. Santa
  Clara Valley under: Water,
  Underground.
--Land.
 sa Land utilization. California.
  Santa Clara Valley.
--Viticulture.
--Water-supply.
 sa Subdivision California. Santa
  Clara Valley under: Water,
  Underground.

Santa Cruz, Argentine Republic (Ter.)
--Agriculture.
 sa Subdivision Argentine Republic.
  Santa Cruz (Ter.) under:
  Colonization, Agricultural.
--Land.
--Paleobotany.
 xx Argentine Republic. Paleo-
  botany.

Santa Cruz, Bolivia (Department)
--Agriculture.
--Botany.
--Economic conditions.
--Social life and customs.

Santa Cruz Co., Calif.
--Agriculture.

Santa Cruz, Danish West Indies. See
 Santa Cruz, Virgin Islands of the
 United States.

Santa Cruz, Virgin Islands of the United
 States.
--Agriculture.
 sa Subdivision Santa Cruz under:
  Cotton.
  Subdivision Virgin Islands of
  the United States. Santa
  Cruz under: Sugar-cane.
--Botany.
--Economic conditions.

Santa Cruz Co., Calif.
--Ornithology.
--Soils.
 xx California. Soils.

Santa Cruz de Tenerife, Spain (Province)
--Statistics.

Santa Cruz Mountains.
--Botany.

Santa Cruz Valley.
--Water-supply.

Santa Fé, Argentine Republic (City)
--Statistics.
 xx Argentine Republic. Statistics.

Santa Fé, Argentine Republic (Province)
--Agriculture.
 sa Subdivision Argentine Republic.
  Santa Fé (Province) under:
  Wheat.
  Agriculture. Economic as-
  pects.
-- --Law.
-- --Periodicals.
-- --Statistics.
 xx Argentine Republic. Agri-
  culture. Statistics.
--Census.
--Dairying.
 sa Subdivision Argentine Republic.
  Santa Fé (Province) under:
  Dairy industry and trade.
--Domestic animals.
-- --Statistics.
--Soils.
 xx Argentine Republic. Soils.
--Water-supply.

Santa Fé Co., N.M.

Santa Fé Expedition, 1841.   See Texan
  Santa Fé Expedition, 1841.

Santa Fé National Forest, N.M.
  sa Bandelier National Monument.

Santa Fé Railroad.   See Atchison, Topeka
  and Santa Fé Railroad Co.

Santa Fé Trail.

Santa Gertrudis cattle.
--Periodicals.

Santa Gertrudis irrigation project.

Santa Lucia.   See Saint Lucia.

Santa Lucia, W.I.   See Saint Lucia.

Santa Margarita River, Calif.

Santa Margherita, Italy (Estate)

Santa Maria del Tule, Oaxaca, Mexico.

Santa María River, Calif.

Santa María River watershed, Calif.

Santa Maura (Island)

Santa Rita Mountains, Ariz.
--Entomology.
      sa Subdivision Arizona. Santa
        Rita Mountains under:
        Orthoptera.
      xx Arizona. Entomology.

Santa Ynez Valley, Calif.
      sa Flood control. Santa Ynez
        Valley.
        Subdivision California. Santa
        Ynez Valley under: Land
        utilization.
        Water. Conservation.

Santalaceae.
      sa Thesium.
        Comandra.
        Santalum.
        Iodina.
        Osyris alba.

Santalum.

Santalum album.   See Sandal-wood.

Santander, Colombia (Dept.)   See Colombia.
  Departamento de Santander.

Santander, Spain (Province)
--Cattle.
--Natural history.

Santee Experimental Forest, S.C.

Santerre region. France.
--Agriculture.

Santiago Chimaltenango, Guatemala.
      xx Guatemala.

Santiago de Chile.
--Description and travel.

Santiago de Chile. Quinta normal de agri-
    cultura.   See Chile. Quinta normal de
    agricultura.

Santiago del Estero, Argentine Republic
  (Province)
      xx Argentine Republic.
--Agriculture.
      sa Subdivision Santiago del
        Estero, Argentine Republic
        (Province) under: Cotton.
      xx Argentine Republic. Agri-
        culture.
--Botany.
--Maps.
      xx Argentine Republic. Maps.
--Statistics.
      xx Argentine Republic. Statistics.
--Zoology.

Santo Domingo.   See Dominican Republic.

Santobane.   See DDT (Insecticide)

Santomerse.
      xx Wetting agents.

Santonin.

Santorini.   See Thera.

Santos (Brazil)
--Commerce.

São Bento (Estate)

São Francisco River, Brazil.   See Río
São Francisco, Brazil.

São Paulo, Brazil (City)
--Description.
--Milk supply.
    xx Brazil. Milk supply.
--Sanitary affairs.
--Statistics.

São Paulo, Brazil (Province)   See São
Paulo, Brazil (State)

São Paulo, Brazil (State)
    x São Paulo, Brazil (Province)
--Agriculture.
    sa Subdivision São Paulo, Brazil
       (State) under: Cotton.
       Mechanized farming.
       Subdivision Brazil. São Paulo
        (State) under: Sugar-cane.
       Coffee.
       Agriculture, Cooperative.
       Maize.
       Field crops.
       Rice.
       Agriculture. Economic as-
        pects.
       Jute.
       Wheat.
       Soy-bean.
       Peanuts.
       Tobacco.
       Farm produce.
-- --Education.
    sa Piracicaba, Brazil. Escola
       agrícola (Luiz de Queiroz)
-- --Periodicals.
-- --Statistics.
    sa São Paulo, Brazil (State)
       Domestic animals. Sta-
       tistics.
--Apiculture.
    sa Subdivision Brazil. São Paulo
       (State) under: Trees.
       Botany, Economic.
       Vegetable pathology.
       Botany, Medical.
--Cattle.
    xx São Paulo. Domestic animals.
--Cattle trade.
--Climate.

São Paulo, Brazil (State) (Continued)
--Commerce.
-- --Directories.
-- --Periodicals.
-- --Statistics.
    sa Subdivision Commerce. Sta-
       tistics under: Santos,
       Brazil.
--Dairying.
    sa Subdivision São Paulo, Brazil
       (State) under: Dairy in-
       dustry and trade.
--Domestic animals.
    sa São Paulo, Brazil (State)
       Cattle.
       São Paulo, Brazil (State)
       Swine.
       São Paulo, Brazil (State)
       Sheep.
-- --Statistics.
--Economic conditions.
    sa Subdivision Brazil. São Paulo
       (State) under: Geography,
       Economic.
--Education.
--Entomology.
    sa Subdivision Brazil. São Paulo
       (State) under: Entomology,
       Economic.
--Fisheries.
--Forestry.
    sa Subdivision Brazil. São Paulo
       (State) under: Trees.
       Timber.
       Silviculture.
--Geography.
    sa Subdivision Brazil. São Paulo
       (State) under: Geography,
       Economic.
--Industries and resources.
--Maps.
--Meteorology.
    sa Subdivision São Paulo, Brazil
       (State) under: Precipita-
       tion (Meteorology)
--Pomology.
    sa Subdivision Brazil. São Paulo
       (State) under: Citrus.
--Population.
--Railroads.
--Roads.
-- --Law.
    xx Brazil. Roads. Law.
--Sericulture.

São Paulo, Brazil (State) (Continued)
--Sheep.
    xx São Paulo, Brazil (State)
        Domestic animals.
--Social life and customs.
--Soils.
    sa Subdivision Brazil. São Paulo
        (State) under: Soil erosion.
          Prevention and control.
          Soil conservation.
    xx Brazil. Soils.
        Soil.
--Statistics.
    sa São Paulo, Brazil (State)
        Agriculture. Statistics.
        São Paulo, Brazil (State)
        Commerce. Statistics.
--Swine.
    xx São Paulo, Brazil (State)
        Domestic animals.
--Viticulture.

São Salvador, Brazil.   See Bahia, Brazil
  (City)

São Thomé (Island) West Africa.   See St.
  Thomas (Island) West Africa.

Sap.
    sa Latex constituents of plants.
        Root-pressure.
--Chloride content.
    xx Chlorides.

Sap, Circulation of.

Sap.
--Oxidase content.
--Phosphorus content.
--Sulphate in.

Sap-rot.

Sap stain in lumber.   See Stain in
  lumber.

Sapanca, Turkey.
--Agriculture.
    sa Subdivision Turkey. Sapanca
        under: Tea.

Saperda.
    x Apple-tree borer.
      Apple. Pests.

Saperda calcarata.
    x Poplar borer.

Saperda candida.

Saperda creata.

Sapindaceae.
    sa Arfeuillea.
      Paullinia.
      Sapindus.
      Atalaya hemiglauca.

Sapindus.

Sapindus utilis.

Sapium.

Sapium anadenum.

Sapium cladogyne.

Sapodilla.
    xx Sapotaceae.
--Propagation.
    xx Plant propagation.

Sapogenin.

Saponification.

Saponin.
--Bibliography.

Sapotaceae.
    sa Argania.
      Butyrospermum.
      Palaquium.
      Mimusops.
      Sideroxylon.
      Pouteria.
      Bassia.
      Sapodilla.

Sapporo, Japan.
--Forestry.
-- --Statistics.

Sapporo, Japan. Institut agronomique.

Saprininae.
    xx Histeridae.

Saprolegnia.

Saprolegniaceae.
    sa Aphanomyces.
       Plectospira.
       Isoachlya.
       Achlya.
    xx Phycomycetes.
--Parasites.

Sapromyza.

Sapromyzidae.
    sa Pallopteridae.
       Lonchaeidae.

Sapropel.

Sapropel as feeding stuff.

Sapropel as fertilizer.

Saprophytes.

Sapstain in lumber.   See Stain in lumber.

Saradzhinsk sheep.
    xx Sheep.

Saragossa (Province)
--Agriculture.
    sa Subdivision Saragossa (Province)
       under: Cotton.
       Flax. Spain.
       Hemp. Spain.
       Tobacco. Spain.

Sarasota Co., Fla.
--Soils.
    sa Subdivision Florida. Sarasota
       Co. under: Soil-surveys.

Saratoga Co., N.Y.
--Geology.
--Soils.
    sa Subdivision New York (State)
       Saratoga Co. under: Soil-
       surveys.

Saratoga reclamation project.

Saratoga spittlebug.   See Aphrophora
  saratogensis.

Saratoga Springs, N.Y.

Saratov (Government)
--Entomology.
    sa Subdivision Russia. Saratov
       (Government) under:
       Entomology, Economic.
       Subdivision Saratov (Govern-
       ment) under: Trees. Pests.
--Statistics.

Saratov Region.
--Agriculture.
    sa Subdivision Saratov Region
       under: Cereals.
       Agriculture. Economic as-
       pects.
       War and agriculture (1939-
       1945)
       Field crops.
       Agricultural laborers.
       Forage plants.
       Crops and climate.
       Agricultural policies and
       programs.
       Irrigation farming.
--Botany.
--Cattle.
--Climate.
    sa Subdivision Saratov Region
       under: Crops and climate.
--Domestic animals.
--Forestry.
    sa Subdivision Saratov Region
       under: Afforestation and
       reforestation.
       Tree planting.
--Industries.
--Soils.
    sa Subdivision Saratov Region
       under: Soil erosion. Pre-
       vention and control.
--Swine.

Sarawak (State)
--Agriculture.
    sa Subdivision Sarawak (State)
       under: Cacao.
       Agricultural policies and
       programs.
--Commerce.
-- --Statistics.
--Economic conditions.
--Economic policy.

Sarawak (State) (Continued)
--Forestry.
        sa Subdivision Sarawak (State)
           under: Forest products.
           Lumber trade.
           War and forestry (1939-1945)
           Forest policy.
--Land.

Sarbagan. See Marmota bobac.

Sarcina.

Sarcina ventriculi.

Sarcobatus vermiculatus.
      x Chico.
        Greasewood.
     xx Poisonous plants.

Sarcocephalus.
     xx Rubiaceae.

Sarcocephalus cordatus.

Sarcocystidia.

Sarcocystis.

Sarcodexia.

Sarcodexia sternodontis.

Sarcodina.
     xx Protozoa.

Sarcoma.

Sarcophaga carnaria.

Sarcophaga kellyi.

Sarcophaga utilis.

Sarcophagidae.
     sa Sarcophaga.
       Miltogrammini.

Sarcophaginae. See Sarcophagidae.

Sarcophila wohlfahrtia.

Sarcoptan.
     xx Benzene hexachloride.

Sarcoptes.

Sarcoptes scabiei.

Sarcoptidae.
     sa Sarcoptes.
       Myialges.
       Hemisarcoptes.
       Psoroptes.
       Cnemidocoptes
       Oribatidae.
     xx Acarida

Sarcosporidia.

Sarcosporidiosis.
     x Scrapie.
     xx Sheep. Diseases.

Sarda. See Bonito.

Sardines.
     sa Pilchards.
--Drying.

Sardinia.
--Agriculture.
        sa Sardinia. Domestic animals.
          Subdivision Sardinia under:Agri-
            culture. Economic aspects.
          Agricultural policies and pro-
            grams.
--Bibliography.
     xx Italy. Bibliography.
--Botany.
--Commerce.
-- --Statistics.
--Domestic animals.
--Entomology.
        sa Subdivision Sardinia under:
          Locusts.
          Culicidae.
          Entomology, Economic.
--Forestry.
        sa Subdivision Sardinia under:
          Forest policy.
     xx Italy. Forestry.
--Industries.
--Land.
        sa Subdivision Sardinia under:
          Land utilization.
--Paleobotany.
--Roads.
--Statistics.
--Viticulture.

Sardinia (Continued)
--Zoology.
  sa Subdivision Sardinia under:
   Vertebrates.

Sardinian sheep.

Sardis Dam and Reservoir project, Miss.
 xx Irrigation projects.

Sarek region, Sweden.
--Botany.
  sa Subdivision Sweden. Sarek region under: Algae.
  xx Sweden. Botany.
--Natural history.

Sargans, Switzerland (District)
--Agriculture.
  sa Subdivision Switzerland.
   Sargans (District) under:
   Agriculture, Cooperative.

Sargassum filipendula.

Sargent Co., N.D.
  sa Subdivision North Dakota.
   Sargent Co. under: County
   surveys.
  xx North Dakota.

Sargent Industrial School, Beacon, N.Y.

Sargentia greggi.
  x Yellow chapote.
   Chapote.
  xx Citrus.

Sarnol.
  xx Tick fever.

Sarocaulon.

Sarola Kasar, India.

Sarothamnus. See Cytisus.

Saroxenus.

Sarpy Co., Neb.
--Soils.
  sa Subdivision Nebraska. Sarpy Co.
   under: Soil-surveys.

Sarracenia.

Sarracenia purpurea.

Sarracenia variolaris.

Sarraceniaceae.

Sarsaparilla.
  sa Drugs.

Sarthe, France. See France. Département
 de la Sarthe.

Sartivellia.
  xx Asteraceae.

Sartwellia flaveriae.

Sary-Chilek, Lake. See Lake Sary-Chilek.

Sasa.

Sashes.
  xx Building.
--Standards.
  xx Standardization.

Saskatchewan.
--Agriculture.
  sa Subdivision Saskatchewan under:
   Agricultural laborers.
   Agriculture. Economic as-
    pects.
   Maize.
   Farms.
   Agricultural outlook.
   Farm management surveys.
   Agricultural indebtedness.
   Farm management.
   Cereals.
   Tenant farming.
   Wheat.
   Agricultural policies and
    programs.
   Agricultural credit.
   Potatoes.
  xx Canada. Agriculture.
-- --Periodicals.
-- --Statistics.
  xx Canada. Agriculture. Statis-
   tics.
--Botany.
  sa Subdivision Saskatchewan under:
   Ferns.
   Fungi.
   Weeds.

Saskatchewan (Continued)
--Boundaries.
--Census.
    xx Canada. Census.
--Census, 1906.
--Commerce.
-- --Directories.
--Dairying.
    sa Subdivision Saskatchewan under:
      Dairy industry and trade.
--Description and travel.
--Domestic animals.
    sa Subdivision Saskatchewan under:
      Livestock cooperatives.
-- --Legislation.
-- --Statistics.
    xx Canada. Domestic animals. Sta-
      tistics.
--Economic conditions.
    sa Subdivision Saskatchewan under:
      Economic surveys.
-- --Periodicals.
--Emigration and immigration.
--Entomology.
--Forestry.
    sa Subdivision Saskatchewan under:
      Lumber trade.
--Industries.
--Land.
    sa Subdivision Saskatchewan under:
      Land. Classification.
      Land utilization.
--Manufactures.
-- --Directories.
--Maps.
--Milk supply.
--Milk trade.
--Ornithology.
--Paleontology.
--Politics and government.
    sa Subdivision Saskatchewan under:
      Local government.
    xx Canada. Politics and government.
--Population.
--Roads.
--Soils.
    sa Subdivision Saskatchewan under:
      Soil-surveys.
--Statistics.
--Water-supply.

Saskatchewan River.
--Explorations.

Saskatchewania.

Sassafras, Australian. See Doryphora
   sassafras.

Sassafras silt loam. See Sassafras soil.

Sassafras oil.

Sassafras soil.
   x Sassafras soil types.
   Sassafras silt loam.

Sassafras soil types. See Sassafras
   soil.

Sassafras tzumu.

Sassari.
--Population.

Sassari (Province)
--Agriculture.
-- --Statistics.

Sassy bark. See Erytrophleum guineense.

Satellites.

Satin moth. See Stilpnotia salicis.

Satinay. See Syncarpia hillii.

Satsuma, Japan.
--Botany.

Satureia.

Saturnia.

Saturniidae.
   sa Samia.
      Philosamia.
      Aglia.
      Hylesia.
      Coloradia.
      Bunaea.
      Telea.
      Callosamia.

Saturnoidea.
   sa Saturniidae.
   xx Lepidoptera.

Satyridae.
   sa Ypthima.
   Erebia.

Satyrites reynesii.

Sauces.
    sa Soy-bean sauce.

Saudi Arabia.
--Agriculture.
--Description and travel.
--Entomology.
    sa Subdivision Saudi Arabia under:
        Entomology, Economic.
--Pomology.
--Water-supply.

Sauer kraut.   See Sauerkraut.

Sauer rüben.

Sauerkraut.
    sa Vitamins in sauerkraut.
    x Sauer kraut.
      Kraut.

Sauerkraut, Canned.
--Grading and standardization.
    xx Sauerkraut. Grading and
       standardization.
      Canned goods. Grading and
       standardization.
      Vegetables, Canned. Grading
       and standardization.
--Statistics.

Sauerkraut.
--Canning.
--Grading and standardization.
    sa Subdivision Grading and stand-
      ardization under: Sauer-
        kraut, Canned.
    xx Vegetables. Grading and stand-
      ardization.
--Statistics.
--Storage.

Sauk Co., Wis.
--Forestry.
    sa Subdivision Wisconsin. Sauk Co.
      under: Wood-lots.
--Soils.
    sa Subdivision Wisconsin. Sauk Co.
      under: Soil-surveys.

Sault Ste. Marie Canal.

Sauna.   See Baths, Finnish.

Sauropoda.
    sa Atlantosaurus.
      Diplodocus.
      Haplocanthosaurus.
    xx Dinosauria.

Saururaceae.
    sa Saururus.
      Houttuynia.

Saururus.

Sausage casings.
    xx Sausages.

Sausages.
    xx Meat.
--Bacteriology.
    xx Meat. Bacteriology.
--Decomposition.
--Prices.

Saussurea.
    xx Aucklandia.

Sauterne.
    xx Wine and wine making.

Savannah (Steamship)

Savannah, Ga.
--Botany.
    sa Subdivision Savannah under:
      Trees. Georgia.
--Commerce.
    sa Subdivision Savannah, Ga.
      under: Wholesale trade.
--Forestry.
    sa Subdivision Savannah under:
      Trees. Georgia.
--Hygiene.
--Maps.
--Markets.

Savannah River.
    sa Subdivision Savannah River
      under: River stages.
--Levees.
    xx Levees.

Savannah-sparrow.   See Passerculus.

Savannas.
    x Grasslands.

Savannas (Continued)
   xx Plains.
      Prairies.

Save the forests week.
   xx U.S. Forestry.

Savenac nursery.
   xx Forest nurseries.

Savin.   See Juniperus sabina.

Saving and thrift.
   sa Forced loans.
   xx Economic development.
      Finance, Personal.
--Bibliography.
   sa Subdivision Bibliography under:
      Forced loans.
--Charts, diagrams, etc.

Savings and loan associations.   See
  Building and loan associations.

Savings bank life insurance.
   xx Insurance, Life.

Savings-banks.   (DIRECT)
   xx Banks and banking.
--Bibliography.
   sa Subdivision Bibliography under:
      Postal savings-banks.
--Periodicals.
   xx Banks and banking. Periodicals.
--Statistics.

Savings bonds.
   sa War bonds.
   xx Bonds.
      War bonds.

Savournon sheep.   See Préalpes du Sud
  sheep.

Savoy, France.
--Agriculture.
--Botany.
--Description and travel.

Saw-fly.   See Tenthredinidae; Tenthredinoidea.

Saw-fly, Hemlock.   See Neodiprion
  tsugae.

Saw-grass.   See Cladium effusum.

Saw mill machinery.   See Sawmill
  machinery.

Saw mills.   See Sawmills.

Saw palmetto.

Saw-toothed grain beetle.   See Oryzae-
  philus surinamensis.

Sawan.   See Panicum frumentaceum.

Sawdust.
   sa Wood flour.
--Abstracts.
--Bibliography.
--Effect on soils.   See Soil. Effect of
  sawdust.
--Moisture content.

Sawdust as building material.
   xx Building materials.

Sawdust as feeding stuff.
   xx Feeding stuffs.

Sawdust as fuel.

Sawdust-cement concrete.   See Sawdust
  composition products.

Sawdust composition products.
   x Sawdust-pulp combinations.
      Sawdust-cement concrete.
      Sawdust-Portland cement com-
      positions.

Sawdust mulches.
   xx Wood waste mulches.

Sawdust-Portland cement compositions.
  See Sawdust composition products.

Sawdust-pulp combinations.   See Sawdust
  composition products.

Sawflies.   See Tenthredinidae; Tenthredinoidea.

Sawfly leaf-miner.   See Profenusa col-
  laris.

Sawing.
　　x Bucking.

Sawmill machinery.
　　sa Lumbering tools.
　　　Saws.
　　　Log frame.
　　x Saw mill machinery.
　　xx Lumbering tools.
　　　Sawmills.

Sawmill workers.　　See Lumbermen.

Sawmills.　　(DIRECT)
　　sa Sawmill machinery.
　　xx Lumbering.
--Accounting.
　　xx Lumbering. Accounting.
--By-products.
　　sa Subdivision By-products under:
　　　Wood.
　　xx Wood. By-products.
　　　Waste products.
--Cost of operation.
　　xx Cost of operation.
　　　Lumbering. Cost.
--Directories.
　　sa Lumbering. Directories.
　　　Sawmills [geographic subdivi-
　　　　sion] Directories, e.g.,
　　　Sawmills. U.S. Directories.
--Maps.
--Periodicals.
--Research.
--Societies.
--Statistics.
--Tables, calculations, etc.
--Work management.
　　xx Work management.

Saws.
　　x Saws, Chain.
　　　Chain saws.
　　　Saws, Frame.
　　　Frame saws.
　　　Bandsaws.
　　　Cross-cut saws.
　　xx Saw mill machinery.
--Catalogs.

Saws, Chain.　　See Saws.

Saws.
--Directories.

Saws, Frame.　　See Saws.

Sawtooth National Forest, Idaho.
　　xx Forest reservations.
　　　Idaho. Forest reservations.

Sawyer Co., Wis.
　　xx Wisconsin.
--Land.
　　sa Subdivision Wisconsin. Sawyer
　　　Co. under: Land. Classifi-
　　　cation.
　　xx Wisconsin. Land.

Saxaol.　　See Saksaul.

Saxe-Altenburg.
--Agriculture.
-- --History.

Saxe-Coburg-Gotha.
--Agriculture.
--Forestry.

Saxe-Weimar-Eisenach.
--Agriculture.

Saxifraga.

Saxifraga crassifolia.　　See Bergenia
　　crassifolia.

Saxifraga florulenta.

Saxifraga granulata.

Saxifraga lantoscana.

Saxifraga lingulata.

Saxifragaceae.
　　sa Argophyllum.
　　　Heuchera.
　　　Philadelphus.
　　　Bergenia.

Saxon Merino sheep.

Saxony.
--Agricultural experiment stations.
--Agriculture.
　　sa Subdivision Agriculture under:
　　　Lützschena, Saxony.
　　　Chemnitz, Saxony.
　　　Frohburg, Saxony (Estate)

Saxony (Continued)
--Agriculture.
　　sa Subdivision Saxony under:
　　　　Agriculture, Cooperative.
　　　　Agriculture. Economic as-
　　　　　　pects.
　　　　Flax.
・--History.
　　xx Agriculture. History.
-- --Statistics.
　　xx Agriculture. Statistics.
--Apiculture.
--Botany.
　　sa Subdivision Botany under:
　　　　Chemnitz.
　　　　Bautzen, Ger.
　　　　Subdivision Saxony under:
　　　　　　Algae.
--Commerce.
　　sa Subdivision Saxony under:
　　　　Farm produce. Marketing.
--Domestic animals.
　　xx Germany. Domestic animals.
--Entomology.
　　sa Subdivision Saxony under:
　　　　Hymenoptera.
--Forestry.
　　sa Olbernhau.
・--History.
　　sa Subdivision Forestry. History
　　　　under: Wernigerode.
--History.
--Milk supply.
　　xx Germany. Milk supply.
--Natural history.
--Ornithology.
--Paleobotany.
--Social life and customs.
--Soils.
　　sa Subdivision Soils under:
　　　　Wingendorf, Saxony.
　　　　Subdivision Saxony under:
　　　　　　Peat.
--Statistics.
　　sa Saxony. Agriculture. Sta-
　　　　tistics.

Saxony. Statisches bureau.
--Publications.

Saxony.
--Swine.
　　sa Subdivision Swine under:
　　　　Schlanstedt, Saxony.
--Water-supply.

Saxony, Lower.　　See Lower Saxony.

Saxony (Province)
　　sa Eastphalia.
--Agriculture.
　　sa Wernigerode. Agriculture.
　　　　Subdivision Saxony (Province)
　　　　under: Agriculture. Eco-
　　　　nomic aspects.
　　　　Sugar-beet.
--Forestry.
　　sa Wernigerode.
--Land.
　　sa Subdivision Saxony (Province)
　　　　under: Land reform.

Saxony sheep.

Say stinkbug.　　See Chlorochroa sayi.

Scab.
　　sa Sheep-dip.
　　x Scabies in sheep.

Scab-mite.　　See Sarcoptes.

Scabby mouth of sheep.　　See Contagious
　　ecthyma of sheep.

Scabies.
　　sa Sarcopties scabiei.
　　　　Mange.

Scabies (Human)

Scabies in cattle.　　See Cattle scab.

Scabies in sheep.　　See Scab.

Scabiosa.
　　sa Knautia.

Scaevola.
　　xx Goodeniaceae.

Scafati. Italy. R. Istituto sperimentale
　　per le coltivazione dei tabacchi.

Scaffolding.
　　xx Carpentry.
　　　　Building.

Scale-insects.　　See Coccidae; Coccoidea.

Scales (Weighing instruments)
    xx Weighing-machines.
       Weights and measures.

Scalidiidae.
    xx Coleoptera.

Scaling.
    sa Subdivision Tables and ready-
       reckoners under: Logs.
    x Log scaling.
      Log measurement.
      Logs. Measurement.
      Logs. Scaling.
    xx Forest mensuration.

Scalp.
 --Diseases.
    sa Alopecia.
    xx Pathology.

Scalpellum.

Scalping.

Scaly leg.

Scandinavia.
    sa Lapland.
      Norway.
      Sweden.
      Denmark.
 --Agriculture.
    sa Subdivision Scandinavia under:
       Forage plants.
       Cereals.
       Wheat.
 - --History.
    sa Scandinavia. Land tenure.
       History.
 -- --Periodicals.
 --Antiquities.
 --Apiculture.
 -- --Periodicals.
 --Botany.
    sa Subdivision Botany under:
       Denmark.
       Norway.
       Sweden.
       Wild flowers.

Scandinavia (Continued)
 --Botany.
    sa Subdivision Scandinavia
       under: Trees.
       Algae.
       Mosses.
       Fresh-water flora.
       Fungi.
 --Cattle.
    xx Cattle.
 --Commerce.
    sa Scandinavia under: Grain
       trade.
 --Dairying.
    sa Subdivision Scandinavia under:
       Dairy industry and trade.
 --Description and travel.
    sa Subdivision Scandinavia under:
       Hunting.
 --Economic conditions.
 --Education.
 --Entomology.
    sa Subdivision Scandinavia under:
       Lepidoptera.
       Hymenoptera.
       Coleoptera.
       Butterflies.
       Orthoptera.
       Diptera.
 --Forestry.
    sa Subdivision Scandinavia under:
       Trees.
       Wood-using industries.
 --History.
 --Land.
    sa Subdivision Land under:
       Denmark.
    xx Europe. Land.
 --Maps.
 --Natural history.
 --Neutrality.
    xx Europe. Neutrality.
 --Ornithology.
 --Politics and government.
    sa Subdivision Politics and
       government under: Sweden.
    xx Europe. Politics and govern-
       ment.
 --Pomology.
 --Research.
 --Social conditions.
 --Soils.
    sa Subdivision Scandinavia under:
       Peat.

Scandinavia (Continued)
--Statistics.
        sa Subdivision Statistics under:
            Norway.
            Sweden.
            Denmark.
            Iceland.
--Zoology.
        sa Subdivision Zoology under:
            Denmark.
            Norway.
            Sweden.
            Subdivision Scandinavia under:
                Fresh-water fauna.

Scandinavian Fisheries Exhibition of
    Trondhjem.   See Trondhjem. Scandina-
    vian Fisheries Exhibition.

Scandinavian literature.
--Bibliography.

Scandinavians in Brazil.

Scandinavians in New Zealand.

Scandium.

Scania, Sweden.
--Botany.
        sa Subdivision Sweden. Scania
            under: Algae.
            Mosses.
--Description and travel.
--Natural history.
--Paleontology.
        xx Sweden. Paleontology.
--Soils.

Scansores.
.

Scantlings.
--Grading and standardization.
        xx Lumber. Grading and standardi-
            zation.
--Testing.

Scapania.

Scaphidiidae.

Scaphoideus.

Scaphoideus luteolus.

Scapteriscus.
        x Mole cricket.

Scapteriscus didactylus.   See Scapteris-
    cus vicinus.

Scapteriscus vicinus.

Scarabaeidae.
        sa Dynastes.
            Allorhina.
            Ligurus.
            Plusiotis.
            Oryctes.
            Onitis.
            Aphodius.
            Anomala.
            Geniatidae.
            Autoserica.
            Phyllophaga.
            Dung beetles.
            Pseudoclinteria.
            Chlaenobia.
            Eupariini.
            Cyclocephala.
            Euchirinae.
            Phaenomerinae.
            Trogiinae.
            Coelorrhina.
            Cetoninae.
            Strategus.
            Oniticellus.
            Pedaria.
            Cetonia.
            Diloboderus.
            Euetheola.
            Popillia japonica.
            Cotinis.
            Aphodiinae.
            Anoxia.
        x Chironinae.
            Geotrupinae.
            Taurocerastinae.
            Coprinae.
            Aegialiinae.
            Rutelidae.
--Parasites.

Scarabaeoidea.

Scarabaeus.

Scarabaeus bettoni.

Scarabaeus quadrifoveatus.   See Strategus
    quadrifoveatus.

Scarabaeus sevoistra.

Scarborough, Eng.
    --Natural history.

Scarcity of labor.   See Labor supply.

Scarecrows.
    x Frightening devices for birds.
    xx Ornithology, Economic.

Scarf clouds.

Scarifiers.
    sa Seed scarifiers.

Scarites.

Scarlatina.

Scarlet runner bean.
    x Phaseolus multiflorus.
    Phaseolus coccineus.
    xx Beans.

Scarlet trefoil.

Scarpanto.
    --Natural history.

Scatomyzides.

Scatophagidae.

Scatopsidae.
    xx Diptera.

Scavenger water beetle.   See Hydrophilus
    triangularis.

Scelidotherium.

Scelionidae.
    sa Phanuropsis.
    Phanurus.

Sceliphron.
    xx Sphegidae.

Sceliphron cementarium.
    x Mud-daubers.

Scellus.
    xx Dolichopodidae.

Scellus virgo.

Sceloporus spinosus floridanus.

Scenedesmaceae.
    sa Scenedesmus.

Scenedesmus.
    xx Scenedesmaceae.

Scenery, Forest.   See Forest scenery.

Scenopinidae.
    sa Scenopinus.
    x Omphralidae.

Scenopinus.

Scent organs.   See Senses and sense
    organs.
    --Insects.   See Smell. Insects.

Schaerbeek, Belgium.

Schaffhausen (Canton)
    --Agriculture.
    --Land.
        sa Subdivision Schaffhausen
            (Canton) under: Land tenure.
    --Roads.

Schardinger reaction.
    xx Aldehydes.
    Milk. Analysis and examination.

Schaumburg (Former County) Germany.
    --Agriculture.

Schaumburg-Lippe, Ger.
    --Agriculture.

Schedius kuvanae.

Schemnitz, Hungary. Konigl.Ungarische
    berg- und forst-akademie.   See
    Schemnitz, Hungary. Magyar királyi bá-
    nyászati és erdészeti akadémia.

Schendylina.

Schenectady Co., N.Y.
--Agriculture.
-- --Periodicals.
--Botany.

Schenley Park Conservatory, Pittsburg, Pa.

Scheuchzeriaceae.
         sa Triglochin.

Schiedea.

Schinus dependens.

Schistocerca.
         sa Acridium.
         x Shistocerca.
         xx Acrididae.
            Acridium.

Schistocerca cancellata.
--Bibliography.

Schistocerca gregaria.
         x Criquet pelerin.
            Schistocerca peregrina.
--Congresses.

Schistocerca migratoria.

Schistocerca paranensis.
--Parasites.

Schistocerca peregrina.   See Schistocerca
   gregaria.

Schistocerca peruviana.

Schistocerca succincta.

Schistoceros.
         x Amphicerus.

Schistoceros bicaudatus.   See Schistoceros
   hamatus.

Schistoceros hamatus.
         x Schistoceros bicaudatus.
            Apple twig borer.

Schistoloma.

Schistosity.

Schistosoma.

Schistosoma mansoni.
         x Schistosomum mansoni.

Schistosomiasis.
--Bibliography.

Schistosomidae.

Schistosomum mansoni.   See Schistosoma
   mansoni.

Schistostega osmundacea.

Schizaeaceae.

Schizomeria.
         xx Cunoniaceae.

Schizomeria ovata.
         x Birch, White Australian.
            Australian white birch.
            White birch, Australian.
--Testing.
         xx Wood. Testing.

Schizomycetes.
         sa Bacteria.
            Streptothryx.
            Sarcina.
            Streptomyces.
         xx Bacteriology.
            Schizophyta.

Schizoneura.   See Eriosoma.

Schizonotus sieboldi.

Schizophora.

Schizophyceae.   See Cyanophyceae.

Schizophyta.
         sa Schizomycetes.
            Cyanophyceae.

Schizosaccharomyces.
         xx Saccharomycetaceae.

Schlalach, Prussia.
         xx Prussia.

Schlangeninsel.
--Ornithology.

Schlanstedt, Saxony.
--Swine.
    xx Saxony. Swine.
        Germany. Swine.

Schlerochroa.   See Scleroderma.

Schleroderma.   See Scleroderma.

Schleswig-Holstein.
--Agriculture.
    sa Subdivision Schleswig-Holstein
       under: Agriculture. Eco-
       nomic aspects.
       Grasses.
       Agricultural laborers.
       Agricultural credit.
       Colonization, Agricultural.
       Reclamation of land.
       Agricultural policies and
        programs.
- --History.
-- --Periodicals.
-- --Statistics.
    xx Germany. Agriculture. Sta-
       tistics.
--Apiculture.
-- --Periodicals.
--Botany.
    sa Subdivision Schleswig-Holstein
       under: Lichens.
-- --Bibliography.
--Cattle.
--Dairying.
-- --Statistics.
--Domestic animals.
    sa Schleswig-Holstein. Cattle.
       Schleswig-Holstein. Swine.
--Forestry.
    sa Subdivision Schleswig-Holstein
       under: Afforestation and
       reforestation.
-- --History.
    xx Germany. Forestry. History.
--Land.
    sa Subdivision Schleswig-Holstein
       under: Land reform.
--Maps.
--Population.
--Statistics.
--Swine.
--Water-supply.
--Zoology.

Schleswig-Holsteiner Rotbuntes.   See Red
    pied Holstein cattle.

Schleswig horse.

Schnauzers.
    xx Terriers.

Schneeberg, Carniola.
--Botany.

Schöckel, Austria (Mountain)
--Botany.

Schoenobius incertellus.

Schoharie Co., N.Y.
    sa Country life. New York (State)
       Schoharie Co.

Scholars.
--Directories.

Scholarships.

Scholasticism.

Schöner von Boskoop apple.

School and community.   See Community
    and school.

School architecture.   See School-houses.

School attendance.   (INDIRECT)

School buildings.   See School-houses.

School buses.
    xx Motor buses.
       School children. Transporta-
       tion.

School cafeterias.   See School lunch-
    rooms.

School centralization.   See Schools.
    Centralization.

School children.
--Food.   See Food for school children.
--Transportation.
    sa School buses.

School children in war.   See World War,
  1939-1945. Children.

School consolidation.   See Schools. Centralization.

School districts.
  sa Special districts.

School fairs.   See Rural school fairs.

School farms.

School finance.
  sa Education. Government aid.
    School taxes.
  xx School taxes.

School forests.
  x Forests, School.
  xx Tree planting.

School gardens.
  sa Children's gardens.
    School farms.
    Gardening. Juvenile literature.
  --Bibliography.
  --Periodicals.
  --Societies.

School grounds.

School-houses.
  sa Teachers' homes.
  x School architecture.
    School buildings.
  xx Architecture.
    Schools.
    Architecture. Designs and
      plans.

School-houses as recreation centers.   See
  Community centers.

School hygiene.
  sa Playgrounds.
  --Congresses.

School lands.
  x School funds.
    Land grants for education.
  xx Public lands.
    Land grants.

School libraries.
  --Bibliography.

School lunch kitchens.   See Kitchens,
  School lunch.

School lunch program (U.S.)   See
  National school lunch program.

School lunches.
  sa National school lunch act.
    National school lunch program.
  xx Food for school children.
    Luncheons.
    Menus.
  --Bibliography.
    xx Food for school children. Bib-
      liography.
    Luncheons. Bibliography.
  --Congresses.
  --Finance.
    xx Finance.
  --Foods list.
  --Government aid.
    xx Government aid.
  --Periodicals.
  --Prices.
    xx Food. Prices.
  --Statistics.

School lunchrooms.
  x School cafeterias.
  xx Restaurants. lunch rooms. etc.
  --Accounting.

School management and organization.
  sa Teaching.
    School districts.
  xx Rural schools.

School milk programs.
  x Special school milk program.
  xx School children. Food.
    Agricultural policies and
      programs.
    Milk.
    Milk for school children.
    Milk programs.

School nurses.

School playgrounds.   See Playgrounds.

School revenues.   See School finance.

School supervision. See School management and organization.

School taxes. (DIRECT)
sa School finance.
xx School finance.
Taxation.

Schoolcraft Co., Mich.
--Soils.
sa Subdivision Michigan. Schoolcraft Co. under: Soil-
surveys.

Schools.
sa Public schools.
Rural schools.
Private schools.
Community schools.
Sunday-schools.
Professional education.
School-houses.
Subdivision Study and teaching
under various subjects.
Subdivision Schools under:
World War, 1939-1945. War
work.
--Advertising.
xx Advertising.
--Centralization.
x Centralization of schools.
Concentration of schools.
Consolidated schools.
Consolidation of schools.
School consolidation.
School centralization.
Schools. Decentralization.

Schools, Community. See Community
schools.

Schools.
--Decentralization. See Schools. Cen-
tralization.
--Directories. See Education. Direc-
tories.
--Exercises and recreations.
xx Games.
--Food service.
x Food service in schools.
--Furniture, equipment, etc.
--Lighting.
xx Electric lighting.

Schools, Public. See Public schools.

Schools, Rural. See Rural schools.

Schools and community. See Community
and school.

Schools in war.
sa World War, 1939-1945. War work.
Schools.

Schopper folder.

Schrenk spruce. See Picea schrenkiana.

Schroders phosphate potash fertilizers.
See Phosphate potash fertilizers.

Schroeteriaster.

Schultz-Lupitz Estate.

Schuyler Co., Ill.
--Soils.
xx Illinois. Soils.

Schuyler Co., N.Y.
--Agriculture.
sa Subdivision New York (State)
Schuyler Co. under:
Land utilization.
Agricultural policies and
programs.
--Land.
sa Subdivision Schuyler Co. under:
Land utilization. New York
(State)
--Soils.
sa Subdivision Schuyler Co. under:
Soil conservation surveys.
New York (State)

Schuylkill Co., Pa.
--Botany.
--Forestry.
sa Subdivision Pennsylvania.
Schuylkill Co. under:
Forest surveys.

Schuylkill River project.

Schwabach, Ger.
--Agriculture.
--Soils.

Schwabisch-Hallisches swine. See
Swabian-Halle swine.

Schwarzbuntes Niederungsvieh. See Black
    pied lowland cattle.

Schwarzburg-Rudolstadt.
--Forestry.

Schwarzburg-Sondershausen.
--Agriculture.
--Botany.
--Forestry.
-- --History.
    xx Germany. Forestry. History.
--Land.
    sa Subdivision Schwarzburg-
      Sondershausen under:
      Land tenure.

Schwarzwald. See Black forest.

Schweitzer system of milling.

Schweizerischer Nationalpark.
    x Parc national suisse.
--Botany.
--Entomology.
--Natural history.

Schwerin.
--Geology.

Sciaenidae.

Sciara.

Sciarinae.

Science.
    sa Agriculture and science.
      Astronomy.
      Bacteriology.
      Biology.
      Botany.
      Chemistry.
      Crystallography.
      Ethnology.
      Geology.
      Mathematics.
      Meteorology.
      Mineralogy.
      Natural history.
      Paleontology.
      Petrology.
      Physics.

Science (Continued)
    sa Physiology.
      Zoology.
      Headings beginning with the
      word Scientific.
--Abbreviations.
    x Scientific abbreviations.
--Abstracts.
-- --Bibliography.
-- --Periodicals.
--Addresses, essays, lectures.
    sa Subdivision Addresses, essays,
      lectures under: Physi-
      ology//

Science, Applied. See Technology.

Science.
--Authorship. See Reports. Preparation;
    Scientific papers.
--Bibliography.
    sa Subdivision Bibliography un-
      der: Science. History.
      Science. Biography.
-- --Periodicals.
--Bio-bibliography.
    x Scientists. Bio-bibliography.
--Biography. See Scientists.
--Classification.
--Collected works.
    sa Science. Addresses, essays,
      lectures.

Science, Communication in. See Communi-
    cations in science.

Science.
--Congresses.
    x Scientific congresses.
-- --Bibliography.
      xx Congresses and conventions.
      Bibliography.
-- --Directories.
--Dictionaries.
-- --Bibliography.
--Directories. See Scientists' direc-
    tories.
--Education. See Science. Study and
    teaching.
--Exhibitions.
    x Scientific exhibits.
    xx Exhibitions.
--Government aid. See Research.
    Government aid.

Science (Continued)
--Graphic methods.
--Handbooks, manuals, etc.
--History.   (INDIRECT)
-- --Bibliography.
-- --Study and teaching.
    xx Science. Study and teaching.
--Information services.
    sa Communication in science.
    xx Communication in science.
-- --Congresses.
-- --Directories.
--Juvenile literature.
--Laboratory manuals.
--Legislation.
    x Scientific legislation.
--Methodology.
    sa Communication in science.
--Museums.   See Scientific museums.
--Periodicals.
    sa Subdivision Periodicals under:
      Entomology.
      Zoology.
      Natural history.
      Science. Bibliography.
      Biology.
      Science. Year-books.
    x Learned periodicals.
-- --Abstracts.
-- --Bibliography.
    sa Biology. Periodicals. Bibliog-
      raphy.
-- --Indexes.
--Philosophy.
    sa Subdivision Philosophy under:
      Physics.
      Biology.

Science, Popular.

Science.
--Research.   See Research.
--Societies.
    sa Learned institutions and
      societies.
    x Scientific societies.
-- --Abbreviations.
-- --Bibliography.
-- --Directories.
    sa Learned institutions and
      societies. Directories.
-- --Rewards (Prizes, etc.)
    xx Rewards (Prizes, etc.)

Science (Continued)
--Study and teaching.
    sa Subdivision Study and teaching
      under: Science. History.
    x Education, Scientific.
      Scientific education.
-- --Bibliography.
-- --Congresses.
-- --Government aid.
    xx Government aid.
--Tables, etc.
    xx Tables (Systematic lists)
--Terminology.
    x Scientific terminology.
    xx Terminology.
-- --Abstracts.
-- --Bibliography.
--Year-books.

Science and agriculture.   See Agri-
    culture and science.

Science and art.

Science and civilization.
    x Civilization and science.
    Science and history.
    History and science.

Science and history.   See Science and
    civilization.

Science and literature.   See Literature
    and science.

Science and religion.   See Religion and
    science.

Science and state.   (DIRECT)
    x State and science.
--Bibliography.

Science and technology act, 1958.

Science and war.   See War and science.

Science as an occupation.
    sa Biology as an occupation.
    xx Occupations.
      Scientists.

Science in poetry.

Science information.   See Communication
    in science.

Science literature searching. See
Information storage and retrieval
systems Science.

Scientific abbreviations. See Science.
Abbreviations.

Scientific apparatus and instruments.
    sa Bacteriological apparatus.
       Biological apparatus and
        supplies.
       Botanical apparatus.
       Chemistry. Apparatus.
       Electric apparatus and
        appliances.
       Engineering instruments.
       Magnetic instruments.
       Mathematical instruments.
       Medical instruments and
        apparatus.
       Meteorological instruments.
       Optical instruments.
       Physiological apparatus.
       Surgical instruments and
        apparatus.
       Entomological apparatus.
       Siltometer.
       Transit-instruments.
       Physical instruments.
       Electronic apparatus and
        appliances.
       Laboratories. Apparatus and
        supplies.
       Names of special instruments,
        e.g., Spectroscope.
    x Apparatus, Scientific.
       Instruments, Scientific.
       Scientific instruments.
       Instruments.
       Instrumentation.
--Abstracts.
--Bibliography.
-- --Periodicals.
--Directories.
--Periodicals.
--Research.

Scientific communication. See Communication in science.

Scientific congresses. See Science.
Congresses.

Scientific education. See Science. Study
and teaching.

Scientific errors. See Errors,
Scientific.

Scientific exchanges. See Exchanges,
Literary and scientific.

Scientific exhibits. See Science.
Exhibitions.

Scientific expeditions.
    sa Challenger Expedition.
       Rurick.
       Sulphur (H.M.S.)//
--Handbooks.

Scientific instruments. See Scientific
apparatus and instruments.

Scientific legislation. See Science.
Legislation.

Scientific literature.
    sa Scientific papers.
    xx Communication in science.

Scientific literature searching. See
Information storage and retrieval
systems. Science.

Scientific management. See Industrial
management.

Scientific manpower. See Scientists.

Scientific museums.
    x Science. Museums.
    xx Museums.

Scientific names.
    sa Subdivision Nomenclature
       under: Botany.
       Entomology.
       Natural history.
       Zoology.

Scientific papers.
    Here are entered works on the
    preparation of technical and
    scientific reports and papers.
    For guides on technical prob-
    lems of writing and works on
    the preparation of manuscripts
    preliminary to printing and
    publication. See Authorship.
    Handbooks, manuals, etc.

Scientific papers (Continued)
    sa Reports. Preparation.
    x Technical writing.
      Medical writing.
      Technology. Authorship.
      Science. Authorship.
      Engineering papers.
      Scientific writing.
    xx Communication in science.
      Scientific literature.
      Reports. Preparation.
--Bibliography.

Scientific research.   See Research.

Scientific societies.   See Science.
  Societies; Learned institutions and
  societies.

Scientific terminology.   See Science.
  Terminology.

Scientific writing.   See Reports. Preparation; Scientific papers.

Scientists.
    sa Anatomists.
      Biologists.
      Botanists.
      Chemists.
      Entomologists.
      Geologists.
      Mathematicians.
      Naturalists.
      Ornithologists.
      Women as scientists.
      Zoologists.
      Science as an occupation.
    x Science. Biography.
      Manpower, Scientific.
      Scientific manpower.

Scientists, American.
--Abstracts.
--Directories.
--Statistics.

Scientists, Argentinean.
--Directories.

Scientists, Australian.

Scientists, Bolivian.
--Directories.

Scientists, British.
--Directories.

Scientists, Chilean.
--Directories.

Scientists, Chinese.

Scientists, Colombian.
--Directories.

Scientists, Dutch.
    x Dutch scientists.
      Netherlands scientists.

Scientists, Dutch East Indies.

Scientists, Egyptian.

Scientists, European.

Scientists, German.
    x German scientists.

Scientists, Greek.

Scientists, Iranian.
    x Iranian scientists.
--Directories.

Scientists, Iraqi.
--Directories.

Scientists, Italian.

Scientists, Japanese.

Scientists, Lebanese.
--Directories.

Scientists, Mexican.
--Directories.

Scientists, New Zealand.
    x New Zealand scientists.
--Directories.

Scientists, Paraguayan.
--Directories.

Scientists, Polish.

Scientists, Puerto Rican.
--Directories.

Scientists, Russian.
--Directories.

Scientists, South American.
--Directories.

Scientists, Swedish.
--Directories.

Scientists, Swiss.

Scientists, Uruguayan.
--Directories.

Scientists, Venezuelan.
--Directories.

Scientists.
--Bibliography.
--Bio-bibliography.   See Science. Bio-
    bibliography.
--Correspondence, reminiscences, etc.
--Directories.   See Scientists' direc-
    tories.
--Statistics.
        sa Subdivision Statistics under
            scientists of a particular
            country, e.g., Scientists,
            American. Statistics.

Scientists' directories.
        sa Subdivision Directories under
            special classes of scien-
            tists, e.g., Botanists. Di-
            rectories.
        Subdivision Directories under
            scientists of a particular
            country, e.g., Scientists,
            American. Directories.
        x Naturalists' directories.
        Scientists. Directories.

Scilla maritima.   See Urginea maritima.

Scilly Isles, Eng.
--Botany.

Scincidae.
        x Lizard.

Sciobius.

Sciomyzidae.

Scioto Co., Ohio.
--History.
--Soils.
        sa Subdivision Ohio. Scioto Co.
            under: Soil-surveys.

Scioto River. Ohio.
        sa Subdivision Ohio. Scioto Valley
            under: Flood control.

Scioto Valley. Ohio.
        sa Subdivision Ohio. Scioto Valley
            under: Flood control.

Scirpophaga nivella.

Scirpus duvallii.

Scirpus lacustris.

Scirrhia acicola.

Scirtothrips aurantii.

Scirtothrips citri.
        xx Citrus. Pests.

Scirtothrips signipennis.
        x Banana rust thrips.
        xx Banana. Pests.

Scitaminaceae.
        sa Costus.

Scitamineae.
        sa Musa.
        Zingiberaceae.
        Thaumatococcus.

Sciuridae.   See Squirrels.

Scleractinia.
        xx Coelenterata.

Scleranthus uncinatus.

Scleroderma.

Scleroderma galapagense.

Scleroproteins.   See Albuminoids.

Sclerospora macrospora.

Sclerospora philippinensis.

Sclerospora sacchari.

Sclerospora spontanea.

Sclerostoma.

Sclerostoma edentatum.

Sclerostoma pinguicola.

Sclerostomidae.

Sclerotinia.

Sclerotinia betulae.

Sclerotinia camelliae.

Sclerotinia carunculoides.

Sclerotinia cinerea.

Sclerotinia fructicola.

Sclerotinia fuckeliana.

Sclerotinia libertiania.

Sclerotinia minor.

Sclerotinia ricini.

Sclerotinia sclerotiorum.
    x Rhizoctonia napi.

Sclerotinia trifoliorum.

Sclerotium delphinii.
    xx Delphinium. Diseases.

Sclerotium oryzae.

Sclerotium rolfsii.
    xx Soil bacteria.

Sclerotium tuliparum.   See Rhizoctonia
  tuliparum.

Sclerurus.

Scobicia declivis.

Scolia.
    xx Scoliidae.

Scolia flavifrons.

Scolia formosa.   See Campsomeris formosa.

Scolia oryctophaga.

Scoliidae.
    sa Brachycistiinae.
       Campsomeris.
       Scolia.

Scoliopus.
    xx Liliaceae.

Scolitus destructor.   See Scolytus
  scolytus.

Scolopendra.

Scolopendra subspinipes.

Scolopendrella.
    sa Scolopendrellidae.

Scolopendrellidae.
    xx Scolopendrella.

Scolopendridae.

Scoloplos armiger.

Scolt Head Island, Eng.
    xx England.
    --Ornithology.

Scolytidae.
    sa Tomicus.
       Dendroctonus.
       Tomicini.
       Hylastinus.
       Phloeotribus.
       Tomicidae.
       Araecerus.
       Stephanoderes.
       Micracinae.
       Pityophthorus.
       Pityogenes.
       Hylastes.
       Pseudohylesinus.
       Sphaerotrypes.
       Xyleborus.
    x Ambrosia beetles.
    xx Scolytoidea.
       Pine. Pests.

Scolytoidea.
    sa Scolytidae.
       Ipidae.
       Dendroctonus.
    x Bark beetles.

Scolytoplataypus hamatus.

Scolytus.
    x Engraver beetles.

Scolytus major.
    xx Deodar. Pests.

Scolytus multistriatus.
    x Smaller European elm bark
      beetle.
      European elm bark beetle,
       Smaller.
      Elm bark beetle.
    xx Elm. Pests.

Scolytus rugulosus.
    x Eccoptogaster.
      Fruit bark beetle.
      Shot-hole borer.

Scolytus scolytus.
  --Parasites.

Scolytus ventralis.

Scoparia.

Scopolamine.
    xx Anaesthetics.

Scoring.
    sa Stock judging.

Scorpio occitanus.

Scorpionida.
    sa Androctonidae.
      Scorpio.
      Proscorpius.
    x Scorpions.
    xx Arachnida.
  --Bibliography.
    xx Arachnida. Bibliography.
  --Parasites.

Scorpions. See Scorpionida.

Scorpions, False. See Chelonethida.

Scorzonera.
    xx Cichoriaceae.

Scorzonera tau-saghyz. See Tau-saghyz.

Scotch pine. See Pinus sylvestris.

Scotch terriers. See Scottish terriers.

Scotia, Calif.

Scotland.
    sa Spay River.
      Dundee, Scot.
      Loch Maree, Scot.//
  --Agricultural experiment stations.
    sa Dalmeny (Scot.) Agricultural
      Station.
  --Agricultural schools. See Scotland.
    Agriculture. Education.
  --Agriculture.
    sa Subdivision Agriculture under:
      Argyleshire.
      Berwickshire.
      Gowrie, Carse of//
      Scotland. Domestic animals.
      Subdivision Scotland under:
      Agricultural laborers.
      Agriculture. Economic
       aspects.
      Flax.
      Farm buildings.
      Poultry.
      Sugar-beet.
      Farm produce. Cost of
       production.
      Colonization, Agricultural.
      Agricultural surveys.
      War and agriculture (1939-
       1945)
      Farms.
      Types of farming.
      Jute.
      Agricultural credit.
      Grassland farming.
  -- --Directories.
  -- --Education.
    sa Edinburgh and East of
      Scotland College of Agri-
      culture.
      West of Scotland Agricultural
      College.
      North of Scotland College of
      Agriculture, Aberdeen//
  --History.

Scotland (Continued)
--Agriculture.
-- --Periodicals.
- --Research.
-- --Statistics.
    xx Agriculture. Statistics.
--Apiculture.
    xx Gt. Brit. Apiculture.
--Appropriations and expenditures.
--Botany.
    sa Subdivision Botany under:
        Banffshire.
        Berwickshire.
        Edinburgh//
        Subdivision Scotland under:
        Trees.
        Shrubs.
        Fungi.
        Mosses.
        Hepaticae.
        Algae.
        Alpine flora.
--Cattle.
-- --History.
    xx Cattle. History.
--Cattle trade.
-- --History.
--Commerce.
    sa Subdivision Scotland under:
        Farm produce. Marketing.
-- --Directories.
    xx Commerce. Directories.
--Dairying.
--Description and travel.
    sa Subdivision Description and
        travel under: Argyleshire,
        Scotland.
        Highlands of Scotland.
--Domestic animals.
--Economic conditions.
    sa Subdivision Scotland under:
        History, Economic.
        Subdivision Economic conditions
        under names of regions, coun- -
        ties, etc.
    xx Gt. Brit. Economic conditions.
--Education.
    sa Scotland. Agriculture. Educa-
        tion.
--Emigration and immigration.
    xx Gt. Brit. Emigration and immi-·
        gration.

Scotland (Continued)
--Entomology.
    sa Subdivision Entomology under:
        Flannan Islands.
        Edinburgh.
        Subdivision Scotland under:
        Coleoptera.
        Hymenoptera.
        Diptera.
--Fisheries.
-- --Statistics.
--Forest reservations.
    sa Argyll National Forest Park.
        Ae, Forest of, Scotland.
        Glen More National Forest
        Park, Scot.//
--Forestry.
    sa Subdivision Forestry under:
        Glenmore, Scot.
        Aberdeenshire, Scot.
        Subdivision Scotland under:
        Afforestation and re-
        forestation.
        Tree planting.
        Trees.
        Forest policy.
-- --History.
-- --Periodicals.
--Geography.
--History.
    sa History, Economic. Scotland.
--Industries.
    sa Subdivision Scotland under:
        Industrial surveys.
--Land.
    sa Subdivision Scotland under:
        Land utilization.
        Land, Marginal.
--Maps.
--Milk supply.
--Milk trade.
    xx Gt. Brit. Milk trade.
--Natural history.
    sa Subdivision Natural history
        under: Benderloch, Scot.
        Highlands of Scotland.
        Tay River.
    xx Gt. Brit. Natural history.
--Ornithology.
    sa Subdivision Ornithology under:
        Dumfriesshire, Scot.
        Perthshire.

Scotland (Continued)
  --Paleobotany.
      sa Subdivision Paleobotany under:
          Sutherland, Scot.
          Berwickshire, Scot.
  --Paleontology.
      sa Ayrshire, Scotland. Paleon-
          tology.
  --Pomology.
  --Population.
      sa Subdivision Scotland under:
          Migration, Internal.
  --Public lands.
  --Research.
      xx Research.
          Gt. Brit. Research.
  --Revenue.
  --Roads.
      sa Subdivision Roads under:
          Haddingtonshire, Scot.
          Peebleshire.
          Renfrewshire.
  - --History.
      sa Highlands of Scotland. Roads.
          History.
  · --Law.
      xx Roads. Legislation.
  --Sheep.
      xx Gt. Brit. Sheep.
  --Social conditions.
  --Social life and customs.
  --Soils.
      sa Subdivision Scotland under:
          Peat.
          Soil-surveys.
      Subdivision Soils under the
          names of individual places,
          e.g., Aberdeenshire, Scot.
          Soils.
  --Statistics.
      sa Scotland. Agriculture. Sta-
          tistics.
  --Transportation.
  --Water-supply.
      sa Subdivision Water-supply under:
          Lanarkshire, Scotland.
  --Zoology.
      sa Subdivision Zoology under:
          Elginshire.
          Argyleshire.
          Dumfriesshire.
          Millport, Scot.

Scott Co., Ark.
  --History.
      xx Arkansas. History.

Scott Co., Ill.
      xx Illinois.

Scott Co., Ind.
  --Soils.
      sa Subdivision Indiana. Scott Co.
          under: Soil-surveys.

Scott Co., Minn.
  --Soils.
      sa Subdivision Minnesota. Scott
          Co. under: Soil-surveys.

Scott Co., Va.
      sa Subdivision Scott Co. under:
          County surveys. Virginia.
      xx Virginia.
  --Economic conditions.
      sa Subdivision Scott Co. under:
          Economic surveys. Virginia.
      xx Virginia. Economic conditions.
  --Industries and resources.
      sa Industrial surveys. Virginia.
          Scott Co.
  --Soils.
      sa Subdivision Virginia. Scott
          Co. under: Soil-surveys.

Scottish Highlands.   See Highlands of
      Scotland.

Scottish terriers.

Scotts Bluff, Neb.
      xx Nebraska.

Scotts Bluff Field Station, Mitchell,
      Neb.
          x U.S. Scotts Bluff Field Sta-
              tion, Mitchell, Neb.
          Mitchell, Neb. Scotts Bluff
              Field Station.
          xx U.S. Dept. of Agriculture.
              Bureau of Plant Industry.
              Field stations.

Scotts Bluff National Monument.
      xx National parks and reserves.

Scottsbluff, Neb.   See Scotts Bluff,
      Neb.

Scottsburg area, Ind.
--Water-supply.
    sa Subdivision Indiana. Scottsburg
        area under: Water, Under-
          ground.

Scouring compounds.
    xx Cleaning.

Scouring disease. See Dysentery in
    cattle.

Scouring lands.

Scrap metal.
    sa Railroads. Scrap material.

Scrap rubber. See Rubber, Scrap.

Scrapbooks.

Scrapie. See Sarcosporidiosis.

Scratches (Pathological)

Scree gardens. See Rock gardens.

Screen printing. See Silk screen
    printing.

Screens.
    sa Wire screens.
    x Insect screens.

Screw-threads.

Screw-worm remedy, EQ 335. See EQ 335
    screw-worm remedy.

Screwbean.
    x Prosopis pubescens.

Screws.
    sa Lag-screws.

Screwworm.
    Prior to 1962, See Callitroga
      americana; beginning 1962,
      See Cochliomyia hominivorax.

Scrip. See Barter and scrip.

Scriptores rei rusticae.

Scrobipalpa ocellatella. See Gnori-
    moschema oscellatella.

Scrophulariaceae.
    sa Collinsia.
       Euphrasia.
       Antirrhinum.
       Linaria.
       Verbascum.
       Calceolaria.
       Castilleja.
       Tretraphacus.
       Rhinanthus.
       Veronica.
       Pentstemon.
       Digitalis purpurea.
       Agalinanae.
       Stemodia.
       Mimulus.
       Orthocarpus.
       Celsia.
       Monochasma.

Scrotum.

Scrub itch mite. See Trombicula de-
    liensis.

Scrub oak. See Quercus ilicifolia;
    Quercus gambellii.

Scrub-pine. See Pinus virginiana.

Sculpin.

Sculpture.
--History.

Scurfy scale. See Chionaspis furfura.

Scurry Co., Tex.
--Soils.
    sa Subdivision Texas. Scurry Co.
       under: Soil-surveys.

Scurvy.
    xx Deficiency diseases.

Scurvy-grass. See Cochlearia offici-
    nalis.

Scutari.
--Botany.

Scutellaria.
  xx Labiatae.

Scutelleridae.
  sa Odontotarsus.

Scutelleroidea.
  sa Scutelleridae.

Scutellista.

Scutellista cyanea.

Scutigera.

Scutigera forceps.

Scutigerella immaculata.

Scutigeridae.
  sa Scutigera.

Scydmaenidae.

Scymnus.

Scyphocrinus.

Scyphophorus acupunctatus.
  xx Curculionidae.

Scythian lamb. See Vegetable lamb.

Scytonemataceae.

Scytonotus.

Scytopetalaceae.

Sea. See Ocean.

Sea angling. See Salt-water fishing.

Sea-bass.
  xx Iethyology.
  Bass.

Sea breeze.

Sea buckthorn. See Hippophae rhamnoides.

Sea-cow. See Sirenia; Rhytina; Meta-
  xytherium floridanum.

Sea fishing. See Salt-water fishing.

Sea food.
  sa Fish as food.
  --Transportation.
    sa Subdivision Sea food under:
      Railroads. Rates.

Sea food cookery. See Cookery (Fish);
  Cookery (Shell-fish)

Sea Island Cotton. See Cotton, Sea
  Island.

Sea Islands, S.C.
  sa Subdivision Sea Islands, S.C.
    under: Negroes.

Sea-kale. See Kale.

Sea level.

Sea-lions. See Seals (Animals)

Sea mud.
  x Mud, Sea.
  xx Mud.

Sea-serpents.
  x Sea-snakes.
    Hydrophiidae.
  xx Serpents.

Sea-snakes. See Sea-serpents.

Sea swallows. See Terns.

Sea terns. See Terns.

Sea-urchins. See Echinoidea.

Sea vegetation. See Marine flora.

Sea-walls.
  sa Dikes (Engineering)

Sea-water.
  x Ocean water.
  xx Saline waters.
  --Bacteriology.
  --Distillation.
    x Desalting of sea-water.
    xx Distillation.
  -- --Bibliography.
  --Effect on building materials.
  --Effect on soils. See Soil. Effect
    of sea-water.

Sea-water (Continued)
--Physiological effect.
-- --Bibliography.
--Purification.
-- --Chlorination.
    xx Water. Purification. Chlorina-
        tion.
--Research.
-- Temperature.
    x.: Temperature.

Sea-weeds.   See Algae.

Sea-wrack.   See Zostera.

Seal oil.

Sealing.
    sa Bering Sea controversy.
       Seals (Animals)
    x Pelagic sealing.
    xx Seals (Animals)
--Periodicals.

Sealing of warehouses.   See Warehouses.
   Sealing.

Sealing-wax.

Seals (Animals)
    sa Sealing.
    x Fur-seals.
      Sea-lions.
    xx Pinnipedia.
      Sealing.
      Fur-bearing animals.
--Parasites.

Seals (Numismatics)
    sa U.S. Dept. of Agriculture.
       Seal.

Sealyham terriers.

Seamen.
    sa Merchant seamen.
--Civil employment.   See Veterans. Employment.

Seamen, Invalid.
--Occupations.   See Disabled. Rehabilitation, etc.

Searing (Cookery)
    xx Cookery.

Searles Lake, Calif.

Searsville Lake, Calif.

Seashore State Park, Cape Henry, Va.
    x Virginia Seashore State Park.
    xx Virginia. Parks.
--Botany.
    sa Subdivision Seashore State
       Park, Cape Henry, Va. under:
       Ferns.
    xx Virginia. Botany.

Seaside planting.
    xx Landscape gardening.

Seasonal migration of domestic animals.
   See Migration of domestic animals.

Seasonal unemployment.   See Unemployment,
   Seasonal.

Seasonal variation.

Seasoning of lumber.   See Lumber. Drying.

Seasoning of wood.   See Lumber. Drying.

Seasonings.   See Condiments.

Seasons.
    sa Summer.
       Winter.
       Autumn.

Seattle. Alaska-Yukon-Pacific Exposition,
   1909.
    x Alaska-Yukon-Pacific Exposi-
       tion, 1909.
--California.
--Japan.
--U.S.

Seattle.
--Commerce.
    xx Commerce.
--Economic conditions.
--Officials and employees.
    xx U.S. Officials and employees.
--Population.
--Social conditions.
--Water-supply.

Seaview Mountain.   See Mount Seaview.

Seaweeds. See Algae.

Sebaceous glands.
    x Glands, Sebaceous.

Sebaea.

Sebastianberg, Bohemia.
--Agriculture.
--Soils.
        sa Subdivision Bohemia. Sebastians-
            berg under: Peat.

Secale.
--Hybrids.

Secale cereale. See Rye.

Sechium edule. See Chayote.

Sechuan. See Szechuan.

Sechura Desert.
    xx Peru.

Secodella.

Secodella argyresthiae.

Second Decontrol act of 1947. See De-
    control act of 1947, Second.

Second war powers act, 1942. See War
    powers act, 1942.

Secondary screwworm. See Callitroga ma-
    cellaria.

Secretaries, Private.
        sa Office management.

Secretion.
        sa Glands.
            Hormones.
        xx Glands.

Secretion (Insect)
    x Insect secretion.
    xx Entomology. Physiology.

Secretion, Internal. See Glands, Ductless.

Secretion of milk. See Lactation.

Section-cutting.
        xx Microscope and microscopy.
            Biology.

Sectionalism (U.S.)
        sa Regionalism.
        xx Regionalism.

Sectonema.

Sectrometer. See Electron beam sectro-
    meter.

Sects.
        sa Church of the Brethren.

Securidaca.

Securipalpi.

Securities.   (DIRECT)
        sa Bonds.
            Investments.
            Mortgages.
            Stocks.
            Dividends.
        x Banks and banking, Investment.
            Investment banking.
--Statistics.
--Taxation. See Taxation of bonds,
    securities, etc.

Securities act of 1933.

Securities exchange act of 1934.

Security, Economic. See Insurance,
    Social.

Security, International.
        sa Arbitration, International.
            Disarmament.
            International law and rela-
                tions.
            Neutrality.
            International organization.
            Mutual security program.
        x International security.
        xx International organization.

Security, Social. See Insurance, Social.

Sedation. See Anesthesia in veterinary
    medicine; Narcosis.

Sedatives.
  sa Anesthetics.
    Tranquilizing drugs.
    Narcotics.
    Names of sedatives.
  xx Anesthetics.
    Tranquilizing drugs.
    Narcotics.

Sedge. See Cyperaceae.

Sedgwick Co., Kan.
  sa Sedgwick Co., Kansas. Social
      conditions.
  xx Kansas.
--Social conditions.
  sa Subdivision Kansas. Sedgwick
     Co. under: Social surveys.
  xx Sedgwick Co., Kan.

Sediment. See Sedimentation and deposition.

Sedimentary petrography. See Rocks,
  Sedimentary.

Sedimentary rocks. See Rocks, Sedimentary.

Sedimentation. See Sedimentation and
  deposition.

Sedimentation and deposition.
  sa Rocks, Sedimentary.
   x Sediment.
    Sedimentation and silt.
    Sedimentation.
  xx Geology.
--Bibliography.
  xx Soil. Bibliography.
--Congresses.

Sedimentation and silt. See Sedimentation and deposition.

Sedoheptose.

Sedum.

Sedum acre.

Seed adulteration and inspection. See
  Seeds. Adulteration; Seeds. Inspection.

Seed analysis. See Seeds. Testing and
  examination.

Seed beds.
  sa Subdivision Seed beds under:
    Wheat.
    Tobacco.
    Grasses//
   x Seedbeds.
--Sterilization.

Seed-borne diseases. See Seeds. Infection.

Seed catalogs. See Nurseries (Horticulture) Catalogs.

Seed certification. See Seeds. Certification.

Seed cleaning. See Seeds. Cleaning.

Seed coats.

Seed collecting. See Seeds. Harvesting.

Seed control.
  sa Seeds. Testing and examination.
    Seeds. Certification.
    Seeds. Inspection.
--Congresses.
--Research.

Seed control stations.

Seed corn. See Maize. Seed.

Seed-corn ground-beetle. See Clivina
  impressifrons.

Seed-corn maggot. See Hylemyia cili-
  crura.

Seed cotton. See Cotton in the seed.

Seed disinfection. See Seeds. Disinfection.

Seed dissemination. See Dissemination
  of plants.

Seed distribution.
   x Seeds. Distribution.

Seed dressing. See Seeds. Disinfection.

Seed driers.
  xx Drying apparatus.

Seed-drill.
  x Spanish sembrador.
  xx Agriculture. Implements and
    machinery.

Seed exchange lists. See Seeds. Exchange
 lists.

Seed fumigation. See Seeds. Fumigation.

Seed gardens.
 --Bibliography.

Seed industry and trade. See Seed trade.

Seed infection.

Seed inspection. See Seeds. Inspection.

Seed laboratories.
 --Apparatus and supplies.
 -- --Directories.

Seed planters.
  x Planters.
  xx Planting tools.
    Seeds. Machinery.

Seed plants. See Spermatophytes.

Seed potatoes. See Potatoes. Seed.

Seed processing. See Seeds. Cleaning.

Seed purchase program.
  xx Purchase programs (Government)

Seed scarifiers.

Seed selection.

Seed separator. See Seeds. Cleaning.
 Implements and machinery.

Seed specifications. See Seeds. Specifications.

Seed spots.
  xx Tree planting.
    Sowing.

Seed standards. See Seeds. Grading and
 standardization.

Seed supply.
  sa Seeds. Statistics.

Seed testing. See Seeds. Testing and
 examination.

Seed time. See Planting time.

Seed trade. (DIRECT)
  x Seed industry and trade.
 --Congresses.
  sa Subdivision Congresses under
    Seed trade [geographic sub-
    division] e.g., Seed trade.
    Europe. Congresses.
 --Directories.
  sa Seed trade [geographic sub-
    division] Directories, e.g.,
    Seed trade. U.S. Direc-
    tories.
  x Seedsmen. Directories.
 --Law and regulation. See Seeds. Legislation.
 --Periodicals. See Seeds. Periodicals.
 --Societies.
 --Tables and ready-reckoners.
  x Seeds. Tables and ready-reck-
    oners.
 --Year-books.
  xx Year-books.

Seed trade catalogs. See Nurseries
 (Horticulture) Catalogs.

Seed treatment. See Seeds. Disinfection

Seed trees.
  xx Trees. Seed.

Seedbeds. See Seed beds.

Seeding. See Sowing.

Seeding time. See Planting time.

Seedlac.
  xx Lac.

Seedless fruit.

Seedlings.
    sa Wheat seedlings.
       Maize seedlings.
       Cotton seedlings//
       Subdivision Seedlings under:
         Populus deltoids.
         Sugar-cane.
         Nicotiana rustica.
         Tomatoes.
         Cabbage.
         Vegetables.
         Citrus.
         Pinus palustris.
         Brassica.
         Weeds.
         Coniferae.
    x Stecklings.
--Diseases.
    sa Subdivision Diseases under:
       Coniferae. Seedlings.
--Fertilizers. See Fertilizers for
    seedlings.
--Physiology and morphology.
--Planting machinery.
    xx Planting machinery.
--Storage.
    xx Nursery stock. Storage.

Seeds.
    sa Subdivision Seed under: Trees.
       Weeds.
       Vegetables//
       Wheat-grass.
       Soy-bean.
       Forage plants//
       Botany. Physiology.
       Germination.
       Plant breeding.
       Seed structure.
       Oil-seeds.
       Hempseed.
    xx Plant propagation.
--Adulteration.
    sa Subdivision Seed. Adulteration
       under: Grasses.
       Clover.
       Vetch, Hairy.
       Soy-bean.
       Alfalfa.
    x Seed adulteration and inspec-
       tion.
--Analysis. See Seeds. Testing and ex-
    amination.

Seeds (Continued)
--Anatomy.
    sa Subdivision Anatomy under:
       Oil-seeds.
    x Carpology.
--Bacteria.
--Bibliography.
    sa Subdivision Bibliography un-
       der: Seeds. Specific gra-
       vity.
       Grasses. Seed.
       Seeds. Testing and examina-
       tion.
--Catalogs. See Nurseries (Horti-
    culture) Catalogs.
--Certification.
    sa Subdivision Certification
       under: Flaxseed.
       Potatoes. Seed.
       Cereals. Seed.
       Clover, Ladino. Seed.
    x Certification of seed.
       Certified seed.
       Seed certification.
       Field crops. Seed. Certifica-
       tion.
    xx Seeds. Testing and examina-
       tion.
       Seed control.
-- --Periodicals.
-- --Statistics.
--Cleaning.
    x Seed processing.
       Seeds. Processing.
       Processing of seed.
-- --Implements and machinery.
    sa Clipper grain and seed clean-
       ing machine.
       Carter disc separator.
       Velvet-roll separator.
    x Deseeding machines.
       Seed separator.
--Collection. See Seeds. Harvesting.
--Color. See Color of seeds.
--Composition.
    sa Subdivision Seed. Composition
       under: Coniferae.
       Trees.
       Leguminosae.
       Turnip.
       Cotton-seed. Composition.

Seeds (Continued)
--Congresses.
    sa Subdivision Congresses under:
      Seeds. Testing and exami-
        nation.
      Seed trade.
--Directories.   See Seed trade. Direc-
   tories.
--Disinfection.
    sa Seeds. Fumigation.
      Formaldehyde as a seed dis-
        infectant. Bibliography.
      Subdivision Disinfection under:
        Cotton-seed.
        Flower seeds.
      Subdivision Seed. Disinfection
        under: Vegetables.
        Cereals.
        Peanuts.
        Sorghum.
        Sugar-beet.
        Rice.
        Coniferae. Seed.
    x Seed disinfection.
      Seed treatment.
      Seed dressing.
    xx Vegetable pathology.
-- --Implements and machinery.
    sa Clipper rocker seed treater.
    xx Seeds. Machinery.
--Dissemination.   See Dissemination of
   plants.
--Distribution.   See Seed distribution.
--Drying.
    xx Drying of farm produce.
--Effect of bisulfid of carbon.
--Effect of environment.
    xx Environment.
--Effect of enzymes.
    xx Enzymes.
--Effect of gases.

Seeds, Effect of heat on.   See Heat.
   Effect on seeds.

Seeds, Effect of humidity on.   See
   Humidity. Effect on seeds.

Seeds, Effect of tanning materials on.
   See Tanning materials. Effect on seeds.

Seeds, Effect of X-rays on.   See X-rays.
   Effect on seeds.

Seeds.
--Electrical treatment.
--Estimating of crops.
--Examination.   See Seeds. Testing and
   examination.
--Exchange lists.
    sa Plants. Exchange lists.
--Exchange lists (Works concerning)
--Exhibitions.
--Financing.

Seeds, Fossil.

Seeds.
--Fumigation.
    sa Seeds. Disinfection.
      Subdivision Fumigation under:
        Vetch. Seed.
    x Seed fumigation.
--Germination.   See Germination.
--Grading and standardization.
    sa Subdivision Grading and
      standardization under:
      Legumes. Seed.
      Oil-seeds.
--Harvesting.
    sa Subdivision Harvesting under:
      Clover. Seed.
      Grasses. Seed.
      Belladonna. Seed//
      Cone gathering.
    x Seeds. Collection.
      Seed collecting.
--Identification.
-- --Bibliography.
--Implements and machinery.   See
   Seeds. Machinery.
--Infection.
    x Seed-borne diseases.
--Injuries.
--Inoculation.
--Inspection.
    x Seed adulteration and
      inspection.
      Seed inspection.
    xx Seeds. Testing and examina-
      tion.
      Seed control.
-- --Bibliography.
    xx Seeds. Testing and examina-
      tion. Bibliography.
-- --Periodicals.
    xx Seeds. Periodicals.
      Farm produce. Inspection.
      Periodicals.

1953

Seeds, Iron in.   See Iron in seeds.

Seeds.
--Juvenile literature.
--Labels.
     sa Subdivision Labels under:
        Vegetables. Seed.
     xx Farm produce. Labels.
--Legislation.
     sa Federal seed act.
        Weeds. Seed.
     x Seed trade. Law and regulation.
--Longevity.   See Seeds. Vitality.
--Machinery.
     sa Seed scarifiers.
        Seed planters.
        Subdivision Seeds under:
        Disinfection. Implements
           and machinery.
        Subdivision Equipment under:
        Cotton-seed. Processing.
     x Seeds. Implements and machinery.

Seeds, Manganese in.   See Manganese in
   seeds.

Seeds.
--Marketing.
--Marketing, Cooperative.
--Moisture content.
--Oil content.
--Origin.
     x Origin of seeds.

Seeds, Pelletized.
     x Pellets.
        Pelletized seeds.

Seeds.
--Periodicals.
     sa Subdivision Periodicals under:
        Seeds. Testing and examina-
           tion.
        Seeds. Inspection.
     x Seed trade. Periodicals.
--Pests.
     sa Subdivision Pests under:
        Coniferae. Seed.
        Trees. Seed.

Seeds, Phosphorus in.   See Phosphorus in
   seeds.

Seeds.
--Physiology.
     x Physiology of seeds.
--Preservation.
     sa Subdivision Preservation un-
        der: Trees. Seed.
--Prices.
     sa Subdivision Seed. Prices un-
        der: Grasses.
        Legumes.
        Field crops.
        Forage plants.
-- --Subsidies.
--Processing.
     sa Seeds. Cleaning.
        Subdivision Seed. Processing
           under: Maize.
        Sugar-beet.
--Proteins in.
--Research.
--Respiration.
     sa Subdivision Respiration under:
        Apple. Seed.
--Ripening.
     sa Leguminosae. Seed. Ripening.
--Societies.
     sa Subdivision Societies under:
        Seed trade.
        Seeds. Testing and examina-
           tion.
        Societies entered under speci-
           fic names.
-- --Directories.
--Sowing.   See Sowing.
--Specific gravity.
-- --Bibliography.
--Specifications.
     x Seed specifications.
--Statistics.
     sa Seed supply.
        Subdivision Statistics under:
        Mustard. Seed.
        Flaxseed.
        Vegetables//
--Sterilization.
--Stimulation.
     sa Yarovization (Botany)
     xx Germination.

Seeds (Continued)
--Storage.
        sa Subdivision Storage under:
           Coniferae. Seed.
           Vegetables. Seed.
           Forage plants. Seed.
           Flaxseed.
           Hempseed.
           Soy-bean. Seed.
--Stratification.
--Swelling.
--Tables and ready-reckoners. See
    Seed trade. Tables and ready-reck-
    oners.
--Terminology.
    xx Botany. Terminology.
--Testing and examination.
    sa Seed control.
       Seeds. Certification.
       Seeds. Inspection.
    x Seed inspection.
       Seed analysis.
       Seeds. Analysis.
-- --Apparatus.
-- --Bibliography.
        sa Subdivision Bibliography under:
           Seeds. Inspection.
    xx Seeds. Bibliography.
-- --Congresses.
    xx Seeds. Congresses.
-- --Periodicals.
    xx Seeds. Periodicals.
-- --Societies.
--Transportation.
--Varieties.
--Viability. See Germination.
--Vitality.
    sa Cotton-seed. Vitality.
       Germination.
-- --Bibliography.
--Water content.
--Weight. See Seeds. Weight and meas-
    ures.
--Weights and measures.
--Yearbooks.

Seedsmen.
--Directories. See Seed trade. Direc-
    tories.

Seedtime. See Planting time.

Seega, Germany.

Seeing eye dogs.

Seeland. See Zealand.

Seethol.

Segenhoe estate irrigation bill.

Seger's cones.

Sego lily. See Calochortus nuttalli.

Segovian horse.

Segrez, France.
--Botany.
        sa Subdivision France. Segrez
           under: Trees.
--Forestry.
        sa Subdivision France. Segrez
           under: Trees.

Segura Valley.
--Water-supply.

Seiches.

Seidlitz powders.
    x Pulvis effervescens composi-
       tus.

Selagineae.
    sa Globularia.

Selaginella.

Selaginella martensii.

Selaginella rupestris.

Selaginellaceae.

Selaginellaceae, Fossil.

Selanaspidus.

Selandria.

Selangor, Federated Malay States.
--Statistics.

Selasphorus torridus.

Selborne, Eng.

Sele Valley.
--Agriculture.
    sa Subdivision Italy. Sele Valley
        under: Reclamation of land.

Selectan.

Selection, Natural. See Natural selection.

Selection of personnel. See Personnel
selection.

Selection system (Forestry)
    sa Selective logging.
    x Continuous inventory system.
    xx Forest management.
    Silviculture.

Selective logging.
    x Selective cutting.
    xx Selection system (Forestry)
    Lumbering.

Selective training and service act of 1940.
    xx U.S. Army. Recruiting, enlist-
    ment, etc.

Seleniferous plants. See Selenium in
plants.

Selenium.
    sa Food, Selenium in.
--Bibliography.
--Determination.
--Effect on plants.
--Toxicity.
    sa Alkali disease.
    Subdivision Toxicity under:
      Sodium selenate.
      Sodium selenite.
    x Toxicity.
-- --Bibliography.

Selenium cells.
    xx Electric batteries.

Selenium compounds.

Selenium disease. See Alkali disease.

Selenium in food. See Food, Selenium in.

Selenium in plants.
    x Seleniferous plants.

Selenium in soil. See Soil, Selenium
in.

Selenium in the body.
    xx Physiological chemistry.

Selenium oxychloride.

Self-determination, National.
    x National self-determination.

Self-feeder (for swine)
    xx Domestic animals. Implements
    and machinery.

Self-help gardens. See Gardens, Subsistence.

Self-service meats. See Meat. Packaging.

Self-service stores.

Self-service stores, Refrigerated.
    x Refrigerated self-service
    stores.
    xx Refrigeration and refrig-
    erating machinery.
    Food, Frozen. Marketing.

Self-sufficiency, Economic. See Nation-
alism and nationality.

Selkirk Range.
    sa Rocky Mountains, Canada.

Selkirk's Red River settlement.

Selkirkshire, Scot.
--Agriculture.

Selling government owned foodstuffs.
    See Sales of government owned food-
    stuffs.

Sellustra Valley.
--Agriculture.
    sa Subdivision Italy. Sellustra
      Valley under: Reclamation
      of land.

Selway Game Preserve.
    xx Game preserves.

Semal. See Bombax malabaricum.

1956

Semantics.
    sa Subdivision Semantics under:
        English language.
        Information theory.

Semantics, General. See General semantics.

Semasia pomonella. See Codling moth.

Semele.

Semen.
    x Sperm.
    xx Spermatozoa.
--Biochemistry.
--Cattle.
--Dogs.
--Effect of temperature.
    x Temperature. Effect on semen.
--Goats.
--Horses.
--Poultry.
--Sheep.
--Swine.

Semesan.
    xx Fungicides.

Semiconductor devices. See Transistors.

Seminal vesicle.

Semipalatinsk, Siberia.
--Soils.
    sa Subdivision Soils under:
        Zaisansk.

Semirech'e.
    x Dzhetysu.
--Botany.
--Natural history.
--Soils.

Semolina.
--Analysis.

Sempervirens Park. See California Redwood Park.

Sempervivum.

Sen Chouen. See Szechuan.

Sen Tchouen. See Szechuan.

Seneca, Ill.
--Social conditions.

Seneca Co., N.Y.
--Agriculture.
    sa Agricultural laborers. New
        York (State) Seneca Co.
--Land.
    sa Subdivision New York (State)
        Seneca Co. under: Land.
        Classification.
--Soils.
    sa Subdivision New York (State)
        Seneca Co. under: Soil-
        surveys.

Seneca Co., Ohio.
--Agriculture.
-- --Periodicals.

Seneca Indians.

Senecio.
    xx Asteraceae.

Senecio poisoning.

Senecio riddellii.
    sa Riddelliine.

Senecionideae.

Senega root.

Senegal.
--Agriculture.
    sa Subdivision Senegal under:
        Agriculture. Economic as-
        pects.
    xx Africa, West. Agriculture.
--Botany.
    sa Subdivision Senegal under:
        Botany, Economic.
    xx Africa. Botany.
--Cattle.
--Commerce.
-- --Statistics.
--Domestic animals.
--Entomology.
    sa Subdivision Senegal under:
        Orthoptera.
        Entomology, Economic.
    xx Africa. Entomology.
--Statistics.

Senegambia.
--Botany.
    xx Africa. Botany.
--Description and travel.

Senna.

Sennatin.

Sennax.

Sensation.   See Senses and sense organs.

Sense organs.   See Senses and sense organs.

Senses and sensation.   See Senses and sense organs.

Senses and sense organs.
    sa Touch.
       Eye.
       Animal psychology.
       Smell.
       Hearing.
       Glands, Odoriferous.
       Taste.
       Pain.
       Chemoreceptors.
    x Animal psychology.
      Sensation.
    xx Glands, Oderiferous.

Senses and sense organs of Arachnida.
--Visual.   See Eye. Arachnida.

Senses and sense organs of insects.
    sa Subdivision Insects under:
           Smell.
           Scent organs.
           Eye.
           Taste.
           Sound production by animals.
           Stridulation.
--Auditory.
    x Ear of insect.
--Olfactory.   See Smell. Insects.
--Smell.   See Smell. Insects.
--Taste.   See Taste.
--Visual.   See Eye. Insects.

Sensitization.
    xx Photographic chemistry.

Seoul, Korea.
    x Keijo.
--Water-supply.

Separators (Machines)
    sa Cream separators.
       Whey separators.
       Centrifuges.

Sepsidae.
    sa Mycetaulus.
    xx Diptera.

Septic tanks.

Septicemia.
    sa Staphylotoxin.
    x Pyosepticemia.
--Preventive inoculation.

Septicemia, Hemorrhagic.   See Hemorrhagic septicemia.

Septicemia (Insect)
    xx Insect diseases.

Septobasidium.
    xx Auriculariaceae.

Septoform.

Septoria.
    xx Ascomycetes.
--Bibliography.

Septoria lycopersici.   See Leaf spot of tomato.

Septoria musiva.

Septoria tritici.
    xx Speckled leaf blotch of wheat.

Sequoia.
       This subject is used for works
       on the botany, description
       and conservation of redwood.
       For works on physical proper-
       ties, technology, lumbering,
       diseases and pests, see Red-
       wood.
    sa Redwood.

Sequoia gigantea.
    x Sierra redwood.
    Sequoia washingtonia.
    Big tree.

Sequoia National Forest, Calif.
    xx California. Forest reserva-
        tions.
--Entomology.
    sa Subdivision California. Sequoia
        National Forest under:
        Trees. Pests.

Sequoia National Park, Calif.
    sa Roosevelt-Sequoia National
        Park.
--Forestry.
--Zoology.

Sequoia sempervirens.
    x Coast redwood.
--Abstracts.
--Bibliography.
    xx Trees. Bibliography.

Sequoia washingtoniana. See Sequoia
  gigantea.

Scradella. See Serradella.

Serb-Croat-Slovene kingdom. See
  Jugoslavia.

Serbia. See Servia.

Serbo-Croatian language. See Croatian
  language; Servian language.

Serebriano-Prudskii Raion.
--Soils.
    xx Moscow Region. Soils.

Serenoa serrulata. See Saw palmetto.

Serfdom. (DIRECT)
    sa Peonage.

Sergestes prehensilis.

Sergestidae.
    sa Sergestes.

Sergipe, Brazil (State)
--Agriculture.
--Industries and resources.
--Statistics.
    xx Brazil. Statistics.

Serial publications.
    sa Periodicals.

Serica.

Sericaria.

Sericea. See Lespedeza sericea.

Sericin.

Sericite.

Sericostomatidae.
    sa Helicopsyche.

Sericulture.
    This subject used for publica-
    tions on the raising of silk-
    worms for the production of
    raw silk. Entomological pub-
    lications on the silkworm as
    an insect are entered under
    the subject. Silkworms.
    sa Silk.
    Silkworm.
    Mulberry.
    Osage orange.
    Cocoons.
    Subdivision Sericulture under:
    Africa.
    Asia.
    Australia//
--Bibliography.
    sa Silk. Bibliography.
--Congresses.
    sa Silk. Congresses.
--Dictionaries.
--Education.
--Exhibitions.
--Juvenile literature.
--Legislation.
--Methodology.
--Periodicals.
--Pictorial works.
--Research.
--Societies.
--Statistics.

Series, Infinite.
    x Infinite series.

Serine.

Seriola.
    xx Carangidae.

Seriola falcata.

Serjania.

Serology.   See Serumtherapy.

Serpentine.

Serpentine superphosphates.
    xx Superphosphates.

Serpents.   (INDIRECT)
    sa Rattlesnake.
       Natrix vibakari.
       Calamaria.
       Sea-serpents.
    x Snakes.
    xx Reptilia.
--Bibliography.
--Parasites.
    xx Parasites.
--Societies.

Serphidae.
    sa Mymaridae.
       Telenomus.

Serphoidea.
    sa Bethylidae.
       Calliceratidae.

Serpulidae.
    xx Annelida.

Serra da Estrella.   See Estrella, Serra
    da.

Serracapriola, Italy.
--Agriculture.

Serradella.
--Digestibility.
--Fertilizers.   See Fertilizers for
    serradilla.
--Germination.
    xx Germination.

Serranidae.

Serrated tussock.   See Nassella tricho-
    toma.

Serricornia.

Serropalpidae.

Serum.
    sa Immunity.
       Serum testing.
       Serumtherapy.
       Toxins and antitoxins.
       Agglutinin.
       Serum diagnosis.
       Precipitins.
       Blood plasma.
       Subdivision Serum under:
          National industrial re-
          covery act, 1933. Codes.
    x Blood. Serum.
    xx Immunity.
--Chemistry.
    xx Chemistry.
--Research.

Serum diagnosis.
    sa Complement.
       Tuberculosis. Serum diagnosis.
    xx Serumtherapy.
--Bibliography.

Serum globulin.

Serum of pregnant mares.
    x Pregnant mare's serum.
       SZHK.
       SPM.

Serum testing.

Serum therapy.   See Serumtherapy.

Serumtherapy.
    sa Allergy.
       Anaphylaxis.
       Antigens and antibodies.
       Immunity.
       Inoculation.
       Opsonins and opsonic index.
       Organotherapy.
       Serum diagnosis.
       Toxins and antitoxins.
       Vaccination.

Serumtherapy (Continued)
  sa Names of special antitoxins,
    e.g., Diphtheria antitoxin;
    Hog cholera antitoxin.
  Subdivision Preventive inocula-
    tion under names of certain
    diseases, e.g., Anthrax.
    Preventive inoculation; Ty-
    phoid fever. Preventive
    inoculation.
  x Serum therapy.
    Preventive inoculation.
    Serology.
  xx Therapeutics.
    Inoculation.
    Toxins and antitoxins.
    Organotherapy.
--Periodicals.
--Societies.

Servants.
  sa Housemaids.
    Waiters.
--Bibliography.
  xx Home economics. Bibliography.

Servia.
--Agriculture.
  sa Subdivision Servia under:
    Agriculture, Cooperative.
    Agriculture. Economic as-
      pects.
    Mechanized farming.
    Servia. Domestic animals.
-- --Education.
-- --History.
  xx Agriculture. History.
-- --Periodicals.
-- --Statistics.
--Apiculture.
-- --Periodicals.
--Botany.
--Cattle.
--Census.
--Description and travel.
--Domestic animals.
--Entomology.
  xx Europe. Entomology.
--Forestry.
-- --Periodicals.
--Geology.
--Paleontology.
--Pomology.
--Sericulture.
--Viticulture.

Servian abbreviations. See Abbreviations,
  Servian.

Servian language.
  x Serbo-Croatian language.
--Abbreviations. See Abbreviations,
  Servian.
--Dictionaries.
  sa Subdivision Dictionaries under:
    Croatian language.

Service, Compulsory non-military. (IN-
  DIRECT)
  x Requisitions of service.

Service industries.
--Directories.

Service rating. See Efficiency rating.

Service-tree. See Pyrus sorbus.

Servicemen, Military. See Soldiers.

Servicemen's readjustment act of 1944.
  x G I bill.
  xx Veterans. Laws and legislation.

Serving.

Servis tie plate.
  xx Railroad ties.

Servitude. See Peonage.

Servitude for debt. See Peonage.

Servitudes. (DIRECT)
  sa Forest rights.
    Pasture, Right of.
    Right of way.
  x Easements.
  xx Real property.

Servo-mechanisms. See Servomechanisms.

Servomechanisms.
  sa Automation.
  x Servo-mechanisms.
  xx Automatic control.
    Automation.

Sesame. See Sesamum.

Sesame cake.

Sesame-oil.
    xx Fats and oils.

Sesamia nonagrioides.

Sesamum.
    x Benne.
      Sesame.
    xx Oleaginous plants.
--Bibliography.
    xx Oil-seeds. Bibliography.
--Breeding.
    xx Plant-breeding.
--Congresses.
--Estimating of crop.
    xx Crop estimating.
--Pests.
--Statistics.

Sesamum as feeding stuff.
    xx Feeding stuffs.

Sesamum indicum.

Sesamum orientale.

Sesbania aculeata.

Sesbania cavanillesii.   See Daubentonia
   longifolia.

Sesbania macrocarpa.

Sesia.

Sesia novaroensis.

Sesia tipuliformis.

Sesiidae.
    sa Synanthedon.
      Sesia.
      Memythrus polistiformis.
      Aegeria.
    x Aegeriidae.

Sesioctonus.

Sesquicentennial International Exposition,
   Philadelphia.   See Philadelphia. Sesquicentennial International Exposition,
   1926.

Sesquioxids in phosphates.

Sesquiterpenes.   See Terpenes.

Sessile oak.   See Quercus petrae.

Setaria.
    x Bristlegrass.
      Chaetochloa.
    xx Gramineae.
--Seed.
    xx Grasses. Seed.

Setaria cernua.

Setaria glauca.   See Pearl millet.

Setaria italica.   See Millet, Foxtail.

Setaria italica mocharium.   See Millet,
   Foxtail.

Setaria lutescens.
    x Chaetochloa lutescens.

Setif, Algeria.
--Agriculture.
--Soils.
    xx Algeria.

Setters (Dogs)
    sa Irish setters.
      English setters.
--Breeding.

Settlement law.   See Domicile.

Settlement of war claims act of 1928.
    x War claims act of 1928.
    xx Commercial law.

Settlements, Social.   See Social settlements.

Sevastopol.   See Sebastopol.

Seventeen-year locust.   See Tibicen
   septendecim.

Severo-Dvinskoe (Government)
--Zoology.
    sa Subdivision Severo-Dvinskoe
      (Government) under:
      Worms. U.S.S.R.
    xx Russia. Zoology.

Sevier Co., Ark.

Sevier Co., Tenn.
--Soils.
    sa Subdivision Tennessee. Sevier
        Co. under: Soil-surveys.

Sevier River, Utah.

Seville, Spain (Province)
--Agriculture.
    sa Subdivision Spain. Seville
        (Province) under: Agri-
        culture, Cooperative.
--Pomology.
    xx Spain. Pomology.

Sewage.
    sa Sewerage.
       Fertilizers.
       Water. Pollution.
--Analysis.
-- --Laboratory manuals.
    xx Laboratory manuals.
--Bacteriology.
    xx Bacteriology.
--Bibliography.
--Disposal. See Sewage disposal.
--Periodicals.
--Purification.

Sewage as fertilizer. See Sewage sludge
  as fertilizer.

Sewage disposal.
    sa Refuse and refuse disposal.
       Septic tanks.
       Sewage irrigation.
       Soil pollution.
       Water. Pollution.
       Sewage sludge as fertilizer.
    x Sewage. Disposal.
      Waste water disposal.
--Bibliography.

Sewage farms. See Sewage irrigation.

Sewage fertilizers. See Sewage sludge
  as fertilizer.

Sewage irrigation.
    x Sewage utilization in agri-
      culture.
      Sewage farms.
    xx Irrigation.
      Sewage disposal.

Sewage purification. See Sewage. Purification.

Sewage sludge as fertilizer.
    x Sewage utilization in agri-
      culture.
      Sewage fertilizers.
      Sewage as fertilizer.
    xx Refuse as fertilizer.
      Sewage disposal.

Sewage utilization in agriculture. See
  Sewage irrigation; Sewage sludge as
  fertilizer.

Sewanee, Tenn.
--Forestry.

Seward Co., Kan.
    xx Kansas.

Seward Peninsula, Alaska.
--Botany.
    xx Alaska. Botany.
--Economic conditions.
    sa Subdivision Alaska. Seward
        Peninsula under: Economic
        surveys.
--Geology.
    xx Alaska. Geology.
--Industries and resources.
--Roads.
--Water-supply.

Sewerage.
    sa Plumbing.
       Refuse and refuse disposal.
       Sewage.
       Sewage irrigation.
       Sewers, Concrete.
       Subdivision Sewerage under:
        New Jersey.
        New South Wales.
        New York (City)//
    x Drainage, House.
      House drainage.
--Bibliography.
--Contracts and specifications.
--Research.

Sewerage, Rural.
    x Rural sewerage.

Sewers, Concrete.

Sewing.
        sa Needlework.
           Embroidery (Machine)
           Dressmaking.
           Fancy work.
--Bibliography.
--Dictionaries.
--Study and teaching.
-- --Congresses.

Sewing machines.
--Statistics.

Sex.
        sa Generative organs.
           Reproduction.
         x Sex of insects.
--Cause and determination.
        sa Poultry. Sexing.
         x Sex determination.
--Congresses.
--Control.   See Sex. Cause and deter-
    mination.

Sex (Biology)
        sa Sex in plants.

Sex determination.   See Sex. Cause and
    determination.

Sex in plants.
        sa Fertilization of plants.
           Subdivision Sexuality under:
              Cotton.

Sex instruction.
        xx Children. Education.

Sex of insects.   See Sex.

Sexava.
        xx Locustidae.

Sexual education.   See Sex instruction.

Sexual ethics.
        sa Prostitution.

Sexual instinct.

Sexual instinct (Perversions and disorders
    of)

Sexual organs.
--Diseases.   See Genito-urinary organs.
    Diseases.

Seychelles Islands.
--Agriculture.
--Botany.
        sa Subdivision Seychelles Islands
              under: Ferns.
--Census.
--Entomology.
        sa Subdivision Seychelles Islands
              under: Lepidoptera.
              Coleoptera.
--Ornithology.

Seymour grass.   See Andropogon pertusus.

Seymour Island.
--Paleobotany.
--Paleontology.

Seymour-Jones anthrax sterilization method.

Shad-flies.   See Ephemeridae.

Shaddock.   See Grape-fruit.

Shade.
--Effect on plants.
        sa Subdivision Shade culture un-
              der: Cacao.
              Tobacco.
              Coffee.
         x Plants, Effect of shade on.
--Effect on soils.

Shade-loving plants.
        xx Floriculture.
           Plants, Ornamental.

Shade trees.   See Trees, Shade.

Shading shelters for plants.   See Plant
    protection from weather.

Shadscale.   See Atriplex confertifolia.

Shagbark hickory.   See Hicoria ovata.

Shakamak State Park, Ind.
        xx Indiana. Parks.

Shakers.

Shakespeare, William.
--Concordance.
    xx Concordances.
--Natural history of the plays.

Shakhrisyabz District.
--Pomology.

Shale.

Shallots. See Onions.

Shallu.

Shama. See Panicum frumentaceum.

Shami cattle. See Damascus cattle.

Shamrock.

Shanghai.
--Botany.
    sa Subdivision China. Shanghai
      under: Weeds.
--Economic conditions.
    xx China. Economic conditions.
--Ornithology.
    xx China. Ornithology.
--Water-supply.
    xx China. Water-supply.
--Zoology.

Shanghai dialect.
--Grammar.

Shanghai Hangchow Highway.
    xx China. Roads.

Shans.

Shansi, China.
--Agriculture.
    sa Subdivision China. Shansi under:
      Agriculture. Economic as-
          pects.
--Domestic animals.
--Physical geography.
--Soils.
    sa Subdivision China. Shansi under:
      Soil-surveys.
    xx China. Soils.

Shantar Islands.
--Botany.
    xx Siberia. Botany.

Shantung, China (Province)
--Botany.
    xx China. Botany.
--Domestic animals.
--Economic conditions.
    xx China. Economic conditions.
--Paleobotany.
    xx China. Paleobotany.
--Social conditions.
--Soils.
    xx China. Soils.
--Water-supply.
    xx China. Water-supply.

Shantung Agricultural and Industrial
    School.
    xx Agriculture. Education.

Sharecroppers.
    Here are entered works on share-
    cropping in the United States.
    For general works and those
    dealing with other countries
    see Métayer system.
    x Farming on shares.
    Sharecropping.
    xx Tenant farming.
--Bibliography.
    xx Tenant farming. Bibliography.
--Statistics.

Sharecropping. See Sharecroppers.

Shares of stocks. See Stocks.

Sharkey Co., Miss.
--Soils.
    sa Subdivision Mississippi. Shar-
      key Co. under: Soil-surveys.

Sharks.
--Parasites.
    xx Nematoda. Parasitic in fishes.

Shasta, Mount. See Mount Shasta.

Shasta National Forest, Calif.
    xx California. Forest reserva-
      tions.

Shasta River. Calif.

Shaving-brushes.

Shavings.

Shavings (as bedding for livestock)

Shaw Botanical Garden.   See Missouri
    Botanical Garden.

Shawano Co., Wis.
    xx Wisconsin.

Shawls.

Shawnee Co., Kan.
    sa Subdivision Shawnee Co., Kansas
        under: Planning, County.
    xx Kansas.

Shchors Collective Farm.

Shea butter.   See Karité.

Shear press.
    xx Measuring instruments.

Sheathing.
    sa Gypsum sheathing.
    xx Building materials.

Sheboygan Co., Wis.
    xx Wisconsin.
    --Soils.
    sa Subdivision Wisconsin. Sheboygan
        Co. under: Soil-surveys.

Sheds.

Sheep.
    sa Flock-book.
        Veterinary medicine.
        De-tailing.
        Names of specific breeds.
        Subdivision Sheep under: Africa.
            Australasia.
            South America//
            Heart.
    x Sheep trade.
        Sheep industry.
    xx Ruminantia.
    --Age.
        xx Domestic animals. Age.
    --Anatomy and physiology.
        sa Subdivision Growth under:
            Sheep.
            Subdivision Sheep under: Heart.

Sheep (Continued)
    --Bibliography.
        sa Subdivision Bibliography under:
            Sheep. Cost of production.
            Sheep. Nutrition.

Sheep, Bighorn.   See Bighorn sheep.

Sheep.
    --Breeders.
    -- --Societies.   See Sheep breeders'
        societies.
    --Breeding.
        sa Subdivision Breeding under:
            Merino sheep.
            Karakul sheep.
            Romney Marsh sheep.
            Subdivision Importation for
                breeding purposes under:
                Sheep.
    -- --Research.
    --Breeds.
        sa Names of specific breeds.
        xx Domestic animals. Breeds.
    --Castration.
        sa Lambs. Castration.
    --Congresses.   See Sheep breeders' con-
        gresses.
    --Control of production.
        xx Farm produce. Control of pro-
            duction.
    --Cost of production.
        sa Subdivision Cost of production
            under: Lambs.
    -- --Bibliography.
        xx Domestic animals. Cost of pro-
            duction. Bibliography.
            Sheep. Bibliography.
    --Diseases.
        sa Veterinary science.
            Scab.
            Foot-rot.
            Gid.
            Braxy.
            Louping-ill.
            Sheep pox.
            Liver-rot.
            Sarcosporidiosis.
            Bighead in sheep.
            Rot (Disease)
            Fascioliasis.
            Pneumonia, Ovine.
            Acetonemia.
            Dysentery in sheep.
            Anemia, Infectious. Sheep.

Sheep (Continued)
--Diseases.
    sa Nodular disease of sheep.
    Brucellosis in sheep.
    Agalactia, Contagious.
    Hemorrhagic septicemia of sheep.
    Pseudotuberculosis in sheep.
    Contagious ecthyma of sheep.
    Enterotoxemia.
    Bluetongue in sheep.
--Economic aspects.
--Effect of climate.
    xx Domestic animals. Effect of
        climate.
--Equipment. See Sheep houses and equip-
    ment.
--Exhibitions.
--Fattening.
    sa Subdivision Fattening under:
        Lambs.
--Fecundity.
    xx Fecundity.
--Feeding.
    sa Subdivision Feeding under:
        Lambs.
--Flock-books. See Flock-book (Sheep)
--Genetics.
    xx Genetics.
--Grading and standardization.
    xx Domestic animals. Grading and
        standardization.
--Grazing.
    sa Ranges, Sheep.
    x Sheep grazing.
    xx Grazing.
--Growth.
    sa Lambs. Growth.
    xx Sheep. Anatomy and physiology.
--History.
--Importation for breeding purposes.
    xx Sheep. Breeding.
        Domestic animals. Importation
        for breeding purposes.
--Judging.
--Juvenile literature.
--Law.
--Marketing.
    sa Lambs. Marketing.
    xx Marketing of live stock.
-- --Bibliography.
    xx Marketing of live stock. Bib-
        liography.
--Marketing, Cooperative.
    sa Subdivision Marketing, Cooper-
        ative under: Lambs.

Sheep (Continued)
--Marketing, Cooperative.
    xx Marketing of live stock,
        Cooperative.
-- --Periodicals.
--Marketing.
-- --Cost.
    xx Marketing of live stock. Cost.
· --Research.

Sheep, Merino. See Merino sheep.

Sheep.
--Metabolism. See Metabolism in sheep.

Sheep, Milch.
    x Milk sheep.

Sheep, Moscia.

Sheep, Negretti. See Negretti sheep.

Sheep.
--Nutrition.
    sa Subdivision Nutrition under:
        Lambs.
    xx Animal nutrition.
-- --Bibliography.
    xx Animal nutrition. Bibliography.
    Sheep. Bibliography.
--Parasites.
    sa Haemonchus contortus.
        Melophagus ovinus.
        Ostertagia circumcincta//
    x Lambs. Parasites.
--Periodicals.
    sa Subdivision Periodicals under:
        Karakul sheep.
        Merino sheep.
        Lambs//
    xx Domestic animals. Periodicals.
--Pests.
--Pictures, illustrations, etc.
--Policies and programs. See Sheep
    policies and programs.
--Prices.
    sa Lambs. Prices.
    xx Domestic animal. Prices.
-- --Subsidies.
    xx Domestic animals. Prices.
        Subsidies.
--Protection from dogs.

Sheep, Rambouillet. See Rambouillet
    sheep.

Sheep.
--Research.
--Shearing.
    x Sheep-shearing.
-- --Machinery.
--Societies.   See Sheep breeders'
    societies.
--Statistics.
    sa Subdivision Statistics under:
      Lambs.
    xx Domestic animals. Statistics.
-- --Maps.
--Tariff.
    sa Subdivision Tariff under: Wool.
      Mutton.
--Transportation.
    xx Domestic animals. Transporta-
      tion.
--Watering.
    xx Watering of animals.
--Weight and measurement.
--Year-books.
    xx Domestic animals. Year-books.

Sheep and lamb production program.
    xx Agricultural policies and
      programs.

Sheep barns.   See Sheep houses and equipment.

Sheep botfly.   See Oestrus ovis.

Sheep breeders' congresses.
    xx Stock breeders' congresses.

Sheep breeders' directories.

Sheep breeders' societies.
    sa Names of individual societies.
    x Sheep. Breeders. Societies.

Sheep brooders, Electric.
    x Electric brooders.
      Electric sheep brooders.
    xx Sheep houses and equipment.

Sheep-dip.
    xx Scab.
      Dipping.

Sheep dogs.   See Shepherd dogs.

Sheep equipment.   See Sheep houses and
   equipment.

Sheep farms.

Sheep fescue.
    x Festuca ovina.

Sheep for mutton.

Sheep grazing.   See Sheep. Grazing.

Sheep houses and equipment.
    sa Sheep brooders, Electric.
    x Sheep barns.
      Sheep equipment.
      Sheep. Equipment.
    xx Barns and stables.
      Farm buildings.
      Farm equipment.

Sheep industry.   See Wool trade and
   industry; Sheep.

Sheep keds.   See Melophagus ovinus.

Sheep lice.
    sa Trichodectes spherocephalus.
    xx Sheep. Parasites.
      Lice.

Sheep loans.
    xx Live stock financing.

Sheep maggot fly.
--Larvae.
    xx Larvae.

Sheep policies and programs.
    x Sheep. Policies and programs.

Sheep-pox.

Sheep ranches.   See Ranges, Sheep.

Sheep stations.   See Ranges, Sheep.

Sheep River, Alberta.
--Geology.

Sheep scab.   See Scab.

Sheep-shearing.   See Sheep. Shearing.

Sheep sorrel.   See Rumex acetosella.

Sheep tick.   See Melophagus ovinus.

Sheep trade.   See Wool trade and in-
    dustry; Sheep.

Sheep's milk.
--Composition.
    xx Milk. Composition.
--Control of production.
    xx Milk. Control of production.

Sheep's milk cheese.   See Cheese, Sheep's
    milk.

Sheepskins.   See Hides and skins.

Sheet-metal.
--Periodicals.

Sheet-metal work.
    sa Punching-machinery.
    xx Metal-work.

Sheeted pig.   See Wessex saddleback pig.

Sheets.

Sheffield, Eng.
--Milk supply.
    xx Gt. Brit. Milk supply.
--Transportation.
    xx Gt. Brit. Transportation.

Shefford Co., Quebec.
--Soils.
    sa Subdivision Quebec (Province)
        Shefford Co. under: Soil-
        surveys.

Shelby Co., Ill.
    xx Illinois.

Shelby Co., Ind.
    xx Indiana.
--Agriculture.
-- --Periodicals.

Shelby Co., Iowa.
    sa Subdivision Iowa. Shelby Co.
        under: County surveys.
    xx Iowa.
--Soils.
    sa Subdivision Iowa. Shelby Co.
        under: Soil-surveys.

Shelby Co., Mo.
    xx Missouri.

Shelby Co., Tenn.
    sa Subdivision Shelby Co., Tenn.
        under: Cities and towns.
        Planning.
--Roads.
    xx Tennessee. Roads.

Shelby County (Tenn.) Penal Farm.
    xx Penal farms.

Shelf-listing (Library science)
    x Notation (for books in
        libraries)

Shell-fish.
    sa Mollusca.
        Oysters.
    x Shellfish.
--Bacteriology.
    xx Bacteriology.
--Bibliography.

Shell-fish fisheries.   (INDIRECT)
    xx Fisheries.

Shell money.

Shell mounds.

Shell roads.   See Roads, Shell.

Shellac.
    sa Lac.
--Arsenic content.
    xx Arsenic.
--Patents.
    xx Patents.

Shelley, Idaho.
    sa Subdivision Idaho. Shelley
        under: Sociology, Rural.
        War and agriculture (1939-
        1945)
--Social conditions.
    sa Subdivision Idaho. Shelley
        under: Community life.

Shellfish.   See Shell-fish.

Shells (Metal work)
    xx Metal-work.
        Iron and steel.

Shelter-belts.   See Wind-breaks; Snow-
    breaks.

Shelter trees.   See Trees. Shelter.

Shelterbelt equipment stations (U.S.S.R.)

Shelters (Horticulture)   See Plant protection from weather.

Shelving (for books) .
    x Book-shelves.
      Bookcases.
      Bookstacks.
      Libraries. Shelving.
      Stacks (for books)
    xx Library fittings and supplies.

Shenandoah Co., Va.
    sa Subdivision Shenandoah Co. under: County surveys. Virginia.
    xx Virginia.
--Economic conditions.
    sa Subdivision Shenandoah Co. under: Economic surveys. Virginia.
    xx Virginia. Economic conditions.
--Industries and resources.
    sa Industrial surveys. Virginia. Shenandoah Co.

Shenandoah National Forest, Virginia-West Virginia.

Shenandoah National Park.

Shenandoah River.

Shenandoah Valley.
--History.
    xx Virginia. History.

Shensi, China.
--Agriculture.
    sa Subdivision China. Shensi under: Wheat.
      Cereals.
      Irrigation.
      Subdivision Shensi, China under: Cotton.
--Forestry.
    sa Subdivision China. Shensi under: Afforestation and reforestation.
--Land.

Shensi, China (Province)
--Soils.
    sa Subdivision China. Shensi under: Soil-surveys.
      Soil conservation.
    xx China. Soils.
--Water-supply.
    sa Subdivision China. Shensi under: Water. Conservation.

Shepherd dogs.
    sa German shepherd dogs.
      Belgian shepherd dogs.
    x Border collie.
    xx Old English sheep-dogs.
      Shetland sheep-dogs.

Shepherds.

Shepherd's purse.   See Capsella bursa-pastoris.

Sheppey, Eng.
--Paleontology.

Sherbet.   See Ices.

Sherbrooke, Que.
    sa Subdivision Sherbrooke, Que. under: Produce trade.
    xx Quebec (Province)

Sherburne Co., Minn.
    xx Minnesota.

Sheridan Co., Kan.
--Land.
    sa Subdivision Kansas. Sheridan Co. under: Land utilization.
--Soils.
    sa Subdivision Kansas. Sheridan Co. under: Soil conservation surveys.

Sheridan Co., Mont.
    sa Subdivision Sheridan Co., Mont. under: School taxes.
    xx Montana.
--Education.
    sa Subdivision Sheridan Co., Mont. under: Rural schools.
    xx Montana. Education.

Sheridan Co., N.D.
      sa Subdivision North Dakota. Sheri-
          dan Co. under: County sur-
          veys.
      xx North Dakota.

Sheridan Co., Wyo.
--Soils.
      sa Subdivision Wyoming. Sheridan
          Co. under: Soil-surveys.

Sherman, Tex.
--Water-supply.

Sherman act.   See Sherman antitrust law,
  1890.

Sherman antitrust law, 1890.
      x Sherman act.

Sherman Co., Kan.
--Land.
      sa Subdivision Kansas. Sherman Co.
          under: Land utilization.
--Soils.
      sa Subdivision Kansas. Sherman Co.
          under: Soil conservation
          surveys.

Sherman Co., Neb.
--Agriculture.
      sa Subdivision Nebraska. Sherman
          Co. under: Rehabilitation,
          Rural.
      xx Nebraska. Agriculture.
--Soils.
      sa Subdivision Nebraska. Sherman
          Co. under: Soil-surveys.

Sherman Co., Or.
--Agriculture.
      sa Subdivision Oregon. Sherman Co.
          under: Farm management sur-
          veys.
      xx Oregon. Agriculture.

Sherry.

Shetland cattle.
      xx Cattle.

Shetland Islands.
--Agriculture.
--Botany.
--Description and travel.

Shetland Islands (Continued)
--Ornithology.
--Social life and customs.
--Statistics.

Shetland pony.

Shetland sheep-dogs.   See Shepherd dogs.

Sheyenne River, N.D.
      xx North Dakota.

Shidzuoka, Japan.
--Agriculture.

Shidzuoka-ken. Japan.
--Agriculture.
-- --Periodicals.
--Forestry.
--Industries.
--Pomology.
      xx Japan. Pomology.

Shifting agriculture.
      x Agriculture, Shifting.
        Shifts in agriculture.

Shifting sands.   See Sand-dunes; Soil-
  drifting.

Shifts in agriculture.   See Shifting
  agriculture.

Shigella.

Shigella flexneri.

Shiitake cortinellus.   See Cortinellus
  edodes.

Shikoku, Japan.
--Land.
      sa Subdivision Japan. Shikoku
          under: Land utilization.

Shima noronhae.

Shimane-ken, Japan.
--Forestry.
-- --Statistics.

Shinano, Japan.
--Botany.
--Forestry.
--Natural history.

Shingles.
    xx Building materials.
       Roofing.
--Statistics.
    xx Lumber. Statistics.

Shinnery oak. See Quercus havardii.

Shinshu. See Chinju, Korea.

Shinto.

Ship-bottom fouling.
    x Fouling of ship-bottoms.
    xx Ships.
--Bibliography.
    xx Ships. Bibliography.

Ship-bottom fouling organisms.
    x Fouling organisms, Ship-bottom.

Ship-building.   (DIRECT)
    sa Boat-building.
    xx Ships.
       Naval architecture.
--Bibliography.
--Dictionaries.

Ship-canals.

Ship painting. See Ships. Painting.
    x Painting, Industrial.

Ship subsidies. See Shipping bounties
  and subsidies.

Ship-worms. See Teredo.

Shipmast locust. See Robinia pseudacacia.

Shipment of goods.
    sa Packing for shipment.
       Lend-lease operations (1941-
)
--Periodicals.
--Societies.
    xx Transportation. Societies.
       Commerce. Societies.

Shippers' guides.

Shipping.   (DIRECT)
    sa Coastwise navigation.
       Inland navigation.
       Insurance.

Shipping (Continued)
    sa Marine.
       Maritime law.
       Merchant marine.
       Shipment of goods.
       Shipping bounties and sub-
         sidies.
       Priorities, Shipping.
       World War. 1939-1945. Shipping.
       Cargo preference act.
    x Marine transportation.
--Accounting.
    xx Accounting.
--Bibliography.
    sa Subdivision Bibliography under:
       Shipping. Periodicals.
--Congresses.
--Law. See Maritime law.
--Periodicals.
-- --Bibliography.
    xx Shipping. Bibliography.
--Rates.
    x Shipping rates.
      Freight rates, Ocean.
      Transportation, Ocean. Freight
        rates.
      Transportation, Water. Rates.
      Ocean freight rates.
-- --Fish, Frozen.
    xx Fish, Frozen. Transportation.
--Registers. See Ships. Registers.
--Statistics.
--Terminology.

Shipping act, 1916.
    xx Maritime law.

Shipping bounties and subsidies.   (IN-
  DIRECT)
    sa Export premiums.
       Merchant marine.
    xx Postal service. Foreign mail.
       Bounties.
       Export premiums.
--Bibliography.
    sa Subdivision Bibliography under
       Shipping bounties and sub-
       sidies [geographic subdivi-
       sion] e.g., Shipping boun-
       ties and subsidies. U.S.
       Bibliography.

Shipping fever of cattle. See Hemorrhagic septicemia.

Shipping priorities.   See Priorities,
  Shipping.

Shipping rates.   See Shipping. Rates.

Shipping register.

Ships.
    sa Submarine boats.
      Steamboat lines.
      Ship-building.
      Ship-bottom fouling.
      Boats.
      Fishing boats.
    x Vessels (Ships)
    xx Boats.
  --Bibliography.
    sa Subdivision Bibliography under:
      Ships. Painting.
  --Cargo.
    sa Load-line.
  --Cold storage.   See Cold storage on
    shipboard.
  --Disinfection.
    xx Fumigation.
  --Fires and fire prevention.
    x Fires in ships.
    xx Fires.
  --Inspection.
    xx Maritime law.

Ships, Iron and steel.
    x Iron and steel ships.
      Steel and iron ships.
    xx Naval architecture.

Ships.
  --Painting.
    x Ship painting.
    xx Painting, Industrial.
  -- --Bibliography.
    xx Painting, Industrial. Bibliog-
      raphy.
      Ships. Bibliography.
  --Registers.
    x Merchant marine. Registration.
      Registration of ships.
      Shipping. Registers.
  --Sanitation.
  --Water-supply.

Ships, Wooden.
    x Wood boats.
      Wooden boats.

Ships, Wooden (Continued)
    x Wooden ships.
      Wooden vessels.
    xx Naval architecture.

Shire horse.

Shirley, Mass.
  --Agriculture.
  -- --History.

Shirts.
    xx Clothing and dress.

Shisham silage.
    xx Dalbergia sissoo.
      Ensilage.

Shistocerca.   See Schistocerca.

Shivers.   See Staggers.

Shizomyces.
    sa Actinomyces.

Shoa, Ethiopia.
  --Description and travel.

Shock.
    sa Electric shock.

Shock therapy.
    x Shock treatment.
    xx Electric shock.
      Therapeutics.

Shock treatment.   See Shock therapy.

Shocking of grain.   See Maize. Shocking.

Shoddy.   See Wool, Reclaimed.

Shoddy manufacture.   See Woolen and
  worsted manufacture.

Shoe industry.   See Shoes. Trade and
  manufacture.

Shoe machinery.
    xx Shoes. Trade and manufacture.

Shoe materials.
    xx Shoes.
  --Testing.
    xx Testing.

Shoe polish.

Shoe repairing.   See Shoes. Repairing.

Shoe trade.   See Shoes. Trade and manu-
    facture.

Shoes.
        sa Shoe materials.
        x Footwear.
    --Repairing.
        x Shoe repairing.
        xx Repairing.
    --Trade and manufacture.   (DIRECT)
        sa Shoe machinery.
        x Shoe trade.
        Shoe industry.

Shonai, Japan.
    --Agriculture.

Shooks.
        sa Staves.
        xx Coopers and cooperage.
        Staves.

Shooting.
        sa Gunnery.
        Trap shooting.
        Duck shooting.
        Fowling.
        Pigeon shooting.

Shooting dogs.   See Hunting dogs.

Shop management.   See Factory management.

Shop work, Farm.   See Farm mechanics.

Shophar (musical instrument)

Shopping.
        sa Marketing (Home economics)
        xx Consumer education.

Shops, Farm.   See Farm workshops.

Shopwork, Farm.   See Farm mechanics.

Shore-birds.   See Limicolae.

Shore-lines.
        sa Shore-protection.

Shore-protection.
        x Coast protective works.
        xx Reclamation of land.
        Shore-lines.
        Hydraulic engineering.

Shorea.
        xx Dipterocarpaceae.

Shorea pauciflora.

Shorea robusta.
    --Pests.
        sa Hoplocerambyx spinicornis.
        Sphaerotrypes siwalikensis.
        xx Trees. Pests.

Shorea smithiana.

Shoring and underpinning.
        x Underpinning.
        xx Building.

Short-circuit beetle.   See Scobicia
    declivis.

Short horn cattle.   See Shorthorn cattle.

Short Mountain Creek, Ark.   See Six Mile
    Creek, Ark.

Short-path distillation.   See Distilla-
    tion, Molecular.

Short selling.   See Future trading.

Short-staple cotton.   See Cotton, Short-
    staple.

Short stories.
        xx Fiction.

Short stories, American.
        xx American fiction.

Short stories, Italian.
        xx Italian fiction.

Short stories, Russian.
        xx Russian fiction.

Short stories, Spanish.
        xx Spanish fiction.

Short story.
    Under this heading are entered
    works on the theory and art of
    short story writing. For col-
    lections of stories, see the
    subject Short stories.
    xx Authorship.
    Story writing.

Short term credit.
    sa Production credit associations.
    National farm loan associations.
    x Production credit.
--Bibliography.

Short-time rural credits.   See Short term
    credit.

Short wave radio.   See Radio, Short wave.

Short waves.   See Ultra high frequency
    waves.

Shortage of labor.   See Labor supply.

Shortening.
    sa Lard.
    Vanaspati.
    xx Fats and oils.
--Prices.
-- --Fixing.
    xx Prices. Fixing.
--Statistics.

Shorthand.
    sa Dictation.
    x Stenography.
--Dictionaries.
--Exercises for dictation.

Shorthand, Left-handedness in.
    xx Left- and right-handedness.

Shorthorn cattle.
    sa Durham cattle.
    Lincolnshire red shorthorn
        cattle.
    Australian Illawarra shorthorn
        cattle.
    x Short horn cattle.
    Milking shorthorn cattle.
    Dairy shorthorn cattle.
    Poll shorthorn cattle.
    Polled shorthorn cattle.

Shorthorn cattle (Continued)
    xx Durham cattle.
    Cattle.
--Breeding.
--History.
    xx Cattle. History.
--Periodicals.
--Societies.

Shortleaf pine.   See Pinus echinata.

Shortleaf pine wood.   See Pinus echinata
    (Wood)

Shoshone Indian Reservation, Wyo.

Shoshone irrigation project.

Shoshone National Forest, Wyo.
    xx Forest reservations.
    Wyoming. Forest reservations.

Shot-guns.
    xx Guns.

Shot-hole borer.   See Scolytus rugu-
    losus.

Shot-hole borer [India]   See Xyleborus
    fornicatus.

Shothead, Scotland, Farm.
    xx Agricultural experiment farms.

Shoulder.

Shovels.
    xx Tools.

Show-cards.   See Advertising cards.

Show-windows.
    x Window-dressing.
    xx Advertising, Outdoor.
    Display of merchandise.

Showa, Japan.
--Agriculture.
-- --Periodicals.

Shower-baths.

Shpola District.
--Agriculture.

Shredded wheat biscuit.

Shrew.   See Soricidae.

Shrewsbury, Eng.
--Ornithology.
--Parks.
    xx England. Parks.

Shrikes.
    x Lanius.
    xx Laniidae.

Shrimps.
    sa Cookery (Shrimps)
       Atyidae.
--Statistics.

Shrink-resistant woolen fabrics.   See
   Woolen fabrics, Shrink resistant.

Shrinkage.
    sa Subdivision Shrinkage under:
       Maize.
       Swine.
       Wool//

Shrinkage of wood.   See Wood. Shrinkage.

Shropshire, Eng.
--Agriculture.
    sa Subdivision England. Shropshire
       under: Agriculture. Economic
         aspects.
       Sugar-beet.
       Mechanized farming.
--Botany.
--Entomology.
    sa Subdivision England. Shropshire
       under: Butterflies.
--Ornithology.
--Soils.
    sa Subdivision England. Shropshire
       under: Soil-surveys.
    x England. Soils.

Shropshire sheep.
--Periodicals.

Shrubs.   (INDIRECT)
    sa Hedges.
       Food plants for wild life.
       Game cover.
    x Ornamental shrubs.
       Woody plants.

Shrubs (Continued)
    x Deciduous shrubs.
       Ligneous plants.
    xx Perennials.
       Arboriculture.
       Plants, Ornamental.
--Bibliography.
    sa Subdivision Bibliography un-
         der: Mate (Shrub)
--Catalogs.
--Diseases.
    sa Clitocybe root rot of woody
         plants.
--Growth.
--Identification.
--Introduction.
--Names.
--Pests.
    sa Subdivision Pests under:
       Sambucus.
       Box (Shrub)
--Physiology and morphology.
--Pictorial works.
    xx Botany. Pictorial works.
--Propagation.
    sa Grafting.
    xx Plant propagation.
--Pruning.
    xx Pruning.
--Seed.
    xx Seeds.
--Transplanting.
    xx Transplanting.

Shrubs in winter.

Shutters, Photographic.
    x Photographic shutters.
    xx Photography. Apparatus and
       supplies.

Shwartzman phenomenon.
    xx Immunity.

Shying in horses.

Sialidae.
    sa Corydalis.
       Raphidia.
       Sialis.
    xx Aquatic insects.

Sialididae.   See Sialidae.

Sialis.
    xx Alder flies.
    Sialidae.
Siam.
    Name changed to Thailand in 1939,
    to Siam in 1945, and once more
    to Thailand in 1949. Author and
    subject entries in this cata-
    log are under Siam.
--Agriculture.
    sa Subdivision Siam under: Rice.
        Agriculture. Economic as-
            pects.
        Poultry.
        Rural surveys.
        Agricultural policies and
            programs.
        Agricultural surveys.
-- --History.
    xx Agriculture. History.
-- --Periodicals.
-- --Statistics.
--Bibliography.
    xx Asia. Bibliography.
--Botany.
    sa Subdivision Siam under: Trees.
        Shrubs.
--Census.
--Commerce.
-- --Directories.
-- --Periodicals.
-- --Statistics.
    sa Subdivision Commerce. Statis-
        tics under: Bangkok.
--Commercial treaties.
    x Commercial treaties.
--Description and travel.
--Domestic animals.
--Economic conditions.
    sa Subdivision Siam under:
        Rural surveys.
--Entomology.
    sa Subdivision Siam under:
        Trichoptera.
        Lepidoptera.
    xx Asia. Entomology.
--Fisheries.
--Forestry.
    sa Subdivision Siam under: Trees.
        Lumbering.
        Timber.
--History.
    xx Asia. History.

Siam (Continued)
--Industries.
-- --Periodicals.
--Language.   See Siamese language.
--Natural history.
--Ornithology.
    xx Asia. Ornithology.
--Pomology.
    sa Subdivision Siam under:
        Citrus.
--Research.
--Roads.
--Social conditions.
    xx Asia. Social conditions.
--Soils.
--Statistics.
    sa Siam. Commerce. Statistics.
--Zoology.
-- --Bibliography.

Siamese cat.
    xx Cats.

Siamese grain beetle.   See Lophocateres
    pusillus.

Siamese language.
    x Siam. Language.
--Dictionaries.

Sibbaldia.   See Potentilla.

Siberia.
    sa Biro-Bidjan.
        Taiga.
--Agricultural experiment stations.
--Agriculture.
    sa Subdivision Agriculture under:
        Amur.
        Tomsk.
        Irkutsk//
        Subdivision Siberia under:Rye.
        Colonization, Agricultural.
        Agricultural laborers.
        Flax.
        Agriculture. Economic
            aspects.
        Forage plants.
        Cereals.
        Cropping systems.
        Mechanized farming.
        Agricultural administration.
        Wheat.
        Agriculture, Cooperative.
        Field crops.

Siberia (Continued)
--Agriculture.
-- --Congresses.
-- --Education.
-- --Periodicals.
--Apiculture.
    sa Subdivision Apiculture under:
      Ural Region.
--Botany.
    sa Subdivision Botany under:
      Lena Valley.
      Amur.
      Altai Mountains//
    Subdivision Siberia under:
      Botany, Economic.
      Algae.
      Hepaticae.
      Vegetable pathology.
      Weeds.
      Botany, Medical.
    xx Asia. Botany.
-- --Bibliography.
    sa Subdivision Botany. Bibliog-
      raphy under: East (Far East)
-- --Research.
--Cattle.
    xx U.S.S.R. Cattle.
--Climate.
    sa Subdivision Climate under: Amur.
--Colonies.
    sa Colonization, Agricultural with
      subdivisions: Siberia.
      Russia.
      Tobolsk (Government)
      U.S.S.R.
--Commerce.
-- --Periodicals.
--Description and travel.
--Domestic animals.
--Economic conditions.
--Entomology.
    sa Subdivision Entomology under:
      Uralsk.
      Primorskaia (Province)
      Tomsk.
    Subdivision Siberia under:
      Lepidoptera.
      Coleoptera.
      Entomology, Economic.
      Diptera.
--Fisheries.
--Forestry.
    sa Subdivision Siberia under:
      Forest industries.

Siberia (Continued)
--Forestry.
    sa Subdivision Forestry under:
      Enisei.
      Tomsk.
      Yakut Republic.
      Krasnoiarsk region.
-- --Research.
--Geology.
-- --Bibliography.
--History.
--Ichthyology.
--Maps.
--Maritime Province.   See Primorskaia
    (Province)
--Natural history.
    sa Subdivision Natural history
      under: Okhotsk, Siberia.
      Primorskaia (Province)
--Ornithology.
    xx Asia. Ornithology.
--Paleobotany.
    sa Subdivision Paleobotany under
      names of districts, regions,
      etc.
--Paleontology.
    sa Subdivision Paleontology un-
      der: Primorskaia (Province)
--Physical geography.
--Pomology.
--Research.
--Roads.
    sa Subdivision Roads under:
      Siberian area.
--Sheep.
--Soils.
    sa Subdivision Soils under:
      Zaisansk.
      Volkhof Valley.
      Amur.
      Saisan region.
--Statistics.
--Swine.
--Water-supply.
    sa Subdivision Siberia under:
      Water. Conservation.
--Zoology.
    sa Subdivision Zoology under:
      Altai Mountains.
      Saisan region.
      Tarbagatai Mountains.
    xx Asia. Zoology.

Siberian cedar.   See Pinus cembra
    sibirica.

Sicily.
--Agriculture.
   sa Sicily. Domestic animals.
     Subdivision Sicily under:
      Agricultural laborers.
      Cotton.
      Colonization, Agricultural.
      Crops and climate.
      Agriculture. Economic as-
        pects.
      Irrigation.
-- --Periodicals.
--Apiculture.
   sa Subdivision Apiculture under:
     Favignana.
--Bibliography.
   xx Italy. Bibliography.
--Botany.
   sa Mount Etna, Sicily. Botany.
     Subdivision Sicily under:
     Mushrooms.
--Cattle.
--Climate.
   sa Subdivision Sicily under:
     Crops and climate.
--Commerce.
   xx Italy. Commerce.
-- --Periodicals.
--Description and travel.
--Domestic animals.
--Economic conditions.
-- --Periodicals.
--Entomology.
   sa Subdivision Sicily under:
     Lepidoptera.
     Orthoptera.
--Forestry.
   sa Subdivision Sicily under:
     Forest policy.
-- --Periodicals.
--Land.
   sa Subdivision Sicily under:
     Land reform.
     Land utilization.
--Learned institutions and societies.
--Natural history.
--Pomology.
   sa Subdivision Sicily under:
     Citrus.
   xx Italy. Pomology.
--Social conditions.
--Soils.
--Statistics.
--Viticulture.
--Water-supply.

Sida.
   xx Malvaceae.

Side chain theory.
   sa Immunity. Mechanism and
     theories.

Side saddle-flower.   See Sarracenia.

Sideroxylon dulcificum.

Sideroxylon novo-zelandicum.

Sidewalks.

Sidi-bel-Abbès, Algeria.
   --Agriculture.

Siebengürgen.   See Transylvania.

Siegen, Prussia.
   --Agriculture.
   --Entomology.

Siegesbeckia orientalis.

Siena (Province)
   --Agriculture.
     sa Subdivision Italy. Siena
       (Province) under: Agri-
       culture, Cooperative.
       Societies.
-- --Periodicals.
   --Botany.
   --Commerce.
-- --Directories.
   --Fairs.
   --Markets.
   --Paleontology.

Sienna Belted Swine.
   x Cinta Senese swine.
     Cinto swine.

Sierola.

Sierozem soils.

Sierra Ancha Experimental Watersheds,
   Ariz.

Sierra Co., N.M.

Sierra de Aralar, Spain.
   --Zoology.

Sierra de Curá-mal.
--Natural history.

Sierra de Valle Fertil, Argentine Republic.
--Geography.
    sa Subdivision Argentine Republic.
        Sierra de Valle Fertil under: Anthropo-geography.

Sierra Forest Reserve, Calif.

Sierra Leone.
--Agriculture.
    sa Subdivision Sierra Leone under:
        Coffee.
        Agricultural policies and programs.
--Botany.
--Census.
--Commerce.
-- --Statistics.
--Economic policy.
--Entomology.
    xx Africa, West. Entomology.
--Forestry.
    sa Subdivision Sierra Leone under:
        Forest policy.
        Timber.
        War and forestry (1939-1945)
    xx Africa, West. Forestry.
--Geology.
--Land.
    sa Subdivision Sierra Leone under:
        Land utilization.
--Maps.
--Pomology.
    sa Subdivision Sierra Leone under:
        Citrus.
    xx Africa. Pomology.
--Sanitary affairs.
--Social life and customs.
--Soils.
    sa Subdivision Sierra Leone under:
        Soil conservation.
    xx Africa, British West. Soils.
--Surveys.

Sierra National Forest, Calif.
    sa Subdivision Sierra National
        Forest under: Fish-culture.
        Stream survey.
--Ichthyology.

Sierra Nevada de Santa Marta.
--Zoology.
    sa Subdivision Sierra Nevada de
        Santa Marta under: Reptilia.
        Batrachia.

Sierra Nevada Mountains.
--Botany.
--Geographic names.
    xx Geographic names.
--Maps.
--Ornithology.
--Paleobotany.
    xx California. Paleobotany.
--Zoology.

Sierra Nevada Mountains, Spain.

Sierra redwood.   See Redwood; Sequoia
    gigantea.

Sieur de Monts National Monument.   See
    Acadia National Park; Wild Gardens of
    Acadia, Bar Harbor, Me.

Sieve-cells.

Sieves.

Siga.   See Schoenobius.

Sigaloëssa.

Sigatoka.   See Cercospora musae.

Sigatoka disease of banana.   See Leaf-
    spot of banana.

Sight.
    sa Eye.
       Stereoscopy.
    x Vision.

Sigillaria.
    sa Syringodendron.

Sigillaria elegans.

Sigillariaceae.

Siginae.

Sigma test.

Sign-boards.   See Signs and sign-boards.

Signals and signaling.
    sa Storm signals.
       Weather signals.
       Wind signals.
    xx Signs and symbols.

Signals and signaling, Automobile.

Signals and signaling, Submarine.

Signatures (Writing)
    sa Initials and pseudonyms.

Signiphorinae.

Signs. See Signs and sign-boards; Signs
  and symbols.

Signs and sign-boards.
    sa Advertising.
       Road marking.
       Bill-posting.
    x Billboards.
      Sign-boards.
      Signs.
    xx Advertising, Outdoor.

Signs and symbols.
    sa Abbreviations.
       Map symbols.
       Signals and signaling.
    x Signs.
      Symbols.
    xx Abbreviations.
  --Bibliography.

Sihl Valley, Switzerland.
  --Botany.
  --Forestry.

Sika.
    x Japanese deer.
    xx Deer.

Sikang, China.
  --Land.
    sa Subdivision Sikang, China under:
       Land tenure.
  --Social conditions.

Sikhim, India.
  --Botany.

Sikhote-Alin Range.
  --Forestry.

Sikkim. See Sikhim.

Siksika Indians.
    x Blackfoot Indians.

Sila Region.
  --Agriculture.
    sa Subdivision Sila Region under:
      Agricultural policies and
        programs.
  --Economic policy.

Silage. See Ensilage.

Silage crops. See Crops for ensilage.

Silage cutters. See Ensilage cutters.

Silage plants. See Crops for ensilage.

Silargel.

Silene.

Silene latifolia.
    x Bladder campion.
      Cowbell.
      Cow bell.
      Rattle weed.
      Bladder weed.
  --Eradication.
    xx Weeds. Eradication.

Sileneae.

Silesia.
  --Agriculture.
    sa Subdivision Agriculture under:
      Waldenburg, Silesia.
      Bunzlau, Silesia.
      Silesia, Lower.
      Breslau region.
      Subdivision Silesia under:
        Agriculture. Economic as-
         pects.
        Colonization, Agricultural.
        Agricultural laborers.
        Farm produce. Cost of pro-
         duction.
        Cereals.
  -- --History.
    xx Germany. Agriculture. History.

Silesia (Continued)
--Botany.
    sa Gleiwitz.
    Subdivision Silesia under:
    Algae.
    Plants, Cultivated.
    xx Austria. Botany.
--Commerce.
    xx Austria. Commerce.
--Domestic animals.
    sa Silesia, Lower. Domestic ani-
      mals.
--Entomology.
    sa Subdivision Silesia under:
    Coleoptera.
    Diptera.
--Forestry.
-- --Bibliography.
--Milk supply.
    xx Germany. Milk supply.
--Natural history.
--Zoology.

Silesia, Lower.
--Agriculture.
    sa Subdivision Silesia, Lower
      under: Agriculture, Coopera-
      tive.
    xx Germany. Agriculture.
    Silesia. Agriculture.
--Domestic animals.
    sa Silesia, Lower. Sheep.
--Sheep.

Silesia, Upper.
--Milk trade.

Silesian horse.

Silica.
--Deficiency in soil.   See Soil, Silica
    deficient.

Silica as a fertilizer.
    xx Fertilizers. -

Silica as an insecticide.

Silica deficient soils.   See Soil, Silica
    deficient.

Silica in plants.

Silica in wood.
    x Siliceous timber.

Silicate of soda.

Silicates.
    sa Soil, Silicates in.
    Zeolite.
--Effect of sulphuric acid on.   See
    Sulphurous acid. Effect on sili-
    cates.

Siliceous timber.   See Silica in wood.

Silicic acid.
    sa Phosphatic slag, Silicic acid
      in.
    Soil, Silicic acid in.

Silicic acid in plants.
    x Plants, Silicic acid in.

Silicoflagellatae.

Silicon.
--Effect on plants.

Silicon compounds.
    sa Tetraethyl silicane.
    x Silicones.

Silicon in plants.
    x Plants, Silicon in.

Silicon-iron.   See Ferro-silicon.

Silicon tetraethyl.   See Tetraethyl
    silicane.

Silicones.   See Silicon compounds.

Silk.
    sa Rayon.

Silk, Artificial.   See Rayon.

Silk.
--Bibliography.
--Classification.   See Silk. Grading
    and standardization.
--Congresses.
    sa Sericulture. Congresses.
--Directories.
    sa Silk, Artificial. Directories.
--Dyeing.
    x Dyes and dyeing. Silk.

Silk, Effect of humidity on.   See Humidity. Effect on silk.

Silk.
--Grading and standardization.
--History.
--Manufacture.   See Silk manufacture and trade.
--Marketing.
     xx Silk manufacture and trade.
· --Costs.
     xx Marketing. Costs.
--Periodicals.   See Sericulture. Periodicals; Silk manufacture and trade. Societies.
--Prices.
--Societies.   See Sericulture. Societies; Silk manufacture and trade. Societies.
--Statistics.
--Tariff.
--Testing.
-- --Law.
     xx Textile industry and fabrics. Testing. Law.

Silk, Tussah.

Silk cotton tree.
     sa Kapok.
     x Kapok tree.
       Randu tree.
       Ceiba pentandra.
--Pests.
     xx Trees. Pests.
--Seed.

Silk cotton tree seed.   See Silk cotton tree. Seed.

Silk cotton tree seed cake.

Silk manufacture and trade.   (DIRECT)
     sa Silk. Marketing.
     x Silk trade.
--Bibliography.

Silk manufacture and trade, Cooperative.

Silk manufacture and trade.
--Exchanges.
     xx Commodity exchanges.
--Periodicals.
--Societies.
--Statistics.

Silk reeling.

Silk screen printing.
     x Screen printing.
       Silk screen process.
       Stencil printing.
     xx Color-printing.
       Stencil work.

Silk screen process.   See Silk screen printing.

Silk spiders.
     sa Nephila.

Silk trade.   See Silk manufacture and trade.

Silk-weed.   See Asclepias.

Silk-worm.   See Silkworms.

Silkworms.
     This subject used for entomological works on the silkworm as an insect. Publications on the raising of silkworms for the production of raw silk are entered under the subject, Sericulture.
     sa Yama-mai.
       Ugimya sericaria.
       Borocera.
       Ailanthus moth.
       Antheraea.
     x Bombyx mori.
     xx Silkworms.
--Bibliography.

Silkworms, Chinese.

Silkworms.
--Diseases.
     sa Muscardine.
       Antheraea pernyi. Diseases.
--Genetics.
     xx Insects. Genetics.

Silkworms, Indian.

Silkworms. Japanese.

Silkworms.
--Larvae.
--Periodicals.

Silkworms (Continued)
--Statistics.

Silky cane weevil.   See Metamasius seri-
ceus.

Silo.   See Silos.

Silos.
          sa Ensilage.
             Compost silos.
          x Silo.
          xx Ensilage.

Silos, Bunker.
          x Bunker silos.

Silos.
--Designs and plans.

Silos, Pit.
          x Pit silos.

Silos.
--Statistics.

Silos, Trench.
          x Trench silos.

Silpha opaca.

Silphidae.
          sa Necrophorus.

Silphium.

Silt.
          sa Sedimentation and deposition.
          x Silting.

Silting.   See Silt.

Siltometer.
          xx Scientific apparatus and in-
             struments.

Silver.
          sa Money.
             Silver purchase act of 1934.
          x Argentum.
          xx Precious metals.
--Physiological effect.
          xx Physiology.
--Prices.
          xx Prices.

Silver as a disinfectant.

Silver Bow Co., Mont.
          xx Montana.

Silver cleaning.

Silver coinage.   See Coinage.

Silver compounds.
          xx Silver oxide.
             Silver salts.

Silver fir.   See Abies alba.

Silver fir beetle.   See Pseudohylesinus
          grandis.

Silver fish.   See Lepismatidae.

Silver fox.
--Diseases.
          sa Distemper in silver foxes.
--Food.
          xx Fur-bearing animals. Food and
             feeding.
--Periodicals.

Silver in veterinary medicine.

Silver leaf diseases of fruit trees.
          xx Fruit diseases.

Silver maple.   See Acer saccharinum.

Silver mines and mining.   (INDIRECT)

Silver oxide.
          sa Silver compounds.

Silver purchase act of 1934.
          xx Silver.

Silver salts.
          sa Silver compounds.

Silver scurf.

Silver Strand Beach State Park, San Diego
          Co., Calif.
          xx California. Parks.

Silver-striped webworms.   See Crambus
          praefectellus.

Silver top ash.　See Eucalyptus sieberiana.

Silverfish.　See Lepismatidae.

Silverton Quadrangle, Colo.
--Geology.

Silvertop ash.　See Eucalyptus sieberiana.

Silverware.

Silvics.　See Forestry. Ecology.

Silvicultural research.　See Forestry.
　Research.

Silviculture.　(INDIRECT)
　　　When subdivided by place, indicate
　　　see also ref.· from name of place
　　　with subdivision: Forestry.
　　sa Litter.
　　　Thinning.
　　　Tree planting.
　　　Arboriculture.
　　　Afforestation and reforestation.
　　　Selection system (Forestry)
　　x Forest planting.
　　xx Arboriculture.
--Bibliography.
　　sa Thinning. Bibliography.
--Exhibitions.
--Laboratory manuals.
--Research.　See Forestry. Research.
--Tropics.
　　xx Tropics. Forestry.

Simalu (Island)
--Entomology.
　　xx Sumatra. Entomology.

Simarubaceae.
　　sa Irvingia.
　　　Koeberlinia.
　　　Picrasma.
　　　Quassia.

Simcoe Co., Ont.
--Agriculture.
　　sa Subdivision Simcoe Co., Ont. un-
　　　　　der: Agriculture, Cooperative.

Simla, India.
--Botany.

Simiidae.
　　sa Primates.
　　　Gorilla.
　　　Monkeys.
　　　Orang-utan.
　　　Chimpanzee.
　　　Colobus.
　　x Apes.

Simmental cattle.
　　x Höhenfleckvieh.
　　　Alpenfleckvieh.
　　　German Simmental.
　　　Red spotted highland cattle.
　　　Spotted mountain cattle.
　　　Spotted cattle (Fleckvieh)
　　　Berner spotted cattle.
　　　Bernese cattle.
　　　Fleckvieh.
　　xx Cattle.

Simmondsia.
　　xx Buxaceae.

Simondsia paradoxa.

Simpheropol.　See Simferopol.

Simplification in industry.　See
　　Standardization.

Simuliidae.
　　sa Simulium.
　　x Buffalo fly.

Simulium.

Simulium (Gigantodax)

Simulium carolinae.

Simulium columbaczense.

Simulium damnosum.

Simulium distinctum.

Simulium mediovittatum.

Simulium nigroparvum.

Simulium nölleri.

Simulium venustum.

Simulium vittatum.

Simultaneous equations.　See Equations,
　　Simultaneous.

Sinai.
　--Botany.

Sinai-Expedition, 1927.

Sinaitic Peninsula.
　--Botany.
　--Description and travel.
　--Geology.
　--Natural history.
　--Zoology.

Sinaloa, Mexico.
　--Agriculture.
　　　xx Mexico. Agriculture.

Sinapis.
　　　sa Mustard.

Sinapis arvensis.　See Charlock.

Sincosta aberrans.

Sind.
　--Agriculture.
　　　sa Subdivision Sind under: Cotton.
　　　　Agricultural policies and
　　　　　programs.
　　　　Agricultural credit.
　-- --Statistics.
　--Economic conditions.
　　　sa Subdivision Sind under:
　　　　Geography, Economic.
　--Forestry.
　　　xx India. Forestry.
　--Geography.
　　　sa Subdivision Sind under:
　　　　Geography, Economic.

Sindangan Bay.
　--Native races.
　　　xx Native races.

Sinea diadema.

Sinestrol.
　　　xx Estrogens.

Singapore.
　--Agriculture.
　--Botanic gardens.
　--Botany.
　　　xx Asia. Botany.
　--Commerce.
　--Domestic animals.
　--Fisheries.
　--Government publications.
　-- --Bibliography.
　--Industries.
　--Land.
　--Statistics.

Singapore (Island)
　--Public works.
　--Sanitary affairs.

Singing and voice culture.
　　　x Voice culture.

Singing sands.
　　　x Musical sands.
　　　　Sand, Singing.
　　　　Sand, Musical.
　　　xx Acoustic phenomena in nature.

Single-leaf piñon.　See Pinus monophylla.

Single tax.
　　　sa Land, Nationalization of.
　　　　Land. Taxation.
　　　　Land tenure.
　　　xx Taxation.
　--Periodicals.

Sinicuiche.

Sinkiang, China.
　--Agriculture.
　　　sa Subdivision China. Sinkiang
　　　　under: Reclamation of land.
　--Economic conditions.
　　　sa Subdivision China. Sinkiang
　　　　under: Geography, Economic.
　--Geography.
　　　sa Subdivision China. Sinkiang
　　　　under: Geography. Economic.
　--Soils.
　　　sa Subdivision China. Sinkiang
　　　　under: Soil conservation.
　--Water-supply.
　　　sa Subdivision China. Sinkiang
　　　　under: Water. Conservation.

Sinnemahoning Creek.
    sa Subdivision Sinnemahoning Creek
       under: Floods.

Sino-Japanese War, 1937. See World War,
   1939-1945. China; World War, 1939-1945.
   Japan.

Sino-Soviet bloc. See U.S.S.R. bloc.

Sinter.

Sinuate pear borer. See Agrilus sinuatus.

Sioux City, Iowa.
  --Social conditions.
    sa Subdivision Sioux City under:
       Social surveys. Iowa.

Sioux Co., Neb.
  --Paleontology.

Sioux Co., N.D.
  --Politics and government.
    sa Subdivision Sioux Co., N.D. un-
       der: Local government.

Sioux Falls, S.D.
    sa Subdivision Sioux Falls, S.D.
       under: Market surveys.
  --Geology.

Sioux Indians. See Dakota Indians.

Siphon.
    x Siphons.

Siphona irritans. See Haematobia irritans.

Siphonales.

Siphonaptera.
    sa Pulicidae.
    Stephanocircus.
    Mesopsylla.
    Palaeopsylla.
    Fleas as carriers of contagion.
    Therevidae.
    Ctenocephalidae.
    Thrassis.
    Echidnophaga gallinacea.
    Micropsylla.
    Malareus.

Siphonaptera (Continued)
    sa Meringis.
    Catallagia.
    Nearctopsylla.
    Corypsylla.
    x Aphaniptera.

Siphonaptera and disease. See Fleas as
   carriers of contagion.

Siphoneae.
    sa Vaucheriaceae.

Siphoneae, Fossil.
    xx Algae, Fossil.

Siphonodon.

Siphonophora.

Siphonotus.

Siphons. See Siphon.

Sipolisia lanaginosa.

Sipunculidae.

Sir Edward Pellew Islands.

Sirenia.
    sa Rhytina.
  --Bibliography.

Sirex.
  --Parasites.

Sirex gigas.

Sirhind Canal.

Siricidae.
    sa Sirex.

Sirth. See Chavica betle.

Sirup. See Syrup.

Sirup scum as fertilizer.
    xx Fertilizers.
      Sugar. By-products.

Sirups. See Syrups.

Sirvel Agricultural Station.
    xx India. Agricultural experiment
        stations.

Sisal.
    x Hemp, Sisal.
      Sisal hemp.
    xx Agave.
  --Bibliography.
  --Congresses.
  --Economic aspects.
  --Estimating of crop.
  --Periodicals.
  --Research.
  --Societies.
  --Statistics.

Sisal bagging.
    xx Bagging.

Sisal hemp.   See Sisal.

Siskiyou Co., Calif.
  --Forestry.
      sa Subdivision California.Siskiyou
        Co. under: Forest surveys.
        Forest industries.
        Timber.
  --Ornithology.
  --Water-supply.
    xx California. Water-supply.
  --Zoology.

Siskiyou National Forest.
    sa Oregon caves.

Sisymbrium altissimum.

Sisymbrium pinnatifidum.

Sisyridae.

Site classification (Forestry)
    x Forestry. Site classification.

Sitgreaves National Forest, Ariz.

Sitka.
  --Botany.

Sitka spruce.   See Picea sitchensis.

Sitka-spruce weevil.   See Pissodes sitchensis.

Sitodiplosis mosellana.
    x Diplosis tritici.
      Thecodiplosis mosellana.
      Wheat midge.

Sitodrepa panicea.

Sitona.
    x Pea weevil.

Sitona hispidula.

Sitona lineata.
    x Pea leaf weevil.

Sitones.   See Sitona.

Sitophilus.
    x Grain weevils.
      Grain beetles.

Sitophilus granarius.
    x Weevils.

Sitophilus linearis.

Sitophilus oryza.
    x Rice weevil.

Sitotroga cereallela.
  --Parasites.
    xx Moths. Parasites.

Sitta.   See Nuthatches.

Sittasomus.

Sium.
   / xx Ammineae.

Sium cicutaefolium.

Siuslaw National Forest, Or.
    xx Oregon. Forest reservations.

Siwa Oasis.
  --Sanitary affairs.

Siwalik Hills, India.
    xx India.

606.   See Salvarsan.

666.   See Benzene hexachloride.

Six Mile Creek, Ark.
      sa Subdivision Six Mile Creek, Ark.
         under: Flood control.
      x Short Mountain Creek, Ark.

Six-spotted leafhopper.   See Macrosteles
  fascifrons.

Sixty-day oats. See Oats.

Size (Biology)

Size in plants.

Size of family. See Family. Size.

Size of farms. See Farms. Size.

Sizing.
      sa Paper. Sizing.

Sizing of garments. See Garment sizes.

Sizing (Textile)
      sa Cotton sizing.

Skagens odde, Denmark.
--Agriculture.
      sa Subdivision Denmark. Skagens
         odde under: Grasses.

Skagit Co., Wash.
      xx Washington (State)
--Agriculture.
      sa Subdivision Washington (State)
         Skagit Co. under: Agri-
           culture. Economic aspects.
--Land.
--Soils.
      sa Subdivision Washington. Skagit
         Co. under: Soil-surveys.

Skagit River, Wash.

Skamania Co., Wash.
--Soils.
      sa Soil surveys. Washington (State)
         Skamania Co.

Skaraborg, Sweden.
      x Mariestad, Sweden (Province)
--Agriculture.
--Geology.
--Soils.

Skates.
--Parasites.

Skatol.

Skeena River district, B.C.
--Pomology.

Skeet. See Trap-shooting.

Skeleton.
      x Osteology.
      xx Bones.
         Anatomy, Comparative.

Skeleton weed. See Chondrilla juncea.

Skew curves.

Ski poles.
      xx Skis and ski-running.

Skidding (Lumbering) See Skidding and
  skidders.

Skidding and skidders.
      x Skidding (Lumbering)
      xx Lumbering.

Skiing. See Skis and ski-running.

Skillet Fork River.
      sa Subdivision Skillet Fork River
         under: Flood control.

Skim milk.
      x Milk, Skim.
--Bibliography.
      xx Milk. Bibliography.

Skim milk, Concentrated sour. See Milk,
  Fermented, Concentrated.

Skim milk, Dried. See Milk, Desiccated.

Skim milk.
--Marketing.
      xx Milk. Marketing.
--Marketing agreements.
      xx Milk. Marketing agreements.
--Nutritive value. See Skim milk as
    food.
--Prices.
      xx Milk. Prices.

Skim milk, Proteins in.
    xx Milk, Proteins in.

Skim milk.
--Statistics.

Skim milk as feeding stuff.
    xx Milk as feeding stuff.

Skim milk as food.
    x Skim milk. Nutritive value.
    xx Milk as food.

Skim milk powder. See Milk, Desiccated.

Skim milk solids, Dried. See Milk, Desiccated.

Skin.
    sa Domestic animals. Identification.
--Diseases.
    sa Acne.
    Dermatomycoses.
    Dermatitis.
    Creeping eruption.
    xx Dermatology.
-- --Periodicals.
--Microbiology.
--Tumors.

Skin-grafting.
    x Grafting of skin.

Skin insects.
    xx Entomology, Economic.

Skin maggot fly. See Cordylobia anthropophaga.

Skins. See Hides and skins.

Skipper butterflies. See Hesperiidae.

Skipper-fly. See Piophila casei.

Skis and ski-running.
    sa Ski poles.
    x Skiing.
    xx Sports.
    Winter sports.

Skogsruss (Pony) See Gotland pony.

Skokholm Island.
--Agriculture.

Skomer Island.
    x Island of Skomer.
--Natural history.

Skopelos (Island)
--Sheep.
    xx Greece. Sheep.
    Greece. Domestic animals.

Skull. See Craniology.

Skunk River Valley.
--Water-supply.

Skunks.
    sa Mephitinae.

Skykomish River.

Skylights.
    xx Windows.
    Building.

Slag.

Slag as a road material.

Slag as fertilizer.
    sa Phosphatic slag.
    x Agricultural slag.

Slang.
    sa Subdivision Slang under:
        English language.

Slash.

Slash disposal.
    sa Brush disposal.
--Bibliography.

Slash pine. See Pinus caribaea.

Slate.

Slaughter-house refuse.

Slaughtering and slaughter-houses.
  (INDIRECT)
    sa Butcher animals.
    Electricity in slaughtering.

Slaughtering and slaughter-houses (Con.)
   sa Subdivision Slaughtering under
      names of animals, e.g.,
      Swine. Slaughtering.
      Subdivision Slaughter-houses
      under names of cities, e.g.,
      Prague. Slaughter-houses.
   x Livestock slaughter establish-
      ments.
   xx Meat industry and trade.
--Bibliography.
   sa Subdivision Bibliography under:
      Electrocution of animals.
--By-products.   See Animal products.

Slaughtering and slaughter-houses, Cooperative.
--Periodicals.

Slaughtering and slaughter-houses.
--Directories.
--Legislation.
--Periodicals.
--Safety measures.
   xx Accidents. Prevention.
--Sanitation.
--Statistics.
   sa Slaughtering and slaughter-
      houses. [geographic subdi-
      vision] Statistics, e.g.,
      Slaughtering and slaughter-
      houses. U.S. Statistics.

Slaughtering as an occupation.

Slaughtering of poultry.   See Poultry.
   Slaughtering.

Slavery.
   sa Peonage.

Slavery in Brazil.

Slavery in Greece.

Slavery in the U.S.
--Florida.
--Kentucky.
--Southern States.
--Virginia.

Slavery in the West Indies, British.
--Bibliography.

Slavic languages.
   sa Names of the various languages
      belonging to the Slavic
      group, e.g., Russian lan-
      guage, Slovenian language.
--Dictionaries.
--Grammar.
--Transliteration.
   x Cyrillic alphabet. Trans-
      literation.
      Russian language. Translitera-
      tion.

Slavonia.
--Agriculture.
--Apiculture.
--Botany.
--Cattle.
   xx Cattle.
--Description and travel.
--Entomology.
   sa Subdivision Slavonia under:
      Coleoptera.
--Forestry.
--Ornithology.
   xx Austria. Ornithology.
--Pomology.
--Zoology.

Slavs.
--History.

Sledges.   See Sleighs and sledges.

Sleep.

Sleepers, Railroad.   See Railroad ties.

Sleeping bags.

Sleeping-sickness.
   sa Trypanosomiasis.
      Encephalo-myelitis.
   xx Trypanosomiasis.
--Bibliography.
   sa Trypanosomiasis. Bibliography.

Sleepy grass.   See Stipa vaseyi.

Sleet.
   sa Glaze.
   xx Meteorology.

Sleighs and sledges.
   x Sledges.

Slickers.   See Lepismidae.

Slide film projectors.
     x Projectors, Slide film.
       Film strip projectors.
     xx Moving-picture projectors.

Slide film scripts.

Slide films.
     sa Lantern slides.
     x Color slides.
       Film slides.
       Films, Photographic.
       Film strips.
     xx Moving-picture films.
       Moving-pictures.
       Lantern slides.
--Abstracts.
--Bibliography.
--Cataloging.   See Cataloging. Slide
     films.
--Catalogs.
     x Slide films. Prices.
     xx Moving-pictures. Catalogs.
--Prices.   See Slide films. Catalogs.

Slide-rule.
     x Calculating rule.
     xx Measuring instruments.

Slime-molds.   See Myxomycetes.

Slings.

Slip covers.

Slippery elm.   See Ulmus pubescens.

Sloan plan.   See Missouri River Basin
     project.

Sloan project in applied economics.

Slogans.
     xx Mottoes.

Slope Co., N.D.
--Soils.
     sa Subdivision North Dakota. Slope
         Co. under: Soil conservation.

Slopes.
--Climatic variations.

Slot-machines.   See Vending machines.

Sloth.
     sa Megalonyx.

Sloths, Fossil.

Slovak abbreviations.   See Abbreviations,
     Slovak.

Slovak language.
--Abbreviations.   See Abbreviations,
     Slovak.
--Dictionaries.
-- --Bibliography.
--Glossaries, vocabularies, etc.
-- --Bibliography.

Slovakia.
--Agriculture.
     sa Subdivision Slovakia under:
         Agriculture, Cooperative.
-- --Periodicals.
--Apiculture.
-- --Periodicals.
--Directories.
--Forestry.
     sa Subdivision Slovakia under:
         Timber.
         Afforestation and reforesta-
           tion.
-- --Directories.
- --History.
-- --Periodicals.
--Gazetteers.
--Land.
     sa Subdivision Slovakia under:
         Waste lands.
--Pomology.
--Sheep.
--Viticulture.

Slovaks in the U.S.
--Food habits.
     xx Food habits.

Slovenia.
--Agriculture.
     sa Subdivision Slovenia under:
         Hops.
-- --Periodicals.
--Apiculture.
--Botany.
--Dairying.

Slovenia (Continued)
--Economic conditions.
-- --Periodicals.
--Forestry.
--Soils.
--Viticulture.

Slovenian language.
--Dictionaries.

Slug caterpillars.   See Limacodidae.

Slug-worms.   See Veronicella.

Slugs, Land.
        x Land slugs.
          Garden slugs.
        xx Limacidae.

Smaland, Sweden.
--Botany.
        xx Sweden. Botany.
--Natural history.

Small business.   See Business. Small
    business.

Small business act of 1953.

Small farms.   See Farms, Small.

Small fruits.   See Berries; Fig; Grapes.

Small loans.   See Loans, Personal.

Small millet.   See Panicum miliare.

Small states.   See States, Small.

Small Yorkshire swine.

Smaller European elm bark beetle.   See
    Scolytus multistriatus.

Smallpox.
--Preventive inoculation.

Smallpox in animals.
--Preventive inoculation.

Smartweed borer.   See Pyrausta ainsliei.

Smell.
--Bibliography.
--Birds.

Smell (Continued)
--Insects.
        x Olfactory sense of insects.
          Scent organs. Insects.
          Senses and sense organs of
            insects. Smell.
        xx Senses and sense organs of
            insects. Olfactory.
          Glands, Odiferous (Insects)
--Mammals.

Smelter fumes.
        sa Soil. Effect of zinc fumes.
--Bibliography.

Smelter waste.

Smelting.
        sa Ore-dressing.

Smelts.

Smicra.

Smicromorpha.

Smieloe, Russia.
--Botany.
        sa Subdivision Russia. Smieloe
            under: Weeds.

Smilaceae.
        sa Smilax.

Smilacina amplexicaulis.

Smilacina racemosa.

Smilax.

Smilax herbacea.

Smilodon.

Sminthuridae.   See Smynthurus.

Smith-Hughes law.

Smith-Lever act.
--Bibliography.

Smith shelling device.
        xx Rice. Grading and standardi-
            zation.

Smithfield club cattle show.

Smithsonian Institution.

Smithsonian Institution. Advisory Committee on the Langley aerodynamical
laboratory.

Smithsonian Institution.
--Bibliography.
--U.S. National Museum.
-- --Bibliography.
-- --Collections.
-- --Turton Collection.

Smoke.
        sa Noxious vapors.
        Tobacco smoke.
--Bibliography.
--Effect on animals.
--Effect on building materials.
--Effect on plants.
        sa Gases. Effect on plants.
        Trees. Smoke and smelter fume
            injury.
--Effect on soil. See Soil. Effect of
    smoke.
--Law.
--Physiological effect.
        xx Physiology.

Smoke and smelter fume injury. See smoke.
    Effect on plants; Gases. Effect on
    plants; Soil. Effect of smoke; Trees.
    Smoke and smelter fume injury.

Smoke houses. See Smokehouses.

Smoke prevention.
        sa Smoke. Effect of plants.
        Smoke. Effect on animals.
        Smoke. Effect on building
            materials.

Smoke tree, Common. See Cotinus coggygria.

Smoked poultry. See Poultry (Meat)
    Smoked.

Smoked turkeys. See Poultry (Meat)
    Smoked.

Smokehouses.
        x Smoke houses.

Smokeless powder.

Smokey Bear.

Smoking.
        x Tobacco smoking.
        xx Tobacco.

Smoky Mountains.   See Great Smoky
    Mountains.

Smoky River Valley, Canada.
--Forestry.

Smöla, Norway.
--Botany.

Smolensk Region.
--Agriculture.
        sa Subdivision Smolensk Region
            under: Agricultural
                policies and programs.
            Wheat.
            Forage plants.
            Agricultural laborers.
--Apiculture.
-- --Botany.
--Cattle.
        xx Smolensk Region. Domestic
            animals.
--Domestic animals.
        sa Subdivision Cattle under:
            Smolensk Region.
--Ichthyology.
--Land.
        sa Subdivision Smolensk Region
            under: Land tenure.
--Politics and government.
--Pomology.
--Soils. . .
--Water-supply.

Smut.
        sa Ustilagineae.
        Barley smut.
        Oat smut.
        Cereal smut.
        Wheat smut.
--Control.
        sa Subdivision Control under:
            Barley smut.
            Cereal smut.
            Oat smut.
            Wheat smut.

Smut fungi.   See Ustilagineae.

Smuticide.
    xx Fungicides.

Smychka State Farm.

Smynthuridae.
    sa Smynthurus.

Smynthurus.
    x Sminthuridae.

Smynthurus viridus.
    x Lucerne flea.

Smyrna.
--Agriculture.
--Commerce.
-- --Periodicals.
-- --Statistics.

Smyth Co., Va.
    sa Subdivision Smyth Co. under:
        County surveys. Virginia.
    xx Virginia.
--Agriculture.
    sa Subdivision Virginia. Smyth Co.
        under: Agricultural policies
        and programs.
--Economic conditions.
    sa Subdivision Smyth Co. under:
        Economic surveys. Virginia.
    xx Virginia. Economic conditions.
--Industries and resources.
    sa Industrial surveys. Virginia.
        Smyth Co.
--Soils.
    sa Subdivision Virginia. Smyth Co.
        under: Soil-surveys.

Snails.   See Helicidae.

Snails, Bilharzia.   See Bilharzia snails.

Snails, Fresh-water.   See Basommatophora.

Snails, Giant African.   See Achatina
fulica.

Snails, Land.   See Helicidae.

Snails, Pond.   See Limnaea.

Snails as food.
    xx Helicidae.

Snake River.
    sa Irrigation. Idaho. Snake
        River.
--Power utilization.
    xx Power (Mechanics)`
        Power utilization.
        Water-power.

Snake River Plains, Idaho.
--Botany.
--Climate.

Snake River Valley.
--Agriculture.
    sa Subdivision Snake River
        Valley under: Wheat.
        Part-time farming.
        Agricultural laborers.

Snake root, White.   See Eupatorium
urticaefolium.

Snakeroot.   See Cicuta.

Snakes.   See Serpents.

Snakeweed.   See Gutierrezia.

Snap beans.   See Beans, Snap.

Snapdragon.   See Antirrhinum.

Sneezeweed.   See Helenium hoopesii.

Snohomish Co., Wash.
--Agriculture.
    sa Subdivision Washington (State)
        under: Agriculture. Eco-
        nomic aspects.
--Forestry.
    sa Subdivision Snohomish Co.,
        Wash. under: Lumbering.
--Land.
    sa Subdivision Washington (State)
        Snohomish Co. under: Land.
        Classification.
    xx Washington (State) Land.
--Soils.
    sa Subdivision Washington (State)
        Snohomish Co. under:
        Soil-surveys.

Snoqualmie National Forest, Wash.

Snoqualmie River.

Snout-beetle.   See Rhynchophora.

Snow.
       sa Railroads. Snow protection and
         removal.
       xx Atmospheric precipitation.
 --Abstracts.
 --Bibliography.
 -- --Periodicals.
 --Congresses.
       xx Meterology. Congresses.
 --Density.

Snow as a fertilizer.

Snow barriers.   See Snowbreaks.

Snow buntings.
       xx Ornithology.

Snow crystals.

Snow damage to trees.   See Trees. Snow
  injury.

Snow fences.   See Snowbreaks.

Snow gage.

Snow injury.
       sa Subdivision Snow injury under:
         Trees.

Snow mold.
       x Fusarium patch disease.

Snow partridge.   See Tetraogallus.

Snow sampler.

Snow surveys.
       xx Water-supply.

Snow-water mosquitoes.   See Aedes.

Snowberry.   See Symphoricarpos.

Snowbreaks.
       sa Field crops as snowbreaks.

Snowbreaks (Continued)
       x Snow fences.
         Snow barriers.
         Shelter-belts.

Snowdonia National Forest Park, Wales.
       xx Wales. Forest reservations.
         Wales. Forestry.

Snowdrop.   See Galanthus nivalis.

Snowshoe hare.
       xx Hares.

Snowy River, Australia.

Snowy tree cricket.   See Oecanthus
  niveus.

Snuff.
       xx Tobacco.

Soap.
       sa Potash soap.
         Cotton-seed oil soap.
         Cleaning compounds.
         Metallic soaps.
       x Soaps.
       xx Cleaning.
 --Analysis.
 --Directories.
 --Effect on lead arsenate.
       x Lead arsenate, Effect of soap
         on.

Soap, Fatty acids in.

Soap, Metallic.   See Metallic soaps.

Soap.
 --Patents.
 -- --Bibliography.
 --Periodicals.
 --Rationing.   See Rationing. Soap.
 --Standards.

Soap as an insecticide.

Soap-bubbles.

Soap-kerosene emulsion.
       sa Kerosene emulsion.
       xx Emulsions.
         Kerosene emulsion.

Soap substitutes.
    xx Substitute products.

Soap trade.
--Congresses.
--Dictionaries.
--Statistics.

Soaps. See Soap.

Soapstone.

Soapweed as feeding stuff.

Sochi.
--Pomology.

Sochi. Sochinskaia sel'sko-khoziaistvennaia
opytnaia stantsiia.
--Bibliography.

Social animals. See Animals, Habits and
behavior of.

Social anthropology. See Anthropology.

Social centers. See Community centers.

Social change.
    Here are entered works on the
theory of social change. General
descriptive works are entered
under the heading Social conditions. Descriptive works on a
particular area are entered
under the name of the place with
subdivision Social conditions.
   x Change, Social.
    Cultural change.
    Cultural evolution.
    Social evolution.
  xx Anthropology.
    Evolution.
    Progress.
    Social sciences.
    Sociology.
--Periodicals.

Social conditions.
   sa Subdivision Social conditions
    under: Africa.
    Asia.
    East Indies (Dutch)//
    Social policy.
    Social surveys.

Social conditions (Continued)
--Bibliography.
   sa Subdivision Social conditions.
    Bibliography under: U.S.
    Gt. Brit.
    Spanish America//
--History.
-- --Bibliography.
--Periodicals.
--Research.

Social credit. See Credit, Social.

Social customs. See Manners and
customs.

Social ecology. See Human ecology.

Social education. See Educational
sociology.

Social ethics.

Social evolution. See Social change.

Social geography. See Anthropo-
geography.

Social group work. See Group work,
Educational and social.

Social insects. See Insect societies.

Social insurance. See Insurance,
Social.

Social life and customs. See Manners
and customs; Social life and customs
under names of places. e.g., U.S.
Social life and customs.

Social planning. See Planning, Social;
Social policy.

Social policy.
   sa Economic policy.
    Subdivision Social policy
    under names of countries,
    states, cities, etc. e.g.,
    Canada. Social policy.
   x Social planning.
  xx Economic policy.
    Social conditions.

Social problems.
  sa Public welfare.
--Addresses, essays, lectures.
  xx Economics. Addresses, essays,
    lectures.
--Bibliography.
--Congresses.
--Research.

Social problems and the church.   See
  Church and social problems.

Social problems in education.   See
  Educational sociology.

Social psychology.
  sa Crowds.
    Prestige.
    Sociometry.
    Economics. Psychological
      aspects.
    Group work, Educational and
      social.
  xx Human ecology.
--Periodicals.
  xx Psychology. Periodicals.
--Research.

Social science.   See Sociology.

Social science research.   See Social
  sciences. Research.

Social sciences.
    Here are entered general and
    comprehensive works dealing
    with sociology, political
    science, and economics. For
    special works see these head-
    ings and the references under
    them to more specific subjects.
  sa Subdivision Social sciences
    under: Subject headings.
    Human ecology.
    Conservatism.
    Social change.
--Abstracts.
--Bibliography.
  sa Subdivision Bibliography under:
    Social sciences. Periodicals.
    Social sciences. Methodology.
    Social sciences. Research.
-- --Periodicals.
  xx Bibliography. Periodicals.
--Classification.

Social sciences (Continued)
--Cyclopedias.   See Social sciences.
  Dictionaries.
--Dictionaries.
  x Social sciences. Cyclopedias.
--History.
-- --Bibliography.
--Methodology.
  sa Sociology. Methodology.
-- --Bibliography.
  xx Social sciences. Bibliography.
--Periodicals.
  sa Subdivision Periodicals
    under: Sociology.
    Social problems.
-- --Bibliography.
  xx Social sciences. Bibliography.
--Research.
  x Social science research.
  xx Research.
-- --Bibliography.
  xx Social sciences. Bibliography.
    Research. Bibliography.
-- --Directories.
--Statistics.
  sa Social statistics.
-- --Congresses.
  sa Subdivision Congresses under:
    Social statistics.
--Study and teaching.
--Year-books.
  xx Year-books.

Social sciences and agriculture.   See
  Agriculture and social sciences.

Social security.   See Insurance, Social;
  Public welfare.

Social security act of 1935.

Social service.
  sa Welfare work in industry.
    Public welfare.
    Community service.
    Federations. Financial
      (Social service)_
    Community organization.
    Social Service, Rural.
    Visiting housekeepers.
--Bibliography.
--Congresses.
--Group work.   See Group work, Edu-
  cational and social.
--Periodicals.

Social service (Continued)
--Public relations.

Social service, Rural.   (INDIRECT)
     x Charities, Rural.
       Public welfare, Rural.
       Rural charities.
       Rural public welfare.
       Rural social programs.
       Rural social service.
     xx Charities.
        Public welfare.
        Social service.

Social service.
--Societies.
-- --Directories.
--Study and teaching.

Social settlements.
     sa Boys. Societies and clubs.
        Community centers.   `
        Day nurseries.
        Girls. Societies and clubs.
        Milk depots.
        Playgrounds.
      x Settlements, Social.
     xx Charities.

Social statistics.
     sa Subdivision Statistics under:
        Hours of labor.
        Housing.
        Population.
      x Statistics, Social.
        Sociology. Statistics.
     xx Social sciences. Statistics.
        Statistics.
--Bibliography.
--Congresses.
     xx Social sciences. Statistics.
        Congresses.
        Statistics.

Social surveys.   (INDIRECT)
     When subdivided by name of place,
     indicate see also ref. from
     name of place with subdivision:
     Social conditions.
     sa Publications of Alabama.
        Industrial development board.
        Youth in rural communities.
--Bibliography.

Social welfare.   See Public welfare.

Social welfare personnel.   See Social
     workers.

Social workers.   (DIRECT)
     x Social welfare personnel.
     xx Public welfare.

Socialism.
     sa National socialism.
        Collectivism.
        Communistic settlements.
        Agriculture and socialism.
        Socialism in Belgium.
        Socialism in Russia.   . ' .
        Socialism in Great Britain//
      x Marxism.

Socialism, Christian.
     sa Church and social problems.
      x Christian socialism.
     xx Church and social problems.
        Sociology, Christian.

Socialism in Belgium.
     xx Socialism.

Socialism in Bulgaria.

Socialism in France.
     xx Socialism.

Socialism in Georgia (Transcaucasia)

Socialism in Germany.
     sa National socialism.

Socialism in Great Britain.
     xx Socialism.

Socialism in India.

Socialism in Italy.

Socialism in Russia.
     xx Socialism.

Socialism in the U.S.
     xx Socialism.

Socialism in White Russia.
     xx Socialism.

Socialized credit.   See Credit, Social.

Socialized medicine. See Medicine, State.

Societies. (INDIRECT)
    sa Subdivision Societies under
        various subjects, e.g.,
        Agriculture. Societies;
        Botany. Societies.
        Boys. Societies and clubs.
        Charitable societies.
        Girls. Societies and clubs.
        Greek letter societies.
        Learned institutions and
          societies.
        Library associations.
        Trade and professional associa-
          tions.
        Trade-unions.
        Woman. Societies and clubs.
        Clubs.
    x Association and Associations.
      Associations.
    xx Clubs.
--Directories.
    sa Societies [geographic subdivi-
        sion] Directories, e.g.,
        Societies. U.S. Directories.
-- --Bibliography.
--Statistics.
    sa Subdivision Statistics under
        Societies [geographic sub-
        division] e.g., Societies.
        Spain. Statistics.

Society, Primitive.
    sa Man, Primitive.
      Village communities.
    x Primitive society.
    xx Civilization.
      Ethnology.
      Sociology.

Society Islands.
--Botany.
    sa Subdivision Botany under:
        Raiatea.
--Entomology.
    sa Subdivision Society Islands
        under: Hymenoptera.
    xx Entomology.

Sociologists.
    sa Comte, Auguste, 1798-1857.
      Marx, Karl, 1818-1883.

Sociologists (Continued)
    sa Pareto, Vilfredo, 1848-1923.
      Ward, Lester Frank, 1841-1913.
    x Sociology. Biography.

Sociology.
    sa Education.
      Criminology.
      Slavery.
      Labor.
      Municipal government.
      Cities.
      Children.
      Sociology, Rural.
      Social service.
      Social psychology.
      Educational sociology.
      Family.
      Public welfare.
      Society, Primitive.
      Community life.
      Human ecology.
      Conservatism.
      Social change.
    xx Human ecology.
--Abstracts.
--Addresses, essays, lectures.
    sa Subdivision Addresses essays.
      lectures under: Sociology,
      Christian.

Sociology, Animal. See Animals, Habits
    and behavior of.

Sociology.
--Bibliography.
    sa Subdivision Bibliography
        under: Social problems.
-- --Periodicals.
--Biography. See Sociologists.

Sociology, Christian.
    sa Socialism, Christian.
      Church and social problems.
    xx Religion.
      Church and social problems.
--Addresses, essays. lectures.
    xx Sociology. Addresses, essays,
      lectures.
--Congresses.
-- --Directories.
--Dictionaries.
--Directories. See Social service.
    Societies. Directories.

Sociology, Educational.   See Educational
    sociology.

Sociology.
--History.
    sa Subdivision History under:
        Family.
--Laboratory manuals.
--Methodology.
    sa Subdivision Methodology under:
        Sociology, Rural.
--Outlines, syllabi, etc.
-- --Periodicals.
    sa Subdivision Periodicals under:
        Social sciences.
        Social problems.

Sociology, Rural.   (INDIRECT)   —
    Here are entered works on social
        organization and conditions in
        rural districts and communities.
        Purely descriptive, popular or
        literary works on living in the
        country are entered under the
        subject Country life.
    sa Rural rehabilitation.
        Rural sociology extension work.
--Bibliography.
    sa Sociology, Rural [geographic
        subdivision] Bibliography,
        e.g., Sociology, Rural. U.S.
        Bibliography.
-- --Periodicals.
    xx Sociology, Rural. Periodicals.
        Bibliography. Periodicals.
--Congresses.
    sa Subdivision Congresses under:
        Sociology, Rural. Research.
        Sociology, Rural. Study and
            teaching.
--Methodology.
    xx Sociology. Methodology.
--Periodicals.
    sa Subdivision Periodicals under:
        Sociology, Rural. Bibliog-
            raphy.
--Research.
    xx Research.
-- --Congresses.
    xx Research. Congresses.
        Sociology, Rural. Congresses.
--Societies.
--Study and teaching.
-- --Congresses.
    xx Sociology, Rural. Congresses.

Sociology.
--Societies.
--Statistics.   See Social statistics.

Sociometry.
    xx Social psychology.
--Periodicals.

Socorro Co., N.M.
--Geology.

Socotra.
--Botany.

Sod and sodding.   See Grasses.

Sod mulches.
    xx Soil mulching.

Soda. Baking.   See Sodium bicarbonate.

Soda, Chloride of.

Soda ash.   See Sodium carbonate.

Soda-fountain.   See Soda-water
    fountains.

Soda industry.

Soda Lakes.

Soda-water.
    xx Bottling.

Soda-water fountains.
--Periodicals.

Södermanland, Sweden.
    x Nyköping, Sweden.
--Agriculture.
--Botany.

Sodium.
    sa Algae. Sodium in.
    x Natrium.
--Effect on plants.
    x Plants, Effect of sodium on.

Sodium acid sulphate.
    x Sodium bisulfate.
--Toxicity.

Sodium amalgam.

Sodium arsenate.
--Effect on soils.

Sodium arsenite.
x Dupont's weed killer.

Sodium benzoate.

Sodium bicarbonate.
x Baking soda.
Soda, Baking.

Sodium bifluoride.
xx Disinfection and disinfectants.

Sodium bisulfate. See Sodium acid
sulphate.

Sodium bisulphite.

Sodium borohydride.

Sodium cacodylate.
xx Arsenic organic compounds.

Sodium carbonate.
x Soda ash.
Carbonate of sodium.

Sodium carboxymethylcellulose.
x Carboxymethylcellulose, Sodium.
CMC.
Cellulose gum.
xx Cellulose.
Colloids.

Sodium chlorate.
xx Chlorates.
--Effect on animals.
--Effect on plants.
xx Chemicals. Effect on plants.

Sodium chlorate in soil. See Soil,
Sodium chlorate in.

Sodium chloride. See Salt.

Sodium chlorite.

Sodium cinnamate. See Hetol.

Sodium citrate.

Sodium cyanid.

Sodium dodecyl sulphate. See Sodium
lauryl sulphate.

Sodium fluoride.

Sodium fluoride as an anthelmintic.
xx Anthelmintics.

Sodium fluoride as an insecticide.

Sodium fluosilicate.

Sodium glutamate. See Monosodium
glutamate.

Sodium hexametaphosphate. See Calgon.

Sodium hydroxide.
x Caustic soda.
--Effect on crude fiber. See Crude
fiber. Effect of sodium hydroxid.

Sodium hypochlorite.

Sodium hypochlorite solutions.

Sodium in animal nutrition.
--Bibliography.

Sodium in animals.

Sodium in plant nutrition.
xx Plant nutrition.
--Bibliography.

Sodium in plants.
x Plants, Sodium in.

Sodium in soils. See Soil, Sodium in.

Sodium lauryl sulphate.
x Sodium dodecyl sulphate.

Sodium meta-silicate. See Sodium
silicate.

Sodium metabisulfite. See Sodium
metabisulphite.

Sodium metabisulphite.
x Sodium metabisulfite.
Sodium metaphyrosulfite.
--Application.

Sodium metaphyrosulfite. See Sodium
  metabisulphite.

Sodium nitrate.
  sa Soil, Sodium nitrate in.
  x Saltpeter, Chile.
    Chile salt-peter.
    Chilean nitrate.
  xx Fertilizers, Nitrogenous.
--Analysis.
--Bibliography.
--Effect on apples.

Sodium nitrate, Perchlorates in.

Sodium nitrate.
--Periodicals.
  sa Sodium nitrate. Statistics.
    Periodicals.

Sodium nitrate, Physiological effect of.

Sodium nitrate.
--Statistics.
-- --Periodicals.

Sodium nitrite.
--Effect on soils. See Soil. Effect of
  sodium nitrite.

Sodium oleate.

Sodium oxalate.

Sodium pentachlorophenolate.

Sodium peroxide.

Sodium rhodonate. See Sodium thiocyanate.

Sodium salicylate.

Sodium salts.

Sodium selenate.
--Toxicity.
  xx Selenium. Toxicity.

Sodium selenite.
--Toxicity.
  xx Selenium. Toxicity.

Sodium silicate.
  sa Silicated surfaces.
    Natrosil.
  x Sodium meta-silicate.

Sodium silicofluoride.
  xx Disinfection and disinfectants.

Sodium soils. See Soil, Sodium in.

Sodium sulphamezathine.

Sodium sulphate.
--Effect on plants.

Sodium sulphate decahydrate.
  x Mirabilite.
    Glauber's salt.

Sodium sulphide.

Sodium sulphite.

Sodium superoxid.

Sodium tartrate.

Sodium thiocyanate.
  x Sodium rhodonate.

Sodium thiosulphate.

Soemba. See Sandalwood Island.

Soerabaia. See Surabaya.

Sofia.
--Description and travel.
-- --Guide books.

Sofia brown cattle.
  x Sofiisko kafiavo cattle.

Sofia Co., Bulgaria.
--Agriculture.
  sa Subdivision Sofia Co. Bulgaria,
    under: Farm organization.
    Subdivision Bulgaria. Sofia
    Co. under: Types of farming.
    Agriculture. Economic
    aspects.

Sofiero (Castle)

Sofiisko kafiavo cattle. See Sofia
 brown cattle.

Soft drinks. See Carbonated beverages.

Soft rot of cabbage. See Bacterial soft
 rot of cabbage.

Soft rot of celery. See Bacterial soft
 rot of celery.

Soft rot of sweet potatoes.
 xx Sweet potatoes. Diseases.

Soft woods.
 x Softwoods.
 --Grading and standardization.
 xx Lumber. Grading and standardization.
 --Growth.
 xx Trees. Growth.
 --Handbooks, manuals, etc.

Softening of water. See Water. Softening.

Softwoods. See Soft woods.

Sognefjord, Norway.
 --Botany.

Soil.
 sa Chemistry, Agricultural.
  Alkali soils.
  Burning of land//
  Vegetable soils.
  Subdivision Soils under names
   of geographic regions, e.g.,
   Africa. Soils.
  Names of geographic locations
   under Soil-surveys, e.g.,
   Soil-surveys. Alabama.
 x Agrology.
  Soils.
  Edaphology.
  Pedology (Soil science)
 --Absorption. See Soil absorption.
 --Abstracts.
 -- --Periodicals.
 --Acid. See Soil acidity.
 --Addresses, essays, lectures.
 --Adsorption. See Soil adsorption.
 --Aeration.

Soil (Continued)
 --Aggregation.
  sa Soil colloids.
  x Soil aggregates.
   Soil particles.
  xx Soil colloids.
   Soil structure.
   Aggregates.

Soil, Alkali. See Alkali soils.

Soil, Alkaloids in.
 xx Alkaloids.

Soil, Aluminum in.
 x Aluminum in soils.

Soil, Ammonia in.
 x Ammonia in soils.
 --Bibliography.

Soil, Ammonium salts in.
 xx Ammonium salts.

Soil.
 --Analysis.
  sa Subdivision Analysis under:
   Alkali soils.
   Moor soils.
   Peat soil.
   Soil. Cleaning.
   Azotobacter.
   Nitrifying bacteria.
   Nitrification.
   Soil inoculation.
   Soil microbiology.
   Sulfofication.
   Soil. Mineral elements.
   Soil microscopy.
   Humus determination.
   Particle size determination.
  x Mechanical analysis of soils.
 -- --Apparatus.
 -- --Bibliography.
 - --Methods.

Soil, Arsenic in.
 xx Arsenic.

Soil, Artificial.

Soil.
 --Bacteriology. See Soil bacteria.

Soil, Barium in.

Soil.
--Bibliography.
  sa Subdivision Soils. Bibliog-
   raphy under: Russia.
   California.
   Europe//
  Subdivision Bibliography under:
   Soil and wind.
   Soil sterilization.
   Soil disinfection.
   Soil fertility.
   Soil protozoa.
   Soil erosion.
   Alkali soils.
   Soil. Analysis.
   Tobacco soils.
   Soil erosion. Prevention
    and control.
   Soil (Engineering)
   Soil series.
   Soil-surveys.
   Sedimentation and deposition.
   Soil percolation.
   Soil moisture.
   Humus.
-- --Periodicals.

Soil, Biotite in.
  xx Soil, Mica in.
  Biotite.

Soil, Black. See Chernozem soils.

Soil, Borax in.
  xx Borax.

Soil, Bundsandstein. See Buntsandstein.

Soil, Calcareous.
  sa Soil, Lime in.
   Soil. Deficient in lime.
--Bibliography.

Soil, Calcium carbonate in.

Soil, Calcium in.

Soil, Carbon dioxide in.
--Bibliography.

Soil, Carbon in.
  x Carbon in soils.

Soil, Carbonates of.

Soil, Celluose in.

Soil, Chlorates in.
  xx Chlorates.

Soil, Chromium in.

Soil.
--Classification. See Soil classification.

Soil, Clay.
  sa Soil, Sandy clay.
  x Clay soil.

Soil, Claypan.
  x Clay pan soil.
  Claypan soil.

Soil.
--Cleaning.

Soil, Cobalt in.
  xx Cobalt.

Soil.
--Compaction. See Soil. Stabiliza-
  tion.
--Congresses.
  sa Subdivision Congresses under:
   Foundations.
   Soil (Engineering)
   Soil erosion. Prevention
    and control.
  xx Soil (Engineering) Congresses.
--Conservation. See Soil conservation.
--Consolidation. See Soil. Stabili-
  zation.

Soil, Copper in.

Soil.
--Corrosive properties. See Soil
  corrosion.

Soil, Creatinin in.

Soil, Desert. See Desert soils.

Soil.
--Dictionaries.

Soil, Diffusion in.

Soil.
--Diseases transmitted by. See Soil
    and disease (Animal, other than
    human); Soil and disease (Human)
--Disinfection. See Soil sterilization.
--Ecology.
        x Soil ecology.
        xx Ecology.
--Education.
--Effect of ammonium sulphate.
--Effect of arsenite of soda.
--Effect of boron.
--Effect of calcium sulphate.
--Effect of carbon disulphide.
        x Carbon disulphide. Effect on
            soil.
--Effect of ferrous oxide.

Soil, Effect of fertilizers on. See
    Fertilizers. Effect on soils.

Soil.
--Effect of frost.
        sa Soil. Freezing.
        x Frost. Effect on soils.
-- --Bibliography.
--Effect of gypsum.
        x Gypsum. Effect on soils.

Soil, Effect of heat on. See Heat.
    Effect on soils.

Soil.
--Effect of hydrogen.
        x Hydrogen. Effect on soil.

Soil, Effect of insecticides on. See
    Insecticides. Effect on soils.

Soil.
--Effect of irrigation.
        x Irrigation. Effect on soils.

Soil, Effect of lime on. See Liming of
    soils.

Soil, Effect of manures on. See Manures.
    Effect on soils.

Soil.
--Effect of phosphates.
        x Phosphates. Effect on soils.
--Effect of plant growth. See Soil and
    plant growth.

Soil (Continued)
--Effect of potash.
        xx Potash as fertilizer.
--Effect of potassium salts.
        x Potassium salts. Effect on
            soils.
--Effect of roots.
--Effect of salts.
        x Salts. Effect on soils.
--Effect of sawdust.
        x Sawdust. Effect on soils.
--Effect of sea-water.
--Effect of smoke.
--Effect of sodium nitrite.
        x Sodium nitrite. Effect on
            soils.
--Effect of sorghum.
--Effect of soybeans.
        x Soy-bean. Effect on soil.
--Effect of sulphur.
-- --Bibliography.
--Effect of tar.

Soil, Effect of tillage on. See
    Tillage. Effect on soil.

Soil.
--Effect of zinc fumes.
--Effect on legumes.
--Effect on nutrition. See Soil and
    nutrition.
--Effect on plant growth. See Soil
    and plant growth.
--Electrical resistance.
--Engineering. See Soil (Engineering)
--Erosion. See Soil erosion.
--Exhibitions.
--Fertility. See Soil fertility.
--Fertilizer requirements.
        sa Aspergillus method of potash
            and phosphorus determina-
            tion.
        Neubauer method.
        Foliar diagnosis.
        x Fertilizer requirements of
            soil.

Soil, Fertilizers in. See Fertilizers.
    Diffusion in soil.

Soil.
--Flocculation.
        sa Clay. Flocculation.
--Formation. See Soil formation.

Soil (Continued)
--Freezing.
    xx Soil. Effect of frost.
--Freezing point.

Soil, Frozen.
    x Permanently frozen ground.
      Permafrost.
      Frozen ground.
      Frozen soil.
    xx Arctic regions. Soils.
      Soil. Effect of frost.
      Freezing.
      Soil (Engineering)
--Abstracts.
--Bibliography.
-- --Periodicals.
--Periodicals.

Soil, Fungi in. See Fungi in soils.

Soil.
--Fungus infection.
    sa Fungi in soils.
--Geography.
    x Soil geography.

Soil, Granitic.

Soil, Gumbo.

Soil.
--History.

Soil, Humus in. See Humus.

Soil.
--Hydrogen ion concentration in. See
    Soil acidity.

Soil, Iodine in.

Soil, Iron in.

Soil, Irrigated.
    x Irrigated soil.

Soil.
--Laboratory manuals.
    sa Subdivision Laboratory manuals
      under specific subjects,
      e.g., Soil fertility.
      Laboratory manuals.
    xx Laboratory manuals.

Soil (Continued)
--Leaching.
    x Leaching of soils.
      Soil leaching.
    xx Soil percolation.

Soil. Lead in.

Soil, Light. See Soil, Sandy.

Soil, Lime deficient.
    x Lime deficient soil.
      Lime. Deficiency in soil.

Soil, Lime in.
    sa Soil, Calcareous.
      Soil. Deficient in lime.
      Moor soils, Lime in.

Soil.
--Lime requirements.
    x Lime requirements of soils.
    xx Liming of soils.

Soil, Limestone.

Soil, Lithium in.

Soil, Magnesia in.

Soil, Magnesium deficient.
    x Magnesium deficient soil.
      Magnesium. Deficiency in soil.

Soil, Magnesium in.

Soil, Manganese in.

Soil, Mannite in.

Soil.
--Maps. See Soil maps.

Soil, Mica in.
    sa Soil, Muscovite in.
      Soil, Biotote in.

Soil.
--Microscopy. See Soil microscopy.
--Mineral elements.
    sa Trace elements.
    x Minerals in soil.
      Mineral constituents in soil.
      Mineral elements.
    xx Soil. Analysis.

Soil (Continued)
--Mineral elements.
-- --Bibliography.

Soil, Mountain.   See Mountain soils.

Soil, Muscovite in.
      xx Soil, Mica in.
      Muscovite.

Soil.
--Museums.   See Soil museums.

Soil, Nickel in.
      xx Nickel.

Soil, Nitrates in.

Soil, Nitre.   See Alkali soils.

Soil, Nitric acid in.

Soil, Nitrogen in.
      sa Humus, Nitrogen in.
      Peat, Nitrogen in.
      Moor soils. Nitrogen in.

Soil.
--Nomenclature.
--Organic content.
--Origin.   See Soil formation.
--Packing.   See Soil. Stabilization.
--Pasteurization.   See Soil steriliza-
   tion.

Soil, Peat.   See Peat soils.

Soil.
--Periodicals.
      sa Subdivision Periodicals under:
      Soil conservation.
      Soil fertility.

Soil, Peptones in.

Soil, Phosphates in.
      sa Moor soils, Phosphates in.

Soil, Phosphoric acid in.
      sa Moor soils, Phosphoric acid in.
      x Phosphoric acid in soil.

Soil, Phosphorus in.
      x Phosphorus in soils.
--Bibliography.

Soil, Phosphorus in (Continued)
--Research.
      xx Phosphorus. Research.

Soil, Plant food in.   See Soil. Fertilizer requirements.

Soil, Potash in.
      sa Moor soils. Potash in.
      x Potash in soil.

Soil, Potassium in.
      x Potassium in soil.
      xx Potassium.

Soil, Potting.   See Potting soil.

Soil, Proteoses in.

Soil, Red.

Soil.
--Research.
      sa Subdivision Research under:
      Soil erosion. Prevention
         and control.
      Soil conservation//
      x Soil research.
      xx Soil conservation. Research.
-- --Bibliography.

Soil, Saline.   See Soil, Salts in.

Soil, Salts in.
      sa Moor soils, Salts in.
      x Soil, Saline.
      Saline soil.
      xx Salinity.

Soil, Sandy.
      x Soil, Light.
      Light soil.

Soil, Sandy clay.
      xx Soil, Clay.

Soil, Sandy loam.
      xx Loam.

Soil.
--Sanitation.
      x Soil sanitation.
--Saturation capacity.   See Soil ab-
   sorption.

Soil, Sick.
xx Soil exhaustion.

Soil, Selenium in.

Soil, Silica deficient.
x Silica deficient soils.
Silica. Deficiency in soil.

Soil, Silicates in.
--Bibliography.

Soil, Silicic acid in.
xx Silicic acid.

Soil.
--Societies.

Soil, Sodium carbonate in.

Soil, Sodium chlorate in.
x Sodium chlorate in soil.

Soil, Sodium in.
x Sodium in soils.
Sodium soils.

Soil, Sodium nitrate in.

Soil.
--Stabilization.
sa Foundations.
Roads, Stabilized.
x Soil compaction.
Compaction of soil.
Consolidation of soil.
Soil consolidation.
Soil packing.
Soil stabilization.
Stabilization of soil.
Soil. Compaction.
Soil. Consolidation.
Soil. Packing.
Subdrainage.
xx Soil mechanics.
Foundations.
Chemical engineering.
Soil (Engineering)
-- --Bibliography.
-- --Congresses.
--Sterilization.   See Soil sterilization.

Soil, Stony.

Soil, Strontium in.
x Strontium in soil.

Soil.
--Study and teaching.

Soil, Submerged.   See Soil, Waterlogged.

Soil, Sulphates in.
xx Sulphates.

Soil, Sulphur in.
sa Sulfofication.

Soil.
--Terminology.
xx Terminology.
--Testing.   See Soil testing.
--Text-books.
--Toxic substances in.

Soil, Tropical.   See Tropics. Soils.

Soil, Vanillin in.

Soil, Volcanic.

Soil.
--Volume-weight.
--Water capacity.
sa Soil, Waterlogged.

Soil, Waterlogged.
sa Rice soils.
x Soil, Submerged.
Submerged soil.
Waterlogged soil.
xx Soil. Water capacity.

Soil.
--Waterproofing.   See Waterproofing of
soils.

Soil, Zinc in.

Soil, Zinc salts in.

Soil.
--Zoology.
x Soil zoology.
xx Zoology.

Soil (Engineering)
    sa Soil mechanics.
       Foundations.
       Earthwork.
       Earth pressure.
       Soil testing.
       Soil sampling.
       Soil, Sandy.
       Soil. Freezing.
       Roads, Soil-cement.
       Soil. Stabilization.
    x Soil Engineering.
    xx Engineering.
--Abstracts.
--Congresses.
--Handbooks, manuals, etc.

Soil absorption.
    sa Soil adsorption.
    x Soil. Saturation capacity.
      Soil saturation.

Soil acidity.
    sa Hydrogen ion concentration.
    x Soil reaction.
--Effect on plants.

Soil adsorption.
    sa Soil absorption.

Soil aeration.   See Soil. Aeration.

Soil aggregates.   See Soil. Aggregation.

Soil air, Carbon dioxide in.

Soil algae.   See Algae in soils.

Soil amendments.
    sa Lime.
       Peat.
       Gypsum.
       Marl.
       Manganese as a fertilizer.
       Sand.
       Manganese sulphate.
       Charcoal.
       Ashes as fertilizer.
       Krilium.
    x Soil conditioners.
      Polyelectrolyte soil condi-
        tioners.

Soil analysis.   See Soil. Analysis.

Soil and animal nutrition.
    sa Soil and nutrition.
    xx Animal nutrition.
      Soil and nutrition.

Soil and climate.
    x Climate and soils.

Soil and crops.
    sa Fruit soils.
       Coffee soils.
       Grape soils.
       Pineapple soils.
       Sugar-cane soils.
       Tea soils.
       Madder soils.
       Hard wood soils.
       Citrus soils.
       Blueberry soils.
       Vegetable soils.
    x Erosion resisting crops.
      Soil improving crops.
      Soil conserving crops.

Soil and disease (animal, other than
    human)
    xx Veterinary medicine.

Soil and disease (Human)
    x Diseases. Transmission from
      soil.

Soil and nutrition.
    sa Soil and animal nutrition.
    x Nutrition and soil.
      Nutrition. Effect of soil.
      Soil. Effect on nutrition.
    xx Soil and animal nutrition.
      Nutrition.
      Soil.

Soil and plant diseases.
    sa Subdivision Effect on plant
       diseases under: Fertilizers.
    xx Plant disease transmission.

Soil and plant growth.
    xx Plant growth.
      Plant nutrition.
--Periodicals.

Soil and society.

Soil and wind.   See Soil drifting; Dust
    storms; Wind erosion.

Soil bacteria.
    sa Nitrifying bacteria.
       Soil, Ammonia in.
       Soil disinfection.
       Azotobacter.
       Nitrification.
       Soil inoculation.
       Soil microbiology.
       Sulfofication.
       Rhizobium meliloti.
       Selerotium rolfsii.
       Bacillus mycoides.
--Effect of climate.
    x Climate. Effect on soil
       bacteria.
--Laboratory manuals.

Soil bacteriology. See Soil bacteria.

Soil bank.
    sa Acreage reserve program.
       Conservation reserve program.
    xx Land utilization.
       Agricultural policies and
          programs.
--Statistics.

Soil bank act.

Soil-binding plants.
    x Erosion controlling plants.
      Vegetative control.
    xx Soil erosion. Prevention and
       control.

Soil biology.
    sa Earthworms.
       Soil microbiology.
    x Biopedology.
    xx Biology.
       Natural history.

Soil block gardening.
    xx Gardening.

Soil blowing. See Soil drifting; Dust
   storms.

Soil capillarity.

Soil catalysis.

Soil-cement.
    xx Cement.
       Road materials.

Soil-cement roads. See Roads, Soil-
   cement.

Soil chemistry.
--Periodicals.
--Text-books.

Soil classification.
    x Soil. Classification.
    xx Soil-surveys.
--Congresses.
--Terminology.

Soil colloids.
    sa Colloids, Humic.
    xx Soil. Aggregation.

Soil color.

Soil compaction. See Soil. Stabilization.

Soil conditioners. See Soil amendments.

Soil conservation. (INDIRECT)
    Whenever used with a geographical
      subdivision, indicate a see
      also ref. from name of place
      with subdivision Soils.
    sa Soil erosion. Prevention and
       control.
       Strip cropping.
       Terracing of land.
       Contour farming.
       Cropping systems.
       Rotation of crops.
       Land utilization.
       Agricultural conservation
         program.
       Drainage.
    xx Soil erosion. Prevention and
       control.
       Southern States. Soils.
       Poland. Soils.
--Abstracts.
--Addresses, essays, lectures.
--Bibliography.
    sa Subdivision Bibliography under
       Soil conservation [geo-
       graphic subdivision] e.g.,
       Soil conservation. U.S.
       Bibliography.
--Biography. See Soil conservationists.
--Biological aspects.

Soil conservation (Continued)
--Charts.
    xx Charts.
--Congresses.
    sa Subdivision Congresses under
      Soil conservation ₍geo-
      graphic subdivision₎ e.g.,
      Soil conservation. U.S. Con-
      gresses.

Soil conservation, Cooperative.
    x Cooperative soil conservation.
    xx Agriculture, Cooperative.
--Law.

Soil conservation.
--Dictionaries.
--Economic aspects.   (DIRECT)
--Education.
--Entomological aspects.   See Insects
    and soils.
--Glossaries.   See Soil conservation.
    Dictionaries.
--Government aid.
    x Federal aid for soil conserva-
      tion.
    xx Government aid.
--History.
--Implements and machinery.
    x Soil conservation machinery.
    xx Agriculture. Implements and
      machinery.
--Juvenile literature.
--Law.
    sa Soil conservation ₍geographic
      subdivision₎ Law, e.g., Soil
      conservation. South Aus-
      tralia. Law.
    x Soil conservation districts.
      Law.
    xx Soil conservation and domestic
      allotment act, 1936.
      Law.
--Periodicals.
--Pictorial works.
--Public opinion.
    xx Public opinion.
--Research.
    sa Subdivision Research under:
      Soil erosion. Prevention and
      control.
    Soil conservation ₍geographic
      subdivision₎ Research, e.g.,
      Soil conservation. U.S. Re-
      search.

Soil conservation (Continued)
--Research.
    xx Soil erosion. Prevention and
      control. Research.
    Soil. Research.
--Study and teaching.
    sa Soil conservation extension
      work.
    Moving-pictures in soil con-
      servation.
    xx Agriculture. Study and teach-
      ing.
    Education.
    Conservation of natural re-
      sources. Study and teaching.
--Subject headings.   See Subject head-
    ings. Soil conservation.

Soil conservation and domestic allotment
    act, 1936.
    sa Soil conservation. Law.
    x Agricultural adjustment act,
      1936.

Soil conservation and domestic allotment
    act, 1938.

Soil conservation as an occupation.

Soil conservation district 4-H club pro-
    gram.   See 4-H soil conservation
    district program.

Soil conservation districts.
    Individual districts may be used
      as subject or author, e.g.,
      Clear Creek Soil Conservation
      District, Ark.
    sa Special districts.
--Accounting.
--Law.   See Soil conservation. Law.
--Maps.

Soil conservation extension work.
    x Extension soil conservation.
      Extension work in soil con-
      servation.
    xx Agricultural extension.
    Soil conservation. Study and
      teaching.

Soil conservation machinery.   See Soil
    conservation. Implements and machinery.

Soil conservation surveys.   (INDIRECT)
     Whenever used with a geographical
     subdivision indicate a see
     also ref. from name of place
     with subdivision Soils.
     sa Soil-surveys.

Soil conservationists.
     x Soil conservation. Biography.
     xx Conservationists.
        Biography, Collected.
   --Directories.

Soil conserving crops.   See Soil and
   crops.

Soil consolidation.   See Soil. Stabilization.

Soil corrosion.
     x Soil. Corrosive properties.

Soil cultivation.   See Tillage.

Soil density.

Soil depletion.   See Soil exhaustion.

Soil disinfection.   See Soil sterilization.

Soil drifting.   (INDIRECT)
     sa Dust storms.
        Wind erosion.
     x Soil blowing.
        Sand shifting.
        Shifting sands.
   --Law.
     sa Subdivision Law under Soil
        drifting [geographic sub-
        division] e.g., Soil drift-
        ing. South Australia. Law.
   --Prevention and control.   (INDIRECT)

Soil dynamics.   See Soil physics.

Soil ecology.   See Soil. Ecology.

Soil engineering.   See Soil (Engineering)

Soil environment.
   --Effect on plant diseases.   See Soil
     and plant diseases.

Soil enzymes.

Soil erosion.   .(INDIRECT)
     Whenever used with a geographical
     subdivision, indicate a see
     also ref. from name of place.
     with subdivision Soils.
     sa Sedimentation and deposition.
        Soil drifting.
        Stream bank erosion.
        Raindrop erosion.
        Wind erosion.
     x Erosion.
   --Control.   See Soil erosion. Prevention
     and control.

Soil erosion, Influence of forests on.
   See Forests and soil erosion.

Soil erosion.   (INDIRECT)
   --Prevention and control.
     Whenever used with a geographical
     subdivision, indicate a see
     also ref. from name of place
     with subdivision Soils.
     sa Terracing of land.
        Strip cropping.
        Contour farming.
        Gully control.
        Soil-binding plants.
        Soil conservation.
        Subdivision Prevention and
          control under: Stream bank
          erosion.
        Highway erosion.
     x Erosion control.
        Erosion engineering.
   -- --Addresses, essays, lectures.
   -- --Charts.
        xx Charts.
   -- --Congresses.
   -- --Pictures, illustrations, etc.
   -- --Research.
   --Research.   See Soil erosion. Pre-
     vention and control. Research.

Soil erosion surveys.   (INDIRECT)
     sa Soil conservation surveys.
     xx Surveys.
   --Indian reservations.
     x Indian reservations.

Soil evolution.
     xx Evolution.

Soil exhaustion.
    sa Soil, Sick.
    x Soil depletion.

Soil ferments. See Nitrifying bacteria.

Soil fertility.
    sa Humus.
    x Soil. Fertility.
--Bibliography.
--Congresses.
--Government aid.
    xx Government aid.
--Indicator plants. See Soil fertility.
    Vegetative indications.
--Laboratory manuals.
--Periodicals.
    xx Soil. Periodicals.
--Plant indicators. See Soil fertility.
    Vegetative indications.
--Research.
--Vegetative indications.
    x Soil fertility. Indicator
      plants.
    Soil fertility. Plant indica-
      tors.
    xx Plant indicators.

Soil formation.
    x Soil genesis.
--Text-books.

Soil fumigation.
    xx Pesticides.
--Implements and machinery.
    xx Agriculture. Implements and
      machinery.

Soil fungi. See Fungi in soils.

Soil gases.
--Effect on fungi.

Soil genesis. See Soil formation.

Soil geography. See Soil. Geography.

Soil heating. See Soil sterilization.

Soil heating, Electric. See Electro-
  horticulture.

Soil husbandry. See Soil; Soil conservation.

Soil hygroscopicity.

Soil improving crops. See Soil and
  crops.

Soil-infesting insects. See Insects and
  soils.

Soil infiltration. See Soil percolation.

Soil-inoculation.
    sa Legume inoculants.
    Nitrification.
    x Legume inoculation.
    Inoculation of legumes.
    Inoculation of soils.

Soil insecticides.
    sa Carbon disulphide emulsions.
--Bibliography.

Soil insects. See Insects and soils.

Soil instruments.
    sa Soil mixing apparatus.
    Lysimeter.
    Soil thermometer.
    Soil testing. Implements and
      machinery.

Soil leaching. See Soil. Leaching.

Soil liming. See Liming of soils.

Soil maintenance. See Soil conservation.

Soil management. See Soil.

Soil maps.
    sa Soil surveys.
--Bibliography.

Soil mechanics.
    sa Soil. Stabilization.
    Earth pressure.
    Earthwork.
    Foundations.
    Soil (Engineering)
    Soil physics.
--Congresses.
--Terminology.

Soil metabolism. See Metabolism in
  soils.

Soil micro-organisms.   See Soil microbiology.

Soil microbiology.
    sa Actinomyces.
      Soil bacteria.
      Soil colloids.
      Soil protozoa.
      Fungi in soils.
      Soil sterilization.
    x Soil micro-organisms.
    xx Soil biology.
      Soil microscopy.
  --Research.
  --Text-books.

Soil microscopy.
    sa Soil microbiology.
    x Soil. Microscopy.
      Micropedology.
      Pedology, Microscopic.
      Microscopic pedology.
    xx Micro-organisms.
      Microscope and microscopy.
      Soil. Analysis.

Soil mixing apparatus.

Soil moisture.
    sa Lysimeter.
      Soil. Water capacity.
      Water, Underground.
    x Moisture conservation.
      Water and soils.
    xx Soil physics.
  --Bibliography.
    xx Soil. Bibliography.
      Water, Underground. Bibliog-
        raphy.
  --Effect on plant diseases.
    x Plant diseases, Effect on soil
      moisture.
    xx Vegetable pathology.
      Soil moisture. Effect on
        plants.
  --Effect on plants.
    sa Soil moisture. Effect on
      plant diseases.
  --Tables and ready-reckoners.

Soil morphology.   See Soil structure.

Soil mulching.   See Mulch and mulching.

Soil museums.

Soil oxidation.

Soil packing.   See Soil. Stabilization.

Soil particles.   See Soil. Aggregation.

Soil pasteurization.   See Soil sterilization.

Soil percolation.
    sa Lysimeter.
      Soil. Leaching.
    x Soil permeability.
    xx Permeability.
  --Bibliography.
    xx Soil. Bibliography.
      Water, Underground. Bibliog-
        raphy.

Soil percolation equipment.
    xx Agriculture. Implements and
      machinery.

Soil permeability.   See Soil percolation.

Soil physics.
    sa Soil mechanics.
      Soil moisture.
      Soil temperature.
    xx Soil mechanics.

Soil pollution.
    sa Soil and disease (human)
      Bacteria, Pathogenic.

Soil profiles.

Soil protozoa.
  --Bibliography.

Soil reaction.
    sa Soil acidity.
      Hydrogen-ion concentration.

Soil reaction diseases.
    xx Vegetable pathology.

Soil research.   See Soil. Research.

Soil resistance recorder.
    xx Agriculture. Implements and
      machinery.

Soil sampling.
    x Sampling of soil.

Soil sanitation.   See Soil. Sanitation.

Soil saturation.   See Soil absorption.

Soil science.   See Soil.

Soil scientists.
--Directories.
    xx Scientists' directories.

Soil series.
    sa Soil types.
--Bibliography.
    xx Soil. Bibliography.

Soil sickness.   See Soil, Sick.

Soil solubility.

Soil solubility, Effect of plants on.

Soil solutions.

Soil stabilization.   See Soil. Stabili-
    zation.

Soil sterilization.
    sa Acetic acid as a soil disin-
        fectant.
    Soil fumigation.
    Zinc oxide as a soil disin-
        fectant.
    Formaldehyde as a soil disin-
        fectant.
    Chloropictin as a soil disin-
        fectant.
    x Soil disinfection.
    Soil pasteurization.
    Soil. Sterilization.
    Soil. Pasteurization.
    Soil warming.
    Soil heat.
    Soil. Disinfection.
    Heating of soils.
    Soil heating.
    xx Disinfection and disinfectants.
    Soil microbiology.
    Sterilization.
--Bibliography.

Soil structure.
    sa Soil. Aggregation.

Soil structure (Continued)
--Bibliography.
--Research.

Soil-surveys.   (INDIRECT)
    Make a see also x-ref. from place
        with subdivision Soils.
    sa Soil maps.
    Soil conservation surveys.
    Soil classification.
    xx Agricultural clubs.

Soil-surveys, Aerial.
    xx Aerial surveys.

Soil-surveys.
--Bibliography.
--Congresses.
    sa Subdivision Congresses under
        Soil-surveys [geographic
        subdivision] e.g., Soil-
        surveys. U.S. Congresses.
--Periodicals.

Soil temperature.
    sa Soil thermometer.
    xx Soil physics.
--Effect on insects.
    x Insects, Effect of soil
        temperature on.
--Effect on plant diseases.
    x Plant diseases, Effect on
        soil temperature.
    xx Vegetable pathology.
    Temperature. Effect on plants.
--Effect on plants.
    sa Soil temperature. Effect on
        plant diseases.
    Soil temperature. Effect on
        wheat.
--Effect on wheat.
--Measurement.

Soil testing.
    x Soil. Testing.
--Implements and machinery.
    xx Soil instruments.

Soil testing laboratories.
--Directories.

Soil texture.

Soil thermometer.
    sa Soil temperature.

Soil types.
    sa Soil series.

Soil valuation.

Soil volume.

Soil warming. See Soil sterilization.

Soil water. See Soil moisture; Water,
Underground; Soil. Water capacity.

Soil water, Phosphoric acid in.

Soil waterproofing. See Waterproofing of
soils.

Soil weathering.

Soil zoology. See Soil. Zoology.

Soiling.
    sa Ensilage.

Soilless culture. See Hydroponics.

Soils. See Soil.

Soils and crops. See Soil and crops.

Soissons, France.
--Agriculture.
    sa Subdivision France. Soissons
        under: Agriculture. Economic
        aspects.

Sokotra.
--Entomology.

Solanaceae.
    sa Capsicum.
        Potato.
        Datura.
        Pallavicinia.
        Hyoscyamus.
        Solanin.
        Mandragora.
        Tropin.
        Petunia.
        Nierembergia.
        Atropa.
        Fabiana.
        Lycopersicon.

Solanaceae (Continued)
--Diseases.
    sa Subdivision Diseases under:
        Capsicum.
        Lycopersicon.
        Nicotiana.
        Solanum.
        Virus diseases of solanaceous
            plants.
    xx Vegetable pathology.

Solanin.

Solano Co., Calif.
--Water-supply.

Solanum.
--Diseases.
    xx Solanaceae. Diseases.

Solanum carolinense.

Solanum commersoni.

Solanum dulcamara.

Solanum melongena. See Egg-plant.

Solanum quitense.

Solanum tuberosum.

Solar atmosphere. See Atmosphere,
Solar.

Solar disturbances.

Solar eclipses. See Eclipses.

Solar energy.
--Bibliography.
--Congresses.

Solar heat method of insect control.
    xx Entomology, Economic.

Solar magnetism. See Magnetism, Solar.

Solar motors. See Motors, Solar.

Solar radiation.
    sa Sun-spots.

Solar radiation (Continued)
    x Atmospheric absorption of solar
      radiation.
    Absorption, Atmospheric.
    xx Radiant heating.

Solar reflectors.
    x Reflectors, Solar.

Solar system.
    xx Astronomy.

Soldanella.

Solder and soldering.
    sa Alloys.
      Welding.
    xx Metal-work.
      Metals.
      Plumbing.
      Welding.

Soldiers.   (DIRECT)
    sa Veterans.
      Armies.
      Military art and science.
      Pensions, Military.
    x Servicemen, Military.
    xx War.
      Military art and science.
      Veterans.
  --Civil employment.   See Veterans. Em-
    ployment.

Soldiers, Discharged.   See Veterans.

Soldiers.
  --Education, Non-military.
    x Education of soldiers.
    xx Military education.

Soldiers, Invalid.
  --Occupations.   See Disabled. Rehabili-
    tation, etc.

Soldiers.
  --Pay, allowances, etc.   See Subdivision
    Army. Pay, allowances, etc. under
    names of countries, e.g., U.S. Army.
    Pay, allowances, etc.

Soldiers' and sailors' civil relief act.
    xx Insurance. Law.

Sole leather.   See Leather.

Soledad, Cuba.
  --Entomology.

Solenodon.

Solenodontidae.
    sa Solenodon.

Solenopsis.
    xx Ants.

Solenopsis geminata.
    x Fire ant.

Solenopsis geminata xyloni.

Solenopsis saevissima richteri.
    x Fire ant, Imported.
      Imported fire ant.

Solid carbon dioxide.   See Dry ice.

Solid solutions.   See Solutions, Solid.

Solidago.   See Goldenrod.

Solids.

Solifuga.   See Solpugida.

Solitaire (Bird)

Solitary wasps.
    xx Wasps.

Soliva anthemidifolia.

Sollinge.
  --Botany.
      xx Brunswick, Ger. Botany.

Solnechnogorsk.
  --Agriculture.
      sa Subdivision Solnechnogorsk
        under: Rehabilitation,
        Rural. U.S.S.R.

Sologne, France.
  --Agriculture.
      sa Subdivision France. Sologne
        under: Agriculture. Eco-
        nomic aspects.
        Agricultural policies and
        programs.
  --Cattle.

Sologne sheep.
    xx Sheep.

Solomon Islands.
--Entomology.
    sa Subdivision Solomon Islands
       under: Moths.

Solomon's seal. See Polygonatum.

Solon goose. See Gannet.

Solonchak soils.

Solonetz soils.

Solothurn (Canton)
--Botany.

Solpugida.
    sa Galeodes.
       Datames.
    x Solifuga.

Sols. See Gels.

Solubea pugnax.
    x Rice stinkbug.

Solubility.

Soluble coffee. See Coffee, Soluble.

Soluble glass.
--Bibliography.

Solution (Chemistry)
    sa Extraction (Chemistry)
       Colloids.

Solutions, Solid.
    x Solid solutions.

Solutions.
--Standardization.

Solvents.
    sa Plasticisers.
--Toxicity.
    xx Toxicology.

Somali Republic.
--Agriculture.
--Economic conditions.

Somalia, East Africa. See Somaliland,
    Italian.

Somaliland.
    This subject is used for publica-
       tions dealing with British,
       French and Italian Somaliland
       collectively.
--Description and travel.
    sa Subdivision Somaliland under:
       Hunting.
--Entomology.
    sa Subdivision Somaliland under:
       Orthoptera.
    xx Africa. Entomology.
--Geology.
--Ornithology.
    xx Africa. Ornithology.
--Zoology.
    sa Subdivision Somaliland under:
       Mammalia.
    xx Africa. Zoology.

Somaliland, British.
--Agriculture.
--Botany.
--Commerce.
--Geology.
--Natural history.
--Water-supply.

Somaliland, Italian.
    x Italian Somaliland.
       Somalia, East Africa.
--Agriculture.
    sa Subdivision Somaliland, Italian
       under: Agriculture. Economic
       aspects.
       Colonization, Agricultural.
-- --Bibliography.
--Bibliography.
--Botany.
    sa Subdivision Somaliland, Italian
       under: Trees.
       Shrubs.
--Domestic animals.
--Economic conditions.
--Entomology.
    sa Subdivision Somaliland, Italian
       under: Entomology, Economic.
--Forestry.
    sa Subdivision Somaliland, Italian
       under: Trees.
       Forest surveys.

Somaliland, Italian (Continued)
--Statistics.
xx Africa. Statistics.

Somateria v - nigrum.

Somatichlora nineana.
xx Odonata.

Somatochlora.
xx Odonata.

Somatochlora calverti.
xx Odonata.

Somatology.
sa Subdivision Constitution under:
Man.
Body measurements.

Somatose.

Somerset, Eng.   See Somersetshire, Eng.

Somerset Co., Md.
--Agriculture.
sa Subdivision Maryland. Somerset
Co. under: Farm management
surveys.
Land utilization.
--Land.
sa Subdivision Maryland. Somerset
Co. under: Land utilization.

Somerset Co., N.J.
--History.

Somersetshire, Eng.
x Somerset, Eng.
--Agriculture.
--Botany.
--Economic conditions.
sa Subdivision England. Somersetshire under: Geography, Economic.
--Geography.
sa Subdivision England. Somersetshire under: Geography, Economic.
--Land.
sa Subdivision England. Somersetshire under: Land. Classification.

Somervell Co., Tex.
xx Texas.
--Water-supply.
xx Texas. Water-supply.

Somerville, Tex.
--Paleobotany.

Somme River, France.
--Geology.

Sonchus arvensis.
x Perennial sow thistle.
Sow thistle, Perennial.
Sowthistle, Perennial.
xx Thistles.
--Eradication.
xx Weeds. Eradication.

Sondershausen.
--Botany.
sa Schwarzburg-Sondershausen.
Botany.

Søndre Bergenhus, Norway.
--Forestry.

Sondrio (Province)
--Agriculture.
--Commerce.
-- --Periodicals.
--Domestic animals.
--Economic conditions.
-- --Periodicals.
--Forestry.
-- --Statistics.

Song sparrow.   See Melospiza.

Songs.
sa State songs.
Folk-songs.

Songs of birds.   See Bird songs.

Sonic engineering.   See Acoustical engineering.

Sonification of insects.   See Stridulation.

Sonoma Co., Calif.
--Social conditions.
sa Subdivision Sonoma Co., Calif.
under: Social surveys.

Sonora, Mexico.
--Agriculture.
--Botany.
--Description and travel.
--Domestic animals.
--History.
--Zoology.
    sa Subdivision Mexico. Sonora
        under: Mammalia.

Sonoran Desert.
    sa Subdivision Sonoran Desert
        under: Precipitation
            (Meteorology)
    xx Deserts.

Sonorella.

Soochow, China.
    sa Subdivision China. Soochow
        under: Gardens.
    xx China.

Soochow-Kashing Highway.

Soodan. See Sudan.

Sooner State. See Oklahoma.

Soot.

Soot as a fertilizer.

Sooty mold.

Sophodermium pinastri.

Sophoreae.
    xx Acrasieae.

Soprocide.

Sopron, Hungary.
--Forestry.
    xx Hungary. Forestry.

Sorbic chloride.

Sorbitol.

Sorbus.
    xx Malaceae.
--Diseases.
--Pests.

Sorbus aucuparia.
    x European mountainash.
    Rowan tree.

Sorbus domestica. See Pyrus sorbus.

Sordaria.

Sordaria uvicola.

Sordariaceae.
    sa Sordaria.

Sore-shin disease of cotton.

Soresina.
--Dairying.
    sa Subdivision Italy. Soresina
        under: Dairy industry and
        trade.

Sorex. See Soricidae.

Sorgho-sugar-cane hybrids. See Sugar-
cane-sorgho hybrids.

Sorghum.
    sa Sugar-cane.
    Feterita.
    Shallu.
    Grohoma.
    Sorgo.
    Cookery (Sorghum)
    Durra.
    Broom-corn.
    x Grain sorghum.
    Sorghum grain.
    Amber cane.
    Andropogon sorghum.
--Abstracts.
--Anatomy.
--Bibliography.
    sa Subdivision Bibliography under:
        Sorghum. Breeding.
--Breeding.
    xx Plant-breeding.
-- --Bibliography.
--Composition.
--Congresses.
--Crop reports.
--Digestibility.
--Disease resistant varieties.
    xx Disease resistant plants.

Sorghum (Continued)
--Diseases.
      sa Sorghum smut.
      Anthracnose of sorghum.
--Effect on soil. See Soil. Effect of
    sorghum.
--Fertilization.
--Financing.
      xx Farm produce. Financing.
--Germination.
      xx Cereals. Germination.
--Grading and standardization.
      xx Farm produce. Grading and
        standardization.
--Growth.
      xx Plant growth.
--Harvesting.
      xx Harvesting.
--History.
      xx Agriculture. History.
--Hybrids.
      sa Sorghum doura-cernum.
      xx Hybrids.
--Hydrocyanic-acid content.
      xx Hydrocyanic acid in plants.
--Implements and machinery.
      xx Agriculture. Implements and
        machinery.

Sorghum, Kaoliang.
    sa Kaocanite.

Sorghum.
--Periodicals.
--Pests.
      xx Entomology, Economic.
--Physiology and morphology.
--Prices.
-- --Subsidies.
--Research.
--Seed.
      xx Seeds.
-- --Disinfection.
      xx Seeds. Disinfection.
--Statistics.
      xx Cereals. Statistics.
--Storage.

Sorghum, Sweet. See Sorgo.

Sorghum, Uses of.

Sorghum.
--Varieties.
--Water requirement.

Sorghum as feeding stuff.
    sa Milo as feeding stuff.
    Hegari as feeding stuff.
    Sorgo as feeding stuff.

Sorghum daura-cernum.
    x Gao-dzhugar.
    xx Sorghum. Hybrids.

Sorghum flour.
    xx Flour.

Sorghum grain. See Sorghum.

Sorghum halepense. See Johnson grass.

Sorghum-midge. See Contarina sorghicola.

Sorghum saccharatum. See Sorgo.

Sorghum sirup. .See Sorgo syrup.

Sorghum smut.

Sorghum sudanénse. See Sudan grass.

Sorghum sugar.

Sorghum syrup. See Sorgo syrup.

Sorghum vulgare. See Durra.

Sorgo.
    sa Sorghum.
    x Sorghum, Sweet.
    Sweet sorghum.
    Sugar-cane, Chinese.
    Chinese sugar-cane.
    Sorghum saccharatum.
--Addresses, essays, lectures.
--Composition.
--Periodicals.

Sorgo as feeding stuff.

Sorgo silage.
    xx Ensilage.

Sorgo syrup.
    x Sorghum sirup.
    Sorghum syrup.
    xx Syrups.

Soria, Spain (Province)
--Agriculture.
-- --Statistics.
--Domestic animals.

Soricidae.
 sa Atophyrax bendirii.
  Atophyrax.
  Crocidura.
--Pests.
 xx Rodentia. Pests.

Soroca, Rumania.
--Botany.

Sorochemyia.

Sorophorae.

Sororities.
 sa Greek letter societies.

Sorosporella.
 xx Moniliaceae.

Sorosporella uvella.

Sorosporium paspali.

Sorption. See Gases. Absorption and adsorption; Vapors. Absorption and adsorption.

Sorrel, Sheep. See Rumex acetosella.

Sotol. See Dasylirion texanum.

Soudan. See Sudan.

Soulanges Co., Que.
--Soils.
 sa Subdivision Quebec (Province)
  Soulanges Co. under: Soil-
  surveys.

Sound.
 sa Acoustic phenomena in nature.
  Architectural acoustics.
  Hearing.
  Noises.
  Phonetics.
  Soundproofing.
  Vibration.
  Electroacoustics.

Sound (Continued)
 sa Acoustical engineering.
  x Acoustics.
  xx Physics.
--Apparatus.
--Bibliography.
--Effect on poultry.
 x Poultry, Effect of sound on.
--Measurement.
 sa Decibels.
--Velocity.
 sa Vibration.

Sound engineering. See Acoustical engineering.

Sound insulation. See Insulation (Sound)

Sound motion pictures. See Moving-pictures, Talking.

Sound pictures. See Moving-pictures, Talking.

Sound production by animals.
 sa Stridulation.
  Senses and sense organs of
   insects.
  Bird-song.
  x Animal sounds.
  Animals, Sound production by.

Sound proofing. See Soundproofing.
 xx Acoustical engineering.

Sound-waves.
 xx Vibration.
  Waves.

Soundings.

Soundproofing.
 x Sound proofing.
 xx Sound.

Soups.
 x Chowders.
--Canning.

Sour cream. See Cream, Fermented.

Sour milk. See Milk, Fermented.

Sour skim milk, Concentrated. See Milk, Fermented, Concentrated.

Sourclover. See Clover, Sweet.

Souris River.

Sousse, Tunis.
--Botany.
    xx Tunis. Botany.

South, The. See Southern States.

South Africa. See Africa, South.

South African black ironwood. See Olea
  laurifolia.

South African citrus thrips. See Scirtothrips aurantii.

South African clawed frog. See Xenopus
  laevis.

South African frog. See Xenopus laevis.

South African literature.

South Africa literature (Afrikaans) See
  Afrikaans literature.

South African literature (English)
    x English literature. South
      Africa.
      English literature. Africa,
      South.
--Bibliography.

South African periodicals.
--Bibliography.

South African War, 1899-1902.
--Medical and sanitary affairs.

South America.
    sa Spanish America.
    xx Spanish America.
--Agriculture.
    sa Subdivision South America under:
      Cotton.
      Colonization, Agricultural.
      Agricultural laborers.
      Agriculture. Economic as-
        pects.
      Cacao.
      South America. Domestic ani-
      mals.

South America (Continued)
--Agriculture.
    sa Subdivision Agriculture under:
      Amazon Valley.
      Brazil.
      Venezuela//
-- --Bibliography.
-- --Education.
    sa Subdivision Agriculture. Edu-
      cation under: Bolivia.
      Brazil.
      Chile//
      Subdivision South America un-
        der: Agricultural extension.
    xx Agriculture. Education.
-- --History.
    sa Subdivision Agriculture. His-
      tory under: Chile.
      Argentine Republic.
    xx Agriculture. History.
. --Maps.
-- --Statistics.
    sa Subdivision Agriculture. Sta-
      tistics under: Bolivia.
    xx Agriculture. Statistics.
--Altitudes.
    xx Altitudes.
--Antiquities.
--Apiculture.
    sa Subdivision Apiculture under:
      Brazil.
      Uruguay.
      Argentine Republic//
    xx Apiculture.
--Bibliography.
    sa Subdivision Bibliography un-
      der: Cotton. South America.
      Amazon Valley.
      Amazon River.
--Biography.
    sa Subdivision Biography under:
      Spanish America.
--Botany.
    sa Bolivia.
      Chile.
      Essequebo//
      Subdivision South America un-
        der: Forage plants.
      Ferns.
      Lichens.
      Mosses.
      Hepaticae.
      Food plants.
      Botany, Medical.
    xx America. Botany.

South America (Continued)
--Botany.
-- --History.
 sa Subdivision Botany. History
   under: Peru.
--Cattle.
 sa Subdivision Cattle under names
   of countries.
 xx Cattle.
--Census.
 sa Subdivision Census under names
   of countries, etc.
--Civilization.
 sa Subdivision South America under:
   Art.
   Subdivision Civilization under
   names of countries, etc.
 xx Civilization.
--Climate.
 sa Argentine Republic. Climate//
--Commerce.
 sa Subdivision Commerce under:
   Amazon Valley.
- --Canada.
-- --Gt. Brit.
- --U.S.
-- --Bibliography.
-- --Directories.
 sa Subdivision Commerce. Directories under: Argentine
   Republic//
· --History.
 sa Subdivision Commerce. History
   under: Brazil.
 xx Commerce. History.
-- --Periodicals.
 sa Subdivision Commerce. Periodicals under: Argentine Republic.
   Brazil.
   Uruguay//
 xx Commerce. Periodicals.
-- --Statistics.
 sa Subdivision Commerce. Statistics
   under: French Guiana.
--Commercial policy.
 sa Subdivision Commercial policy
   under: Argentine Republic//
 xx Commercial policy.
--Commercial treaties.
 sa Subdivision Commercial treaties
   under: Argentine Republic.
   Brazil.
   Peru.
 xx Commercial treaties.

South America (Continued)
--Dairying.
 sa Subdivision Dairying under:
   Argentine Republic.
   Brazil.
   Chile//
   Subdivision South America un-
   der: Dairy industry and
   trade.
 xx Dairying.
--Description and travel.
 sa Subdivision Description and
   travel under: Bolivia?
   Patagonia.
   Tierra del Fuego//
--Domestic animals.
 sa Subdivision Domestic animals
   under: Argentine Republic.
   Peru.
   Ecuador//
   South America. Sheep.
-- --History and origin.
 sa Subdivision Domestic animals.
   History and origin under:
   Argentine Republic.
 xx Domestic animals. History and
   origin.
--Economic conditions.
 sa Subdivision Economic condi-
   tions under: Venezuela.
   Argentine Republic.
   Ecuador//
   Geography, Economic. South
   America.
--Economic policy.
 sa Subdivision Economic policy
   under: Uruguay.
   Venezuela.
   Argentine Republic//
 xx Economic policy.
   Spanish America. Economic
   policy.
--Education.
-- --Statistics.
 sa Subdivision Education. Sta-
   tistics under: Peru.
 xx Education. Statistics.
--Emigration and immigration.
 sa Subdivision Emigration and
   immigration under: Brazil.
   Bolivia//

South America (Continued)
--Entomology.
    sa Subdivision Entomology under:
      Amazon Region.
      British Guiana.
      Buenos Ayres (Province)//
    Subdivision South America un-
      der: Moths.
      Hymenoptera.
      Orthoptera.
      Lepidoptera.
      Coleoptera.
      Diptera.
      Wasps.
      Hemiptera.
      Locusts.
      Culicidae.
-- --Bibliography.
    sa Subdivision Entomology. Bib-
      liography under: Brazil.
--Foreign relations.
    sa Subdivision Foreign relations
      under: Brazil.
      Argentine Republic.
      Bolivia//
    xx International law and rela-
      tions.
--Forestry.
    sa Subdivision Forestry under:
      Bolivia//
--Geographic names.
--Geography.
    sa Subdivision South America un-
      der: Geography, Economic.
    Subdivision Geography under:
      Brazil.
      Dutch Guiana//
--Geology.
-- --Bibliography.
--Government publications.
    sa Colombia. Government publica-
      tions.
    xx Government publications.
--History.
    sa Subdivision History under:
      Brazil.
      Spanish America.
      Argentine Republic.
--Horse.
--Ichthyology.
    sa Subdivision Ichthyology under
      names of countries, etc.

South America (Continued)
--Industries and resources.
    sa Subdivision Industries and re-
      sources under names of
      countries, etc.
--Land.
    sa Subdivision Land under:
      Brazil//
    Subdivision South America un-
      der: Land reform.
    xx Land.
--Libraries.
    sa Subdivision Libraries under:
      Argentine Republic//
    xx Libraries.
--Manufactures.
    sa Subdivision Manufactures un-
      der: Brazil//
    xx Manufactures.
--Maps.
    sa Subdivision Maps under:
      Argentine Republic.
      Bolivia.
      Brazil//
    xx Spanish America. Maps.
-- --Bibliography.
--Meat supply.
    sa Subdivision Meat supply under
      names of countries, cities,
      etc.
--Meteorology.
    sa Precipitation (Meteorology)
      South America.
    Subdivision Meteorology under:
      Dutch Guiana.
      Chile//
--Milk supply.
    sa Subdivision Milk supply under:
      Brazil.
--Milk trade.
    sa Subdivision Milk trade under:
      Venezuela//
    xx Milk trade.
--Museums.
    sa Subdivision Museums under:
      Argentine Republic.
--Ornithology.
    sa Subdivision Ornithology un-
      der: Argentine Republic.
      Paraguay.
      Puna Island, Ecuador//
--Natural history.
    sa Argentine Republic.
      Brazil.
      Chile//

South America (Continued)
--Natural history.
    xx Natural history.
        America. Natural history.
--Paleobotany.
    sa Subdivision Paleobotany under:
        Patagonia.
        Tierra del Fuego.
        Bolivia.
--Paleontology.
    sa Patagonia.
        Bolivia.
--Physical geography.
    sa Subdivision Physical geography
        under: Chile.
        Venezuela.
        Paraguay//
--Politics and government.
    sa Subdivision Politics and gov-
        ernment under: Bolivia.
        Caribbean Region.
        Argentine Republic//
    xx Political science.
--Pomology.
    sa Subdivision Pomology under:
        Brazil.
        British Guiana.
        Paraguay//
--Population.
    sa Subdivision Population under:
        Colombia.
        Peru.
--Public lands.
    sa Subdivision Public lands under:
        Venezuela.
        Argentine Republic.
        Brazil.
    xx Public lands.
--Public works.
    sa Subdivision Public works under:
        Argentine Republic.
        Colombia.
        Ecuador//
--Railroads.
--Roads.
    sa Subdivision Roads under:
        Bolivia.
        Spanish America.
--Sericulture.
    sa Subdivision Sericulture under:
        Argentine Republic.
        Brazil.
        Chile//
    xx Sericulture.

South America (Continued)
--Sheep.
    sa Subdivision Sheep under:
        Argentine Republic.
        Brazil//
    xx Sheep.
--Social conditions.
    sa Subdivision Social conditions
        under: Chile.
        Venezuela.
        Argentine Republic//
    xx Social conditions.
--Social life and customs.
    sa Subdivision Social life and
        customs under: Brazil//
    xx Social life and customs.
--Soils.
    sa Subdivision Soils under:
        Argentine Republic.
        Colombia.
        Parahiba, Brazil (State)//
    xx Soil.
--Surveys.
--Swine.
    sa Subdivision Swine under names
        of countries, etc.
--Transportation.
    sa Subdivision Transportation
        under names of countries,
        etc.
    xx Transportation.
--Viticulture.
    sa Subdivision Viticulture under:
        Brazil.
        Chile.
        Peru//
    xx Viticulture.
--Water-supply.
    sa Subdivision Water-supply un-
        der: Peru.
        Brazil.
--Zoology.
    sa Subdivision Zoology under:
        Brazil.
        Colombia.
        Dutch Guiana//
        Subdivision South America un-
        der: Mammalia.
        Araneida.
        Batrachia.
        Reptilia.

South American leaf disease of rubber.
    x Leaf blight of Hevea
      rubbertrees.
    xx Hevea brasiliensis. Diseases.

South Australia.
    x Australia, South.
    xx Australia.
--Agricultural experiment stations.
--Agriculture.
    sa Subdivision South Australia
      under: Cotton.
      Wheat.
      Forage plants.
      Farm buildings.
      Poultry.
      Sugar-beet.
      Agriculture. Economic
      aspects.
      Colonization, Agricultural.
      Rehabilitation, Rural.
      Crops and climate.
      Grassland farming.
    xx Australia. Agriculture.
-- --Statistics.
    xx Agriculture. Statistics.
--Botany.
    sa Subdivision South Australia
      under: Fungi.
      Trees.
    xx Australia. Botany.
-- --History.
--Climate.
    sa Subdivision South Australia
      under: Crops and climate.
--Commerce.
    sa Subdivision South Australia
      under: Farm produce.
      Marketing.
--Dairying.
-- --Statistics.
--Description and travel.
--Domestic animals.
    sa South Australia. Swine.
      South Australia. Sheep.
--Economic conditions.
    sa Subdivision South Australia
      under: Economic surveys.
--Entomology.
    sa Subdivision South Australia
      under: Lepidoptera.
      Entomology, Economic.

South Australia (Continued)
--Forestry.
    sa Subdivision South Australia
      under: Afforestation and
      reforestation.
      Trees.
    xx Australia. Forestry.
--Geology.
--Industries.
-- --Statistics.
--Land.
    sa Subdivision South Australia
      under: Land utilization.
      Land, Marginal.
    xx Australia. Land.
--Law.
--Maps.
    sa Subdivision Maps under:
      Australia, Southeastern.
--Museums.
--Natural history.
--Paleontology.
--Pomology.
    sa Coonawarra fruit colony,
      Penola, South Australia.
    xx Australia. Pomology.
--Public lands.
--Sheep.
--Soils.
    sa Subdivision Soils under:
      Renmark irrigation
      district, South
      Australia.
      Waikeri irrigation area,
      South Australia.
      Subdivision South Australia
      under: Soil-surveys.
      Soil drifting.
      Wind erosion.
      Soil erosion.
      Soil conservation.
--Statistics.
    sa South Australia. Census.
--Swine.
--Water-supply.
    sa Subdivision South Australia
      under: Water, Underground.

South Bend, Ind.
--Milk trade.

South Carolina.
    sa Southern States.
    Georgetown Co., S.C.
    Columbia, S.C.//

South Carolina (Continued)
--Agriculture.
    sa Subdivision South Carolina
       under: Cotton.
       Rice.
       Colonization, Agricultural.
       Maize.
       Cropping systems.
       Agricultural outlook.
       Agricultural policies and
        programs.
       Agriculture. Economic
        aspects.
       Rural surveys.
       Agricultural credit.
       Farm produce. Cost of
        production.
       Tobacco.
       Subdivision Agriculture under:
        Anderson Co.//
-- --Education.
    sa Penn Normal, Industrial and
       Agricultural School.
 - --History.
-- --Periodicals.
--Botany.
    sa Hartsville, S.C. Botany.
       Brookgreen Gardens, Brookgreen,
        S.C.
       Horry Co., S.C. Botany//
--Census.
--Description and travel.
-- --Guide-books.
--Domestic animals.
    sa South Carolina. Sheep.
       South Carolina. Horse.
--Economic conditions.
    sa Subdivision Economic conditions
       under: Chesterfield Co.,
        S.C.
       Dillon Co., S.C.
       Florence Co., S.C.//
       Subdivision South Carolina
       under: Rural surveys.
       History, Economic.
--Education.
    sa Subdivision South Carolina
       under: Rural schools.
--Entomology.
    sa Subdivision South Carolina
       under: Entomology, Economic.
--Fisheries.

South Carolina (Continued)
--Forest reservations.
    sa Francis Marion National
       Forest, S.C.
       Sumter National Forest, S.C.
--Forestry.
    sa Subdivision Forestry under:
       Beaufort Co., S.C.
       Hampton Co., S.C.
       Nantahala National Forest.
       Subdivision South Carolina
       under: Forest surveys.
       Trees.
       Forest fires. Prevention.
       Lumber.
       Forest industries.
       Timber.
       Forest policy.
       Wood-lots.
-- --Statistics.
--Geology.
    sa Subdivision South Carolina
       under: Mines and mineral
        resources.
--History.
    sa Subdivision South Carolina
       under: History, Economic.
    xx U.S. History.
-- --Colonial period.
    xx U.S. History. Colonial period.
 --Sources.
    sa Subdivision South Carolina
       under: Archives.
    xx U.S. History. Sources.
--Horse.
    sa Subdivision South Carolina
       under: Horses. Breeding.
    xx South Carolina. Domestic ani-
       mals.
--Industries and resources.
    sa Subdivision South Carolina
       under: Conservation of
       natural resources.
-- --Directories.
    xx Southern States. Industries
       and resources. Directories.
--Land.
    sa Subdivision South Carolina
       under: Land reform.
       Subdivision Land under names
       of counties, etc.
--Libraries.
    xx U.S. Libraries.
--Maps.
--Meat supply.

South Carolina (Continued)
--Natural history.
--Occupations.
--Ornithology.
--Paleobotany.
--Paleontology.
--Parks.
    xx U.S. Parks.
--Politics and government.
    xx U.S. Politics and government.
--Pomology.
--Public lands.
    xx U.S. Public lands.
--Railroads.
--Roads.
--Sheep.
--Social conditions.
    sa Subdivision South Carolina
        under: Cost and standard of
        living.
        Social surveys.
--Social life and customs.
    sa Subdivision Social life and
        customs under: Dutch Fork.
    xx U.S. Social life and customs.
--Soils.
    sa Subdivision Soils under:
        Lancaster Co., S.C.
        Darlington Co., S.C.//
        Subdivision South Carolina un-
        der: Soil-surveys.
        Soil erosion.
        Soil conservation.
        Soil conservation. Piedmont
        region (S.C.)
--Statistics.
--Water-supply.
    xx U.S. Water-supply.
--Zoology.

South Carolina Agricultural Loan Associa-
    tion.

South Carolina State Agricultural Society.

South Central States.
    xx Central States.
--Agriculture.
    sa Subdivision South Central States
        under: Agricultural surveys.
        War and agriculture (1939-
        1945)
-- --Statistics.
--Land.
-- --Prices.

South Central States (Continued)
--Maps.

South Cholla, Korea.
--Agriculture.
--Soils.
    sa Subdivision Korea. South Cholla
        under: Soil-surveys.

South Dakota.
    sa Harding County, S.D.
        Big Sioux River.
        James River, S.D.//
--Agriculture.
    sa Subdivision South Dakota under:
        Wheat.
        Maize.
        Agricultural outlook.
        Agriculture. Economic as-
        pects.
        Rural surveys.
        War and agriculture (1939-
        1945)
        Farm management surveys.
        Cereals.
        Crops and climate.
        Agricultural conservation
        program.
        Grassland farming.
        Irrigation farming.
        Subdivision Agriculture under:
        Brown Co., S.D.
 · --History.
    sa Subdivision Agriculture. His-
        tory under: Brown Co., S.D.
-- --Periodicals.
-- --Statistics.
    sa Subdivision Statistics under:
        Brown Co., S.D.
--Altitudes.
--Botany.
    sa Subdivision South Dakota under:
      \ Trees.
        Shrubs.
        Vegetable pathology.
        Wild flowers.
-- --Bibliography.
--Cattle trade.
    xx U.S. Cattle trade.
--Census.
--Climate.
    sa Subdivision Climate under:
    ·   Hand Co., S.D.
        Subdivision South Dakota under:
        Crops and climate.

South Dakota (Continued)
--Commerce.
    sa Subdivision South Dakota under:
      Farm produce. Marketing.
--Dairying.
--Description and travel.
--Domestic animals.
-- --Legislation.
-- --Research.
-- --Statistics.
--Economic conditions.
    sa Subdivision Economic conditions
      under: Day Co., S.D.
      McCook Co., S.D.
      Clay Co., S.D.//
      Subdivision South Dakota under:
      Economic surveys.
      Rural surveys.
-- --Periodicals.
    xx U.S. Economic conditions. Peri-
      odicals.
--Education.
    sa Subdivision South Dakota under:
      Rural schools.
-- --Statistics.
    xx U.S. Education. Statistics.
--Entomology.
--Fisheries.
--Forest reservations.
--Forestry.
    sa Subdivision South Dakota under:
      Trees.
--Geology.
    sa Subdivision Geology under:
      Sioux Falls, S.D.
      Black Hills, S.D.
    Subdivision South Dakota under:
      Water, Underground.
      Mines and mineral resources.
-- --Bibliography.
    sa Subdivision Geology. Bibliog-
      raphy under: Black Hills.
    xx U.S. Geology. Bibliography.
--History.
    sa Subdivision History under:
      Miner Co., S.D.
      McPherson Co., S.D.
· --Sources.
    sa Subdivision South Dakota under:
      Archives.
    xx U.S. History. Sources.
--Industries and resources.
-- --Directories.

South Dakota (Continued)
--Land.
    sa Subdivision Land under:
      Haakon Co., S.D.
      Perkins Co., S.D.
    xx U.S. Land.
--Libraries.
    xx U.S. Libraries.
--Manufactures.
--Maps.
--Meteorology.
    sa Subdivision South Dakota under:
      Precipitation (Meteorology)
--Ornithology.
-- --Bibliography.
--Paleobotany.
--Paleontology.
--Parks.
--Politics and government.
    xx U.S. Politics and government.
--Population.
    xx U.S. Population.
--Public lands.
--Public works.
    xx U.S. Public works.
--Railroads.
--Roads.
-- --Law.
    xx Roads. Legislation.
    U.S. Roads. Law.
--Social conditions.
    sa Social surveys. South Dakota
      with subdivisions: Clay Co.
      Day Co.
      Grant Co.
      Hamlin Co.
      Jerauld Co.
      McCook Co.
    Cost and standard of living.
      South Dakota.
    Subdivision Social conditions
      under: Beadle Co.
--Soils.
    sa Subdivision South Dakota under:
      Soil-surveys.
      Soil erosion. Prevention
        and control.
      Soil erosion.
      Soil erosion surveys.
      Soil conservation surveys.
      Soil conservation.
    Subdivision Soils under names
      of counties. etc.

South Dakota. State College of Agriculture
    and Mechanic Arts, Brookings.

South Dakota.
--Statistics.
--Transportation.
    xx U.S. Transportation.
--Water-supply.
    sa Subdivision Water-supply under:
        Black Hills, S.D.
        Huron, S.D.//
    Subdivision South Dakota under:
        Water, Underground.
--Zoology.
    sa Subdivision South Dakota under:
        Mammalia.

South Devon, Eng.
--Agriculture.
    sa Rural surveys. South Devon, Eng.
        Agriculture. Economic aspects.
        Gt. Brit. South Devon.
    xx England. Agriculture.
--Botany.
--Dairying.
--Economic conditions.
    sa Subdivision South Devon, Eng.
        under: Rural surveys.
    xx Gt. Brit. Economic conditions.

South Devon cattle.

South Georgia.
--Entomology.
--Ornithology.

South Holland, Ill.
--Social conditions.
    sa Subdivision Illinois. South
        Holland under: Social
        surveys.

South Indian Agricultural Workers' Union.
    xx Farmers' unions.

South Island, N.Z.
--Agriculture.
    sa Subdivision New Zealand. South
        Island under: Grasses.
--Botany.
--Zoology.

South Ossetia (Region)
    x Ossetia.
--Botany.

South Ossetia (Region) (Continued)
--Research.

South Pacific area.
    sa Oceania.

South Platte Valley.
--Agriculture.
--Geology.
    sa Subdivision South Platte Valley
        under: Water, Underground.
--Water-supply.
    sa Subdivision South Platte
        Valley under: Water, Under-
        ground.

South Pole.

South Saskatchewan River development
    project (Proposed)

South Sea.   See Pacific Ocean.

South Sea Islands.   See Islands of the
    Pacific.

South Tyrol.
    x Upper Adige.
    Alto Adige.
    Adige, Upper.
--Agriculture.
    sa Subdivision Italy. South Tyrol
        under: Reclamation of land.
        Colonization, Agricultural.
--Botany.
    sa Subdivision Italy. South Tyrol
        under: Vegetable pathology.
--Civilization.
--Economic conditions.
--Pomology.

Southampton, Eng.
--History.

Southampton Botanic Garden.

Southampton Co., Va.
    sa Subdivision Southampton Co.,
        Va. under: Negroes.
    xx Virginia.
--Agriculture.
    xx Virginia. Agriculture.
--History.
    xx Virginia. History.

Southampton Co., Va. (Continued)
--Social conditions.
    xx Virginia. Social conditions.
--Soils.
    sa Subdivision Virginia. Southampton Co. under: Soil-surveys.

Southampton Island.
--Botany.
--Entomology.
    sa Subdivision Southampton Island under: Lepidoptera.
    xx Hudson Bay. Entomology.
--Ornithology.

Southboro, Mass.
    sa Deerfoot Farm, Southboro, Mass.

Southdown sheep.

Southeast Asia.   See Asia, Southeastern.

Southeastern Asia.   See Asia, Southeastern.

Southeastern States.
--Agriculture.
    sa Subdivision Southeastern States under: Part-time farming.
    Maize.
    Agricultural laborers.
    Agriculture. Economic aspects.
    Irrigation.
    Cotton.
    Agricultural policies and programs.
    Crops and climate.
    Mechanized farming.
    Agricultural credit.
    Poultry.
-- --Statistics.
--Botany.
    sa Subdivision Southeastern States under: Trees.
    Ferns.
    Shrubs.
    Botany, Medical.
    Vegetable pathology.
--Climate.
    sa Subdivision Southeastern States under: Crops and climate.

Southeastern States (Continued)
--Economic conditions.
    sa Subdivision Southeastern States under: Agriculture. Economic aspects.
--Entomology.
    sa Subdivision Southeastern States under: Entomology, Economic.
    xx U.S. Entomology.
--Forestry.
    sa Subdivision Southeastern States under: Trees.
    Lumbering.
    Forest surveys.
    Wood-lots.
    Forest management.
-- --Bibliography.
--Land.
    sa Subdivision Southeastern States under: Land. Classification.
    Land utilization.
-- --Prices.
--Libraries.
--Maps.
--Markets.
--Pomology.
--Research.
--Roads.
    xx U.S. Roads.
--Social conditions.
    sa Subdivision Southeastern States under: Cost and standard of living.
--Soils.
    sa Subdivision Southeastern States under: Soil erosion. Prevention and control.
    Soil conservation.
--Statistics.

Southern army-worm.   See Prodenia eridania.

Southern Asia.   See Asia, Southern.

Southern beet web-worm.   See Pachyzancla bipunctalis.

Southern blight of tomato.
    x Blight diseases of tomato.
    Tomato blights.

Southern California.   See California, Southern.

Southern cattle fever.   See Texas fever.

Southern cone rust.   See Cone rust.

Southern corn rootworm.   See Diabrotica undecimpunctata howardi.

Southern cornstalk borer.   See Diatraea crambidoides.

Southern Cross (Ship)

Southern fusiform rust of pines.   See Fusiform rust of pines.

Southern Great Plains.   See Great Plains.

Southern green plant-bug.   See Nezara viridula.

Southern high plains.   See High plains.

Southern highlanders.   See Mountain whites (Southern States)

Southern moss.   See Tillandsia usneoides.

Southern Nigeria.   See Nigeria, Southern.

Southern pine.   See Pinus palustris.

Southern pine beetle.   See Dendroctonus frontalis.

Southern red oak.   See Quercus falcata.

Southern red oak wood.   See Quercus falcata (Wood)

Southern regional beef cattle breeding project.
  xx Cattle, Beef. Breeding. Research.

Southern Rhodesia.   See Rhodesia, Southern.

Southern States.
  sa Subdivision Southern States under: Mountain whites.
   Soil erosion surveys.
   Gulf States.
  xx Gulf States.

Southern States (Continued)
--Agriculture.
  sa Subdivision Southern States under: Cotton.
   Agriculture. Economic aspects.
   Wheat.
   Grasses.
   Forage plants.
   Rice.
   Sugar-cane.
   Maize.
   Farm buildings.
   Poultry.
   War and agriculture (1939-1945)
   Agricultural outlook.
   Part-time farming.
   Types of farming.
   Rural rehabilitation.
   Rural surveys.
   Agricultural extension.
   Potatoes.
   Mechanized farming.
   Grassland farming.
   Sweet potatoes.
   Field crops.
   Agricultural industries.
   Peanuts.
   Crops and climate.
   Agricultural laborers.
   Agricultural credit.
   Colonization, Agricultural.
   Ranges.
   Flax.
-- --Biography.
  xx Southern States. Biography.
   Agriculture. Biography.
-- --Education.
  sa Subdivision Southern States under: Agricultural extension.
-- --History.
  sa Subdivision Agriculture. History under: Virginia.
-- -- --Bibliography.
  xx U.S. Agriculture. History. Bibliography.
-- --Statistics.
  sa Mississippi. Agriculture. Statistics.
--Apiculture.
  xx U.S. Apiculture.

Southern States (Continued)
--Geology.
 sa Subdivision Southern States
  under: Water, Underground.
--History.
 sa Subdivision Southern States
  under: History, Economic.
-- --Colonial period.
 xx U.S. History. Colonial period.
--Horse.
 xx Southern States. Domestic ani-
  mals.
--Ichthyology.
--Industries.
 sa Subdivision Southern States
  under: Rural industries.
  Agricultural industries.
  Industrial surveys.
  Chemical industries.
-- --Directories.
--Intellectual life.
--Land.
 sa Subdivision Southern States
  under: Waste lands.
  Land. Classification.
  Land utilization.
--Libraries.
 xx U.S. Libraries.
--Manufactures.
 xx U.S. Manufactures.
--Maps.
--Milk trade.

Southern Riverina irrigation project.

Southern States.
--Natural history.
--Occupations.
 xx U.S. Occupations.
--Ornithology.
 sa Subdivision Ornithology under:
  Southwestern States.
--Paleobotany.
--Periodicals.
-- --Bibliography.
 xx Periodicals. Bibliography.
--Pomology.
 sa Gulf States. Pomology.
 xx U.S. Pomology.
--Population.
 sa Subdivision Southern States
  under: Rural population.
  Migration, Internal.

Southern States (Continued)
--Race question.
 sa Subdivision Race question under: Mississippi.
 xx U.S. Race question.
--Railroads.
--Religion.
--Research.
 x Utilization of natural resources.
 xx U.S. Research.
--Roads.
 xx Roads.
--Sheep.
--Social conditions.
 sa Subdivision Social conditions
  under: Appalachian Moun-
  tains, Southern.
  Subdivision Southern States
  under: Social surveys.
-- --Bibliography.
--Social life and customs.
 xx U.S. Social life and customs.
--Soils.
 sa Subdivision Southern States
  under: Soil erosion. Pre-
  vention and control.
  Soil conservation. Economic
  aspects.
  Soil erosion surveys.
  Subdivision Soils under:
  Gulf States.
  Soil conservation.
--Statistics.
 sa Southern States. Agriculture.
  Statistics.
--Swine.
--Tariff.
--Transportation.
-- --History.
 xx U.S. Transportation. History.
--Viticulture.
--Water-supply.
 sa Subdivision Southern States
  under: Water, Underground.
  Water. Conservation.
--Zoology.
 sa Subdivision Zoology under:
  Southwestern States.
  Subdivision Southern States
  under: Wild life.

Southern Territories of Algeria.
 x Algeria, Southern.

Southern Territories of Algeria (Continued)
--Zoology.

Southington, Conn.
--Botany.

Southport, Eng.
--Natural history.

Southwest, New.   See Southwestern States.

Southwest, Old.   See Southwestern States.

Southwest, Pacific.   See Southwestern
States; Pacific Coast.

Southwest Intermountain region.   See
Southwestern States.

Southwestern corn borer.   See Diatraea
grandiosella.

Southwestern States.
    x Southwest, Old.
      Southwest, New.
      Southwest Intermountain region.
      Intermountain region. Southwest.
      Southwest, Pacific.
      Pacific Southwestern States.
--Agriculture.
    sa Subdivision Southwestern States
        under: Ranges.
      Agriculture. Economic as-
        pects.
      War and agriculture (1939-
        1945)
      Agricultural laborers.
      Agricultural policies and
        programs.
      Cotton.
      Rehabilitation, Rural.
-- --Conferences.
 · --History.
    xx U.S. Agriculture. History.
-- --Periodicals.
-- --Statistics.
    xx U.S. Agriculture. Statistics.
      Southwestern States. Statistics.
--Antiquities.
--Bibliography.
    xx U.S. Bibliography.

Southwestern States (Continued)
--Botany.
    sa Subdivision Southwestern
        States under: Weeds.
      Botany. Economic.
      Botany, Medical.
      Wild flowers.
      Ethnobotany.
      Forage plants.
      Shrubs.
--Cattle.
-- --History.
--Cattle trade.
    sa Subdivision Cattle trade un-
        der: Texas.
    xx Cattle trade.
      U.S. Cattle trade.
--Census. ·
--Civilization.
--Climate.
--Commerce.
--Description and travel.
--Domestic animals.
    sa Subdivision Southwestern
        States under: Sheep.
      Ranges.
    xx U.S. Domestic animals.
--Economic conditions.
--Entomology.
    sa Subdivision Southwestern
        States under: Orthoptera.
--Forest reservations.
    xx Forest reservations.
--Forestry.
    sa Subdivision Southwestern
        States under: Timber.
      Forest fires. Prevention.
      Wood-lots.
      Afforestation and re-
        forestation.
      Lumber trade.
    xx U.S. Forestry.
-- --Bibliography.
-- --Periodicals.
-- --Statistics.
    xx U.S. Forestry. Statistics.
      Southwestern States. Sta-
        tistics.
--Geology.
--History.
    xx U.S. History.
-- --Bibliography.
-- --Chronology.
--Horse.
    xx U.S. Horse.

Southwestern States (Continued)
--Industries.
--Land.
    sa Subdivision Southwestern States
       under: Land. Classification.
       Land utilization.
--Maps.
--Markets.
--Natural history.
--Ornithology.
    sa Subdivision Southwestern States
       under: Game-birds.
--Pomology.
    sa Subdivision Southwestern States
       under: Citrus.
    xx U.S. Pomology.
--Railroads.
    sa Subdivision Southwestern States
       under: Railroad land grants.
--Roads.
    xx Southern States. Roads.
       U.S. Roads.
--Sheep.
    xx Southwestern States. Domestic
       animals.
--Social life and customs.
--Soils.
    sa Subdivision Southwestern States
       under: Soil conservation.
       Soil erosion.
       Soil erosion. Prevention
       and control.
    xx U.S. Soils.
--Statistics.
    sa Subdivision Statistics under:
       Southwestern States. Agri-
       culture.
       Southwestern States. For-
       estry.
    xx U.S. Statistics.
--Water-supply.
    sa Subdivision Southwestern States
       under: Water. Conservation.
--Zoology.
    sa Mammalia. Southwestern States.
       Subdivision Southwestern States
       under: Game.

Soviet bloc.   See U.S.S.R. bloc.

Soviet Far East.   See U.S.S.R., Asiatic.

Soviet Georgia.   See Georgia (Transcaucasia)

Sow thistle, Perennial.   See Sonchus
   arvensis.

Sow-thistles.   See Thistles.

Sowbugs.

Sowing.
    sa Seed-drill.
       Seed spots.
       Subdivision Sowing under:
       Forage plants. Seed.
       Tomatoes. Seed.
       Nicotiana rustica. Seed//
    x Direct seeding.
       Seeds. Sowing.
       Planting.
       Seeding.
--Bibliography.

Sows.   See Swine.

Sowthistle, Perennial.   See Sonchus
   arvensis.

Soy-bean.   (INDIRECT)
    sa Cookery (Soy-bean)
    x Soya.
--Analysis.
--Bibliography.
    sa Subdivision Bibliography un-
       der: Soy-bean meal.
--Breeding.
--Canning.
    xx Vegetables. Canning.
--Composition.
    sa Soy-bean, Proteins in.
--Congresses.
--Cost of production.
    xx Farm produce. Cost of produc-
       tion.
--Digestibility.
--Directories.
--Disease resistant varieties.
--Diseases.
    sa Mosaic disease of soybean.
       Anthracnose of soy bean.
       Brown spot of soy bean.
       Root-rot of soy-bean.
       Heterodera glycines.
--Economic aspects.

Soy-bean, Effect of fertilization on.
   See Fertilizers. Effect on soy-bean.

Soy-bean.
--Effect on soil. See Soil. Effect of
      soybeans.
--Fermentation.
--Financing.
      xx Farm produce. Financing.
--Futures.
--Genetics.
--Germination.
      xx Germination.
--Grading and standardization.
      xx Agricultural products. Grading
            and standardization.
--Growth.
      xx Plant growth.
--Harvesting.
      xx Harvesting.
--Hybrids.
--Implements and machinery.
      xx Agriculture. Implements and
            machinery.
--Industrial uses. See Soy-bean prod-
      ucts.
--Inspection.
      xx Farm produce. Inspection.

Soy-bean, Lecithin in.
      x Soy-bean lecithin.
      xx Lecithin.

Soy-bean.
--Marketing.
      sa Subdivision Marketing under:
            Soy-bean oil.
            Soy-bean meal.
      xx Beans. Marketing.
--Marketing agreements.
      xx Marketing agreements.
--Nutritive value. See Soy-bean as
      food.
--Periodicals.
--Pest resistant varieties.
      xx Pest resistant plants.
--Pests.
      sa Anticarsia gemmatilis.
      xx Entomology, Economic.
--Physiology and morphology.
      xx Vegetables. Physiology and
            morphology.
--Planting time.
--Prices.
      xx Beans. Prices.
-- --Subsidies.
--Processing.
      xx Processing (Industrial)

Soy-bean (Continued)
--Processing.
-- --Bibliography.
-- --Congresses.

Soy-bean, Proteins in.
      sa Subdivision Proteins in under:
            Soy-bean flour.
      x Soy-bean protein.
      xx Proteins.
            Soy-bean. Composition.

Soy-bean.
--Research.
      sa Soy-bean [geographic subdi-
            vision] Research, e.g.,
            Soy-bean. Japan. Research.
      xx Agriculture. Research.
--Respiration.
--Seed.
-- --Adulteration.
-- --Germination.
-- --Storage.
      xx Seeds. Storage.
--Societies.
--Statistics.
      xx Beans. Statistics.
--Storage.
--Testing.
--Transportation.
      sa Railroads. Rates. Soy-bean.
      xx Vegetables. Transportation.
--Varieties.

Soy-bean, Vitamins in. See Vitamins in
      soy-beans.

Soy-bean.
--Year-books.

Soy-bean as a cause of disease. See
      Soy-bean meal poisoning.

Soy-bean as feeding stuff.
      sa Subdivision Effect of soy-bean
            under: Butter.
            Milk.

Soy-bean as food.
      x Soy-bean. Nutritive value.

Soy-bean cake.
--Statistics.

Soy-bean caterpillar.   See Anticarsia
  gemmatilis.

Soy-bean cheese.

Soy-bean competitions.

Soy-bean cyst nematode.   See Heterodera
  glycines.

Soy-bean flour.
    sa Soyolk.
    x Soy flour.
  --Digestibility.

Soy-bean flour, Proteins in.
    xx Soy-bean, Proteins in.
    Flour, Proteins in.

Soy-bean glue.
    xx Glue and paste.

Soy-bean grits.

Soy-bean hay.
    xx Hay.

Soy-bean lecithin.   See Soy-bean, Lecithin
  in.

Soy-bean meal.
    x Soy-bean oilmeal.
    xx Meal.
  --Bibliography.
    xx Soy-bean. Bibliography.
    Feeding stuffs. Bibliography.
  --Marketing.
    xx Soy-bean. Marketing.
  --Statistics.

Soy-bean meal as feeding stuff.

Soy-bean meal poisoning.
    x Soy-bean as a cause of disease.
    Düren disease,
    Brabant disease.

Soy-bean meal trade.
  --Futures.
  -- --Statistics.

Soy-bean milk.
    xx Vegetable milk.
  --Bibliography.

Soy-bean mills.
    x Soy-bean oil mills.

Soy-bean mills, Cooperative.
    x Cooperative soy-bean mills.
    Soy-bean oil mills, Coopera-
      tive.
    xx Cooperation. Societies.
  --Congresses.

Soy-bean mills.
  --Cost of operation.

Soy-bean oil.
  --Analysis.
  --Bibliography.
  --Futures.   See Soy-bean oil trade.
    Futures.
  --Marketing.
    xx Fats and oils. Marketing.
    Soy-bean. Marketing.
  --Prices.
  -- --Subsidies.
    xx Prices subsidies.
  --Processing.
  -- --Directories.
  --Statistics.

Soy-bean oil mills.   See Soy-bean mills.

Soy-bean oil mills, Cooperative.   See
    Soy-bean mills, Cooperative.

Soy-bean oil trade.
  --Futures.
    x Soy-bean oil. Futures.
  -- --Statistics.
  --Statistics.

Soy-bean oilmeal.   See Soy-bean meal.

Soy-bean products.
    x Soya products.
    Soy-bean. Industrial uses.
    xx Chemurgy.
  --Advertising.
    xx Food. Advertising.
  --Analysis.
  --Marketing.
  --Prices.

Soy-bean products as food.

Soy-bean proteins.   See Soy-bean, Proteins in.

Soy-bean sauce.
    x Japanese bean sauce.
      Soy sauce.
    xx Sauces.
--Bibliography.
--Fermentation.

Soy-bean seed.
--Adulteration.

Soy-bean silage.
    xx Ensilage.

Soy-bean sprouts.
    x Sprouted soy-beans.

Soy-bean trade.
--Futures.
    xx Future trading.
--Statistics.

Soy flour.   See Soy-bean flour.

Soy sauce.   See Soy-bean sauce.

Soya.   See Soy-bean.

Soya products.   See Soy-bean products.

Soybean.   See Soy-bean.

Soyolk.

Spaarn-Berg.   See Hortus Spaarn-Bergensis.

Space and time.
    sa Relativity (Physics)
    xx Time.

Space flight.
    x Astronautics.
      Rocket flight.
      Space travel.

Space travel.   See Space flight.

Spacing.   See Plant spacing.

Spade vs. plow.

Spaerotheca mors uvae.   See Powdery mildew of gooseberries.

Spaghetti.   See Macaroni.

Spain.
    sa Guadalcacin, Spain//
--Agricultural experiment stations.
    sa Madrid. Instituto agrícola
        de Alfonso 12. Estación
        agronómica.
      Murcia, Spain (City) Estación
        sericicola de.
      Barcelona. Agricultural ex-
        periment stations//
--Agriculture.
    sa Subdivision Agriculture under:
        Santander.
        Valencia.
        Andalusia//
      Subdivision Spain under:
        Cotton.
        Agriculture, Cooperative.
        Wheat.
        Rice.
        Colonization, Agricultural.
        Agricultural laborers.
        Cereals.
        Sugar-cane.
        Farm buildings.
        Poultry.
        Sugar-beet.
        Agricultural administration.
        Potatoes.
        Onions.
        Forage plants.
        Maize.
        Agriculture. Economic as-
          pects.
        Farm produce.
        Cropping systems.
        Agricultural industries.
        Crops and climate.
        Grassland farming.
-- --Bibliography.
-- --Directories.
-- --Education.
    sa Subdivision Agriculture. Edu-
        cation under: Catalonia.
        Barcelona.
      Pamplona, Spain. Escuela de
        peritos agrícolas de
        Navarra.
      Palencia, Spain. Granja es-
        cuela práctica de agri-
        cultura.
    xx Europe. Agriculture. Educa-
        tion.

Spain (Continued)
--Agriculture.
-- --History.
    sa Subdivision Agriculture.
       History under names of
       provinces, etc.
    xx Agriculture. History.
- --Maps.
-- --Periodicals.
-- --Statistics.
    sa Subdivision Statistics under:
       Spain. Domestic animals.
       Spain. Forestry.
       Spain. Horticulture.
       Spain. Pomology.
       Albacete, Spain. Agricul-
         ture.
       Valencia, Spain. Agriculture.
    x Agriculture. Statistics.
--Apiculture.
    sa Subdivision Apiculture under
       names of provinces, etc.
-- --Periodicals.
--Bibliography.
    xx Europe. Bibliography.
--Botany.
    sa Gibraltar.
       Catalonia.
       Madrid (Province)//
       Subdivision Spain under: Trees.
       Fungi.
       Vegetable pathology.
       Plants, Cultivated.
       Botany, Economic.
       Weeds.
       Fresh-water flora.
       Honey-bearing plants.
       Botany, Medical.
       Mosses.
       Mushrooms.
--Cattle.
    sa Subdivision Cattle under:
       Galicia, Spain//
    xx Cattle.
--Census.
    sa Subdivision Census under:
       Catalonia.
--Climate.
    sa Subdivision Spain under:
       Crops and climate.
    xx Europe. Climate.
       Crops and climate.
--Colonies.
-- --Administration.
-- --Statistics.

Spain (Continued)
--Commerce.
    sa Subdivision Commerce under
       names of provinces, cities,
       etc.
       Subdivision Spain under:
       Oil-seed trade.
       Citrus trade.
    xx Europe. Commerce.
-- --Directories.
-- --History.
    sa Subdivision Commerce. History
       under: Castile.
       Leon (Kingdom)//
-- --Periodicals.
-- --Statistics.
--Dairying.
    sa Subdivision Spain under:
       Dairy industry and trade.
--Description and travel.
--Directories.
--Domestic animals.
    sa Spain. Poultry.
       Spain. Sheep.
       Spain. Swine.
       Subdivision Domestic animals
       under: Corunna, Spain//
-- --Statistics.
--Economic conditions.
    sa Subdivision Economic condi-
       tions under: Barcelona
       (Province)//
       Subdivision Spain under:
       History, Economic.
       World War 1939-1945.
       Economic aspects.
-- --Periodicals.
-- --Statistics.
--Economic policy.
    xx Europe. Economic policy.
--Entomology.
    sa Subdivision Entomology under:
       Andalusia.
       Catalonia//
       Subdivision Spain under:
       Entomology, Economic.
       Diptera.
       Orthoptera.
       Neuroptera.
       Coleoptera.
       Hemiptera.
       Locusts.
       Trees. Pests.
-- --Periodicals.
-- --Societies.

Spain (Continued)
--Fairs.
--Fisheries.
-- --Statistics.
--Foreign relations.
--Forestry.
    sa Subdivision Spain under: Trees.
      Timber.
      Afforestation and reforesta-
        tion.
      Community forests.
      Forest policy.
      Forest products.
      Forest management.
      Subdivision Forestry under:
        Andalusia.
- --Research.
-- --Statistics.
--Gazetteers.
--Geography.
    sa Subdivision Spain under:
      Geography, Economic.
-- --Bibliography.
--Geology.
    sa Valencia.
--Goats.
--History.
    sa Spanish-American War.
      Subdivision History under:
      Spain. Commerce.
      Spain. Prices.
      Subdivision Spain under:
      History, Economic.
      Subdivision History under names
      of provinces, etc.
--Horse.
    sa Subdivision Spain under:
      Horses. Breeding.
--Horticulture.
-- --Statistics. See Gardening. Spain.
      Statistics.
--Ichthyology.
--Industries.
    sa Subdivision Spain under:
      Agricultural industries.
--Land.
    sa Subdivision Spain under:
      Land reform.
      Land laws.
      Land utilization.
      Farm valuation.
--Language. See Spanish language.
-- --Readers. See Spanish language.
    Chrestomathies and readers.
--Literature. See Spanish literature.

Spain (Continued)
--Maps.
--Markets.
    xx Markets.
--Meat supply.
--Meteorology.
--Milk supply.
--Milk trade.
--Natural history.
    sa Subdivision Natural history
      under: Valencia, Spain.
--Ornithology.
--Paleobotany.
--Paleontology.
    sa Subdivision Palentology under:
      Balearic Isles.
      Majorca.
--Parks.
    sa Subdivision Parks under:
      Murcia, Spain.
      Lisbon. Parque de liberdade.
--Politics and government.
--Pomology.
    sa Subdivision Pomology under:
      Murcia, Spain (Province)
      Rioja, Spain.
      Majorca.
      Sevilla, Spain (Province)
      Balearic Islands//
      Subdivision Spain under:
      Orange.
      Citrus.
-- --Statistics.
--Population.
    sa Subdivision Population under:
      Catalonia.
--Prices.
-- --History.
    xx Spain. History.
      Prices. History.
--Public lands.
--Research.
    sa Subdivision Research under:
      Catalonia.
--Roads.
--Sericulture.
--Sheep.
    sa Subdivision Sheep under:
      Palencia.
      Andalusia//
--Social conditions.
-- --Statistics.

Spain (Continued)
--Soils.
    sa Subdivision Spain under:
       Soil erosion. Prevention
        and control.
       Soil conservation.
       Soil erosion.
       Soil-surveys.
--Statistics.
    sa Subdivision Statistics under:
       Spain. Agriculture.
       Spain. Commerce.
       Spain. Domestic animals.
--Swine.
    sa Subdivision Swine under names
       of provinces, etc.
    xx Spain. Domestic animals.
--Viticulture.
    sa Subdivision Viticulture under:
       Andalusia.
       Malaga//
-- --Statistics.
--Water-supply.
    sa Subdivision Water-supply under:
       Madrid (Province)
       Segura Valley.
--Zoology.
    sa Subdivision Zoology under:
       Andalusia.
       Galicia//
       Subdivision Spain under:
       Fresh-water fauna.
       Marine fauna.

Spalax.

Span-worm.   See Geometridae.

Spaniards in America.

Spaniels.
    sa Pekingese spaniels.
    x Cocker spaniel.
      Springer spaniels.
    xx Dogs.
--Periodicals.

Spanish America.
    sa America, Tropical.
      South America.
    x Hispanic America.
      Latin America.
    xx South America.

Spanish America (Continued)
--Agricultural experiment stations.
-- --Directories.
    xx Agricultural experiment sta-
       tions. Directories.
--Agriculture.
    sa Subdivision Spanish America
       under: Rice.
       Cereals.
       Coffee.
       Agricultural policies and
        programs.
       War and agriculture (1939-
        1945)
       Agriculture. Cooperative.
       Agriculture. Economic as-
        pects.
       Fiber plants and vegetable
        fibers.
       Tobacco.
       Agricultural laborers.
       Agricultural surveys.
       Agricultural credit.
       Colonization, Agricultural.
       Agricultural extension.
-- --Bibliography.
-- --Congresses.
-- --Education.
    sa Subdivision Spanish America
       under: Agricultural ex-
       tension.
-- -- --Directories.
    xx Agriculture. Education. Direc-
       tories.
       Spanish America. Education.
        Directories.
-- --Statistics.
--Apiculture.
-- --Periodicals.
--Bibliography.
-- --Periodicals.
--Botany.
    sa Subdivision Spanish America
       under: Botany, Economic.
       Ferns.
       Oleaginous plants.
       Vegetable pathology.
-- --History.
--Boundaries.
-- --Bibliography.
    xx Boundaries. Bibliography.
--Civilization.
    sa Subdivision Civilization under:
       West Indies.

Spanish America (Continued)
--Civilization.
    sa Subdivision Spanish America
        under: Art.
    xx Civilization.
--Commerce.
    sa Subdivision Spanish America
        under: Fruit trade.
        Coffee trade.
- --Europe.
- --U.S.
-- --Directories.
-- --History.
    xx Commerce. History.
-- --Statistics.
--Commercial policy.
--Commercial treaties.
    xx Commercial treaties.
--Cyclopedias.
--Dairying.
-- --Bibliography.
--Defenses.
    xx Defenses.
-- --Bibliography.
    xx Defenses. Bibliography.
--Description and travel.
--Economic conditions.
    sa Subdivision Spanish America
        under: Geography, Economic.
        History, Economic.
        World War, 1939-1945. Eco-
          nomic aspects.
        Economic surveys.
-- --Bibliography.
    xx Economic conditions. Bibliog-
        raphy.
-- --Congresses.
-- --Periodicals.
    xx Economic conditions. Peri-
        odicals.
--Economic policy.
    sa Subdivision Economic policy
        under: South America.
--Education.
-- --Directories.
    sa Subdivision Education. Direc-
        tories under: Spanish
        America. Agriculture.
--Emigration and immigration.
    sa Japanese in Spanish America.
        Chinese in Spanish America.
--Entomology.
    sa Subdivision Spanish America
        under: Locusts.
--Fisheries.

Spanish America (Continued)
--Foreign relations.
-- --Periodicals.
-- --Treaties.
--Forestry.
    sa Subdivision Spanish America
        under: Timber.
        Forest policy.
-- --Bibliography.
-- --Periodicals.
-- --Research.
--Geographic names.
--Geography.
    sa Subdivision Spanish America
        under: Geography, Economic.
--Government publications.
-- --Bibliography.
    xx Spanish America. Bibliography.
    Government publications. Bib-
        liography.
--History.
    sa Subdivision Spanish America
        under: History, Economic.
        Geography, Historical.
-- --Bibliography.
    sa History, Economic. Spanish
        America. Bibliography.
-- --Sources.
    sa Subdivision Spanish America
        under: Archives.
--Industries.
-- --Bibliography.
--Intellectual life.
--Land.
    sa Subdivision Spanish America
        under: Land tenure.
        Land reform.
--Language.
    sa Subdivision Language under:
        Portugal.
        Spain.
--Law.
--Laws, statutes, etc.
--Learned institutions and societies.
    xx Learned institutions and
        societies.
-- --Bibliography.
    xx Learned institutions and
        societies. Bibliography.
--Libraries.
    xx America. Libraries.
--Literature.   See Spanish-American
    literature.

Spanish America (Continued)
--Maps.
 sa Subdivision Maps under:
  South America.
-- --Bibliography.
 xx America. Maps. Bibliography.
--Natural history.
 sa Subdivision Natural history
  under: Central America.
  South America.
 xx America. Natural history.
--Parks.
 sa Subdivision Spanish America
  under: National parks and
  reserves.
--Periodicals. See Spanish-American
 periodicals.
--Politics and government.
--Pomology.
 xx Pomology.
--Population.
 xx Population.
--Public lands.
--Relations (general) with the U.S.
--Research.
 xx Research.
--Roads.
 sa Inter-American highway.
--Social conditions.
 xx Social conditions.
-- --Bibliography.
 xx Social conditions. Bibliography.
 Spanish America. Bibliography.
--Soils.
-- --Bibliography.
 sa Spanish America. Bibliography
  under: Soil conservation.
 xx Soil. Bibliography.
--Statistics.
-- --Bibliography.
--Transportation.
 xx Transportation.
-- --Bibliography.
 xx Spanish America. Bibliography.
 America. Transportation. Bib-
  liography.

Spanish-American literature.
 sa Cuban literature.
 Mexican literature.
 Peruvian literature.
 Venezuelan literature.
 x Spanish America. Literature.
--Bibliography.
-- --Periodicals.

Spanish-American literature (Continued)
--Bio-bibliography.
--History and criticism.
 xx Literature. History and
  criticism.
--Translations into English.
-- --Bibliography.

Spanish-American newspapers.
--Directories.

Spanish-American periodicals.
 sa Ecuadorean periodicals.
 Venezuelan periodicals.
 x Spanish America. Periodicals.
--Abstracts.
--Bibliography.

Spanish-American War.
 x U.S. History. Spanish-American
  War.

Spanish-Americans in Colorado.

Spanish-Americans in the U.S.
--Food habits.
 xx Food habits.

Spanish broom. See Spartium junceum.

Spanish chestnut trees. See Castanea
 sativa.

Spanish drama.
 xx Drama.

Spanish fiction.
 sa Short stories, Spanish.
 xx Spanish literature.

Spanish fir. See Abies Pinsapo.

Spanish flies, Tincture of. See
 Cantharides, Tincture of.

Spanish Fork River, Utah.
 sa Subdivision Utah. Spanish
  Fork River under:
  Irrigation.

Spanish grass. See Alfa.

Spanish Guinea.
--Agriculture.

Spanish Guinea (Continued)
--Botany.
--Climate.
--Commerce.
--Economic conditions.
--Entomology.
    sa Subdivision Spanish Guinea
        under: Coleoptera.
--Forestry.
    sa Subdivision Spanish Guinea
        under: Timber.
        Forest policy.
--Native races.
--Natural history.
--Ornithology.
--Physical geography.
--Soils.
--Statistics.
--Zoology.
    xx Guinea. Zoology.

Spanish language.
    x Spain. Language.
--Chrestomathies and readers.
    x Spain. Language. Readers.
--Composition and exercises.
--Dictionaries.
--Glossaries, vocabularies, etc.
--Grammar.
--Idioms, corrections, errors.
--Provincialisms.   (DIRECT)

Spanish literature.
    sa Spanish fiction.
    x Spain. Literature.
--Addresses, essays, lectures.
--Bibliography.
--Translations into English.
-- --Bibliography.

Spanish missions of California.

Spanish moss.   See Tillandsia usneoides.

Spanish newspapers.
--Bibliography.

Spanish paprika.   See Red pepper.

Spanish periodicals.
--Bibliography.
--Indexes.
--Statistics.

Spanish sembrador.   See Seed-drill.

Spanish walnut oil.   See Kukui oil.

Spanish West Africa.
    This form is used only as an
    author entry for official pub-
    lications of the government
    of Spanish West Africa."Sub-
    ject entries are under Africa,
    Spanish West.

Sparganiaceae.
    sa Sparganium.
    Typha.

Sparganium.

Sparganothis pilleriana.

Sparganum.

Sparganum mansoni.

Sparganum proliferum.

Sparidae.

Spark arresters.
    xx Fire prevention.

Sparks and spark arresters.
    sa Locomotive sparks.

Sparrows.
    sa English sparrow.
    Fringillidae.
    Acanthidops.
    xx Passeres.
--Diseases.
    xx Birds. Diseases.

Sparteine.   See Lupine alkaloids.

Spartina.

Spartina townsendii.   See Rice grass.

Spartium junceum.
    x Spanish broom.

Spartopyge.
    xx Cicadellidae.

Spasmolysis.   See Antispasmodics.

Spasskii district.
--Agriculture.
    sa Subdivision Spasskii district
       under: Agriculture. Economic
       aspects.

Spatallopsis.

Spathe borer.   See Tirathaba trichogramma.

Spavin.
    xx Hock. Diseases.

Spavinaw, Lake.
    xx Oklahoma.

Spaying.
    sa Castration.
    xx Veterinary surgery.
       Castration.

Speaking.   See Oratory.

Spear fishing.
    xx Fishing.

Spear grass.   See Andropogon contortus.

Spearmint.
--Statistics.

Spearmint oil.

Special book collections in libraries.
   See Libraries, Special collections.

Special collections in libraries.   See
   Libraries. Special collections.

Special districts.   (DIRECT)
    Special districts are governmental
    units established by local ac-
    tion in accordance with au-
    thorizing State laws or direct-
    ly by State legislation. Most
    of them are responsible for
    performing only a single func-
    tion. Special districts are,
    in most instances, set up only
    to serve certain areas or to
    provide facilities at parti-
    cular locations.
    x Districts, Special.

Special districts (Continued)
    xx Local government.
       School districts.
       Soil conservation districts.

Special libraries.   See Libraries,
   Special.

Special school milk program.   See
   School milk programs.

Species.
    sa Evolution.
       Mutation theory.
       Type species.

Species, Extinction of.

Species, Origin of.   See Species.

Specific gravity.
    sa Subdivision Specific gravity
       under: Seeds.
       Wheat.
       Eggs.
       Wood.
       Turpentine.
       Veneer.
       Plywood.
--Tables.   See Specific gravity tables.

Specific gravity of plant substances.

Specific gravity tables.
    x Specific gravity. Tables.

Specific heat.
    sa Vaporization, Heats of.
       Thermal diffusivity.
    x Heat, Specific.
    xx Calorimeters and calorimetry.

Specifications.
    sa Building. Estimates.
       Subdivision Contracts and
         specifications or Speci-
         fications under special
         subjects, e.g., Building.
         Contracts and specifica-
         tions; Commercial products.
         Specifications.
--Congresses.

Specimens.
--Preservation. See Natural history.
Technique; Pathological specimens.
Collection and preservation.

Speckled leaf blotch of wheat.
sa Septoria tritici.
x Leaf blotch of wheat.
xx Wheat. Diseases.

Spectra color temperature meter.

Spectrochemical analysis. See Spectrochemistry.

Spectrochemistry.
x Spectrochemical analysis.
xx Chemistry, Analytic.
Spectrum analysis.
--Bibliography.
--Periodicals.

Spectrograph.
xx Spectroscope.

Spectroheliograph.

Spectrometer.
sa Mass spectrometry.

Spectrometry. See Spectrum analysis.

Spectrophotometry.
--Abstracts.
--Bibliography.

Spectroscope.
sa Spectrograph.
xx Spectrum analysis.

Spectroscopy. See Spectrum analysis.

Spectrum.

Spectrum, Infra-red.
sa Infra-red rays.
x Ultra-red spectrum.
Spectrum. Ultra-red.
Infra-red spectrum.
Light, Invisible.
Rays, Invisible.
xx Spectrum analysis.

Spectrum, Microwave.
x Microwave spectroscopy.

Spectrum, Ultra-red. See Spectrum,
Infra-red.

Spectrum, Ultra-violet.
sa Ultra-violet rays.
--Indexes.

Spectrum analysis.
sa Optical analysis.
Astrophysics.
Raman effect.
Spectrum, Infra-red.
Spectroscope.
Spectrochemistry.
Mass spectrometry.
x Spectroscopy.
Spectrometry.
--Abstracts.
--Bibliography.
--Congresses.
--Periodicals.
xx Physics. Periodicals.
--Tables, etc.

Spectrum femoratum.

Speculation (in business)
sa Subdivision Speculation under:
Cotton.
Wheat.
Tobacco.
Future trading.
Produce trade.
Stock exchange.
Produce exchange.
Land speculation.
Commodity exchanges.
x Corners, Commercial.
xx Commodity exchanges.
--Bibliography.
sa Subdivision Bibliography un-
der: Future trading.
--Graphic methods.
xx Graphic methods.

Speculation (in land) See Land speculation.

Speech.

Speech, Disorders of.

Speech.
--Terminology.

Speech correction.   See Speech therapy.

Speech of insects.   See Communication
among insects.

Speech preparation.   See Speeches, addresses, etc. Preparation.

Speech therapy.
x Speech correction.

Speeches, addresses, etc.
sa Oratory.
Subdivision Addresses, essays,
lectures, under particular
subjects, e.g., Agriculture.
Addresses, essays, lectures.
x Orations.
Addresses.
--Preparation.
x Speech preparation.
xx Manuscript preparation.

Speleology.   See Caves.

Spellers.

Spelling.   See Subdivision Orthography
and spelling under names of languages,
e.g., Dutch language. Orthography and
spelling.

Spelling reform.
xx Orthography.

Spelt.
x Triticum spelta.

Spelter.   See Zinc.

Spence bill.   See Economic stability act
of 1949.

Spencer Co., Ind.
--Agriculture.
-- --Periodicals.

Spengler's tuberculin (I.K. immunkörper)

Sperda populeana.

Spergon.
x Tetrachloro-para-benzoquinone.

Spergula.
sa Spurry.

Sperm.   See Semen.

Spermaceti.

Spermacoce.

Spermatic duct.   See Vas deferens.

Spermatochnaceae.

Spermatogenesis.
sa Ovogenesis.

Spermatophytes.
sa Gymnosperms.
Angiospermae.
x Seed plants.
Phanerogams.

Spermatozoa.
sa Semen.

Spermogonium.

Spermophilus.   See Ground-squirrels.

Spessart Mountains.
--Forestry.
sa Subdivision Spessart Mountains
under: Afforestation and
reforestation.
--Social conditions.
sa Subdivision Germany. Spessart
Mountains under: Social
surveys.

Sphacelariaceae.
xx Algae.

Sphaceloma.

Sphaceloma perseae.

Sphacelotheca cruenta.

Sphacelotheca sorghi.

Sphaeria typhina.

Sphaeriaceae.
  sa Nummularia.
   Glomerella.
   Phaeosporae.
   Melanops.
   Trichosphaeria.
   Dilophia.
   Physalospora.
   Venturia inequalis.
   Rosellinia.

Sphaeriales.

Sphaeriidae.

Sphaeriodesminae.

Sphaeritidae.

Sphaerocarpos.

Sphaerocarpos donnellii.

Sphaeroceridae. See Borboridae.

Sphaerococcaceae.
  sa Hypnea.
   Gracilaria.
  xx Algae.

Sphaerococcoideae.
  sa Sphaerococcus.

Sphaerococcus confervoides.

Sphaerococcus coronopifolius.

Sphaeroidaceae.
  sa Ascochyta.
   Sphaeronema.

Sphaeromidae.

Sphaeronema fimbriatum. See Ceratostom-
ella fimbriata.

Sphaeropleaceae.

Sphaeropsidaceae.
  sa Glutinium.
   Sphaeropsis.
   Macrophoma.
   Nectrioidaceae.
   Trichoseptoria.
   Excipulaceae.

Sphaeropsidaceae (Continued)
  sa Plenodomus.
   Septoria.
   Dendrophoma.
   Vermicularia.
   Pimulus.
   Phomopsis.
   Stagonospora.

Sphaeropsidales.
  sa Sphaeropsidaceae.
   Excipulaceae.
  xx Deuteromycetes.

Sphaeropsis malorum.

Sphaeropsis tumefaciens.

Sphaerosoma.

Sphaerotheca castagnei.

Sphaerotheca mors uvae.

Sphaerotherium.

Sphaerotrypes.
  xx Scolytidae.

Sphaerotrypes siwalikensis.
  x Sal bark-borer.
  xx Shorea robusta. Pests.

Sphagnaceae.
  sa Sphagnum.

Sphagnum.
  x Sphagnum moss.
  --Diseases.

Sphagnum moors.

Sphagnum moss. See Sphagnum.

Spharagemon.
  xx Acridiidae.

Spheariaceae.
  sa Titania.
   Prosthecium.

Sphecidae.
  sa Ampulex.
   Sphex.
   Sceliphron.

Sphecidae (Continued)
  sa Dindineis.
   Pseninae.
   Eucerceris.
   Sphecius.
  x Sphegidae.
  xx Sphecoidea.

Sphecius.
  xx Sphecidae.

Sphecius speciosus.
  x Cicada-killer wasp.

Sphecodes gibbus.

Sphecoidea.
  sa Sphecidae.
  x Sphegoidea.
   Digger wasps.
   Fossores.
   Hymenoptera, Fossorial.
   Wasps, Fossorial.

Sphegidae. See Sphecidae.

Sphegoidea. See Sphecoidea.

Spheniscidae. See Penguins.

Sphenoclea zeylanica.

Sphenophorus. See Calendra.

Sphenodontidae.
  sa Opisthias.

Sphenophyllaceae.

Spherarmadillo.

Sphere.
  sa Trigonometry, Spherical.
  xx Trigonometry, Spherical.

Spherical trigonometry. See Trigonometry,
  Spherical.

Sphex.

Sphex fervens.

Sphingidae.
  sa Sphinx.
   Protoparce.
   Ceratomia.
   Acherontia.
   Cephonodes.
   Dilophonota.
   Phlegethontius.
   Thyreus.

Sphingine.
  xx Sphingosine.

Sphingosine.
  sa Sphingine.
  x Dihydrosphingosine.

Sphinx vespiformis.

Sphygmomanometer.

Sphyriidae.

Sphyroncotaenia.

Sphyrorrhina.

Spices.
  sa Cardamoms.
   Nutmeg.
   Pepper.
   Cinnamon.
   Ginger.
   Paprika.
   Clove.
   Red pepper.
   Condiments.
   Aromatic plants.
  xx Condiments.
 --Ash analysis.
  xx Ash analysis.
 --Bibliography.
  sa Subdivision Bibliography under:
   Pepper.
 --Dictionaries.
 --Grading and standardization.
  sa Spices. Inspection.
  xx Spices. Standards.
 --Inspection.
  sa Subdivision Inspection under:
   Clove.
 --Periodicals.
 --Prices.
  sa Subdivision Prices under:
   Clove.

Spices (Continued)
--Societies.
--Standards.   See Spices. Grading and
     standardization.   :
--Statistics.
     sa Subdivision Statistics under:
          Clove.
--Year-books.

Spiciformis.   See Brachystegia spici-
     formis.

Spider beetles.   See Ptinus.

Spider-crabs.
     x Oxyrhyncha.
     xx Crabs.

Spider mite.   See Tetranychus telarius.

Spider venom.
     xx Arachnolysin.

Spider-webs.
     xx Araneida.

Spider-wort.   See Commelinaceae; Trades-
     cantia.

Spiderlilies, Red.
--Parasites.   See Lycoris radiata. Para-
     sites.

Spiders.   See Araneida.

Spigelia.

Spigelia anthelmia.

Spigelia marilandica.

Spike-disease of sandal.

Spike-horned leaf-miner.   See Cerodonta
     dorsalis.

Spilanthes.

Spilanthes acmella.

Spilanthes uliginosa.

Spillways.
     xx Hydraulic engineering.

Spilographa electa.
     x Pepper maggot.

Spilonota ocellana.
     x Bud-moth.
          Eye-spotted bud-moth.
          Tmetocera.ocellano.

Spilosoma.   See Diacrisia.

Spinach.
     sa Vitamins in spinach.
          Cookery (Spinach)

Spinach, Canned.
     xx Greens, Canned.
--Grading and standardization.
     xx Vegetables, Canned. Grading
          and standardization.
--Statistics.

Spinach, Canning.

Spinach.
--Diseases.

Spinach, Frozen.
--Grading and standardization.
     xx Vegetables, Frozen. Grading
          and standardization.
          Spinach. Grading and stand-
               ardization.

Spinach.
--Grading and standardization.
     sa Subdivision Grading and stand-
          ardization under: Spinach,
          Frozen.
     xx Vegetables. Grading and stand-
          ardization.
--Inspection.
--Marketing.
     xx Vegetables. Marketing.
--Packaging.
     xx Packaging.
--Prices.
     xx Vegetables. Prices.
--Statistics.
     xx Vegetables. Statistics.

Spinach leaf miner.   See Pegomyia vicina;
     Pegomyia hyoscyami.

Spinal cord.
xx Nervous system.
--Diseases.
sa Azoturia.

Spinal meningitis.   See Meningitis.

Spindle shaped fruit trees.·
x Fruit trees, Spindle shaped.
xx Dwarf fruit trees.
Pomology.

Spindle-tree.   See Evonymus europaeus;
Evonymus verrucosa.

Spindle worm.   See Achatodes zeae.

Spindles.
--Statistics.
xx Spinning machinery. Statistics.

Spindling tuber.

Spine.

Spined soldier bug.   See Podisus macu-
liventris.

Spines (Botany)

Spiniger rubropictus.

Spinning.
sa Flax spinning.
Yarn strength.
Cotton spinning.
Wool spinning.
Rayon spinning.
--Bibliography.
--Periodicals.
sa Subdivision Periodicals under:
Cotton spinning.
--Societies.

Spinning machinery.
sa Spinning-wheel.
x Cotton spinning machinery.
xx Cotton. Implements and machinery.
--Periodicals.
xx Machinery.
--Repairing.
xx Textile machinery. Repairing.

Spinning machinery (Continued)
--Statistics.
sa Subdivision Statistics under:
Spindles.
xx Machinery. Statistics.

Spinning tackle.   See Fishing. Implements and appliances.

Spinning tests.
sa Subdivision Spinning tests
under: Cotton.

Spinning-wheel.
xx Spinning machinery.

Spinose ear tick.   See Ornithodoros
megini.

Spinturnix.

Spiny citrus white fly.   See Aleurocan-
thus woglumi.

Spiny pocket mouse.   See Heteromys;
Liomys.

Spioniformia.
xx Annelida.

Spiraea.

Spiral flag.   See Costus speciosus.

Spiral grain.   See Grain·in wood.

Spiral gutters.   See Gutters.

Spirillaceae.

Spirillosis.   See Spirochaetosis.

Spirits.   See Liquors.

Spirits, Distilled.   See Liquors,
Distilled.

Spirits of turpentine.   See Turpentine
oil.

Spiritual life.
xx Religion.

Spirobolus.

Spirochaeta cytophaga.

Spirochaeta recurrentis.

Spirochaetaceae.
    sa Spirochaeta.

Spirochaetae.

Spirochaetal jaundice.   See Leptospirosis.

Spirochaetosis.
    sa Framboesia.
    x Spirochetal diseases.
  --Bibliography.
  --Maps.

Spirochaetosis (Poultry)

Spirochaetosis (Rabbits)

Spirochetal diseases.   See Spirochaetosis.

Spirocladia barodensis.

Spirodela polyrhiza.
    x Spirodela polyrrhizza.   .

Spirodela polyrrhizza.   See Spirodela
    polyrhiza.

Spirogyra.
    xx Algae.

Spirogyra longata.

Spironoura.
    xx Nematoda.

Spiroptera.

Spiroptera obtusa.

Spirorbis.
    xx Annelida.

Spirotrichonympha polygyra.

Spitsbergen.   See Spitzbergen.

Spittle insects.   See Cercopidae.

Spitz (Dogs)

Spitzbergen.
    x Spitsbergen.
  --Botany.
    sa Subdivision Spitzbergen under:
        Fungi.
    xx Arctic regions. Botany.
  --Description and travel.
  --Entomology.
  --Ornithology.
  --Paleontology.
  --Zoology.
    sa Subdivision Spitzbergen under:
        Marine fauna.
        Arachnida.
    xx Arctic regions. Zoology.

Splachnaceae.
    sa Splachnum.

Splachnum.

Splanchnology.   See Viscera.

Spleen.
  --Diseases.

Spleenwort.   See Asplenium.

Splenic fever.   See Tick fever.

Splices.   See Knots and splices.

Split-peas.   See Peas, Split.

Spodoptera abyssinia.
    x Lawn caterpillar.

Spodoptera mauritia.

Spogostylum.
    x Argyramoeba.

Spogostylum oedipus.

Spokane Co., Wash.
  --Agriculture.
    sa Subdivision Washington (State)
        Spokane Co. under: Agri-
        cultural credit.
        Agriculture. Economic as-
        pects.
  --Land.
    sa Subdivision Washington (State)
        Spokane Co. under: Land
        utilization.

Spokane River.
       sa Subdivision Spokane River
           under: Flood control.

Spokane Valley project (Wash. and Idaho)

Spöl River.
   --Power utilization.
       xx National parks and reserves.

Spondylidae.
       sa Parandra.

Spondylocladium cladium.

Sponge spicules.

Sponges.

Sponges, Fossil.

Sponges, Vegetable.   See Luffa.

Sponsor (Insects)
       xx Buprestidae.

Spontaneous combustion.   See Combustion,
   Spontaneous.

Spoon River Valley, Ill.
       xx Illinois.

Spoonbills.
       sa Roseata spoonbills.

Sporangia.

Sporangium.
       sa Microsporangia.

Sporeforming bacteria.   See Bacteria,
   Sporeforming.

Spores.
       sa Ascospores.
          Asci.
          Sporangia.
          Gametogenesis.
          Microsporangia.
          Zygospores.
          Fungi. Spore germination.
          Fungus spores.
          Bacteria, Sporeforming.
   --Bibliography.
   -- --Periodicals.

Spores (Continued)
   --Periodicals.

Sporobolus.
       x Dropseed grass.

Sporobolus flexuosus.
       x Mesa dropseed grass.

Sporochnaceae.

Sporodesmium scorzonerae.

Sporodesmium warsowiensis.

Sporogenes test.   See Milk. Sporogenes
   test.

Sporolithon.

Sporotrichiella.

Sporotrichum densum.   See Isaria densa.

Sporotrichosis.

Sporotrichum globuliferum.

Sporozoa.
       sa Cnidosporidia.
          Zygocyctis cometa.
          Plasmodium.
          Leucocytozoon.
   --Bibliography.

Sports.
       sa Fishing.
          Hunting.
          Horse racing.
          Skis and ski-running.
          Winter sports.
          Games.
       xx Games.
   --Bibliography.
   --Bio-bibliography.
   --Dictionaries.
   --Medical treatment and training.
   --Periodicals.
   --Societies.

Sports stories.
       sa Fishing stories.
          Hunting stories.

Spot analysis.   See Spot tests (Chemistry)

Spot disease of violet.   See Alternaria
    violae.

Spot reactions.   See Spot tests
    (Chemistry)

Spot tests (Chemistry)
    x Drop tests (Chemistry)
      Spot analysis.
      Spot reactions.
    xx Chemical tests and reagents.
      Chemistry, Analytic. Qualita-
        tive.
      Microchemistry.

Spotsylvania Co., Va.
--Economic conditions.
    sa Economic surveys. Virginia.
      Spotsylvania Co.
    xx Virginia. Economic conditions.
--Social conditions.
    sa Subdivision Virginia. Spot-
      sylvania Co. under: Social
      surveys.

Spotted alfalfa aphid.   See Ptero-
    callidium trifoli.

Spotted beet webworm.   See Hymenia per-
    spectalis.

Spotted boil-worm of cotton.   See Earias
    fabia; Earias insulana.

Spotted cattle (Fleckvieh)   See Simmental
    cattle.

Spotted cucumber beetle.   See Diabrotica
    undecimpunctata howardi.

Spotted-fever tick.   See Dermacentor
    venustus.

Spotted fever of the Rocky mountains.
    See Rocky mountain spotted fever.

Spotted garden slug.   See Limax maximus.

Spotted gum.

Spotted mountain cattle.   See Simmental
    cattle.

Spotted Poland-China swine.
--Congresses.

Spotted wilt of tomatoes.
    xx Tomato wilt.
      Tomatoes. Diseases.
      Virus diseases of tomatoes.

Spotting (Cleaning)   See Stains. Re-
    moval.

Sprat.

Spray injury.   See Spraying. Injurious
    effects.

Spray irrigation.
    x Irrigation, Spray.
      Irrigation, Overhead.
      Sprinkler irrigation.
    xx Irrigation.
      Rainfall. Artificial.
--Periodicals.

Spray residue.   See Spraying and dusting
    residues.

Spray vaccine.
    xx Vaccine.

Sprayed fruits.
--Analysis.
-- --Bibliography.

Spraying.
    sa Copper sulphate.
      Nicotine-sulphate spray.
      Water as a spray.
      Bordeaux-oil emulsion.
      Dusting.
      Sulphuric acid.
      Black leaf 40.
      Oil as an insecticide.
      Fungicides.
      Insecticides.
      Pyrethrum as an insecticide.
      Herbicides.
    xx Entomology, Economic.
      Vegetable pathology.

Spraying, Airplane.   See Airplanes in
    weed eradication; Airplanes in insect
    control.

Spraying.
--Apples.
          x Apple. Spraying.
            Apple spraying.
--Banana.
          x Banana. Spraying.
            Banana spraying.
--Beans, Lima.
-- --Seed.
          x Beans, Lima. Seed. Spraying.
--Berries.
          x Berries. Spraying.
--Cacao.
--Cherry.
          x Cherry. Spraying.
--Coffee.
--Costs.
--Cotton.
          x Cotton. Spraying.
--Effect on citrus.
--Effect on peaches.
--Egg-plant.
--Equipment.   See Spraying apparatus.
--Evergreens.
          x Evergreens. Spraying.
--Field crops.
--Fruit.
          x Fruit. Spraying.
            Fruit spraying.
--Grapes.
          x Grapes. Spraying.
--Injurious effects.
          sa Spraying and dusting residues.
            Subdivision Spray injury under:
                Cherry.
                Ginseng.
                Peach.
                Prune.
                Cucumbers.
                Apple.
                Grapes.
                Kidney bean.
--Maize.
          x Maize. Spraying.
--Olive.
          x Olive. Spraying.
--Peach.
--Pear.
          x Pear. Spraying.
            Pear spraying.
--Plants, Ornamental.
--Plum.
          x Plum. Spraying.
--Potatoes.
          x Potatoes. Spraying.

Spraying (Continued)
--Roses.
          x Roses. Spraying.
--Tobacco.
          x Tobacco. Spraying.
--Tomatoes.
          x Tomatoes. Spraying.
--Vegetables.
          x Vegetables. Spraying.
--Weeds.
          x Weeds. Spraying.

Spraying and dusting residues.
          sa Spraying. Injurious effects.
            Food. Insecticide contamina-
              tion.
          x Fungicide residues.
            Residues from spraying and
              dusting.
            Pesticide residues.
            Insecticide residues.
            Spray residues.
          xx Insecticides.
--Abstracts.
--Bibliography.
--Congresses.
--Effect on field crops.
--Patents.
          xx Patents.
--Research.
--Testing.

Spraying apparatus.
          sa Mist blowers.
            Aerosol machines.
          x Insecticides. Equipment.
            Insecticides. Apparatus and
              equipment.
            Spraying. Equipment.
            Spraying equipment.
            Spraying machine.
          xx Agriculture. Implements and
              machinery.

Spraying apparatus, Airplane.
          x Airplanes in insect control.
            Apparatus.
--Bibliography.
--Congresses.

Spraying apparatus, Tractor.
          xx Traction-engines in agri-
              culture.

Spraying equipment.   See Spraying appa-
    ratus.

Spraying machine.   See Spraying apparatus.

Spraying pumps.

Spreading fruit trees.
    x Spreading orchards.
      Near-the-ground growing trees.
    xx Pomology.
      Dwarf fruit trees.

Spreading orchards.   See Spreading fruit
trees.

Spring adonis.   See Adonis vernalis.

Spring Co., N.Y. Benevolent and Moral
    Institutions and Societies.
    xx Charitable societies.

Spring Creek Valley, Minn.
    sa Subdivision Minnesota. Spring
      Creek Valley under: Flood
      control.

Spring Mill State Park, Ind.

Spring season.

Spring tails.   See Collembola.

Spring wheat.   See Wheat.

Springer spaniels.   See Spaniels.

Springfield, Idaho.
    --Entomology.
      sa Subdivision Idaho. Springfield
        under: Orthoptera.

Springfield, Ill.
    --Politics and government.
      xx Municipal government. Illinois.

Springfield, Mass. Art Museum.

Springfield, Mass.
    --Botany.
      xx Massachusetts. Botany.
    --History.
      xx Massachusetts. History.
    --Hygiene.
    --Ornithology.

Springfield, Mo.
    --Milk trade.

Springfield, Ohio.
    --Milk trade.

Springs.
    xx Water-supply.

Springs (Mechanism)

Springtail insects.   See Collembola.

Sprinkler irrigation.   See Spray
    irrigation.

Sprout forests.

Sprout prevention.
    sa Subdivision Sprout prevention
      under: Potatoes.
      Root-crops//

Sprouted soy-beans.   See Soy-bean
    sprouts.

Sprouting.
    Used for works dealing with some
      extension of germination. For
      materials limited to germi-
      nation and viability of seeds,
      See Germination.
    sa Subdivision Sprouting under:
      Potatoes.
      Wheat.
    xx Germination.

Sprouts, Brussels.   See Brussels
    sprouts.

Spruce.
    sa Picea excelsa.
      Picea engelmanni.
      Picea sitchensis.
      Pseudotsuga macrocarpa.
      Picea canadensis.
      Picea breweriana.
      Picea mariana.
      Picea parryana.
      Picea rubens.
      Picea omorica.
    xx Arboriculture.
    --Bibliography.
      sa Picea sitchensis. Bibliog-
        raphy.

Spruce, Black.   See Picea mariana.

Spruce.
--Diseases.
    sa Subdivision Diseases under:
        Picea engelmanni.
        Picea sitchensis.
        Picea abies.
        Spruce canker.
--Growth.
    sa Coniferae. Growth.
        Trees. Growth.
--Pests.
    sa Dendroctonus piceaperda.
        Chermes abietis.

Spruce, Red.   See Picea rubens.

Spruce, Schrenk.   See Picea schrenkiana.

Spruce.
--Seed.
    sa Subdivision Seed under:
        Picea rubens.
        Picea abies.
        Picea mariana.
--Seedlings.
--Utilization tables.
    xx Wood. Utilization tables.

Spruce bark beetle.   See Dendroctonus
    piceaperda.

Spruce budworm.   See Choristoneura fumi-
    ferana.

Spruce canker.
    xx Spruce. Diseases.

Spruce gall-aphid.   See Chermes abietis.

Spruce gum.
    xx Gums and resins.

Spruce sawfly.   See Neodiprion abietis.

Spruce sawfly, Small.   See Pristiphora
    abietina.

Spruce sawfly, Yellow-headed.   See
    Pikonema alaskensis.

Sprue, Tropical.   See Aphthae tropicae.

Spumaria alba.

Spurge, Leafy.   See Euphorbia esula.

Spurge nettle.   See Jatropha stimulosa.

Spurry.   See Spergula.

Sputum.

Squabs.   See Pigeons.

Squalls.

Squamariaceae.

Squares.

Squash.
    x Marrow, Vegetable.
        Marrow squash.
        Vegetable marrow.
        Acorn squash.
        Squash, Acorn.

Squash, Acorn.   See Squash.

Squash, Canned.
--Grading and standardization.
    xx Vegetables, Canned. Grading
        and standardization.
--Statistics.

Squash.
--Freezing and frost injury.

Squash, Frozen.
    xx Vegetables, Frozen.
--Grading and standardization.

Squash.
--Grading and standardization.
    xx Vegetables. Grading and
        standardization.
--Statistics.
--Storage.

Squash-bug.   See Anasa tristis.

Squash lady-bird beetle.   See Epilachna
    borealis.

Squash-vine borer.   See Melittia saty-
    riniformis.

Squids.

Squill, Red.   See Urginea maritima.

Squirrel-corn.   See Bikukulla canadensis.

Squirrel traps.
    xx Squirrels. Eradication.
       Trapping.

Squirrels.
    x Tree squirrels.
      Fox squirrels.
      Sciuridae.
      Gray squirrel.
      Squirrels, Tree.
  --Eradication.
      sa Squirrel traps.

Squirrels, Ground.   See Ground-squirrels.

Squirrels.
  --Parasites.

Squirrels, Tree.   See Squirrels.

Sredniaia Aziia.   See Asia, Central.

Ssuch'uan.   See Szechuan.

Stabilization act of 1942.

Stabilization of soil.   See Soil. Stabi-
    lization.

Stabilizers.   See Stabilizing agents.

Stabilizing agents.
    x Food stabilizers.
      Stabilizers.

Stable fly.   See Stomoxys calcitrans.

Stables.   See Barns and stables.

Stachyose.

Stachys.
    xx Menthaceae.

Stachys affinis.

Stachys tuberifera.   See Stachys affinis.

Stachyuraceae.

Stackhousiaceae.

Stacking of lumber.   See Lumber. Piling.

Stacks (for books)   See Shelving (for
    books)

Stacks (Hay, grain, etc.)

Stade, Ger. (Regierungsbezirk)
  --Cattle.
  --Domestic animals.

Stadia tables.
    xx Leveling.
       Surveying. Tables, etc.

Stafford Co., Kan.
  --Land.
      sa Subdivision Kansas. Stafford
          Co. under: Land utilization.
  --Soils.
      sa Subdivision Kansas. Stafford
          Co. under: Soil conserva-
          tion surveys.

Staffordshire, Eng.
  --Agriculture.
  --Botany.
  --Natural history.
  --Paleobotany.

Staffordshire bull terriers.   See
    Staffordshire terriers.

Staffordshire terriers.
      x Staffordshire bull terriers.
      xx Bull-terriers.

Stagger grass.   See Chrosperma muscae-
    toxicum.

Staggers.
      sa Grass tetany.

Stagmomantis.

Stagonospora.
      xx Sphaeropsidaceae.

Stain in lumber.
      sa Ceratostomella.
         Wood staining fungi.
       x Blue stain in lumber.
         Sap stain in lumber.
         Lumber stain.
         Log blue.

Stain in lumber (Continued)
    x Molds in wood.
      Sapstain in lumber.
    xx Wood staining fungi.

Stain removal. See Stains. Removal.

Staining methods. See Stains and
  staining (Microscopy)

Stainless steel. See Steel, Stainless.

Stains.
 --Removal.
      sa Cleaning.
      x Spotting (Cleaning)
        Stain removal.

Stains and staining.
      sa Cleaning.
        Polishes.
        Wood finishing.
      xx Finishes and finishing.

Stains and staining (Microscopy)
      xx Dyes and dyeing.
        Microscope and microscopy.
 --History.
 --Research.

Stains of wood. See Wood staining fungi.

Stair building.
      x Wooden stair building.
        Stairs.
        Staircases.
      xx Building.
        Carpentry.

Staircases. See Stair building.

Stairs. See Stair building.

Stakhanovets Collective Farm.

Stalin Collective Farm.

Stalin constitution. See U.S.S.R.
  Constitution.

Stalin five-year plan. See U.S.S.R.
  Economic policy. Five-year plan,
  Fourth (1946-1950)

Stalin plan to change nature.
      sa Travopol'naia sistema zemle-
        deliia.

Stalin prizes.
      xx Rewards (Prizes, etc.)

Stalingrad.

Stalingrad (Government)
 --Domestic animals.
      sa Stalingrad (Government) Goats.
 --Goats.
      xx Stalingrad (Government) Do-
        mestic animals.

Stalingrad Region.
 --Agriculture.
      sa Subdivision Stalingrad Region
        under: Field crops.
        Forage plants.
        Agricultural laborers.
 -- --Statistics.
 --Climate.
 --Domestic animals.
 --Pomology.
 --Soils.
 --Statistics.
 --Viticulture.

Stall vs. out-of-door feeding.

Stallions.

Stalls.
      xx Barns and stables.
 --Ventilation.

Stamens.
      sa Anthers.

Stamp plan. See Food commodity stamps;
  Trading stamps.

Stamps, Commodity. See Commodity
  stamps.

Stamps, Food. See Food commodity
  stamps.

Stand improvement.
      x Timber stand improvement.
      xx Forest management.

Stand tables.   See Volume and yield
    tables.

Standard container act.
    xx Containers. Legislation.

Standard of living.   See Cost and
    standard of living.

Standardization.   (DIRECT)
    sa Subdivision Grading and stand-
        ardization under: Biological
        products.
        Confectionery.
        Farm produce//
        Subdivision Standards under:
        Oil-cakes.
        Bread.
        Chemical industries//
    x Grade labeling.
        Simplification in industry.
        Standards.
    --Bibliography.
    --Congresses.
        sa Subdivision Congresses nnder:
        Fruit standardization.
        Vegetables. Grading and
            standardization.
    --Periodicals.

Standardization of agricultural implements
    and machinery.   See Agriculture. Im-
    plements and machinery. Standards.

Standardization of farm products.   See
    Farm produce. Grading and standardiza-
    tion.

Standards.   See Standardization.

Standards, Electric.   See Electric
    standards.

Standards.
    --Engineering.   See Engineering standards

Standards of length.
    sa Length measurement.
    x Length, Standards of.
    xx Mensuration.
        Weights and measures.

Standards of performance.
    xx Work standards.
        Efficiency rating.

Stanislaus Co., Calif.
    sa County surveys. California.
        Stanislaus Co.
    xx California..
    --Social conditions.

Stanislaus National Forest, Calif.

Stanislaus River.

Stanley Co., S.D.
    --Soils.
        sa Subdivision South Dakota.
            Stanley Co. under: Soil
            conservation.

Stanton Co., Kan.
    --Soils.
        sa Subdivision Kansas. Stanton
            Co. under: Soil-surveys.

Stanton Co., Neb.
    --Soils.
        sa Subdivision Nebraska. Stanton
            Co. under: Soil-surveys.

Stantonville, Tenn.
    xx Tennessee.

Stapelia.
    xx Asclepiadaceae.

Stapelia gigantea.

Stapelieae.
    sa Stapelia.

Stapfia.

Staphyleaceae.
    sa Tapiscia.

Staphylinidae.
    sa Aleocharini.
        Apocellus.
        Osoriini.
        Atemeles.
        Tachyporinae.
        Weiserianum.
        Cordylaspis.
        Atheta.
    xx Coleoptera.

Staphylococcal infection in dogs.
    xx Dogs. Diseases.

Staphylococcus.
    sa Staphylotoxin.
       Septicaemia.

Staphylococcus aureus.

Staphylococcus botryogenes.

Staphylococcus in milk.

Staphylokinase.

Staphylotoxin.

Star-gazer.

Starch.
    For the commercial product see
       Corn-starch.
    sa Amyliferous sheath.
       Canna starch.
       Rice starch//
       Cassava starch.
       Sago.
    For chemical studies see subdivi-
       sion Starch content under:
       Barley.
       Beet.
       Carrots//
    xx Polysaccharides.
--Analysis.
--Bibliography.
    sa Subdivision Bibliography under:
       Sweet potato starch.
--By-products.
--Chemistry.
--Determination.
--Digestibility.

Starch, Effect of cold on. See Cold. Effect on starch.

Starch.
--Periodicals.
--Prices.
    sa Subdivision Prices under:
       Corn-starch.
    xx Prices.
--Quality.
    xx Quality.
--Research.
--Statistics.
    sa Subdivision Statistics under:
       Corn-starch.

Starch (Continued)
--Tariff.
    xx Tariff.

Starch content of feeding stuffs. See
   Feeding stuffs. Starch content.

Starch industry.
--Bibliography.
--Periodicals.

Starch iodide.

Starfishes   See Asteroidea.

Stargard.
--Botany.

Starke Co., Ind.
--Agriculture.
-- --Periodicals.
--Soils.
    sa Subdivision Indiana. Starke
       Co. under: Soil-surveys.
    xx Indiana. Soils.

Starkenburg, Ger.
--Pomology.
--Population.
    xx Germany. Population.
--Soils.

Starkenburger goats. See Goats, Starkenburger.

Starlings. See Sturnidae.

Starr Co., Tex.
--Water-supply.
    sa Subdivision Texas. Starr Co.
       under: Water, Underground.

Stars.
    xx Astronomy.

Starters (Dairy)

Starvation.
    sa Hunger.
       Famines.
       Malnutrition.
--Experimental studies.

Starved Rock, Ill.

Stassfurt salts.

State, The.
    sa Political science.
    xx Political science.

State aid for education.   See Education.
    Government aid.

State and agriculture.   See Agriculture
    and state.

State and insurance.   See Insurance,
    Social.

State and local relations.   See State-
    local relations.

State and science.   See Science and
    state.

State birds.

State bonds.

State control.   See Industry and state.

State debts.   See Debts, Public. U.S.
    States.

State departments of agriculture.   See
    Agricultural administration.

State farm colonies.   See Farm colonies
    (correction farms)

State farms.
    This heading used for state-owned
        farms in the U.S.S.R. only.
        Publications on state farms of
        the individual republics given
        individual headings, e.g.,
        State farms (U.S.S.R.); State
        farms (Ukraine) Regions are
        given direct subdivision, e.g.,
        State farms. Omsk region. For
        state farms in other countries,
        See appropriate general subject
        headings, e.g., Farm manage-
        ment; Agriculture and socialism;
        Agriculture and state.
    sa Machine-tractor stations
        (Russian)
    xx Farm management.

State farms (Estonia)

State farms (Kazakstan)

State farms (Kirghiz Republic)

State farms (Latvia)

State farms (Ukraine)

State farms (U.S.S.R.)
    sa Collective farming.
        Names of individual farms,
            e.g., Sukhanovo state farm.
        Kuban state farm.
        Lesnye Poliany state farm//
    xx Collective farming.
        Large-scale farming.
--Accounting.
    xx Agriculture. Accounting.
-- --Periodicals.
--Economic aspects.
    xx Agriculture. Economic aspects.
--Exhibitions.
--Finance.
    xx Finance.
-- --Periodicals.
--History.
--Legislation.
--Periodicals.
--Statistics.

State farms (Uzbekistan)

State farms (White Russia)

State-federal relations.   See Federal-
    state relations.

State finance.   See Finance. U.S.
    States.

State flowers.
    xx National flowers.

State forests.
    For general works only. For pub-
        lications on forests of
        special states see name of
        each state, with subdivision
        Forest reservations.
    sa Northern State Forest.
    xx Forest reservations.
--Law.
    xx Forestry. Law.

State governments.
    sa States, Creation of.
       State-local relations.
       Federal-state-local relations.
  --Bibliography.
    sa Subdivision Bibliography under:
       State governments. Reorgani-
       zation.
  --Finance. See Finance. U.S. States.
  --Officials and employees.
    xx U.S. Officials and employees.
  -- --Statistics.
  --Reorganization. (DIRECT)
    x Reorganization of state govern-
      ment.
  -- --Bibliography.
    xx State governments. Bibliography.
  --Year-books.
    xx Year-books.

State insecticide, fungicide and rodenticide act (Proposed)

State institutions.
  --Farms.
  --Finance.

State lands.
    xx Public lands.
  --Statistics.

State laws, Uniform. See Uniform state
  laws.

State libraries. See Libraries. Govern-
  mental, administrative, etc.

State-local relations.
    sa Federal-state-local relations.
    x State and local relations.
      Local-state relations.
    xx Public administration.
      Local government.
      State governments.
      Federal-state-local relations.

State medicine. See Medicine, State.

State ownership. See Government ownership.

State parks.
  For publications on parks in the
    United States in general, in-
    cluding State parks, See U.S.
    Parks. For parks of individ-
    ual states, See name of State
    with subdivision Parks, e.g.,
    Ohio. Parks.

State planning. See Economic planning;
  Planning, State.

State publications.
    xx Government publications.
  --Bibliography.
    sa Subdivision State publica-
      tions. Bibliography under:
      Virginia.
      Ohio.
      Nebraska.
      Utah.
      Washington.
  --Preservation.
    x Preservation of state pub-
      lications.

State Redwood Park. Calif.

State rights.
  --Bibliography.

State school lunch act.

State separation. See States, Creation
  of.

State songs.
    xx Songs.

State taxation. See Taxation, State.

State trading. See Government trading.

State trees.
    x Trees, State.
    xx National trees.
      Trees.

Staten Island, N.Y.
  --Botany.
    sa Subdivision New York (State)
      Staten Island under:
      Algae.

Staten Island, N.Y. (Continued)
--Entomology.
    sa Subdivision Staten Island
        under: Butterflies.

States, Creation of.

States, Small.
    x Small states.
    xx Political science.

States' rights.   See State rights.

Statesmen.

Statesmen, American.
    x American statesmen.

Static electricity.   See Electrostatics.

Statice.

Statice limonium.

Statics.

Station agronomique de l'est.

Stationary engineering.   See Steam engineering.

Stationery.
    sa Paper.
       Ink.
    xx Book industries and trade.
--Testing.
    xx Paper. Testing.
       Testing.

Statistical classification.   See Statistics. Classification.

Statistical control.
    x Statistics. Control.

Statistical curves.   See Curves, Statistical.

Statistical decisions.
    x Decision problems.
    xx Statistics.

Statistical diagrams.   See Statistics.
    Charts, tables, etc.

Statistical mathematics.   See Mathematical statistics.

Statistical mechanics.
    xx Mechanics.

Statistical methods.   See Statistics.
    Graphic methods; Statistics. Meth-
    odology; Subdivision Statistical
    methods under various subjects, i.e.,
    Entomology.

Statistical methods (Biology)   See Biometry.

Statisticians.
--Directories.
--Education.
    xx Professional education.

Statistics.
    sa Subdivision Statistics under:
        Names of countries.
        Agriculture.
        Commerce//
        Almanacs.
        Census.
        Year-books.
        Vital statistics.
        Medical statistics.
        Index numbers (Economics)
        Sampling (Statistical methods)
        Correlation (Statistics)
        Econometrics.
        Medical statistics.
        Factor analysis.
        Time series analysis.
        Social statistics.
        Social statistics. Congresses.
        Mathematical statistics.
        Gross national product.
--Abstracts.
-- --Periodicals.
--Addresses, essays, lectures.
--Bibliography.
    sa Subdivision Statistics. Bib-
        liography under: U.S.
        Italy.
        Wheat//
        Subdivision Bibliography un-
        der: Sampling (Statistics)
        Statistics. Graphic
          methods.
          Statistics. Methodology//
-- --Periodicals.

Statistics (Continued)
--Charts, tables, etc.
    sa Tabulating machines.
    x Diagrams, Statistical.
      Statistical diagrams.
-- --Bibliography.
--Classification.
    x Statistical classification.
--Congresses.
    sa Subdivision Statistics. Con-
      gresses under: Agriculture.
      Labor and laboring classes.
      Subdivision Congresses under:
      Industrial statistics.
      Statistics. Graphic methods.
--Control. See Statistical control.
--Dictionaries.
--Graphic methods.
    sa Statistics. Methodology.
      Correlation (Statistics)
-- --Bibliography.
    xx Statistics. Bibliography.
-- --Congresses.
    xx Statistics. Congresses.
--History.

Statistics, Mathematical. See Mathematical statistics.

Statistics, Medical. See Medical statistics.

Statistics.
--Methodology.
    sa Statistics. Graphic methods.
      Subdivision Statistical methods
      under: Entomology.
      Chemistry.
      Agriculture//
    x Experimental design.
      Design, Experimental.
-- --Abstracts.
-- -- --Periodicals.
-- --Bibliography.
    xx Statistics. Bibliography.
-- -- --Periodicals.
-- --Periodicals.
--Periodicals.
    sa Statistics. Year-books.
      Subdivision Periodicals under:
      Econometrics.
      Subdivision Statistics. Periodi-
      cals under: Agriculture.
      Domestic animals.
      Cotton.

Statistics (Continued)
--Periodicals.
-- --Bibliography.

Statistics, Pictorial. See Statistics.
  Graphic methods.

Statistics.
--Research.
--Societies.
--Study and teaching.
    xx Education.
--Tables, etc. See Statistics. Charts,
  tables, etc.
--Terminology.

Statistics, Vital. See Vital statistics.

Statistics.
--Year-books.

Statistics of sampling. See Sampling
  (Statistics)

Statocysts.
    xx Anatomy, Comparative.

Staunton, Va.
--Natural history.

Staurojoenina assimilis.

Stauroneis.

Stauronotus.
    xx Acridiidae.

Stauronotus maroccanus.

Stavanger, Norway.
--Botany.
--Forestry.

Stave pipe.

Staves.
    sa Shooks.
    xx Coopers and cooperage.
    Shooks.

Stavropol.
--Botany.
    sa Subdivision Stavropol under:
      Weeds.

Stavropol (Continued)
--Entomology.
    sa Subdivision Stavropol under:
        Entomology, Economic.

Stavropol Merino sheep.

Stavropol Region.
--Agriculture.
    sa Subdivision Stavropol Region
        under: Rice.
        Wheat.
--Apiculture.
--Domestic animals.
--Sheep.

Staybwood.   See Heat-stabilized wood.

Staypak.   See Compressed wood.

Stealing.

Steam.
    sa Exhaust steam.
--Tables, calculations, etc.
    x Tables (Systematic lists)

Steam-boilers.
    sa Autoclaves.
       Feed-water.
       Furnaces.
       Steam-engines.
       Stokers, Mechanical.
       Insurance, Boiler.
       Pressure-gages.
    xx Boilers.
--Handbooks, manuals, etc.
--Incrustations.   See Boiler scale.
--Periodicals.

Steam-boilers, Water-tube.
    x Water-tube boilers.

Steam-carriages.
    sa Automobiles.

Steam cookers.

Steam ejectors.   See Steam jets.

Steam engineering.
    x Engineering, Steam.
      Stationary engineering.
    xx Engineering.
      Mechanical engineering.

Steam-engines.
    sa Farm engines.
      Horse-power (Mechanics)
      Indicators for steam-engines.
      Locomotives.
      Steam-boilers.
      Steam-turbines.
      Traction-engines.
    xx Steam-boilers.

Steam jets.
    x Steam ejectors.
    xx Ejectors.

Steam navigation.

Steam-pipes.

Steam power-plants.

Steam pressure canners.   See Pressure
    cookers.

Steam pressure cookers.   See Pressure
    cookers.

Steam-shovels.
    xx Roads. Implements and
        machinery.

Steam skidders.

Steam-traps.

Steam-turbines.
    xx Turbines.

Steamboat lines.
    sa Baltimore Mail Line.
      Cunard White Star Line.
--Maps.

Steamship lines.   See Steamboat lines.

Stearic acid.
    sa Rye, Stearic acid in.
      Butter fat. Stearic acid
        content.

Stearin.

Stearns Co., Minn.
    xx Minnesota.

Stearns Co., Minn. (Continued)
--Agriculture.
    sa Subdivision Stearns Co. under:
        Agricultural policies and
        programs. Minnesota.
        Rural rehabilitation.
        Minnesota.

Stecklings. See Seedlings.

Steel. See Iron and steel.

Steel, Stainless.
    x Stainless steel.
    xx Iron and steel.
    Steel alloys.

Steel, Structural.
    sa Building, Iron and steel.
    Plates, Iron and steel.
    x Construction, Steel.
    xx Building, Iron and steel.
    Iron and steel.
--Agricultural uses.
--Tables, calculations, etc.

Steel alloys.
    sa Steel, Stainless.
    xx Alloys.
    Iron and steel.
--Patents.
    xx Patents.

Steel and iron plates. See Plates, Iron
    and steel.

Steel and iron ships. See Ships, Iron
    and steel.

Steel construction. See Steel, Struc-
    tural.

Steel-piling. See Sheet-piling.

Steel plates. See Plates, Iron and
    steel.

Steel roofing. See Roofing, Steel.

Steel substitutes.
    x Iron and steel. Substitutes.
    xx Substitute products.

Steel tanks. See Tanks, Steel.

Steel-track roads. See Roads, Steel-
    track.

Steelhead. See Trout.

Steeplechasing. See Horse-racing.

Steeprock Lake Ont.
--Geology.

Steers.
    xx Cattle.
--Feeding.
--Grading and standardization.
--Growth.
--Prices.

Steesow, Ger.
--Agriculture.
    sa Subdivision Brandenburg.
    Steesow under: Coloniza-
    tion, Agricultural.

Steganopodes.
    sa Gannet.

Stegodyphus sarsinorum.

Stegomyia. See Aedes.

Stegomyia calopus.

Stegomyia fasciata. See Stegomyia
    calopus.

Stegomyia taeniata. See Stegomyia
    calopus.

Stegosaurus.

Steiermark. See Styria.

Steiroxys hendersoni. See Tettigoniidae

Stele.
    xx Botany. Morphology.

Stellaria aquatica.

Stellaria media.
--Eradication (Chemical)

Stelleroidea, Fossil.

Steller's sea-cow. See Rhytina.

Stellite.
xx Alloys.

Stem rust.
xx Rye. Diseases.
Uredineae.

Stem rust of barley.   See Barley rust.

Stem rust of cereals.   See Cereal rust.

Stem rust of wheat.   See Wheat rust.

Stemmatoiulidae.

Stemodia.

Stemonaceae.

Stemphylium.
xx Dematiaceae.

Stemphylium solani.

Stems.
sa Culm (Botany)

Stenamma gallorum.

Stenares completus.

Stencil printing.   See Silk screen
printing.

Stencil work.
sa Silk screen printing.
xx Arts and crafts movement.

Stende, Latvia. Valsts selekcijas stacija.

Stenelmis sulcata.

Stenini.

Stenodiplosis geniculati.

Stenodiplosis panici.
xx Millet, Proso. Pests.

Stenographers.

Stenography.   See Shorthand.

Stenopelmatidae.

Stenopelmatus.
--Parasites.

Stenopelmatus fuscus.

Stenosis disease of cotton.
xx Cotton. Diseases.

Stenostomum incaudatum.

Stenotaphrum secundatum.
x St. Augustine grass.
--Pests.
xx Grasses and forage plants.
Pests.
--Seed.

Stenotarsia punctiventris.

Stenus.

Stephaniaceae.
sa Radula.

Stephanidae.
xx Hymenoptera.

Stephanocircus.
xx Siphonaptera.

Stephanocircus dasyuri.

Stephanoderes.
--Parasites.
sa Subdivision Parasites under:
Stephanoderes hampei.
xx Parasites.

Stephanoderes coffeae.   See Stephanoderes hampei.

Stephanoderes hampei.
x Stephanoderes coffeae.
Broca do café.
Hypothenemus hampei.
Coffee berry borer.
xx Coffee, Pests.
--Parasites.
xx Stephanoderes. Parasites.

Stephanofilariasis.   See Dermatitis,
Verminous.

Stephenson Co., Ill.
xx Illinois.

Stephenson Co., Ill. (Continued)
--Soils.
    sa Subdivision Illinois. Stephen-
        son Co. under: Soil con-
        servation.

Steppes.   (DIRECT)
    sa Forest steppes.
    xx Llanos.
       Pampas.
       Plains.
       Prairies.

Sterculia alexandri.

Sterculia rhinopetala.

Sterculia urens.
    sa Gum karaya.

Sterculiaceae.
    sa Helicteres.
       Heritiera.
       Theobroma.
       Tribroma.
       Sterculia.
       Abroma.
       Melochia.
       Hermannia.
       Ayenia.

Sterculic acid.

Stereo-comparagraph.
    xx Surveying instruments.
       Stereoscope.
       Optical instruments.

Stereo vision. See Stereoscopy.

Stereochemistry.
    sa Atoms.
       Chemistry, Organic.
       Chemistry, Physical and
         theoretical.
    x Molecular asymmetry.
    xx Chemistry, Physical and
        theoretical.
       Atoms.

Stereophotogrammetry. See Photographic
  surveying.

Stereopticon. See Lantern projection.

Stereoscope.
    sa Stereo-comparagraph.

Stereoscopic sight. See Stereoscopy.

Stereoscopy.
    x Stereo vision.
      Stereoscopic sight.
    xx Optics, Physiological.
       Sight.

Stereosimplex.
    xx Photography. Apparatus and
       supplies.

Stereum.
    xx Thelephoraceae.

Stereum hirsutum.

Stereum sanguinolentum.

Sterides. See Steroids.

Sterids. See Steroids.

Sterility.

Sterility in animals.
    sa Subdivision Sterility under:
       Cattle.
       Goats.
       Horses.
       Dogs.
  --Congresses.

Sterility in insects.
    xx Insect diseases.

Sterility in plants.

Sterilization.
    sa Subdivision Sterilization
       under: Must.
       Dairy. Implements and
         machinery.
       Canned goods.
       Milk. Pasteurization and
         sterilization.
       Soil sterilization.
       Radiation sterilization.
       Food. Preservation.
       Wine. Pasteurization.

Sterna wilsonii.

Sternberg, Ost.   See Ost-Sternberg.

Sternechus.
        x Plectromodes.
        xx Coleoptera.

Sternechus paludatus.
        x Beanstalk weevil.
        xx Beans. Pests.

Sternochetus.
        xx Curculionidae.

Sternochetus lapathi.
        x Cryptorhynchus lapathi.
        Poplar and willow borer.
        Willow borer.

Sternum.

Steroid nomenclature.   See Steroids.
    Nomenclature.

Steroids.
        x Sterides.
        Sterids.
        xx Lipoids.
    --Metabolism.
    --Nomenclature.
        x Steroid nomenclature.

Sterols.
        sa Ergosterol.
        Amyrin.
        xx Alcohols.

Stethynium cinctiventris.

Stettin, Ger.
    --Botany.

Stettin. Stadtisches museum.

Steuben Co., Ind.
    --Description and travel.
    --Soils.
        sa Subdivision Indiana. Steuben Co.
            under: Soil-surveys.

Steuben Co., N.Y.
    --Agriculture.
    -- --Periodicals.

Steuben Co., N.Y. (Continued)
    --Soils.
        sa Subdivision New York (State)
        Steuben Co. under: Soil-
            surveys.
    --Viticulture.

Stevens Co., Kan.
    --Soils.
        sa Subdivision Kansas. Stevens
        Co. under: Soil-surveys.

Stevens Co., Wash.
    --Geology.

Stewards.
        xx Waiters.
        Caterers and catering.

Stewart Co., Tenn.
    --Soils.
        sa Subdivision Tennessee. Stewart
        Co. under: Soil-surveys.

Stewart's disease of maize.

Stibasoma.

Stichococcus.
        xx Algae.

Stichococcus bacillaris.

Stichocotyle.

Stichostemma eilhardi.

Stick-lac.   See Shellac.

Stickfast flea.   See Echidnophaga galli-
    nacea.

Sticta.

Stictaceae.

Stictis Panizzei.

Stictocephala festina.

Stiff sickness.   See Three-day sickness.

Stigmatophyllon.

Stigmonose.

Stigonema.

Stigonemataceae.
  sa Stigonema.

Stikine River.

Stilbaceae.
  sa Graphium.
     Isaria.
     Stilbeae.
     Pilacre.
     Epidermophyton.

Stilbamidine.   See 4,4'-Diamidinostilbene.

Stilbella flavida.   See Omphalia flavida.

Stilbene.

Stilbestrol.   See Diethylstilbestrol.

Still-birth.
  xx Veterinary obstetrics.

Stilling basins.
  xx Hydraulic engineering.

Stillingia sebifera.   See Tallow tree.

Stills.   See Distilling apparatus.

Stillwater, Minn.
  --Social conditions. ·
     sa Subdivision Minnesota. Still-
        water under: Social surveys.

Stillwater, Okla.
     sa Subdivision Stillwater, Okla.
        under: Market surveys.
  xx Oklahoma.

Stilophoraceae.

Stilpnomelane.

Stilpnotia salicis.
  --Parasites.

Stilts.
  --Food.
     xx Birds. Food.

Stimulants.
  sa Cardiazol.
  xx Therapeutics.

Stimulus.

Stinchfield Woods, Mich.
  xx Demonstration forests.
     Michigan. University. School
        of Forestry and Conserva-
        tion.

Sting (Bees)   See Sting (Insects)

Sting (Insects)
  x Sting (Bees)
     Bee stings.

Stingless bees.   See Melipona.

Stink bugs.   See Pentatomidae.

Stinking smut of wheat.
  sa Tilletia tritici.
     Tilletia levis.
  --Control.
     xx Wheat smut. Control.
  --Research.

Stinkwood.   See Ocotea bullata.

Stipa.

Stipa capillata.

Stipa tenacissima. ` See Alfa.

Stipa vaseyi.
  x Sleepy grass.

Stipules.

Stirlingshire, Scot.
  --Agriculture.
     xx Scotland. Agriculture.

Stizolobium deeringiana.   See Florida
  velvet bean.

Stizolobium pruriens.   See Mucuna
  pruriens.

Stock (Flowers)   See Stocks (Flowers)

Stock and stock-breeding.　See Domestic
　animals; Domestic animals. Breeding.

Stock breeders' congresses.
　　sa Cattle breeders' congresses.
　　Sheep breeders' congresses.
　　Horse breeders' congresses.
　　Rabbits. Congresses.
　　Goat breeders' congresses.
　　x Domestic animals. Breeding.
　　Congresses.

Stock breeders' directories.
　　sa Cattle breeders' directories.
　　xx Stock breeders' societies.
　　Directories.

Stock breeders' societies.
　　sa Names of individual Stock
　　　breeders' societies.
　　x Stockbreeders' societies.
　　Domestic animals. Breeding.
　　Societies.
　　Live stock associations.
　--Directories.
　　sa Stock breeders' directories.

Stock-breeding.　See Domestic animals.
　Breeding.

Stock companies.　See Corporations; Joint
　stock companies.

Stock-exchange.
　　sa Speculation (in business)
　　Produce trade.
　　New York stock exchange.
　　Live stock exchanges.
　--Law.

Stock exchange firms.

Stock farms.

Stock inspection.　　(INDIRECT)
　　sa Quarantine, Veterinary.
　　Veterinary hygiene.
　　x Domestic animals. Inspection.
　　Inspection of live stock.
　　xx Inspection.
　　Quarantine, Veterinary.
　　Veterinary medicine.
　　Veterinary medicine. Legislation.
　　Veterinary hygiene.

Stock inspection (Continued)
　--Fees and fee-bills.
　　xx Veterinary medicine. Fees and
　　　fee bills.

Stock-judging.
　　sa Subdivision Judging under:
　　Horse.
　　Swine.
　　Sheep.
　　Cattle.
　　Judging.
　　Guenon system.

Stock-ranges.　See Ranges.

Stock-taking.　See Inventories.

Stock waterer, Automatic.　See Electric
　stock waterer.

Stock-yards.
　　sa Subdivision Stock-yards under
　　　names of cities, e.g.,
　　　Kansas City, Mo. Stock-
　　　yards.
　　xx Abattoirs.
　--Bibliography.
　　sa Subdivision Bibliography under:
　　　Stock-yards. Legislation.
　　xx Meat industry and trade. Bib-
　　　liography.
　--Legislation.
　　sa Packers and stockyards act.
　-- --Bibliography.
　　sa Subdivision Bibliography under:
　　　Packers and stockyards act.
　　xx Stock-yards. Bibliography.
　　Law. Bibliography.
　-- --Periodicals.
　　xx Meat industry and trade. Peri-
　　　odicals.
　--Rates.

Stockpiling.

Stockach, Ger.
　--Forestry.
　　xx Baden. Forestry.

Stockbreeders' societies.　See Stock
　breeders' societies.

Stockbreeding.　See Domestic animals.
　Breeding.

Stockholm.
--Botany.
--Milk supply.
    xx Sweden. Milk supply.

Stockholm (Province)
--Agriculture.

Stockings. See Hosiery.

Stocks.
    sa Securities.
       Dividends.
    x Shares of stocks.
--Bibliography.

Stocks (Flowers)
--Diseases.
    sa Mosaic disease of stocks
       (Flowers)

Stocks (Fruit-culture) See Fruit stocks.

Stockyards. See Stock-yards.

Stokers, Mechanical.
    x Mechanical stokers.
    xx Steam-boilers.

Stokes Co., N.C.
--Soils.
    sa Subdivision North Carolina.
       Stokes Co. under: Soil-
         surveys.

Stokes's theorem.

Stolberg-Wernigerode. See Wernigerode.

Stolbur.
--Congresses.

Stomach.
    sa Abomasum.
       Rumen.
--Diseases.
    sa Tympanites.

Stomach, Foreign objects in.

Stomach worm in rabbits. See Obelis-
coides cuniculi.

Stomach worm in sheep. See Haemonchus
contortus.

Stomata.

Stomatitis, Mycotic. See Mycotic stomatitis.

Stomatitis, Necrotic. See Necrotic sto-
matis.

Stomatitis, Proliferative. See X disease in cattle.

Stomoxys.

Stomoxys calcitrans.

Stomoxys nigra.

Stone.
    sa Sandstone.
       Soapstone.
       Soil, Stony.
       Rocks.
       Building stones.

Stone, Artificial.

Stone, Crushed.
    sa Roads, Crushed stone.
--Specification.

Stone.
--Effect of plant growth on.
--Testing.

Stone age.

Stone age, United States.

Stone and quarry products.
    x Quarry products.
       Stone products.
    xx Quarries and quarrying.
--Quarantine.

Stone as a road material.

Stone-building plants. See Rock-forming
plants.

Stone-flies. See Plecoptera.

Stone fruit.
    sa Particular stone fruits, e.g.,
       apricot, peach.

Stone fruit (Continued)
    xx Fruit.
      Pomology.

Stone houses.
--Bibliography.

Stone implements.
    xx Implements, utensils, etc.

Stone meal.

Stone mulches.
    xx Mulch and mulching.

Stone products.   See Stone and quarry
   products.

Stoner wheat.   See Wheat, Stoner.

Stoneworts.   See Characeae.

Stoney Creek, Calif.

Stongyloides intestinalis.

Stony Brook Reservation, Mass.

Stooling of grain.   See Cereals. Stooling.

Storage and transportation diseases and
   injuries.
      sa Stored products. Pests.
     x Farm produce. Transportation.
       Diseases and injuries.
      Storage of farm produce. Dis-
       eases and injuries.
      Storage diseases.
      Storage injuries.
      Transportation diseases.
      Transportation injuries.
    xx Stored products. Pests.
      Vegetables. Diseases.
      Vegetables. Marketing.
      Entomology, Economic.
      Cattle. Injuries.
      Transportation of animals.
      Domestic animals. Transporta-
       tion.
   --Bibliography.

Storage cellars.   See Storage houses and
   cellars.

Storage diseases.   See Storage and
   transportation diseases and injuries.

Storage houses and cellars.
    x Storage cellars.
    xx Farm buildings.
      Cellars.
  --Aeration.
    xx Aeration systems.
  --Fumigation.
    xx Fumigation.

Storage injuries.   See Storage and
   transportation diseases and injuries.

Storage libraries.   See Libraries
   Storage.

Storage of farm produce.
      sa Subdivision Storage under:
       Butter.
       Fruit.
       Cotton//
       Granaries.
       Grain elevators.
       Cold storage.
     x Agricultural products. Stor-
       age.
      Storage of food.
    xx Warehouses.
      Food. Storage.
  --Accounting.
    xx Accounting.
  --Bibliography.
      sa Subdivision Bibliography un-
       der: Fruit. Storage.
       Granaries.
       Vegetables. Storage.
       Cereals. Storage.

Storage of farm produce, Cooperative.

Storage of farm produce.
  --Diseases and injuries.   See Storage
    and transportation diseases and
    injuries.
  --Financing.
  --Legislation.
    xx Agriculture. Law.
  --Periodicals.
  --Prices.
  -- --Subsidies.
  --Research.
  --Statistics.

Storage of food.   See Refrigeration and
refrigerating machinery; Storage of
farm produce; Cold storage; Food. Storage.

Storage of household textiles.   See
Household textiles. Storage.

Storage of limestone.   See Limestone.
Storage.

Storage of lumber.   See Wood. Storage.

Storage of wood.   See Wood. Storage.

Storage reservoirs.   See Ponds; Reservoirs.

Storage warehouses.   See Warehouses.

Storax.
    sa Liquid storax.

Store-door delivery.
--Bibliography.

Stored grains.   See Cereals. Storage.

Stored palm kernels.   See Palm kernels.
Storage.

Stored products.
    xx Food. Storage.
--Congresses.
--Fumigation.
    xx Fumigation.
--Pests.
    sa Tenebroides mauritanicus.
       Storage and transportation
          diseases and injuries.
       Subdivision Pests under:
          Flour.
          Cocoa.
          Chocolate.
          Milk, Desiccated.
          Cereals. Storage.
          Peanuts.
    xx Storage and transportation
       diseases and injuries.
--Ventilation.

Stores, Chain.   See Chain stores.

Stores, Cooperative.   See Cooperative
stores.

Stores (retail trade)
    xx Retail trade.
       Grocery trade.
       Chain stores.
       Department stores.

Storks.

Storm damage to trees.   See Trees.
    Storm injury.

Storm insurance.   See Insurance, Tornado.

Storm movement.

Storm-proof construction.
    sa Earthquakes and building.
    x Building, Storm-proof.

Storm relief.

Storm signals.

Storm warnings.

Storms.
    sa Hail.
       Hurricane.
       Monsoons.
       Tornadoes.
       Rain.
       Cyclones.
       Thunder storms.
       Ice storms.
       Blizzards.
    xx Disasters.

Stornaro, Italy.
--Agriculture.
    sa Subdivision Italy. Stornaro
       under: Reclamation of land.

Story Co., Iowa.
--Agriculture.
    sa Agriculture. Economic aspects.
       Iowa. Story Co.
--Soils.
    sa Subdivision Iowa. Story Co.
       under: Soil-surveys.

Story-telling.

Story writing.   See Short story.

Stovaine.

Stoves.
    sa Oven temperatures.

Stoves, Camp.
    x Camp stoves.

Stoves, Electric.
    sa Electric cookery.
       Electric heating.
       Electric water heaters.
    x Ranges, Electric.
       Electric ranges.
       Electric stoves.
    xx Electric cookery.
--Bibliography.
    xx Electric apparatus and ap-
       pliances, Domestic. Bib-
       liography.
--Rates.
    xx Electric power. Rates.

Stoves, Gas.
    x Gas ranges.
       Gas stoves.

Stoves, Oil.
    x Oil stoves.

Stoves.
--Statistics.

Stoves, Wood.
    x Wood stoves.

Stow Township, Summit Co., Ohio.
--Soils.

Stowe House.

Strafford Co., N.H.
--Soils.
    sa Subdivision New Hampshire.
       Strafford Co. under: Soil-
       surveys.

Strain gages.
    xx Gages.
       Strains and stresses.

Strains and stresses.
    sa Elasticity.
       Graphic statics.
       Strength of materials.
       Wind-pressure.
       Impact.

Strains and stresses (Continued)
    sa Photoelasticity.
       Deformations (Mechanics)
       Buckling.
       Creep.
       Strain gages.
    xx Structural engineering.
       Mechanics.
--Bibliography.

Strait of Magellan.   See Magellan, Strait
of.

Straits Settlements.
    sa Christmas Island.
       Cocos Island.
       Providence Wellesley, Straits
          Settlements.
--Agriculture.
    sa Penang Island. Straits Settle-
       ments. Agriculture.
       Subdivision Straits Settle-
       ments under: Coffee.
-- --Bibliography.
--Bibliography.
--Commerce.
-- --Statistics.
--Politics and government.
    xx Asia. Politics and government.
--Public works.
    sa Subdivision Public works under:
       Singapore (Island)
       Dindings, Straits Settle-
          ments.
       Penang Island, Straits
          Settlements.
--Sanitary affairs.
--Statistics.
--Zoology.
    sa Subdivision Zoology under:
       Penang Island, Straits
          Settlements.

Stramonium.   See Datura stramonium.

Strand flora, Marine.   See Coast flora.

Strangles.   See Distemper in horses.

Strasbourg.   See Strassburg.

Strassburg.
--Botany.

Strassburg plan.

Strategic materials.
 x Critical materials.
 xx Raw materials.
--Directories.
--Prices.

Strategus.
 xx Scarabaeidae.

Strategus quadrifoveatus.
 x Coconut rhinoceros beetle.
 Scarabaeus quadrifoveatus.
 xx Coconut. Pests.

Strategy.
 sa Atomic warfare.
 x Strategy, Military.
 Military strategy.
 xx Military art and science.

Strategy, Military. See Strategy.

Strathspey, Scot.
--Agriculture.

Strathyre Forest, Scot.

Stratigraphic geology. See Geology,
 Stratigraphic.

Stratiomyidae.

Stratosphere.

Strauss method.

Straw.
 sa Flax straw.
 Rye straw.
 Wheat straw.
 x Cereal straw.
--Abstracts.
--Analysis.
--Bibliography.
 sa Subdivision Bibliography under:
 Straw. Marketing.
--By-products.
 sa Gas, Straw.
--Care and handling.
--Effect on plants.
--Grading and standardization.
--Harvesting.
--Industrial uses.
 x Straw. Utilization, Industrial.
 xx Chemurgy.

Straw (Continued)
--Marketing.
-- --Bibliography.
 xx Marketing. Bibliography.
 Straw. Bibliography.
--Patents.
-- --Bibliography.
--Utilization, Industrial. See Straw.
 Industrial uses.

Straw as feeding stuff.

Straw as a fertilizer.

Straw as food for man.

Straw braid.

Straw gas. See Gas, Straw,

Straw industries.
 xx Hats.

Straw itch.

Straw manure. See Straw as a fertilizer.

Straw mulches.

Straw pulps.
 xx Paper materials.

Straw removal equipment.
 xx Harvesting machinery.

Straw votes. See Public opinion polls.

Strawberries.
 sa Strawberry industry and trade.
 Fragaria.
 Cookery (Strawberries)
--Bibliography.
--Breeding.
 xx Plant breeding.

Strawberries, Canned.

Strawberries.
--Canning and preserving.
 xx Fruit preservation.
--Composition.
--Congresses.

Strawberries (Continued)
--Cost of production.
    xx Berries. Cost of production.
-- --Statistics.
--Disease resistant varieties.
    xx Strawberries. Varieties.
--Diseases.
    sa Leather rot of strawberries.
        Strawberry leaf-blight.
        Crinkle disease of strawberries.
        Strawberry dwarf.
        Virus diseases of strawberries.
--Fertilizers. See Fertilizers for
   strawberries.

Strawberries, Frozen.
--Grading and standardization.
    xx Berries, Frozen. Grading and
        standardization.

Strawberries.
--Grading and standardization.
    xx Farm produce. Grading and
        standardization.
--Harvesting.
    xx Fruit harvesting and marketing.
--History.
--Inspection.
    xx Fruit inspection.
--Marketing.
--Marketing, Cooperative.
    xx Fruit harvesting and marketing,
        Cooperative.
--Periodicals.
    xx Berries. Periodicals.
--Pest resistant varieties.
    xx Strawberries. Varieties.
--Pests.
    sa Anthonomus signatus.
        Aphis forbesi.
        Synanthedon bibionipennis.
        Tarsonemus pallidus.
--Physiology and morphology.
    xx Botany. Physiological and
        structural.
        Berries. Physiology and mor-
        phology.
--Precooling.
    xx Fruit. Precooling.
--Prices.
    xx Farm produce. Prices.
        Berries. Prices.
 --Fixing.
    xx Prices. Fixing.

Strawberries (Continued)
--Processing.
    xx Berries. Processing.
        Fruit. Processing.
--Statistics.
--Storage.
    xx Fruit. Storage.
--Transportation.
-- --Costs.
    xx Fruit transportation. Costs.
        Vegetables. Transportation.
        Costs.
--Varieties.

Strawberry clover. See Clover, Strawberry.

Strawberry Creek, Calif.

Strawberry crown moth. See Synanthedon
   bibionipennis.

Strawberry dwarf.
    xx Strawberries. Diseases.

Strawberry filer. See Emphytus ful-
   vipes.

Strawberry industry and trade. (DI-
   RECT)
    xx Strawberries.

Strawberry leaf blight.

Strawberry leaf roller. See Ancylis
   comptana.

Strawberry products.
    xx Fruit products.

Strawberry root rot. See Ascochyta
   fragaricola.

Strawberry rootworm. See Paria canella.

Strawberry tree. See Arbutus unedo.

Strawberry Valley irrigation project.

Strawberry-weevil. See Anthonomus
   signatus.

Streak disease of roses.
    xx Roses. Diseases.

Stream bank erosion.
    xx Soil erosion.
--Prevention and control.
    xx Soil erosion. Prevention and
        control.

Stream control. See Stream regulation.

Stream discharge. See Rivers.

Stream dynamics. See Fluids; Sedimentation and deposition.

Stream flow. See Stream measurements;
Hydraulics.

Stream-gaging equipment. See Stream
measurements. Equipment.

Stream improvement. See Stream regulation.

Stream load.

Stream management. See Stream regulation.

Stream measurements.
    sa Run-off.
       Flow meters.
    x Water measurement.
--Bibliography.
--Equipment.
    x Stream-gaging equipment.
    xx Hydraulic engineering. Instru-
        ments.

Stream pollution. See Water. Pollution.

Stream regulation.
    x River management.
       River and stream improvement.
       Stream improvement.
       Stream management.
    xx Flood control.
--Research.

Stream surveys. (INDIRECT)

Streariinae.

Streblidae.
    sa Nycteribosca africana.
    xx Diptera.
       Parasitic and predaceous insects.

Streblomastix strix.

Streblota.

Street-cleaning.
--Bibliography.

Street-lighting.
    sa Subdivision Lighting under:
       Bridges.
       Roads.
    xx Roads. Lighting.

Street railroads.
    sa Philadelphia. Railroads.
       Electric railroads.
       New York (City) Railroads.
--Periodicals.

Street sweepings.

Street traffic regulations. See Traffic
regulations.

Street trees. See Trees in cities.

Streets.
    sa Traffic regulations.
       Subdivision Streets under names
        of cities, towns, etc.
--Finance.
--Periodicals.

Strengnäs, Sweden.
--Botany.

Strength of materials.
    sa Mechanics.
       Timber physics.
       Building materials. Testing.
       Elasticity.
       Strains and stresses.
       Buckling.
       Wood. Properties and uses.
    xx Structural engineering.
--Bibliography.
--Periodicals.

Strepsiptera. See Stylopidae.

Streptanthus.

Streptobacillus moniliformis.

Streptocarpus.

Streptococcus.
  xx Bacteriology.

Streptococcus agalactiae.

Streptococcus angina.
  xx Angina.
     Veterinary medicine.

Streptococcus equi.

Streptococcus in milk.
  x Streptoccus lactis.

Streptococcus lactis.   See Streptococcus
  in milk.

Streptococcus pyogenes equi.

Streptomyces.
  xx Schizomycetes.

Streptomyces aureofaciens.

Streptomycin.
  x Dihydrostreptomycin.
  xx Antibiotics.
  --Bibliography.

Streptomycin as a fungicide.

Streptomycin in agriculture.
  --Bibliography.

Streptomycin in veterinary medicine.
  xx Veterinary materia medica and
     pharmacy.
     Antibiotics in veterinary
       medicine.
  --Bibliography.

Streptoneura.
  sa Prosobranchia.
  xx Gasteropoda.

Streptothricin.
  xx Antibiotics.

Streptothrix.
  sa Nocardia.

Streptothrix pyaemiae canis.

Stresses.   See Strains and stresses.

Striariaceae.

Striariidae.

Stridulation.
    x Insects, Sound production by.

Striga asiatica.
    x Witchweed.

Strigeidae.

Strigops habroptilus.

Strikes and lockouts.
    sa Anthracite coal strike.
       Farmers' strikes.
    xx Collective bargaining.
       Industrial relations.
  --Agricultural laborers.   See Farmers'
    strikes.
  --Bibliography.
    sa Farmers' strikes. Bibliography.
  --Farm machinery.   (DIRECT)
    xx Agriculture. Implements and
       machinery. Trade and manu-
       facture.
  --Packing-houses.
    xx Packing-houses.
  --Potash industry.

String.   See Cordage.

Stringybark, Brown.   See Eucalyptus
  capitellata.

Stringybark, White.   See Eucalyptus
  eugenioides.

Strip coal mining.   See Coal mines and
  mining. Stripping operations.

Strip cropping.
    x Strip farming.
    xx Soil erosion. Prevention and
       control.
  --Statistics.

Strip farming.   See Strip cropping.

Stripe disease of barley.

Stripe disease of rice.

Stripe rust.   See Puccinia glumarum.

Striped beet caterpillar.   See Mamestra
  trifolii.

Striped blister beetle.   See Epicauta
  lemniscata.

Striped cucumber beetle.   See Diabrotica
  vittata.

Striped garden caterpillar.   See Mamestra
  legitima.

Striped harvest-spider.   See Liobunum
  vittatum.

Striped peach worm.   See Gelechia con-
  fusella.

Striped sod webworm.   See Crambus muta-
  bilis.

Striphonopterygidae.

Stripping operations.   See Coal mines
  and mining. Stripping operations.

Stroboscope.
     xx Physical instruments.

Stromatium fulvum.
     xx Cerambycidae.

Stromatocystites walcotti.

Stromboli, Eruption of, 1912.

Strongilina.

Strongylidae.
     sa Uncinaria.
        Strongylus.
        Haemonchus.
        Sclerostomidae.
        Syngamus.
        Metastrongylus.
        Dictyocaulus.
        Trichostrongylus.
        Ostertagia.
        Camelostrongylus.

Strongylium.

Strongyloides ransomi.
     xx Swine. Parasites.

Strongylose pulmonaire.   See Verminous
  bronchitis.

Strongylosis.

Strongylosomatidae.

Strongylus.
   --Larvae.
     xx Larvae.

Strongylus contortus.   See Haemonchus
  contortus.

Strongylus edentatus.

Strongylus equinus.
     xx Horses. Parasites.

Strongylus paradoxus.   See Metastrongylus
  apri.

Strongylus quadriradiatus.   See Orni-
  thostrongylus quadriradiatus.

Strongylus subtilis.

Strontium.
   --Effect on plants.
   --Metabolism.
   -- --Abstracts.
   -- --Bibliography.

Strontium in animal nutrition.

Strontium in plant nutrition.
     xx Plant nutrition.

Strophanthus.
     xx Apocynaceae.

Stropharia.

Structural design.   See Structural engineering.

Structural drawing.
      x Drawing, Structural.
     xx Mechanical drawing.

Structural engineering.
     sa Framing (Building)
        Structures, Theory of.
        Building, Iron and steel.
        Strength of materials.

Structural engineering (Continued)
    sa Strains and stresses.
        Framing, Continuous.
    x Engineering, Structural.
    xx Engineering.
--Bibliography.
--Periodicals.

Structural geology. See Geology, Struc-
    tural.

Structural materials. See Building
    materials.

Structural steel. See Steel, Structural.

Structural timbers. See Wood as building
    material.

Structures, Theory of.
    sa Structural engineering.

Strumella coryneoidea.

Struthiolithus chersonensis.

Struthiopteris.

Struthiopteris germanica.

Strychnos.

Strychnos, Alkaloids in.
    xx Alkaloids.

Strychnos tienté.

Stuart Forest Nursery.
    xx Forest nurseries.

Stubble crops.

Stubble mulches.
    xx Soil mulching.
--Research.

Stucco.

Stud-book (Ass and mule)

Stud-book (Cat)

Stud-book (Dog)

Stud-book (Fox)
    xx Fox.

Stud-book (Horse)
    sa Stallions.

Stud-book (Mule) See Stud-book (Ass and
    mule)

Stud-book (Pigeon)

Stud-book (Pony)
    xx Ponies.

Stud-book (Sheep)

Stud books.

Student cooperative associations.
    xx Virginia. Education.

Student home economics clubs. See Home
    economics student clubs.

Students.
    sa Subdivision Students under
        names of universities,
        colleges, and schools, e.g.,
        Indiana. University. Stu-
        dents.
    xx Biography, Collected.
        Universities and colleges.
--Grading and marking. See Grading and
    marking (Students)

Student's methods.

Study and teaching. See Education;
    Teaching; Subdivision Study and teach-
    ing under various subjects.

Study groups to foreign countries. See
    International visits.

Stump killing. See Stumps.

Stump pulling. See Stumps. Removal.

Stumpage appraisal.

Stumpage prices.
    sa Subdivision Prices under:
        Pulp-wood.
    x Stumps. Prices.
      Timber. Prices.

Stumpage prices (Continued)
    xx Wood. Prices.

Stumps.
    sa Stumpage appraisal.
    x Stump killing.
--Prices.   See Stumpage prices.
--Removal.
    x Stump pulling.
    xx Clearing of land.

Sturmia inconspicua.

Sturmia rhodesiensis.

Sturnidae.
    sa Sturnus.

Sturnus vulgaris.

Sturtevant Prelinnean Library.

Stutsman Co., N.D.
--Agriculture.
    sa Subdivision North Dakota.
        Stutsman Co. under: Agri-
            cultural credit.
--Land.
    sa Subdivision North Dakota.
        Stutsman Co. under: Land.
        Classification.

Stuttgart.
--Milk supply.
    xx Germany. Milk supply.
--Paleobotany.

Stuttgart disease.   See Black tongue.

Stuttgarter Hundeseuche.   See Black
   tongue.

Stygeoclonium.
    xx Algae.

Stylarioides papillosa.

Stylasteridae.
    x Hydrocorals.
    xx Coral.

Style book (Printing)   See Printing,
   Practical. Style manuals.

Style manuals.   See Printing, Practical.
   Style manuals.

Stylidiaceae.   See Candolleaceae.

Stylocerus.

Stylogaster.

Stylopidae.
    sa Elenchinus.

Stylosanthes.

Stylurus.
    xx Gomphidae.

Styphlodora bascaniensis.

Styracaceae.
    sa Styrax.

Styrax.
    sa Liquid storax.
    xx Styracaceae.

Styrax officinalis.

Styrene.
    sa Vinyltoluene.
    xx Chemistry, Organic.

Styrene dibromide.

Styria.
--Agriculture.
    sa Subdivision Styria under:
        Agricultural laborers.
        Agriculture. Economic as-
            pects.
-- --Maps.
-- --Periodicals.
--Apiculture.
--Botany.
    sa Subdivision Styria under:
        Mosses.
--Cattle.
--Dairying.
--Entomology.
    sa Subdivision Styria under:
        Coleoptera.
        Butterflies.
--Forestry.
--Industries and resources.

Styria (Continued)
--Natural history.
xx Austria. Natural history.
--Pomology.
xx Austria. Pomology.
--Poor, The.
--Statistics.
--Viticulture.
-- --Periodicals.
--Zoology.

Suahili language. See Swahili language.

Sub-soil water. See Water, Underground.

Sub-surface plowing. See Subsoiling.

Sub-surface tillage. See Subsoiling.

Subanuns.

Subarctic regions. See Arctic regions.

Subconsciousness.
xx Psychology.

Subcutaneous injections. See Injections,
Hypodermic.

Subdivision of land. See Land subdivision.

Subdrainage. See Drainage; Soil.
Stabilization.

Subhumid regions.
sa Subdivision Subhumid regions
under: Soil erosion. Pre-
vention and control.

Subirrigation.
x Irrigation, Underground.
Irrigation, Subterranean.
Subterranean irrigation.

Subject catalogs. See Catalogs, Subject.

Subject headings.
Whenever used with subject subdivision, make see also reference from that subject.
--Aeronautics.
x Aeronautics. Subject headings.
--Agricultural engineering.
xx Agricultural engineering.

Subject headings (Continued)
--Agriculture.
--Atomic energy.
xx Atomic energy.
--Bibliography.
--Business.
--Chemistry.
--Cities and towns.
--European war, 1914-1918.
--Fisheries.
x Fisheries. Subject headings.
--Forestry.
--Landscape gardening.
--Language.
--Law.
--Literature.
--Medicine.
--Naval art and science.
xx Naval art and science.
--Nuclear physics.
xx Nuclear physics.
--Physics.
x Physics. Subject headings.
--Public administration.
xx Public administration.
--Science.
--Social sciences.
xx Social sciences.
--Soil conservation.
x Soil.conservation. Subject
headings.
--Technology.
x Technology. Subject headings.
--Textile industry and fabrics.
x Textile industry and fabrics.
Subject headings.
--World War, 1939-1945.
xx World War, 1939-1945.

Sublette, Kan.
--Social conditions.
sa Subdivision Kansas. Sublette
under: Community life.

Sublimate.

Sublimed blue lead.

Submarginal lands. See Land, Marginal.

Submarine boats.
--Cargo.
xx Cargo.

Submarine forests.   See Forests, Submarine.

Submarine geology.
sa Ocean bottom.
x Marine geology.
Geology, Submarine.
Geology, Marine.
xx Geology.

Submarine photography. See Photography,
Submarine.

Submerged soil.   See Soil, Waterlogged.

Subsidies.   See Bounties; Government aid;
Price subsidies.

Subsistence farms.   See Farms, Small.

Subsistence gardens.   See Gardens, Subsistence.

Subsistence homesteads.   See Homesteads,
Subsistence.

Subsoiling.
--Bibliography.

Substations, Electric.   See Electric
power-plants. Substations.

Substitute fibers.

Substitute products.
sa Feeding stuffs. Substitutes.
Sugar substitutes.
Wheat substitutes//
x Alternate materials.
Substitutes.
--Cyclopedias.
--Dictionaries.
--Periodicals.

Substitutes.   See Substitute products.

Substitutes for pyrethrum.   See Pyrethrum
substitutes.

Subterranean clover.
x Clover, Subterranean.
Trifolium subterraneum.
xx Clover.
--Effect on sheep.
xx Clover as feeding stuff.

Subterranean irrigation.   See Subirrigation.

Subtilin.
xx Antibiotics.
--Bibliography.

Subtropical fruit.   See Tropical fruit.

Subulurinae.

Suburban life.
--Congresses.
xx Country life. Congresses.

Subversive activities.   See Sabotage.

Subways.   (DIRECT)
sa Subways. New York (City)
Subways. Pittsburgh.
Subways. Detroit.

Success.
sa Ability.
Applications for position.
Business.
Profession, Choice of.
Saving and thrift.
Conduct of life.
Prediction of scholastic
success.
x Business success.

Succinic acid.

Succory.   See Chicory.

Succotash, Canned.
--Grading and standardization.
xx Vegetables, Canned. Grading
and standardization.
Canned goods. Grading and
standardization.
--Statistics.

Succotash, Frozen.
--Grading and standardization.

Succulent plants.
sa Cactaceae.
Ceropegia.
--Effect on milk.   See Milk. Effect of
succulent plants.
--Periodicals.

Succulent plants (Continued)
--Pictorial works.
  xx Botany. Pictorial works.
--Societies.

Suchuan. See Szechuan.

Suckfly. See Dicyphus minimus.

Sucking lice. See Anoplura.

Sucre, Venezuela.
--Agriculture.
--Soils.

Sucrose.
--Bibliography.
--Inversion. See Sugar. Inversion.

Suctoria.
 sa Ephelotidae.
 xx Infusoria.

Sudan.
 sa Haussa.
 Bahr-el-Ghazal, Sudan
  (Province)//
 x Sudan, Egyptian.
 Egyptian Sudan.
 xx Africa.
--Agriculture.
 sa Sudan. Domestic animals.
 Subdivision Sudan under:
  Cotton.
  Agriculture. Economic aspects.
  Agricultural policies and
   programs.
  Mechanized farming.
 xx Africa, West. Agriculture.
-- --Bibliography.
--Botany.
 sa Subdivision Sudan under: Fungi.
  Trees.
  Botany, Economic.
--Census.
--Commerce.
-- --Statistics.
--Description and travel.
--Domestic animals.
--Economic conditions.
 sa Subdivision Sudan under:
  History, Economic.

Sudan, Egyptian. See Sudan.

Sudan.
--Entomology.
--Fisheries.
--Forestry.
 sa Subdivision Sudan under:
  Forest products.
  Lumber trade.
  War and forestry (1939-1945)
  Trees.
-- --Periodicals.
--Geographic names.
 xx Geographic names.
--History.
 sa Subdivision Sudan under:
  History, Economic.
--Industries.
--Meteorology.
--Natural history.
--Ornithology.
--Population.
--Research.
--Social life and customs.
--Soils.
 sa Subdivision Sudan under:
  Soil conservation.
  Soil erosion.
--Water-supply.
--Zoology.

Sudan, French.
 x French Sudan.
--Agriculture.
 sa Subdivision Sudan, French under: Rice.
--Domestic animals.
--Entomology.
 sa Subdivision Sudan, French under:
  Entomology, Economic.

Sudan grass.
--Diseases.
--Research.
--Seed.

Sudan grass as feeding stuff.
 xx Feeding stuffs.

Sudan grass silage.
 xx Ensilage.

Sudetes.
--Botany.

Sudetic Mountains. See Sudetes.

Suez Canal.
--Commerce.
-- --Statistics.

Suffolk, Eng.
     sa Subdivision Suffolk, Eng. under:
        Planning, Regional.
     xx England.
--Agriculture.
-- --Periodicals.
--Botany.
--Natural history.
--Ornithology.

Suffolk, Va.
--Economic conditions.
--Industries and resources.
     sa Industrial surveys. Virginia.
        Suffolk.

Suffolk Co., Mass.
--Politics and government.

Suffolk Co., N.Y.
--Agriculture.
--Botany.

Suffolk Co., Va.
     sa Subdivision Suffolk Co. under:
        County surveys. Virginia.
     xx Virginia.
--Economic conditions.
     sa Subdivision Suffolk Co. under:
        Economic surveys. Virginia.
     xx Virginia. Economic conditions.

Suffolk horse.

Suffolk sheep.

Suffrage.   (INDIRECT)
--U.S.
     sa Negroes. Politics and suffrage.
     xx U.S. Politics and government.
--Virginia.
     xx Virginia. Politics and govern-
        ment.

Sugar.   (INDIRECT)
     sa Sugar-beet.
        Saccharimeter.
        Glucose.
        Sorghum.
        Maple sugar.
        Palm sugar.

Sugar (Continued)
     sa Levulose.
        Sugar bounties.
        Maize sugar.
        Molasses.
        Arabinose.
        Peach gum sugar.
        Quince seed sugar.
        Galactose.
        Potato. Sugar content.
        Grape leaves, Sugar in.
        Sucrose.
        Vegetables, Sugar in.
        Malt sugar.
        Fehling's solution.
        Date sugar.
        Coffee, Sugar in.
        Jaggery.
        Sugar substitutes.
        Sugar-cane.
        Rationing. Sugar.
     x Sugar, Raw.
--Abstracts.
--Advertising.
--Analysis and testing.
     sa Subdivision Analysis and
        testing under: Wood sugar.
     x Sugar analysis.
        Sugar testing.
        Sugar scale.
     xx Chemistry. Analysis.
-- --Congresses.
     xx Sugar. Congresses.
--Bacteriology.
--Bibliography.
     sa Subdivision Bibliography under:
        Maple sugar.
        Sugar-cane. Varieties.
        Palm sugar.
        Sugar-cane. Breeding.
        Sugar trade.
-- --Periodicals.
--Color.
     sa Dutch standard of color.
--Competitive commodities.
--Congresses.
     sa Subdivision Congresses under:
        Sugar-cane.
        Sugar-beet.
        Sugar. Analysis and testing.
        Sugar. Legislation.
--Consumption. See Sugar consumption.
--Control of production. See Sugar-cane
     Acreage adjustments; Sugar-beet.
     Acreage adjustments.

Sugar (Continued)
--Cost of production.
    sa Subdivision Cost of production
        under: Maple sugar.
-- --Bibliography.

Sugar, Date. See Date sugar.

Sugar.
--Determination.
--Directories. See Sugar trade. Direc-
    tories.
--Economic aspects.
    xx Agriculture. Economic aspects.
--Expositions.
--Fermentation.
    sa Molasses. Fermentation.
--Food value. See Sugar as food.
--History.
    sa Sugar. Manufacture and refining.
        History.
--Hydrolysis. See Sugar. Inversion.
--Industrial uses.
    xx Chemurgy.
--Inversion.
    x Inversion of sugar.
      Sugar. Hydrolysis.
      Sucrose. Inversion.
    xx Fructose.
      Glucose.
      Invertase.
      Hydrolysis.
-- --Bibliography.
--Juvenile literature.
    xx Agriculture. Juvenile litera-
      ture.
--Legislation.
    sa Subdivision Legislation under:
      Sugar-beet.
      Sugar act of 1934.
      Sugar act of 1937.
      Sugar act of 1948.
-- --Congresses.
    xx Sugar. Congresses.

Sugar, Liquid.
    x Liquid sugar.
--Grading and standardization.
--Marketing.
    xx Sugar. Marketing.
--Statistics.

Sugar.
--Machinery. See Sugar machinery.

Sugar (Continued)
--Manufacture and refining.   (DIRECT)
    sa Sugar machinery.
    x Cane milling.
      Milling (of sugar)
      Sugar-refining.
      Sugar-beet. Manufacture.
      Sugar manufacturing.
-- --Abstracts.
-- --Accounting.
-- --Bibliography.
-- --By-products.
-- --Directories. See Sugar trade. Di-
    rectories.
-- --Handbooks, manuals, etc.
· --History.
-- --Implements and machinery. See
    Sugar machinery.
-- --Laboratory manuals.
-- --Maps.
-- --Periodicals.
-- --Statistics.
    sa Sugar. Manufacture and re-
      fining. ₍geographical sub-
      division₎ Statistics. e.g.
      Sugar. Manufacture and re-
      fining. British Guiana. Sta-
      tistics.
· --Waste.
    xx Factory and trade waste.
--Marketing.
    sa Sugar, Liquid. Marketing.
    xx Marketing.
· --Control.
    sa Subdivision Marketing. Control
      under: Sugar-beet.
--Marketing, Cooperative.
--Marketing agreements.
    xx Marketing agreements.
--Marketing quotas.
    xx Marketing quotas.
--Metabolism.
--Nutritive value. See Sugar as food.
--Periodicals.
    sa Sugar trade. Periodicals.
      Sugar ₍geographic subdivision₎
      Periodicals, e.g., Sugar.
      Formosa. Periodicals.
--Pests.
--Physiological effect.
    xx Physiology.
--Prices.
    sa Sugar-beet. Prices.
· --Fixing.
    xx Prices. Fixing.

Sugar (Continued)
--Processing tax.
  sa Subdivision Processing tax un-
    der: Sugar-cane.
--Production, Control of. See Sugar-
  cane. Acreage adjustments.
--Rationing. See Rationing. Sugar.

Sugar, Raw. See Sugar.

Sugar.
--Refining. See Sugar. Manufacture and
  refining.
--Research.
  sa Sugar [geographic subdivision]
    Research, e.g., Sugar. Ar-
    gentine Republic. Tucuman
    (Province) Research.
--Societies.
--Statistics.
  sa Subdivision Statistics under:
    Sugar trade.
    Sugar-beet.
    Sugar-cane.
    Maple sugar.
    Sugar supply.
    Sugar [geographic subdivision]
    Statistics, e.g., Sugar.
    Peru. Statistics.
-- --Bibliography.
--Storage.
--Tables and ready-reckoners.
--Tariff.
--Taxation.
--Technology.
  x Sugar-beet. Technology.
-- --Periodicals.
--Testing. See Sugar. Analysis and
  testing.
--Trade. See Sugar trade.
--Transportation.
  sa Railroads. Rates. Sugar.
--Utilization in the manufacture of to-
  bacco products. See Sugar utili-
  zation in the manufacture of to-
  bacco products.
--Year-books.
  xx Year-books.

Sugar act of 1934.
  x Jones-Costigan act of 1934.
  xx Sugar. Legislation.

Sugar act of 1937.
  xx Sugar. Legislation.

Sugar act of 1948.
  xx Sugar. Legislation.

Sugar agreement act.
  x Export sugar agreement.
    Commonwealth sugar agreement
    act.

Sugar analysis. See Sugar. Analysis and
  testing.

Sugar as feeding stuff.
  sa Molasses. Massecuite.

Sugar as food.
  x Sugar. Food value.
    Sugar. Nutritive value.

Sugar-beet.   (INDIRECT)
  sa Beet.
    Cookery (Sugar-beet)
    Subdivision Sugar-beet under:
      Rotation of crops.
  xx Sugar.
--Acreage adjustments.
  x Sugar-beet. Control of pro-
    duction.
  xx Farm produce. Control of pro-
    duction.
--Analysis.
--Ash analysis.
  xx Ash analysis.
--Bibliography.
--Breeding.
--By-products.
--Chemistry.
  xx Chemistry, Vegetable.

Sugar-beet, Chlorin in.
  xx Chlorin in plants.
    Sugar-beet. Composition.

Sugar-beet.
--Claims.
  xx Claims and adjustments.
--Composition.
--Control of production. See Sugar-
  beet. Acreage adjustments.
--Cost of production.
--Dictionaries.
--Disease resistant varieties.
  xx Disease resistant plants.

Sugar-beet (Continued)
--Diseases.
    sa Curly-top of sugar-beet.
       Leaf-spot of sugar-beet.
       Mosaic disease of sugar-beet.
       Crown-gall of sugar-beet.
       Virus diseases of sugar-beets.
       Fusarium diseases of sugar-
         beet.
       Sugar-beet rots.
--Economic aspects.

Sugar-beet, Effect of climate on.
    x Climate. Effect on sugar-beet.
    xx Climate and vegetation.

Sugar-beet, Effect of fertilizers on.
    See Fertilizers. Effect on sugar-beet.

Sugar-beet, Effect of nitrogen on.   See
    Nitrogen. Effect on sugar-beet.

Sugar-beet.
--Fertilization.
--Fertilizers.   See Fertilizers for
    sugar-beet.
--Germination.
--Growth.
--Harvesting.
    xx Harvesting.
--Hybrids.
    xx Hybridization.
--Implements and machinery.   See Sugar-
    beet. Machinery.
--Industry and trade.   See Sugar trade.
--Injuries.
--Inoculation.
--Irrigation.
--Legislation.
    xx Sugar. Legislation.
       Agriculture. Law.
--Loading and unloading equipment.
    xx Loading and unloading equip-
       ment.
--Machinery.
    sa Sugar-beet harvester.
    xx Sugar machinery.
       Sugar-beet harvester.
--Manufacture.   See Sugar. Manufacture
    and refining.
--Marketing.
-- --Control.
    xx Farm produce. Marketing. Con-
       trol.
       Sugar. Marketing. Control.

Sugar-beet (Continued)
--Marketing.
-- --Cost.
    xx Farm produce. Marketing. Cost.

Sugar-beet, Nitrogen in.

Sugar-beet.
--Periodicals.
--Pests.
    sa Heterodera schachtii.
       Monoxia puncticollis.
       Hulstea undulatella.
       Loxostege sticticalis.
       Mamestra trifolii.
       Hymenia perspectalis.
       Limonius californicus.
       Pemphigus betae.
       Eutettix tenellus.
       Gnorimoschema ocellatella.
--Physiology and morphology.
    xx Botany. Physiology.
       Botany. Morphology.
--Planting time.
--Prices.
-- --Subsidies.
    xx Farm produce. Prices. Subsi-
       dies.
--Processing.
    xx Processing (Industrial)
--Research.
    sa Sugar-beet [geographic subdi-
       vision] Research, e.g.,
       Sugar-beet. Kirghiz Re-
       public. Research.
--Seed.
-- --Disinfection.
    xx Seeds. Disinfection.
-- --Processing.
    xx Seeds. Processing.
--Spacing.
--Starch content.
    xx Starch.
--Statistics.
    sa Sugar-beet [geographic subdi-
       vision] Statistics, e.g.,
       Sugar-beet. California.
       Statistics.
--Storage.
--Technology.   See Sugar. Technology.
--Testing.
    xx Vegetables. Testing.
--Utilization.
    xx Chemurgy.
--Valuation.

Sugar-beet (Continued)
--Varieties.
--Water requirements.
    xx Water requirements of crops.
--Weed control.

Sugar-beet as feeding stuff.
    sa Sugar-beet silage.
    x Sugar-beet pulp as feeding
      stuff.

Sugar-beet crown-borer.   See Hulstea un-
   dalatella.

Sugar-beet harvester.

Sugar-beet juice.

Sugar-beet leaf-beetle.   See Monoxia
   puncticollis.

Sugar-beet leaf-spot.   See Leaf-spot of
   sugar-beet.

Sugar-beet leafhopper.   See Circulifer
   tenellus.

Sugar-beet leaves.

Sugar-beet nematode.   See Heterodera
   schachtii.

Sugar-beet pulp as feeding stuff.   See
   Sugar-beet as feeding stuff.

Sugar-beet root-louse.   See Pemphigus
   betae.

Sugar-beet rots.
    xx Sugar-beet. Diseases.

Sugar-beet seed.   See Sugar-beet. Seed.

Sugar-beet silage.
    xx Ensilage.
    Sugar-beet as feeding stuff.

Sugar-beet sirup.   See Sugar-beet syrup.

Sugar-beet soils.

Sugar-beet syrup.

Sugar-beet thrips.   See Heliothrips
   femoralis.

Sugar-beet trade.   See Sugar trade.

Sugar-beet waste.
    xx Factory and trade waste.

Sugar-beet web-worm.   See Loxostege
   sticticalis.

Sugar-beet wireworm.   See Limonius
   californicus.

Sugar bounties.

Sugar bush.   See Maple sugar.

Sugar-cane.   (INDIRECT)
    sa Tropical agriculture.
    Bagasse.
    x Cane sugar.
    Saccharum officinarum.
    xx Sugar.
--Acreage adjustments.
    x Sugar. Control of production.
    Sugar. Production, Control of.
--Analysis.
    x Sugar-cane. Testing.
--Bibliography.
    sa Subdivision Bibliography un-
      der: Sugar-cane soils//
--Breeding.
-- --Bibliography.
--By-products.
    xx Waste products.
-- --Industrial uses.

Sugar-cane, Chinese.   See Sorgo.

Sugar-cane.
--Cleaning.
    xx Cleaning.

Sugar-cane, Colloids in.

Sugar-cane.
--Composition.
--Congresses.
    sa Sugar. Congresses.
--Control of production.   See Sugar-
   cane. Acreage adjustments.
--Cost of production.
    xx Farm produce. Cost of pro-
      duction.
--Cytology.

Sugar-cane (Continued)
--Description.
x Sugar-cane. Deterioration.
Sugar-cane. Spoilage.
xx Depreciation.
--Deterioration.   See Sugar-cane. De-
preciation.
--Disease resistant varieties.
xx Disease resistant plants.
--Diseases.
sa Red rot of sugar-cane.
Mosaic disease of sugar-cane.
Root-rot of sugar-cane.
Ringspot of sugar-cane.
Virus diseases of sugar-cane.
Chlorotic streak of sugar-cane.
Leaf scald of sugar-cane.
Sugar-cane wilt.
-- --Bibliography.
--Effect of burning on.
x Burning. Effect on sugar-cane.
--Effect of potash on.   See Potash. Ef-
fect on sugar-cane.

Sugar-cane, Effect of temperature on.   See
Temperature. Effect on sugar-cane.

Sugar-cane.
--Effect of weather on.
--Estimating of crop.
--Fertilizers.   See Fertilizers for
sugar-cane.
--Growth.
--Hybrids.
--Implements and machinery.   See Sugar
machinery.
--Inspection.
--Irrigation.
-- --Bibliography.

Sugar-cane, Kavangire.   See Sugar-cane,
Uba.

Sugar-cane.
--Legislation.
--Marketing.
-- --Research.
--Milling tests.
xx Milling tests.
--Periodicals.
sa Sugar-cane ₍geographic subdivi-
sion₎ Periodicals, e.g.,
Sugar-cane. West Indies
(French) Periodicals.

Sugar-cane (Continued)
--Pests.
sa Ligyrus rugiceps.
Castinia licus.
Diatraea saccharalis.
Sugar-cane weevil.
Ripersia radicicola.
Diaprepes abbreviatus.
Tomaspis.
xx Parasites.
-- --Bibliography.
--Physiology and morphology.
xx Botany. Morphology.
--Planting time.
xx Planting time.
--Prices.
xx Farm produce. Prices.
--Processing tax.
xx Sugar. Processing tax.
Processing tax.
--Propagation.
xx Plant propagation.
--Research.
sa Sugar-cane ₍geographic subdi-
vision₎ Research, e.g.,
Sugar-cane. Argentine Re-
public. Tucumán (Province)
Research.
--Ripening.
--Seed.
--Seedlings.
x Sugar-cane seedlings.
xx Seedlings.
--Societies.
--Soils.   See Sugar-cane soils.
--Spoilage.   See Sugar-cane. Deprecia-
tion.
--Statistics.
sa Subdivision Statistics under
Sugar-cane ₍geographic sub-
division₎ e.g., Sugar-cane.
Jamaica. Statistics.
xx Sugar. Statistics.
--Storage.
--Testing.   See Sugar-cane. Analysis.

Sugar-cane, Uba.

Sugar-cane.
--Varieties.
sa Sugar-cane, Uba.
-- --Bibliography.

Sugar-cane, Vitamins in.   See Vitamins in
sugar-cane.

Sugar-cane.
--Weed control.

Sugar-cane beetle. See Eutheola rugiceps;
Alissonotum crassum.

Sugar-cane borer. See Diatraea saccharalis.

Sugar-cane borer beetle. See Rhabdocnemis obscura.

Sugar-cane factories.
    x Sugar mills.
    xx Factories.
--Directories. See Sugar trade. Directories.

Sugar-cane fiber. See Bagasse.

Sugar-cane mosaic disease. See Mosaic
disease of sugar-cane.

Sugar-cane moth borer. See Diatraea
saccharalis.

Sugarcane production control associations.

Sugar-cane seedlings. See Sugar-cane.
Seedlings.

Sugar-cane soils.
    xx Soil.
--Bibliography.

Sugar-cane-sorgho hybrids.

Sugar-cane syrup.
    xx Syrups.
--Grading and standardization.
--Inspection.
--Statistics.

Sugar-cane wax.

Sugar-cane wilt.
    xx Wilt diseases.
        Sugar-cane. Diseases.

Sugar-cane yields.
    xx Crop yields.

Sugar consumption.
    x Sugar. Consumption.
    xx Food consumption.

Sugar control extension act of 1947.

Sugar equivalents. See Sugar substitutes.

Sugar growing. See Sugar-beet; Sugar-
cane.

Sugar-growing industry employees. See
Sugar workers.

Sugar in animals.

Sugar in blood. See Blood. Sugar.

Sugar in plants.
    sa Tobacco, Sugar in.

Sugar industry and trade. See Sugar
trade.

Sugar laborers. See Sugar workers.

Sugar lactones.

Sugar machinery.
    sa Sugar-beet. Machinery.
        Sugar-beet harvester.
        Maple sugar. Machinery.
    x Sugar. Manufacture and re-
        fining. Implements and
        machinery.

Sugar manufacturing. See Sugar. Manufacture and refining.

Sugar maple. See Acer saccharum.

Sugar-maple borer. See Glycobius speciosus.

Sugar mills. See Sugar cane factories.

Sugar pine. See Pinus lambertiana.

Sugar pine wood. See Pinus lambertiana
(Wood)

Sugar plants.
    sa Agave americana.
        Sorghum.
        Sugar beet.
        Sugar-cane.
    x Sugar producing plants.

Sugar policies and programs.
    xx Agricultural policies and
        programs.

Sugar producing plants. See Sugar plants.

Sugar-refining. See Sugar. Manufacture
  and refining.

Sugar scale. See Sugar. Analysis and
  testing.

Sugar substitutes.
    sa Flour hydrolyzate.
    x Sugar equivalents.
      Cookery without sugar.
      Sugarless cookery.
    xx Toxicology.
      Food substitutes.
      Sugar.
      Substitute products.
--Toxicity.

Sugar supply.
    sa Sugar. Statistics.

Sugar testing. See Sugar. Analysis and
  testing.

Sugar trade.   (DIRECT)
    sa Sugar. Tariff.
      Cipher and telegraph codes.
      Sugar trade.
      Sugar speculation.
      Molasses trade.
      Syrup trade.
    x Sugar-beet. Industry and trade.
      Sugar-beet trade.
--Directories.
    x Sugar-cane factories.
--Exchanges.
    xx Exchanges.
-- --Directories.
--Futures.
--History.
--Periodicals.
    sa Subdivision Periodicals under
      Sugar trade [geographic sub-
      division] e.g., Sugar trade.
      Cuba. Periodicals.
--Statistics.
    sa Subdivision Statistics under
      Sugar trade [geographic sub-
      division] e.g., Sugar trade.
      Peru. Statistics.

Sugar utilization in the manufacture of
  tobacco products.
    x Sugar. Utilization in the manu-
      facture of tobacco products.
    xx Tobacco manufacture and trade.

Sugar workers.
    x Sugar laborers.
      Sugar-growing industry em-
      ployees.
    xx Labor and laboring classes.
      Agricultural laborers.
--Statistics.

Sugarberry. See Celtis laevigata.

Sugarcane. See Sugar-cane.

Sugarless cookery. See Sugar substitutes.

Sugars.
    sa Sedoheptose.
      Birch sugar.
    xx Polysaccharides.
--Bibliography.

Sugars, Compound.

Sugars.
--Effect on plants.
--Metabolism.
    xx Metabolism.

Sugars, Reducing.

Suggestion systems.
    sa Rewards (Prizes, etc.)
    x Employee suggestions.
    xx Efficiency, Industrial.
      Employment management.
      Rewards (Prizes, etc.)
--Bibliography.
--Congresses.

Suggestive therapeutics. See Therapeutics, Suggestive.

Suicides.

Suidae.
    sa Hylochoerus.

Suislaw National Forest.

Sukhanovo state farm.

Sukkur barrage canals project.

Sula. See Gannet.

Sulfamethazine. See Sulfamezathine.

Sulfamezathine.
    x Sulfamethazine.

Sulfanilamide and sulfanilamide deriva-
    tives.
        x Sulfathiazole.
        Sulphanilamide.
        Sulfapyridine.
        Sulfonilamide.
        Sulfonamide compounds.
        Sulphonamides.
        Sulphathiazole.
        Sulfisoxazole.
        Prontosil.
        xx Drugs.
    --Bibliography.
        xx Drugs. Bibliography.

Sulfanilamide and sulfanilamide derivatives
    in veterinary medicine.

Sulfapyridine. See Sulfanilamide and
    sulfanilamide derivatives.

Sulfaquinoxaline.
    --Bibliography.

Sulfarsenol.

Sulfate process (Paper making) See
    Paper making and trade. Sulphate
    process.

Sulfates. See Sulphates.

Sulfathiazole. See Sulfanilamide and
    sulfanilamide derivatives.

Sulfides. See Sulphides.

Sulfigen.
    xx Drugs.

Sulfinates. See Sulphinates.

Sulfinic acids.
    x Acids, Sulfinic.

Sulfisoxazole. See Sulfanilamide and
    sulfanilamide derivatives.

Sulfite process (Paper making) See
    Paper making and trade. Sulphite
    process.

Sulfite pulping. See Paper making and
    trade. Sulphite process.

Sulfites. See Sulphites.

Sulfochloramide.

Sulfofication.
    xx Soil, Sulphur in.

Sulfonamide compounds. See Sulfanila-
    mide and sulfanilamide derivatives.

Sulfones. See Sulphones.

Sulfonilamide. See Sulfanilamide and
    sulfanilamide derivatives.

Sulfonyl compounds.

Sulfoxides. See Sulphoxides.

Sulfur. See Sulphur.

Sulfuric acid. See Sulphuric acid.

Sullivan Co., N.H.
    --Soils.
        sa Subdivision New Hampshire.
        Sullivan Co. under: Soil-
        surveys.

Sullivan Co., N.Y.
    --Agriculture.
        sa Subdivision New York (State)
        Sullivan Co. under: Farms.
    --Soils.
        sa Subdivision New York (State)
        Sullivan Co. under: Soil-
        surveys.

Sullivan Co., Pa.
    --Forestry.
        sa Subdivision Pennsylvania. Sul-
        livan Co. under: Forest
        surveys.

Sullivan Co., Tenn.
    sa Subdivision Tennessee. Sullivan
        Co. under: County surveys.
        Subdivision Sullivan Co., Tenn.
        under: Taxation.
    xx Tennessee.
--Economic conditions.
--Politics and government.
    xx Tennessee. Politics and govern-
        ment.
--Social conditions.
    sa Subdivision Tennessee. Sullivan
        Co. under: Social surveys.
--Soils.
    sa Subdivision Tennessee. Sullivan
        Co. under: Soil-surveys.

Sullys Hill National Park.

Sulphanilamide.   See Sulfanilamide and
    sulfanilamide derivatives.

Sulphanilyl sulphanilamide.
    xx Drugs.

Sulphapyridine.   See Sulfanilamide and
    sulfanilamide derivatives.

Sulphate black liquor soap.   See Tall oil.

Sulphate of ammonia.   See Ammonium sul-
    phate.

Sulphate of copper.   See Copper sulphate.

Sulphate of iron.   See Iron sulphate.

Sulphate of potash.   See Potassium sul-
    phate.

Sulphate process (Paper making)   See Paper
    making and trade. Sulphate process.

Sulphate pulping.   See Paper making and
    trade. Sulphate process.

Sulphated oils.   See Sulphonated oils.
    xx Fats and oils.

Sulphates.
    sa Soil, Sulphates in.
        Anabasine sulphate.
        Nicotine-sulphate.
        Paper making and trade. Sulphate
        process.

Sulphates (Continued)
    x Sulfates.
--Effect on plants.
    x Plants, Effect of sulphates
        on.

Sulphathiazole.   See Sulfanilamide and
    sulfanilamide derivatives.

Sulphides.
    sa Soil, Sulphides in.
        Zinc sulphide.
        Tetrasulphide.
    x Sulfides.
        Disulphides.

Sulphinates.
    x Sulfinates.

Sulphite liquor.
    x Cellulose liquor.
        Sulphite waste liquor.
        Waste sulphite liquor.
    xx Wood. By-products.
        Sulphites.
        Paper making and trade. By-
        products.
        Waste products.
--Bibliography.
--Fermentation.

Sulphite pitch.

Sulphite pulping.   See Paper making and
    trade. Sulphite process.

Sulphite waste as feeding stuff.

Sulphite waste as fertilizer.

Sulphite waste liquor.   See Sulphite
    liquor.

Sulphites.
    sa Paper making and trade. Sul-
        phite process.
        Sulphite liquor.
    x Sulfites.
--Bibliography.
--Effect on plants.

Sulphocyanates.   See Thiocyanates.

Sulphocyanide of ammonia.

Sulphonamides.   See Sulfanilamide and
    sulfanilamide derivatives.

Sulphonated oils.
    x Sulphated oils.
    xx Fats and oils.
--Analysis.
    xx Fats and oils. Analysis.

Sulphones.
    x Sulfones.

Sulphonic acids.

Sulphosteatite.

Sulphotoluic acid, Ortho.
    x Ortho-sulphotoluic acid.
    xx Acids.

Sulphoxides.
    x Sulfoxides.

Sulphur.
        sa Soil, Sulphur in.
           Onions, Sulphur in.
           Mineral waters, Sulphurous.
           Precipitation (Meteorology)
              Sulphur in.
           Air, Sulphur in.
        x Sulfur.
           Sulphuration.
--Bibliography.
--Biochemistry.
--Determination.
--Effect on plants.
-- --Bibliography.
--Effect on wool.
    x Wool. Effect of sulphur.
--Effect on soils.   See Soil. Effect of
    sulphur.
--Therapeutic use.
    xx Materia medica and therapeutics.

Sulphur as a fertilizer.

Sulphur as a fungicide.
    xx Fungicides.

Sulphur as an insecticide.
    x Sulphur dusts.
    xx Insecticides.

Sulphur bacteria.
    xx Bacteria.

Sulphur compounds.
        sa Mercaptans.
--Bibliography.
--Metabolism.

Sulphur dioxide.
        sa Subdivision Sulphur dioxide
           process under: Paper making
           and trade.
           Subdivision Effect of sulphur
           dioxide under: Alfalfa hay.
           Alfalfa silage.
           Wheat.
        x Sulphurous anhydride.
--Effect on trees.
        x Trees, Effect of sulphur
           dioxide on.
        xx Trees. Smoke and smelter fume
           injury.

Sulphur dusts.   See Sulphur as an in-
    secticide.

Sulphur dyes.

Sulphur in plants.

Sulphur mines and mining.

Sulphur residue.

Sulphur trioxide.

Sulphuration.   See Sulphur.

Sulphured grain.
        sa Subdivision Bleaching under:
           Barley.
           Oats.

Sulphuric acid.
        sa Germination. Effect of sul-
           phuric acid.
        x Sulfuric acid.
        xx Acids.
--Determination.
--Statistics.

Sulphuric anhydrid.

Sulphuring of fruits and vegetables.
        x Fruit. Sulphuring.
           Vegetables. Sulphuring.
           Desulphuring of fruits and
           vegetables.

Sulphuring of fruits and vegetables (Con.)
  xx Drying of fruits and vegetables
Sulphurous acid.
  --Effect on plants.
  --Effect on silicates.

Sulphurous anhydride. See Sulphur
  dioxide.

Sulphuryl chloride.

Sultan River.

Sultanas. See Grapes.

Sulu Islands.

Sumac.
  sa Rhus.

Sumadija.
  --Forestry.

Sumatra.
  sa Pedir, Sumatra.
  --Agriculture.
    sa Deli, Sumatra. Agriculture.
    Subdivision Sumatra under:
      Colonization, Agricultural.
  -- --Statistics.
  --Botany.
    sa Subdivision Sumatra under:
      Ferns.
      Trees.
  --Commerce.
  -- --Statistics.
  --Description and travel.
  --Economic conditions.
  --Entomology.
    sa Subdivision Entomology under:
      Simalu (Island)
    Subdivision Sumatra under:
      Diptera.
      Hemiptera.
  --Forestry.
  --Geology.
  --Maps.
    xx East Indies (Dutch) Maps.
  --Meteorology.
  --Ornithology.
  --Soils.
    sa Subdivision Soils under:
      Deli, Sumatra.

Sumatra (Continued)
  --Statistics.
    sa Subdivision Statistics under:
      Sumatra. Agriculture.
  --Water-supply.
    sa Subdivision Water-supply un-
      der: Medan, Sumatra.
  --Zoology.
    sa Subdivision Sumatra under:
      Mammalia.

Sumava. See Bohemian Forest.

Sumava Mountains.
  --Botany.

Sumba. See Sandalwood Island.

Sumida River.
  xx Japan. Rivers.

Summer.

Summer resorts.

Summers Co., W. Va.
  --Soils.
    sa Subdivision West Virginia.
      Summers Co. under: Soil-
      surveys.

Summit Co., Ohio.
  xx Ohio.

Sumter Co., Ala.
  --Soils.
    sa Subdivision Alabama. Sumter
      Co. under: Soil-surveys.

Sumter Co., Fla.
  --Markets.

Sumter Co., Ga.
    sa Subdivision Georgia. Sumter
      Co. under: County surveys.
    xx Georgia.
  --Agriculture.
    sa Subdivision Georgia. Sumter
      Co. under: Agriculture.
      Economic aspects.
      Farm management surveys.
  --Land.
    sa Subdivision Sumter Co., Ga.
      under: Land tenure.

Sumter Co., S.C.
--Economic conditions.
--Social conditions.
 sa Subdivision South Carolina.
  Sumter Co. under: Social
   surveys.
--Soils.
 sa Subdivision South Carolina.
  Sumter Co. under: Soil-
   surveys.

Sumter National Forest, S.C.
 xx South Carolina. Forest reservations.

Sun.
 sa Atmosphere, Solar.
  Sun-spots.
 xx Astronomy.

Sun-baths.
 xx Therapeutics, Physiological.

Sun-birds. See Nectariniidae.

Sun dials.

Sun River irrigation project.

Sun River Valley, Mont.
--Soils.
 sa Subdivision Montana. Sun River
  Valley under: Soil conservation.

Sun-spots.
 x Sunspots.
 xx Magnetism, Terrestrial.
  Meteorology.
  Solar radiation.
  Sun.
--Effect on animals.
 x Animals. Effect of sun-spots.

Sunbirds.

Sunburn.

Sunda Islands.
 sa Lesser Sunda Islands.
--Geology.
--Paleontology.
--Zoology.
 sa Araneida. Sunda Islands.

Sundarbans, India.
--Botany.
 sa Chakaria Sundarbans, Bengal.
  Botany.

Sunday-schools.
 xx Schools.

Sundays River Valley, Natal.
--Pomology.
 sa Subdivision Sundays River
  Valley under: Citrus. Natal.
--Soils.
 xx Natal. Soils.

Sunderbuns. See Sundarbans.

Sundri. See Heritiera minor.

Sundribuns. See Sundarbans.

Sunfish.
 sa Lepomis.

Sunflower.
 xx Oleaginous plants.
--Bibliography.
--Breeding.
--Composition.
--Growth.
--Harvesting.
--Implements and machinery.
--Physiology and morphology.
--Seeds. See Sunflower seed.
--Statistics.
--Weather influences.
 xx Crops and climate.

Sunflower as a feeding stuff.

Sunflower Co., Miss.
--Soils.
 sa Subdivision Mississippi. Sunflower Co. under: Soil-
  surveys.

Sunflower seed.
 xx Sunflower. Seeds.
--Estimating of crop.
 xx Crop estimating.
--Prices.
 xx Oil-seeds. Prices.

Sunflower seed cake.

Sunflower seed oil.
--Processing.
-- --Equipment.
    xx Fats and oils. Processing.
       Equipment.

Sunflower silage.
--Bibliography.

Sungaria.
--Botany.
--Description and travel.

Sunlight.
--Therapeutic use.   See Sun-baths.

Sunlight recorder.   See Light recorder.

Sunn hemp.   See Sann.

Sunnerbo, Sweden.
--History.

Sunshine.
--Bibliography.

Sunshine recorder.

Sunshine tables.

Sunspots.   See Sun-spots.

Suomi.   See Finland.

Supella supellectilium.
    x Brown-banded cockroach.
    xx Blattidae.

Super markets.
    x Food stores.
       Grocery stores.
       Market stores.
       Supermarkets.
       Food marketing.
    xx Markets.
--Directories.
--Periodicals.
-- --Indexes.

Superb plant bug.   See Adelphocoris
  superbus.

Superfinish.   See Metals. Finishing.

Superhighways.   See Roads. Superhighways.

Superior, Lake.   See Lake Superior.

Superior, Wis.
--Milk trade.

Superior-Courtland Diversion Dam.

Superior National Forest, Minn.
    xx Minnesota. Forest reserva-
       tions.
--Maps.

Supermarkets.   See Super markets.

Superphosphates.
       sa Oberphos.
       Serpentine superphosphates.

Superphosphates, Ammoniated.
    xx Ammonia.

Superphosphates, Bone.

Superphosphates, Phosphoric acid in.

Superphosphates, Granulated.
    xx Fertilizers. Granulation.

Superphosphates.
--Prices.
--Reversion.
--Statistics.

Supersonics.   See Ultrasonics; Ultrasonic testing.

Superstition.

Supervisors.
    xx Efficiency, Industrial.
       Employment management.
--Bibliography.
--Congresses.

Supplies, Laboratory.   See Laboratories.
    Apparatus and supplies.

Supplies, Military.   See Military
  supplies.

Supplies and stores.   See U.S. Executive
    departments. Equipment and supplies.

Supply and demand.
    sa Overproduction.
    Domestic allotment plan.
    x Demand (Economics)
    Production (Economics)
--Bibliography.

Supply and demand curves.   See Curves,
  Statistical.

Support prices. See Price subsidies.

Suprarenal glands. See Adrenal glands.

Suprarenin. See Adrenalin.

Suptol.

Surabaya.
--Geology.
--Maps.

Surat. Experimental Farm.

Suretyship and guaranty.

Surf fishing. See Salt-water fishing.
  \
Surface active agents.
    x Surfactants.
    xx Chemistry, Organic.
    Surface tension.

Surface chemistry.
    sa Capillarity.
    Catalysis.
    Colloids.
    Surface tension.
    x Chemistry, Surface.
    Surface phenomena.
    Surfaces (Chemistry)
    Chemisorption.
    xx Capillarity.
    Chemistry, Physical and
      theoretical.
    Surface tension.
--Congresses.

Surface phenomena. See Surface chemistry.

Surface tension.
    sa Capillarity.
    Surface active agents.
    Surface chemistry.

Surface tension (Continued)
    xx Surface chemistry.
    Capillarity.

Surfaces.
    sa Subdivision Surfaces under:
      Roads.
--Areas and volumes.

Surfaces (Chemistry) See Surfaces
  chemistry.

Surfaces (Metallurgy) See Surfaces
  (Technology)

Surfaces (Technology)
    x Surfaces (Metallurgy)
    xx Friction.
    Testing.
--Congresses.

Surfactants. See Surface active agents.

Surge (Electricity) See Transients
  (Electricity)

Surge pressure. See Water hammer.

Surgery.
    sa Anaesthetics.
    Surgical instruments.
    Antisepsis.
    Autopsy.
    Veterinary surgery.
    Fractures.
    Neurotomy.
    Neurectomy.
--Dictionaries.

Surgery, Experimental.

Surgery, Orthopedic. See Orthopedia.

Surgery.
--Periodicals.

Surgical instruments and apparatus.

Surgical knots. See Sutures.

Surinam. See Dutch Guiana.

Surinam cherry. See Eugenia uniflora.

Surnadal, Norway.

Suroide.
  xx Germany.

Surplus agricultural commodities. See
  Agricultural surpluses.

Surplus cereals. See Cereals. Surplus.

Surplus farm products. See Agricultural
  surpluses.

Surplus government property.
  sa Surplus war property.
  xx U.S. Government property.

Surplus grain. See Cereals. Surplus.

Surplus materials. See Surplus products.

Surplus potatoes. See Potatoes. Surplus.

Surplus products.
  sa Surplus war property.
    Agricultural surpluses.
  x Surplus materials.
    Surplus property.

Surplus property. See Surplus products.

Surplus property act, 1944.

Surplus war property.   (DIRECT)
  x War surpluses.
  xx World War, 1939-1945. Supplies.
    Surplus products.
    Surplus government property.
  --Bibliography.

Surra.
  sa Tsetse-flies.
    Trypanosoma.

Surra américain. See Mal de caderas.

Surrey, Eng.
  sa Subdivision Surrey, Eng. under:
    Planning, Regional.
  --Agriculture.
  --Botany.
    sa Subdivision England. Surrey un-
      der: Trees.
      Shrubs.
  --Dairying.

Surrey, Eng. (Continued)
  --Entomology.
    sa Subdivision England. Surrey
      under: Lepidoptera.
  --Forestry.
    sa Subdivision England. Surrey
      under: Trees.
  --Natural history.

Surrol.
  xx Antibiotics.

Surry Co., N.C.
  --Soils.
    sa Subdivision North Carolina.
      Surry Co. under: Soil-
      surveys.

Surveying.
  sa Geodesy.
    Cadastral surveys.
    Egypt. Cadastral surveys.
    Azimuth.
    Photographic surveying.
    Topographical surveying.
    Railroad surveying.
    Surveying.
    Public lands.
    Aerial surveys.
    Hydrographic surveying.
    Area measurement.
  xx Geodesy.
  --Congresses.
  --Dictionaries.
  --Handbooks, manuals, etc.
  --Law.

Surveying, Marine.   See Hydrographic
  surveying.

Surveying.
  --Periodicals.

Surveying, Photographic. See Photographic surveying.

Surveying.
  --Study and teaching.
    xx Education.
  --Tables, etc.
    sa Stadia tables.
  --Terminology.
  --Text-books.

Surveying fees.
   x Fees.

Surveying instruments.
   sa Stereo-comparagraph.
      Tachymeter.

Surveyors.
   --Gt. Brit.
   -- --Directories.

Surveys.
   sa Rural surveys.
      Social surveys.
      Farm management surveys.
      Topographical surveying.
      Food surveys.
      Traffic surveys.
      Aerial surveys.
      Business surveys.
      Educational surveys.
      Industrial surveys.
      Health surveys.
      Housing surveys.
      Soil-surveys.
      Evaluation surveys.
      Economic surveys.
      Market surveys.
      Home economics surveys.
      Agricultural surveys.
      Flood surveys.
      Entomological surveys.
      Subdivision Surveys under:
        U.S.//
   --Bibliography.
     sa Subdivision Bibliography under:
       Marketing surveys.

Surveys, Library. See Library surveys.

Surveys.
   --Methodology.
     xx Methodology.

Survival (after aeroplane accidents, ship-
  wrecks, etc.)
     sa Survival planning.
     xx Survival planning.
       Outdoor life.
       Life-saving.

Survival and emergency equipment. See
  Survival planning.

Survival and emergency rations. See
  Survival planning.

Survival kits. See Survival planning.

Survival planning.
   sa Survival (after aeroplane
      accidents, shipwrecks, etc.)
   x Survival and emergency rations.
     Survival and emergency equip-
      ment.
     Survival kits.
   xx Survival (after aeroplane
      accidents, shipwrecks, etc.)
     Civilian defense.

Sus scrofa. See Wild swine.

Susitna River, Alaska.

Suslik. See Spermophilus citillus.

Suspended load. See Sedimentation and
  deposition.

Suspension bridges. See Bridges, Suspension.

Susquehanna Boom Co.

Susquehanna Co.

Susquehanna Co., Pa.
   sa Subdivision Pennsylvania. Sus-
     quehanna Co. under:
     County surveys.
     Rural churches.
   xx Pennsylvania.
   --Agriculture.
   --Forestry.
     sa Subdivision Pennsylvania. Sus-
     quehanna Co. under: Forest
     surveys.

Susquehanna fine sandy loam.

Susquehanna region.
   --Botany.

Susquehanna River.
   sa Subdivision Susquehanna River
     under: Flood control.

Susquehanna Valley.
--History.
    xx Pennsylvania. History.

Sussex, Eng.
--Agriculture.
--Botany.
    sa Subdivision England. Sussex
        under: Mosses.
--Natural history.
--Social life and customs.

Sussex cattle.
    xx Cattle.

Sussex fowl.

Sustained yield management (Forestry)
    x Continuous forest.
      Forests, Continuous.
    xx Forest management.
--Bibliography.

Sutherland, Scot.
--Agriculture.
--Paleobotany.

Sutroa rostrata.

Sutter Basin, Calif.
--Soils.

Sutter Co., Calif.

Sutton's Island, Me.

Sutures.
    x Knots, Surgical.
      Surgical knots.
      Ligatures, Surgical.

Suwannee Co., Fla.
--Agriculture.
    sa Subdivision Florida. Suwannee Co.
      under: Agricultural laborers.
      Agriculture. Economic as-
        pects.
      Cropping systems.
    xx Florida. Agriculture.

Suwannee River.

Suye Mura, Japan.
    xx Japan.

Suye Mura, Japan (Continued)
--Social life and customs.
    xx Japan. Social life and customs.

Svaert horse.
    xx Horses.

Svalbard.   See Spitzbergen.

Svalöf method.

Svealand, Sweden.
--Botany.

Svendborgamt, Denmark.
--Agriculture.

Sverdlovsk Region.
--Agriculture.
    sa Subdivision Sverdlovsk Region
      under: Forage plants.

Sverige.   See Sweden.

Sveriges riksbank.   See Sweden; Riks-
    banken.

Swabia.
--Agriculture.
    sa Subdivision Swabia under:
      Farm mangement.
--Forestry.
--Pharmacy.
-- --Bio-bibliography.
--Viticulture.

Swabian-Halle swine.
    x Schwäbisch-Hällisches swine.

Swahili language.
--Dictionaries.

Swain Co., N.C.
--Soils.
    sa Subdivision North Carolina.
      Swain Co. under: Soil-surveys.

Swaledale sheep.

Swallows.
    x Hirundinidae.

Swamp bay.   See Persea pubescens.

Swamp beaver.   See Coypou.

Swamp cottonwood.   See Populus hetero-
    phylla.

Swamp fever.   See Anemia, Infectious.

Swamp gardens.   See Water gardens.

Swamp plants.   See Aquatic plants.

Swamp rabbit.   See Rabbits.

Swamp sumach.
    sa Rhus venenata.

Swamps.   See Bogs; Marshes.

Swan Hill irrigation district, Victoria,
    Australia.
  --Soils.

Swan River Colony.
  --Botany.
        xx Australia. Botany.

Swans.
        xx Water-fowl.

Swansea, Wales.
  --Agriculture.
  --Entomology.
        xx Wales. Entomology.
  --Natural history.

Swant.   See Panicum frumentaceum.

Swat canal.   See Upper Swat canal.

Swaziland.
  --Agriculture.
        sa Subdivision Swaziland under:
            Colonization, Agricultural.
        xx Africa, South. Agriculture.
  --Botany.
        xx Africa, South. Botany.
  --Cattle.
        xx Swaziland. Domestic animals.
  --Census.
  --Domestic animals.
        sa Swaziland. Cattle.
  --Economic conditions.
  --Forestry.
  --Native races.
  --Statistics.

Sweaters.

Sweating of fruit.
    sa Subdivision Sweating under:
        Orange.

Sweden.
    sa Kloten, Sweden (Lake)
        Sarek region, Sweden.
        Götaland, Sweden.
        Gotland (Island)
  --Agricultural experiment stations.
    sa Halmstad, Kemiska station.
        Hernösand.
        Kemiska station//
  --Agricultural schools.   See Sweden.
        Agriculture. Education.
  --Agriculture.
    sa Subdivision Agriculture under:
        Norrland, Sweden.
        Skaraborg, Sweden.
        Dalarne, Sweden//
        Bjärka Säby (estate)
        Subdivision Sweden under:
        Gardening.
        Agriculture, Cooperative.
        Agriculture. Economic as-
            pects.
        Agricultural laborers.
        Maize.
        Farm buildings.
        Sugar-beet.
        Farm produce. Cost of
            production.
        Field crops.
        Flax.
        Farm management surveys.
        Vegetable gardening.
        War and agriculture (1939-
            1945)
        Hemp.
        Potatoes.
        Forage plants.
        Hops.
        Irrigation.
        Drug plants.
        Mechanized farming.
        Agricultural indebtedness.
        Farms.
        Agricultural credit.
        Types of farming.
    -- --Bibliography.
        xx Agriculture. Bibliography.

Sweden (Continued)
--Agriculture.
-- --Education.
  sa Akarp. Folkhögskolan och lant-
    mannaskolan, Hvilan.
  Gardsjö, Sweden. Lantbruks-
    skolan.
  Landtbruks-akademien,
    Stockholm//
  x Sweden. Agricultural schools.
-- --Directories.
- --History.
  xx Agriculture. History.
-- --Periodicals.
-- --Statistics.
  sa Agricultural laborers. Sweden.
    Statistics.
--Apiculture.
--Biography.
-- --Dictionaries.
--Botany.
  sa Subdivision Botany under:
    Dalarne, Sweden.
    Göteborg.
    Scania, Sweden//
  Subdivision Sweden under:
    Trees.
    Shrubs.
    Botany, Economic.
    Fungi.
    Algae.
    Grasses.
    Plants, Cultivated.
    Lichens.
    Mosses.
    Mushrooms.
    Weeds.
    Food plants.
    Botany, Medical.
    Oleaginous plants.
    Fresh-water flora.
    Vegetable pathology.
-- --Bibliography.
-- --History.
--Cattle.
  xx Cattle.
--Civilization.
--Climate.
--Commerce.
  sa Subdivision Sweden under:
    Oil-seed trade.
    Citrus trade.
- --Brazil.
- --Iran.
-- --Directories.

Sweden (Continued)
--Commerce.
-- --Periodicals.
-- --Statistics.
  sa Göteborg. Commerce. Statistics.
--Commercial policy.
--Dairying.
  sa Subdivision Dairying under:
    Norrland.
  Subdivision Sweden under:
    Dairy industry and trade.
-- --Societies.
-- --Statistics.
--Description and travel.
  sa Subdivision Sweden under:
    Hunting.
  Subdivision Description and
    travel under: Scania.
    Gotland (Island)
--Directories.
--Domestic animals.
  sa Sweden. Cattle.
    Sweden. Swine.
    Sweden. Horse.
-- --Legislation.
-- --Research.
-- --Statistics.
--Economic conditions.
  sa Subdivision Economic condi-
    tions under: Norrland,
    Sweden.
  Subdivision Sweden under:
    History, Economic.
    World War, 1939-1945. Eco-
      nomic aspects.
    Economic surveys.
-- --Periodicals.
--Economic policy.
--Education.
  sa Subdivision Sweden under:
    Rural schools.
--Emigration and immigration.
  xx Emigration and immigration.
--Entomology.
  sa Subdivision Sweden under:
    Entomology, Economic.
    Coleoptera.
    Lepidoptera.
    Hymenoptera.
    Orthoptera.
    Diptera.
    Heteroptera.
    Butterflies.
    Trees. Pests.

Sweden (Continued)
--Fisheries.
    sa Subdivision Fisheries under
      names of provinces, etc.,
      e.g., Gotland, Sweden
      (Island) Fisheries.
--Forest reservations.
--Forestry.
    sa Subdivision Forestry under:
      Kopparberg, Sweden.
      Norrland.
      Wermland//
    Subdivision Sweden under: Trees.
      Forest surveys.
      Forest industries.
      Lumber trade.
      Timber.
      Forest products.
      Lumbering.
      Forest policy.
      Forest management.
-- --Bibliography.
    xx Forestry. Bibliography.
- --History.
-- --Periodicals.
-- --Societies.
-> --Statistics.
--Geology.
    sa Subdivision Geology under:
      Skaraborg, Sweden.
      Halland, Sweden.
--Government publications.
-- --Bibliography.
    xx Government publications.
      Bibliography.
--History.
    sa Subdivision Sweden under:
      History, Economic.
--Horse.
    sa Subdivision Sweden under:
      Horses, Breeding.
    xx Sweden. Domestic animals.
--Ichthyology.
--Industries.
-- --Statistics.
--Land.
    sa Subdivision Sweden under:
      Waste lands.
      Farm valuation.
      Farm land values.
      Land reform.
      Land utilization.
    Subdivision Land under names of
      districts, etc.
--Language. See Swedish language.

Sweden (Continued)
--Markets.
    sa Subdivision Markets under:
      Malmo, Sweden.
--Meteorology.
--Milk supply.
    sa Subdivision Milk supply under:
      Stockholm.
    xx Milk supply.
--Milk trade.
--Monopolies.
--Museums.
--Natural history.
    sa Subdivision Natural history
      under: Norrland.
      Sarek region, Sweden.
      Scania, Sweden//
--Officials and employees.
-- --Directories.
--Ornithology.
    sa Subdivision Ornithology under:
      Götland, Sweden.
--Paleobotany.
--Paleontology.
    sa Subdivision Paleontology under:
      Gotland.
      Scania, Sweden.
--Politics and government.
    xx Scandinavia. Politics and
      government.
--Pomology.
    sa Subdivision Sweden under:
      Berries.
--Population.
    sa Subdivision Population under
      names of provinces, etc.
    Subdivision Sweden under:
      Migration, Internal.
    xx Population.
-- --Bibliography.
--Public lands.
    sa Subdivision Public lands under:
      Norrland, Sweden.
--Public works.
    xx Public works.
--Railroads.
    xx Sweden. Transportation.
-- --History.
--Religion.
    xx Religion.
--Research.
    xx Research.
--Roads.
-- --Law.
    xx Roads. Legislation.

Sweden (Continued)
--Roads.
-- --Periodicals.
-- --Societies.
--Seed control stations.
    sa Borås.
      Christianstad.
      Gefleborg//
--Social conditions.
    sa Subdivision Sweden under:
      Community life.
    xx Europe. Social conditions.
--Social life and customs.
    sa Subdivision Social life and
      customs under: Götland,
        Sweden.
--Soils.
    sa Subdivision Soils under:
      Scania.
      Skaraborg//
      Subdivision Sweden under:
      Peat.
      Soil conservation.
      Soil erosion.
    xx Europe. Soils.
-- --Periodicals.
--Statistics.
    sa Sweden, Commerce. Statistics.
--Statistics, Vital.
-- --Bibliography.
--Swine.
--Transportation.
    sa Subdivision Sweden under:
      World War, 1939-1945. Trans-
        portation.
      Railroads.
--Water-supply.
    sa Subdivision Sweden under:
      Water, Underground.
--Zoology.
    sa Subdivision Zoology under:
      Hjälmar, Sweden.
      Lappmark, Sweden.
      Subdivision Sweden under:
      Araneida.
      Vertebrates.
      Fur-bearing animals.
      Fresh-water fauna.
      Mammalia.

Sweden, N.Y.
--Statistics.
    xx Monroe Co., N.Y. Statistics.

Swedes (Vegetable) See Rutabaga.

Swedes in the U.S.
--Bibliography.
--Biography.
    xx Sweden. Biography.

Swedish botanists. See Botanists,
    Swedish.

Swedish Friesian cattle.
    x SLB.
      Svensk läglands boskap.
      Black-and white Swedish cattle.
      Swedish lowland cattle.
    xx Friesian cattle.

Swedish landrace swine.
    xx Landrace swine.

Swedish language.
    x Sweden. Language.
--Dictionaries.
--Glossaries, vocabularies, etc.
--Grammar.

Swedish literature.
--Bibliography.
-- --Periodicals.

Swedish periodicals.
--Bibliography.

Swedish red and white cattle.
    x SRB (Sweden)

Swedish select oats. See Oats.

Swedish turnip. See Rutabaga.

Sweeping compounds.
    x Floor-sweeping compounds.
    xx Cleaning compounds.

Sweet clover. See Clover, Sweet.

Sweet clover disease.
    xx Cattle. Diseases.

Sweet clover silage.
    xx Clover, Sweet.
      Ensilage.

Sweet corn. See Maize, Sweet.

Sweet gum. See Liquidambar styraciflua.

Sweet peas.
--Breeding.
--Diseases.
--Seed.

Sweet pepper.   See Red pepper.

Sweet potato flakes.
    xx Potato flakes.

Sweet potato internal cork.
    x Internal cork disease of
        sweet potatoes.

Sweet potato leaf beetle.   See Typophorus
    viridicyaneus.

Sweet potato leaf-folder.   See Pilocrocis
    tripunctata.

Sweet potato scurf.

Sweet potato sirup.   See Sweet potato
    syrup.

Sweet potato starch.
    xx Starch.
        Sweet potatoes, Uses of.
--Bibliography.
    xx Sweet potatoes. Bibliography.
        Starch. Bibliography.

Sweet potato stem rot.

Sweet potato syrup.

Sweet potato weevil.   See Cylas formi-
    carius.

Sweet potato wilt.

Sweet potato yields.
    xx Crop yields.

Sweet potatoes.   (INDIRECT)
    sa Food plants.
        Vitamins in sweet potatoes.
        Cookery (Sweet potatoes)
    x Sweetpotatoes.
    xx Vegetables. By-products.
--Acreage adjustments.
    x Sweet potatoes. Control of
        production.
--Analysis.
    xx Food. Analysis.

Sweet potatoes (Continued)
--Anatomy.
    xx Botany. Anatomy.
--Bibliography.
    sa Subdivision Bibliography
        under: Sweet potato starch.
--By-products.
    xx By-products.

Sweet potatoes, Canned.
--Grading and standardization.
    xx Sweet potatoes. Grading.
        Vegetables, Canned. Grading
        and standardization.
--Statistics.

Sweet potatoes.
--Canning.
--Composition.
--Consumption.
    xx Vegetables. Consumption.
--Control of production.   See Sweet
    potatoes. Acreage adjustments.
--Cost of production.
--Curing.
    xx Curing.
--Disease resistant varieties.
    xx Disease resistant plants.
--Diseases.
    sa Sweet potato scurf.
        Sweet potato stem rot.
        Root-rot of sweet potatoes.
        Black rot of sweet potatoes.
        Charcoal rot of sweet pota-
            toes.
        Soft rot of sweet potatoes.

Sweet potatoes, Dried.   See Dried
    sweet potatoes.

Sweet potatoes.
--Drying.
    xx Potatoes. Drying.
        Drying of fruits and
            vegetables.

Sweet potatoes, Effect of humidity on.
    See Humidity. Effect on sweet pota-
    toes.

Sweet potatoes, Effect of potash on.
    See Potash. Effect on sweet potatoes.

Sweet potatoes, Effect of temperature on.
See Temperature. Effect on sweet potatoes.

Sweet potatoes.
--Estimating of crop.
--Fertilizers.   See Fertilizers for
   sweet potatoes.
--Financing.
      xx Farm produce. Financing.
--Fumigation.
      xx Fumigation.
--Grading and standardization.
      sa Subdivision Grading and
         standardization under:
         Sweet potatoes, Canned.
         Dried sweet potatoes.
      xx Vegetables. Grading and
         standardization.
--Harvesting.
-- --Costs.
--Harvesting time.
--Injuries.
--Inspection.
--Marketing.
      xx Marketing of farm produce.
         Potato. Marketing.
         Vegetables. Marketing.
--Marketing, Cooperative.
      xx Vegetables. Marketing,
         Cooperative.
--Nutritive value.   See Sweet potatoes
   as food.
--Periodicals.
--Pests.
      sa Typophorus viridicyaneus.
         Cylas formicarius.
         Pilocrocis tripunctata.
--Planting time.
      xx Planting time.
         Vegetables. Planting time.
--Prices.
      xx Vegetables. Prices.
         Potatoes. Prices.
         Prices.
-- --Subsidies.
      xx Food. Prices. Subsidies.
--Processing.
--Propagation.
      xx Plant propagation.
--Research.
--Seed.
-- --Cost of production.

Sweet potatoes (Continued)
--Seed.
-- --Disinfection.
      xx Disinfection and disinfect-
         ants.
         Vegetables. Seed. Disinfec-
         tion.
--Spacing.
      xx Plant spacing.
--Statistics.
      sa Sweet potatoes [geographic
         subdivision] Statistics,
         e.g., Sweet potatoes.
         Japan. Okayama-ken.
         Statistics.
      xx Vegetables. Statistics.
-- --Maps.
--Storage.
--Transplanting.
      xx Transplanting.

Sweet potatoes, Uses of.
      sa Sweet potatoes as feeding
         stuff.
         Sweet potato starch.
      x Sweet potatoes. Utilization.

Sweet potatoes.
--Utilization.   See Sweet potatoes,
   Uses of.
--Varieties.
-- --Pictorial works.
--Wounds.
      xx Wounds in plants.

Sweet potatoes as feeding stuff.
      xx Sweet potatoes, Uses of.

Sweet potatoes as food.
      x Sweet potatoes. Nutritive
         value.
      xx Food. Nutritive value.

Sweet sorghum.   See Sorgo.

Sweet tussac.   See Tussac, Sweet.

Sweet vernal grass.

Sweeteners, Synthetic.
      sa Saccharin.
         Saccharine products.
      x Synthetic sweeteners.
         Artificial sweeteners.
      xx Synthetic products.

Sweetgum.   See Liquidambar styraciflua.

Sweetpotato weevil.   See Cylas formi-
carius.

Sweetpotatoes.   See Sweet potatoes.

Sweetwater Co., Wyo.
--Economic conditions.

Swick Dam, Or.

Swietenia.
sa Mahogany.

Swifts.

Swimming pools.
xx Pools.

Swindlers and swindling.

Swine.
sa Bacon.
Blood. Swine.
Herd-book (Swine)
Pachydermata.
Pork.
Wild swine.
Subdivision Swine under names
of countries, etc.
Duroc-Jersey swine.
Hampshire swine.
Lincolnshire curly-coated pig//
x Pigs.
Sows.
Hogs.
xx Domestic animals.
--Age.
xx Domestic animals. Age.
--Anatomy and physiology.
sa Shield (Swine)
Eye. Swine.
Subdivision Swine under:
Embryology.
xx Anatomy.
-- --Laboratory manuals.
--Bibliography.
sa Subdivision Bibliography under:
Swine. Prices.
xx Domestic animals. Bibliography.
--Breeding.
sa Swine testing.
Swine. Performance records and
registration.

Swine (Continued)
--Breeding.
-- --Periodicals.
- --Research.
xx Domestic animals. Breeding.
Research.
--Breeds.
sa Names of specific breeds
listed under Swine, e.g.,
Hampshire swine.
xx Domestic animals. Breeds.
--Castration.
--Composition.
--Congresses.
--Control of production.
-- --Periodicals.
--Cost of production.
xx Cost of production.
--Damage to forests.
xx Trees. Animal injury.
--Diseases.
sa Veterinary medicine.
Trichinosis.
Swine plague.
Hog cholera.
Scabies.
Necrotic stomatitis.
Mesenteric emphysema.
Swine erysipelas.
Scurvy.
Embryonal adenosarcoma.
Swine dysentery.
East African swine fever.
Brucellosis in swine.
Rhinitis (Swine)
Vesicular exanthema of swine.
Encephalo-myelitis. Swine.
Meningitis. Swine.
Pneumonia, Swine.
Swine influenza.
Vesicular stomatitis.
--Effect of hormones.   See Hormones.
Effect on swine.
--Exhibitions.
-- --Prizes.
--Fatness.
xx Fatness of animals.
--Fattening.
-- --Bibliography.
--Fecundity.
xx Fecundity.
--Feeding.

Swine, Fossil.

Swine.
--Genetics.
--Grading and standardization.
    xx Domestic animals. Grading and
        standardization.
--Grazing.
--Growth.
--History.
    sa Subdivision History under:
        Missouri. Swine//

Swine, Infectious paralysis of.   See
   Encephalo-myelitis. Swine.

Swine.
--Judging.
--Leanness.
    x Meat-type hog.
    xx Leanness of animals.
--Legislation.
--Marketing.
    xx Marketing of live stock.
 --Control.
    xx Marketing of live stock.
        Control.
--Marketing, Cooperative.
    xx Marketing of live stock,
        Cooperative.
-- --Societies.
    x Swine. Societies.
--Marketing.
-- --Cost.
    xx Marketing of live stock. Cost.
- --Research.
    xx Marketing. Research.
--Metabolism.
    sa Metabolism in swine.
--Nutrition.
    xx Animal nutrition.
-- --Bibliography.
--Parasites.
    sa Strongyloides ransomi.
--Performance records and registration.
    x Performance records (Swine)
      Record of performance (Swine)
      Advanced registry (Swine)
    xx Live stock records.
      Swine. Breeding.
--Periodicals.
    sa Subdivision Periodicals under:
      Poland China swine.
      Duroc-Jersey swine.
      Hampshire swine//
--Pests.
    sa Haematopinus adventicius.

Swine (Continued)
--Policies and programs. See Swine
   policies and programs.
--Prices.
-- --Bibliography.
    xx Prices. Bibliography.
      Swine. Bibliography.
 --Fixing.
    xx Prices. Fixing.
-- --Subsidies.
    xx Domestic animals. Prices.
      Subsidies.
--Processing tax.
--Research.
--Shrinkage.
    xx Shrinkage.
--Slaughtering.
--Societies. See Swine breeders'
   societies; Swine. Marketing,
   Cooperative. Societies//
--Statistics.
    sa Subdivision Swine. Statis-
      tics. under: Canada.
      Europe//
    xx Domestic animals. Statistics.
-- --Maps.
--Sterility.
--Study and teaching.
--Tariff.
    sa Pork. Tariff.
--Transportation.
--Watering.
    xx Water requirements of
      animals.
      Watering of animals.
--Weight and measurement.

Swine, Wild. See Wild swine.

Swine breeders' directories.

Swine breeders' societies.

Swine bristles. See Hog bristles.
    xx Bristles.

Swine brooders, Electric.
    x Electric brooders.
      Electric pig brooders.
      Electric swine brooders.
      Pig brooders, Electric.
    xx Swine houses and equipment.

Swine clubs. See Pig clubs.

Swine crates.

Swine dysentery.
    sa Vibrionic dysentery.
    x Dysentery in swine.

Swine equipment. See Swine houses and
equipment.

Swine erysipelas.
    x Diamond-skin disease of swine.
--Preventive inoculation.

Swine farms.

Swine fever. See Hog cholera.

Swine fever, East African. See East
African swine fever.

Swine houses and equipment.
    sa Swine brooders, Electric.
    x Hog houses.
      Hog slaughtering equipment.
      Swine equipment.
      Swine-lot equipment.
    xx Farm buildings.
      Farm equipment.
--Designs and plans.
    xx Farm buildings. Designs and
      plans.
--Sanitation.
--Ventilation.
    xx Ventilation.

Swine influenza.
    x Influenza, Swine.
    xx Swine. Diseases.

Swine-lot equipment. See Swine houses
and equipment.

Swine-milk.

Swine plague.
    sa Bruschettini's swine plague
      serum.

Swine policies and programs.
    x Swine. Policies and programs.

Swine records. See Swine. Performance
records and registration.

Swine roundworms. See Ascaris lumbri-
coides.

Swine testing.

Swine's milk cheese. See Cheese,
Swine's milk.

Swiss Alps. See Alps, Swiss.

Swiss cattle. See Brown Swiss cattle;
Simmental cattle.

Swiss cheese. See Cheese, Swiss.

Swiss in Tennessee.
    xx Switzerland. Emigration and
      immigration.

Swiss in the U.S.
    xx Switzerland. Emigration and
      immigration.

Swiss literature.
    x Switzerland. Literature.
--Bibliography.
-- --Periodicals.

Swiss periodicals.
--Bibliography.

Swiss rye grass.
    x Lolium rigidum.
      Wimmera rye grass.

Switzerland.
    sa Chippis, Switzerland.
      Lake Brienz, Switzerland.
--Agricultural experiment stations.
    sa Switzerland. Schweizerische
      agrikulturchemische
      anstalt.
      Oerlikon. Schweizerische
      landwirtschaftliche
      versuchsanstalt.
--Agricultural schools. See Switzer-
land. Agriculture. Education.
--Agriculture.
    sa Subdivision Agriculture under:
      Churfirsten Mountains.
      Lausanne.
      Zurich//

Switzerland (Continued)
--Agriculture.
  sa Subdivision Switzerland under:
    Agriculture, Cooperative.
    Agriculture. Economic
      aspects.
    Wheat.
    Grasses.
    Agricultural engineering.
    Cereals.
    Colonization, Agricultural.
    Forage plants.
    Tobacco.
    Farm buildings.
    Agricultural policies and
      programs.
    Agricultural surveys.
    Agricultural indebtedness.
    Potatoes.
    Poultry.
    War and agriculture (1939-
      1945)
    Fiber plants and vegetable
      fibers.
    Reclamation of land.
    Sugar-beet.
    Farm management.
    Agricultural laborers.
    Agricultural credit.
    Switzerland. Domestic animals.
-- --Bibliography.
  xx Agriculture. Bibliography.
-- --Education.
  sa Lausanne, Institut agricole du
    Champ-de-l' Air á.
    Wadensivil, Deutsch-schweizeri-
    sche versuchsstation
    undschulefurobst, wein-und-
    gartenbaw in.
 · --History.
  xx Agriculture. History.
-- --Periodicals.
-- --Statistics.
  sa Bern (Canton) Agriculture.
    Statistics.
  xx Agriculture. Statistics.
-- -- --Bibliography.
--Apiculture.
-- --Periodicals.
--Bibliography.
--Biography.
-- --Dictionaries.

Switzerland (Continued)
--Botany.
  sa Subdivision Botany under:
    Saint-Bernard, Great.
    Alps, The.
    Ticino, Switzerland//
    Subdivision Switzerland under:
    Trees.
    Shrubs.
    Fungi.
    Algae.
    Mosses.
    Lichens.
    Hepaticae.
    Mushrooms.
    Weeds.
    Botany, Economic.
    Vegetable pathology.
    Honey-bearing plants.
    Botany, Medical.
    Oleaginous plants.
    Wild flowers.
    Flowers.
-- --Bibliography.
--Cadastral surveys.
--Cattle.
  sa Simmental cattle.
    Brown Swiss cattle.
    Subdivision Cattle under names
      of Cantons, etc., e.g.,
      Grisons (Canton) Cattle.
  xx Switzerland. Domestic animals.
-- --Statistics.
  xx Cattle. Statistics.
    Switzerland. Domestic animals.
    Statistics.
--Cattle trade.
-- --History.
--Census.
  sa Subdivision Census under:
    Bern (Canton)
--Civilization.
--Commerce.
  sa Subdivision Switzerland under:
    Oil-seed trade.
-- --Periodicals.
-- --Statistics.
--Constitution.
--Dairying.
  sa Subdivision Dairying under:
    Zürich (Canton)
    Vaud (Canton)
    Subdivision Switzerland under:
    Dairy industry and trade.
-- --Societies.

Switzerland (Continued)
--Description and travel.
   sa Subdivision Description and
     travel under: Alps.
--Domestic animals.
   sa Switzerland. Cattle.
     Switzerland. Swine.
     Switzerland. Goats.
     Switzerland. Sheep.
     Subdivision Domestic animals
      under: Valais (Canton)
-- --Legislation.
-- --Statistics.
   sa Subdivision Statistics under:
     Switzerland. Cattle.
     Switzerland. Swine.
--Economic conditions.
   sa Subdivision Switzerland under:
     World War, 1939-1945.
     Economic aspects.
-- --Bibliography.
-- --Periodicals.
--Economic policy.
--Education.
   sa Switzerland. Agriculture.
     Education.
--Emigration and immigration.
   sa Swiss in the U.S.
     Swiss in Tennessee.
--Entomology.
   sa Subdivision Entomology under:
     Basel.
     Zürich (Canton)
     Lake Geneva region. Switzer-
      land//
     Subdivision Switzerland under:
     Entomology, Economic.
     Lepidoptera.
     Coleoptera.
     Hymenoptera.
     Orthoptera.
     Diptera.
     Neuroptera.
     Wasps.
     Trees. Pests.
     Moths.
--Forestry.
   sa Subdivision Forestry under:
     Alps.
     Bern.
     St. Gall//

Switzerland (Continued)
--Forestry.
   sa Subdivision Switzerland under:
     Lumber trade.
     Forest management.
     Lumbering.
     Forest policy.
-- --Bibliography.
- --History.
   sa Subdivision Forestry. History
     under: Bern (Canton)
     Switzerland.
     xx Forestry. History.
-- --Periodicals.
-- --Statistics.
--Geology.
--Goats.
     xx Switzerland. Domestic animals.
--Government publications.
-- --Bibliography.
--History.
--Horse.
   sa Subdivision Switzerland under:
     Horses. Breeding.
--Horticulture.
-- --History. See Gardening. Switzer-
     land. History.
--Ichthyology.
--Industries.
-- --Periodicals.
--Insurance.
--Land.
   sa Subdivision Switzerland
     under: Land laws.
-- --Prices.
--Learned institutions and societies.
--Literature. See Swiss literature.
--Maps.
--Meteorology.
   sa Subdivision Meteorology
     under: Caléves, Switzer-
     land.
--Milk trade.
--National history.
-- --Bibliography.
--Natural history.
   sa Vevey.
--Ornithology.
   sa Subdivision Ornithology
     under: Geneva.
     Grisons.
--Paleobotany.
   sa Subdivision Paleobotany
     under: Basel.
--Physical geography.

Switzerland (Continued)
--Politics and government.
    xx Europe. Politics and govern-
        ment.
--Pomology.
    sa Subdivision Pomology under:
        Bern (Canton)//
        Subdivision Switzerland under:
        Berries.
--Population.
    sa Bern (Canton) Population.
-- --Bibliography.
--Revenue.
--Roads.
    sa Subdivision Roads under:
        Schaffhausen (Canton)
        Grisons.
--Scientific societies. See Schaff-
    hausen.
--Seed control stations.
    sa Zurich, Schweiz samen-control
        stations.
--Sheep.
    xx Switzerland. Domestic animals.
--Social conditions.
--Soils.
    sa Subdivision Switzerland under:
        Peat.
--Statistics.
    sa Subdivision Statistics under:
        Aargau.
        Töss.
        Veltheim.
        Winterthur.
        Switzerland. Commerce.
        Switzerland. Domestic
          animals.
        Switzerland. Forestry.
        Switzerland. Census.
--Statistics, Vital.
--Swine.
-- --Statistics.
    xx Swine. Statistics.
        Switzerland. Domestic animals.
        Statistics.
--Viticulture.
    sa Subdivision Viticulture under:
        Schaffhausen, Switzerland.
-- --Periodicals.
--Water-supply.
    sa Subdivision Water-supply under:
        Basel.

Switzerland (Continued)
--Zoology.
    sa Subdivision Zoology under:
        Lake St. Moritz.
        Basel.
        Subdivision Switzerland under:
        Vertebrates.
        Mammalia.
-- --Bibliography.

Switzerland Co., Ind.
--Agriculture.
-- --Periodicals.

Swollen shoot disease of cocoa. See
    Virus diseases of cacao.

Sword bean.

Swordfish.
    xx Fish.

Sycamore.
    x American plane tree.
    Platanus occidentalis.
    xx Platanus.

Sycamore fig. See Ficus sycomorus.

Sycosoter lavagnei.

Sydney.
--Botanic gardens.
--Description.
--Parks.

Sydney area, Nova Scotia.
    sa Subdivision Sydney area, Nova
        Scotia under: Produce
        trade.
        Farm produce. Marketing.
    xx Nova Scotia.

Syenite.

Syke, Germany.
--Soils.
    xx Germany. Soils.

Sylene National Park, Norway.
--Botany.

Syllabication.
    x Division of words.
      Syllabification.
      Word division.

Syllabification. See Syllabication.

Syllidae.

Sylt.
--Land.
    sa Subdivision Sylt under: Land
        tenure.

Sylvic acid. See Abietic acid.

Sylviculture. See Silviculture.

Sylvietta.

Sylviidae.

Sylvinite. See Sylvite.

Sylvite.
    Sylvinite.
    xx Potassium chloride.
--Effect on plants.
    x Plants, Effect of sylvite on.

Symbiosis.
    sa Mycorhiza.
      Insect microbiology.
      Plants and insects.
--Bibliography.

Symbolism.
    sa Emblems.

Symbols. See Signs and symbols.

Symbols (in science and industry, etc.)
  See Abbreviations.

Symmetry.

Symmetry (Biology)

Symolocaceae.

Sympetrum.

Sympherobius amicus.
    xx Parasitic and predaceous
        insects.

Symphoremaceae. -

Symphoricarpos alba.
    x Snowberry.
      Symphoricarpus racemosus.

Symphoricarpos racemosus. See Symphoricarpos alba.

Symphoricarpos rotundifolius.

Symphoricarpos vaccinioides.
    x Snowberry.

Symphoromyia.

Symphya.

Symphyla.
    sa Scolopendrella.
      Myriapoda.

Symphyogyna.

Symphyogyna aspera.

Symphyta.
    sa Tenthredinidae.
    xx Hymenoptera.

Symphytum. See Comfrey.

Sympus.

Synagris.

Synanthedon.
    sa Aegeria.

Synanthedon bibionipennis.

Synapsis.

Synaptomys.
    xx Lemmings.
      Microtinae.

Syncarpia.

Syncarpia hillii.
    x Satinay.

Synchloe.

Synchronous dynamos.   See Dynamos,
    Synchronous.

Synchronous generators.   See Dynamos,
    Synchronous.

Synchytriaceae.
        sa Synchytrium.

Synchytrium endobioticum.
        sa Potato wart.
        xx Potatoes. Diseases.

Syndactylism.

Syndesmon thalictroides.
        x Anemone thalictroides.

Syndicalism.

Syndicalism, Agricultural.   (INDIRECT)
        x Agricultural syndicalism.
          Agrarian syndicalism.
        xx Agriculture, Cooperative.
--Legislation.
        xx Agriculture, Cooperative.
          Legislation.

Synedra.
        xx Diatomaceae.

Synema.
        xx Thomisidae.

Syngamus laryngeus.

Syngamus tracnealis.   See Gape worm.

Synklor 5-D.   See Chlordane.

Synonyms.
        sa Subdivision Synonyms under:
          English language.
          France. Language.

Syntexidae.

Syntexis libocedrii.

Synthesis.   See Chemistry, Organic.
    Synthesis.

Synthetic albumin.   See Albumin, Synthe-
    tic.

Synthetic chemicals.   See Chemicals,
    Synthetic.

Synthetic detergents.   See Cleaning
    compounds. Synthetic.

Synthetic drugs.   See Drugs, Synthetic.

Synthetic egg white.   See Albumin,
    Synthetic.

Synthetic fats.   See Fats and oils,
    Synthetic.

Synthetic fuel.   See Fuel, Synthetic.

Synthetic manures.   See Manures,
    Synthetic.

Synthetic motor fuels.   See Motor fuels,
    Synthetic.

Synthetic perfumes.   See Perfumery,
    Synthetic.

Synthetic petroleum.   See Petroleum,
    Synthetic.

Synthetic products.
        sa Artificial food.
          Gums and resins, Artificial.
          Rubber, Artificial.
          Wool, Artificial.
          Plastic materials.
          Chemicals, Synthetic.
          Drugs, Synthetic.
          Fuel, Synthetic.
          Motor fuels, Synthetic.
          Latex, Synthetic.
          Vitamins, Synthetic.
          Waxes, Synthetic.
          Textile fibers, Synthetic.
          Petroleum, Synthetic.
          Perfumery, Synthetic.
          Sweeteners, Synthetic.
        x Materials, Synthetic.
          Artificial products.
        xx Chemistry, Organic.
          Synthesis.
          Chemistry. Technology.
          Chemurgy.
          Plastic materials.
--Bibliography.
        sa Subdivision Bibliography
          under: Plastic materials.

Synthetic products (Continued)
--Cyclopedias.
--Dictionaries.
--Periodicals.
    x Products, Synthetic.

Synthetic protein fibers.   See Protein
    fibers, Synthetic.

Synthetic resins.   See Gums and resins,
    Artificial.

Synthetic rubber.   See Rubber, Artificial.

Synthetic sweeteners.   See Sweeteners,
    Synthetic.

Synthetic tannins.   See Tannins, Synthe-
    tic.

Synthetic textile fibers.   See Textile
    fibers, Synthetic.

Synthine process.
    x Fischer-Tropsch process.
      Petroleum. Synthine process.
    xx Hydrocarbons.

Synthliboramphus.   See Alcidae.

Syntomaspis druparum.
    x Apple-seed chalcid.
    xx Apple. Pests.

Syntomidae.

Syon House, Brentford, Eng.

Syphilis.
    sa Sigma test.
       Wassermann test.
  --Periodicals.
    xx Pathology. Periodicals.
       Venereal diseases. Periodicals.

Syr-Darya region.
--Botany.
--Soils.

Syracosphaera.
    xx Coccolithophoridaceae.

Syracosphaera carterae.

Syracuse, N.Y.
--Airports.   See Airports. New York
    (State) Syracuse.

Syrbula.
    xx Acridiidae.

Syrbula admirabilis.

Syria.
--Agriculture.
    sa Subdivision Syria under:
       Agricultural policies and
         programs.
       Agriculture. Economic
         aspects.
-- --Statistics.
--Botany.
    sa Subdivision Syria under:
       Fungi.
       Vegetable pathology.
--Commerce.
-- --Statistics.
--Description and travel.
    sa Subdivision Description under:
       Aleppo.
--Economic conditions.
    sa Subdivision Economic condi-
       tions under: Lebanon.
--Entomology.
    sa Subdivision Syria under:
       Entomology, Economic.
--Forestry.
--Geographic names.
--Geography.
    sa Subdivision Syria under:
       Anthropo-geography.
--Land.
    sa Subdivision Syria under:
       Land tenure.
--Roads.
    sa Diocletian road.
--Soils.
    sa Subdivision Syria under:
       Soil erosion.
    xx Asia. Soils.
--Statistics.
--Zoology.

Syringa vulgaris.   See Lilacs.

Syringodendron.

Syrinx (of birds)

Syros, Aegean Islands.
--History.

Syrphidae.
    sa Cheilosia.
       Merodon.
       Volucella.
       Eristalis.
       Temnostoma.
       Callicera.
       Eumerus.
       Brachyopa.
       Brachypalpus.
       Merapioidus.
       Microdon.
       Pipiza.
       Helophilus.
       Chrysotozum.
       Xylotini.
       Xanthgramma.
       Lathyrophthalmus.
       Mesogramma marginata.
    xx Diptera.

Syrphus.

Syrup. See Syrups.

Syrup trade.
    xx Sugar trade.

Syrups.
    sa Maize syrup.
       Maple syrup.
       Sorgo syrup.
       Apple syrup.
       Tamarind syrup.
       Flavoring extracts.
       Sweet potato syrup.
       Sugar beet syrup.
       Cookery (Syrups)
       Grape sirup.
       Birch syrup.
       Glucose syrup.
       Maltose syrup.
       Fruit syrup.
       Sugar-cane syrup.
--Bacteriology.
--Bibliography.
    sa Subdivision Bibliography under:
       Maple syrup.
--Composition.
-- --Bibliography.
--Grading and standardization.
--Legislation.

Syrups (Continued)
--Statistics.
    sa Subdivision Statistics under:
       Maple syrup.
--Storage.
    xx Storage of farm produce.

Systena frontalis.
    x Red-headed flea beetle.

Systena taeniata.
    x Pale-striped flea beetle.
      Banded flea beetle.

Systole coriandri.
    xx Coriander. Pests.
      Eurytomidae.

Systox.

Syvde Parish, Norway.

Syzran region.
--Soils.

Syzygium.

Szechuan, China. See Szechwan, China.

Szechuen. See Szechwan.

Szechwan, China.
--Agriculture.
    sa Subdivision Szechwan, China
      under: Agriculture.
       Economic aspects.
       Farm management surveys.
       Sugar-cane.
       Tobacco.
       Rice.
      Subdivision China. Szechwan
      under: Agriculture.
       Economic aspects.
    xx China. Agriculture.
--Botany.
    sa Subdivision China. Szechwan
      under: Vegetable pathology.
--Description and travel.
--Domestic animals.
    sa Szechwan, China. Swine.
--Economic conditions.
    sa Subdivision China. Szechwan
      under: Geography, Economic
-- --Periodicals.

Szechwan, China (Continued).
--Entomology.
    sa Subdivision China. Szechwan
        under: Entomology, Economic.
--Forestry.
    sa Subdivision China. Szechwan
        under: Timber.
--Geography.
    sa Subdivision China. Szechwan
        under: Geography, Economic.
--Industries.
--Land.
    sa Subdivision China. Szechwan
        under: Land utilization.
        Land. Classification.
--Maps.
--Sericulture.
--Soils.
    sa Subdivision China. Szechwan
        under: Soil-surveys.
--Swine.
    xx Szechwan, China. Domestic ani-
        mals.

Tankage as feeding stuff.

TDE (Insecticide)

Tabanidae.
    sa Chrysops.
       Tabanus.
       Stibasoma.
       Diachlorinae.
    x Pangoniinae.
    xx Diptera.
--Parasites.
    xx Parasites.

Tabanus.

Tabanus mexicanus.

Tabanus punctifer.

Tabanus rubidus.

Tabanus stantoni.

Tabasco, Mexico.

Tabasco sauce.

Tabernaemontana. See Rubber producing
  plants, Miscellaneous.
    xx Apocynaceae.

Tabio, Colombia.
    sa Subdivision Colombia. Tabio
        under: Social surveys.
        Sociology, Rural.
--Census.
    xx Colombia. Census.

Table.
    sa Stewards.

Table etiquette.
    xx Etiquette.
--Bibliography.

Table grapes. See Grapes.

Table Mountain, Cape of Good Hope.
--Botany.

Table-top photography. See Photography,
  Table-top.

Tables, Interest. See Interest and
  usury. Tables, etc.

Tables, Mathematical. See Mathematics.
  Tables, etc; Ready-reckoners.

Tables (Systematic lists)
    sa Subdivision Tables and ready-
       reckoners under: Agri-
       culture.
       Cattle trade.
       Coal trade//
       Subdivision Tables, calcula-
       tions, etc. under:
       Engineering.
       Excavation.
       Hydraulics//
       Subdivision Tables, etc. under:
       Biology.
       Chemistry.
       Coffee//

Tables, Computing. See Ready-reckoners.

Tabletop photography. See Photography,
  Table-top.

Tablets (Medicine)

Tabulating.

Tabulating machines.
    sa Calculating machines.
    x Business machines.

Tacagua, Venezuela.
--Forestry.
    sa Subdivision Venezuela. Tacagua
        under: Afforestation and re-
        forestation.
--Soils.
    sa Subdivision Venezuela. Tacagua
        under: Soil conservation.

Tacamahaca.

Tacarigua, Lake.   See Lake Valencia.

Taccaceae.

Tachardia.

Tachardia lacca.
    xx Tachardininae.
--Larvae.

Tachardininae.
    sa Tachardia lacca.
    xx Lacciferidae.

Tacheometer (Surveying instrument)   See
   Tachymeter.

Tachinidae.   –
    sa Blepharipeza.
       Talarocera.
       Exorista.
       Exoristoides.
       Argyrophylax.
       Chaetophleps.
       Myiophasia.
       Saskatchewania.
       Mauromyia.
       Exoristidae.
       Winthemia.
       Compsilura concinnata.
       Eubiomyia calosoma.
       Zygobothria.
       Archytas.
       Microphthalma.
       Belvosia.
       Digonochata.
       Rhacodineura.

Tachinidae (Continued)
    sa Achaetoneura.
       Sturmia.
       Siphosturmiini.
       Lydella.
       Zenillia.
       Paradexodes.
       Metagonistylum.

Tachira, Venezuela.
--Agriculture.
    sa Subdivision Venezuela. Tachira
        under: Agricultural surveys.
--Roads.

Tachkent.   See Tashkent.

Tachymeter.
    x Tacheometer (Surveying in-
       strument)
    xx Surveying instruments.

Tachypeza.

Tachyporinae.
    xx Staphylinidae.

Tachypterellus.
    xx Cherry. Pests.

Tachypterellus quadrigibbus.
    x Apple curculio.
      Anthonomus quadrigibbus.

Tachypterus.   See Tachypterellus.

Tachytrechus.

Tacoma, Wash.
--Parks.

Taconic system.

Tacony-Palmyra Bridge.

Tadarida.

Tadjikistan.
--Agriculture.
    sa Subdivision Tadjikistan under:
        Potatoes.
-- --Periodicals.
--Botany.
-- --Bibliography.
-- --Research.

Tadjikistan (Continued)
--Domestic animals.
-- --Research.
--Entomology.
    sa Subdivision Entomology under:
        Alai Mountains.
        Pamir.
--Forestry.
    sa Subdivision Tadjikistan under:
        Silviculture.
--Geography.
--Geology.
--Ichthyology.
--Industries and resources.
    sa Mines and mineral resources.
        Tadjikistan.
--Natural history.
-- --Periodicals.
--Pomology.
--Sheep.
--Social conditions.
--Soils.
    xx U.S.S.R. Soils.
--Viticulture.
--Zoology.
    xx U.S.S.R. Zoology.

Tadshikistan.   See Tadjikistan.

Tadzhikistan.   See Tadjikistan.

Tadzhiksko-Pamirskaia ekspeditsiia.
    xx Scientific expeditions.

Taenia.
    sa Cestode.
        Cysticercus.

Taenia chamissonii.

Taenia coenurus.
    sa Gid.

Taenia echinococcus.

Taenia grimaldii.

Taenia nana.

Taenia saginata.

Taenia teniaeformis.

Taenia serialis.
    x Coenurus serialis.
        Multiceps serialis.

Taeniasis, Nodular.   See Nodular
    taeniasis.

Taeniothrips gladioli.   See Taeniothrips
    simplex.
    x Gladiolus thrips.
    xx Gladiolus. Pests.

Taeniothrips inconsequens.
    x Taeniothrips pyri.
        Pear thrips.
        Euthrips pyri.

Taeniothrips pyri.   See Taeniothrips in-
    consequens.

Taeniothrips simplex.
    x Taeniothrips gladioli.
        Gladiolus thrips.
    xx Gladiolus. Pests.

Taft-Hartley act.   See Labor-Management
    relations act of 1947.

Tag-Heppenstall moisture meter.
    xx Moisture tester.

Tagasaste.   See Cytisus proliferus.

Tagii cattle.
    xx Cattle. Breeds.

Tagua.   See Phytelephas.

Tagus River and Valley.

Tahiti.
--Agriculture.
--Botany.
    sa Subdivision Tahiti under:
        Fungi.
        Algae.
        Lichens.
        Ferns.
        Mosses.
        Marine flora.
--Entomology.
--Pomology.
--Zoology.

Tahltan Indians.
  xx Indians of Canada.

Tahoe, Lake. See Lake Tahoe.

Tahoe National Forest, Calif.
  xx California. Forest reservations

Taichung, China.
  --Agriculture.

Taiga.

Tail.
  --Dogs.
  -- --Trimming.

Tailor-birds.

Tailoring.
  sa Garment cutting.
  x Garment making.
    Cutting.
  xx Clothing and dress.

Tailoring (Women's)

Taimyr.
  --Botany.
    xx U.S.S.R. Botany.
      Arctic regions. Botany.

Taitou, China.
  --Social life and customs.

Taiwan (Formosa) See Formosa.

Takao-ken, Japan.
  --Industries.
    xx Japan. Industries.

Takara River.

Take-all disease.
  xx Cereals. Diseases.
    Grasses and forage plants.
      Diseases.

Take-all of wheat. See Mosaic disease of
  wheat.
    xx Wheat. Diseases.

Takosis.

Takyr soils.

Talarocera nigripennis.

Talas Region.
  --Sheep.

Talbot Co., Md.
  --Geology.
  --Soils.
    sa Subdivision Maryland. Talbot
      Co. under: Soil-surveys.

Taliaferro Co., Ga.
  --Education.

Talinum.
    xx Portulacaceae.

Tall fescue. See Meadow fescue.

Tall oil.
    x Tallöl.
      Black liquor soap.
      Sulphate black liquor soap.
    xx Liquid rosin.
      Pine-oil.
  --Bibliography.
  --Refining.

Talladega Co., Ala.
  --Economic conditions.
  --Industries and resources.
    sa Industrial surveys. Alabama.
      Talladega Co.

Tallahatchie Co., Miss.
    sa Subdivision Tallahatchie Co.,
      Miss. under: Negroes.
      Subdivision Mississippi.
        Tallahatchie Co. under:
        County surveys.
  --Social conditions.
    sa Subdivision Mississippi.
      Tallahatchie Co. under:
      Social surveys.
    xx Mississippi. Social conditions.

Tallahatchie River, Miss.
    sa Subdivision Tallahatchie River,
      Miss. under: Flood control.
    x Little Tallahatchie River.

Tallahatchie Valley, Miss.
--Soils.
    sa Subdivision Tallahatchie
        Valley, Miss. under: Soil
        erosion. Prevention and
        control.
    xx Mississippi. Soils.

Tallianine.

Tallöl. See Tall oil.

Tallow.
    xx Animal products.
        Fats and oils.
--Prices.
    xx Animal products. Prices.
        Prices.
--Societies.
--Statistics.

Tallow trade.
--Futures.

Tallow tree.

Talons. See Claws.

Talorchestia longicornis.
    xx Amphipoda.

Talpidae.
    sa Myogale.

Taltal, Chile.
--Geology.

Tama Co., Iowa.
--Land.
    sa Subdivision Iowa. Tama Co. un-
        der: Land utilization.
    xx Iowa. Land.
--Soils.
    sa Subdivision Iowa. Tama Co. un-
        der: Soil conservation sur-
        veys.
        Soil-surveys.
    xx Iowa. Soils.

Tamalpais, Mount, Calif.

Tamandua.
    xx Anteater.

Tamarack. See Larix laricina.

Tamaricaceae.
    sa Myricaria.
        Tamarix.

Tamarind.
--Pests.

Tamarind pod-borer. See Sitophilus
    linearis.

Tamarind sirup. See Tamarind syrup.

Tamarind syrup.

Tamarindicus indica.

Tamariscineae. See Tamaricaceae.

Tamarisk manna.

Tamarix.

Tamarix aphylla.
    x Athel.
        Tamarix articulata.

Tamarix articulata. See Tamarix aphylla.

Tamarix gallica.
    x Salt cedar.

Tamaulipas, Mexico.
--Domestic animals.
-- --Legislation.
--Geology.
--Paleontology.

Tambelan Islands.
--Ornithology.

Tambov Region.
--Agriculture.
-- --Education.
--Pomology.

Tamerlanea.
    xx Trematoda.

Tamerlanea bragai.

Tamil language.
--Dictionaries.

Tamil Nattuvivasayathozilalar Sangham.
 xx Farmers' unions.

Tamilnad.
 --Economic conditions.

Tampa, Fla.
 --Commerce.
 sa Subdivision Tampa, Fla. under:
  Produce trade.
 --Harbor.
 xx Harbors.
 --Industries.
 sa Subdivision Tampa, Fla. under:
  Cigar manufacture and trade.
 xx Florida. Industries and re-
  sources.
 --Markets.

Tamus communis.

Tamus elephantipes.
 sa Testudinaria elephantipos.

Tamworth swine.
 --Periodicals.

Tan-bark. See Tanbark.

Tana River.
 xx Kenya colony and protectorate.

Tanacetum.
 xx Anthemidae.

Tanagridae.
 sa Procniatidae.

Tanaidacea.

Tanalith.
 x Wolman salts.

Tananá River.

Tananarive, Madagascar. Parc botanique et
 zoologique.
 xx Zoological gardens.

Tanbark.
 xx Tanning materials.

Tanbark oak. See Quercus densiflora.

Tandu. See Pseudomonas tritici.

Tanganyika, Lake. See Lake Tanganyika.

Tanganyika Territory.
 --Agricultural experiment stations.
 sa East African Agricultural
  Research Station. Amani,
  Tanganyika Territory.
 --Agriculture.
 sa Subdivision Tanganyika Terri-
  tory under: Peanuts.
  Colonization, Agricultural.
  Crop reports.
  Agriculture. Economic as-
   pects.
  Coffee.
  Agriculture. Research.
 xx Africa. Agriculture.
 --Apiculture.
 --Botany.
 sa Subdivision Tanganyika Terri-
  tory under: Shrubs.
  Trees.
 --Census.
 --Commerce.
 -- --Periodicals.
 -- --Statistics.
 --Description and travel.
 --Domestic animals.
 --Economic conditions.
 -- --Statistics.
 --Entomology.
 sa Subdivision Tanganyika Terri-
  tory under: Locusts.
 --Forestry.
 sa Subdivision Tanganyika Terri-
  tory under: Trees.
  Lumber.
  Timber.
 --Geographic names.
 --Geography.
 sa Subdivision Tanganyika Terri-
  tory under: Geography, Eco-
  nomic.
 --Land.
 sa Subdivision Tanganyika Terri-
  tory under: Land utiliza-
  tion.
 --Maps.
 --Native races.
 --Ornithology.
 sa Subdivision Ornithology under:
  Dar-es-Salaam.
 --Politics and government.
 --Social conditions.

Tanganyika Territory (Continued)
--Soils.
    sa Subdivision Tanganyika Terri-
        tory under: Soil erosion.
           Prevention and control.
--Water-supply.
--Zoology.

Tangelo.

Tangerine.
    sa Tangelo.
    x Mandarin orange.
      Chinese orange.
      Japanese mandarin orange.
--Composition.
    xx Citrus. Composition.
--Diseases.
    xx Citrus. Diseases.

Tangerine, Effect of moisture on.
    xx Moisture. Effect on plants.

Tangerine.
--Grading and standardization.
    xx Citrus. Grading and standardi-
        zation.
--Marketing.
    xx Citrus. Marketing.
--Physiology and morphology.
    xx Citrus. Physiology and mor-
        phology.
--Statistics.
    xx Citrus trade. Statistics.

Tangerine juice, Canned.
--Grading and standardization.
    xx Fruit juices, Canned. Grading
        and standardization.

Tangerine juice, Concentrated.
--Grading and standardization.
    xx Fruit juices, Concentrated.
        Grading and standardization.

Tanghinia venenifera.
    xx Apocynaceae.

Tangier Island, Va.
    xx Virginia.

Tangipahoa Parish, La.

Tangüis cotton.   See Cotton, Tangüis.

Tania.
    sa Food plants.

Tanier.   See Yautia.

Tank-cars.

Tank farming.   See Hydroponics.

Tankage as feeding stuff.
--Statistics.

Tanks.

Tanks, Steel.
    x Steel tanks.

Tanks, Wood.
    x Wood tanks.
    xx Containers.

Tankage.

Tannan.   See Pseudomonas tritici.

Tannalbinum veterinarium.

Tanner's dock.   See Canaigre.

Tannia beetle.   See Ligyrus ebenus.

Tannic acid.
--Fermentation.

Tannin.   See Tannins.

Tannin as a fertilizer.

Tannin determination.   See Tannins. De-
    termination.

Tanning.
    sa Caesalpinia brevifolia.
    x Tanning industry and trade.
--Bibliography.
    sa Tanning materials. Bibliog-
        raphy.
--By-products.
--Dictionaries.
--Periodicals.
--Waste.

Tanning extract.

Tanning industry and trade.   See Tanning.

Tanning materials.
        sa Tanbark.
    --Analysis.
    --Bibliography.
    --Economic aspects.
    --Effect on seeds.
        x Seeds, Effect of tanning
            materials on.
    --Periodicals.
    --Tariff.
        xx Tariff.

Tannins.
        sa Rhus coriaria.
            Cotinus coggygria.
            Wattle tannin.
            Quebracho tannin.
    --Analysis.
    --Bibliography.
    --Estimation.

Tannins, Synthetic.
    --Patents.
    -- --Abstracts.

Tansy.   See Tanacetum vulgare.

Tantalum.

Tantalus.   See Storks; Ibis.

Tanyderidae.

Tanypezidae.

Tanytarsus.
        xx Tendipedidae.

Taos Co., N.M.
        sa Subdivision New Mexico. Taos
            Co. under: Rehabilitation,
            Rural.
            Subdivision Taos Co., N.M. un-
            der: Diet.
            Planning, County.
    --Economic conditions.
        xx New Mexico. Economic condi-
            tions.
    --Water-supply.

Tapa.

Tape, Measuring.   See Measuring tape.

Tape recordings (Data storage)   See
    Recording systems (Data storage)

Tape recordings in agriculture.

Tape recordings in home economics.

Tapes, Industrial.   See Industrial
    tapes.

Tapestry.
        xx Textile industry and fabrics.
            Arts and crafts movement.

Tapeworms.   See Cestoda.

Taphrina.
        xx Exoascaceae.

Taphrina deformans.
        x Exoascus deformans.

Taphrocerus gracilis.
        xx Buprestidae.

Tapinoma sessile.

Tapinostola musculosa.

Tapioca.
        sa Cassava.
        xx Cassava.
    --Bibliography.
        sa Subdivision Bibliography
            under: Tapioca starch.
            Tapioca flour.
    --Tariff.

Tapioca flour.
    --Bibliography.

Tapioca industry and trade.

Tapioca plant.   See Cassava.

Tapioca starch.
    --Bibliography.

Tapir.

Tapiscia.

Tappoons.
        xx Dams.
            Irrigation. Machinery.

Tar.
    sa Wood-tar.
--Distillation.
    xx Distillation.
--Effect on soil.   See Soil. Effect of
    tar.
--Specifications.
--Testing.

Tar as a road material.
--Congresses.
    xx Roads. Congresses.

Tar-weeds.   See Madia.

Taranto, Italy (Province)
--Agriculture.
-- --Statistics.
--Commerce.
-- --Periodicals.
--Economic conditions.
-- --Periodicals.

Tarantula (common name)
    This term used as a common name
    refers to the large spiders be-
    longing to the family Avi-
    culariidae (super-family Avi-
    cularioidea) found in south and
    west of the U.S. and Puerto
    Rico. For publications in this
    catalog see Aviculariidae.
    Tarantula as a generic name be-
    longs to the family Taran-
    tulidae (the whip-scorpions)

Tarantula (generic name)
    This term as a generic name be-
    longs to the family Tarantuli-
    dae (the whip-scorpions) No en-
    tries in this catalogue at
    present.

Tarantula, European.   See Lycosa
    tarentula.

Tarantula, Haitian.   See Phormictopus
    cancerides.

Tarascon. Cavernes de.

Tarascon Indians.

Taraxacum.

Taraxacum gymnanthum.
    x Krym-saghyz.

Taraxacum kok-saghyz.
    x Kok-saghyz.
    Dandelion, Russian.
    Russian dandelion.
    xx Rubber.
    Rubber producing plants, Mis-
    cellaneous.
--Bibliography.
--Harvesting.
    xx Harvesting.
--Implements and machinery.
    xx Agriculture. Implements and
    machinery.
--Physiology and morphology.

Taraxacum officinale.

Tarbagan.   See Marmota bobac.
    x Tarabagon.
    Sarbagan.
    Haitian.

Tarbagatai Mountains.
--Zoology.

Tarboro, N.C.
--Milk supply.
    xx North Carolina. Milk supply.

Tardigrada.
    sa Echinus.
    xx Arachnida.

Tare.
    sa Cotton tare.

Tarentaise cattle.

Tarentula.
    x Wolf-spider.
    xx Lycosidae.

Target leaf spot of Hevea brasiliensis.
    xx Pellicularia filamentosa.
    Hevea brasiliensis. Diseases.

Targhee National Forest, Idaho.
    xx Idaho. Forest reservations.

Tariff.   (INDIRECT)
    sa Subdivision Tariff under:
        Cereals.
        Cotton.
        Hops//
        Fruit tariff.
        Dingley law.
        Free trade and protection.
        Reciprocity.
        Balance of trade.
        Trade barriers.
        Customs unions.
    x Duties.
        Customs tariff.
        Customs (Tariff)
        Exports.
        Imports.
        Protective tariff.
    xx Economic policy.
--Bibliography.
    sa Subdivision Bibliography under:
        Tariff. Gt. Brit.
        Tariff. U.S.
--Congresses.
    sa Subdivision Congresses under:
        Tariff. Mexico.
        Tariff. U.S.
--Cyclopedias.   See Tariff. Dictionaries.
--Dictionaries.
    x Tariff. Cyclopedias.
--History.
    sa Tariff [geographic subdivision]
        History, e.g., Tariff. U.S.
        History.
--Law.
    sa Subdivision Law under:
        Tariff. Argentine Republic.
        Tariff. Bolivia.
        Tariff. Brazil//
--Nomenclature.   See Tariff. Terminology.
--Periodicals.
    sa Tariff. U.S. Periodicals.
--Terminology.
    x Tariff. Nomenclature.
    xx Commerce. Terminology.
Tarija, Bolivia (Province)
--Agriculture.
--Forestry.
    sa Subdivision Tarija, Bolivia
        (Province) under: Af-
        forestation and reforesta-
        tion.
--Paleontology.

Tarnished plant bug.   See Lygus pra-
    tensis.

Taro.
    sa Dasheen.
    x Colocasia esculenta.
    xx Food plants.
--Diseases.
--Processing.
    xx Processing (Industrial)

Tarpaulin.

Tarrant Co., Tex.
--Geology.
--Roads.

Tarred roads.   See Roads, Tar for.

Tarrietia argyrodendron var. peralata
    (Wood)
    x Red tulip oak wood.

Tarsiidae.

Tarsonemidae.
    sa Tarsonemus.
        Disparipes.
    xx Acarida.

Tarsonemus.

Tarsonemus pallidus.
    xx Strawberries. Pests.

Tarsonemus waitei.

Tarsostenus univittatus.

Tartar emetic.
    x Potassium antimonyl tartrate.

Tartaric acid.
    xx Acids.
        Argol.
--Determination.

Tartarus stibiatus.   See Tartar emetic.

Tartrates.
--Bibliography.

Tarweed.   See Madia sativa.

Tashkent.
--Agriculture.
    sa Subdivision Tashkent under:
        Irrigation.
--Entomology.
--Viticulture.

Tasmania.
    xx Australasia.
--Agriculture.
    sa Subdivision Tasmania under:
        Cereals.
        Colonization, Agricultural.
        Crops and climate.
-- --Statistics.
    xx Tasmania. Statistics.
        Agriculture. Statistics.
--Apiculture.
--Botany.
    sa Subdivision Tasmania under:
        Ferns.
        Vegetable pathology.
--Census.
--Climate.
    sa Subdivision Tasmania under:
        Crops and climate.
--Dairying.
--Domestic animals.
    sa Subdivision Sheep under:
        Tasmania.
-- --Statistics.
--Economic conditions.
    sa Subdivision Tasmania under:
        Geography, Economic.
    xx Australia. Economic conditions.
--Entomology.
    sa Subdivision Tasmania under:
        Entomology, Economic.
--Forestry.
    sa Subdivision Tasmania under:
        Timber.
--Geography.
    sa Subdivision Tasmania under:
        Geography, Economic.
--Industries and resources.
    sa Subdivision Tasmania under:
        Fruit trade.
--Maps.
--Natural history.
--Ornithology.
--Paleobotany.
--Public lands.
    xx Australia. Public lands.
--Roads.

Tasmania (Continued)
--Sheep.
    xx Tasmania. Domestic animals.
--Social life and customs.
--Soils.
    sa Subdivision Soils under:
        Huonville district,
        Tasmania.
        King Island, Tasmania.
--Statistics.
    sa Tasmania. Agriculture. Sta-
        tistics.
--Water-supply.
--Zoology.

Tassel, Maize. See Maize. Anatomy.

Taste.
    x Senses and sense organs of
        insects. Taste.
    xx Senses and sense organs.
--Bibliography.

Taste testing of food. See Food. Flavor.
    Testing.

Tatar Republic.
--Agriculture.
    sa Subdivision Tatar Republic
        under: Grasses.
        Agricultural policies and
        programs.
        Field crops.
        Mechanized farming.
-- --Statistics.
--Botany.
    sa Subdivision Tatar Republic
        under: Botany, Medical.
        Weeds.
--Entomology.
    sa Subdivision Tatar Republic
        under: Entomology, Economic.
--Forestry.
--Geography.
--Pomology.
    sa Subdivision Tatar Republic
        under: Berries.
--Statistics.
--Swine.

Tatihou Island, France.
--Zoology.
    sa Subdivision France. Tatihou
        Island under: Araneida.

Tatocheila.

Tatoosh Island, Wash.

Tatra Mountains.
--Botany.

Tatrzański Park Narodowy.
    x Tatranský Národný Park.

Tatranský Národný Park.   See Tatrzański
    Park Narodowy.

Tau-saghyz.
--Pests.

Taunton, Mass.
--Parks.

Tauorga, Tripolitania.
--Soils.
        sa Subdivision Tripolitania.
            Tauorga under: Soil-surveys.

Taurida (Government)
--Description and travel.
--Entomology.
        sa Subdivision Russia. Taurida
            (Government) under:
            Entomology, Economic.

Taurin.

Taurocerastinae.   See Scarabaeidae.

Tautomerism.
        sa Mesomerism.
        xx Mesomerism.

Tavricheskaia Gubernii.   See Taurida.

Tax accounting.
        x Taxation. Accounting.
        xx Accounting.

Tax collection.   (DIRECT)
        x Taxation. Collection.
            Collection of taxes.

Tax delinquency.   (DIRECT)
        xx Taxation.

Tax exemption.   See Taxation, Exemption
    from.

Tax sales.   (DIRECT)
        xx Taxation.

Taxaceae.
        sa Yew.
            Dacrydium.
            Phyllocladus.

Taxation.   (DIRECT)
        sa Subdivision Taxation under:
            Breadstuffs.
            Liquor traffic.
            Gasoline.
            Banks and banking.
            Land.
            Automobiles.
            Sugar.
            Vehicles.
            Corporations.
            Beverages.
            Railroads.
            Cotton.
            Marihuana.
            Fats and oils.
            Retail trade.
            Natural resources.
            Beer.
            Insurance companies.
            Cooperation. Societies.
            Wine and wine making.
            Occupations.
            Water-power electric plants.
            Carriers.
            Income tax.
            Inheritance and transfer tax.
            Forestry. Valuation and taxa-
                tion.
            Single tax.
            Farm taxation.
            Assessment.
            Tithes.
            Sales tax.
            Taxation of personal property.
            Internal revenue.
            Revenue.
            Taxation of bonds, securities,
                etc.
            Poll-tax.
            School taxes.
            Tax collection.
            Excess profits tax.
            Tax delinquency.
            Tax sales.
        x Real property. Taxation.
        xx Assessment.

Taxation (Continued)
--Accounting. See Tax accounting.
--Bibliography.
    sa Subdivision Bibliography under:
        Taxation, State.
        Gasoline. Taxation.
        Automobiles. Taxation//
    Subdivision Bibliography under:
        Taxation. District of
            Columbia//
--Periodicals.
    xx Bibliography. Periodicals.
--Collection. See Tax collection.
--Congresses.
    sa Subdivision Taxation. Congresses
        under: Land.
        Assessment.

Taxation, Double.   (DIRECT)
    sa Taxation, Exemption from.
    x Double taxation.
    xx Taxation, Exemption from.

Taxation, Exemption from.   (DIRECT)
    sa Taxation, Double.
    x Tax exemption.
        Income tax, Exemption from.
    xx Taxation, Double.
--Bibliography.
    xx Taxation. Bibliography.
--Law.
    sa Taxation, Exemption from
        ₍geographic subdivision₎
        Law, e.g., Taxation, Ex-
        emption from. U.S. Law.

Taxation.
--History.
    sa Subdivision History under:
        Taxation. U.S.
--Law.
    sa Revenue laws.
        Farm taxation. Law.
        Gasoline. Taxation. Law.
        Subdivision Law under Taxation
        ₍geographic subdivisions₎
        e.g., Taxation. Arizona.
        Law.

Taxation, Local.   (DIRECT)
    x Local taxation.
        Municipal taxation.
        Taxation, Municipal.

Taxation, Municipal. See Taxation, Local

Taxation.
--Periodicals.
    sa Subdivision Periodicals under:
        Assessment.
        Land.
--Societies.
    sa New Hampshire Federation of
        Taxpayers Association, Inc.

Taxation, State.
    x State taxation.
--Bibliography.
    xx Taxation. Bibliography.

Taxation in kind.
--Legislation.

Taxation in kind (Milk)
    xx Milk. Taxation.

Taxation in kind (Oil-seeds)
    xx Oil-seeds. Taxation.

Taxation of bonds, securities, etc.
    (DIRECT)
    x Taxation of securities.
        Securities. Taxation.
    xx Taxation.
--Bibliography.
    xx Taxation. Bibliography.

Taxation of capital gains. See Capital
    gains tax.

Taxation of excess profits. See Excess
    profits tax.

Taxation of industrial corporations.
    See Corporations. Taxation.

Taxation of insurance companies. See
    Insurance companies. Taxation.

Taxation of personal property.   (DI-
    RECT)
    x Personal property. Taxation.
    xx Taxation.

Taxation of securities. See Taxation
    of bonds, securities, etc.

Taxidermy.
    sa Fur.
        Zoological specimens. Col-
        lection and preservation.

Taxidermy (Continued)
--Periodicals.

Taxin.

Taxodium.
    xx Abietineae.
--Diseases.

Taxodium distichum.   See Bald cypress.

Taxodium mucronatum.

Taxoideae, Fossil.
    sa Nageiopsis.

Taxonomy.   See Botany, Systematic-
    Entomology, Systematic; Biology Classi-
    fication; Zoology. Classification.

Taxonus nigrisoma.   See Ametastegia
    glabrata.

Taxus baccata.
    sa Yew.

Taxus canadensis.

Tay River.

Taylor Co., Ky.
--Agriculture.
    sa Subdivision Kentucky. Taylor
        Co. under: Agricultural
        credit.
    xx Kentucky. Agriculture.

Taylor Co., W. Va.
    xx West Virginia.

Taylor Co., Wis.
    xx Wisconsin.
--Land.
    sa Subdivision Wisconsin. Taylor
        Co. under: Land. Classifi-
        cation.
    xx Wisconsin. Land.

Taylor grazing act.
    xx Agriculture. Law.

Taylors Fold farm, Matley Hyde, Eng.
    xx Farms.

Tazewell, Va.
--Economic conditions.

Tazewell Co., Ill.
--Soils.
    xx Illinois. Soils.

Tazewell Co., Va.
--Forestry.
--Industries and resources.
    sa Industrial surveys. Virginia.
        Tazewell Co.
--Soils.
    sa Subdivision Virginia. Taze-
        well Co. under: Soil-
        surveys.

Tchad, Africa.   See Chad, Africa.

Tchè Li.   See Chih-li.

Tchernigof, Russia.   See Chernigof,
    Russia.

Tchuguiev.   See Chuguev.

Tea.   (INDIRECT)
    sa Tropical agriculture.
        Matè.
    x Green tea.
--Adulteration.
--Advertising.
    xx Beverages. Advertising.
--Analysis.
--Bibliography.
--Biochemistry.
--Breeding.
    xx Plant-breeding.
--Composition.
--Congresses.
--Diseases.
    sa Blister blight of tea.
--Economic aspects.
--Fermentation.
--Fertilizers.   See Fertilizers for
    tea.
--Handbooks, manuals, etc.
--History.
    sa Tea trade. History.
--Implements and machinery.
    xx Agriculture. Implements and
        machinery.
--Legislation.

Tea, Paraguay.   See Mate.

Tea.
--Periodicals.
--Pests.
        sa Helopeltis theivora.
           Tetranychus bioculatus.
           Helopeltis.
--Prices.
--Processing.
--Pruning.
--Research.
        sa Tea ₍geographic subdivision₎
           Research. e.g., Tea. Formosa.
           Research.
        xx Research.
--Statistics.
        sa Tea ₍geographic subdivision₎
           Statistics, e.g., Tea.
           Africa, East. Statistics.
        xx Beverages. Statistics.
--Substitutes.   See Tea substitutes.
--Tables, etc.

Tea-bug.   See Helopeltis theivora.

Tea chests.

Tea consumption.   (DIRECT)

Tea industry and trade.   See Tea trade.

Tea-mite.   See Tetranychus bioculatus.

Tea preservation.

Tea soils.

Tea substitutes.
        x Tea. Substitutes.
        xx Food substitutes.

Tea trade.   (DIRECT)
        x Tea industry and trade.
--Directories.
--History.
--Periodicals.
--Societies.
--Statistics.
        sa Tea trade ₍geographic subdivi-
           sion₎ Statistics. e.g., Tea
           trade. Asia. Statistics.

Tea tree.   See Melaleuca; Leptospermum.

Teachers.
        sa Home economics teachers.
           Rural teachers.
        xx Education.
--Biography.
--Directories.

Teachers, Interchange of.
        x Exchange teaching.
          Interchange of teachers.
          International exchange of
             teachers.
        xx Educational exchanges.

Teachers.
--Salaries, pensions, etc.
        xx Salaries.

Teachers, Training of.

Teachers' colleges.   See Normal
  schools.

Teachers' homes.

Teaching.
        sa Child study.
           Education.
           Children. Education.
           Examinations.
           Normal schools.
           School management and
              organization.
           Radio in education.
        x Study and teaching.
--Aids and devices.
        sa Moving-pictures in education.
           Radio in education.
           Visual instruction.
           Teaching. Demonstration
              method.
           Phonograph records in
              education.
           Audio-visual instruction.
           Television in education.
        x Teaching aids.
          Training aids.
        xx Educational materials.
-- --Bibliography.
        sa Subdivision Bibliography
           under: Education of
              adults. Teaching aids
              and devices//

Teaching (Continued)
--Aids and devices.
-- --Directories.
       sa Subdivision Directories under:
          Education of adults. Teach-
          aids and devices.
--Demonstration method.
       x Demonstration method of
         teaching.
       xx Teaching. Aids and devices.
--Periodicals.

Teaching aids. See Teaching. Aids and
  devices.

Teak.
       x Tectona grandis.
--Congresses.
--Diseases.
--Pests.
       sa Pyrausta machaeralis.
         Hyblaea puera.

Teak defoliator. See Hyblaea puera.

Teak skeletonizer. See Pyrausta
  machaeralis.

Teara.

Teasel.
       x Fuller's teasel.
         Dipsacus fullonum.

Tebessa, Algeria.
       xx Algeria.

Technical abbreviations. See Technology.
  Abbreviations.

Technical assistance. See Technical
  assistance program.

Technical assistance program.
       sa Underdeveloped areas.
       x Productivity and technical
         assistance program.
         United Nations. Technical
          assistance.
         Technical assistance.
         Point four program.
         Technical cooperation.
       xx Economic assistance.
         Economic cooperation.

Technical assistance program (Continued)
       xx Industrialization.
         International cooperation.
--Addresses, essays, lectures.
--Bibliography.
--Congresses.
--Directories.
--Periodicals.
--Statistics.

Technical chemistry. See Chemistry.
  Technology.

Technical cooperation. See Technical
  assistance program.

Technical education.   (INDIRECT)
       sa Apprentices.
         Correspondence schools and
          courses.
         Evening and continuation
          schools.
         Manual training.
         Mining schools and education.
         Textile schools.
         Vocational education.
         Professional education.
         Arts and crafts movement.
         Names of technical schools.
         Subdivision Education under:
          Agriculture.
          Forestry.
         Subdivision Study and teaching
          under: Baking.
          Confectionery.
          Home economics.
       x Training, Mechanical.
         Mechanical training.
         Industrial education.
--Bibliography.
--Curricula.
       xx Education. Curricula.
--Legislation.
--Periodicals.

Technical journalism. See Journalism,
  Technical.

Technical laboratories.

Technical libraries.

Technical plants.   See Food plants;
Oleaginous plants; Aromatic plants;
Commercial products; Drug plants;
Botany, Economic; Potatoes for techni-
cal use.

Technical schools.

Technical terms.   See Technology.
Dictionaries.

Technical writing.   See Reports. Preparation; Scientific papers.

Technicians in industry.
    x Industrial technicians.
    xx Technologists.

Technique, Bacteriological.   See
Bacteriology. Technique.

Technique, Botanical.
    x Laboratory technique (botanical)
    Botany. Technique.
    Botanical technique.

Technique, Laboratory.   See Laboratory
technique.

Technique, Mycological.
    sa Fungi. Culture media.
    x Laboratory technique (myco-
      logical)

Technique, Pathological.   See Pathology.
Laboratory manuals; Medicine, Clinical.
Laboratory manuals; Histology, Patho-
logical. Laboratory manuals.

Technocracy.
    xx Over-production.

Technological chemistry.   See Chemistry.
Technology.

Technological museums.   See Industrial
museums.

Technological processing.   See Processing
(Industrial)

Technological unemployment.   See Unemployment, Technological.

Technologists.
    sa Technicians in industry.

Technology.
    sa Printing.
    Wool technology.
    Chemistry. Technology.
    Brick.
    Handicraft.
    Plastic materials.
    Industrial arts.
    Paint.
    Cotton technology.
    Rubber technology.
    x Applied science.
    Science, Applied.
    Arts, Useful.
--Abbreviations.
    x Technical abbreviations.
--Abstracts.
-- --Periodicals.
--Addresses, essays, lectures.
--Authorship.   See Reports. Prepara-
    tion; Scientific papers.
--Bibliography.
    sa Subdivision Bibliography
      under: Plastic materials.
-- --Periodicals.
    xx Bibliography. Periodicals.

Technology, Chemical.   See Chemistry.
Technology.

Technology.
--Classification.
--Congresses.
    sa Subdivision Congresses under:
      Research, Industrial.
--Dictionaries.
    x Technical terms.
-- --Bibliography.
--Education.   See Technical education.
--Exhibitions.
--History.
-- --Bibliography.
--Information services.

Technology (Continued)
--Language.
 Here are entered works in which
 the language of technology is
 discussed and exemplified. For
 works on the vocabulary of
 technology, See Technology.
 Terminology. For guides to
 writing technical reports and
 papers, See Reports. Prepara-
 tion; Scientific papers; For
 works on the technical problems
 of writing and the preparation
 of manuscripts preliminary to
 printing and publication, See
 Authorship. Handbooks, manuals,
 etc.
 xx Reports. Preparation.
-- --Bibliography.
-- --Periodicals.
--Periodicals.
-- --Abstracts.
-- --Bibliography.
-- --Indexes.
--Philosophy.
 xx Philosophy.
--Research.
--Societies.
-- --Abbreviations.
-- --Bibliography.
-- --Directories.
-- --Rewards (Prizes, etc.)
 xx Rewards (Prizes, etc.)
--Study and teaching.
--Subject headings. See Subject head-
 ings. Technology.
--Terminology.
-- --Bibliography.
--Year-books.

Technology of food. See Food technology.

Technomyrmex albipes.

Teckel. See Dachshund.

Tecoma mollis.

Tectona grandis. See Teak.

Teesta Bridge. See Anderson Bridge,
 Bengal, India.

Teeth.
--Care and hygiene.
 x Dental hygiene.
 Hygiene, Dental.
--Diseases.
 x Caries, Dental.
 Dental caries.
--Effect of diet. See Diet. Effect on
 teeth.

Teff.

Teflon.
 x Tetrafluoroethylene resin.
 Ethylene, Tetrafluoro.
 Polymerized tetrafluoro
 ethylene.

Tegenaria.
 xx Agelenidae.

Tehipite Valley, Calif.

Tehuacan, Mexico.
--Botany.

Tehuantepec, Isthmus of.
--Agriculture.

Tekke. See Ashkabad.

Tel Aviv.
 xx Jews. Restoration.
 Palestine. Colonies.

Telangiectasis.

Telea polyphemus.
 x Polyphemus moth.

Telegeusidae.
 xx Coleoptera.

Telegony.

Telegraph. (DIRECT)
--Laws and regulations.
 sa Subdivision Laws and regulations under Telegraph
 [geographic subdivision]
 e.g., Telegraph. Alabama.
 Laws and regulations.
--Picture transmission.
--Rates.

Telegraph, Wireless.
    sa Radio.
    x Wireless telegraph.
      Radio telegraph.
      Radiotelegraph.

Telegraph poles. See Telephone and
  telegraph poles.

Telegraphic codes. See Cipher and
  telegraph codes.

Telegraphy.
    sa Cables.

Telemark, Norway.
--Cattle.
--Forestry.

Telemeter.
    xx Distances. Measurement.

Telenomus.
    xx Hymenoptera.
      Parasitic and predaceous
        insects.

Telenomus cosmopelae.

Telenomus sokolovi.
    xx Parasitic and predaceous
        insects.

Teleology.
    xx Natural theology.

Teleosts.

Telephone.   (DIRECT)
--Apparatus and supplies.
-- --Catalogs.
-- --Directories.

Telephone, Automatic.
    x Automatic telephone.
      Dial telephone.
      Telephone, Dial.

Telephone, Dial. See Telephone, Automatic.

Telephone.
--Directories.

Telephone (Continued)
--Laws and regulations.
    sa Subdivision Laws and regula-
      tions under Telephone
      [geographic subdivision]
      e.g., Telephone. Alabama.
      Laws and regulations.
--Periodicals.
--Rates.

Telephone, Rural.
    sa Rural telephone cooperatives.
    x Farm telephone.
      Rural telephone.
    xx Country life.
--Rates.
--Statistics.

Telephone.
--Statistics.

Telephone, Wireless.
    sa Radio.
    x Wireless telephone.
      Radio telephone.
      Radiotelephone.

Telephone and telegraph poles.
--Congresses.
--Inspection.
-- --Statistics.
--Specifications.

Telephone engineers.
    xx Electric engineers.

Telephone lines.
--Construction.

Telephone wire.

Telephone wire, Insulated.

Telephonograph.

Telephonography.

Telephotography.

Telescope.
    xx Astronomy.

Telescope fish.
    xx Goldfish.

Telethermoscope.

Teletypewriters.
    xx/Type-writers.

Television.
    sa Radio facsimile.
--Bibliography.
--Broadcasting.   See Television broad-
    casting.
--Dictionaries.
--Periodicals.
--Research.
--Terminology.

Television advertising.
    xx Advertising.
       Television broadcasting.

Television authorship.
    x Television writing.
    xx Authorship.

Television broadcasting.
    sa Television advertising.
       Television broadcasting of
        films.
    x Television. Broadcasting.
      Radio broadcasting.
--Agricultural applications.
    sa Television in extension work.
--Economic applications.
--Films. See Television broadcasting
    of films.
--History.
--Moving pictures. See Television
    broadcasting of films.
--Yearbooks.

Television broadcasting in home demon-
    stration work.

Television broadcasting of films.
    x Television broadcasting. Films.
      Television broadcasting. Mov-
       ing pictures.
    xx Television broadcasting.
--Agricultural applications.

Television in education.
    xx Radio in education.
      Audio-visual instruction.
      Visual instruction.
      Teaching. Aids and devices.

Television in extension work.
    xx Television broadcasting.
       Agricultural applications.

Television scripts.
    xx Radio scripts.

Television writing. See Television
    authorship.

Telkwa River.

Tell el-Amarna.

Tellervo.

Tellow, Ger. (Estate)

Tellurides.

Tellurium.

Tellurium compounds.

Telman Collective Farm.
    xx Collective farms.

Telopea speciosissima.
    x Waratah.

Teloschistaceae. See Theloschistaceae.

Telpherage.

Teltow.
--Agriculture.

Temiskaming.

Temnocephala.

Temnochilidae.

Temnostoma bombylans.

Temperament.
    sa Subdivision Constitution
      under: Man.

Temperance and intemperance.
    xx Alcoholic liquors.

Temperature.
     sa Cold.
        Ocean temperature.
        Plant respiration, Temperature
          in.
        Thermo-regulator.
        Telethermoscope.
        Earth temperature.
        Evaporation. Effect on
          temperature.
        Cover crops. Effect on
          temperature.
        High temperature research.
        Plant temperature.
        Low temperature research.
        Subdivision Temperature under:
          Lakes.
          Valleys.
          Sea water.
          Leaves.

Temperature, Animal and human.
     sa Animal heat.
     x Temperature, Body.
     xx Animal heat.

Temperature.
  --Bibliography.

Temperature, Body.   See Temperature,
  Animal and human.

Temperature.
  --Effect on animals.
  --Effect on bacteria.
      x Bacteria, Effect of tempera-
        ture on.
  --Effect on beans.
  --Effect on canned goods.
      x Canned goods. Effect of
        temperature on.
  --Effect on carrots.
  --Effect on cellulose.
      x Cellulose. Effect of tempera-
        ture on.
  --Effect on cereals.
      sa Cereals. Freezing and frost
        injury.
  --Effect on cherries.
  --Effect on coniferae.
      x Coniferae. Effect of tempera-
        ture on.
  --Effect on cotton.

Temperature (Continued)
  --Effect on dairy cattle.
      x Cattle, Dairy, Effect of
        temperature on.
  --Effect on eggs.
      x Eggs, Effect of temperature
        on.
  --Effect on enzymes.
  --Effect on food.
      x Food, Effect of temperature
        on.
  --Effect on fruit.
      sa Heat. Effect on fruit.
        Fruit. Freezing and frost
          injury.
        Temperature. Effect on
          cherries.
        Temperature. Effect on papaya.
  --Effect on fungi.
      x Fungi, Effect of temperature
        on.
      xx Temperature. Effect on plants.
  --Effect on germination.   See Germi-
    nation. Effect of temperature.
  --Effect on gipsy-moth.
  --Effect on grasses.
      x Grasses. Effect of tempera-
        ture.
  --Effect on ice cream.
  --Effect on insects.
      x Insects, Effect of tempera-
        ture on.
        Heat. Effect on insects.
        Cold. Effect on insects.
      xx Entomology. Economics.
        Entomology. Ecology.
  --Effect on lemons.
      x Lemon. Effect of temperature.
  --Effect on maize.
  --Effect on meat.
      x Meat, Effect of temperature
        on.
  --Effect on metals.   See Metals.
    Effect of temperature.
  --Effect on olive-oil.
      x Olive-oil, Effect of tempera-
        ture on.
  --Effect on oranges.
      x Orange, Effect of temperature
        on.
  --Effect on papaya.
      x Papaya. Effect of temperature
        on.
      xx Temperature. Effect on fruit.

Temperature (Continued)
--Effect on parasites.
    ' xx Parasites.
--Effect on peaches.
    x Peach, Effect of temperature
      on.
--Effect on pears.
    x Pear, Effect of temperature on.
--Effect on plants.
    sa Freezing of plants.
      Soil temperature. Effect on
        plant diseases.
      Cold. Effect on plants.
      Heat. Effect on plants.
      Temperature with subdivisions:
        Effect on fungi.
        Effect on maize.
        Effect on beans.
        Effect on sorghum.
        Effect on soy-bean.
        Effect on sugar beet.
        Effect on sweet potatoes.
        Effect on tomatoes.
        Effect on cereals.
        Effect on carrots.
        Effect on wheat.
        Effect on coniferae.
        Effect on trees.
    xx Cold. Physiological effect.
      Hardiness.
-- --Bibliography.
--Effect on potatoes.
    x Potatoes, Effect of tempera-
      ture on.
--Effect on poultry.
    x Poultry, Effect of temperature
      on.
--Effect on semen. See Semen. Effect of
    temperature.
--Effect on sorghum.
--Effect on soy-bean.
--Effect on sugar-cane.
    x Sugar-cane, Effect of tempera-
      ture on.
--Effect on surface measurement of body.
--Effect on textile fabrics.
    x Textile industry and fabrics.
      Effect of temperature on.
-- --Bibliography.
--Effect on tomatoes.
--Effect on trees.
    x Trees. Effect of temperature.
    xx Temperature. Effect on plants.
--Effect on Uredineae.

Temperature (Continued)
--Effect on vegetables.
    sa Vegetables. Freezing and
      frost injury.
    x Vegetables, Effect of tempera-
      ture on.
--Effect on wheat.
    sa Subdivision Effect on wheat
      under: Cold.
--Effect on wines.
    sa Subdivision Effect on wines
      under: Cold.
--Effect on wood.
    x Wood, Effect of temperature
      on.

Temperature, Human. See Temperature,
  Animal and human.

Temperature, Low. See Low temperature
  research.

Temperature, Minimum.

Temperature, Nocturnal.

Temperature.
--Physiological effect.
    sa Subdivision Physiological
      effect under: Cold.
    xx Cold. Physiological effect.

Temperature, Plant. See Plant temperature.

Temperature.
--Research.
--Tables, etc.
--Variations.

Temperature and food products.

Temperature gradients.

Temperature inversions.

Temperature observations.

Temples.
    sa Mut (Temple)

Tenagobia.
    xx Heteroptera.
      Corixidae.

Tenancy.   See Tenant farming.

Tenant farming.   (INDIRECT)
     When subdivided by place, indicate
     see also ref. from name of
     place with subdivision: Agri-
     culture.
     sa Land tenure.
        Large-scale farming.
        Landlord and tenant.
        Sharecroppers.
        Métayer system.
     x Crofting.
     xx Agriculture. Economic aspects.
--Bibliography.
     sa Subdivision Bibliography under:
        Tenant farming. U.S.
        Sharecroppers.
--Congresses.
     xx Agriculture. Economic aspects.
        Congresses.
--Legislation.
     sa Tenant farming [geographic sub-
        division] Legislation, e.g.,
        Tenant farming. France.
        Legislation.
     xx Agriculture. Law.

Tenant rights.

Tenderization of meat.   See Meat. Tenderi-
     zation.

Tenderness of meat.   See Meat. Tenderness.

Tendipedidae.
     sa Psamathiomya.
        Tanytarsus.
        Eutanytarsus.
        Culicoides.
        Tendipes.
        Gymnometriocnemus.
     x Midges.
        Chironomidae.
     xx Diptera.
--Larvae.

Tendipes.
     x Chironomus.
     xx Tendipedidae.

Tendipes pusio.

Tendons.
--Diseases.

Tendrils.

Tenebrio ferrugineus.

Tenebrio molitor.
     x Yellow mealworm.

Tenebrionidae.
     sa Diaperia.
        Tenebrio.
        Latheticus.
        Mercantha.
        Tribolium.
        Gonocephalum.
        Embaphion.
        Eleodes.
        Opatrinae.
        Cossyphini.
        Araucaricola.
        Palorus.

Tenebroides mauritanicus.
     x Cadelle.
     xx Stored products. Pests.

Teneriffe.
     sa Santa Cruz de Tenerife.
--Botany.
--Commerce.
-- --Statistics.
--Entomology.
     sa Subdivision Teneriffe under:
        Lepidoptera.
--Statistics.

Tennessee.
     sa Nashville.
        Forked River, Tenn.
        Obion River, Tenn//
--Agriculture.
     sa Tennessee. Domestic animals.
        Subdivision Agriculture under:
        Rugby, Tenn.
        Overton Co., Tenn.
        Knox Co., Tenn//

Tennessee (Continued)
--Horse.
--Ichthyology.
--Industries.
-- --Directories.
--Land.
    sa Subdivision Tennessee under:
      Land. Classification.
      Subdivision Land under: Memphis.
      Jefferson Co.
      Hamilton Co.//
    xx U.S. Land.
--Maps.
    sa Subdivision Maps under:
      Memphis, Tenn.
      Tennessee Valley.
--Markets.
    sa Subdivision Markets under:
      Knoxville, Tenn.
    xx U.S. Markets.
--Milk supply.
    sa Memphis. Milk supply.
--Milk trade.
    sa Subdivision Milk trade under:
      Memphis.
--Ornithology.
--Paleobotany.
--Paleontology.
--Parks.
    sa Subdivision Parks under:
      Chattanooga.
    xx U.S. Parks.
--Politics and government.
    sa Subdivision Tennessee under:
      County government.
      Municipal government.
      Local government.
      Subdivision Politics and
      government under: Hamilton
        Co., Tenn.
      Sullivan Co., Tenn.
--Pomology.
    sa Subdivision Tennessee under:
      Berries.
--Population.
    sa Subdivision Tennessee under:
      Rural population.
    xx U.S. Population.
--Prices.
    sa Knoxville, Tenn. Prices.
--Public works.
    xx U.S. Public works.

Tennessee (Continued)
--Roads.
    sa Subdivision Roads under:
      Hamilton Co., Tenn.
      Shelby Co., Tenn.
-- --Law.
    xx Roads. Legislation.
      U.S. Roads. Law.
--Social conditions.
    sa Subdivision Social conditions
      under: Cumberland Co.,
      Tenn.//
-- --Bibliography.
--Soils.
    sa Subdivision Soils under:
      Rutherford Co., Tenn.//
      Subdivision Tennessee under:
      Soil erosion. Prevention
      and control.
      Soil-surveys.
      Soil conservation.
-- --Bibliography.
--Statistics.
    sa Subdivision Statistics under:
      Tennessee. Agriculture.
--Transportation.
    sa Subdivision Transportation
      under: Nashville.
--Water supply.
    sa Subdivision Tennessee under:
      Water, Underground.
      Water. Conservation.
      Subdivision Water supply
      under: Tennessee Valley.
--Zoology.
    sa Subdivision Tennessee under:
      Myriapoda.

Tennessee River.
    xx Alabama.
      Mississippi.
      Tennessee.
--Floods. See Floods. Tennessee
  River.

Tennessee-Tombigbee Waterway.
    x Tombigbee-Tennessee Waterway.

Tennessee Valley.
    sa Subdivision Tennessee Valley
      under: Planning, Regional.
      Bridges.
      Hygiene, Public.

Tennessee Valley (Continued)
--Agriculture.
    sa Subdivision Tennessee Valley
      • under: Agriculture,
        Cooperative.
      Market gardening.
      Agricultural policies and
        programs.
      Agriculture. Economic
        aspects.
-- --Bibliography.
--Description and travel.
    xx Tennessee. Description and
        travel.
--Education.
    xx U.S. Education.
--Forestry.
    sa Subdivision Tennessee Valley
      under: Afforestation and
        reforestation.
      Forest fires. Prevention.
      Wood-using industries.
      Forest management.
      Forest products.
    xx U.S. Forestry.
--Geology.
    xx Tennessee. Geology.
--History.
--Ichthyology.
--Industries.
--Libraries.
--Maps.
    xx U.S. Maps.
--Politics and government.
    sa County government. Tennessee
        Valley.
--Public lands.
--Soils.
    sa Subdivision Tennessee Valley
      under: Terracing of land.
      Soil erosion.
      Soil erosion. Prevention
        and control.
    xx U.S. Soils.
--Water supply.
    xx Tennessee. Water supply.
--Zoology.
    sa Subdivision Tennessee Valley
      under: Wild life.

Tennessee walking horse.
    xx Horses.

Tension.
 --Effect on plants.

Tensor analysis.　See Calculus of
    tensors.

Tent-building ant.　See Cremastogaster
    lineolata.

Tent-caterpillar.　See Malacosoma.

Tenthredinidae.
    sa Hoplocampa.
      Pamphilius.
      Caliroa.
      Eriocampoides.
      Pristiphora.
      Diprion.
      Messinae.
      Dimorphopteryx.
      Ametastegia.
      Emphytus.
      Empria.
      Neodiprion.
      Itycorsia.
      Janus.
      Metallus.
      Monophadnoides.
      Phyllotoma.
      Tenthredo.
      Pristiphora abietina.
    x Dolerinae.
      Cladiinae.
      Perreyiinae.
    xx Tenthredinoidea.
--Parasites.
    xx Parasitic and predaceous
        insects.

Tenthredinoidea.
    sa Lydidae.
      Tenthredinidae.
    x Saw-fly.
      Sawflies.

Tenthredo.

Tenthredo truncatus.　See Emphytus
    fulvipes.

Tenthredocerris.

Tenuipalpus bioculatus.

Tenure of land.　See Land tenure.

Teosinte.
--Diseases.
  xx Cereals. Diseases.
--Hybrids.
  sa Teosinte-maize hybrids.
--Teratology.
  xx Abnormalities (Plants)

Teosinte-maize hybrids.

Teotihuacan, Mexico.

Tepary bean.
--Digestibility.
  xx Beans. Digestibility.

Tephritidae.
  sa Trupanea.
   Fruit flies.
  xx Diptera.
   Fruit flies.

Tephritis.

Tephritis cerasi. See Ortales cerasi.

Tephritis onopordinis.

Tephrosia as an insecticide.
  xx Insecticides.

Tephrosia candida.

Tephrosin.
  xx Chemistry, Vegetable.

Tepic, Mexico.
--Entomology.

Tepoztlan, Mexico.
  sa Subdivision Tepoztlan, Mexico
   under: Land tenure.
  xx Mexico.

Tepulidae.
  x Limoniidae.
   Cylindrotomidae.
  xx Diptera.

Ter, Russia.
--Agriculture.

Ter Meulen bond plan.
  xx Credit.

Teracolus.

Teramo, Italy (Province)
--Agriculture.
-- --Statistics.
--Commerce.
-- --Periodicals.
--Economic conditions.
-- --Periodicals.

Teras minuta.
  x Apple leaf-roller.
--Parasites.

Teratology. See Abnormalities
  (Animals); Abnormalities (Plants);
  Abnormalities (Insects); Polydacty-
  lism; Syndactylism.

Teratornis.

Terbium.

Terebellidae.

Terebinthaceae.
  sa Turpentine.
   Anacardiaceae.

Teredinidae.
  sa Teredo.

Teredo.
  xx Teredinidae.

Teredo navalis.

Terek, Russia.
--Economic conditions.
--Entomology.
  sa Subdivision Russia. Terek
   under: Entomology,
   Economic.

Terephthalic acid.

Tereshchenko Estates, Russia.

Termes flavipes.

Termes gestroi.

Termes lactis.

Termes lucifugus.

Termes taprobanes.

Termimaliaceae.
    sa Conocarpus.

Terminal markets.   See Markets, Terminal.

Terminalia.
    xx Combretaceae.

Terminalia chebula.

Terminalis paniculata.
    x Hongal.
      Kindal.

Terminalia superba.
    x Afara.
      Frake.
      Korina.
      Limba.

Terminalia tomentosa.

Termination of war contracts.   See War
   contracts. Termination.

Terminology.
    sa Subdivision Terminology under:
      Botany.
      Meteorology.
      Biology//

Termiteproofing.
    xx Insect proofing.
      Termites.

Termites.
    sa Termes.
      Termopsis.
      Nasutitermes.
      Cryptotermes.
      Leucotermes.
      Reticulitermes.
      Kalotermitidae.
      Amitermes.
      Zootermopsis.
      Rhinotermitidae.
      Termiteproofing.
    x Termitidae.
      White ants.
    xx Insect societies.
  --Bibliography.

Termites, Fossil.

Termites, Parasites.

Termitgas.

Termitidae.   See Termites.

Termitophilous insects.

Termitoxenia.
    xx Phoridae.

Termitoxenia assmuthi.

Termoprecipitine.

Termopsis.

Termopsis angusticollis.

Ternopol Region.
  --Agriculture.
  -- --History.

Terns.
    sa Sterna wilsonii.
    xx Longipennes.

Ternstroemiaceae.
    sa Camellia.
      Actinidia.
      Schima.

Terpenes.
    x Sesquiterpenes.
      Triterpenes.
      Polyterpenes.
      Monocyclic terpenes.

Terrace furnishings.   See Garden
   ornaments and furniture.

Terrace outlet ditches.
    xx Ditches.

Terraces and terracing.   See Terracing
   of land.

Terracing machinery.   See Agriculture.
   Implements and machinery.

Terracing of land.   (DIRECT)
    sa Soil erosion.
      Contour farming.

Terracing of land (Continued)
    x Broad base terraces.
      Hillside drainage.
      Level terracing.
      Terraces and terracing.
    xx Drainage.
      Erosion engineering.
      Soil conservation.
--Costs.
    xx Cost.

Terrapin.

Terrapin scale. See Lecanium nigro-
fasciatum.

Terrariums. See Gardens, Miniature.

Terrebonne Co., Que.
--Soils.
    sa Subdivision Quebec (Province)
      Terrebonne Co. under:
      Soil-surveys.

Terrebonne Parish, La.
    xx Louisiana.
--Soils.
    sa Subdivision Louisiana.
      Terrebonne Parish under:
      Soil-surveys.

Terrell Co., Tex.
--Geology.
--Roads.

Terrestial magnetism. See Magnetism,
Terrestial.

Terric bacteria. See Iron bacteria.

Terriers.
    sa Boston terriers.
      Fox-terriers.
      Sealyham terriers//

Territorial jurisdiction. See Jurisdiction, Territorial.

Terror (Ship) See Erebus and Terror
(Ship)

Terry Co., Tex.
--Soils.
    sa Subdivision Texas. Terry Co.
      under: Soil-surveys.

Tertiary period. See Paleontology.
Tertiary; Paleobotany. Tertiary.

Teruel, Spain (Province)
--Botany.
    sa Subdivision Teruel, Spain
      (Province) under: Trees.
--Domestic animals.
--Forestry.
    sa Subdivision Teruel, Spain
      (Province) under: Trees.
--Statistics.

Teschen disease. See Encephalo-myelitis
Swine.

Tessin (Canton) See Ticino (Canton)

Testicle.
--Diseases.

Testing.
    sa Strength of materials.
      Testing machines.
      X-rays. Industrial applica-
      tions.
      Electric testing.
      Surfaces (Technology)
      Ultrasonic testing.
      Retailers' testing league.
      Subdivision Testing under:
      Automobiles.
      Machinery.
      Building materials//

Testing laboratories.
    xx Engineering laboratories.
--Directories.
    xx Laboratories. Directories.

Testing machines.
    x Building materials. Testing.
      Apparatus.
    xx Machinery.

Tests and reagents, Chemical. See
Chemical tests and reagents.

Tests and scales.
    sa Employment tests.

Testudinaria elephantipes.

Testudo.   See Turtles.

Tetandysin.

Tetaniidae.
        sa Oscinella.

Tetanus.

Tetanus antitoxin.

Tetany.

Tethelin.

Teton Co., Idaho.
        xx Idaho.
    --Agriculture.
        sa Subdivision Idaho. Teton Co.
            under: Agricultural
                laborers.
    --Water-supply.
        sa Subdivision Idaho. Teton Co.
            under: Water-rights.

Teton Co., Mont.
    --Agriculture.
        sa Subdivision Montana. Teton Co.
            under: Farms.

Teton Co., Wyo.
    --Water-supply.
        sa Subdivision Wyoming. Teton Co.
            under: Water-rights.

Teton Forest Reserve.

Teton National Forest, Wyo.
        xx Wyoming. Forest reservations.

Teton River.

Tetothoracidae.

Tetraarylmethanes.
        xx Methanes.

Tetracarbonimid.

Tetracarboxylic acids.
        x Acids, Tetracarboxylic.

Tetrachlorethane as a fungicide.
        xx Fungicides.

Tetrachlorethylene.
        xx Chemistry.
    --Physiological effect.

Tetrachloro-para-benzoquinone.   See
    Spergon.

Tetracycline.
        xx Antibiotics.

Tetradenia.   See Neolitsea.

Tetradymia glabrata.
        x Horsebrush.
        xx Poisonous plants.

Tetraethyl lead gasoline.
        xx Gasoline.

Tetraethyl pyrophosphate.
        x Tetraethylpyrophosphate.

Tetraethyl silicane.
        x Silicon tetraethyl.
        xx Silicon organic compounds.

Tetraethylpyrophosphate.   See Tetra-
    ethyl pyrophosphate.

Tetrafluoroethylene resin.   See Teflon.

Tetrahit.   See Galeopsis.

Tetrahydrocannabinol.
        xx Cannabinol.

Tetrahydroindanones.

Tetrahydronaphthalene.
        x Tetralol.
          Tetralin.

Tetrahydropyridines.

Tetralin.   See Tetrahydronaphthalene.

Tetralol.   See Tetrahydronaphthalene.

Tetramera.
        sa Cassididae.
           Hispidae.
           Phytophaga.

Tetramethyldiphenylendisulfid.
   x Catilan.

Tetramethylglucose.

Tetraneura ulmi.

Tetranychidae.
   sa Bryobia.
     Tenuipalpus.
     Paratetranychus.
   x Bryobiidae.
   xx Acarina.

Tetranychus althaeae. See Tetranychus
   telarius.

Tetranychus atlanticus.

Tetranychus bimaculatus.
   x Two-spotted mite.

Tetranychus bioculatus.

Tetranychus citri.

Tetranychus gloveri.

Tetranychus humuli.

Tetranychus lapidus.

Tetranychus pacificus.
   x Pacific mite.

Tetranychus telarius.
   x Spider mite.
   Tetranychus urticae.

Tetranychus urticae. See Tetranychus
   telarius.

Tetranychus viennensis.

Tetranychus yothersi.

Tetraonidae.
   sa Grouse.
     Tympanuchus.

Tetraopes femoratus.

Tetraphacus.

Tetraphosphates.

Tetraphyllidea.
   xx Cestoidea.

Tetrapoda.

Tetrarhynchidae.
   sa Dibothriorhynchus.

Tetrasporaceae.

Tetrastichus.
   xx Eulophidae.

Tetrastichus asparagi.

Tetrastichus brevistigma.

Tetrastichus bruchophagi.

Tetrasulphide.
   xx Sulphides.

Tetrazolium compounds.

Tetriginae.
   xx Acridiidae.

Tetrogallus.

Tetropium luridum.

Tetschen.
  --Cattle.

Tetschen, Bohemia. Höhere landwirtschaft-
   liche landeslehranstalt Tetschen-
   Liebwerd.

Tettigellinae.
   xx Cicadellidae.

Tettigidae.

Tettigidae lateralis.

Tettigonia.

Tettigoniidae.
   For Tettigoniidae as a family of
     Orthoptera, see Tettigoniidae.
   For Tettigoniidae as a family of
     Homoptera, see Cicadellidae.

Texas (Continued)
--Cattle.
-- --History.
    xx Cattle. History.
-- --Periodicals.
--Cattle trade.
    xx Cattle trade.
    Southwestern States. Cattle
      trade.
    U.S. Cattle trade.
--Census.
--Climate.
    sa Subdivision Texas under:
      Crops and climate.
--Commerce.
    sa Subdivision Texas under: Farm
      produce. Marketing.
      Poultry industry and trade.
      Produce trade.
-- --Periodicals.
    sa Subdivision Commerce. Periodi-
      cals under: Corpus Christi,
      Tex.//
    xx U.S. Commerce. Periodicals.
--Dairying.
-- --Periodicals.
--Description and travel.
--Domestic animals.
    sa Subdivision Texas under:
      Live stock reports.
--Economic conditions.
    sa Houston, Tex. Economic condi-
      tions.
    Subdivision Texas under: Rural
      surveys.
    Economic surveys.
    History, Economic.
-- --Periodicals.
--Education.
    sa Subdivision Education under:
      Travis Co., Tex.
    Subdivision Texas under:
      Rural schools.
--Entomology.
    sa Subdivision Entomology under:
      Brownsville, Tex.
      Brazos Co., Tex.
    Subdivision Texas under: Wasps.
      Lepidoptera.
      Hymenoptera.
      Orthoptera.
      Hemiptera.
      Diptera.
      Butterflies.
--Fisheries.

Texas (Continued)
--Forest reservations.
--Forestry.
    sa Subdivision Texas under:
      Lumbering.
      Wood-using industries.
      Forest surveys.
      Wood-lots.
      Tree planting.
      Forest fires. .
      Forest products.
      Forest policy.
      Afforestation and
        reforestation.
      Timber.
-- --Periodicals.
-- --Research.
-- --Statistics.
--Geology.
    sa Subdivision Geology under:
      Brewster Co., Tex.
      Runnels Co., Tex.
      Terrell Co., Tex.//
    Subdivision Texas under:
      Water, Underground.
      Mines and mineral
        resources.
-- --Bibliography.
--History.
    sa Subdivision Texas under:
      History, Economic.
    xx U.S. History.
-- --Sources.
    sa Subdivision Texas under:
      Archives.
    xx U.S. History. Sources.
--Horticulture.
    sa Texas. Pomology.
--Industries.
-- --Maps.
--Insurance.
--Land.
    sa Subdivision Texas under:
      Land laws.
      Terracing of land.
      Land tenure.
      Land utilization.
    Subdivision Land under:
      El Paso Co., Tex.//
    xx U.S. Land.
--Legislative manuals.
--Legislature.
-- --Rules and practice.
--Manufactures.
    xx U.S. Manufactures.

Texas (Continued)
--Maps.
    sa Subdivision Maps under:
        Dallas, Tex.
        Houston, Tex.
--Meteorology.
--Milk supply.
    sa Subdivision Milk supply under:
        Austin.
--Natural history.
    xx U.S. Natural history
--Ornithology.
    sa Subdivision Ornithology under:
        McLennan Co., Tex.
        Bexar Co., Tex.
        Brewster Co., Tex.
        Subdivision Texas under:
        Game-birds.
--Paleobotany.
--Paleontology.
    sa Subdivision Paleontology under:
        Somerville, Tex.
--Parks.
    sa Subdivision Parks under:
        Houston.
    xx U.S. Parks.
--Periodicals.
--Petrology.
--Politics and government.
    sa Subdivision Texas under:
        County government.
        Local government.
--Pomology.
    sa Subdivision Texas under: Citrus.
-- --History.
--Population.
    sa Subdivision Texas under:
        Rural population.
        Migration, Internal.
    xx U.S. Population.
--Public lands.
--Public schools.
    xx Public schools.
--Public works.
    xx U.S. Public works.
--Research.
    xx U.S. Research.
--Revenue.
--Roads.
    sa Subdivision Roads under:
        Tarrant Co., Tex.
        Terrell Co., Tex.
        Guadalupe Co., Tex.//

Texas (Continued)
--Roads.
-- --Law.
    xx Roads. Legislation.
        U.S. Roads. Law.
--Sericulture.
--Sheep.
    xx U.S. Sheep.
--Social conditions.
    sa Subdivision Texas under:
        Social surveys.
--Soils.
    sa Subdivision Texas under:
        Soil-surveys.
        Soil conservation surveys.
        Soil conservation.
        Soil erosion. Prevention
          and control.
        Subdivision Soils under:
        Pecos Valley.
        Trinity Valley.
        Red River Valley, Tex.//
--Statistics.
    sa Subdivision Statistics under:
        Houston, Tex.
--Swine.

Texas. University. Biological Labora--
  tory.

Texas.
--Water-supply.
    sa Subdivision Texas under:
        Water, Underground.
        Subdivision Water-supply
        under: Somervell Co., Tex.
        Pecos Valley//
-- --Congresses.
--Zoology.
    sa Subdivision Texas under:
        Batrachia.
        Game.
        Subdivision Zoology under
        names of regions, counties,
        etc.

Texas City, Tex. Fire, 1947.

Texas Co., Okla.
--Agriculture.
    sa Subdivision Texas Co., Okla.
        under: Agricultural
        credit.
--Geology.
    xx Oklahoma. Geology.

Texas Co., Okla. (Continued)
--Soils.
    sa Subdivision Oklahoma. Texas
        Co. under: Soil-surveys.
--Water-supply.
    xx Oklahoma. Water-supply.

Texas Farm Life Commission.

Texas fever. See Tick fever.

Texas High Plains. See High Plains.

Texas leaf-cutting ant. See Atta
texana.

Texas longhorn cattle. See Longhorn
cattle.

Texas root-rot fungus. See Phymato-
trichum omnivorum.

Texcoco, Lake.
    sa Drainage. Mexico. Texcoco,
        Lake.

Texcoco.
--Soils.

Texel.

Texel sheep.
    xx Sheep.

Text-books.
    sa Subdivision Text-books under
        various subjects.
    xx Handbooks, vade-mecums, etc.

Textile bacteriology.
    sa Subdivision Bacteriology
        under: Cotton fabrics.
    x Textile industry and fabrics.
      Bacteriology.
    xx Bacteriology.

Textile chemistry.
    x Textile fibers. Chemistry.
--Abstracts.
--Research.

Textile design.
    sa Textile painting.

Textile deterioration.
    sa Bacterial deterioration of
        textiles.
       Fungus deterioration of
        textiles.
       Subdivision Deterioration
        under: Canvas.
       Cotton fabrics.
    x Textile disintegration.
    xx Deterioration.

Textile dictionaries. See Textile
industries and fabrics. Dictionaries.

Textile disintegration. See Textile
deterioration.

Textile education. See Textile
schools.

Textile engineering as an occupation.

Textile fabrics. See Textile industry
and fabrics.

Textile factories.
    sa Naumkeag Steam Cotton Co.,
        Salem.
    x Textile mills.
      Cotton pressing factories.
      Cotton factories.
--Air conditioning.
    xx Factories. Air conditioning.
--Heating.
    xx Factories. Heating.
--Lighting.
    xx Lighting, Industrial.
--Management. See Textile factory
    management.
--Safety measures.
--Ventilation.

Textile factory management.
    x Textile factories. Manage-
      ment.
    xx Factory management.

Textile fibers.
    sa Fiber plants and vegetable
        fibers.
       Mohair.
       Camel's hair.
       Rayon.
       Silk.

Textile fibers (Continued)
    sa Wool.
       Animal fibers.
       Cordage.
       Nylon.
       Cellulose fibers.

Textile fibers, Artificial. See Textile
    fibers, Synthetic.

Textile fibers.
--Chemistry. .See Textile chemistry.
--Effect of moisture. See Moisture.
    Effect on textile fibers.
--Patents.
    sa Subdivision Patents under:
        Textile fibers, Synthetic.
    xx Patents.
--Periodicals.
--Research.

Textile fibers, Synthetic.
    sa Rayon.
       Nylon.
       Wool, Artificial.
       Protein fibers, Synthetic.
       Acetylated cotton.
    x Textiles, Synthetic.
       Textile substitutes.
       Textile fibers, Artificial.
       Artificial textile fibers.
       Synthetic textile fibers.
    xx Fibers, Synthetic.
       Synthetic products.
--Abstracts.
--Congresses.
--Dyeing.
    xx Dyes and dyeing.
--Manufacture and trade. (DIRECT)
-- --Statistics.
--Patents.
    xx Textile fibers. Patents.
--Periodicals.
--Shrinkage.
    xx Textile industry and fabrics,
       Shrink-resistant.
--Statistics.

Textile fibers.
--Testing.
    xx Testing.

Textile finishing.
    sa Cotton finishing.
    xx Finishes and finishing.

Textile industry. See Textile industry
    and fabrics.

Textile industry and fabrics.   (DIRECT)
    sa Bleaching.
       Tapa.
       Cotton fabrics.
       Woolen fabrics.
       Textile substitutes.
       Paper as a textile material.
       Rayon.
       Calico-printing.
       Color in the textile industries
       Cotton. Manufacture.
       Cotton trade.
       Dry-goods.
       Dyes and dyeing.
       Mercerization.
       Silk manufacture and trade.
       Spinning.
       Weaving.
       Woolen and worsted manufacture.
       Wool trade and industry.
       Yarn.
       Textile chemistry.
       Vicuña.
       Wool, Artificial.
       Bunting (Cloth)
       Household textiles.
       National industrial recovery
         act, 1933. Codes. Textiles.
       Clothing and dress.
       Waterproofing of fabrics.
       Jute bagging.
       Nylon.
       Tapestry.
       Rayolanda.
       Ribbon.
       Mothproofing.
       Mohair.
       Indians of Mexico. Textile in-
         dustry and fabrics.
       Fillers (in paper, paint, etc.)
       Insectproofing.
       Automobile fabrics.
       Indians, North American. Tex-
         tile industry and fabrics.
       Canvas.
    x Cloth.
       Textiles.
       Fabrics.
       Flock.
       Textile trade.
       Textile industry.
--Abstracts.

Textile industry and fabrics (Continued)
--Accounting.
    xx Cost. Accounting.
      Accounting.
--Advertising.
--Bacteriology.   See Textile bacteriology.
--Bibliography.
--Chemistry.   See Textile chemistry.
--Congresses.
    sa Subdivision Congresses under
      Textile industry and fabrics
      [geographic subdivision] e.g.,
      Textile industry and fabrics.
      Spain. Congresses.
--Dictionaries.
--Directories.
    sa Subdivision Directories under
      Textile industry and fabrics
      [geographic subdivision]
      e.g., Textile industry and
      fabrics. France. Directories.
--Drying.
    sa Subdivision Drying under:
      Clothing and dress.
      Drying apparatus. Textile
      fabrics.
--Effect of humidity.   See Humidity.
    Effect on textile fabrics.
--Effect of temperature.   See Temperature.
    Effect on textile fabrics.
--Encyclopedias.   See Textile industry
    and fabrics. Dictionaries.
--Exhibitions.
--Fireproofing.   See Fireproofing of
    textiles.
--Fungus proofing.   See Fungus proofing
    of textiles.
--Grading and standardization.
    sa Subdivision Grading and stand-
      ardization under: Household
      textiles.
      Garment sizes.
--History.
    sa Subdivision History under Tex-
      tile industry and fabrics
      [geographic subdivision] e.g.,
      Textile industry and fabrics.
      U.S. History.

Textile industry and fabrics, Household.
    See Household textiles.

Textile industry and fabrics.
--Juvenile literature.

Textile industry and fabrics (Continued)
--Labels.
    sa Subdivision Labels under:
      Woolen fabrics.
    xx Labels.
--Law.
--Marketing.
    sa Subdivision Marketing under:
      Cotton fabrics.
-- --Research.
--Marketing agreements.
--Outlines, syllabi, etc.
--Patents.
--Periodicals.
    sa Subdivision Periodicals under
      Textile industry and fabrics
      [geographic subdivision]
      e.g., Textile industry and
      fabrics. France. Periodicals
      Subdivision Periodicals under:
      Dry-goods.
--Pictorial works.
--Preservation.   See Textile industry
    and fabrics. Protective treatments.
--Prices.
    sa Subdivision Prices under:
      Cotton fabrics.
      Jute bagging.
--Private collection.
--Protective treatments.
    sa Waterproofing of fabrics.
      Mildewproofing of fabrics.
      Fungus proofing of textiles.
      Fireproofing of textiles.
      Subdivision Protective treat-
      ments under: Cotton fabrics.
    x Textile industry and fabrics.
      Preservation.
      Preservation of fabrics.
      Preservation of textiles.
      Protective treatments of
      fabrics.
      Protective treatments of tex-
      tiles.
-- --Bibliography.
--Research.
    sa Textile industry and fabrics
      [geographic subdivision] Re-
      search, e.g., Textile in-
      dustry and fabrics. Belgium.
      Research.
-- --Bibliography.
-- --Periodicals.
-- --Societies.   See Textile industry
    and fabrics. Societies.

Textile industry and fabrics (Continued)
--Schools.   See Textile industry and
    fabrics. Study and teaching.

Textile industry and fabrics, Shrink-
    resistant.
        sa Woolen fabrics, Shrink-
            resistant.
            Textile fibers, Synthetic.
            Shrinkage.

Textile industry and fabrics.
--Societies.
        sa Textile industry and fabrics
            ₍geographic subdivision₎
            Societies, e.g., Textile
            industry and fabrics.
            Ahmedabad, India (City)
            Societies.
        x Textile industry and fabrics.
            Research. Societies.
--Statistical methods.
--Statistics.
        sa Subdivision Statistics under
            Textile industry and fabrics
            ₍geographic subdivision₎
            e.g., Textile industry and
            fabrics. France. Statistics.
--Subject headings.   See Subject head-
    ings. Textile industry and fabrics.
--Substitutes.   See Textile substitutes.
--Tables, calculations, etc.
        sa Subdivision Tables, calcula-
            tions, etc. under: Yarn.
--Tariff.
        sa Subdivision Tariff under:
            Cotton. Manufacture.
--Terminology.
--Testing.
        sa Subdivision Testing under:
            Woolen fabrics.
            Cotton fabrics.
            Linen.
            Canvas.
 - --Law.
        sa Subdivision Testing. Law under:
            Silk.
--Trade-marks.
        xx Trade-marks.
--Waste.
        xx Factory and trade waste.
--Waterproofing.   See Waterproofing of
    fabrics.

Textile industry as an occupation.

Textile machinery.
        sa Cotton, Implements and
            machinery.
            Looms.
            Spinning machinery.
            Doubling machinery.
            Carding-machines.
--Directories.
--Repairing.
        sa Subdivision Repairing under:
            Spinning machinery.
        xx Repairing.
--Tariff.

Textile mills.   See Textile factories.

Textile museums.
--Directories.

Textile painting.
        xx Art.
            Textile design.

Textile plants.   See Fiber plants and
    vegetable fibers.

Textile printing.
        sa Calico-printing.
        x Printing, Textile.

Textile research.   See Textile industry
    and fabrics. Research.

Textile schools.
        sa Textile industry and fabrics.
            Study and teaching.
        x Textile education.
            Textile industry and fabrics.
            Study and teaching.
        xx Technical education.

Textile standards.   See Textile industry
    and fabrics. Grading and standardiza-
    tion.

Textile substitutes.   See Textile fibers,
    Synthetic.

Textile testing.   See Textile industry
    and fabrics. Testing.

Textile trade.   See Textile industry
    and fabrics.

2161

Textile workers.   (DIRECT)
     sa Cotton textile workers.
        Woolen and worsted manufacture.
        Employees.
        Wages, Textile.

Textiles.   See Textile industry and
    fabrics.

Textiles, Synthetic.   See Textile fibers,
    Synthetic.

Thaï.   See Siam.

Thailand.
        Long known as Siam. Name changed
        to Thailand in 1939, to Siam
        in 1945, and once more to
        Thailand in 1949. Subject en-
        tries are under Siam.

Thal, West Punjab.
--Agriculture.

Thalamus opticus.   See Optic thalamus.

Thalassema neptuni.

Thalassocrinus.

Thallium.
--Effect on animals.
--Effect on plants.
        x Plants, Effect of thallium on.
--Toxicity.
        xx Toxicology.

Thallium salts.

Thallophyta.

Thallus.

Thames River.
        sa Floods. Thames River.

Thames Valley, Eng.
--Natural history.

Thamnophilus.

Thanatopsyche chilensis.

Thanite.

Thaon-les-Vosges.
--Agriculture.
-- --History.

Thatched roofs.   See Roofs, Thatched.

Thaumaleidae.
        x Orphnepholidae.
        xx Diptera.

Thaumasite.

Thaumatococcus danielli.

Thayer Co., Neb.
--Soils.
        sa Subdivision Nebraska. Thayer
        Co. under: Soil-surveys.

Theaceae.

Theater.   See Theatre.

Theatre.
        sa Acting.
        x Theater.

Theces ternus.

Thecodiplosis brachyptera.

Thecodiplosis mosellana.   See Sito-
    diplosis mosellana.

Thecothens.
        xx Ascobolaceae.

Thecotheus pelletieri.

Theileriasis.   See Theileriosis.

Theileriosis in cattle.
        x African coast fever.
        Bovine theileriosis.
        East African coast fever.
        Piroplasmosis, Bovine.
        Bovine piroplasmosis.
        East coast fever.
        xx Cattle. Diseases.

Theine.   See Caffein.

Theiss River.
        sa Subdivision Theiss River under:
        Flood control.

Thelazia.
 xx Nematoda.

Thelazia rhodesi.

Thelaziasis.
 xx Eye. Diseases.

Thelephoraceae.
 sa Stereum.
  Corticium.

Thelle, France.
 sa France. Département de l'Oise.
--Agriculture.

Thelocarpaceae.
 xx Lichens.

Thelon Game Sanctuary.

Theloschistaceae.
 xx Lichens.

Thelyphonidae.
 sa Thelyphonus.

Thelyphonus.

Thelyphonus caudatus.

Thelyphonus maximus.

Thelypodium.

Theobroma bicolor.

Theobroma cacao. See Cacao.

Theobroma grandiflorum.

Theobromine.
 sa Agurin.

Theodolite board.

Theodora speciosa.

Theodore Roosevelt National Memorial
 Park, N.D.

Theology, Natural. See Natural theology.

Theophrastaceae.

Theophylline compounds.
 --Physiological effect.

Theoretical physics. See Mathematical
 physics.

Theory of equations. See Equations,
 Theory of.

Theory of errors. See Errors, Theory of.

Theory of groups. See Groups, Theory of.

Theory of numbers. See Numbers, Theory
 of.

Thera.
 --Botany.

Therapeutic effect of work. See
 Occupational therapy.

Therapeutics.
 sa Chemistry, Medical and
  pharmaceutical.
  Chemotherapy.
  Counter-irritants.
  Diet in disease.
  Dosiology.
  Drugs.
  Homeopathy. Materia medica and
   therapeutics.
  Inhalation (Therapeutics)
  Injections, Hypodermic.
  Materia medica.
  Medicine. Formulae, receipts
   prescriptions.
  Malariotherapy.
  Mineral waters.
  Narcotics.
  Nurses and nursing.
  Nutrition.
  Organotherapy.
  Prescription writing.
  Purgatives.
  Serumtherapy.
  Stimulants.
  Shock therapy.
  Subdivision Therapeutic use
   under: Radium.
   X-rays.
   Antimony//
 xx Materia medica.
  Medicine. Practice.
--Bibliography.

Therapeutics, Dental.
    x Dental medicine.
      Dental therapeutics.
      Medicine, Dental.
    xx Materia medica and therapeutics.

Therapeutics, Experimental.
    x Experimental therapeutics.
  --Periodicals.

Therapeutics.
  --Periodicals.

Therapeutics, Physiological.
    Under this heading are entered
    comprehensive or general works
    dealing with non-medicinal
    therapeutics. Specific works
    are entered under appropriate
    headings, e.g., Diet in disease,
    Phototherapy, Physical therapy,
    etc.
    sa Diet in disease.
      Mineral waters.
      Music, Physical effect.
      Nature, Healing power of.
      Radiotherapy.
      Sun-baths.
      Occupational therapy.
      Physical therapy.
      Phototherapy.
    x Physiological therapeutics.

Therapeutics, Suggestive.
    sa Animal magnetism.
    x Psychotherapy.
      Suggestive therapeutics.
    xx Mental healing.
      Mental suggestion.

Theraphosidae.
    sa Citharoscelus.
    xx Araneida.

Therapogen.

Theresia ampelophaga.   See Procris ampelophaga.

Theresimina ampelophaga.
    x Ino ampelophaga.

Therevidae.
    xx Siphonaptera.

Therica.

Theridiidae.
    sa Latrodectus.
    xx Arachnida.

Theridion.
    x Theridium.

Theridion triste.

Theridium.   See Theridion.

Therioaphis maculata.   See Pterocallidium
  trifoli.

Therisimina.
    xx Zygaenidae.

Thermal analysis.
  --Bibliography.

Thermal conductivity.
    x Conductivity, Thermal.

Thermal constants.

Thermal diffusivity.
    x Diffusivity, Thermal.
    xx Heat. Conduction.
      Specific heat.

Thermal expansion.   See Expansion (Heat)

Thermal waters.

Thermionic tubes.   See Vacuum-tubes.

Thermionic valve circuits.   See Vacuum-
  tube circuits.

Thermobia domestica.
    x Fire brat.

Thermochemistry.
    sa Low temperature research.
      Pyrolysis.
  --Research.

Thermocouples.
    xx Thermometers and thermometry.
      Thermo-electricity.

Thermodynamics.
    sa Heat.
       Heat-engines.
       Quantum theory.
       Heat pumps.
    xx Chemistry, Physical and
        theoretical.
--Tables, etc.

Thermo-electricity.
    sa Pyro- and piezo-electricity.
       Thermocouples.
    x Thermoelectricity.
    xx Electricity.
       Heat.

Thermoelectricity.   See Thermo-electricity.

Thermo-gen.

Thermograph.

Thermography.

Thermoisopleths.

Thermometer exposure.

Thermometers and thermometry.
    sa Soil thermometer.
       Radiation thermometer.
       Katathermometer.
       Thermocouples.

Thermometry.

Thermophiles.
    xx Micro-organisms.

Thermophilic bacteria.   See Bacteria,
   Thermophilic.

Thermopiles.

Thermoregulator.

Thermosbaena mirabilis.

Thermostat.

Thermotherapy.
    xx Materia medica and therapeutics.
       Physical therapy.

Thersilochus conotracheli.

Thescelosaurus.

Theses.
--Abstracts.
    Whenever this subject is used,
    also assign subject Theses.
    Bibliography (or Theses. Bib-
    liography. Periodicals. if
    publication is an abstract
    periodical)
    sa Theses. Bibliography.
    xx Theses. Bibliography.
       Theses. Bibliography. Peri-
       odicals.
--Bibliography.
    sa Theses. Abstracts.
    xx Theses. Abstracts.
-- --Periodicals.
    sa Theses. Abstracts.

Thesium.

Thessaly.
--Maps.

Thetford Chase Forest, Eng.

Thiamin chloride.   See Vitamins (B_1)

Thiamine.   See Vitamins (B_1)

Thiamine hydrochloride.   See Vitamins
   (B_1)

Thian-Shan Mountains.   See Celestial-
   Shan Mountains.

Thiazines as anthelmintics.
    xx Anthelmintics.

Thiazol.

Thibaudieae.
    sa Vacciniaceae.

Thibet.   See Tibet.

Thiela viopsis paradoxa.   See Thielaviopsis paradoxa.

Thielavia basicola.

Thielaviopsis ethaceticus. See Thiela-
    viopsis paradoxa.

Thielaviopsis paradoxa.
        x Thiela viopsis paradoxa.

Thieves.

Thingan. See Hopea odorata.

Thinking. See Thought and thinking.

Thinner (Paint mixing)
        sa Vinyltoluene.

Thinnfeldia.

Thinning.
        x Trees. Thinning.
            Release cuttings.
    --Bibliography.
        xx Sylviculture. Bibliography.

Thinning of fruit. See Fruit thinning.

Thinning sprays. See Growth substances
    for plants.

Thinolite.

Thiocyanates.
        x Sulphocyanates.
            Rhodanates.
    --Physiological effect.

Thiodiphenylamine. See Phenothiazine.

Thiokol. See Rubber, Artificial.

Thiols. See Mercaptans.

Thiophene.
        xx Chemistry, Organic.

Thiophosphates.

Thiophosphoric acids.

Thiosulphates.
    --Effect on plants.

Thiouracil.

Thiourea.
        sa Alpha napthylthiourea.
        xx Urea.

Thira. See Thera.

Thismia americana.

Thistle, Canada. See Carduus arvensis.

Thistle, Russian. See Russian thistle.

Thistles.
        sa Carduus arvensis.
            Sonchus arvensis.
        x Sow-thistles.

Thistles, Artichoke. See Cardoon.

Thistles, Cardoon. See Cardoon.

Thistles.
    --Eradication.
        xx Weeds. Eradication.
    --Toxicity.

Thixotropy.
        xx Colloids.
            Gels.

Thlaspideae.
        sa Biscutella.

Tholen, Netherlands.

Thomas Co., Ga.
    --Entomology.
        sa Subdivision Georgia. Thomas
            Co. under: Orthoptera.
    --Social conditions.
        sa Housing, Rural. Georgia.
            Thomas Co.
        xx Georgia. Social conditions.

Thomas meal. See Phosphatic slag.

Thomas meal sickness.

Thomas phosphate. See Phosphatic slag.

Thomas slag. See Phosphatic slag.

Thomisidae.
        sa Synema.

Thomomys.   See Pocket gophers.

Thompsonella.

Thonga Tribe.
         x Tonga Tribe.
           Tsonga Tribe.

Thoracic duct.

Thoracostraca.

Thorax.
  --Insects.
  --Mammals.

Thoreaceae.

Thorictidae.

Thorictus.

Thorictus foreli.

Thorin (Farm)

Thorium.
  --Bibliography.

Thorn-apple.   See Datura stramonium.

Thorn-headed worms.   See Macracanthoryn-
    chus hirudinaceus.

Thorns.

Thornthwaite Forest, Eng.

Thorocaphis umbellulariae.
         xx Aphididae.

Thoroughbred horse.
         sa Race horses.
  --Breeding.
         xx Horses. Breeding.
  --Periodicals.

Thought and thinking.
         sa Logic.
            Reasoning.
          x Thinking.
         xx Philosophy.
            Psychology.

Thought-transference.
         xx Psychical research.

Thousand-legs.   See Diplopoda.

Thrace.
  --Agriculture.

Thrasher Demonstration Farm, Frederick
    Co., Md.
         xx Demonstration farms.

Thrassis.
         xx Siphonaptera.

Thread.

Threadworms.   See Cestoidea.

Three-banded grape leafhopper.   See
    Erythroneura tricincta.

Three-cornered alfalfa hopper.   See
    Stictocephala festina.

Three-day sickness.
          x Ephemeral fever.
            Dengue fever of cattle.
            Stiff sickness.
         xx Cattle. Diseases.

Three Rivers, Que.
         sa Subdivision Three Rivers, Que.
                under: Produce trade.
         xx Quebec (Province)

Threonine.
         xx Amino acids.

Threshing.
         xx Agriculture. Implements and
                machinery.
  --Costs.
         xx Costs.
  --Work management.
         xx Work management.

Threshing injuries.   See Farm produce.
    Injuries.

Threshing machines.
         sa Bates aspirator.
  --Design.
         xx Machinery. Design.

Threshing machines, Electric.
      x Electric threshing machines.
      xx Electric farm machinery.

Threshing machines.
--History.
      xx Agriculture. Implements and
        machinery. History.
--Maintenance and repair.
      xx Agriculture. Implements and
        machinery. Maintenance and
        repair.
--Safety measures.
      xx Agriculture. Implements and
        machinery. Safety measures.
--Statistics.

Threshing record books.
      xx Farm record books.

Thrift.   See Saving and thrift.

Thripidae.
      sa Frankliniella.
      xx Thysanoptera.

Thrips.
      This is used only for works on
      the genus Thrips. For popular
      works on thrips see Thysanop-
      tera.

Thrips pisivora.

Thrips tabaci.
      xx Onions. Pests.

Throat.
--Diseases.

Throat botfly.   See Gasterophilus
  nasalis.

Thrombocytes.

Thrombosis.
      x Thrombus formation.

Thrombus formation.   See Thrombosis.

Throscidae.

Throscoryssa citri.

Thrushes.   See Turdidae.

Thryomanes.

Thuja.   See Thuya.

Thule, Greenland.
--Climate.
--Physical geography.

Thulium.

Thunder.

Thunder-storms.
      xx Acoustic phenomena in nature.

Thunderstorm-recorders.

Thurberia weevil.

Thüringer Wald.
--Domestic animals.

Thuringia.
--Agriculture.
      sa Subdivision Thuringia under:
        Agriculture. Economic as-
         pects.
--Apiculture.
--Botany.
      sa Reuss.
--Cattle.
      xx Cattle.
--Entomology.
      sa Subdivision Thuringia under:
        Coleoptera.
        Lepidoptera.
        Butterflies.
--Forestry.
      sa Schwarzburg.
        Rodolstadt.
        Subdivision Thuringia under:
         Lumber trade.
--History.
      xx Germany. Forestry. History.
--Paleobotany.
--Soils.
--Statistics.

Thuringian Forest.   See Thüringer Wald.

Thurins, France.

Thurn und Taxis Domains.

Thurston Co., Wash.
--Soils.
    sa Subdivision Washington (State)
        Thurston under: Soil-surveys.

Thuya.
    x Thuja.
    xx Cedar.
    Arborvitae.

Thuya gigantea. See Thuya plicata.

Thuya occidentalis.
    x Northern white cedar.
    xx Arbor Vitae.

Thuya orientalis.

Thuya plicata.
--Seed.
    xx Trees. Seed.
- --Sowing.
    xx Sowing.

Thuya plicata (Wood)
    x Western red cedar wood.

Thyca.

Thymalus marginicollis.

Thymelaeaceae.
    sa Aguilaria.
    Daphne.
    Lagetta.
    Edgeworthia chrysantha.

Thymol.

Thymus.
    xx Menthaceae.

Thymus gland.

Thymus mastichina.

Thymus oils.
    xx Essences and essential oils.

Thynnidae.
    sa Methoca.

Thyreocorinae.

Thyreus abbotii.

Thyrididae.
    xx Lepidoptera.

Thyridopteryx.

Thyridopteryx ephemeraeformis.

Thyroid gland.
    sa Parathyroid gland.
--Diseases.
    sa Graves' disease.
    Goiter.

Thyroprotein.

Thyroxine.

Thysanoptera.
    sa Melanothrips.
    Prosopothrips.
    Phloeothripidae.
    Euthrips.
    Physopus.
    Anaphothrips.
    Phloeothrips.
    Thrips.
    Taeniothrips.
    Bregmatothrips iridis.
    Aeolothripidae.
    Thripidae.

Thysanura.
    sa Collembola.
    Poduridae.
    Aptera.
    Campodea.
    Lepidocampa.
    Machilidae.
    Lepismatidae.
    Symphyla.
    Myrientomata.
    Iapygidae.

Thysonotis.

Tia Juana River.
    x Tijuana River.

Tian-Shan Mountains. See Celestial-
  Shan Mountains.

Tiber River and Valley.
--Agriculture.
    sa Subdivision Italy. Tiber River
        and Valley under: Farms.

Tiber River and Valley (Continued)
--Soils.

Tibet.
      xx Asia.
--Bibliography.
      xx Asia. Bibliography.
--Botany.
      xx Asia. Botany.
--Commerce.
--Description and travel.
--Ethnology.
--Geology.
-- --Bibliography.
--History.
--Paleontology.
--Zoology.
      xx Asia. Zoology.

Tibetans.

Tibicen erratica.　See Cicada erratica.

Tibicen septendecim.
    x Cicada septendecim.
      Periodical cicada.
      Seventeen-year locust.

Tibidaba Mountains, Spain.
--Botany.

Ticino (Canton)
--Agriculture.
--Apiculture.
-- --Periodicals.
--Botany.
--Forestry.
--Pomology.
    sa Subdivision Switzerland. Ticino
      (Canton) under: Berries.

Tick fever.
      This subject used for Tick fever
        in cattle. For other tick
        fevers see African tick fever;
        Rocky Mountain spotted fever;
        Sarnol.
    x Splenic fever.
      Texas fever.
      Bovine piroplasmosis.
      Piroplasmosis, Bovine.
      Tristeza.
    xx Cattle. Diseases.

Tick trefoil.　See Desmodium.

Ticks.　See Ixodidae.

Ticks as carriers of contagion.
      xx Animals as carriers of con-
        tagion.
      Ixodidae.
      Acarina.

Tide marshes.　See Marshes, Tide.

Tides.

Tierra del Fuego.
--Botany.
--Domestic animals.
-- --Statistics.
--Entomology.
--Ornithology.
--Paleobotany.
--Soils.
      sa Subdivision Tierra del Fuego
        under: Peat.

Ties, Railroad.　See Railroad ties.

Tiflis. Kavkazskii muzei i tiflisskaia
  publichnaia biblioteka.

Tiflis, Russia. Kaukasisches museum.

Tift Co., Ga.
--Soils.
      sa Subdivision Georgia. Tift Co.
        under: Soil-surveys.

Tigai sheep.　See Tsigai sheep.

Tiger-beetles.　See Cicindelidae.

Tiger swallow-tail butterfly.　See
  Papilio glaucus.

Tigris River.

Tijuana River.　See Tia Juana River.

Tilapia.

Tilefish.

Tiles.

Tiles, Drain.　See Drain-tiles.

Tiles.
--Floor.
-- --Statistics.

Tiles, Roofing.

Tilia.

Tilia americana.
        x Basswood.
 --Diseases.

Tilia cordata.

Tiliaceae.
        sa Triumfetta.
            Grewia.
            Tilia.
            Corchoropsis.

Tillage.
        sa Plowing.
            Mulch and mulching.
        x Cultivation of soils.
            Soil cultivation.
        xx Agriculture.
 --Charts, diagrams, etc.
 --Effect on plants.
 --Effect on soil.
        x Soil, Effect of tillage on.
 --Research.

Tillage machinery.
        sa Harrow.
            Cultivators.
            Plow.
            Rollers (Tillage)
        xx Agriculture. Implements and
            machinery.
 --Congresses.
 --Design.
        xx Machinery. Design.
 --Research.
 -- --Bibliography.
 --Terminology.
        xx Agriculture. Implements and
            machinery. Terminology.

Tillamook Co., Or.
        xx Oregon.
 --Agriculture.
        sa Agriculture. Economic aspects.
            Oregon. Tillamook Co.
 --Forestry.
 -- --Statistics.

Tillamook Co., Or. (Continued)
 --Land.
        sa Subdivision Oregon. Tillamook
            Co. under: Land. Classifi-
                cation.
        xx Oregon. Land.
 --Soils.
        sa Subdivision Oregon. Tillamook
            Co. under: Soil conserva-
                tion.

Tillamook Co. (Or.) Creamery Association.

Tillandria recurvate.

Tilletia.

Tilletia caries.

Tilletia horrida.

Tilletia in feeding stuffs.   See Feeding
    stuffs, Tilletia in.

Tilletia levis.

Tilletia tritici.
        sa Stinking smut of wheat.
 --Bibliography.
        xx Wheat. Diseases. Bibliography.

Tilletiaceae.
        sa Entyloma.
            Entorrhiza.
        xx Ustilagineae.

Tillman Co., Okla.
 --Soils.
        sa Subdivision Oklahoma. Tillman
            Co. under: Soil-surveys.

Tilopteridaceae.

Tilsiter cheese.   See Cheese, Tilsiter.

Timber.   (INDIRECT)
        sa Timber physics.
            Wood preservation.
            Lumber.
            Wood.
            Mine timbers.
            Pile timbers.
            Beech.
            Mahogony.
            Oak.

Timber (Continued)
    sa Pine.
       Redwoods.
       Hemlock.
       Pulpwood.
    xx Connecticut. Forestry.
--Bibliography.
    sa Timber ₍geographic subdivision₎
       Bibliography, e.g., Timber.
       Australia. Bibliography.

Timber, Building. See Wood as building
  material.

Timber.
--Congresses.
--Cost of production.
    sa Subdivision Cost of production
       under: Pulpwood.
    xx Farm produce. Cost of produc-
       tion.
--Deterioration.
    sa Collapse of timber.
       Subdivision Deterioration under:
       Wood.
    xx Deterioration.
       Wood. Deterioration.
--Drying. See Lumber. Drying.
--Felling.
    x Cutting of timber.
       Timber cutting.
       Felling.
       Tree felling.
       Timber felling.
       Tree cutting.
       Wood cutting.
    xx Lumbering.
--Exhibitions. See Lumber. Exhibitions.

Timber, Fire killed. See Fire-killed
  timber.

Timber.
--Fireproofing. See Wood. Fireproofing.
--Grading and standardization. See
    Lumber. Grading and standardization;
    Trees. Grading and standardization.
--Identification. See Wood. Identifi-
    cation; Trees. Identification.
--Law. See Forestry. Law.
--Marketing.
    sa Subdivision Marketing under:
       Lumber.
       Forest products.
       Wood as fuel.

Timber (Continued)
--Marketing.
    sa Timber sales.
    xx Lumber. Marketing.
--Marking.
    sa Subdivision Marking under:
       Trees.
--Mensuration. See Forest mensuration.
--Names. See Trees. Names.
--Pests. See Wood. Pests.
--Preservation. See Wood preservation.
--Prices. See Stumpage prices.

Timber, Reinforced. See Lumber, Reinforced.

Timber.
--Seasoning. See Lumber. Drying.
--Statistics.
    sa Lumber. Statistics.
       Timber ₍geographic subdivi-
       sion₎ Statistics, e.g.,
       Timber. U.S. Statistics.
    x Timber statistics.
    xx Lumber. Statistics.
       Forestry. Statistics.
--Tariff.
    sa Timber ₍geographic subdivi-
       sion₎ Tariff, e.g., Timber.
       Australia. Tariff.
--Theft.
    xx Forestry. Law.
       Crime and criminals.
--Transportation. See Log transporta-
    tion.

Timber as building material. See Wood
  as building material.

Timber brands. See Log brands.

Timber columns. See Columns, Wooden.

Timber-connector joints. See Joints,
  Timber-connector.

Timber cruising. See Timber estimating.

Timber culture act.

Timber cutting. See Timber. Felling.

Timber diseases. See Trees. Diseases.

Timber drying. See Lumber. Drying.

Timber drying kilns. See Kilns.

Timber estimating.
 sa Forest mensuration.
 x Cruising.
  Timber cruising.
  Forest estimating.
  Forestry. Appraisal.
  Forestry. Estimating.
  Forest appraisal.

Timber felling. See Timber. Felling.

Timber fireproofing. See Wood. Fireproofing.

Timber for airplanes. See Wood as airplane material.

Timber for mining. See Mine timbering.

Timber joints. See Joints, Timber-
connector.

Timber line.

Timber management. See Forest management.

Timber marks. See Log brands.

Timber physics.
 sa Wood. Hardness.
  Wood. Testing.
  Temperature. Effect on wood.
 x Wood. Physics.
  Wood physics.
 xx Wood technology.
 --Research.
  xx Forest products. Research.

Timber preservation. See Wood preservation.

Timber products. See Forest products.

Timber sales.
 xx Timber. Marketing.

Timber seasoning. See Lumber. Drying.

Timber slides. See Log slides.

Timber stand improvement. See Stand
improvement.

Timber statistics. See Timber. Statistics.

Timber tests. See Wood. Testing.

Timber trade. See Lumber trade.

Timber workers. See Lumbermen.

Timberland valuation. See Forestry.
Valuation and taxation.

Timbers for airplanes. See Wood as airplane material.

Timbo. See Lonchocarpus; Paullinia pin-
nata.

Timbuktu.

Time.
 sa Space and time.

Time measurements.

Time of planting. See Planting time.

Time series (Statistics) See Time
series analysis.

Time series analysis.
 sa Harmonic analysis.
 x Time series (Statistics)
 xx Statistics.

Time study.
 sa Motion study.
 x Timestudy.
 xx Employment management.
  Factory management.
  Job analysis.
  Efficiency, Industrial.
  Motion study.
 --Bibliography.

Time-tables. See Motor buses. Time-
tables; Railroads. Time-tables; Air
lines. Time-tables; Transportation.
Time-tables.

Timekeepers.

Timeliidae.
 sa Cisticola.

Timestudy.   See Time study.

Timgad.
--Description.
-- --Guide books.

Timiskaming Co., Que.
--Geology.

Timmiaceae.
        sa Timmia.

Timor (Province)
--Agriculture.
-- --Statistics.
--Botany.
        sa Subdivision Timor under: Trees.
--Commerce.
-- --Statistics.
--Forestry.
        sa Subdivision Timor under: Trees.

Timorlaut Islands.
--Ornithology.

Timothy.
        x Phleum.
          Phleum pratense.
--Diseases.
        sa Timothy rust.
        xx Grasses and forage plants.
--Growth.
--Seed.
        x Timothy seed.
-- --Statistics.

Timothy as feeding stuff.
        xx Feeding stuffs.

Timothy hay.

Timothy rust.

Timothy seed.   See Timothy. Seed.

Timothy silage.
        xx Ensilage.

Timothy stem-borer.   See Mordellistena
   ustulata.

Timpanogos Cave National Monument, Utah.
        xx National parks and reserves.

Timur.   See Timor.

Tin.
        sa Food, Tin in.
           Milk, Tin in.
--Bibliography.
--Compounds.
--Effect on plants.
--Periodicals.
--Statistics.
--Substitutes.   See Tin substitutes.
--Year-books.
        xx Year-books.

Tin cans.
        x Metal cans.
          Cans, Tin.
        xx Containers.
--Bibliography.

Tin in food.   See Food, Tin in.

Tin in milk.   See Milk, Tin in.

Tin substitutes.
        x Tin. Substitutes.
        xx Substitute products.

Tinamidae.
        sa Nothura.

Tinamous.   See Tinamidae.

Tinea ambiguella.   See Cochylis ambiguella.

Tinea granella.

Tinea imbricata.

Tinea pellionella.   See Clothes moths.

Tinea spretella.

Tinea vastella.

Tineidae.
        sa Blastobasidae.
           Tischeria.
           Agdistidae.
           Gracilaria.
           Phthorimaea.
           Prodoxus.
           Pronuba.
           Lampronia.
           Tinea.
           Incurvaria.

Tineidae (Continued)
    sa Ornix.
        Bucculatrix.
        Ectoedemia.
        Marmara.
        Acrocercops.
        Nepticula.
        Neopseustis.

Tineina.

Tineoidea.

Tineola biselliella.

Tinghsien, China.
--Social conditions.

Tingidae.   See Tingitidae.

Tingitidae.
    sa Gargaphia.
        Piesma.

Tingitoidea.

Tinned foods.   See Canned goods.

Tinnevelly, India.
--Botany.

Tinoporus.

Tintern Forest, Eng.
    xx England. Forest reservations.

Tintinnopsis nucula.

Tintinnus neriticus.

Tioga Co., N.Y.
--Agriculture.
--Soils.
    sa Subdivision New York (State)
        Tioga Co. under: Soil-
            surveys.

Tioga Co., Pa.
--Soils.
    sa Subdivision Pennsylvania.
        Tioga Co. under: Soil-
            surveys.

Tionesta Dam, Tionesta Creek, Pa.
    xx Dams.

Tip-burn.

Tiphia.

Tiphiidae.

Tippecanoe Co., Ind.
    xx Indiana.
--Agriculture.
-- --Periodicals.
--Soils.
    sa Subdivision Indiana. Tippe-
        canoe Co. under: Soil-
            surveys.

Tipperary (South riding) Ireland (County)
--Agriculture.

Tipton Co., Ind.
    xx Indiana.
--Soils.
    sa Subdivision Indiana. Tipton
        Co. under: Soil-surveys. a

Tipton Co., Tenn.
    xx Tennessee.

Tipula.

Tipula culiciformis.

Tipula infuscata.

Tipula oleracea.

Tipula paludosa.

Tipulidae.
    sa Ptchoptera.
        Limnobinae.
        Polymera.

Tiranë, Albania.
--Entomology.
    xx Albania. Entomology.

Tirathaba rufivena.

Tirathaba trichogramma.
    x Coconut spike moth.
        Spathe borer.
    xx Pyralididae.

Tire conservation.   See Tires, Rubber.
    Conservation.

Tire cords. See Tire fabrics.

Tire fabrics.
   x Tire cords.
 --Bibliography.
 --Statistics.

Tire rationing. See Rationing. Tires,
 Rubber.

Tires.
   sa Tire fabrics.

Tires, Rubber.
   x Automobiles. Tires.
    Rubber tires.
    Tracks, Rubber.
 --Bibliography.
 --Conservation.
   x Conservation of tires.
    Tire conservation.
 --Prices.
   xx Rubber. Prices.
 --Rationing. See Rationing. Tires,
  Rubber.
 --Tariff.
 --Testing.

Tires, Steel.

Tiresias serra Fabr.

Tirlemont. Hortus thenensis.

Tirol. See Tyrol.

Tischeria.

Tischeria complanella.

Tischeria malifoliella.

Tishomingo Co., Miss.
 --Soils.
   sa Subdivision Mississippi.
    Tishomingo Co. under:
    Soil-surveys.

Tishomingo State Park, Miss.
   xx Mississippi. Parks.

Tissue culture. See Tissues. Culture.

Tissue fluids. See Sap.

Tissue respiration.
   xx Tissues.

Tissue therapy.
   xx Veterinary medicine.

Tissues.
   sa Plant cells and tissues.
    Tissue respiration.
    Polarity (Biology)
 --Culture.
   x Tissue culture.

Tissues, Vegetable. See Plant cells
 and tissues.

Tisza River. See Theiss River.

Titania.
   xx Spheariaceae.

Titanite.

Titanium.
 --Metallurgy.

Titanium alloys.
   xx Alloys.

Titanium in plants.
   x Plants, Titanium in.

Titanium oxide.

Titanium sulphate.

Titer test.

Tithes.

Titicaca, Lake. See Lake Titicaca.

Title insurance. See Insurance, Title.

Titles, Land. See Land titles.

Titles of address.
   x Address, Titles of.
   xx Letter-writing.

Titmouse. See Paridae.

Titration. See Volumetric analysis.

Tittaniidae. See Chloropidae.

Tlingit Indians.
    xx Indians of Alaska.

Tmetocera ocellano. See Spilonota
  ocellana.

TNT. See Trinitrotoluene.

Toad bug. See Gelastocoris oculatus.

Toad flax. See Linaria vulgaris.

Toad venom.

Toadbug. See Gelastocoris oculatus.

Toads.
    x Bufo.
 --Anatomy and physiology.
 --Parasites.

Toadstools. See Mushrooms.

Toasters.
    sa Electric toasters.

Toasts. See Oratory.

Tobacco.   (INDIRECT)
    sa Nicotiana.
      Tropical agriculture.
      Nicotiana alata.
      Snuff.
      Smoking.
      Tobacco pipes.
      Subdivision Tobacco under:
        Rotation of crops.
 --Abstracts.
 -- --Periodicals.
 --Acreage adjustments.
    x Tobacco. Production, Control of.
      Tobacco. Control of production.
    xx Farm produce. Control of pro-
        duction.
 --Advertising.
 --Aging.
 --Analysis. See Tobacco. Chemistry.
 --Bibliography.
    sa Subdivision Bibliography under:
      Tobacco. Curing.
      Fertilizers for tobacco.
      Tobacco soils.
      Tobacco. Breeding.
      Tobacco as an insecticide.
 -- --Periodicals.

Tobacco (Continued)
 -- Breeding.
    xx Plant-breeding.
 -- --Bibliography.
    xx Tobacco. Bibliography.

Tobacco, Bright-leaf. See Tobacco, Flue-
  cured.

Tobacco, Burley.
 --Chemistry.
    xx Tobacco. Chemistry.
 --Diseases.
    xx Tobacco. Diseases.
 --Estimating of crop.
    xx Tobacco. Estimating of crop.
 --Grading and standardization.
    xx Tobacco. Grading and stand-
        ardization.
 --Marketing.
 -- --Control.
    xx Tobacco. Marketing. Control.·
 --Marketing quotas.
 --Pests.
    xx Tobacco. Pests.
 --Statistics.

Tobacco.
 --Burning quality.
 --By-products.
    xx Waste products.
 --Chemistry.
    sa Tobacco, Nicotine in.
      Subdivision Chemistry under:
        Tobacco, Burley.
        Tobacco, Flue-cured.
    x Tobacco. Analysis.
      Tobacco. Composition.
    xx Chemistry, Vegetable.
 --Composition. See Tobacco. Chemistry.
 --Congresses.
 --Consumption. See Tobacco consumption.
 --Control of production. See Tobacco.
    Acreage adjustments.
 --Cost of production.
    sa Subdivision Cost of production
        under: Tobacco, Flue-cured.
    xx Agricultural products. Cost
        of production.
 --Crop insurance.
    xx Crop insurance.
 --Crop reports.
    xx Crop reports.

Tobacco (Continued)
--Curing.
    x Tobacco. Stringing.
    xx Curing.
-- --Bibliography.
    xx Tobacco. Bibliography.
--Cytology.
    xx Plant cells and tissues.

Tobacco, Dark air-cured.
--Grading and standardization.
    xx Tobacco. Grading and standardi-
       zation.
--Marketing quotas.

Tobacco.
--Dictionaries.
--Disease resistant varieties.
    sa Subdivision Disease resistant
       varieties under: Tobacco,
       Flue-cured.
    xx Disease resistant plants.
--Diseases.
    sa Mosaic disease of tobacco.
       Blue-mold disease of tobacco.
       Sand-drown.
       Leaf-spot of tobacco.
       Root-rot of tobacco.
       Ringspot of tobacco.
       Virus diseases of tobacco.
       Curly-top of tobacco.
       Angular leaf spot of tobacco.
       Black shank of tobacco.
       Tobacco wilt.
       Subdivision Diseases under:
       Tobacco, Burley.
--Drying.
    x Tobacco drying.
--Economic aspects.
    xx Agriculture. Economic aspects.

Tobacco, Effect of ethylene on. See
    Ethylene. Effect on tobacco.

Tobacco, Effect of maleic hydrazide on.
    See Maleic hydrazide. Effect on tobacco.

Tobacco, Effect of potash on. See
    Potash. Effect on tobacco.

Tobacco.
--Estimating of crop.
    sa Subdivision Estimating of crop
       under: Tobacco, Burley.
    xx Crop estimating.

Tobacco, Effect of nitrogen on. See
    Nitrogen. Effect on tobacco.

Tobacco.
--Exhibitions.
--Fermentation.
--Fertilization.
--Financing.

Tobacco, Fire-cured.
--Grading and standardization.
    xx Tobacco. Grading and stand-
       ardization.
--Marketing quotas.
--Prices. See Tobacco. Prices.

Tobacco, Flue-cured.
    x Flue-cured tobacco.
       Tobacco, Bright-leaf.
--Chemistry.
    xx Tobacco. Chemistry.
--Cost of production.
    xx Tobacco. Cost of production.
--Disease resistant varieties.
    xx Tobacco. Disease resistant
       varieties.
--Grading and standardization.
    xx Tobacco. Grading and stand-
       ardization.
--Marketing.
    xx Tobacco. Marketing.
-- --Control.
    xx Tobacco. Marketing. Control.
--Marketing quotas.
    xx Tobacco. Marketing quotas.
--Prices. See Tobacco. Prices.
--Statistics.

Tobacco.
--Fumigation.
    xx Fumigation.
--Genetics.
--Germination.
--Grading and standardization.
    sa Subdivision Grading and
       standardization under:
       Tobacco, Burley.
       Tobacco, Fire-cured.
       Tobacco, Dark air-cured.
       Tobacco, Flue-cured.
--Growth.
--Hail injury.
    xx Hail injury.
--Hardiness.

Tobacco (Continued)
--Harvesting.
    xx Harvesting.
--History.   (DIRECT)
-- --Bibliography.
-- --Pictorial works.
--Hybrids.   See Nicotiana. Hybrids.
--Implements and machinery.
    x Tobacco. Machinery.
    xx Agriculture. Implements and
        machinery.
-- --Congresses.
--Inspection.
    xx Farm produce. Inspection.
--Irrigation.
    xx Irrigation.
--Legislation.

Tobacco, Light air-cured.

Tobacco.
--Machinery.   See Tobacco. Implements
    and machinery.
--Manufacture and trade.   See Tobacco
    manufacture and trade.
--Marketing.
    sa Dark Tobacco Growers' Coopera-
        tive Association.
    Subdivision Marketing under:
        Tobacco, Flue-cured.
    xx Tobacco manufacture and trade.
-- --Bibliography.
- --Control.
    sa Subdivision Marketing. Control
        under: Tobacco, Burley.
        Tobacco, Flue-cured.
    xx Farm produce. Marketing.
        Control.
--Marketing, Cooperative.
    xx Marketing, Cooperative.
-- --Bibliography.
    xx Marketing, Cooperative. Bib-
        liography.
-- --Periodicals.
-- --Societies.
    sa American Tobacco Co.
        Imperial Tobacco Co.
--Marketing.
-- --Costs.
    xx Farm produce. Marketing. Costs.
- --Research.
-- --Study and teaching.
--Marketing agreements.
    xx Marketing agreements.

Tobacco (Continued)
--Marketing quotas.
    sa Subdivision Marketing quotas
        under: Tobacco, Flue-cured.
    xx Marketing quotas.
-- --Legislation.
--Mineral elements.
    xx Plants. Mineral elements.
--Morphology and physiology.   See
    Tobacco. Physiology and morphology.

Tobacco, Nicotine in.
    xx Tobacco. Chemistry.

Tobacco, Oriental.

Tobacco.
--Periodicals.
    sa Subdivision Periodicals under
        Tobacco [geographic subdi-
        vision] e.g., Tobacco.
        Austria. Periodicals.
--Pests.
    sa Protoparce carolina.
        Epitrix parvula.
        Trichobaris mucorea.
        Crambus caliginosellus.
        Euthrips nicotianae.
        Lasioderma serricorne.
        Prodenia littoralis.
        Phlegethontius carolina.
        Myzus persicae.
        Ephestia elutella.
        Elater segetis.
        Dicyphus minimus.
    Subdivision Pests under:
        Tobacco, Burley.
--Physiological effect.
--Physiology and morphology.
--Planting time.
    xx Planting time.
--Price policy.
--Prices.
    x Tobacco, Flue-cured. Prices.
        Tobacco, Fire-cured. Prices.
    xx Farm produce. Prices.
- --Fixing.
    xx Prices. Fixing.
-- --Subsidies.
    xx Farm produce. Prices. Subsi-
        dies.
--Processing.
    xx Processing (Industrial)

Tobacco (Continued)
--Processing tax.
    xx Processing tax.
       Tobacco. Taxation.
--Production, Control of. See Tobacco.
    Acreage adjustments.
--Quality.
-- --Terminology.
--Research.
    sa Tobacco ₍geographic subdivi-
       sion₎ Research, e.g., To-
       bacco. U.S. Research.
    xx Research.
--Seed.
-- --Directories.
--Seed beds.
--Shade culture.
--Societies.
    x Tobacco Dealers and Growers
       Association.
--Speculation.
    xx Speculation (in business)
--Spraying. See Spraying. Tobacco.
--Statistics.
    sa Subdivision Statistics under
       various types of tobacco,
       i.e., Tobacco, Burley. Sta-
       tistics. Tobacco, Flue-cured.
       Statistics.
--Storage.
--Stringing. See Tobacco. Curing.
--Substitutes. See Tobacco substitutes.

Tobacco, Sugar in.
    xx Sugar in plants.

Tobacco.
--Tariff.
--Taxation. (DIRECT)
    sa Subdivision Processing tax
       under: Tobacco.
    x Cigarette taxation.
--Transportation.
    sa Subdivision Tobacco under:
       Railroads. Rates.
    xx Farm produce. Transportation.
--Varieties.
--Weather influences.
    xx Crops and climate.

Tobacco, Wild. See Nicotiana attenuata;
    Nicotiana trigonophylla.

Tobacco aphid. See Myzus persicae.

Tobacco as an insecticide.
--Bibliography.
    xx Tobacco. Bibliography.
       Insecticides. Bibliography.

Tobacco barns.
--Designs and plans.
    xx Barns and stables. Designs and
       plans.
--Heating and ventilation.
    xx Farm buildings. Heating and
       ventilation.
       Barns and stables. Ventilation.

Tobacco beetle. See Lasioderma serri-
    corne.

Tobacco blue mold. See Blue-mold dis-
    ease of tobacco.

Tobacco budworm. See Heliothis vires-
    cens.

Tobacco caterpillar. See Prodenia
    littoralis.

Tobacco consumption. (DIRECT)
    x Tobacco. Consumption.

Tobacco cooperatives.
    x Tobacco growers cooperative
       associations.
    xx Agriculture, Cooperative.
       Societies.

Tobacco dealers and growers associations.
    See Tobacco. Societies.

Tobacco downy mildew. See Blue-mold
    disease of tobacco.

Tobacco driers.
    xx Drying apparatus.

Tobacco drying. See Tobacco. Drying.

Tobacco exchanges.
    xx Commodity exchanges.
       Tobacco manufacture and trade.

Tobacco flea-beetle. See Epitrix
    parvula.

Tobacco growers cooperative associations.
    See Tobacco cooperatives.

Tobacco hornworm.   See Protoparce sexta.

Tobacco industry.   See Tobacco manufacture and trade.

Tobacco inspection act of 1935.

Tobacco leaves.

Tobacco louse.   See Myzus persicae.

Tobacco manufacture and trade.   (DI-
RECT)
  sa Cigar manufacture and trade.
   Cigarette manufacture and
    trade.
   Tobacco exchanges.
   National industrial recovery
    act, 1933. Codes. Tobacco.
   Sugar utilization in the manu-
    facture of tobacco products.
   Subdivision Marketing under:
    Tobacco.
   Subdivision Tobacco industry
    under: Collective labor
    agreements.
  x Tobacco trade.
--Accounting.
--Bibliography.
--Directories.
  sa Subdivision Directories under
   Tobacco manufacture and
   trade [geographic subdivi-
   sion] e.g., Tobacco manu-
   facture and trade. India.
   Directories.
--Employees.   See Tobacco workers.
--Futures.
--History.
  sa Subdivision History under:
   Tobacco manufacture and
   trade. Maryland.
   Tobacco manufacture and
   trade. Virginia.
--Periodicals.
  sa Tobacco manufacture and trade
   [geographic subdivision]
   Periodicals, e.g., Tobacco
   manufacture and trade.
   Greece. Periodicals.
--Societies.
--Statistics.
--Tables and ready-reckoners.

Tobacco mosaic.   See Mosaic disease of
tobacco.

Tobacco moth.   See Ephestia elutella.

Tobacco pipes.
  xx Tobacco.

Tobacco root-rot.   See Root-rot of
tobacco.

Tobacco seedlings.
  xx Seedlings.

Tobacco smoke.
  x Cigar smoke.
  xx Smoke.

Tobacco smoking.   See Smoking.

Tobacco soils.
  --Bibliography.

Tobacco standards.   See Tobacco. Grading
and standardization.

Tobacco substitutes.
  x Tobacco. Substitutes.

Tobacco-thrips.   See Euthrips nicotianae.

Tobacco trade.   See Tobacco manufacture
and trade.

Tobacco types.

Tobacco wildfire.

Tobacco wilt.
  x Granville tobacco wilt.
   Bacterial wilt of tobacco.
  xx Tobacco. Diseases.

Tobacco workers.   (DIRECT)
  x Tobacco manufacture and trade.
   Employees.

Tobacco worm.   See Phlegethontius carolina.

Tobago.
--Agriculture.
    sa Subdivision Tobago under:
        Agricultural policies and
        programs.
        Agriculture. Economic as-
        pects.
--Botany.
    sa Subdivision Tobago under: Trees.
--Cattle.
--Census.
--Commerce.
-- --Statistics.
--Dairying.
--Economic conditions.
    sa Subdivision Tobago under:
        Economic surveys.
--Economic policy.
-- --Five-year plan (1956-1960)
--Entomology.
--Fisheries.
--Forestry.
    sa Subdivision Tobago under:
        Lumber.
        Timber.
        Forest products.
        War and forestry (1939-1945)
--Industries and resources.
--Maps.
--Physical geography.
    xx Physical geography.
--Roads.
--Statistics.
--Zoology.

Tobi Island, Japan.
--Botany.

Tobolsk (Government)
--Colonies.
    sa Colonization, Agricultural.
        Russia. Tobolsk (Government)

Tobosa grass.   See Hilaria mutica.

Tochigi.
--Soils.

Tochigi-ken, Japan.
--Agriculture.
-- --Education.
-- --Periodicals.

Tocopherol.   See Vitamins (E)

Tocuyo region, Lara, Venezuela.

Togo.
--Statistics.

Togoland.
--Census.
--Forestry.
    xx Africa. Forestry.
--Water-supply.
--Zoology.
    sa Subdivision Togoland under:
        Worms.
    xx Africa. Zoology.

Toilet preparations.
--Societies.

Tokay, Hungary.
--Viticulture.

Tokay grapes.   See Grapes, Tokay.

Tokay wine.

Tokelau Islands.
--Economic conditions.

Tokushima-ken, Japan.
--Forestry.
-- --Statistics.

Tokyo.
--Agriculture.
-- --Maps.
--Commerce.
-- --Directories.
    xx Japan. Commerce. Directories.
--Forestry.
-- --Statistics.
--Libraries.
--Markets.
    xx Markets.
--Paleontology.
--Statistics.

Toledo, Iowa. Indian Training School.

Toledo, Ohio.
--Commerce.
--Economic conditions.
-- --Periodicals.
    xx Ohio. Economic conditions.
        Periodicals.
--Markets.

Toledo, Ohio (Continued)
--Milk trade.
--Transportation.
    xx Ohio. Transportation.

Tolerance in trees. See Light. Effect
on trees.

Toll bridges. See Bridges, Toll.

Tolland, Colo. Mountain Laboratory. See
Colorado. University. Mountain Laboratory, Tolland.

Tolls.

Tollymore Forest Park, Northern Ireland.
    x Tollymore Park, Northern
      Ireland.

Tollymore Park, Northern Ireland. See
Tollymore Forest Park, Northern
Ireland.

Toluene.

Toluol. See Toluene.

Tom Green Co., Tex.
    sa Subdivision Tom Green Co. under:
      Flood control. Texas.
      County surveys. Texas.
--Water-supply.
    sa Subdivision Texas. Tom Green
      Co. under: Water, Under-
        ground.

Tom Newman Memorial Award.
    xx Newman, Tom.
    Poultry. Research. Rewards
      (Prizes, etc.)

Tomas Barrera (Ship)

Tomaspis.
    xx Hemiptera.
    Sugar-cane. Pests.

Tomaspis liturata.

Tomaspis postica.
--Diseases.
    xx Insect diseases.

Tomatin.
    xx Antibiotics.

Tomato and corn pack. See Canned goods.

Tomato blights. See Curly-top of tomato; Late blight of tomato; Leaf-spot
of tomato; Tomato wilt; Southern
blight of tomato.

Tomato canneries.
--Waste.

Tomato catsup. See Ketchup.

Tomato fruitworm. See Heliothis armi-
gera.

Tomato fruitworm (American) See
Heliothis zea.

Tomato hornworm. See Protoparce quin-
quemaculatus.

Tomato juice.
    xx Juices.
    Tomato products.

Tomato juice, Canned.
--Grading and standardization. See
    Tomato juice. Grading and stand-
    ardization.
--Statistics.

Tomato juice.
--Grading and standardization.
    x Tomato juice, Canned. Grading
      and standardization.
    xx Juices. Grading and standardi-
      zation.
    Tomatoes. Grading and stand-
      ardization.

Tomato ketchup. See Ketchup.

Tomato late blight. See Late blight of
tomato.

Tomato leaf mold. See Leaf-mold of
tomato.

Tomato leaf-spot. See Leaf-spot of
tomato.

Tomato paste.
    xx Tomato products.

Tomato paste, Canned.
--Grading and standardization.
    xx Tomatoes. Grading and stand-
        ardization.
--Statistics.

Tomato peelings as fertilizer.
    xx Tomatoes. By-products.

Tomato pinworm.   See Keiferia lycoper-
sicella.

Tomato pomace.
    xx Tomatoes. By-products.
       Pomace.

Tomato pomace as feeding stuff.
    xx Pomace as feeding stuff.

Tomato products.
    sa Tomato juice.
       Ketchup.
       Tomato paste.
       Tomato puree.
       Chili sauce.
       Tomato sauce.
    xx Tomatoes. By-products.
       Tomatoes. Utilization.
--Analysis.
--Grading and standardization.
    sa Subdivision Grading and stand-
        ardization under: Tomato
        pulp, Canned.
    x Tomatoes. Grading and stand-
        ardization.
--Spoilage.
    xx Tomatoes, Canned.
--Statistics.
    xx Tomatoes. Statistics.

Tomato psyllid.   See Paratrioza cockerelli.

Tomato pulp, Canned.
--Grading and standardization.
    xx Tomato products. Grading and
        standardization.
--Statistics.

Tomato puree.
    xx Tomato products.

Tomato puree, Canned.
--Statistics.

Tomato ripening.   See Tomatoes. Ripening.

Tomato rots.
    x Rot of tomato.
      Rots of tomato.
    xx Tomatoes. Diseases.

Tomato sauce.
    xx Tomato products.

Tomato sauce, Canned.
--Statistics.

Tomato sauce.
--Grading and standardization.

Tomato wilt.
    sa Spotted wilt of tomatoes.
    x Blight diseases of tomato.
      Tomato blights.
    xx Tomatoes. Diseases.

Tomato worm.   See Phlegethontius.

Tomato yellows.   See Curly-top of tomato.

Tomatoes.
    xx Vegetables. By-products.
--Analysis.
--Bibliography.
    sa Subdivision Bibliography un-
        der: Tomatoes. Canning//
--Breeding.
    xx Vegetables. Breeding.
--By-products.
    sa Tomato products.
       Tomatoes. Utilization.
       Tomato peelings as fertilizer.
       Tomato pomace.
    xx Waste products.

Tomatoes, Canned.
    sa Tomato products. Spoilage.
--Grading and standardization.
    xx Vegetables, Canned. Grading
        and standardization.
--Inspection.
    xx Canned goods. Adulteration and
        inspection.
--Prices.
    xx Vegetables, Canned. Prices.

Tomatoes, Canned (Continued)
--Statistics.
    sa Tomato products. Statistics.
    xx Tomatoes. Statistics.

Tomatoes.
--Canning.
-- --Bibliography.
    xx Tomatoes. Bibliography.
--Composition.
    sa Tomatoes. Starch content.
    xx Vegetables. Composition.
--Cost of production.
    xx Vegetables. Cost of production.
--Disease resistant varieties.
    xx Disease resistant plants.
--Diseases.
    sa Mosaic disease of tomato.
       Leaf-spot of tomato.
       Virus diseases of tomatoes.
       Curly-top of tomatoes.
       Leaf-mold of tomato.
       Damping-off diseases. Tomatoes.
       Buckeye rot of tomato.
       Tomato wilt.
       Spotted wilt of tomatoes.
       Late blight of tomato.
       Tomato rots.
       Bacterial canker of tomato.
       Witches' broom disease of
         tomato.
       Collar-rot of tomato.
       Big bud of tomatoes.
       Bacterial diseases of tomatoes.
--Estimating of crop.
--Fertilization.
--Fertilizers. See Fertilizers for
    tomatoes.
--Freezing and frost injury.
--Fumigation.
    xx Fumigation.
--Genetics.
--Germination.
--Grading and standardization.
    sa Subdivision Grading and stand-
       ardization under: Tomato
       juice.
       Tomato paste, Canned.
       Tomato products.
    xx Agricultural products. Grading
       and standardization.
       Vegetables. Grading and stand-
       ardization.
--Growth.

Tomatoes (Continued)
--Hardiness.
    xx Vegetables. Hardiness.
--Harvesting.
-- --Cost.
    xx Vegetables. Harvesting. Cost.
--Hybrids.
-- --Bibliography.
--Implements and machinery.
--Injuries.
    xx Vegetables. Injuries.
--Inspection.
    xx Vegetables. Inspection.
--Marketing.
-- --Bibliography.
    xx Vegetables. Marketing. Bib-
       liography.
--Marketing agreements.
    xx Vegetables. Marketing agree-
       ments.
--Morphology and physiology. See
    Tomatoes. Physiology and morphology.
--Nutritive value. See Tomatoes as
    food.

Tomatoes, Packaged. See Tomatoes.
    Packaging.

Tomatoes.
--Packaging.
    x Tomatoes, Prepackaging.
      Tomatoes, Packaged.
--Packing.
    xx Vegetables. Packing.
--Periodicals.
--Pests.
    sa Gnorimoschema.
      Paratrioza cockerelli.
      Keiferia lycopersicella.
      Heliothis zea.
      Heliothis armigera.
--Physiology and morphology.
    x Tomatoes. Morphology and
      physiology.
--Prepackaging. See Tomatoes. Pack-
    aging.
--Preservation.
    xx Vegetables. Preservation.
--Prices.
    xx Vegetables. Prices.
--Propagation.
    xx Plant propagation.
--Pruning.
    xx Pruning.

Tomatoes (Continued)
--Ripening.
  x Tomato ripening.
--Seed.
-- --Disinfection.
  xx Vegetables. Seed. Disinfection.
- --Sowing.
  xx Sowing.
--Seedlings.
  xx Seedlings.
-- --Transportation.
--Societies.
--Spraying. See Spraying. Tomatoes.
--Starch content.
  xx Tomatoes. Composition.
   Starch.
--Statistics.
  sa Subdivision Statistics under:
   Tomato products.
   Tomatoes, Canned.
  xx Vegetables. Statistics.
--Storage.
  xx Vegetables. Storage.
--Tariff.
--Transportation.
  xx Vegetables. Transportation.
-- --Costs.
  xx Vegetables. Transportation.
   Costs.
--Utilization.
  sa Tomato products.
   Tomatoes. By-products.
   Tomatoes as food.
  xx Tomatoes. By-products.
--Varieties.
--Year-books.

Tomatoes as food.
  sa Vitamins in tomatoes.
  x Tomatoes. Nutritive value.
  xx Vegetables as food.
   Tomatoes. Utilization.

Tombigbee River.
  xx Alabama.
   Mississippi.

Tombigbee River Valley.

Tombigbee-Tennessee Waterway. See
 Tennessee-Tombigbee Waterway.

Tombillo, Chile.
--Entomology.

Tomicidae.

Tomicini.

Tomicus.

Tomicus ribbentropi.
  xx Pinus excelsa. Pests.

Tomicus typographus.

Tomocerodes americana.

Tomopteridae.

Tomosis.

Tompkins Co., N.Y.
  sa Subdivision Tompkins Co., N.Y.
   under: Planning, County.
   Subdivision New York. Tompkins
    Co. under: County surveys.
  xx New York (State)
--Agriculture.
  sa Subdivision New York (State)
   Tompkins Co. under: Agri-
   cultural conservation
   program.
--Directories.
  xx New York (State) Directories.
--Politics and government.
  sa Local government. Tompkins Co.,
   N.Y.
--Roads.
--Sanitary affairs.
--Social conditions.
  sa Planning, County. Tompkins Co.,
   N.Y.
--Soils.

Tompkinsville, Nova Scotia.
  xx Nova Scotia.

Tomsk.
  sa Taiga.
--Agriculture.
--Botany.
--Entomology.
  xx Siberia. Entomology.
--Forestry.

Tonduzia.
  xx Apocynaceae.

Tone River.
       sa Subdivision Tone River under:
          Flood control.

Toned milk. See Milk, Toned.

Tonga Islands.
--Agriculture.
--Census.
--Geographic names.
--Statistics.

Tonga language.
      x Tongan language.
--Dictionaries.

Tonga Tribe. See Thonga Tribe.

Tongan language. See Tonga language.

Tongariro National Park, N.Z.

Tongass National Forest, Alaska.

Tongking. See Tonkin.

Tongue.
--Diseases.
      xx Veterinary medicine.

Tongue River Valley, Wyo.
--Economic conditions.

Tonka bean.
      sa Coumarin.
--Grading and standardization.

Tonka bean tree. See Dipteryx odorata.

Tonkin.
--Agriculture.
      sa Agriculture. Economic aspects.
          Indo-China, French, Tonkin.
--Botany.
--Forestry.
--Ichthyology.
--Population.
      xx Indo-China, French. Population.
--Zoology.

Tonquin. See Tonkin.

Tonsils.
--Diseases.
      xx Veterinary medicine.

Tonto National Forest, Ariz.

Tooele Co., Utah.
--Statistics.
--Water-supply.

Tooele Valley, Utah.

Toola, Russia. See Tula, Russia.

Toole Co., Mont.
      xx Montana.

Tools.
      sa Agriculture. Implements and
          machinery.
          Machine-tools.
          Machinery.
          Machinists' tools.
          Carpentry. Tools.
          Shovels.
          Implements, utensils, etc.
      xx Implements, utensils, etc.
--Care and repair. See Tools. Mainte-
    nance and repair.
--Maintenance and repair.
      x Tools. Repairing.
          Tools. Care and repair.
--Repairing. See Tools. Maintenance and
    repair.
--Statistics.

Toombs Co., Ga.
--Soils.
      sa Subdivision Georgia. Toombs
          Co. under: Soil-surveys.

Toon wood. See Cedrela toona.

Toonu. See Tunu.

Top-knot (Poultry) See Crest (Poultry)

Top-lopping. See Lopping (Lumbering)

Top-minnow.

Topeka, Kan.
--Milk supply.
      xx Kansas. Milk supply.
--Milk trade.

Topiary work.

Topographic drawing.   See Topographical
    drawing.

Topographical drawing.
        x Topographic drawing.

Topographical surveying.
        xx Surveying.
    --Periodicals.

Toponar, Hungary.
    --Agriculture.
        xx Hungary. Agriculture.

Tori horse.
        xx Horses.

Torino.   See Turin.

Tornadoes.
        sa Insurance, Tornado.

Toronto.
    --Libraries.
    --Markets.
        xx Markets.
    --Natural history.

Toronto. University. Dept. of Botany.
    --Botanical Laboratories.

Torpedinidae.

Torquatellidae.

Torrance Co., N.M.
        xx New Mexico.

Torrens system.
        xx Land titles. Registration and
            transfer.
    --Bibliography.

Torrents.   See Floods.

Torres Strait.
    --Entomology.

Torrey pine.   See Pinus torreyana.

Torrington, Conn.
    --Milk trade.

Torrubia.   See Cordyceps.

Tortoise-beetles.   See Cassidinae.

Tortoise burrow insects.

Tortoises.   See Turtles.

Tortola Island, W.I.
    --Agricultural Experiment Station.

Tortricidae.
        sa Enarmonia.
            Cochylis.
            Polychrosis.
            Teras.
            Tortrix.
            Codling moth.
            Sparganothis.
            Archips.
            Olethreutes.
            Ancylis.
            Laspeyresia.
            Eucosma.
            Eulia.
            Homona.
            Spilonota.
            Rhyacionia.
            Sparagnothis.
            Argyrotaenia.
            Grapholitha.
        xx Leaf-rollers.

Tortrix.

Tortrix ambiguella.   See Cochylis am-
    biguella.

Tortrix citrana.
        x Orange tortrix.
            Orange worm.

Tortrix fumiferana.   See Choristoneura
    fumiferana.

Tortrix murinana.

Tortrix paleana.

Tortrix pinicolana.

Tortrix pomonella.   See Codling moth.

Tortrix viridana.

Torts.

Tortugas, Fla.   See Dry Tortugas.

Tortula.   See Barbula.

Torula.

Torula utilis, Dried.   See Food yeast.

Torymidae.
     sa Ditropinotus.

Töss, Switzerland.
  --Statistics.

Total state.   See Totalitarianism.

Totalitarian state.   See Totalitarianism.

Totalitarianism.
        Under this heading are entered
        works discussing (in theory and
        in its various manifestations)
        a highly centralized govern-
        ment under the control of a
        political group permitting no
        rival loyalties or parties.
     sa Communism.
        Dictators.
        Fascism.
        National socialism.
      x Totalitarian state.
        Total state.

Totara.   See Podocarpus totara; Podocarpus hallii.

Totems.

Tottenville, N.Y.
  --Bridges.

Tottori-ken, Japan.
  --Forestry.
  -- --Research.

Touaregs.   See Tuaregs.

Toucans.   See Ramphastidae.

Touch.

Touchet Valley, Wash. (State)

Toulon.
  --Botany.

Toulouse.
  --Agriculture.
        xx France. Agriculture.

Toulouse. Jardin des plantes.

Toumeyella numismaticum.

Touraine, France.
  --Paleontology.

Tourist camps.
        x Tourists' camps.
        xx Camping.
           Hotels, taverns, etc.
  --Bibliography.

Tourist trade.

Tourists' camps.   See Tourist camps.

Tourmalin.

Tournaments.

Tours.

Tous-les-mois.
     .   sa Food plants.

Tovariaceae.

Towels.

Towers, Packed.   See Packed towers.

Towhee.   See Pipilo.

Towing.
        xx Tugboats.

Town and country planning act, 1943.

Town and country planning act, 1944.

Town and country planning act, 1947.

Town and country planning act, 1953.

Town and country planning bill, 1947.

Town forests.   See Community forests.

Town government.   See Municipal govern-
        ment.

Town-meeting. See Local government.

Town planning. See Cities and towns.
  Planning.

Towns. See Cities and towns.

Towns Co., Ga.
  --Soils.
      sa Subdivision Georgia. Towns Co.
         under: Soil-surveys.

Townsend old-age pension plan.
  --Bibliography.
      xx Old age pensions.

Townsendia exscapa.

Toxaphene.
      x Chlorinated camphene.
  --Bibliography.
  --Effect on milk composition.
      xx Milk. Composition.
         Insecticides. Effect on milk
            composition.
  --Effect on parasites.

Toxascaris leonina.

Toxemia.
      xx Toxicology.

Toxic chemicals. See Chemicals. Toxicity.

Toxic effect of herbicides. See Herbicides. Toxicity.

Toxic effect of insecticides. See Insecticides. Toxicity.

Toxic plants. See Poisonous plants.

Toxic salts. See Salts, Toxic.

Toxic substances.
      xx Salts, Toxic.

Toxic substances (in botany) See Poison.
  Effect on plants.

Toxicity. See Toxicology.

Toxicology.
    sa Aconitum.
       Antidotes.
       Arsenin.
       Chloroform.
       Coal-tar colors.
       Curari.
       Derris elliptica.
       Food as a cause of disease.
       Food poisoning.
       Fish poisons.
       Lead-poison.
       Lupinus.
       Oxalic acid.
       Paullinia pinnata.
       Poison. Effect on plants.
       Poisonous plants.
       Tanghin.
       Serpents.
       Toxics and antitoxins.
       Vegetable technology.
       Venom.
       Alkaline metals, Physiological
          effect of.
       Ricinin.
       Feeding stuffs as a cause of
          disease.
       Trinitrotoluene as a cause of
          disease.
       Poisonous animals.
       Animal poisons.
       Toxemia.
       Arsenic poisoning.
       Poisonous plants (to fish)
       Dihydrodeguelins.
       Poisonous plants (to bees)
       Cresol.
       Poisoning of domestic animals.
       Poisoning of fish.
       Poisoning of dogs.
       Sugar substitutes.
       Bee venom.
       Subdivision Toxicity under:
          Copper.
          Cotton-seed.
          Cotton-seed meal//
      x Physiological effect of toxins.
     xx Materia medica.
  --Bibliography.
  --Dictionaries.
  --Directories.
  --Legislation.
      sa Subdivision Legislation under:
         Caustic poison.

Toxins and antitoxins.
    sa Anaphylaxis.
    Antigens and antibodies.
    Immunity.
    Ptomaines.
    Serumtherapy.
    Names of special antitoxins,
      e.g., Diphtheria antitoxin;
      Spider venom; Staphylo-
      toxin//
    x Antitoxins.
    xx Serumtherapy.

Toxocara.
    xx Ascaridae.

Toxocara canis.

Toxochelys.

Toxodontia.

Toxoplasmosis.

Toxoptera.

Toxoptera coffeae.
    xx Coffee. Pests.

Toxoptera graminum.
    --Biological control.
      xx Biological control of insects.
    --Parasites.

Toxostoma rufum.

Toxotrypana curvicauda.

Toxylon pomiferum. See Osage orange.

Toy Manchester terriers. See Manchester
    terriers.

Toyama-ken, Japan.
    --Agriculture.
    --Soils.
      sa Subdivision Japan. Toyama-ken
        under: Soil-surveys.

Toys.

Trace elements.
    sa Subdivision Mineral consti-
      tuents under: Feeding stuffs.
      Food.

Trace elements (Continued)
    sa Subdivision Mineral elements
      under: Animals.
      Plants.
      Soil.
    x Minor elements.
    Micro-elements.
    Rarer elements.
    Trace metals.
    Trace minerals.
    Minor minerals.
    Micro-nutrients.
    Micronutrient elements.
    xx Mineral fertilizer.
    Auxiliary elements.
    Chemical elements.
    --Bibliography.
    --Congresses.

Trace metals. See Trace elements.

Trace minerals. See Trace elements.

Tracers (Biology)
    sa Hydrogen. Isotopes.
    xx Radioactive tracers.
    Radioactivity.
    Radiotherapy.

Tracers (Chemistry)

Tracers, Radioactive. See Radioactive
    tracers.

Trachea.
    sa Injections, Intratracheal.
    --Diseases.
      xx Veterinary medicine.
    --Insects.
      xx Entomology. Anatomy.

Tracheid.
    sa Cells.

Trachelomonas.

Trachelus tabidus. See Cephus tabidus.

Tracheophonae.
    sa Sittasomus.

Tracheophytum.

Trachoma. See Conjunctivitis, Granular.

Trachyderini.

Trachykele blondeli.
  x Western cedar pole borer.
    Powder worm.

Trachyphloeus.

Tracing paper.

Tracking and trailing.
  xx Animals, Habits and behavior of.
    Hunting.

Tracks, Rubber. See Tires, Rubber.

Traction-engines.
  sa Machine-tractor stations
      (Russian)
    Cultivators, Motor.
  x Tractors.
    Caterpillar tractors.
  --Bibliography.
    xx Agriculture. Implements and
      machinery. Bibliography.
  --Care and repair. See Traction-engines.
    Maintenance and repair.
  --Congresses.
  --Cost of operation.
    sa Subdivision Cost of operation
      under: Traction-engines in
        lumbering.
      Traction-engines in agri-
        culture.
    xx Cost of operation.
  --Design.
    xx Machinery. Design.
  --Directories.
    xx Agriculture. Implements and
      machinery. Directories.
  --Electric equipment.
    xx Electric apparatus and
      appliances.
  --History.
    xx Agriculture. Implements and
      machinery. History.
  --Maintenance and repair.
    x Traction-engines. Care and
      repair.
      Traction-engines. Repairing.
    xx Agriculture. Implements and
      machinery. Maintenance and
      repair.
  -- --Work management.
    xx Work management.

Traction-engines (Continued)
  --Parts.
  --Periodicals.
    x Traction-engines in agri-
      culture. Periodicals.
  --Prices.
  --Repairing. See Traction-engines.
    Maintenance and repair.
  --Research.
  -- --Bibliography.
  --Statistics.
    xx Agriculture. Implements and
      machinery. Statistics.
  --Study and teaching.
  --Tariff.
  --Terminology.
  --Testing. See Traction tests.

Traction-engines in agriculture.
  sa Spraying apparatus, Tractor.
  x Traction farming.
    Tractor farming.
  xx Mechanized farming.
  --Cost of operation.
    x Tractor costs on farms.
    xx Traction-engines. Cost of
      operation.
  -- --Research.
  --History.
  --Lubrication.
    xx Automobiles. Lubrication.
  -- --Statistics.
  --Periodicals. See Traction-engines.
    Periodicals.
  --Statistics.

Traction-engines in forestry.
  xx Forestry. Implements and
    machinery.

Traction-engines in lumbering.
  xx Mechanized lumbering.
    Lumbering.
    Logging machinery.
  --Cost of operation.
    xx Traction-engines. Cost of
      operation.

Traction-engines in orchard cultivation.
  xx Pomology.

Traction farming. See Traction-engines
  in agriculture.

Traction tests.
    x Tractor trials.
    Tractor tests.
    Traction-engines. Testing.
    xx Agriculture. Implements and
      machinery. Testing.

Tractive resistance.

Tractor costs on farms. See Traction-
engines in agriculture. Cost of operation.

Tractor cultivators. See Cultivators,
Motor.

Tractor farming. See Traction-engines
in agriculture.

Tractor plow. See Plow, Motor.

Tractor tests. See Traction tests.

Tractor trials. See Traction tests.

Tractors. See Traction-engines.

Trade. See Commerce.

Trade acceptance.
    x Acceptances.
    xx Credit.

Trade agreements. See Commercial treaties; Marketing agreements.

Trade agreements act.

Trade agreements extension act.

Trade and professional associations.
    (INDIRECT)
    x Labor and laboring classes.
      Societies.
--Bibliography.
    sa Subdivision Bibliography under
      Trade and professional as-
      sociations [geographic sub-
      division] e.g., Trade and
      professional associations.
      U.S. Bibliography.

Trade and professional associations (Con.)
--Directories.
    sa Subdivision Directories under
      Trade and professional as-
      sociations [geographic sub-
      division] e.g., Trade and
      professional associations.
      California. Directories.
--Statistics.
    sa Subdivision Statistics under
      Trade and professional as-
      sociations [geographic sub-
      division] e.g., Trade and
      professional associations.
      Portugal. Statistics.

Trade areas. See Market areas.

Trade associations. See Trade and professional associations.

Trade barriers.
    xx Commercial policy.
      Tariff.

Trade barriers, State.
    x Interstate trade barriers.
    xx Interstate commerce.
      U.S. Commercial policy.
--Bibliography.
    xx Interstate commerce. Bibliog-
      raphy.
      U.S. Commercial policy. Bib-
      liography.

Trade cycles. See Business cycles.

Trade fairs. See Agriculture. Fairs and
expositions; Commercial products.
Fairs and expositions.

Trade labels. See Labels.

Trade-marks.
    sa Subdivision Trade-marks under:
      Textile industry and
        fabrics.
      Poultry industry and trade.
      Bakers and bakeries.
      Paper making and trade.
      Water-marks.
      Trade names.
--Directories.
--Law.
--Periodicals.

Trade names.
　x Brand names.
　xx Business names.
　　Trade-marks.
--Bibliography.
--Indexes.

Trade names (Firm names)　See Business
　names.

Trade privileges.　See Privileges (Grain
　futures)

Trade relations (Retail trade)
　xx Retail trade.

Trade routes.

Trade stamps.　See Trading stamps.

Trade terms.　See Commerce. Terminology.

Trade union agreements.　See Labor con-
　tract.

Trade-unions.　(DIRECT)
　sa Arbitration, Industrial.
　　Farmers' unions.
　　Foresters' unions.
　　Labor and wages, Societies.
　　Trade and professional as-
　　　sociations.
　　Congress of industrial organi-
　　　zations.
　x Labor and laboring classes.
　　　Societies.
　　Unionism.
　xx Collective bargaining.
--Bibliography.
　xx Labor and laboring classes.
　　　Bibliography.
--Congresses.
--Directories.
　sa Trade unions ₍geographic sub-
　　　division₎ Directories, e.g.,
　　　Trade unions. U.S. Direc-
　　　tories.
--History.
　sa Subdivision History under Trade-
　　　unions ₍geographic subdivi-
　　　sion₎ e.g., Trade-unions.
　　　U.S. History.
--Periodicals.

Trade waste.　See Factory and trade waste.

Tradescantia.

Tradescantia Virginica.

Tradewater River area, Ky.
--Land.
　sa Subdivision Kentucky. Trade-
　　　water River area ·under:
　　　Land grants.

Trading areas.　See Market areas.

Trading stamps.
　x Trade stamps.
　　Stamp plan. ·

Trading with the enemy act.
　xx Commercial law.

Traditions.　See Folk-lore.

Traffic.　See Communication and traffic.

Traffic accidents.　See Automobiles.
　Accidents.

Traffic census.　See Traffic surveys.

Traffic control.　See Traffic regula-
　tions.

Traffic regulations. .　(DIRECT)
　x Traffic control.
--Bibliography.
--Congresses.
　sa Subdivision Congresses under:
　　　Traffic congestion.
--Study and teaching.
　sa New England Traffic Officers'
　　　Training School. ·

Traffic signals.　See Road marking.

Traffic surveys.　(INDIRECT)
　x Traffic census.
　xx Transportation. Statistics.
　　Surveys.

Tragacanth.　See Gum tragacanth.

Tragidion fulvipenne.

Tragopogon porrifolius.　See Salsify.

Tragulidae.　See Mouse-deer.

Trailers.　See Automobiles. Trailers.

Traill Co., N.D.
　　sa Subdivision North Dakota.
　　　　Traill Co. under: County
　　　　　surveys.
　　xx North Dakota.
--Agriculture.
　　sa Subdivision North Dakota.
　　　　Traill Co. under: Farm
　　　　　management surveys.

Trails.　　(DIRECT)
　　sa Nature trails.
　　　　Names of trails, e.g., Appa-
　　　　　lachian Trail.
--Implements and machinery.
　　xx Roads. Implements and machinery.

Training, Mechanical.　See Technical
　education.
Training aids.　See Teaching. Aids and
　devices.

Training films.　See Moving-pictures in
　personnel training.

Training of animals.　See Animals, Train-
　ing of.

Training of personnel.　See Personnel
　training.

Training within industry.　See Personnel
　training.

Trait, France.

Trakehnen horse.

Traktor Collective Farm.

Trametes pini.　See Fomes pini.

Trametes radiciperda.

Trametes serialis.

Trametes setotus.

Trametes suaveolens.

Trametes subrosea.

Tramps.

Tranquilizers.　See Tranquilizing drugs.

Tranquilizing drugs.
　　sa Sedatives.
　　x Tranquilizers.
　　xx Sedatives.
　　　　Anesthetics.
　　　　Narcotics.

Trans-Jordan.
　　x Transjordan.
　　　　Jordan.
　　　　Hashemite Kingdom of Jordan.
--Agriculture.
　　sa Subdivision Trans-Jordan under:
　　　　Colonization, Agricultural.
　　　　Irrigation.
　　　　Agriculture, Cooperative.
--Botany.
-- --Bibliography.
--Climate.
--Commerce.
--Economic conditions.
--Economic policy.
--Geographic names.
　　xx Geographic names.
--Geology.
--Land.
　　sa Subdivision Trans-Jordan under:
　　　　Land laws.
　　　　Land tenure.
--Soils.
--Statistics.
--Water-supply.

Transaminase.
　　xx Enzymes.

Transbaikalia, Siberia.
--Botany.
--Soils.
--Zoology.

Transbay Bridge, San Francisco.　See San
　Francisco Bay Bridge.

Transcarpathian Region.
--Agriculture.
-- --Addresses, essays, lectures.
--Geography.
--Viticulture.

Transcaspian district. See Transcaspian
Province.

Transcaspian Province.
--Agriculture.
    xx Asia. Agriculture.
--Botany.
--Maps.

Transcaucasia.
    sa Georgia (Transcaucasia)
--Agriculture.
    sa Subdivision Transcaucasia under:
      Cotton.
      Crops and climate.
      Subdivision Agriculture under:
      Colonization, Agricultural.
-- --Statistics.
--Botany.
    sa Subdivision Transcaucasia under:
      Weeds.
--Climate.
    sa Subdivision Transcaucasia under:
      Crops and climate.
--Commerce.
-- --Periodicals.
--Economic conditions.
-- --Periodicals.
--Entomology.
    sa Subdivision Transcaucasia under:
      Coleoptera.
--Physical geography.
--Soils.
    sa Subdivision Soils under:
      Georgia (Transcaucasia)
--Viticulture.
--Zoology.

Transcription (Transliteration) See
Transliteration.

Transducers.
    sa Geiger-Müller counters.
    xx Electric apparatus and appli-
      ances.
    Electronic apparatus and appli-
      ances.

Transfer, Heat. See Heat. Transmission.

Transfer of ova. See Ovum. Transplantation.

Transfer of population. See Population
transfers.

Transference of labor. See Labor supply.

Transformation, Laplace. See Laplace
transformation.

Transformations (Mathematics)
    sa Laplace transformation.

Transformers, Electric. See Electric
transformers.

Transhumance. See Migration of domestic
animals.

Transient camps.
    sa Labor camps.

Transient workers. See Migrant labor.

Transients (Electricity)
    x Electric surge.
    Electric transient phenomena.
    Surge (Electricity)
    xx Electric currents.
    Electric waves.
    Lightning.
    Oscillators, Electric.

Transistors.
    x Semiconductor devices.
    xx Electronics.

Transit-instruments.
    xx Instruments.

Transit of Venus (Ship)

Transjordan. See Trans-Jordan.

Transkeian Territories.
    x United Transkeian Territories.
--Agriculture.

Translating.
    sa Machine translating.

Translating services. See Translations.
Directories.

Translations.
>Here are entered works about trans-
lations, e.g., works on the
comparative values of different
translations, etc. For works on
the techniques and methods of
preparing translations, see
Translating.
--Bibliography.
-- --Periodicals.
--Directories.
>x Translating services.

Transliteration.
>sa Subdivision Transliteration
under names of languages,
e.g., Slavic languages.
Transliteration.
>x Transcription (Transliteration)

Translocation in plants.   See Plant
translocation.

Transmission belts.   See Belts and
belting.

Transmission lines.   See Electric lines.

Transmission of plant diseases.   See
Plant disease transmission.

Transmutation (Chemistry)

Transpiration of plants.   See Plant
transpiration.

Transpirometer.

Transplantation (Biology)

Transplantation (Botany)   See
Grafting.

Transplantation (Physiology)
>sa Subdivision Transplantation
under:
Ovum.
Pituitary body.

Transplanting.
>sa Subdivision Transplanting un-
der: Trees.
Shrubs.
Cotton.
Sweet potatoes.
Evergreens.
Vegetables.
Guayule.
>xx Planting.

Transplanting machines.

Transport workers.   (DIRECT)
>xx Labor and laboring classes.

Transportation.
>sa Subdivision Transportation un-
der: Cattle.
Europe.
Agriculture. Implements and
machinery//
Railroads.
Subways.
Grain transportation.
Bills of lading.
Electric railroads.
Pack transportation.
Fruit transportation.
Motor trucks.
Motor trucks in freight
service.
Railroads. Motor vehicle com-
petition.
Inland waterways.
Rapid transit.
War and transportation.
Freight and freightage.
>x Transportation surveys.

Transportation, Air.   See Aeronautics,
Commercial.

Transportation, Automotive.
>sa Motor trucks in freight
service.
Railroads. Motor vehicle com-
petition.
Automobiles.
Motor buses.
Motor-trucks.
>x Highway transportation.
Transportation, Highway.
--Laws and regulations.

Transportation.
--Bibliography.
    sa Subdivision Transportation.
        Bibliography under: Food.
        Farm produce.
        France.
        Germany.
        America.
        Transportation, Automotive.
--Catalogs and collections.
--Congresses.
    sa Subdivision Congresses under:
        Transportation, Automotive.
        Railroads.

Transportation, Cooperative.
    sa Subdivision Transportation, Co-
        operative under: Farm
        produce.
    x Cooperative transportation.
    xx Cooperation.

Transportation.
--Costs.
    sa Subdivision Transportation.
        Costs under: Farm produce.
--Dictionaries.
    sa Subdivision Dictionaries under:
        Commerce.
--Directories.
    sa Subdivision Directories under.
        Transportation, Automotive.
--Economic aspects.
--Government aid.
    sa Subdivision Government aid
        under: Railroads.

Transportation, Highway. See Transporta-
    tion, Automotive.

Transportation.
--History.
    sa Subdivision History under:
        Roads.
        Communication and traffic.
        Transportation, Water.
        Subdivision Transportation.
        History under: U.S.
        Canada.
--Law.
    sa Subdivision Law under:
        Plants. Transportation.
        Transportation, Automotive.
        U.S. Transportation.
        Transportation act.

Transportation (Continued)
--Maps.
    sa Subdivision Maps under:
        Railroads.

Transportation, Military. See Military
    transportation.

Transportation, Motor. See Transporta-
    tion, Automotive.

Transportation, Ocean.
--Freight rates. See Shipping. Rates.
--Legislation.

Transportation, Passenger.
    sa Railroads. Passenger traffic.
    x Passenger transportation.

Transportation.
--Periodicals.
    sa Subdivision Periodicals under:
        Transportation, Water.
        Subdivision Transportation.
        Periodicals under: Farm
        produce.

Transportation, Railroad. See Railroads.

Transportation.
--Rates.
    sa Subdivision Rates under:
        Railroads.
        Shipping.
        Motor-trucks in freight
        service.
        Subdivision Rates and tolls
        under: Canals.
--Research.
    x Transportation research.
--Societies.
    sa Shipment of goods. Societies.
--Statistics.
    sa Subdivision Statistics under:
        Fruit transportation.
        Vegetables. Transportation.
        Grain transportation.
        Traffic surveys.
--Taxation.
    x Transportation tax.
--Time-tables.
    x Time-tables.

Transportation, War. See War and trans-
    portation.

Transportation, Water.
    sa Canals.
        Ferries.
        Harbors.
        Inland navigation.
        Merchant marine.
        Shipping.
        Shipping bounties and subsi-
          dies.
        Steam-navigation.
        Steamboat lines.
        Waterways.
        Transportation, Ocean.
    x Water transportation.
--History.
    sa Subdivision History under:
        Inland navigation.
    xx Transportation. History.
--Laws.
    sa Inland navigation. Legislation.
--Periodicals.
    xx Transportation. Periodicals.
--Rates. See Shipping. Rates.
--Statistics.

Transportation act, 1920.
    xx Transportation. Law.

Transportation act, 1939.

Transportation act, 1940.

Transportation and war. See War and
    transportation.

Transportation diseases. See Storage
    and transportation diseases and in-
    juries.

Transportation injuries. See Storage and
    transportation diseases and injuries.

Transportation of animals.
    sa Domestic animals. Transporta-
        tion.
        Storage and transportation
          diseases and injuries.
    x Animals. Transportation.

Transportation of farm produce. See
    Farm produce. Transportation.

Transportation of grain. See Grain trans-
    portation.

Transportation of logs. See Log trans-
    portation.

Transportation of pupils. See School
    children. Transportation.

Transportation research. See Transporta-
    tion. Research.

Transportation surveys. See Transporta-
    tion.

Transportation tax. See Transportation.
    Taxation.

Transudation. See Exudation and tran-
    sudation.

Transvaal.
    sa Great Marico River. Transvaal.
        Veld.
        Kruger National Park, Transvaal
    xx Africa.
        Africa. South.
--Agriculture.
    sa Subdivision Transvaal under:
        Colonization, Agricultural.
    xx Africa, South. Agriculture.
        Africa. Agriculture.
-- --Education.
--Botany.
    xx Africa. Botany.
--Census.
--Commerce.
--Dairying.
--Description and travel.
    sa Subdivision Transvaal under:
        Hunting.
    xx Africa, South. Description and
        travel.
--Entomology.
    xx Africa. Entomology.
        Africa, South. Entomology.
--Forestry.
--Geology.
--Land.
    sa Subdivision Transvaal under:
        Land utilization.
    xx Africa, South. Land.
--Law.
--Natural history.
--Pomology.
--Roads.
-- --Law.
    xx Roads. Legislation.

Transvaal (Continued)
--Statistics.
--Water-supply.
    sa Witwatersrand, Transvaal.
        Water-supply.
--Zoology.
    xx Africa. Zoology.
        Africa, South. Zoology.

Transvaal daisy. See Gerbera jamesonii.

Transylvania.
    x Siebenbürgen.
--Agriculture.
--Botany.
--Cattle.
--Domestic animals.
    sa Transylvania. Sheep.
--Economic conditions.
--Entomology.
    sa Subdivision Hungary. Transyl-
      vania under: Coleoptera.
      Subdivision Transylvania under:
      Entomology, Economic.
--Geology.
--Land.
    sa Subdivision Transylvania under:
      Land reform.
    xx Hungary. Land.
--Politics and government.
--Sheep.
    xx Transylvania. Domestic animals.

Transylvania Co., N.C.
--Soils.
    sa Subdivision North Carolina.
      Transylvania Co. under:
      Soil-surveys.

Trap.

Trap-door spiders.
    xx Arachnida.

Trap lanterns. See Insect traps.

Trap nests. See Poultry. Nests.

Trap-shooting.
    x Skeet.
    xx Shooting.

Trapa natans.

Trapaceae.

Trapani, Sicily (Province)
--Agriculture.
-- --Congresses.

Trapezium (anatomy)
    xx Anatomy.

Trapogon orientalis.

Trapping.
    sa Hunting.
      Insect traps.
      Beaver traps.
      Rabbit traps.
      Fox traps.
      Squirrel traps.
--Law. See Game-laws.
--Periodicals.

Trashy fallow. See Stubble mulches.

Trass cement.
    xx Portland cement.
      Cement.

Traumatic gastro-peritonitis.

Traumatic wood.

Traumatism in plants. See Wounds in
    plants.

Traumatisms.

Traum's disease in swine. See
    Brucellosis in swine.

Travancore.
--Botany.
    sa Subdivision India. Travancore
      under: Trees.
--Entomology.
    sa Subdivision India. Travancore
      under: Entomology, Economic.
--Famines.
--Forestry.
    sa Subdivision India. Travancore
      under: Trees.
--Statistics, Vital.

Travel etiquette.
    xx Etiquette.

Traveling libraries. See Libraries,
    Traveling.

Travels. See Voyages and travels.

Traverse Co., Minn.
    xx Minnesota.

Travertine.

Travis Co., Tex.
    sa Subdivision Texas. Travis Co.
        under: County surveys.
--Education.
    sa Subdivision Texas. Travis Co.
        under: Rural schools.
--Milk supply.
    sa Subdivision Milk supply under:
        Austin, Texas.
--Social conditions.
    sa Subdivision Texas. Travis Co.
        under: Social surveys.
--Water-supply.

Travopol'naia sistema zemledeliia.
    x Trawopolnaja System der
        Landwirtschaft.
    xx Rotation of crops.
        U.S.S.R. Agriculture.
        Stalin plan to change nature.

Trawls and trawling.
    xx Fishing.

Trawopolnaja System der Landwirtschaft.
    See Travopol'naia sistema zemledeliia.

Tray agriculture. See Hydroponics.

Tre Venezie. See Veneto.

Treaders.
    xx Agriculture. Implements and
        machinery.

Treated wood. See Wood preservation.

Treaties.
    sa Commercial treaties.
        Congresses and conventions.
        Arbitration, International.
        Brest-Litovsk, Treaty of,
           March 3, 1918.
        Versailles, Treaty of.
        Indians. North American. Trea-
           ties.

Treaties (Continued)
    sa Subdivision Foreign relations.
        Treaties under the names of
        countries, e.g., Spanish
        America. Foreign relations.
        Treaties.
--Bibliography.
--Collections.

Trebizond, Turkey (Vilayet)
--Botany.

Trechinae.

Trechus fulvus.

Tree breeding. See Trees. Breeding.

Tree classes. See Trees. Classifica-
    tion.

Tree-creepers. See Certhia.

Tree crickets. See Oecanthinae.

Tree crown. See Trees. Crowns.

Tree cutting. See Timber. Felling.

Tree farms.
    Woodlands managed under industrial
        sponsorship (or the Tree Farm
        movement) to supply specific
        industries in a timber·shed.
    x Trees as crops.
    xx Forest management.
--Juvenile literature.
--Periodicals.
--Societies.
--Study and teaching.

Tree felling. See Timber. Felling.

Tree ferns. See Cyatheaceae.

Tree-frog. See Hylidae.

Tree growth. See Trees. Growth.

Tree-hoppers. See Membracidae.

Tree identification. See Trees.
    Identification.

Tree impregnation. See Tree injections.

Tree injections.
    x Injections, Tree.
    Tree impregnation.
    Impregnation of trees.

Tree injuries. See Trees. Injuries.

Tree introduction. See Trees. Introduction.

Tree killing. See Trees. Killing.

Tree lore. See Folk-lore of trees.

Tree measurement. See Forest mensuration.

Tree names. See Trees. Names.

Tree nuts. See Nuts.

Tree of heaven. See Ailanthus altissima.

Tree photography. See Photography of trees.

Tree planting. (INDIRECT)
    sa Trees. Transplanting.
    Seed spots.
    School forests.
    Subdivision Planting machinery
      under: Trees.
    x Forest planting.
    xx Forestry.
    Planting.
--Bibliography.
--Periodicals.
--Societies.
--Statistics.
    sa Subdivision Statistics under
      Tree planting [geographic
      subdivision] e.g., Tree
      planting. U.S. Statistics.

Tree planting machinery. See Trees.
  Planting machinery.

Tree preservation. See Forest preservation.

Tree rat.
    xx Cacao rats.

Tree reproduction. See Forest reproduction.

Tree-rings.
    x Annual rings.
    Dendrochronology.
    xx Trees. Growth.
--Bibliography.

Tree seedlings.
--Effect of heat on. See Heat. Effect
    on tree seedlings.
--Effect of nitrogen on. See Nitrogen.
    Effect on tree seedlings.
--Statistics.

Tree seeds as feeding stuffs.

Tree shelters. See Trees, Shelter.

Tree squirrels. See Squirrels.

Tree surgery.
    sa Tree injections.
    Pruning.
    Tree wounds.
    xx Trees, Care of.
--Bibliography.

Tree-toad. See Hylidae.

Tree-worship.
    x Trees, Sacred.
    xx Trees.

Tree wounds.
    sa Subdivision Wounds under:
      Apple.
      Trees. Injuries.
    x Plant wounds.
    Pruning wounds.
    xx Trees. Injuries.
    Tree surgery.
    Wounds in plants.

Trees. (INDIRECT)
    sa Acacia.
    Basket willow.
    Beech.
    Birch.
    Catalpa.
    Camphor tree.
    Coconut palm.
    Coniferae.
    Eucalyptus.

Trees (Continued)
 sa Evergreens.
  Fir.
  Larch.
  Mahogany.
  Oak.
  Palm.
  Pine.
  Spruce.
  Poplar.
  Wattles.
  Mulberry.
  Yew.
  Ginkgo.
  Cedar.
  Hemlock.
  Red gum.
  Arboriculture.
  Pruning.
  Shrubs.
  Sylviculture.
  Transplanting.
  Bamboo.
  Tupelo.
  Plane tree.
  Chestnut.
  Walnut.
  Locust.
  Hackberry.
  Hicoria ovata.
  Gleditsia triacanthos.
  Deodar.
  Tallow tree.
  Tolerance in trees.
  Christmas trees.
  Balsa.
  Chaulmugra.
  Hornbeam.
  Tree-worship.
  Trees, Ornamental.
  Fruit trees.
  Dwarf potted trees.
  State trees.
 x Forest trees.
  Woody plants.
  Ligneous plants.
  Dendrology.
 xx Germination.
  Plants, Ornamental.
--Addresses, essays, lectures.
--Analysis.
 sa Acer saccharum. Composition.
--Anatomy.
 sa Wood structure.

Trees (Continued)
--Anatomy.
 sa Subdivision Anatomy under
  names of trees; e.g., Coniferae. Anatomy.
--Animal injury.
 sa Subdivision Damage to forests
  under: Deer.
  Swine.
  Rabbits.
 x Trees. Injuries.
  Animal injuries to trees.
 xx Trees. Pests.
--Bibliography.
 sa Subdivision Bibliography
  under: Trees. Growth.
  Trees. Diseases.
  Coconut palm. Diseases//
--Biochemistry.
 sa Subdivision Biochemistry un-
  der: Pecan.
 xx Chemistry, Vegetable.
--Botany. See Trees.
--Breeding. .
 sa Forest nurseries.
  Subdivision Breeding under:
  Pine.
  Oak.
 x Tree breeding.
 xx Plant-breeding.
  Forest genetics.
-- --Bibliography.
-- --Congresses.
-- --Research.
-- --Terminology.

Trees, Care of.
 sa Tree surgery.
 xx Arboriculture.
  Silviculture.

Trees.
--Catalogs.
--Chemical injections. See Tree injections.
--Classification.
 x Tree classes.
  Tree classification.
--Construction work injuries.
 x Construction work injuries to
  trees.
 xx Trees. Injuries.
--Crowns.
 x Tree crown.

Trees, Curious.
    x Curious trees.
    xx Trees, Notable.

Trees.
--Decay.
    sa Wood decay.
    x Fungus deterioration of trees.
      Decay of trees.
    xx Wood decay.
--Diseases. (INDIRECT)
    sa Entomology, Economic.
      Fruit diseases.
      Lightning. Effect on trees.
      Sap-rot.
      Tree surgery.
      Trees. Weather injuries.
      Weather. Effect on tree dis-
        eases.
      Clitocybe root rot of woody
        plants.
      Subdivision Diseases under:
        Basket-willow.
        Birch.
        Catalpa//
    x Forest phytopathology.
    xx Arboriculture.
      Forest protection.
-- --Bibliography.
-- --Text-books.
--Distribution. See Forest geography.

Trees, Dwarf potted. See Dwarf potted
  trees.

Trees, Effect of carbon dioxide on. See
  Carbon dioxide. Effect on trees.

Trees, Effect of climate on. See Climate,
  Effect on trees.

Trees.
 --Effect of droughts. See Droughts.
    Effect on trees.

Trees, Effect of fire on. See Trees.
  Fire damage.

Trees, Effect of light on. See Light.
  Effect on trees.

Trees, Effect of lightning on. See
  Lightning. Effect on trees.

Trees.
--Effect of lime on. See Lime. Effect
  on trees.
--Effect of logging damage. See
  Logging damage. Effect on trees.

Trees, Effect of nitrogen on. See
  Nitrogen. Effect on trees.

Trees, Effect of sulphur dioxide on.
  See Sulphur dioxide. Effect on trees.

Trees.
--Effect of temperature. See Tempera-
  ture. Effect on trees.
--Effect of weather. See Trees.
  Weather influences.
--Effect of wind. See Winds. Effect
  on trees.
--Eradication. See Trees. Killing.

Trees, Famous. See Trees, Notable.

Trees.
--Fertilizers. See Fertilizers for
  trees.
--Fire damage.
    sa Fire-killed timber.
    x Trees, Effect of fire on.
      Fire damage to trees.
      Fire injury to trees.
      Forest fires. Effect on trees.
      Forest fires. Damage.
      Forest fires. Effect on re-
        production of trees.
    xx Forest fires.
      Fire and vegetation.
-- --Bibliography.

Trees, Folk-lore of. See Folk-lore of
  trees.

Trees, Fossil.
    sa Prepinus viticetensis.
      Woodworthia arizonica.
      Nicolia.
      Platanus.
      Araucarioxylon.
      Cheirolepis.
      Hirmeriella.

Trees, Freak. See Trees, Curious.

Trees.
--Freezing and frost injury.
    sa Subdivision Freezing and frost
      injury under: Fruit.
      Coniferae.
--Gas pressure.
    xx Plant respiration.
      Trees. Physiology and mor-
      phology.
--Genetics. See Forest genetics.
--Geographic distribution. See Forest
    geography.
--Glaze injuries.
    x Glaze injury to trees.
--Grading and standardization.
    x Timber. Grading and standardi-
      zation.
-- --Bibliography.
--Growth.
    sa Forest accretion and yield.
      Longevity of plants.
      Tree rings.
      Dendrographs.
      Subdivision Growth under:
      Pseudotsuga taxifolia.
      Oak.
      Eucalyptus.
      Pinus radiata.
      Coniferae.
      Pine.
      Poplar.
      Pinus strobus.
      Beech.
      Spruce.
      Pinus taeda.
      Hard woods.
      Robinia pseudo-acacia.
      Iuercus rubra.
      Populus deltoides.
      Hemlock.
      Bark.
      Soft woods.
    xx Growth.
      Forest accretion and yield.
-- --Abnormal.
    xx Abnormalities (Plants)
-- --Bibliography.
    xx Trees. Bibliography.
--Hail injury.

Trees, Historic. See Trees, Notable.

Trees.
--Hybrids.
    sa Subdivision Hybrids under:
      Poplar.
--Identification.
    sa Wood. Identification.
    x Tree identification.
      Identification of trees.
-- --Bibliography.
--Injuries.
    sa Trees with subdivisions:
      Hail injury.
      Snow injury.
      Smoke and smelter fume
      injury.
      Animal injury.
      Construction work injuries.
      Storm injury.
      Wind injury.
      Tree wounds.
      Wood. Injuries.
      Logging damage. Effect on
      trees.
    x Damage to trees.
      Tree injuries.
    xx Tree wounds.
--Introduction.
    x Tree introduction.
--Juvenile literature.
    xx Forestry. Juvenile literature.
--Killing.
    sa Poisoning of trees.
    x Trees. Eradication.
      Tree killing.
      Killing trees.
    xx Clearing of land.
--Marking.
    x Marking trees.
      Timber. Marking.
--Measurement. See Forest mensuration.
--Morphology. See Trees. Physiology
    and morphology.
--Names.
    x Trees. Nomenclature.

Trees, National. See National trees.

Trees.
--Nomenclature. See Trees. Names.

Trees, Notable.
    sa Trees, Curious.
    x Famous trees.
      Historic trees.
--Bibliography.

Trees.
--Nutrition.   See Plant nutrition.

Trees, Ornamental.
      sa Cherry, Ornamental.
      x Ornamental trees.
      xx Trees.
        Plants, Ornamental.
--Diseases.
      xx Trees. Diseases.
--Pests.
      xx Trees. Pests.
--Pictorial works.
--Periodicals.
      xx Forestry. Periodicals.
--Pests.   (INDIRECT)
      sa Subdivision Pests under: Birch.
        Acer campestre.
        Acer negundo.
        Bamboo.
        Casuarina.
        Chestnut.
        Cypress.
        Elm.
        Locust (Tree)
        Maple.
        Oak.
        Pine.
        Pinus gerardiana.
        Redwood.
        Sandal-wood.
        Spruce.
        Teak.
        Abies.
        Populus canadensis.
        Pinus ponderosa.
        Larch.
        Fir.
        Crataegus.
        Juglans.
        Robinia pseudacacia.
        Picea morinda.
        Poplar.
        Salix.
        Hickory.
        Larix europaea.
        Abies balsamea.
        Catalpa.
        Wood.
        Crataegus.
        Betula.
        Evergreens.
        Trees, Shade.
        Silk cotton tree.
        Catalpa speciosa.

Trees (Continued)
--Pests.
      sa Subdivision Pests under:
        Shorea robusta.
        Mora.
        Horse-chestnut.
        Juniperus bermudiana.
        Trees, Ornamental.
        Fruit pests.
        Gipsy moth.
        Lymantria monacha//
-- --Bibliography.
-- --Periodicals.
- --Research.
      sa Trees. Pests [geographic sub-
        division] Research, e.g.,
        Trees. Pests. U.S. Research.
--Photographs and photography.   See
      Photography of trees.
--Physiology and morphology.
      sa Trees. Gas pressure.
        Trees. Water content.
        Subdivision Physiology and
          morphology under: Mulberry.
        Eucalyptus.
        Rest period of trees.
        x Trees. Morphology.
-- --Bibliography.
-- --Text-books.
--Pictorial works.
      sa Subdivision Pictorial works
        under: Oak//
      xx Botany. Pictorial works.
--Planting.   See Tree planting.
--Planting machinery.
      x Mechanization of forest plant-
        ing.
        Tree planting machinery.
      xx Forestry. Implements and
        machinery.
        Planting machinery.
        Tree planting.
--Planting time.
      sa Subdivision Planting time
        under: Abies grandis.
        Pinus ponderosa.
      xx Planting time.
--Poisoning.   See Poisoning of trees.
--Preservation.   See Forest preserva-
      tion.
--Propagation.
      sa Subdivision Propagation under:
        Hard woods.
        Acer rubrum.
        Grafting.

Trees (Continued)
--Propagation.
    xx Plant propagation.
-- --Bibliography.
--Pruning. See Pruning.
--Removal.
    x Tree removal.
    xx Pomology.
--Reproduction. See Forest reproduction.
--Roots. See Roots.

Trees, Sacred. See Tree-worship.

Trees.
--Seed.
    sa Forest nurseries.
    Seed trees.
    Subdivision Seed under:
      Pine.
      Pseudotsuga taxifolia.
      Spruce//
-- --Composition.
-- --Disinfection.
    xx Disinfection and disinfectants.
-- --Germination.
    sa Subdivision Seed. Germination
      under: Coniferae.
-- --Harvesting.
    xx Seeds. Harvesting.
- --Pests.
    sa Subdivision Seed. Pests under
      names of trees, e.g., Coni-
      ferae. Seed. Pests.
    xx Seeds. Pests.
-- --Preservation.
    xx Seeds. Preservation.
- --Research.
-- --Testing and examination.
-- -- --Bibliography.

Trees, Shade.
    sa Trees in cities.
    Trees, Shelter.
    x Shade trees.
    xx Trees in cities.
    Forestry.
--Congresses.
--Diseases.
    xx Trees. Diseases.
    Vegetable pathology.
--Periodicals.
--Pests.
    xx Trees. Pests.
    Entomology, Economic.

Trees, Shelter.
    sa Wind-breaks.
    x Shelter trees.
    Tree shelters.
    xx Wind-breaks.
    Trees, Shade.
    Air raids. Protective measures.
    Camouflage (Military science)

Trees.
--Smoke and smelter fume injury.
    sa Subdivision Effect on trees
      under: Sulphur dioxide.
--Snow injury.
    x Snow damage to trees.
    xx Trees. Injuries.
--Spacing.
    xx Plant spacing.

Trees, State. See State trees.

Trees.
--Storm injury.
    x Storm damage to trees.
    xx Trees. Injuries.

Trees, Street. See Trees in cities.

Trees.
--Temperature.
--Thinning. See Thinning.
--Transpiration.
    xx Plant transpiration.
--Transplanting.
    xx Tree planting.
--Transportation.
--Valuation.
    x Fruit trees. Valuation.
--Water content.
--Water requirements.
-- --Bibliography.
    xx Water requirements of crops.
    Bibliography.
--Weather influences.
    x Weather. Effect on trees.
    Trees. Effect of weather.
--Wind injury.
    x Wind damage to trees.
    xx Winds. Effect on trees.
    Trees. Injuries.
--Wire clearance.
    x Wire clearance from trees.
    xx Roadside planting.

Trees as crops. See Tree farms.

Trees as feeding stuff.
    x Fodder trees.

Trees in cities.
    sa Trees, Shade.
    x City trees.
    Street trees.
    Trees, Street.
    xx Trees, Shade.

Trees in literature.
    sa Forestry. Poetry.
    xx Forestry. Poetry.

Trees in poetry.   See Forestry. Poetry.

Trees in winter.

Trefoil, Big.   See Lotuṣ tenuis.

Trefoil, Narrowleaf.   See Lotus tenuis.

Trefoil, Scarlet.   See Scarlet trefoil.

Tre Fontane.

Trehala.

Trehalose.

Treleasea.

Trellises.

Tremandraceae.

Tremandreae.

Trematoda.
    The Trematoda are divided into
    three large sub-classes: Mono-
    genea (mostly external parasites
    on fish and other aquatic ver-
    tebrates; Aspidogastrea (para-
    sites of cold-blooded animals,
    including fish) and Digenea
    (internal parasites which de-
    velop through a complex series
    of stages involving an alterna-
    tion of hosts, one of which is
    always a mollusc) All trema-
    todes parasitic in man, as well
    as those of economic importance
    in the lower vertebrates belong
    in the subclass, Digenea.

Trematoda (Continued)
    sa Amphistoma.
    Aspidogaster.
    Cercaria.
    Cotylogaster.
    Diplodiscus.
    Distoma.
    Epidella.
    Fasciola.
    Holostomata.
    Opisthotrema.
    Temnocephala.
    Bathycolyle.
    Hirudinella.
    Bilharzia.
    Gastrodiscus.
    Gyrodactylus elegans.
    Levinseniella.
    Stichocotyle.
    Watsonius.
    Allocreadium.
    Fasciola-hepatica.
    Prosthogonimus cuneatus.
    Styphlodora bascaniensis.
    Hemiurus.
    Opisthorchis.
    Parorchis.
    Hasstilesia.
    Monocotyle floridana.
    Monostomidae.
    Heterophyidae.
    Gyrodactylidae.
    Megalodiscus.
    Paragonimus edwardsi.
    Parametorchis.
    Zygocotyle.
    Schistosomidae.
    Multivitellaria.
    Echinostomidae.
    Strigeidae.
    Bucephalidae.
    Polystomidae.
    Eucotyle.
    Onchocotylinae.
    Urotrema.
    Digenea.
    Paramphistomidae.
    Cotylophoron.
    Posthodiplostomum.
    Gyrodactyloidea.
    Infidum.
    Paragonimus.
    Tamerlanea.
--Bibliography.

Trematoidea. See Trematoda.

Trembles and milk-sickness.
    sa Alkali disease.
    xx Alkali disease.

Trembling. See Louping ill.

Tremella.

Tremella nostoch.

Tremellineae.
    sa Tremella.

Trempealeau Co., Wis.
    xx Wisconsin.
--Education.
    xx Wisconsin. Education.
--Soils.
    sa Subdivision Wisconsin.
        Trempealeau Co. under:
        Soil-surveys.

Trench fever.

Trench silos. See Silos, Trench.

Trenching machines. See Excavating
   machinery.

Trent (Province)
--Agriculture.
    sa Subdivision Italy. Trent
       (Province) under: Agri-
       culture. Economic as-
       pects.
-- --Periodicals.
--Commerce.
-- --Directories.
-- --Periodicals.
--Economic conditions.
-- --Periodicals.
--Pomology.
--Viticulture.

Trentepohlia.

Trentino.
--Botany.
    sa Subdivision Trentino under:
       Fungi.

Trentino-Alto Adige.
--Economic conditions.

Trentino-Alto Adige (Continued)
--Forestry.
--Social conditions.
--Statistics.

Trenton, N.J.
--Markets.
    xx New Jersey. Markets.
--Water-supply.

Trepang.

Tres Marias Islands.
--Botany.
--Natural history.

Trespass. (DIRECT)

Trespass on national forests.
    xx Forest reservations.

Trestles. See Bridges, Trestle.

Treves.
--Agriculture.
-- --History.
--Forestry.

Treviso (Province)
--Agriculture.
    sa Subdivision Italy. Treviso
       (Province) under: Agri-
       culture. Economic as-
       pects.
-- --Statistics.
    xx Italy. Agriculture. Statistics.
--Commerce.
-- --Periodicals.
--Economic conditions.
-- --Periodicals.

Triacanthagyna.

Trialeurodes.
    xx Aleurodidae.

Trialeurodes vaporariorum.
    x Greenhouse white fly.
    Aleurodes vaporariorum.

Triangulation.
    xx Geodesy.

Triarylpyridylmethanes.
    xx Methanes.

Triassic period.   See Geology, Stratigraphic. Triassic.

Triatoma.
      x Conorhinus.

Triatoma infestans.
      x Barbeiro.

Triatoma maculata.

Triatoma megista.   See Panstrongylus
  megistus.

Triatoma sanguisuga.
  --Bibliography.

Triatominae.   See Reduviidae.

Triazines.

Tribolium.
      x Flour beetles.

Tribolium confusum.
      x Tubelium confusum.
        Confused flour beetle.

Tribolium ferrugineum.

Tribonema.

Tribonemaceae.
        sa Tribonema.

Triborough Bridge.
        xx New York (City) Bridges.

Tribroma bicolor.   See Patashte.

Tricalcium phosphate.

Triceratops.

Tricercomitus.

Trichiidae.   See Trichiinae.

Trichiinae.

Trichina.

Trichinella spiralis.
      x Muscle worm.

Trichinellosis.   See Trichinosis.

Trichinosis.
      x Trichinellosis.
  --Bibliography.
  --Diagnosis.

Trichiotinus.
        xx Coleoptera.

Trichlorethylene.

Trichloroacetic acid in veterinary
  medicine.

Trichlorophenoxyacetic acid, 2,4,5-.
      x 2,4,5-T.
        xx Herbicides.

Trichobaris mucorea.

Trichocephalus.   See Worms, Intestinal
  and parasitic.

Trichocera regelationis.
  --Larvae.
        xx Larvae.

Trichoceridae.

Trichodectes hermsi.

Trichodectes scalaris.

Trichodectes spherocephalus.
        xx Sheep lice.

Trichodectidae.
        sa Trichodectes.

Trichoderma.
        xx Moniliaceae.

Trichoderma lignorum.

Trichodesma.

Trichogramma.
  --Parasites.
        xx Parasitic and predaceous in-
            sects.

Trichogramma evanescens.

Trichogramma minutum.
    xx Parasitic and predaceous in-
       sects.

Trichogrammatidae.
    sa Trichogramma.
       Pseudobrachysticha.

Trichogrammidae.
    sa Trichogramma.

Tricholaena rosea. See Natal grass.

Trichomes.

Trichomitus parvus.

Trichomonas.
    xx Veterinary medicine.
  --Congresses.

Trichomonas buccalis.

Trichomonas foetus.
    x Trichomonas vaginalis bovis.
      Trichomonas genitalis.
      Trichomonas utero-vaginalis
       vitulae.
      Trichomonas Mazzanti.

Trichomonas gallinarum.

Trichomonas genitalis. See Trichomonas
  foetus.

Trichomonas hepatica.

Trichomonas Mazzanti. See Trichomonas
  foetus.

Trichomonas utero-vaginalis vitulae. See
  Trichomonas foetus.

Trichomonas vaginalis.

Trichomonas vaginalis bovis. See
  Trichomonas foetus.

Trichomoniasis, Bovine.
    x Bovine trichomoniasis.
    xx Cattle. Diseases.

Trichonympha.

Trichophyton.
    xx Moniliaceae.

Trichophyton interdigitale.

Trichoptera.   (INDIRECT)
    sa Limnephilidae.
      Sericostomatidae.
      Leptoceridae.
      Limnophilus.
      Hydropsychidae.
      Leptenema.

Trichopterygidae.

Trichoscelidae.

Trichoseptoria fructigena.

Trichosomoides.
    xx Nematoda.

Trichosomoides crassicauda.

Trichosphaeria saccharin.

Trichosporon pullulans.

Trichostibas.

Trichostomum.

Trichostrongylidae.
    sa Obeliscoides.

Trichostrongylus.
    xx Strongylidae.
      Nematoidea.
      Parasites.

Trichosurus vulpecula.

Trichothecium plasmoparae.

Trichuris.

Trichuris trichiura.

Trick photography. See Photography,
  Trick.

Triclada.
    sa Polycladodes.

Tricorythus.

Tri-County irrigation project, Neb.
  (Proposed)

Tricrania sanguinipennis.

Trictenotomidae.
    xx Coleoptera.

Tricuspidaria.

Tricyrtis hirta.

Tridactylus.

Tri-Dam project.

Trier, Ger.
  --Agriculture.
        sa Subdivision Germany. Trier un-
            der: Agriculture. Economic
                aspects.
  --Forestry.

Trieste.
  --Botany.
        sa Subdivision Austria. Trieste
            under: Marine flora.
  --Commerce.

Trieste (Free Territory)
    xx Venezia Giulia, Italy.
  --Agriculture.
  --Biography.
  --Commerce.
  -- --Periodicals.
  -- --Statistics.
  --Economic conditions.
  -- --Periodicals.
  --Fisheries.
  --Forestry.
  --Statistics.

Trieste, Gulf of.
  --Botany.

Triethanolamines.
    xx Ethanolamines.

Triethylene glycol. See Glycols.

Trifolium.
        sa Clover.
        xx Fabaceae.

Trifolium alexandrinum. See Berseem.

Trifolium angulatum.

Trifolium barbeyi.

Trifolium fragiferum. See Clover,
    Strawberry.

Trifolium hybridum. See Alsike.

Trifolium incarnatum. See Clover,
    Crimson.

Trifolium lappaceum.
        x Lappa clover.
        Clover, Lappa.

Trifolium parviflorum.

Trifolium pratense. See Clover.

Trifolium repens. See Clover, White.

Trifolium resupinatum. See Clover,
    Persian.

Trifolium subterraneum. See Subter-
    ranean clover.

Triglochin.

Triglochin maritima.
        x Arrow grass.

Triglops.

Trigno Valley.
  --Agriculture.
        sa Subdivision Italy. Trigno
            Valley under: Reclamation
                of land.

Trigona.

Trigonalidae.

Trigonantheae. See Jungermanniaceae.

Trigonella.

Trigonella phoenum graecum. See
    Fenugreek.

Trigoniaceae.

Trigoniastrum.

Trigoniulus goësii.

Trigonometopus.

Trigonometry.
    sa Logarithms.

Trigonometry, Plane.
    x Plane trigonometry.

Trigonometry, Spherical.
    sa Sphere.
    x Spherical trigonometry.
    xx Sphere.

Trigonometry.
  --Tables, etc.
    xx Mathematics. Tables, etc.

Trigonophymus arrogans.

Trillium.

Trillium grandiflorum.

Trilobita.
    xx Crustacea, Fossil.

Trimeria.

Trimerotropis.
    xx Acridiidae.

Trimesitylvinyl alcohol.
    xx Vinyl alcohol.

Trimethylene chlorobromide.

Trincomali wood.   See Berrya ammonilla.

Trinidad.
    sa Subdivision Trinidad under:
      Trees.
  --Agriculture.
    sa Subdivision Trinidad under:
      Sugar-cane.
      Coffee.
      Agricultural policies and
        programs.
      Agriculture. Economic as-
        pects.

Trinidad (Continued)
  --Agriculture.
    sa Trinidad. Domestic animals.
  -- --Education.
    sa St. Augustine, Trinidad. Im-
      perial College of Tropical
      Agriculture.
  --Botany.
    sa Subdivision Trinidad under:
      Trees.
      Fungi.
      Vegetable pathology.
  --Cattle.
  --Census.
  --Commerce.
  -- --Brazil.
  -- --Statistics.
  --Dairying.
  --Description and travel.
  --Domestic animals.
  --Economic conditions.
    sa Subdivision Trinidad under:
      Economic surveys.
  -- --Periodicals.
  --Economic policy.
  -- --Five-year plan (1956-1960)
  --Entomology.
    sa Subdivision Trinidad under:
      Entomology, Economic.
      Butterflies.
      Moths.
      Hymenoptera.
  --Fisheries.
  --Forestry.
    sa Subdivision Trinidad under:
      Lumber.
      Timber.
      Forest products.
      War and forestry (1939-1945)
  --Geology.
  --History.
  --Industries and resources.
  --Maps.
  --Natural history.
    xx West Indies. Natural history.
  --Ornithology.
  --Paleobotany.
  --Paleontology.
  --Physical geography.
    xx Physical geography.
  --Pomology.
    sa Subdivision Trinidad under:
      Citrus.

Trinidad (Continued)
--Precipitation (Meteorology)   See
    Precipitation (Meteorology)
    Trinidad.
--Roads.
--Soils.
        sa Subdivision Trinidad under:
            Soil-surveys.
        xx West Indies (British) Soils.
--Statistics.
        sa Trinidad. Commerce. Statistics.
--Zoology.

Trinitrotoluene as a cause of disease.

Trinity clay.

Trinity Co., Calif.
--Geography.
--History.

Trinity National Forest, Calif.

Trinity River, Calif.

Trinity River, Tex.
        sa Subdivision Trinity River,
            Tex. under: Flood control.

Trinity Valley, Tex.
--Soils.
        sa Subdivision Trinity Valley,
            Tex. under: Soil conserva-
            tion.
        xx Texas. Soils.
--Water-supply.
        sa Subdivision Texas. Trinity
            Valley under: Water. Con-
            servation.

Triodes.   See Vacuum-tubes.

Triolith.
        x Wolman salts.

Trional.

Trioxane.
        x Alpha-trioxymethylene.

Trioxynaphthalene.

Trioza alacris.

Trioza cockerelli.

Tripang.   See Trepang.

Tripanosomiasis.   See Trypanosomiasis.

Tripe.

Triphenylmethane dyes.

Triphenylmethyl.

Triphleps insidiosus.

Triphylite.

Triploidy.   See Polyploidy.

Tripoli (Province)   See Tripolitania.

Tripoli (Silica)
        xx Silica.

Tripolitania.
        Tripolitania is a province or
            district of Libya.
        x Tripoli (Province)
--Agriculture.
        sa Subdivision Tripolitania un-
            der: Poultry.
            Agricultural policies and
            programs.
            Agriculture. Economic as-
            pects.
            Subdivision Agriculture under:
            Barka, Africa.
        xx Africa. Agriculture.
- --History.
-- --Statistics.
--Antiquities.
--Botany.
        sa Subdivision Tripolitania un-
            der: Botany, Economic.
            Algae.
--Domestic animals.
--Economic conditions.
--Entomology.
        sa Subdivision Tripolitania un-
            der: Locusts.
--Forestry.
        sa Subdivision Tripolitania un-
            der: Afforestation and re-
            forestation.
--History.
-- --British occupation, 1942-

Tripolitania (Continued)
--Land.
    sa Subdivision Tripolitania un-
        der: Land utilization.
--Maps.
--Statistics.
--Water-supply.

Tripp Co., S.D.
--Population.
    sa Subdivision South Dakota.
        Tripp Co. under: Rural
          exodus.

Trirhabda.

Trisema wagapii.

Trissocladius equitans.

Tristan da Cunha (Islands)
--Botany.
--Natural history.

Tristania.
    xx Myrtaceae.

Tristania conferta.
    x Brush box.

Tristellateia.

Tristeza. See Tick fever.

Tristeza of citrus.
    xx Citrus. Diseases.

Tristoma.

Triterpenes. See Terpenes.

Triticum.
--Hybrids.

Triticum aestivum.

Triticum compactum. See Triticum
  vulgare.

Triticum dicoccum. See Emmer.

Triticum durum. See Wheat, Durum.

Triticum monococcum. See Einkorn.

Triticum polonicum. See Wheat, Polish.

Triticum sativum dicoccum. See Emmer.

Triticum sativum spelta. See Spelt.

Triticum spelta. See Spelt.

Triticum vulgare.
    sa Wheat.

Tritium.
    xx Hydrogen. Isotopes.
--Congresses.

Triton.

Triumfetta cordifolia.

Triuridaceae.

Trivandrum public gardens.

Trixis.

Trobriand Islands.

Trochidae.
    sa Trochus.

Trochilidae.
    sa Goldmania.
       Atthis.
       Selasphorus.

Trochodendraceae.
    sa Eucommia.

Trochodendron.

Trochus niloticus.

Troctes divinatorius.

Trogiinae.
    xx Scarabaeidae.

Troglodytes.

Troglodytes gorilla. See Gorilla.

Trogoderma.
    xx Dermestidae.
--Larvae.

Trogoderma granarium.
    x Khapra beetle.

Trogones.

Trogosita.

Trogositidae.
    sa Lophocateres.

Trogulidae.

Trolleys. See Electric railroads.

Trombicula.
    xx Trombiculidae.

Trombicula deliensis.
    x Scrub itch mite.

Trombicula tlalzahuatl.

Trombiculidae.
    sa Trombicula.
    Acomatacarus.
    x Harvest bugs.
    Chiggers (Mites)
    Trombiculinae.
    Trombidium.
    xx Acarina.
    Arachnida.

Trombiculidae as carriers of contagion.
    xx Arachnida as carriers of con-
        tagion.

Trombiculinae. See Trombiculidae.

Trombidium. See Trombiculidae.

Trombidiidae.
    sa Alophus.
    xx Acarina.
    Arachnida.

Tromsø, Norway. Museum.
--Bibliography.

Trona, Calif.

Tronch.

Trondhjem (District) Norway.
--Agriculture.

Trondhjem Fiord.
--Botany.
    sa Subdivision Norway. Trondhjem
        Fiord under: Algae.
    xx Norway. Botany.

Tropaeolaceae.
    sa Magallana.
    Tropaeolum.

Tropaeolum.
    sa Nasturtium.

Tropaeolum majus.

Tropaeolum patagonicum.

Trophodiscus.

Tropical Africa. See Africa, Tropical.

Tropical agriculture. See Tropics.
    Agriculture.

Tropical America. See America,
    Tropical.

Tropical cookery. See Cookery, Tropi-
    cal.

Tropical deterioration.
    xx Deterioration.

Tropical diet. See Diet, Tropics.

Tropical diseases. See Tropical
    medicine.

Tropical fish.
    x Ornamental fish.
    Fish, Ornamental.
    Fish, Tropical.
    xx Ichthyology.

Tropical forestry. See Tropics.
    Forestry.

Tropical fowl mite. See Liponyssus
    bursa.

Tropical fruit.
    sa East Indies (Dutch) Pomology.
    Tropics. Pomology.
    Names of specific tropical
        fruits, e.g., Data; Fig.

Tropical fruit (Continued)
    x Subtropical fruit.
    xx Tropical plants.
--Bibliography.
--Breeding.
--Diseases.
    xx Fruit diseases.
       Tropical plant diseases.
--Pests.
    xx Fruit pests.
--Text-books.
--Varieties.

Tropical geography.   See Tropics. Geography.

Tropical horticulture.   See Gardening. Tropics.

Tropical hygiene.   See Tropical medicine.

Tropical kudzu.   See Kudzu, Tropical.

Tropical medicine.
    sa Framboesia tropica.
       Tinea imbricata.
       Tropical veterinary medicine.
       Names of specific tropical
          diseases, e.g., Sleeping-
          sickness.
    x Hygiene, Tropical.
       Tropics. Hygiene.
       Tropical diseases.
       Tropical hygiene.
    xx Acclimatization.
       Climate and health.
       Hygiene.
       Military hygiene.
--Bibliography.
    xx Medicine. Bibliography.
--Congresses.
--History.
    xx Medicine. History.
--Periodicals.
    sa Subdivision Periodicals under:
       Tropical veterinary medicine.
-- --Bibliography.
--Research.
--Schools.
--Societies.

Tropical meteorology.   See Tropics. Meteorology.

Tropical plant diseases.
    sa Tropical fruit. Diseases.

Tropical plants.
    sa Tropical fruit.
       Names of specific tropical
          plants, e.g., Rubber.
    x Plants, Tropical.
    xx Botany.
       Tropics. Botany.
--Bibliography.
--Congresses.
--Pictorial works.

Tropical soils.   See Tropics. Soils.

Tropical trees.   See Trees. Tropics.

Tropical vegetables.   See Vegetables. Tropics.

Tropical veterinary medicine.
    x Veterinary medicine, Tropical.
    xx Veterinary medicine.
--Bibliography.
--Periodicals.
--Societies.

Tropical woods.
    xx Wood.
--Mechanical properties.   See Tropical
       woods. Properties and uses.
--Nomenclature.
    xx Wood. Nomenclature.
--Periodicals.
--Physical properties.   See Tropical
       woods. Properties and uses.
--Properties and uses.
    x Tropical woods. Mechanical
         properties.
       Tropical woods. Physical pro-
         perties.
       Tropical woods. Utilization.
    xx Wood. Properties and uses.
--Testing.
    xx Wood. Testing.
--Utilization.   See Tropical woods.
       Properties and uses.

Tropics.
    sa Africa, Tropical.
       America, Tropical.

Tropics (Continued)
--Agriculture.
    sa Names of tropical countries
      with subdivision Agriculture,
      e.g., America, Tropical.
      Agriculture; East Indies
      (Dutch) Agriculture.
      Phrases beginning with the word
      Tropical; and other subdi-
      visions under Tropics, e.g.,
      Tropics. Domestic animals;
      Tropics. Soils.
      Subdivision Tropics under:
      Gardening.
      Colonization, Agricultural.
      Agriculture. Economic as-
        pects.
      Coffee.
      Poultry.
      Maize.
      Mechanized farming.
      Agricultural laborers.
-- --Bibliography.
    sa Subdivision Bibliography under:
      Cassava.
-- --Congresses.
-- --Exhibitions.
- --History.
-- -- --Abstracts.
-- -- --Bibliography.
-- --Periodicals.
- --Research.
    xx Agriculture. Research.
-- --Societies.
--Apiculture.
--Bibliography.
--Botany.
    sa Subdivision Tropics under: Trees.
      Vegetable pathology.
      Botany, Economic.
      Shrubs.
      Fungi.
      Subdivision Botany under:
      America, Tropical.
      Tropical plants.
--Cattle.
    xx Cattle.
      Tropics. Domestic animals.
--Climate.
--Colonies.
    xx Colonies and colonization.
--Description and travel.
--Diet. See Diet. Tropics.
--Diseases. See Tropical medicine.

Tropics (Continued)
--Domestic animals.
    sa Tropics. Cattle.
    xx Domestic animals.
      Agriculture, Tropical.
--Economic conditions.
    sa Subdivision Tropics under:
      Geography, Economic.
    xx Economic conditions.
--Entomology.
    sa Subdivision Tropics under:
      Butterflies.
      Wasps.
      Trees. Pests.
      Entomology, Economic.
--Forestry.
    sa Subdivision Forestry under:
      Caribbean region.
      Africa, Tropical.
      Subdivision Tropics under:
      Trees.
      Timber.
      Lumber trade.
      Silviculture.
    x Forests, Tropical.
-- --Bibliography.
-- --Periodicals.
-- --Research.
--Geography.
    sa Subdivision Tropics under:
      Geography, Economic.
    x Tropical geography.
--Geology.
--Horticulture. See Gardening. Tropics.
-- --Periodicals.
--Hygiene. See Tropical medicine.
--Industries.
--Land. See Land utilization. Tropics.
--Meteorology.
    sa Precipitation (Meteorology)
      Tropics.
    x Tropical meteorology.
      Meteorology, Tropical.
--Natural history.
--Ornithology.
--Periodicals.
--Pomology.
    sa Subdivision Pomology under:
      Federated Malay States.
      Tropical fruits.
--Poultry. See Poultry. Tropics.
--Research.

Tropics (Continued)
--Soils.
    sa Laterite.
    x Soil, Tropical.
      Tropical soils.
--Study and teaching.
--Viticulture.
--Zoology.

Tropidocarpum.

Tropidophorus.

Tropin.
    xx Alkaloids.
      Atropin.

Tropism.
    sa Chemotropism.
      Phototropism.
      Plant irritability and move-
        ment.

Troposphere.

Troppau.
    x Opava.

Trosiinae.
    xx Megalopygidae.

Trotting. See Horse-racing.

Trousdale Co., Tenn.
--Politics and government.

Trout.
    x Rainbow-trout.
      Steelhead.
--Diseases.

Trout Creek Watershed, Colo.

Trout fishing.   (INDIRECT)
    xx Fishing.
      Fly-casting.

Truck (Vegetables) See Vegetables.

Truck-crops. See Berries; Melons;
  Vegetables.

Truck farming. See Market gardening;
  Vegetable gardening.

Truck gardening. See Market gardening;
  Vegetable gardening.

Truckee-Carson Experiment Farm. See
  Newlands Experiment Farm.

Truckee-Carson irrigation project. See
  Newlands Experiment Farm.

Truckee River.

Truckee River General Electric Co.

Truckee Valley (Nev.)
--Botany.

Trucks. See Motor-trucks.

Trudovaia Armiia Collective Farm.
    xx Collective farms.

Truffles.
--Bibliography.

Trujillo, Venezuela (State)
--Agriculture.
    sa Subdivision Venezuela.
      Trujillo (State) under:
      Sugar-cane.
--Forestry.
--Goats.
--Maps.
--Soils.

Truk Islands.
--Geology.
--Physical geography.

Trumbull, Conn.
--Mineralogy.

Trunk-fish. See Ostraciontidae.

Trupanea.
    xx Tephritidae.

Trusses.
    x Roof-trusses.

Trust Territory of the Pacific Islands.
    sa Caroline Islands.
      Ladrone Islands.
      Marshall Islands.

Trust Territory of the Pacific Islands
(Continued)
--Agriculture.
    sa Subdivision Trust Territory of
       the Pacific Islands under:
       Agriculture. Economic as-
        pects.
--Economic conditions.
--Politics and government.
--Social conditions.

Trustees. See Trusts and trustees.

Trusteeships, International. See International trusteeships.

Trusts, Industrial.   (DIRECT)
    sa Competition.
       Corporations.
       Government ownership.
       Interstate commerce.
       Monopolies.
       Railroads.
       Restraint of trade.
       Sherman antitrust law.
       Tariff.
       Lumber trust.
       Consolidation and merger of
        corporations.
       Cartels.
    xx Big business.
       Consolidation and merger of
        corporations.
--Bibliography.
--History.
    sa Subdivision History under:
       Corporations.
--Law.
    sa Subdivision Law under Trusts,
       Industrial [geographic sub-
       division] e.g., Trusts, In-
       dustrial. Canada. Law.
    x Antitrust laws.
      Anti-trust laws.

Trusts, Philanthropic. See Endowments.

Trusts and trustees.
    x Trustees.
    xx Executors and administrators.
--Law.

Truth.

Truxalinae.
    xx Acridiidae.

Trycaraballylic acid.

Trypanidae.

Trypanosoma.
    sa Surra.

Trypanosoma americanum.

Trypanosoma brucei.

Trypanosoma criceti.

Trypanosoma cruzi.

Trypanosoma elmassiani.
    sa Mal de caderas.

Trypanosoma equiperdum.

Trypanosoma kirdanii.

Trypanosoma lewisi.

Trypanosoma neotomae.

Trypanosoma triatomae.

Trypanosoma venezuelense.

Trypanosomiasis.
    sa Nagana.
       Surra.
       Sleeping sickness.
       Chagas' disease.
       Dourine.
    x Derrengadera.
      Murrina.
      Tripanosomiasis.
--Abstracts.
--Bibliography.
--Congresses.

Trypanosomidae.

Trypanosomo vivax.

Tryparsamide.
    xx Drugs.

Trypeta.

Trypeta cardui.

Trypeta ludens.

Trypeta pomonella.   See Rhagoletis
pomonella.

Trypetidae.   See Euribiidae.

Trypodendron lineatus.   See Xyloterus
lineatus.

Trypsin.

Tryptophane.

Tsad, Africa.   See Chad, Africa.

Tsao.   See Zizyphus jujuba.

Tschernigow, Russia.   See Chernigof,
Russia.

Tschishinsk.   See Chizhinsk.

Tsetse-flies.
       sa Surra.
          Glossina.
   --Abstracts.
   --Bibliography.
   --Congresses.

Tsetse-flies as carriers of contagion.

Tsigai sheep.
       x Tigai sheep.

Tsinghai (Province) China.
   --Botany.

Tsonga Tribe.   See Thonga Tribe.

Tsuga canadensis.
       sa Hemlock.
       xx Abietineae.

Tsuga heterophylla.
       sa Black streak in western
          hemlock.
          Brown streak in western
          hemlock.
       x West coast hemlock.
   --Diseases.
       xx Trees. Diseases.

Tsuga heterophylla (Continued)
   --Testing.
       xx Wood. Testing.

Tsuga heterophylla (Wood)
       x West Coast hemlock wood.

Tsuga mertensiana.

Tu-Kiang irrigation project.
       x Tukiangyien irrigation project.

Tuaregs.
       x Touaregs.
       xx Berbers.

Tub gardening.
       xx Gardens.
   --Periodicals.

Tuba auditiva.   See Eustachian tube.

Tubelium confusum.   See Tribolium
confusum.

Tuber formation.   See Tubers.

Tuberaceae.
       sa Elaphomyces.
          Truffles.
          Tugui.
       xx Ascomycetes.

Tubercle.

Tubercle bacilli.   See Tuberculosis,
Bacilli.

Tubercles.
       sa Root-tubercles.

Tuberculariaceae.
       sa Strumella.
          Fusarium.

Tuberculin.
       sa Tuberculol.
          Tuberculosan.

Tuberculin test.
   --Legislation.

Tuberculol.

Tuberculosan.

Tuberculosis.
    sa Subjects beginning with the
        word Tuberculosis, e.g.,
        Tuberculosis in animals;
        Tuberculosis of bovine
        origin.
    x Consumption.
      Miliary tuberculosis.
      Phthisis.
      Pulmonary tuberculosis.
      Tuberculous caries.
      Pott's disease.
--Bacilli.
    sa Calmette-Guérin bacillus.
      Vole acid-fast bacillus.
    x Mycobacterium tuberculosis.
    xx Mycobacterium.
--Bibliography.

Tuberculosis, Bovine.   See Tuberculosis
   in cattle.

Tuberculosis.
--Congresses.

Tuberculosis, Contagiousness of.   See
   Tuberculosis. Transmission.

Tuberculosis.
--Diagnosis.
    sa Complement fixation.

Tuberculosis, Diet in.

Tuberculosis.
--Hospitals and sanataria.
--Legislation.
    sa Tuberculosis in cattle. Legis-
      lation.
--Periodicals.
-- --Bibliography.
--Preventive inoculation.
--Societies.
--Transmission.
    sa Tuberculosis of bovine origin.
    x Tuberculosis, Contagiousness
      of.

Tuberculosis in animals.
    sa Tuberculosis in camels.
      Tuberculosis in cats.
      Tuberculosis in cattle//
--Diagnosis.
--Preventive inoculation.

Tuberculosis in apes.

Tuberculosis in buffaloes.
    xx Tuberculosis in animals.

Tuberculosis in camels.

Tuberculosis in cats.

Tuberculosis in cattle.
    x Bovine tuberculosis.
      Tuberculosis in cattle.
        Eradication.
--Claims and adjustments.
    xx Claims and adjustments.
--Diagnosis.
-- --Agglutination reaction.
--Eradication.   See Tuberculosis in
    cattle.
--Legislation.
    xx Cattle. Legislation.
--Preventive inoculation.
--Transmission to man.   See Tubercu-
    losis of bovine origin.

Tuberculosis in dogs.

Tuberculosis in goats.
    xx Goats. Diseases.

Tuberculosis in hamsters.

Tuberculosis in horses.
--Diagnosis.

Tuberculosis in monkeys.

Tuberculosis in poultry.
    sa Tuberculosis in turkeys.
--Diagnosis.

Tuberculosis in rabbits.
    xx Rabbits. Diseases.
      Tuberculosis in animals.

Tuberculosis in sheep.
    xx Sheep. Diseases.

Tuberculosis in swine.
--Diagnosis.

Tuberculosis in turkeys.
    xx Tuberculosis in poultry.
      Turkeys. Diseases.

Tuberculosis in voles.
    xx Voles. Diseases.

Tuberculosis of bovine origin.
    x Bovine tuberculosis in man.
    Tuberculosis in cattle. Trans-
      mission to man.
    xx Milk in relation to disease.
    Tuberculosis. Transmission.
    Diseases. Transmission from
      animal to man.

Tuberculosis transmission. See Tuberculosis. Transmission.

Tuberculous caries. See Tuberculosis.

Tuberineae.

Tuberous rooted plants. See Bulbous and
  tuberous rooted plants.

Tubers.
    x Tuber formation.

Tubes.
    sa Radio tubes.

Tubicaulis.

Tubifex rivulorum.

Tubinares.
    sa Petrels.

Tübingen, Ger.
  --Botany.

Tubulifera.
    xx Hymenoptera.

Tucumán, Argentine Republic (Province)
  --Agriculture.
    sa Subdivision Argentine Republic.
      Tucumán (Province) under:
      Irrigation.
  --Botany.
  --Climate.
  --Domestic animals.
  --Entomology.
    xx Argentine Republic. Entomology.
  --Forestry.
  --Statistics.

Tuff. See Volcanic ash, tuff, etc.

Tug Fork of Big Sandy River.

Tug Hill Plateau, N.Y.
  --Botany.

Tugboats.
    sa Towing.

Tugui.
    xx Tuberaceae.

Tugwell-Copeland bill.
    xx Drugs. Legislation.
  --Bibliography.

Tuileries. See Paris. Tuileries.

Tukiangyien irrigation project. See
  Tu-Kiang irrigation project.

Tula (Gpvernment)
  --Entomology.
    sa Subdivision Russia. Tula
      (Government) under:
      Entomology, Economic.

Tula Region.
  --Agriculture.
  --Apiculture.

Tulare Co., Calif.
  --Dairying.
  -- --**Statistics.**
    xx California. Dairying. Sta-
      tistics.
  --Water-supply.

Tulare Valley, Calif.

Tularemia.

Tulaselaktin.

Tule River Basin, Calif.

Tulip fire.

Tulip tree. See Liriodendron tulipifera.

Tulipa gesneriana.

Tulips.
  --Diseases.
    sa Tulip fire.
    Anthracnose of tulips.

Tulips (Continued)
--Periodicals.
--Societies.
-- --Directories.

Tulostomataceae.
        sa Queletia.

Tulsa, Okla.
--Commerce.
        sa Subdivision Tulsa, Okla. under:
           Produce trade.
           Wholesale trade.
--Markets.

Tulsa Co., Okla.
--Soils.
        sa Subdivision Oklahoma. Tulsa Co.
           under: Soil-surveys.

Tumacacori National Monument.

Tumalo irrigation project.

Tumamoca.

Tumbleweed. See Russian thistle.

Tumbling mustard. See Sisymbrium altissimum.

Tumbu fly. See Cordylobia anthropophaga.

Tumors.
        sa Myxoma.
          Lymphadenoma.
          Adenoma.
          Cancer.
          Keloids.
          Neurinomatosis.
          Subdivision Tumors under names
            of organs and regions of the
            body, e.g., Skin. Tumors.
        x Oncology.
--Bibliography.
--Diagnosis.
        xx Veterinary medicine. Diagnosis.
--Nomenclature.
--Periodicals.
--Spinal cord. See Myelosis.

Tumors (Plant)

The tuna as food for man.

Tuna fish.
        x Tunny.

Tuna fish, Canned.
        xx Fishery products. Preservation.

Tuna fish.
--Tariff.

Tunbridge Wells, Eng.
--Botany.

Tundras.
        xx Llanos.
          Pampas.
          Prairies.

Tung farming. See Tung oil and tung oil tree.

Tung leaves.
        xx Leaves.
          Tung oil and tung oil tree.
--Mineral elements.
        xx Plants. Mineral elements.

Tung nut.
        xx Tung oil and tung oil tree.
          Nuts.
--Congresses.
--Marketing.
--Policies and programs.
--Processing.
--Statistics.

Tung nuts, Proteins in.
        xx Proteins.

Tung oil and tung oil tree.
        sa Tung leaves.
          Tung nut.
        x Aleurites cordata.
          Japanese wood oil.
          Chinese wood oil tree.
          Aleurites fordii.
          Aleurites montana.
          Tung tree.
          Wood oil tree.
          Tung farming.
        xx Wood oil.
--Abstracts.
--Bibliography.
--Policies and programs.
--Societies.

Tung oil and tung oil tree (Continued)
--Statistics.
   xx Fats and oils. Statistics.

Tung tree. See Tung oil and tung oil
 tree.

Tungsten.
   xx Wolframite.

Tungstic acid.
   xx Acids.

Tungurahua, Ecuador (Province)
--Agriculture.
--Soils.
   sa Subdivision Ecuador. Tungurahua
    (Province) under: Soil
    conservation.

Tunica Co., Miss.
--Soils.
   sa Subdivision Mississippi. Tunice
    Co. under: Soil-surveys.

Tunicata.
   sa Ascidians.
--Bibliography.

Tunis.
   x Tunisia.
   xx Africa.
    Africa, French North.
--Agricultural experiment stations.
-- --Directories.
   xx Agricultural experiment sta-
    tions. Directories.
--Agriculture.
   sa Subdivision Tunis under:
    Agriculture. Economic as-
     pects.
    Cereals.
    Potatoes.
    Drug plants.
-- --Education.
-- --Periodicals.
-- --Statistics.
--Apiculture.
--Botany.
   sa Subdivision Botany under:
    Sousse, Tunis.
    Subdivision Tunis under: Trees.
    Shrubs.
    Botany, Medical.
   xx Africa. Botany.

Tunis (Continued)
--Cattle.
--Climate.
--Commerce.
   sa Subdivision Tunis under:
    Grain trade.
    Wool trade and industry.
-- --Directories.
-- --Periodicals.
-- --Statistics.
--Commercial treaties.
   xx Commercial treaties.
--Description and travel.
-- --Guide-books.
--Economic conditions.
   xx Africa. Economic conditions.
-- --Periodicals.
--Entomology.
   sa Subdivision Tunis under:
    Diptera.
    Hymenoptera.
--Forestry.
   sa Subdivision Tunis under: Trees.
   xx Africa. Forestry.
--Industries and resources.
--Land.
   sa Subdivision Tunis under:
    Land laws.
   xx Africa. Land.
--Maps.
--Meteorology.
   sa Precipitation (Meteorology)
    Tunis.
--Ornithology.
--Physical geography.
--Politics and government.
--Pomology.
--Roads.
--Sheep.
--Statistics.
   sa Tunis. Commerce. Statistics.
--Viticulture.
-- --Periodicals.

Tunisia. See Tunis.

Tunnels. (DIRECT)
   sa Rock excavation.
    Holland Tunnel.
    Cascade Tunnel//
--Ventilation.

Tunny. See Tuna fish.

Tunu.

Tuolumne Co., Calif.

Tuolumne River, Calif.

Tupaiidae.

Tupelo.

Tur. See Cajanus indicus.

Turanga. See Populus pruinosa.

Turbellaria.
    sa Rhabdocoela.
       Dendrocoela.
       Planoceridae.
       Convoluta.
       Polycladida.
       Polycladodes.
       Paravortex gemellipara.
       Planaria.
       Prorhynchidae.

Turbidae.

Turbine wheels.

Turbines.
    sa Steam-turbines.
       Water-wheels.
       Gas-turbines.
       Air-turbines.

Turbinolia, Fossil.

Turbo-generators. See Air-turbines.

Turbulence, Atmospheric. See Atmospheric
   turbulence.

Turdidae.
    sa Shama.
       Geocichla.
       Catharus.

Turén, Venezuela.
  --Agriculture.
    sa Subdivision Venezuela. Turén
       under: Colonization, Agri-
       cultural.

Turf. See Lawns; Golf-links.

Turf-closets.

Turfing. See Lawns; Grasses.

Turgai, Russia.
  --Entomology.

Turgidity.

Turgor.

Turin.
  --Botanic gardens.
    sa Turin. Università. Orto
       botanico.
  --Botany.

Turin (Province)
    x Torino (Province)
  --Agriculture.
    sa Subdivision Italy. Turin
       (Province) under: Wheat.
       Cropping systems.
    xx Italy. Agriculture.
  -- --Statistics.
  --Domestic animals.
  --Economic conditions.
  --Entomology.
  --Forestry.
  -- --Statistics.

Türkenschanzpark, Vienna. See Vienna.
   Türkenschanzpark.

Turkestan.
    x Turkistan.
  --Agriculture.
    sa Subdivision Agriculture under:
       Turkestan, West.
       Subdivision Turkestan under:
       Cereals.
  --Botany.
    sa Subdivision Turkestan under:
       Trees.
    xx Asia. Botany.
  --Description and travel.
  --Domestic animals.
    sa Turkestan. Sheep.
  --Economic conditions.
  --Entomology.
    sa Subdivision Entomology under:
       Kirghiz Steppe.
       Uzbekistan.

Turkestan (Continued)
--Entomology.
    sa Subdivision Turkestan under:
      Lepidoptera.
      Hemiptera.
      Neuroptera.
      Orthoptera.
      Entomology, Economic.
    xx Asia. Entomology.
--Land.
    sa Subdivision Turkestan under:
      Land tenure.
--Maps.
    sa Subdivision Maps under:
      Turkestan, West.
--Natural history.
    sa Subdivision Natural history
      under: Turkestan, Chinese.
--Politics and government.
--Population.
--Sheep.
--Soils.
--Statistics.
--Viticulture.
    sa Subdivision Viticulture under:
      Samarkand.
      Tashkent.
--Zoology.
    sa Subdivision Turkestan under:
      Serpents.

Turkestan, Chinese.
    x Chinese Turkestan.
    xx Turkestan.
--Commerce.
    xx China. Commerce.
--Description and travel.
    xx China. Description and travel.
--Entomology.
    sa Subdivision Turkestan, Chinese
      under: Hemiptera.
--Natural history.
    xx Turkestan. Natural history.

Turkestan, East.

Turkestan, West.
    x West Turkestan.
--Agriculture.
--Description and travel.
--Maps.
--Soils.

Turkestan Range.
--Botany.

Turkey.
    sa Subdivision Agriculture under:
      Albania.
      Macedonia.
      Subdivision Turkey under: Rice.
      Agriculture, Cooperative.
      Sugar-cane.
      Field crops.
      Sugar-beet.
      Wheat.
      Rye.
      Potatoes.
      Agricultural policies and
        programs.
      Agricultural credit.
      Colonization, Agricultural.
      Mechanized farming.
      Agricultural extension.
-- --Education.
    sa Subdivision Turkey under:
      Agricultural extension.
-- --Periodicals.
-- --Statistics.
    sa Farm produce. Turkey. Sta-
      tistics.
--Apiculture.
-- --Periodicals.
--Bibliography.
--Botany.
    sa Subdivision Botany under:
      Albania.
      Trebizond, Turkey (Vilayet)
      Scutari.
    Subdivision Turkey under:
      Fungi.
      Vegetable pathology.
--Cattle.
--Census.
    xx Turkey. Statistics.
--Climate.
--Commerce.
-- --Periodicals.
    sa Subdivision Commerce. Peri-
      odicals under: Smyrna.
-- --Statistics.
    sa Smyrna. Commerce. Statistics.
--Commercial treaties.
    xx Commercial treaties.
--Description and travel.
--Domestic animals.
    xx Europe. Domestic animals.
-- --Periodicals.
--Economic conditions.
-- --Periodicals.
--Economic policy.

Turkey (Continued)
--Emigration and immigration.
--Entomology.
 sa Subdivision Turkey under:
  Coleoptera.
  Trees. Pests.
  Entomology, Economic.
--Foreign relations.
-- --U.S.
--Forestry.
-- --Research.
-- --Statistics.
--Geographic names.
--Horse.
--Industries.
-- --Statistics.
--Maps.
--Ornithology.
 sa Subdivision Ornithology under:
  Mesopotamia.
--Sericulture.
--Sheep.
--Social life and customs.
--Statistics.
 sa Turkey. Agriculture. Statistics.
  Turkey. Commerce. Statistics.
  Turkey. Census.
--Zoology.
 sa Subdivision Zoology under:
  Mesopotamia.

Turkey, Asiatic.
 sa Asia Minor.
--Agricultural experiment stations.
 sa Adana, Turkey. Agricultural
  Experiment Station.
--Agriculture.
 sa Subdivision Agriculture under:
  Anatolia, Asia Minor.
--Botany.
 sa Subdivision Botany under:
  Armenia.
  Palestine.
  Mesopotamia//
--Entomology.
 sa Subdivision Entomology under:
  Mesopotamia.
--Forestry.
 sa Subdivision Forestry under:
  Anatolia, Asia Minor.
 xx Asia Minor. Forestry.
--Irrigation.

Turkey breeders. See Turkey industry and
 trade. Directories.

Turkey financing. See Turkeys. Financing.

Turkey houses and equipment.
 xx Poultry houses and equipment.

Turkey improvement plan. See National
 turkey improvement plan.

Turkey industry and trade. (DIRECT)
--Directories.
 x Turkey breeders.
  Turkeys. Directories.
--Periodicals.

Turkey plan. See National turkey improvement plan.

Turkey plants. See Poultry plants.

Turkey Run State Park, Ind.

Turkeys. (INDIRECT)
 sa Eggs, Turkey.
  Cookery (Turkeys)
--Bibliography.
--Breeding.
 xx Poultry. Breeding.
--Castration.
 xx Castration.
--Directories. See Turkey industry
 and trade. Directories.
--Diseases.
 sa Pullorum disease in turkeys.
  Tuberculosis in turkeys.
  Enterohepatitis.

Turkeys, Dressed.
 x Dressed turkeys.
--Grading and standardization.
 xx Poultry, Dressed. Grading and
  standardization.
--Prices.

Turkeys, Dressing of.
 xx Poultry, Dressing of.

Turkeys.
--Effect of carbon dioxide. See Carbon
 dioxide. Effect on turkeys.
--Feeding.
 xx Feeding stuffs.
--Financing.
 x Turkey financing.

Turkeys, Frozen.
    x Frozen turkeys.
    xx Poultry, Frozen.
--Containers.
--Transportation.

Turkeys.
--Grading and standardization.
    xx Poultry. Grading and
        standardization.
--History.
    xx Poultry. History.
--Inspection.
    xx Poultry. Inspection.
--Marketing.
    xx Marketing of farm produce.
        Poultry. Marketing.
- --Control.
    xx Poultry. Marketing. Control.
--Marketing, Cooperative.
    xx Poultry. Marketing, Coopera-
        tive.
--Marketing.
-- --Costs.
    xx Marketing of live stock. Costs.
--Marketing agreements.
    xx Poultry. Marketing agreements.
--Parasites.
    xx Poultry. Parasites.
--Performance records and registration.
--Periodicals.
--Pests.
--Prices.
    xx Poultry. Prices.
-- --Subsidies.
--Slaughtering.
    xx Poultry. Slaughtering.

Turkeys, Smoked.   See Poultry (Meat)
  Smoked.

Turkeys.
--Societies.
--Statistics.
    sa Turkeys [geographic subdi-
       vision] Statistics, e.g.,
       Turkeys. U.S. Statistics.
    xx Poultry. Statistics.

Turkeys, Wild.
    x Wild turkeys.
    xx Game-birds.

Turkish language.
--Dictionaries.
--Grammar.

Turkish periodicals.
--Bibliography.

Turkistan.   See Turkestan.

Turkmenistan.
    sa Turkestan.
--Agriculture.
-- --Periodicals.
-- --Statistics.
--Botany.
    sa Subdivision Turkmenistan
        under: Botany, Economic.
--Cattle.
--Domestic animals.
    sa Turkmenistan. Sheep.
--Economic conditions.
-- --Periodicals.
    xx U.S.S.R. Economic conditions.
        Periodicals.
--Entomology.
    sa Subdivision Entomology under:
        Ashkabad.
    xx U.S.S.R. Entomology.
--Horse.
--Industries and resources.
--Natural history.
    xx U.S.S.R. Natural history.
--Paleontology.
--Pomology.
--Sheep.
    xx Turkmenistan. Domestic
        animals.
--Soils.
--Statistics.
--Water-supply.
--Zoology.
    xx Zoology.

Turlock Irrigation District, Calif.

Turmeric.
    sa Dyes.
    x Curcuma longa.
    xx Zingiberaceae.

Turneraceae.

Turners Lake, Isle-au-Haut, Me.
--Natural history.

Turnicidae.

Turning.
    x Wood turning.

Turnip aphid.   See Rhopalosiphum
  pseudobrassicae.

Turnip club root.   See Clubroot of
  turnips.

Turnip leaves.
    xx Leaves.

Turnip mud-beetle.   See Holophorus
  rugosus.

Turnips.
    sa Rutabaga.
       Brassica.
 --Breeding.
    xx Vegetables. Breeding.
 --Composition.
    xx Vegetables. Composition.
 --Diseases.
    sa Clubroot of turnips.
       Mosaic disease of turnips.
       Black rot of turnips.
 --Effect on butter.   See Butter. Effect
    of turnips.
 --Effect on milk.   See Milk. Effect of
    turnips.
 --Grading and standardization.
    xx Vegetables. Grading and stand-
       ardization.
 --Marketing.
    xx Vegetables. Marketing.
 --Pests.
    sa Phyllotreta nemorum.
       Rhopalosiphum pseudobrassicae.
 --Seed.
 -- --Composition.

Turnips as feeding stuff.

Turnips as food.
    xx Sauer rüben.

Turnover of employees.   See Labor turnover.

Turnover of labor.   See Labor turnover.

Turnus butterfly.   See Papilio glaucus.

Turpentine.
    sa Terebinthaceae.
       Wood turpentine.
       Naval stores.
    x Turpentine orcharding.
       Turpentining.
 --Analysis.
 --Legislation.
 --Periodicals.
 --Societies.
 --Specific gravity.
    xx Specific gravity.
 --Statistics.

Turpentine, Uses of.

Turpentine borer.   See Buprestis apri-
  cans.

Turpentine oil.
    x Oil of turpentine.
       Spirits of turpentine.

Turpentine orcharding.   See Turpentine.

Turpentine stills.
    xx Distilling apparatus.

Turpentine timber.

Turpentining.   See Turpentine.

Turquino, Pico.
    x Pico Turquino.

Turrialba, Costa Rica.
 --Agriculture.
 --Population.
 --Social conditions.

Turribaicaliinae.
    xx Helicidae.

Turricaspiinae.
    xx Helicidae.

Tursiops.

Turtle Mountain, Frank, Alberta.
    xx Alberta.

Turtle Mountain Forest Reservation.

Turtles.
--Bibliography.
--Parasites.

Turtles, Fossil.

Turtles as food.

Turtur risorius.

Tusayan National Forest, Ariz.

Tusayan religion.

Tuscan Archipelago.

Tuscany.
--Agriculture.
    sa Subdivision Tuscany under:
        Agriculture. Economic as-
            pects.
        Agricultural laborers.
        Reclamation of land.
-- --Congresses.
--Botany.
    sa Subdivision Tuscany under:
        Trees.
        Botany, Medical.
--Commerce.
--Entomology.
--Forestry.
--Geography.
    sa Subdivision Tuscany under:
        Geography, Economic.
--Industries.
--Natural history.
--Paleobotany.
--Statistics.

Tuscarawas Co., Ohio.
--Soils.
    sa Subdivision Ohio. Tuscarawas
        Co. under: Soil-surveys.

Tuscola Co., Mich.
--Soils.
    sa Subdivision Michigan. Tuscola
        Co. under: Soil-surveys.

Tusks.

Tussac grass.   See Poa flabellata.

Tussock grass.   See Poa flabellata.

Tussock moths.   See Hemerocampa; Notolo-
    phus.

Tussore silk moth.   See Antheraea
    pernyi.

Tutira, New Zealand.
--Ornithology.

Tutu.   See Coriaria.

Tutuila.
--Natural history.

Tuva Autonomous Region.
--Bibliography.
--Botany.

Tver, Russia.
--Entomology.
    sa Subdivision Russia. Tver under:
        Butterflies.

Tvorchestvo Collective Farm.
    xx Collective farms.

Tweedale, Scot.
--Agriculture.

Twentieth century.

Twenty-eight hour law.

Twig-borer.   See Anarsia lineatella.

Twig pruner.   See Hypermallus villosus.

Twigs as feeding stuff.

Twilight.

Twin Falls Canal Co.

Twin Falls Co., Idaho.
--Agriculture.
    sa Subdivision Idaho. Twin Falls
        Co. under: Agriculture.
            Economic aspects.
        Agricultural conservation
            program.

Twine.   See Cordage.

Twining of plants.
    sa Climbing plants.

Twins.
     sa Free-martins.

Twist, Ark.
--Agriculture.
     sa Subdivision Twist under:
          Rural rehabilitation.
          Arkansas.

2, 4-D.   See Dichlorophenoxyacetic acid,
     2, 4-.

2,4,5-T.   See Trichlorophenoxyacetic
     acid, 2,4,5-.

Two Mountains Co., Que.
--Soils.
     sa Subdivision Quebec (Province)
          Two Mountains Co. under:
          Soil-surveys.

Two price system.
     sa Food commodity stamps.
          Cotton commodity stamps.

Two-spotted mite.   See Tetranychus bi-
     maculatus.

Two-spotted red spider.   See Tetranychus
     bimaculatus.

Tyan-Shan Mountains.   See Celestial-Shan
     Mountains.

Tychea phaseoli.
     xx Aphididae.

Tychius.
     xx Curculionidae.

Tychius picirostris.
     x Clover head weevil.
          Clover seed weevil.
     xx Clover. Pests.

Tydeidae.

Tydeus molestus.

Tygart River Reservoir Dam, W.Va.
     xx Dams.

Tylenchus.
     xx Anguillulidae.
          Nematoda.

Tylenchus angustus.

Tylenchus devastatrix.

Tylenchus devastatrix Kühn.

Tylenchus dipsaci.

Tylenchus hordei.

Tylenchus pratensis.

Tylenchus scandens.

Tylenchus similis.

Tylenchus tritici.
     x Anguillula tritici.

Tyler, Tex.
--Markets.

Tylidae.

Tyloses.

Tylostomeae.

Tympanal organ.

Tympanis pinastri.

Tympanites.
     sa Bloat in cattle.
          Bloat in ruminants.
     xx Stomach. Diseases.
          Intestines. Diseases.

Tympanuchus cupido.   See Prairie-hens.

Tympanuchus cupido cupido.   See Heath
     hen.

Tyne River region, Eng.
     sa Subdivision Tyne River region,
          Eng. under: Planning,
          Regional.

Type and type-founding.
     sa Composition (Printing)
     xx Composition (Printing)

Type-setting.   See Composition
     (Printing)

Type species.

Type-writers.
 sa Varitypers.
  Teletypewriters.
  Typists.
 x Typewriters.
 xx Office supplies.
  Typists.

Type-writing.
 x Typing.
  Typewriting.

Types of farming. (INDIRECT)
 Whenever used with a geographical
  subdivision, indicate a see
  also ref. from name of place
  with subdivision Agriculture.
 x Kinds of farming.
 xx Farm management.
--Bibliography.

Typewriters. See Type-writers.

Typewriting. See Type-writing.

Typha.

Typha latifolia.

Typhaceae.
 sa Sparganium.
  Typha.

Typhlocyba.
 xx Leaf-hoppers.

Typhlocyba comes. See Erythroneura
 comes.

Typhlocyba rosae.
 x Rose leaf-hopper.

Typhlocybidae.

Typhlocybinae.

Typhoid fever.
 --Preventive inoculation.

Typhoons.
 --Effect on rice.

Typhus. See Typhus fever.

Typhus fever.
 sa Murrine typhus.
 x Typhus.
--Bibliography.
--Congresses.

Typing. See Type-writing.

Typists.
 sa Type-writers.

Typography. See Printing.

Typophorus.
 xx Chrysomelidae.

Typophorus viridicyaneus.
 x Sweet potato leaf beetle.

Typotheria.

Typus gilmorei.

Tyrannidae.
 sa Myiarchus.
  Contopus.

Tyroglyphidae.
 sa Glyciphagus.
  Tyroglyphus.
 xx Acarina.

Tyroglyphus.

Tyrol.
 --Agriculture.
  xx Austria. Agriculture.
 --Botany.
  xx Austria. Botany.
 --Cattle.
  xx Cattle.
 --Entomology.
  sa Subdivision Tyrol under:
   Diptera.
   Lepidoptera.
   Orthoptera.
   Coleoptera.
 --Forestry.
  sa Alps, The. Forestry.
  xx Austria. Forestry.
 . --History.

Tyrol (Continued)
--Land.
    sa Subdivision Austria. Tyrol
        under: Land utilization.
--Maps.
--Natural history.
    xx Austria. Natural history.
--Paleobotany.
    xx Austria. Paleobotany.
--Paleontology.
--Pomology.
--Social conditions.
--Soils.
--Viticulture.
--Zoology.
    sa Subdivision Tyrol under:
        Arachnida.
-- --Bibliography.

Tyrone, Ireland (County)
--Agriculture.

Tyrophagus.
    xx Acarina.

Tyrophagus lintneri.
    x Mushroom mite.
    xx Mushrooms. Pests.

Tyrosin.

Tyrosinase.

Tyrothricin.
    xx Antibiotics.

Tyrrell Co., N.C.
    sa Subdivision Tyrrell Co., N.C.
        under: Consumers' coopera-
          tion.
        Credit unions.

Tyumen Region.
--Forestry.

U-H-F radio. See Radio, Short wave.

Ubangi-Shari.
--Botany.
    xx Africa, French Equatorial.
        Botany.

Ubaye Valley, France.
--Agriculture.

Ubaye Valley, France (Continued)
--Forestry.
    sa Subdivision France. Ubaye
        Valley under: Afforestation
        and reforestation.

Ucuhuba. See Virola surinamensis.

Udder.
    xx Mammary gland.
--Bacteriology.
--Diseases.
    sa Mastitis.
    Galactophoritis.

Udine, Italy (City)

Udine, Italy (Province)
    x Friuli, Italy (Province)
--Agriculture.
    sa Subdivision Italy. Udine
        (Province) under:
        Irrigation.
        Agriculture. Economic
          aspects.
-- --Periodicals.
-- --Statistics.
--Botany.
--Cattle.
--Description and travel.
--Economic conditions.
--Sericulture.
--Soils.
--Statistics.

Udo.
--Diseases.
    xx Vegetable pathology.

Ufa (Government)
--Agriculture.
    sa Subdivision Ufa (Government)
        under: Colonization, Agri-
        cultural. Russia.
-- --Statistics.

Uganda.
    xx Africa.

Uganda (Continued)
--Agriculture.
    sa Subdivision Uganda under:
        Cotton.
        Agricultural surveys.
        Agriculture. Economic
          aspects.
        Agricultural policies and
          programs.
        Coffee.
-- --Periodicals.
--Botany.
    sa Subdivision Uganda under:
        Trees.
        Shrubs.
--Commerce.
    sa Subdivision Uganda under:
        Cotton trade.
-- --Periodicals.
-- --Statistics.
--Description and travel.
    xx Africa. Description and travel.
--Economic conditions.
--Economic history.
--Economic policy.
--Entomology.
    sa Subdivision Uganda under:
        Entomology, Economic.
    xx Africa. Entomology.
--Forest reservations.
--Forestry.
    sa Subdivision Uganda under:
        Trees.
        Timber.
        War and forestry (1939-1945)
        Lumber trade.
-- --Research.
--Geography.
--Industries.
-- --Directories.
-- --Periodicals.
--Land.
    sa Subdivision Uganda under:
        Land tenure.
--Natural history.
    xx Africa. Natural history.
--Ornithology.
    xx Africa, British East. Orni-
        thology.
--Soils.
    sa Subdivision Uganda under:
        Soil erosion.
        Soil conservation.
        Soil-surveys.

Uganda (Continued)
--Statistics.
    sa Subdivision Statistics under:
        Uganda. Commerce.
--Surveys.

Uganda Railway.

Ugimya sericaria.

Ugly-nest caterpillar.   See Archips
    cerasivorana.

Uintah Co., Utah.
    xx Utah.
--Agriculture.
    sa Subdivision Utah. Uintah Co.
        under: Irrigation.
--Water-supply.

Uinta Co., Wyo.
--Soils.
    sa Subdivision Wyoming. Uinta Co.
        under: Soil-surveys.

Uinta Mountains, Utah.
--Geology.
--Zoology.

Uinta National Forest, Utah.

Uitenhage, South Africa (District)
--Botany.

Ukermünde.   See Uckermünde.

Ukhtomskii district.
--Agriculture.
    sa Subdivision Ukhtomskii
        district under:
        Potatoes.
        Vegetable gardening.

Ukraina Collective Farm.
    xx Collective farms.

Ukraine.
--Agricultural experiment station.
    sa Drabovskaia sel'skokhoziaist-
        vennaia opytnaia stantsiia.

Ukraine (Continued)
--Agriculture.
 sa Subdivision Ukraine under:
  Agriculture. Economic as-
   pects.
  Sugar-beet.
  Agricultural policies and
   programs.
  Maize.
  Cropping systems.
  Farm management.
  Agriculture, Cooperative.
  Agricultural credit.
  Cereals.
  Forage plants.
  Grasses.
  Potatoes.
  Poultry.
  Mechanized farming.
  Field crops.
  Drug plants.
  Reclamation of land.
  Irrigation farming.
  Subdivision Agriculture under:
   Melitopol region.
-- --Bibliography.
-- --Education.
-- --History.
 sa Subdivision Agriculture. His-
  tory under: Melitopol
   region.
 - --Maps.
-- --Periodicals.
-- --Statistics.
--Apiculture.
-- --Research.
--Bibliography.
--Botany.
 sa Subdivision Ukraine under:
  Vegetable pathology.
  Lichens.
  Trees.
  Oleaginous plants.
  Botany, Medical.
  Subdivision Botany under names
   of regions, etc.
-- --Bibliography.
 xx Botany. Bibliography.
-- --Research.
--Cattle.
 xx Ukraine. Domestic animals.
--Climate.
--Commerce.
 sa Subdivision Ukraine under:
  Farm produce. Marketing.

Ukraine (Continued)
--Dairying.
--Domestic animals.
 sa Subdivision Ukraine under:
  Swine.
-- --History and origin.
-- --Research.
--Economic conditions.
--Economic policy.
 xx U.S.S.R. Economic policy.
--Entomology.
 sa Subdivision Ukraine under:
  Entomology, Economic.
  Coleoptera.
  Trees. Pests.
--Famines.
--Forestry.
 sa Subdivision Ukraine under:
  Trees.
  Lumbering.
  Forest policy.
  Silviculture.
  Afforestation and re-
   forestation.
--Geography.
-- --Research.
--Geology.
--History.
 xx U.S.S.R. History.
--Horse.
--Industries.
-- --Statistics.
--Land.
 sa Subdivision Ukraine under:
  Land utilization.
--Maps.
--Meteorology.
--Natural history.
--Paleobotany.
--Parks.
--Physical geography.
--Pomology.
 sa Subdivision Pomology under:
  Volhynia.
  Subdivision Ukraine under:
   Citrus.
--Prices.
--Research.
--Sericulture.
--Sheep.
--Social conditions.
 sa Subdivision Social conditions
  under: Melitopol region.

Ukraine (Continued)
--Soils.
    sa Subdivision Soils under:
       Kief (Government)//
      Subdivision Ukraine under:
       Soil erosion. Prevention
       and control.
--Statistics.
    sa Ukraine. Agriculture. Sta-
      tistics.
--Swine.
    xx Ukraine. Domestic animals.
--Viticulture.
--Water-supply.
    sa Subdivision Ukraine under:
      Water, Underground.
--Zoology.
    sa Subdivision Ukraine under:
      Mammalia.
- --Research.

Ukrainian language.
    x Ruthenian language.
--Dictionaries.

Ukrainian literature.
--Bibliography.

Ukrainian newspapers.

Ukrainian periodicals.
--Bibliography.

Ukrainian Red cattle.   See Red German
  cattle.

Ukrainian White Head cattle.
    xx Cattle, Breeds.

Ulex europaeus.

Ulidiidae.

Ulithi, Caroline Islands.
    xx Caroline Islands.

Ullage.

Ullucus.

Ulm.
--Milk supply.
    xx Germany. Milk supply.

Ulmaceae.

Ulmin compounds.

Ulmus americana.
--Pests.

Ulmus campestris.

Ulmus glabra.

Ulmus glabra var.
    x Augustine ascending elm.
      Wych elm.

Ulmus montana.

Ulmus pubescens.

Uloborus geniculatus.

Ulota.

Ulothricaceae.

Ulster.
--Agriculture.
    sa Subdivision Ulster under:
      Agriculture, Cooperative.
      Northern Ireland.
--Botany.
--Land.
    sa Subdivision Northern Ireland.
      Ulster under: Land utiliza-
      tion.

Ulster Co., N.Y.
    xx New York (State)
--Agriculture.
-- --Periodicals.
--Soils.
    sa Subdivision New York (State)
      Ulster Co. under: Soil-
      surveys.

Ultracentrifuges.   See Centrifuges.

Ultra-high-frequency radio.   See Radio,
  Short wave.

Ultra high frequency waves.
--Effect on insects.
    x Short waves.
    xx Entomology, Economic.
      Radioactivity.

Ultramarine.

Ultramicroscopic objects.

Ultra-microscopy.　See Ultramicroscopic
objects.

Ultra-red spectrum.　See Spectrum, Infra-
red.

Ultra-short wave radio.　See Radio, Short
wave.

Ultrasonic testing.
　　xx Testing.
　　　Ultrasonics.

Ultrasonic waves.
　--Effect on animals.
　--Physiological effect.
　--Therapeutic use.

Ultrasonic waves as an antiseptic.

Ultrasonics.
　　sa Ultrasonic testing.
　　x Supersonics.
　　xx Vibration.
　--Bibliography.

Ultra-violet photography.　See Photography, Ultra-violet.

Ultra-violet rays.
　　sa Spectrum, Ultra-violet.
　　　Bees. Effect of ultra-violet
　　　　rays on.
　　　Mitogenetic rays.
　　xx Radiant heating.
　--Effect on domestic animals.
　　x Domestic animals, Effect of
　　　ultra-violet rays on.
　--Effect on insects.
　　xx Light. Effect on insects.
　--Effect on micro-organisms.
　　xx Micro-organisms.
　--Effect on plants.
　　xx Light. Effect on plants.
　--Effect on poultry.
　　x Poultry. Effect of ultra-
　　　violet rays on.
　　xx Light. Effect on poultry.

Ultuna landtbruksinstitut.

Ulu de la coca.　See Eloria noyesi.

Ulva.

Ulva latissima.

Ulvaceae.

Ulvella.
　　sa Dermatophyton.

Umatilla Dam.
　　xx Dams.

Umatilla Experiment Farm.　See Umatilla
reclamation project. Experiment farm.

Umatilla irrigation project.　See
Umatilla reclamation project.

Umatilla Rapids.

Umatilla reclamation project.
　　x Umatilla irrigation project.

Umatilla reclamation project. Experiment
farm.
　　x Umatilla Experiment Farm.
　　xx Agricultural experiment farms.

Umbelliferae.
　　sa Physocaulos.
　　　Bupleurum.
　　　Carum.
　　　Harperella.
　　　Ferula.
　　　Hydrocotyle.
　　　Heracleum.
　　　Cymopterus.
　　　Anthriscus.
　　　Zizia.
　　　Leptotaenia.
　　　Endressia.
　　　Deringa.
　　　Cryptotaenia.
　　　Levisticum officinale.
　　x Ammiaceae.
　　　Apiaceae.

Umbellula.

Umbellularia californica Nutt.

Umbilicariaceae.　See Gyrophoraceae.

Umbilicus.
　　x Umbilical cord.

Umbrella ants. See Atta.

Umbria.
--Agriculture.
    sa Subdivision Umbria under:
      Agricultural laborers.
      Agriculture. Economic as-
        pects.

Umea, Sweden.
--Forestry.
    sa Subdivision Sweden. Umea under:
      Timber.
    xx Sweden. Forestry.

Umpqua Basin. See Umpqua Valley.

Umpqua National Forest, Or.
    xx Oregon. Forest reservations.

Umpqua Valley.
--Water-supply.

Un-American propaganda. See Propaganda,
    Un-American.

Unaka National Forest.

Uncinaria.
    x Anchylostoma.
      Ancylostoma.
      Hookworm.

Uncinaria americana.
    sa Uncinariasis.
    x Hookworm larva.

Uncinaria brasiliense.

Uncinariasis.
    x Ankylostomiasis.
--Bibliography.

Uncinula.

Uncinula necator.
    x Oidium tuckeri.

Uncompahgre irrigation project.

Uncompahgre National Forest, Colo.
    xx Colorado. Forest reservations.

Uncompahgre Valley.
--Agriculture.

Uncompahgre Valley irrigation project.

Uncooked food. See Food, Uncooked.

Underground water. See Water, Under-
    ground.

Underdeveloped areas.
    x Backward areas.
    xx Economic development.
      Technical assistance program.
      Economic assistance.
      Economic conditions.
      Industrialization.

Undernutrition. See Malnutrition.

Underpinning. See Shoring and under-
    pinning.

Underwear.
    sa Garment cutting.
      Corset.
--Periodicals.
--Statistics.

Undulant fever.
    sa Brucella melitensis.
      Brucella.
      Brucella abortus.
    x Malta fever.
      Mediterranean fever.
      Brucellosis in man.
    xx Brucella abortus.
      Brucella.
      Brucella melitensis.
--Abstracts.
--Diagnosis.
    xx Diagnosis.

Unearned increment.

Unemployed. (DIRECT)
    sa Employment exchanges.
      Insurance, Employment.
      Business depression.
      Right to labor.
      Work camps.
      Unemployment and roads.
      Public works as relief
        measure.
      Employment.
      Labor turnover.
      Labor supply.
      Public welfare.

Unemployed. (Continued)
    xx Employment.
--U.S.
        This subject is to be used for
        general works on unemployment.
        For road building or, public
        works for the unemployed see
        Unemployment and roads and
        Public works as relief measure.
        This system will be used for
        state and local publications
        also.
--Bibliography.
    sa Unemployed. U.S. Bibliography.
-- --Periodicals.
    xx Economics. Bibliography. Peri-
        odicals.
--Congresses.
    sa Unemployed. Argentine Republic.
       Congresses.
--Relief work. See Relief work.
--Statistics.
        Used only for general statistics.
        For statistics of a special
        country see Unemployed with
        country subdivision, as Unem-
        ployed. U.S.

Unemployment. See Unemployed.

Unemployment, Seasonal.   (DIRECT)
    sa Subdivision Annual wage under:
       Wages.
    x Seasonal unemployment.

Unemployment, Technological.
    x Technological unemployment.

Unemployment and public works. See
    Public works as relief measure.

Unemployment and roads.
    xx Public works as relief measure.
       Roads.

Unemployment benefit plans. See In-
    surance, Unemployment.

Unemployment compensation. See In-
    surance, Unemployment.

Unemployment insurance. See Insurance,
    Unemployment.

Unemployment relief. See Relief work.

Unemployment reserves. See Insurance,
    Unemployment.

Unfair competition. See Competition,
    Unfair.

Unfair trade practices. See Competition,
    Unfair.

Unfederated Malay States. See Malay
    States, Unfederated.

Unfermented wines. See Wines, Un-
    fermented.

Ungarisch-Altenburg. See Altenburg.
    Hungary.

Ungava. See New Quebec.

Unguents. See Fats and oils; Ointments.

Ungulata.
    sa Names of ungulate animals,
        e.g., Camels; Deer; Horses.
    x Herbivora.
--Feeding.

Ungulata, Fossil.
    sa Leptauchenia.
       Preptoceras.
       Euceratherium.

Unicellular organisms.
    sa Protozoa.
       Coenobic plants.
    x Protistology.
       Protista.
    xx Micro-organisms.
--Periodicals.

Unicorn.

Unicorn plant. See Martynia louisiana.

Uniform grain storage agreement.
    sa Rice. Storage.
    xx Contracts, Agricultural.

Uniform rice storage agreement.
    xx Uniform grain storage agree-
       ment.

Uniform state laws.
    sa Interstate agreements.

Uniforms.
    xx Clothing and dress.

Uniforms, Military.
    x Uniforms, Naval.
    Clothing and dress, Military.

Uniforms, Naval. See Uniforms, Military.

Union catalogs. See Catalogs, Union.

Union City, Tenn.
--Economic conditions.
    sa Subdivision Tennessee. Union
        City under: Economic surveys.

Union Co., Ga.
--Soils.
    sa Subdivision Georgia. Union Co.
        under: Soil-surveys.

Union Co., Ill.
--Agriculture.
-- --Periodicals.

Union Co., Ind.
--Agriculture.
-- --Periodicals.
--Soils.
    sa Subdivision Indiana. Union Co.
        under: Soil-surveys.

Union Co., Iowa.
--Geology.
--Soils.
    sa Subdivision Iowa. Union Co.
        under: Peat.
        Soil-surveys.

Union Co., Miss.
--Bibliography.
    xx Mississippi. Bibliography.

Union Co., N.J.
--Botany.

Union Co., N.M.
    xx New Mexico.

Union Co., Ohio.
    sa Subdivision Union Co. under:
        County surveys. Ohio.
    xx Ohio.
--Social conditions.

Union Co., Pa.
--Soils.
    sa Subdivision Pennsylvania.
        Union Co. under: Soil-
        surveys.

Union Co., S.C.
--Economic conditions.
--Social conditions.
    sa Subdivision South Carolina.
        Union Co. under: Social
        surveys.

Union Co., Tenn.
    sa Subdivision Tennessee. Union
        Co. under: County surveys.
    xx Tennessee.
--Economic conditions.
--Social conditions.
    sa Subdivision Tennessee. Union
        Co. under: Social surveys.

Union lists. See Catalogs, Union.

Union lists of serials. See Periodicals.
    Bibliography. Union lists.

U.S.S.R.
    Used for subjects concerning
        Soviet Russia (1923-   ) For
        subjects concerning the
        Russian Empire (to Mar. 1917)
        the provisional governments
        (Mar. 1917-1922) and the
        Russian Socialist Federated
        Soviet Republic (RSFSR) use
        Russia.
--Agricultural experiment stations.
    sa Subdivision Agricultural ex-
        periment stations under:
        Russia.
--Agriculture.
    sa Subdivision Agriculture under:
        Russia.
        Georgian Republic.
        Turkmenistan//
        Collective farming.
        Machine tractor stations
        (Russian)
        State farms (U.S.S.R.)
        Travopol'naia sistema zemle-
        deliia.

2241

U.S.S.R. (Continued)
--Agriculture.
 sa Subdivision U.S.S.R. under:
  Agriculture. Economic as-
   pects.
  Rice.
  Colonization, Agricultural.
  Agricultural laborers.
  Maize.
  Tobacco.
  Flax.
  Farm buildings.
  Sugar-beet.
  Poultry.
  War and agriculture (1939-
   1945)
  Ranges.
  Mechanized farming.
  Agricultural policies and
   programs.
  Grassland farming.
  Tea.
  Types of farming.
  Hemp.
  Onions.
  Soy-bean.
  Drug plants.
  Rye.
  Grasses.
  Agricultural extension.
  Agricultural industries.
  Crops and climate.
  Cropping systems.
  Agricultural administration.
  Irrigation farming.
--Bibliography.
 sa Subdivision Agriculture. Bib-
  liography under: Ukraine.
  Russia//
  Subdivision Bibliography under:
   Collective farming.
-- --Congresses.
-- -- --Bibliography.
-- --Education.
 sa Subdivision U.S.S.R. under:
  Agricultural extension.
- --History.
 sa Subdivision Agriculture. His-
  tory under: Russia.
  Ukraine.
  White Russia.
- - --Maps.
-- --Periodicals.

U.S.S.R. (Continued)
--Agriculture.
-- --Statistics.
 sa Subdivision Agriculture. Sta-
  tistics under: Russia.
  Caucasus.
  Subdivision Statistics under:
   Collective farming.
   Farm produce. U.S.S.R.
--Apiculture.
 sa Subdivision Apiculture under:
  Ural Region.
  Siberia//
-- --Bibliography.
-- --Education.
-- --Periodicals.
-- --Research.
--Bibliography.
 sa Subdivision Bibliography under:
  Nova Zembla.
--Bio-bibliography.
--Biography.
-- --Dictionaries.
--Botanic gardens.
--Botany.
 sa Subdivision Botany under:
  Russia.
  Volkhof Valley.
  Lake Ilmen Region.
  Yakut Republic//
  Subdivision U.S.S.R. under:
   Botany, Economic.
   Vegetable pathology.
   Weeds.
   Shrubs.
   Mushrooms.
   Plants, Cultivated.
   Fungi.
   Honey-bearing plants.
   Botany, Medical.
   Food plants.
   Poisonous plants.
   Algae.
-- --Bibliography.
 sa Subdivision Botany. Bibliog-
  raphy under: East (Far
  East//
-- --History.
-- --Research.
--Camels.
--Cattle.
 sa Subdivision Cattle under:
  Yakut Republic.
  Caucasus.
  Siberia//

U.S.S.R. (Continued)
--Cattle.
-- --Bibliography.
-- --Periodicals.
--Census.
  sa Subdivision Census under:
    White Russia//
--Civilization.
--Climate.
  sa Subdivision Climate under
    various regions, etc.,
    e.g., Kazakstan. Climate.
  Subdivision U.S.S.R. under:
    Crops and climate.
--Commerce.
  sa U.S.S.R. Commercial treaties.
  Subdivision U.S.S.R. under:
    Farm produce. Marketing.
    Oil-seed trade.
- --U.S.
-- --Periodicals.
  sa Subdivision Commerce. Periodi-
    cals under: Transcaucasia.
    Ukraine.
  xx Europe. Commerce. Periodicals.
-- --Statistics.
  sa Subdivision Commerce. Sta-
    tistics under: Russia.
--Commercial policy.
--Constitution.
  x Stalin constitution.
--Constitutional history.
--Cyclopedias.
--Dairying.
  sa Subdivision U.S.S.R. under:
    Dairy industry and trade.
  Subdivision Dairying under
    names of regions, republics,
    etc.
--Description and travel.
--Domestic animals.
  sa Subdivision Domestic animals
    under names of various
    republics, regions, etc.
  U.S.S.R. Cattle.
  U.S.S.R. Horse.
  U.S.S.R. Goats.
  Subdivision U.S.S.R. under:
    Ranges.
    Swine.
-- --Addresses, essays, lectures.
-- --Bibliography.
-- --Legislation.
-- --Periodicals.
- --Research.

U.S.S.R. (Continued)
--Domestic animals.
-- --Statistics.
  xx Domestic animals. Statistics.
--Economic conditions.
  sa Subdivision Economic condi-
    tions under: Russia.
    Turkestan//
  Subdivision U.S.S.R. under:
    Geography, Economic.
    World War, 1939-1945. Eco-
    nomic aspects.
    History, Economic.
    Economic surveys.
-- --Bibliography.
-- --Periodicals.
  sa Subdivision Economic condi-
    tions. Periodicals under:
    Asia, Central.
    Turkmenistan.
--Economic policy.
  sa Subdivision Economic policy
    under: Russia.
  U.S.S.R. Commercial policy.
-- --Five-year plan (1928-1932)
  xx Planning, National.
-- --Five-year plan, Second (1933-1937)
-- --Five-year plan, Third (1938-1942)
  xx Planning, National.
-- --Five-year plan, Fourth (1946-1950)
  x First postwar five-year plan.
    Fourth Stalin five-year plan.
    Stalin five-year plan.
-- --Five-year plan, Fifth (1951-1955)
-- --Five-year plan, Sixth (1956-1960)
-- --Seven-year plan (1959-1965)
-- --Three-year plan (1949-1951)
--Education.
--Emigration and immigration.
--Entomology.
  sa Subdivision Entomology under:
    Russia.
    Uzbekistan.
    Turkmenistan//
  Subdivision U.S.S.R. under:
    Entomology, Economic.
    Trees. Pests.
    Locusts.
-- --Bibliography.
  sa Subdivision Entomology. Bib-
    liography under: Russia.
-- --Dictionaries.
-- --Periodicals.

U.S.S.R. (Continued)
--Finance.
 sa Russia. Finance.
  Credit. U.S.S.R.
--Fisheries.
 sa Subdivision Fisheries under:
  Murman Coast.
--Foreign relations.
 x Russia. Foreign relations.
-- --East (Far East)
-- --Europe, Western.
-- --U.S.
--Forest reservations.
 xx U.S.S.R. Forestry.
--Forestry.
 sa Subdivision Forestry under:
  Russia.
  Caucasus.
  White Russia//
  Subdivision U.S.S.R. under:
  Forest surveys.
  Forest industries.
  Timber.
  Forest fires.
  Forest fires. Prevention.
  Lumber.
  Lumbering.
  Forest policy.
  Forest reservations.
  Afforestation and reforesta-
   tion.
  Tree planting.
  Forest products.
  Silviculture.
-- --Congresses.
- --History.
-- --Periodicals.
-- --Research.
-- --Statistics.
 sa Subdivision Forestry. Sta-
  tistics under: Russia.
  Yakut Republic.
--Geographic names.
--Geography.
 sa Subdivision U.S.S.R. under:
  Geography, Economic.
  Geography, Historical.
  Subdivision Geography under
   names of republics, etc.
-- --Bibliography.
--Geology.
-- --Bibliography.
 xx Europe. Geology. Bibliography.

U.S.S.R. Glavzagotsortzerno.

U.S.S.R.
--Goats.
 xx U.S.S.R. Domestic animals.
--Government publications.
-- --Bibliography.
--Grain trade.
 sa Grain trade. Russia.
--History.
 sa Subdivision History under:
  Russia.
  Ukraine.
  Subdivision U.S.S.R. under:
  History, Economic.
  Geography, Historical.
  History, Economic. Russia.
-- --Chronology.
-- --Revolution.
 x Revolution, Russian.
--Horse.
 sa Subdivision Horse under:
  Asia, Central//
  Subdivision U.S.S.R. under:
  Horses. Breeding.
-- --History.
--Ichthyology.
-- --Research.
--Industries.
 sa Subdivision U.S.S.R. under:
  Agricultural industries.
  Subdivision Industries under
   the Republics and regions
   of the USSR; e.g.,Moldavian.
   Republic. Industries.
--Land.
 sa Subdivision U.S.S.R. under:
  Land reform.
  Land. Classification.
  Subdivision Land under names
   of republics, etc.
--Learned institutions and societies.
 xx Europe. Learned institutions
  and societies.
--Libraries.
 sa Names of special libraries,
  e.g., Saratov. Gosudarst-
  vennyi universitet. Nauch-
  naia biblioteka.
  Subdivision Libraries under
   names of cities.
-- --Directories.
--Manufactures.
--Maps.
 sa Subdivision Maps under:
  Russia.
  Siberia//

U.S.S.R. (Continued)
--Markets.

U.S.S.R. Mashino-traktornaia stantsiia.
See Machine tractor stations (Russian)

U.S.S.R.
--Meteorology.
    sa Subdivision Meteorology under
      names of countries, regions,
      etc.
--Milk supply.
--Milk trade.
--Natural history.
    sa Subdivision Natural history
      under: White Russia.
      Primorskaia (Province)
      Kazakstan//
-- --Bibliography.
--Ornithology.
    sa Subdivision Ornithology under:
      Russia.
      Tiumen//
      Subdivision U.S.S.R. under:
      Game-birds.
--Paleobotany.
--Paleontology.
    xx Paleontology.
--Parks.
--Periodicals. See Russian periodicals.
--Physical geography.
    sa Subdivision Physical geography
      under: Transcaucasia//
    xx Europe. Physical geography.
--Politics and government.
    sa Subdivision U.S.S.R. under:
      Administrative and politi-
      cal divisions.
-- --Bibliography.
--Pomology.
    sa Subdivision Pomology under:
      Russia.
      Caucasus.
      Georgia (Transcaucasia)//
      Subdivision U.S.S.R. under:
      Berries.
      Citrus.
      Orange.
-- --Bibliography.
-- --Study and teaching.
--Population.
    sa Subdivision U.S.S.R. under:
      Rural population.
      Migration, Internal.
    xx Europe. Population.

U.S.S.R. (Continued)
--Prices.
    sa Subdivision Prices under:
      Ukraine.
--Railroads.
--Research.
    xx Research.
-- --Periodicals.
--Rewards (Prizes, etc.)
--Roads.
    sa Subdivision Roads under:
      Russia.
-- --Maps.
--Sericulture.
    sa Subdivision Sericulture under:
      Transcaucasia.
      Caucasus.
    xx Asia. Sericulture.
      Europe. Sericulture.
--Sheep.
    sa Subdivision Sheep under:
      Russia.
      Uzbekistan.
      Tadzhikistana//
--Social conditions.
    sa Subdivision Social conditions
      under: Russia.
      Ukraine.
--Soils.
    sa Subdivision Soils under:
      Russia.
      Volkhof Valley.
      Transbaikalia//
      Subdivision U.S.S.R. under:
      Peat.
      Soil erosion. Prevention
      and control.
      Soil conservation.
--Statistics.
    sa Subdivision Statistics under:
      Russia.
      White Russia.
      Irkutsk//
--Swine.
    xx U.S.S.R. Domestic animals.
--Transportation.
-- --Statistics.
--Viticulture.
    sa Subdivision Viticulture
      under: Azerbaijan.
      Caucasus//
-- --Bibliography.
-- --Periodicals.
 - --Research.

U.S.S.R. (Continued)
--Water-supply.
    sa Subdivision Water-supply under
       names of regions, etc.
       Water, Underground.
--Zoology.
    sa Subdivision Zoology under:
       Russia.
       Daghestan.
       White Russia//
       Subdivision U.S.S.R. under:
       Mammalia.
       Fur-bearing animals.
       Fresh-water fauna.
       Marine fauna.
       Game.
- --Research.

U.S.S.R., Arctic.
--Agriculture.
    sa Subdivision U.S.S.R., Arctic
       under: Agricultural policies
       and programs.
--Botany.
    sa Subdivision U.S.S.R., Arctic
       under: Mushrooms.
--Census.
--Economic conditions.
--Industries.
-- .--Statistics.
--Natural history.
--Physical geography.
--Research.
--Soils.

U.S.S.R., Asiatic.
    x Asiatic Russia.
      Russia, Asiatic.
      Soviet Far East.
      Far eastern region, U.S.S.R.
      Russia in Asia.
--Agriculture.
    sa Subdivision U.S.S.R., Asiatic
       under: Colonization, Agri-
       cultural.
       Cereals.
       Agriculture. Economic as-
         pects.
-- --Congresses.
--Botany.
    sa Subdivision U.S.S.R., Asiatic
       under: Botany, Economic.
--Cattle.
--Economic conditions.

U.S.S.R., Asiatic (Continued)
--Entomology.
    sa Subdivision U.S.S.R., Asiatic
       under: Entomology, Economic.
--Forestry.
    sa Subdivision U.S.S.R., Asiatic
       under: Lumbering.
       Afforestation and reforest-
         ation.
-- --Research.
--Geography.
-- --Research.
--History.
--Physical geography.
--Soils.
--Viticulture.
--Zoology.

U.S.S.R. bloc.
    Here are entered works which
      deal collectively with Russia,
      the communist countries of
      Eastern Europe, and those of
      the Far East.
    x Iron curtain lands.
      Soviet bloc.
      Communist countries.
      Sino-Soviet bloc.
      Russian satellites.
      Intrabloc.
--Abstracts.
--Agriculture.
-- --Periodicals.
--Bibliography.
--Commerce.
--Economic conditions.
--Economic policy.
--Periodicals.
-- --Bibliography.
--Research.
-- --Bibliography.
--Statistics.
--Swine.

Union of Soviet Socialist Republics.
    See U.S.S.R.

Union parish, La.

Unionidae.
--Parasites.

Unionism. See Trade-unions.

United Arab Republic.
--Agriculture.
    sa Subdivision United Arab Re-
       public under: Agricultural
       policies and programs.
--Economic conditions.
    sa Subdivision United Arab Re-
       public under: Geography,
       Economic.
--Maps.

United farm women.

United Farmers of Ontario.

United Fruit Co., Boston.

United Irishwomen.

United Kingdom.　See Great Britain.

United Kingdom colonial development and
   welfare acts.

United Nations.
    xx World politics.
       World War, 1939-1945.
--Bibliography.
--Charter.
    x United nations charter.
--Directories.
--Officials and employees.
-- --Directories.
- --Pensions.
    x United Nations. Pensions.
    xx Pensions.
--Pensions.　See United Nations. Offi-
   cials and employees. Pensions.
--Periodicals.
--Privileges and immunities.
--Technical assistance.　See Technical
   assistance program.

United nations charter.　See United
   Nations. Charter.

United Nations Conference on Food and
   Agriculture, Hot Springs, Va., 1943.
    x Hot Springs Food Conference.

United Nations Relief and Rehabilitation
   Administration.
--History.

United-Otto system.　See United Coke and
   Gas Co., New York.

United Provinces of Agra and Oudh.
   Name changed in 1949 to Uttar
   Pradesh.
--Agriculture.
    sa Subdivision India. United
       Provinces of Agra and Oudh
       under: Wheat.
       Rice.
       Agricultural laborers.
       Sugar-cane.
       Cereals.
       Maize.
       Field crops.
       Subdivision United Provinces
       of Agra and Oudh under:
       Agricultural policies and
       programs.
       Cotton.
-- --Statistics.
--Domestic animals.
--Economic conditions.
--Entomology.
    sa Entomology, Economic. India.
       United Provinces of Agra
       and Oudh.
--Forestry.
    sa Subdivision United Provinces
       of Agra and Oudh under:
       Afforestation and reforesta-
       tion.
       Forest industries.
    xx India. Forestry.
--Industries and resources.
--Land.
    sa Subdivision United Provinces
       of Agra and Oudh under:
       Land. Taxation.
       Land laws.
       Land tenure.
       Land utilization.
--Social conditions.
    sa Subdivision United Provinces
       of Agra and Oudh under:
       Cost and standard of living.
    xx India. Social conditions.
--Soils.
    sa Subdivision United Provinces
       of Agra and Oudh under:
       Soil erosion. Prevention
       and control.
--Statistics.
--Veterinary services.

U.S.
   sa Names of states and territories.
    Rivers.

U.S. Agricultural Adjustment Administra-
  tion.
--Appropriations and expenditures.
   sa Benefit payments.
   xx U.S. Dept of Agriculture. Ap-
    propriations and expendi-
    tures.
--Bibliography.
--Claims and adjustments.
   xx Claims and adjustments.
   U.S. Dept.of Agriculture.
    Claims and adjustments.
--Codes. See National industrial re-
  covery act, 1933. Codes.
--Legislation.
--Officials and employees.
   xx U.S. Dept. of Agriculture.
    Officials and employees.

U.S. Bureau of Agricultural Chemistry and
  Engineering.
--Bibliography.

U.S. Bureau of Agricultural Economics.
  sa Subdivision Bibliography under:
    U.S. Bureau of Agricultural
    Economics. Division of
    Cotton Marketing.
--Division of Cotton Marketing.
-- --Bibliography.
   xx U.S. Bureau of Agricultural
    Economics. Bibliography.
--Directories.
   xx U.S. Dept of Agriculture. Em-
    ployees.
--Library.
-- --Bibliography.
--Reorganization.
   xx U.S. Executive departments.
    Reorganization.
--War work.
   xx U.S. Dept. of Agriculture. War
    work.

U.S. Agricultural experiment stations.
  sa U.S. Office of experiment sta-
    tions.
    Names of experiment stations in
    various states.

U.S. Agricultural experiment stations
  (Continued)
--Bibliography.
   sa Subdivision Agricultural Ex-
    periment Station. Bibliog-
    raphy under: Connecticut.
    Massachusetts.
    Utah//
--Legislation.
   xx Agriculture. Law.

U.S. Agricultural Marketing Administration.
--Directories.
   xx U.S. Dept. of Agriculture.
    Directories.
--Officials and employees.
   xx U.S. Dept. of Agriculture.
    Officials and employees.

U.S. Agricultural Marketing Service.
--Division of Agricultural Statistics.
-- --Directories.
   xx U.S. Agricultural Marketing
    Service. Directories.
--Bibliography.
--Directories.
   sa Subdivision Directories under:
    U.S. Agricultural Marketing
    Service. Division of
    Agricultural Statistics.
   xx U.S. Dept. of Agriculture.
    Directories.
--Officials and employees.
--Marketing Research Division.
-- --Directories.

U.S. Agricultural Research Administration.
--Field stations.

U.S. Agricultural research centers.

U.S. Agricultural Research Service.
--Advisory committees.
--Animal Inspection and Quarantine
  Branch.
-- -- Officials and employees.
--Field stations.
--Human Nutrition and Home Economics
  Research.
-- --Bibliography.
--Officials and employees.

U.S. Agricultural Stabilization and Conservation Committees.
--Appropriations and expenditures.

U.S. Office for Agricultural War
Relations.
--Officials and employees.
xx U.S. Dept. of Agriculture.
Officials and employees.

U.S.
--Agriculture.
sa Subdivision Agriculture under
state names, e.g., Connecti-
cut. Agriculture, and under
names of counties, e.g.,
Chester Co., Pa.Agriculture.
U.S. Domestic animals.
Subdivision U.S. under:
Rural surveys.
Farm produce. Cost of
production.
Part-time farming.
Cropping systems.
Agricultural surveys.
Mechanized farming.
Agricultural industries.
Market gardening.
Crop reports.
Field crops.
Grassland farming.
Agricultural outlook.
Farm organization.
Agriculture. Economic
aspects.
Gardening.
Agriculture. Cooperative.
Colonization, Agricultural.
Agricultural laborers.
Farm produce.
Farms.
Farm buildings.
Farm management surveys.
Agricultural policies and
programs.
Crops and climate.
Agricultural credit.
Reclamation of land.
Agricultural conservation
program.
-- --Bibliography.
sa U.S. Dept. of Agriculture.
Bibliography.
Subdivision U.S. Bibliography
under: Part-time farming.

U.S. (Continued)
--Agriculture.
-- --Bibliography.
sa Subdivision Agriculture. Bib-
liography under: Virginia.
New England.
Colorado//
-- --Biography.
xx Agriculture. Biography.
-- --Congresses.
-- --Directories.
sa Subdivision Agriculture.
Directories under:
Colorado.
Maryland.
Wisconsin//
-- --Education.
sa Subdivision Agriculture. Edu-
cation under: Georgia.
Minnesota.
Pennsylvania//
Land grant colleges.
xx North America. Agriculture.
Education.
-- -- --Directories.
xx U.S. Education. Directories.
-- --History.
sa Subdivision Agriculture. His-
tory under: Southern
States.
Virginia.
Minnesota//
Subdivision U.S. History
under: Agricultural credit.
Agricultural laborers.
xx North America. Agriculture.
History.
-- -- --Bibliography.
sa Subdivision Bibliography
under: Southern States.
Agriculture. History.
- --Maps.
-- --Periodicals.
x Food. Research. Periodicals.
-- --Periodicals (Works concerning)
-- --Statistics.
sa Subdivision Agriculture. Sta-
tistics under: Kansas.
New York (State)
Nebraska//
Subdivision Statistics under:·
Farm produce. U.S.
Field crops. U.S.
Agricultural laborers. U.S.
xx Agriculture. Statistics.

U.S. (Continued)
--Agriculture.
-- --Statistics.
-- -- --Bibliography.
    sa Subdivision Agriculture. Sta-
      tistics. Bibliography under:
      Alabama.
      Idaho.
      Oklahoma.
      Oregon.
      California.

U.S. Dept. of Agriculture.
--Accounting.
    sa Subdivision Accounting under:
      U.S. Agricultural Adjust-
        ment Administration.
      U.S. Forest Service.
      U.S. Rural Electrification
        Administration//
--Division of Agrostology.
-- --Bibliography.
--Appointments, etc.
--Appropriations and expenditures.
    sa Subdivision Appropriations and
      expenditures under: U.S.
      Agricultural Adjustment
      Administration.
      U.S. Bureau of Animal in-
        dustry.
      U.S. Forest Service//
      Agriculture. Appropriations
      and expenditures.
--Bibliography.
    xx Agriculture. Bibliography.
-- --Periodicals.
--Division of Botany.
-- --Bibliography.
--Buildings.
    sa County agricultural centers.
--Chemical work.
--Chicago field offices.
    xx U.S. Dept. of Agriculture.
      Field stations.
--Claims and adjustments.
    sa Subdivision Claims and
      adjustments under:
      U.S. Agricultural Adjust-
        ment Administration.
--Directories.
--Economic Research Service.
-- --Officials and employees.
--Employees. See U.S. Dept. of Agri-
    culture. Officials and employees.
--Exhibits.

U.S. Dept. of Agriculture (Continued)
--Expenditures. See U.S. Dept. of
    Agriculture. Appropriations and
    expenditures.
--Field laboratories.
    This subject used for publica-
      tions on the field labora-
      tories of all the bureaus of
      the Department. For publica-
      tions on the four Regional
      research laboratories of the
      Bureau of Agricultural and
      Industrial Chemistry see U.S.
      Regional research laboratories.
      For publications on all other
      special laboratories of the
      bureaus see the name of the
      laboratory under the bureau,
      e.g., U.S. Bureau of Animal
      Industry. Regional Poultry Re-
      search Laboratory, East
      Lansing, Mich.
--Field stations.
    sa Sacaton, Arizona. Cooperative
      Testing Station.
      U.S. Bureau of Plant Industry.
      Field stations.
      U.S. Dry Land Field Station,
      Ardmore, S.D.//
--Flag.
    xx Flags.
--History. See U.S. Dept. of Agri-
    culture.
--Office of Information.
-- --Division of Photography.
-- -- --Bibliography.
--Legislation.
    sa Subdivision Legislation under
      names of various bureaus
      of the Department.
--Library.
- --Appropriations and expenditures.
--Officials and employees.
    sa Subdivision Officials and
      employees under: U.S.
      Bureau of Animal in-
      dustry.
      U.S. Forest Service.
      U.S. Bureau of Biological
      Survey//
    x U.S. Dept. of Agriculture.
      Personnel.
    xx U.S. Dept. of Agriculture.
      Directories.

U.S. Dept. of Agriculture (Continued)
--Officials and employees.
-- --Awards. See U.S. Dept. of Agri-
culture. Officials and employee.
Rewards (Prizes, etc.)
-- --Portraits.
xx Portraits.
-- --Recruiting, enlistment, etc.
-- --Rewards (Prizes, etc.)
sa William A. Jump Memorial Award.
x U.S. Dept. of Agriculture.
Officials and employees.
Awards.
xx Rewards (Prizes, etc.)
-- --Statistics.
--Organization.
--Patents.
xx Patents.
--Personnel. See U.S. Dept. of Agri-
culture. Officials and employees.
--Public relations.
--Publications. See U.S. Dept. of
Agriculture. Bibliography.
--Records and correspondence.
--Recreational activities.
--Reorganization.
xx U.S. Executive Department.
Reorganization.
--Seal.
xx Seals (Numismatics)
--Statistical Reporting Service.
-- --Officials and employees.
--War work.
sa Subdivision War work under:
U.S. Bureau of Markets.
U.S. Forest Service.
U.S. Bureau of Agricultural
Economics//

U.S.
--Air defenses. See Air raids. Protec-
tive measures.
--Altitudes.
sa Subdivision Altitudes under:
California.
Louisiana.
New York (State)//
xx Altitudes.

U.S. Bureau of Animal Industry.
--Appointments.
--Bibliography.
--Officials and employees.
xx U.S. Dept. of Agriculture.
Officials and employees.

U.S. Bureau of Animal Industry (Continued)
--Project symbols.
--Record and correspondence files.

U.S.
--Annexation.
xx Annexation.
--Antiquities.
sa Subdivision Antiquities under:
Alaska.
Mississippi Valley.
New York (State)//
xx Archaeology.
--Apiculture.
sa Subdivision Apiculture under:
Texas.
California.
Arizona//
xx Apiculture.
--Appropriations and expenditures.
sa Subdivision Appropriations
and expenditures under:
U.S. Dept. of Agriculture.
U.S. Dept. of Commerce.
U.S. Dept. of Interior//
xx U.S. Expenditures.
--Arbitration.
--Archaeology.

U.S. Armed Forces.
--Commissariat.
--Organization.

U.S. Armed Services Technical Information
Agency.
--Bibliography.

U.S. Army.
--Artillery.
-- --Drill and tactics.
--Biography.
--Cavalry.
-- --Drill and tactics.
--Commissariat.
xx Armies. Commissariat.
--Education.
xx U.S. Education.
--Food supply.
xx U.S. Army. Supplies and stores.
--History.
-- --Civil War.
xx U.S. History. Civil War.
--Medical Service.
-- --Drill regulations.
--Organization.

U.S. Army (Continued)
--Pay, allowances, etc.
    x Soldiers. Pay, allowances, etc.
--Rations.
--Recruiting, enlistment, etc.
-- --European war, 1914-1918.
    xx European war, 1914-1918. Re-
      cruiting, enlistment, etc.
-- --World War, 1939-1945.
    sa Military service, Compulsory.
      Selective training and service
      act of 1940.
    x World War, 1939-1945. Re-
      cruiting, enlistment, etc.
    xx U.S. Selective service.
      Military service, Compulsory.
--Research.
--Sanitary affairs.
--Supplies and stores.
    sa U.S. Army. Food supply.
    xx Military supplies.
--Surgeons.
--Terminology.
--Transportation.
--Uniforms.

U.S. Atomic Energy Commission.
--Bibliography.

U.S.
--Bibliography.
--Biography.
    sa Subdivision Biography under:
      U.S. Congress.
      Eastern States.
      Iowa//
--Dictionaries.

U.S. Bureau of Biological Survey.
--Bibliography.
--Field stations.
    xx U.S. Dept. of Agriculture.
      Field stations.
--Officials and employees.
    xx U.S. Dept. of Agriculture. Em-
      ployees.

U.S.
--Botany.
    sa Subdivision Botany under:
      Arkansas.
      Black Hills.
      California//

U.S. (Continued)
--Botany.
    sa Subdivision U.S. under:
      Trees.
      Shrubs.
      Grasses.
      Forage plants.
      Botany, Economic.
      Fungi.
      Vegetable pathology.
      Algae.
      Plants, Cultivated.
      Honey-bearing plants.
      Food plants.
      Botany, Medical.
      Orchidaceae.
      Poisonous plants.
      Wild flowers.
      Palmae.
-- --Bibliography.
    sa Subdivision Botany. Bibliog-
      raphy under: Colorado.
      Texas.
      Ohio//
-- --History.
    sa Subdivision Botany. History
      under: Colorado//
--Boundaries.
    sa Subdivision Boundaries under:
      Alaska.
      California.
--Capitol.
--Cattle.
    sa Subdivision Cattle under:
      Texas.
      Southern States.
      Northwestern States//
    xx Cattle.
 · --History.
    sa Subdivision Cattle. History
      under: Texas.
      Iowa.
      Western States//
-- --Statistics.
    sa Subdivision Cattle. Statistics
      under names of states, etc.
--Cattle trade.
    sa Subdivision Cattle trade
      under: Texas.
      Southwestern States.
      Illinois//
 · --History.

U.S. (Continued)
--Census.
    sa Subdivision Census under:
      U.S. Insular possessions.
      Arizona.
-- --History.
--Census, 18th, 1960.

U.S. Bureau of the Census.
--Bibliography.
    xx U.S. Dept. of Commerce. Bib-
      liography.
--Census of distribution.

U.S. Bureau of Chemistry.
--Exhibits.

U.S. Children's Bureau.
--Bibliography.

U.S. Civil Service Commission.
--Officials and employees.

U.S. Civilian Conservation Corps.
--Appropriations and expenditures.
    xx U.S. Appropriations and
      expenditures.
--Bibliography.

U.S.
--Civilian defense. See Civilian
   defense.
--Civilization.
    sa Civilization, American.
    Subdivision Civilization under:
      Southern States//
    Subdivision U.S. under: Art.
--Climate.
    sa Subdivision Climate under:
      Pacific Coast.
      New Mexico.
      California//
    Subdivision U.S. under:
      Crops and climate.
-- --Bibliography.
    sa Subdivision Bibliography
      under: Western States.
      Climate.
    xx Climate. Bibliography.

U.S. Coast and Geodetic Survey.
--Bibliography.

U.S.
--Colonial question.
-- --Bibliography.
--Colonies.
    sa U.S. Insular possessions.
--Commerce.
    sa Subdivision Commerce under
      names of states, etc.
    Interstate commerce.
    Lend-lease operations
      (1941-1945)
    Subdivision U.S. under:
      Farm produce. Marketing.
      Produce trade.
      Oil-seed trade.
      Onion industry and trade.
      Export control.
      Food industry and trade.
      Fruit trade.
      Egg industry and trade.
      Wholesale trade.
· --Africa.
-- --Argentine Republic.
-- --Asia, Western.
-- --Australasia.
· --Belgium.
· --Canada.
-- --Caribbean region.
· --Chile.
· --China.
· --Cuba.
-- --East Indies (Dutch)
· --Europe.
-- --France.
-- --Gt. Brit.
· --Hawaii.
-- --Indonesia.
· --Italy.
-- --Japan.
· --Levant.
-- --New Zealand.
-- --Philippine Islands.
-- --Puerto Rico.
-- --South America.
-- --Spanish America.
-- --Switzerland.
· --Turkey.
- --U.S.S.R.
- --Uruguay.
-- --Bibliography.
    sa Subdivision Commerce. Bibliog-
      raphy under: Northwest,
      Pacific.
-- --Directories.

U.S. (Continued)
--Commerce.
-- --History.
    sa Embargo.
       Merchant marine. U.S. History.
       Subdivision Commerce. History
         under: Southern States.
         North Carolina.
-- --Periodicals.
    sa Subdivision Commerce. Periodi-
       cals under: Southern States.
       Mississippi Valley.
       Pacific Coast.
       Texas.
    xx Commerce. Periodicals.
-- --Statistics.
    sa Subdivision Commerce. Sta-
       tistics under: Great Lakes.
       Iowa.
       Georgia//
       Subdivision Statistics under:
         Farm produce. U.S.
-- --Bibliography.

U.S. Dept. of Commerce.
--Bibliography.
    sa U.S. Bureau of Foreign and
       Domestic Commerce (Dept. of
       Commerce) Bibliography.
       U.S. Bureau of the Census. Bib-
       liography.
--Officials and employees.
    xx U.S. Officials and employees.

U.S. Dept. of Commerce and labor.
--Bibliography.
--Statistics.

U.S.
--Commercial policy.
    sa Subdivision U.S. under:
       Import quotas.
       Export control.
       U.S. Economic policy.
       Trade barriers, State.
    xx North America. Commercial
       policy.
-- --Bibliography.
    sa Subdivision Bibliography under:
       Trade barriers, State.
--Commercial treaties.
    xx North America. Commercial
       treaties.

U.S. Commodity Credit Corporation.
--Officials and employees.

U.S. Commodity Exchange Administration.
--Bibliography.

U.S. Commodity Stabilization Service.
--Appropriations and expenditures.
--Officials and employees.
-- --Rewards (Prizes, etc.)
--Records and correspondence.

U.S. Congress.
--Bibliography.
--Biography.
--Directories.
--History.
    xx U.S. History.
--Portraits.
--Powers and duties.
--Rules and practice.

U.S. Constitution.
    sa Cabinet system.
       U.S. Executive depts.
       U.S. Politics and government.
       Constitutional law.
--Amendments.
--Bibliography.

U.S.
--Constitutional history.
    xx U.S. History.
       Constitutional history.
--Constitutional law. See Constitu-
    tional law.
--Consular service. See U.S. Diplo-
    matic and consular service.

U.S. Continental Congress.
--Bibliography.

U.S. Council of National Defense.
--Advisory Commission.
-- --Directories.

U.S.
--Courts. See Courts. U.S.

U.S. Crop Corps.
    sa U.S. Women's land army.
       Victory farm volunteers.
    x U.S. Crop corps.

U.S.
--Cyclopedias.
    sa Subdivision Cyclopedias under:
       Idaho.
--Dairying.
    sa Subdivision Dairying under:
       Arizona.
       California.
       Indiana//
       Subdivision U.S. under:
       Dairy industry and trade.
       Dairy policies and programs.
-- --Bibliography.
    sa Subdivision Bibliography under:
       Virginia. Dairying.
-- --Credit guides.
-- --Periodicals.
-- --Research.
-- --Societies.
    sa Subdivision Dairying. Socie-
       ties under: California.
       New York (State)//
-- --Statistics.
    sa Subdivision Dairying. Sta-
       tistics under: New England.
       Vermont.
       Western States//
--Defenses.
    sa Defense savings program.
       Subdivision Defenses under:
       New England.
       District of Columbia.
       California//
    x National defenses.
       U.S. National defenses.
    xx North America. Defenses.
-- --Appropriations and expenditures.
    xx U.S. Appropriations and ex-
       penditures.
-- --Bibliography.
    xx North America. Defenses. Bib-
       liography.
       War. Bibliography.
-- --Congresses.
    xx Defenses. Congresses.
-- --Law.
-- --Periodicals.
--Departmental salaries. See U.S.
    Government salaries.
--Departments. See U.S. Executive
    departments.

U.S. (Continued)
--Description and travel.
    sa Subdivision Description and
       travel under: Southern
       States.
       Pacific Coast.
       Atlantic Coast.
       Names of various states
       and territories.
-- --Guide-books.
--Diplomacy. See U.S. Foreign rela-
    tions.
--Diplomatic and consular service.
-- --Bibliography.
-- --Directories.
--Distances, etc.
--Domestic animals.
    sa Subdivision Domestic animals
       under: Massachusetts.
       Tennessee.
       Southern States//
       Subdivision U.S. under:
       Turkeys.
       Live stock reports.
       U.S. Horse.
       U.S. Sheep.
       U.S. Swine.
    xx North America. Domestic
       animals.
-- --History and origin.
    sa Subdivision Domestic animals.
       History and origin under:
       Missouri.
       Ohio//
    xx Domestic animals. History and
       origin.
-- --Legislation.
-- --Research.
-- --Statistics.
    sa Subdivision Domestic animals.
       Statistics under:
       Minnesota.
       Pennsylvania.
       Southern States//
--Economic conditions.
    sa Subdivision Economic condi-
       tions under: Montana.
       North Dakota.
       Minnesota//

U.S. (Continued)
--Economic conditions.
    sa Subdivision U.S. under:
        Economics. History.
        Geography, Economic.
        History, Economic.
        European war, 1914-1918.
        Economic aspects.
        World War, 1939-1945. Eco-
          nomic aspects.
        Business depression.
        Economic surveys.
        Rural surveys.
        Natural resources.
-- --Bibliography.
    sa Subdivision Economic conditions.
        Bibliography under: Alabama.
        Massachusetts.
        Great Plains//
-- --Congresses.
-- --Periodicals.
    sa Subdivision Economic conditions.
        Periodicals under: Oregon.
        Texas.
        New England//
--Economic policy.
    sa U.S. Commercial policy.
        Subdivision U.S. under:
          Postwar planning (1939-   )
    xx Economic policy.
-- --Bibliography.
    sa Subdivision U.S. Bibliography
        under: Postwar planning
          (1939-   )
--Education.
    sa Subdivision Education under:
        Alabama.
        Appalachian Mountains.
        Arizona//
        U.S. Agriculture.
        U.S. Officials and employees.
        U.S. Army//
        Subdivision U.S. under:
        Rural schools.
        Universities and colleges.
        Professional education.
        Community schools.
        National University for the
          U.S.
    xx North America. Education.
-- --Bibliography.

U.S. (Continued)
--Education.
-- --Directories.
    sa Subdivision Education. Direc-
        tories under: Illinois.
        District of Columbia.
        Michigan.
        Indiana.
        Wisconsin.
        U.S. Agriculture.
    xx Education. Directories.
- --History.
    xx History. Education.
-- --Statistics.
    sa Subdivision Education. Sta-
        tistics under: South
        Dakota.
    xx Education. Statistics.

U.S. Bureau of Education.
--Bibliography.

U.S. Office of Education.
--Appropriations and expenditures.
    xx U.S. Appropriations and ex-
        penditures.
--Bibliography.
--Cooperating Committee on School
    Lunches. See U.S. Interagency
    Committee on School Lunches.

U.S.
--Emigration and immigration.
    sa Subdivision Emigration and
        immigration under: Hawaii.
        Connecticut.
        Oregon//
        Americans in Canada.
        U.S. Foreign population.
-- --Bibliography.
-- --History.
    xx North America. Emigration
        and immigration. History.
-- --Periodicals.
--Employees. See U.S. Officials and
    employees.
--Entomology.
    sa Subdivision Entomology under:
        Southwestern States.
        Western States.
        Mississippi Valley//

U.S. (Continued)
--Entomology.
    sa Subdivision U.S. under:
        Entomology, Economic.
        Orthoptera.
        Hymenoptera.
        Butterflies.
        Coleoptera.
        Lepidoptera.
        Diptera.
        Neuroptera.
        Hemiptera.
        Trees. Pests.
        Grasshoppers.
        Aphididae.
-- --Bibliography.
- --History.
    sa Subdivision Entomology. His-
        tory under: Massachusetts.
-- --Periodicals.

U.S. Bureau of Entomology.
--Bibliography.
    sa U.S.
        Bureau of Entomology.
        Division of Cereal and Forage
        Insect Investigations. Bib-
        liography.
--Division of Cereal and Forage Insect
    Investigations.
-- --Bibliography.

U.S. Bureau of Entomology and Plant
    Quarantine.
--Bibliography.
    sa Subdivision Bibliography under:
        U.S. Bureau of Entomology
        and Plant Quarantine.
        Forest Insect Field
        Laboratory.
        U.S. Bureau of Entomology
        and Plant Quarantine.
        Division of Insecticide
        Investigations.
--Division of Cereal and Forage Insect
    Investigations.
-- --Directories.
--Directories.
    sa Subdivision Directories under:
        U.S. Bureau of Entomology
        and Plant Quarantine.
        Division of Foreign
        Plant Quarantine.
--Field stations.

U.S. Bureau of Entomology and Plant
    Quarantine (Continued)
--Division of foreign plant quarantines.
-- --Directories.
    xx U.S. Bureau of Entomology and
        Plant Quarantines. Direc-
        tories.
--Forest Insect Field Laboratory.
-- --Bibliography.
--Division of Insecticide Investigations.
-- --Bibliography.
    xx U.S. Bureau of Entomology and
        Plant Quarantine. Bibliog-
        raphy.

U.S.
--Executive departments.
    sa Subdivision Executive depart-
        ments under: Ohio.
        Kansas.
        Alabama//
    U.S. Officials and employees.
    x Federal departments.
-- --Accounting.
    sa Subdivision Accounting under
        names of various executive
        departments, e.g., U.S.
        Dept. of Agriculture.
        Accounting.
    xx Cost. Accounting.
-- --Appropriations and expenditures.
    See U.S. Appropriations and
        expenditures.
-- --Bibliography.
    sa Subdivision Bibliography
        under: U.S. Executive
        departments. Reorgani-
        zation.
-- --Directories.
-- --Equipment and supplies.
    x Government supplies.
        Equipment, Government.
        Supplies and stores.
    xx U.S. Government property.
-- -- --Terminology.
- --History.
-- -- --Bibliography.
-- --Management.
-- --Public relations.
-- --Records and correspondence.

U.S. (Continued)
--Executive departments.
-- --Reorganization.
    sa Subdivision Reorganization
      under: U.S. Dept. of Agri-
      culture.
    U.S. Bureau of Agricultural
      Economics.
    U.S. Commission on Organization
      of the Executive Branch of
      the Government.
    x Federal reorganization.
    Reorganization of government
      departments.
    Reorganization of executive
      departments.
-- --Bibliography.
    xx U.S. Politics and government.
      Bibliography.
    U.S. Executive departments.
      Bibliography.
--Expenditures. See U.S. Appropriations
  and expenditures.
--Experiment stations. See U.S. Agri-
  cultural experiment stations.

U.S. Office of Experiment stations.
--Bibliography.

U.S.
--Explorations.
    sa Colorado River.
    Lady Franklin Bay.
    Montana.
    Wyoming.
-- --Bibliography.

U.S. Extension Service.
--Bibliography.
--Directories.
--Division of Extension Research and
  Training.
-- --Directories.
-- --Officials and employees.
--Officials and employees.
    xx U.S. Dept. of Agriculture.
      Officials and employees.
--Public relations.
    xx Public relations.

U.S. Farm Credit Administration.
--Appropriations and expenditures.
    xx U.S. Dept. of Agriculture.
      Appropriations and expendi-
      tures.

U.S. Farm Credit Administration (Con.)
--Bibliography.
--Directories.
    xx U.S. Dept. of Agriculture.
      Directories.
--Officials and employees.
    xx U.S. Officials and employees.
--War work.
    xx U.S. Dept. of Agriculture.
      War work.

U.S. Office of Farm Management and Farm
  Economics.
--Bibliography.

U.S. Farm Security Administration.
--Appropriations and expenditures.
    xx U.S. Dept. of Agriculture.
      Appropriations and ex-
      penditures.
--Bibliography.
--Directories.
    xx U.S. Dept. of Agriculture.
      Employees.
--Officials and employees.
    xx U.S. Officials and employees.
--War work.
    xx U.S. Dept. of Agriculture.
      War work.

U.S. Farmer Cooperative Service.
--Bibliography.

U.S. Farmers' Home Administration.
--Loans.
    xx Agricultural credit.
      Loans.
--Officials and employees.
-- --Rewards (Prizes, etc.)

U.S. Federal Civil Works Administration.
--Appropriations and expenditures.
    xx U.S. Appropriations and ex-
      penditures.

U.S. Federal Crop Insurance Corporation.
--Directories.
    xx U.S. Dept. of Agriculture.
      Directories.

U.S. Federal Emergency Administrations.
--Legislation.
-- --Bibliography.

U.S. Federal Emergency Relief Administration.
--Appropriations and expenditures.
xx U.S. Appropriations and expenditures.
--Bibliography.

U.S.
--Federal departments.   See U.S. Executive departments.

U.S. Federal Loan Agency.

U.S. Federal Security Agency.
--Appropriations and expenditures.
xx U.S. Appropriations and expenditures.

U.S. Federal Trade Commission.
--Bibliography.

U.S.
--Ferries.
sa Subdivision Ferries under:
Alabama.

U.S. Fish and Wildlife Service.
--Bibliography.
x U.S. Fish and Wildlife Service.
Publications.
xx Wild life. Conservation. Bib-
liography.
Fisheries. Bibliography.
--Publications.   See U.S. Fish and
Wildlife Service. Bibliography.

U.S.
--Fisheries.
sa Subdivision Fisheries under:
Maryland.
Washington (State)
Georgia//
Columbia River fisheries.
-- --Directories.

U.S. Bureau of Fisheries.
--Bibliography.

U.S.
--Flag.   See Flags.

U.S. Food Administration.
--Appropriations and expenditures.

U.S. Food Distribution Administration.
--Accounting.
xx U.S. Dept. of Agriculture.
Accounting.
--Directories.
xx U.S. Dept. of Agriculture.
Directories.
--Officials and employees.
xx U.S. Dept. of Agriculture.
Officials and employees.

U.S. Foreign Agricultural Service.
--Officials and employees.

U.S. Foreign Economic Administration.
--Appropriations and expenditures.

U.S.
--Foreign mail.   See Postal service.
Foreign mail.
--Foreign policy.   See U.S. Foreign
relations.
--Foreign population.
xx U.S. Population.
U.S. Emigration and immi-
gration.
-- --Agriculture.
-- --Periodicals.
-- --Statistics.
sa Subdivision Statistics under:
Japanese in the U.S.
Germans in the U.S.
Italians in the U.S.
xx Population. Statistics.
--Foreign relations.
sa Subdivision Foreign relations
under: Confederate States
of America.
U.S. Relations (general) with
foreign countries.
x U.S. Foreign policy.
xx North America. Foreign rela-
tions.
-- --Africa, South.
-- --Argentine Republic.
· --Canada.
- --Cuba.
- --Europe.
- --Germany.
· --Gt. Brit.
· --Greece.
-- --Spanish America.
· --Turkey.
-- --Yugoslavia.
-- --Bibliography.

U.S. (Continued)
--Foreign relations.
-- --Treaties.
--Forest reservations.   See Forest re-
    servations.

U.S. Forest Service.
--Accounting.
    xx Cost. Accounting.
--Appropriations and expenditures.
--Bibliography.
    sa Subdivision Bibliography under:
    U.S. Forest Service. Forest
    Products Laboratory,
    Madison.
    U.S. Forest Experiment Sta-
    tion, Central States,
    Columbus, Ohio.
    U.S. Forest Experiment Sta-
    tion, Northern Rocky
    Mountain, Missoula,
    Mont.//
--Directories.
    xx U.S.Dept. of Agriculture.
    Directories.
--Eastern Tree Seed Laboratory, Macon,
    Ga.   See U.S. Eastern Tree Seed
    Laboratory, Macon, Ga.
--Field stations.
    xx U.S. Dept. of Agriculture.
    Field stations.
--Forest products laboratory, Madison.
-- --Records and correspondence.
    xx Records and correspondence.
--Intermountain Forest and Range Ex-
    periment Station.
-- --Bibliography.
--Northern Rocky Mountain Forest and
    Range Experiment Station.
-- --Bibliography.
--Officials and employees.
    xx U.S. Dept. of Agriculture.
    Officials and employees.
-- --Rewards (Prizes, etc.)
--Public relations.
    xx Public relations.
--Records and correspondence.

U.S. Forest Service. Southern Region.
--Eastern Tree Seed Laboratory, Macon,
    Ga.   See U.S. Eastern Tree Seed
    Laboratory, Macon, Ga.
--Tree Seed Testing Laboratory, Macon,
    Ga.   See U.S. Tree Seed Testing
    Laboratory, Macon, Ga.

U.S. Forest Service.
--Tree Seed Testing Laboratory, Macon,
    Ga.   See U.S. Tree Seed Testing
    Laboratory, Macon, Ga.
--War work.
    xx U.S. Dept. of Agriculture.
    War work.

U.S.
--Forestry.
    sa Subdivision Forestry under:
    California.
    Chicago.
    Colorado//
    Save the forests week.
    Indians, North American.
    Forestry.
    U.S. Dept. of Agriculture.
    Division of Forestry.
    Subdivision U.S. under:
    Timber.
    Trees.
    Lumber trade.
    Wood-lots.
    Forest fires. Prevention.
    Forest products.
    War and forestry (1939-
    1945)
    Afforestation and reforest-
    ation.
    Forest industries.
    Forest surveys.
    Forest policy.
    War and forestry.
    Forest management.
    Tree planting.
-- --Bibliography.
    sa Subdivision Forestry. Bib-
    liography under:
    Tennessee//
-- --Directories.
-- --History.
    sa Subdivision Forestry. History
    under: Western States.
-- --Periodicals.
-- --Research.
-- --Statistics.
    sa Subdivision Forestry. Sta-
    tistics under: Oregon.
    Pacific Coast.
    Washington (State)//

U.S. Fuel Administration.
--Appropriations and expenditures.

U.S.
--Gazetteers.
    sa Subdivision Gazetteers under:
        Washington (State)
        New Hampshire.
        Hawaii.
        Maryland.
        California.
--Geographic names.
    sa Subdivision Geographic names
        under: Pennsylvania.
        Sierra Nevada Mountains,
        Calif.
        Oregon//
--Geography.
    sa Subdivision Geography under:
        Ohio.
        Oregon.
        Oklahoma//
        Geography, Economic.
        Subdivision U.S. under:
        Geography, Historical.
        Anthropo-geography.
    xx North America. Geography.

U.S. Geological Survey.
--Bibliography.
--Publications.

U.S.
--Geology.
    sa Subdivision Geology under:
        Black Hills.
        Alabama.
        Buffalo Peaks//
        Subdivision U.S. under:
        Water, Underground.
        Mines and mineral resources.
-- --Bibliography.
    sa Subdivision Geology. Bibliog-
        raphy under: Alabama.
        California.
        Iowa//
    xx North America. Geology. Bib-
        liography.
--Government employees. See U.S.
    Officials and employees.

U.S. Government information services.
--Directories.

U.S.
--Government positions.

U.S. (Continued)
--Government positions.
-- --Classification.
    xx Civil service.
    Occupations. Classification.
-- -- --Bibliography.
--Government property.
    sa U.S. Executive departments.
    Equipment and supplies.
    Surplus government property.
    Surplus war property. U.S.
    x Government property.
--Fires and fire prevention.
    xx Fires.
--Government publications.
    sa Subdivision Government publi-
        cations under: Minnesota.
    xx Government publications.
-- --Bibliography.
    sa Subdivision Bibliography
        under: U.S. Temporary
        National Economic
        Committee.
        U.S. Dept. of Agriculture.
        State publications//
        U.S. Dept. of Commerce.
-- -- --Bibliography.
-- --Indexes.
-- -- --Bibliography.
-- --Policies and programs.
--Government publications (Counties)
-- --Bibliography.
--Government publications (Municipal
    governments)
    x Municipal publications.
-- --Bibliography.
--Government publications (State
    governments) See State publica-
    tions.
--Government reorganization. See
    U.S. Executive departments.
--Government salaries.
    sa Subdivision Government salaries
        under: Utah.
    Pay readjustment act.
    Ramspeck act.
    Pay readjustment act, 1942.
    x Salaries of Government em-
        ployees.
--Historic houses, etc.
    xx Historic houses, etc.

U.S. (Continued)
--History.
    sa Subdivision History under:
      California.
      Connecticut.
      Kansas//
    Subdivision U.S. under:
      Economics. History.
      History, Economic.
      Geography, Historical.
      Political science. History.
      U.S. Annexations.
      U.S. President.
      Postal service. U.S. History.
      U.S. Constitutional history.
-- --Bibliography.
    sa Subdivision History. Bibliog-
      raphy under: Western States.
      Oklahoma//
    Subdivision Bibliography under:
      History, Economic. U.S.
      U.S. History. Colonial
      period.
-- --Chronology.
-- --Civil war.
    sa Reconstruction.
    Subdivision Civil war under:
      U.S. Army. History.
    xx War.
-- -- --Causes.
-- --Colonial period.
    sa Subdivision History. Colonial
      period under: Washington,
      D.C.
      New England.
      Southern States//
    x Colonial period (U.S.) His-
      tory.
-- --Bibliography.
    xx U.S. History. Bibliography.
-- --Confederation, 1783-1789.
-- --Dictionaries.
    xx History. Dictionaries.
-- --Periodicals.
    sa Subdivision History. Periodi-
      cals under: Iowa.
      Georgia.
-- --Revolution.
    sa Subdivision History. Revolu-
      tion under: Virginia.
      Maryland//
    x Revolution, American.
    xx War.
- --Sources.
    sa Archives. U.S.

U.S. (Continued)
--History.
-- --Sources.
    sa Subdivision History. Sources
      under: New Jersey.
      North Dakota.
      Oregon//
-- --Bibliography.
-- --Spanish-American War. See
      Spanish-American War.
-- --War with Mexico, 1845-1848.
    x Mexican War, 1845-1848.
-- -- --Personal narratives.

U.S. Bureau of Home Economics.
--Bibliography.

U.S.
--Horse.
    sa Subdivision Horse under:
      Maine.
      New England.
      Pennsylvania//
    Subdivision U.S. under:
      Horses. Breeding.
--Horticulture.
-- --History. See Gardening. U.S.
    History.

U.S. Bureau of Human Nutrition and Home
    Economics.
--Directories.

U.S.
--Hygiene. See Hygiene, Public. U.S.
--Ichthyology.
    sa Subdivision Ichthyology under:
      Northeastern States//
    xx Ichthyology.
-- --Bibliography.
--Industries.
    sa Subdivision U.S. under:
      Rural industries.
      Agricultural industries.
      Machinery. Trade and
      manufacture.
-- --Bibliography. See U.S. Economic
    conditions. Bibliography.
-- --Directories.
    sa Subdivision Industries.
      Directories under:
      Southern States.
      New York (State)//
- --History.
-- --Statistics.

U.S. (Continued)
--Inland navigation.
--Insular possessions.
    xx U.S. Territories.
-- --Bibliography.
    sa Subdivision Bibliography under:
      Guam.
      U.S. Territories.
    xx U.S. Territories. Bibliography.
 · --Census.
    xx U.S. Census.
-- --Commerce.
-- --Periodicals.
--Intellectual life.

U.S. Interstate Commerce Commission.
--Bibliography.
--Officials and employees.
    xx U.S. Officials and employees.
--Land.
    sa Subdivision Land under:
      California.
      Iowa.
      Kentucky//
    Subdivision U.S. under:
      Waste lands.
      Land utilization.
      Farm valuation.
      Land, Marginal.
      Land. Classification.
      Farm land values.
-- --Bibliography.
    sa Subdivision Bibliography under:
      Land utilization. U.S.
      New York (State) Land.
    xx Land. Bibliography.
      U.S. Bibliography.
 · --Prices.
    sa Subdivision Land. Prices under:
      Kentucky//
--Learned institutions and societies.
    sa Subdivision Learned institu-
      tions and societies under:
      Washington, D.C.//
      Names of societies.
    xx North America. Learned insti-
      tutions and societies.
-- --Bibliography.
    xx North America. Learned insti-
      tutions and societies. Bib-
      liography.
-- --Directories.

U.S. (Continued)
--Libraries.
    sa Subdivision Libraries under:
      North Carolina.
      Mississippi.
      Washington, D.C.//
--Literature.   See American literature.
--Manufactures.
    sa Subdivision Manufactures
      under: Wyoming.
      Nevada.
      South Dakota//
 - --History.
-- --Statistics.
    sa Subdivision Manufactures.
      Statistics under: Iowa//
--Maps.
    sa Subdivision Maps under:
      District of Columbia.
      Tennessee Valley.
      Southern States//
      Subdivision Maps under the
      names of the various
      states and territories.
-- --Bibliography.
    sa Subdivision Maps. Bibliography
      under: California.
      Virginia.
      Alaska//
    xx North America. Maps. Bibliog-
      graphy.
--Markets.
    sa Subdivision Markets under:
      Boston.
      California.
      Chicago//
      New York (State) Dept. of
      Farms and Markets. Division
      of Agriculture.
-- --Bibliography.
    xx North America. Markets. Bib-
      liography.

U.S. Bureau of Markets.
--War work.
    xx U.S. Dept. of Agriculture.
      War work.

U.S.
--Meat supply.
    sa Subdivision Meat supply under:
      New York (City)//
-- --Statistics.

U.S. (Continued)
  --Meteorology.
    sa Subdivision Meteorology under:
      California.
      Colorado.
      Massachusetts//
      Subdivision U.S. under:
      Precipitation (Meteorology)
  -- --Bibliography.
    xx Meteorology. Bibliography.
  --Milk supply.
    sa Subdivision Milk supply under:
      Washington, D.C.
      New England.
      Illinois//
  --Milk trade.
    sa Subdivision Milk trade under:
      New York (State)
      Massachusetts.
      Tennessee//
  -- --Bibliography.
  -- --Directories.
    xx Milk trade. Directories.

U.S. Bureau of Mines.
  --Bibliography.

U.S.
  --Monopolies.
    xx Monopolies.
  --Museums.

U.S. National Agricultural Advisory
  Commission.
  --Directories.

U.S.
  --National defenses. See U.S. Defenses.

U.S. National Library of Medicine.
  --Bibliography.

U.S. National Recovery Administration.
  --Codes. See National industrial
    recovery act, 1933. Codes.

U.S. National Youth Administration.
  --Appropriations and expenditures.
    xx U.S. Appropriations and ex-
      penditures.

U.S.
  --Nationality.
    xx Nationalism and nationality.

U.S. (Continued)
  --Natural history.
    sa Subdivision Natural history
      under: Alabama.
      California.
      Colorado//
    xx North America. Natural his-
      tory.
  -- --Bibliography.

U.S. Naval Academy, Annapolis.
  --Milk supply.
    xx Annapolis, Md. Milk supply.

U.S. Navy.
  --Education.
    xx U.S. Education.
  --Meteorological Service.
  --Recruiting, enlistment, etc.
  --Safety measures.

U.S. Navy Dept.
  --Officials and employment.
    xx U.S. Officials and employees.

U.S.
  --Neutrality.
    sa Subdivision Neutrality under:
      Great Lakes.
    xx North America. Neutrality.
  --Occupations.
    sa Subdivision Occupations under:
      Iowa.
      Florida.
      Southern States//
    xx Occupations.
  --Officials and employees.
    sa Subdivision Officials and em-
      ployees under:
      Rochester, N.Y.//
      U.S. Dept. of Agriculture.
      U.S. Dept. of Commerce.
      U.S. Farm Security Adminis-
        tration.
      U.S. National Bureau of
        Standards.
      U.S. Navy Dept.
      U.S. Dept. of State.
      State governments.
      U.S. Interstate Commerce
        Commission.
      U.S. Farm Credit Adminis-
        tration.
      U.S. Rural Electrification
        Administration.

U.S. Bureau of Plant Industry, Soils and
Agricultural Engineering.
--Directories.
    xx U.S. Dept. of Agriculture.
        Directories.
--Field stations. See U.S. Bureau of
    Plant Industry. Field stations.

U.S. Plant Quarantine and Control Administration.
--Field stations.
    xx U.S. Dept. of Agriculture.
        Field stations.

U.S.
--Politics and government.
    sa Subdivision U.S. under:
        Legislative bodies.
        Administrative and political
          divisions.
        Nationalism and nationality.
        Suffrage.
        Subdivision Politics and govern-
          ment under: Georgia.
          Texas.
          Virgin Islands of the U.S.//
        U.S. Constitutional history.
        Farmer-labor party.
        State rights.
        Local government.
        State governments.
        Government competition with
          business.
        Lobbying.
        Federal-state-local relations.
-- --Addresses, essays, lectures.
    xx Political science. Addresses,
        essays, lectures.
-- --Bibliography.
    sa Subdivision Bibliography under:
        U.S. Elections.
        Western States. Politics and
          government.
        U.S. Executive departments.
          Reorganization.
        Kansas. Politics and govern-
          ment.
        New deal.
-- --Constitutional period, 1789-1800.
-- --Handbooks, manuals, etc.

U.S. (Continued)
--Pomology.
    sa Subdivision Pomology under:
        Eastern States.
        Central States.
        Southern States//
        Names of states and terri-
          tories.
        Subdivision U.S. under: Citrus.
        Berries.
-- --Bibliography.
-- --History.
    sa Subdivision Pomology. History
        under: Connecticut.
        Pennsylvania.
        Virginia//
-- --Research.
-- --Statistics.
    sa Subdivision Pomology. Sta-
        tistics under: California//
    xx Pomology. Statistics.
-- --Bibliography.
    sa Subdivision Pomology. Sta-
        tistics. Bibliography under:
        California.
--Population.
    sa Subdivision Population under:
        Names of states, cities,etc.
        U.S. Foreign population.
        Subdivision U.S. under:
        Rural population.
        Migration, Internal.
-- --Bibliography.

U.S. Post Office Dept.
--Accounting.
    xx Accounting.
--Public buildings.
    sa Subdivision Public buildings
        under: Washington, D.C.
        Colorado.
--Public documents.
    sa U.S. Government publications.
--Public lands.
    sa Subdivision Public lands
        under: Arkansas.
        Washington (State)
        Michigan//
-- --Bibliography.
    xx Land. Bibliography.
  --History.
    sa Subdivision Public lands.
        History under: Ohio.
        Iowa//
-- --Periodicals.

U.S. (Continued)
--Public lands.
-- --Statistics.

U.S. Bureau of Public Roads.

U.S.
--Public schools.
    xx Public schools.
--Public work reserve.
-- --Officials and employees.
    xx U.S. Officials and employees.
--Public works.
    This subject is to be used for
    general works on public works.
    For unemployment and public
    works see Public works as re-
    lief measure. An additional
    subject for U.S. Public works
    will not be made. This system
    will be used for state and
    local publications also.
    sa Subdivision Public works under:
        New York (State)
        Ohio.
        Delaware//
    Works financing act of 1939.
-- --Bibliography.
    xx Public works. Bibliography.

U.S. Public Works Administration.
--Appropriations and expenditures.
    xx U.S. Appropriations and ex-
        penditures.
--Race question.
    sa Subdivision Race question under:
        Southern States.
        Subdivision U.S. under:
        Discrimination in employ-
            ment.
    xx Race problems.
--Railroads.
    sa Subdivision Railroads under:
        New England.
        California.
        Southern States//
        Illinois Central Railroad.
-- --Bibliography.
    xx Railroads. Bibliography.
- --History.
    sa Subdivision Railroads. History
        under: California.
        Nevada//
    xx Railroads. History.
        U.S. History.

U.S. (Continued)
--Railroads.
-- --Statistics.

U.S. Bureau of Reclamation.
--Recreational activities.

U.S. Reclamation Service.
--Bibliography.

U.S. Regional research laboratories.
    This subject used for the four
    regional laboratories of the
    Bureau of Agricultural and
    Industrial Chemistry. For
    other field laboratories of
    the Dept. of Agriculture see
    U.S. Dept. of Agriculture.
    Field laboratories.
    sa U.S. Southern Regional Re-
        search Laboratory, New
        Orleans, La.
    x U.S. Dept. of Agriculture.
        Regional research labora-
        tories.
    xx Laboratories.
        Agricultural laboratories.

U.S.
--Relations (general) with Asia, Western.
--Relations (general) with foreign
    countries.
    xx U.S. Foreign relations.
--Relations (general) with Germany.
--Relations (general) with Nicaragua.
--Relations (general) with Spanish
    America.
--Religion.
-- --Bibliography.
--Research.
    sa Subdivision Research under:
        Minnesota.
        North Carolina.
        New England//
- --Costs.
    xx Research. Costs.
--Revenue.
    sa Subdivision Revenue under:
        Georgia.
        Kentucky.
        Texas//

U.S. (Continued)
--Roads.
    sa Pacific wagon roads.
    Subdivision Roads under names
      of individual States and
      areas, e.g., Alabama.
      Roads; Yellowstone National
      Park. Roads; Southeastern
      States. Roads.
      Names of specific roads, e.g.,
      Cumberland Road; Mt. Vernon
      Memorial Highway.
-- --Bibliography.
- --History.
    sa Subdivision Roads. History
      under: New England.
      Middle States.
      Alabama//
    xx Roads. History.
- --Law.
    sa Subdivision Roads. Law under:
      Alabama.
      Arkansas.
      California//
      Highway right of-way act,
      1940.
-- --Statistics.
    sa Subdivision Roads. Statistics
      under: Arkansas.

U.S. Rural Electrification Administra-
    tion.
--Accounting.
    xx U.S. Dept. of Agriculture.
      Accounting.
--Appropriations and expenditures.
    xx U.S. Dept. of Agriculture.
      Appropriations and ex-
      penditures.
--Loans.
    xx Loans.
--Officials and employees.
    xx U.S. Officials and employees.
--Projects.   See Electric cooperative
    associations, Rural.
--War work.

U.S.
--Sanitary affairs.
    sa Hygiene, Public. U.S.
--Scientific bureaus.

U.S. Selective Service.   See U.S. Army.
    Recruiting, enlistment, etc.

U.S. Selective service system.
--Appropriations and expenditures.
    xx U.S. Appropriations and ex-
      penditures.

U.S.
--Sericulture.
    sa Subdivision Sericulture under:
      California.
      Southern States.
      Florida.
      Ohio.
    xx North America. Sericulture.
--Sewerage.
    sa Subdivision Sewerage under:
      Mississippi.
      Ohio.
--Sheep.
    sa Subdivision Sheep under:
      Kansas.
      Montana.
      Western States//
-- --History.
--Social conditions.
    sa Subdivision Social conditions
      under: Minnesota.
      New Jersey.
      Washington//
    Subdivision U.S. under:
      Social surveys.
      Community life.
      Rural surveys.
-- --Bibliography.
    sa Great Plains. Social condi-
      tions. Bibliography//
-- --Periodicals.
--Social life and customs.
    sa Subdivision Social life and
      customs under: Idaho.
      South Carolina.
      New England//

U.S. Social Security Board.
--Appropriations and expenditures.
    xx U.S. Appropriations and ex-
      penditures.

U.S. Soil Conservation Service.
--Appropriations and expenditures.
--Bibliography.
--Directories.
    sa Subdivision Directories under:
      Soil conservation districts.
    xx U.S. Dept. of Agriculture.
      Directories.

U.S. Soil Conservation Service (Continued)
--Officials and employees.
    xx U.S. Dept. of Agriculture.
      Officials and employees.
-- --Rewards (Prizes, etc.)
--Public relations.
    xx Public relations.
--War work.
    xx U.S. Dept. of Agriculture. War
      work.

U.S.
--Soils.
    sa Subdivision Soils under:
      Names of states.
      Eastern States.
      Great Plains//
      Subdivision U.S. under:
      Soil erosion. Prevention
        and control.
      Soil conservation.
      Soil-surveys.
      Peat.
      Soil conservation. Economic
        aspects.
      Soil erosion surveys.
      Soil erosion.
      Soil conservation surveys.
-- --Bibliography.
    sa Subdivision Soils. Bibliography
      under: Tennessee.
      Illinois.

U.S. Bureau of Soils.
--Bibliography.

U.S. Solicitor of the Dept. of Agriculture.
--Directories.
    xx U.S. Dept. of Agriculture.
      Directories.

U.S. National Bureau of Standards.
--Officials and employees.
    xx U.S. Officials and employees.

U.S. Dept. of State.
--Officials and employees.
    xx U.S. Officials and employees.

U.S. States Relations Service.
--Home demonstration work. See Home
    demonstration work.

U.S.
--Statistics.
    sa Subdivision Statistics under:
      Pacific Coast.
      Southwestern States.
      Washington. D.C.//
      Names of various states and
        territories.
      U.S. Agriculture.
      U.S. Census.
-- --Bibliography.
    sa Subdivision Statistics. Bib-
      liography under:
      California//
--Statistics, Medical.
--Statistics, Vital.

U.S. Bureau of Statistics.
--Bibliography.
--Cotton estimates.

U.S.
--Surveys.
    sa Subdivision Surveys under:
      District of Columbia.
      California//
--Swine.
    sa Subdivision Swine under:
      Texas.
      Southern States.
      Iowa//
-- --Statistics.

U.S. Temporary National Economic
    Committee.
--Bibliography.
    xx U.S. Government publications.
      Bibliography.

U.S. Tennessee Valley Authority.
--Appropriations and expenditures.
    xx U.S. Appropriations and ex-
      penditures.
--Bibliography.
--Libraries.
    xx Libraries.
--Officials and employees.

U.S.
--Territorial expansion.
--Territories.
    sa U.S. Insular possessions.

U.S. (Continued)
--Territories.
-- --Bibliography.
 sa Subdivision Bibliography
  under: U.S. Insular pos-
  sessions.
 xx U.S. Insular possessions. Bib-
  liography.
-- --Commerce.
-- -- --Statistics.
--Transportation.
 sa Subdivision Transportation
  under: Ohio Valley.
  New Hampshire.
  Minnesota//
  World War, 1939-1945. Trans-
  portation. U.S.
 xx Transportation.
- --History.
 sa Subdivision Transportation.
  History under: Southern
  States//
- --Law.
 xx Transportation. Law.

U.S. Tree Seed Testing Laboratory, Macon,
 Ga.
  Established as U.S. Tree Seed
  Testing Laboratory, Macon, Ga.
  Name changed in 1961 to U.S.
  Eastern Tree Seed Laboratory,
  Macon, Ga.

U.S.
--Universities and colleges. See
 Universities and colleges. U.S.
--Viticulture.
 sa Subdivision Viticulture under:
  California.
  Idaho.
  Ohio//
 xx North America. Viticulture.
-- --Periodicals.
-- --Statistics.
--Water-supply.
 sa Subdivision Water-supply under:
  Names of various states and
  regions.
  Subdivision U.S. under:
  Water, Underground.
  Water. Conservation.

U.S. (Continued)
--Water-supply.
-- --Bibliography.
 sa Subdivision Water-supply. Bib-
  liography under:
  Washington (State)
  New England.
  Western States//
-- --Congresses.

U.S. Waterways Experiment Station.
--Bibliography.

U.S. Weather Bureau.
--History. See U.S. Weather Bureau.

U.S. Women's Army Auxiliary Corps.
 xx World War, 1939-1945. Women's
  work.

U.S. Women's Land Army.
 x World War, 1939-1945. Women's
  work.
  Women's Land Army.
 xx U.S. Crop Corps.
  Women in agriculture.

U.S. Work Projects Administration.
--Bibliography.

U.S.
--Zoology.
 sa Subdivision Zoology under:
  Black Hills.
  Indian Territory.
  New Mexico//
  Subdivision U.S. under:
  Araneida.
  Mammalia.
  Vertebrates.
  Natrachia.
  Reptilia.
  Marine fauna.
  Wild life.
  Game.
  Fresh-water fauna.
  Game. North America.

United States cotton standards act.
 See Cotton standards act.

United States Crop Corps. See U.S.
 Crop Corps.

United States Foreign Relief Program.
  sa Technical assistance program.
    European recovery program.
  xx Technical assistance program.
    Foreign relief program.
--Accounting.

United States grain standards act. See
  Grain standards act, 1916.

United States housing act.
  sa National housing act.
  xx Housing.
    National housing act.

United States housing act of 1936.
  xx Housing.

United States Naval Expedition to Japan,
  1852-1854.
    x Japan Expedition of the
      American Squadron, 1852-
      1854.

United States of Europe (proposed)
  x European federation.

United States Steel Corporation.

United States Touring Bureau. See U.S.
  Tourist Bureau.

United States Travel Commission.

United States Warehouse act. See Warehouse act.

United Transkeian Territories. See
  Transkeian Territories.

Units.
  sa Metric system.
    Weights and measures.

Universal decimal classification. See
  Classification, Decimal.

Universal language. See Language, Universal.

Universal military training. See
  Military service, Compulsory.

Universe. See Cosmology.

Universe, Destruction of.
  xx Cosmogony.

Universities and colleges.   (INDIRECT)
  sa Names of universities and
    colleges.
    Classical education.
    Coeducation.
    Degrees, Academic.
    Greek letter societies.
    Land grant colleges.
    Libraries, University.
    Scholarships.
    Students.
    Theses.
    Education, Higher.
    University extension.
    Normal schools.
--Bibliography.
  sa Subdivision Bibliography
    under Universities and
    colleges [geographic sub-
    division] e.g., Universi-
    ties and colleges. Spanish-
    America. Bibliography.
--Curricula.
  sa Subdivision Curricula under:
    Land-grant colleges.
    Universities and colleges
      [geographic subdivision]
      e.g., Universities and
      colleges. U.S. Curricula.
  xx Education. Curricula.
--Directories. See Education. Directories.
--Examinations.
  sa Subdivision Examinations un-
    der: Michigan. State
    College of Agriculture
    and Applied Science,
    Lansing.
  xx Examinations.
--Finance.
  sa Subdivision Finance under:
    Land-grant colleges.
--Graduate work.
--Research.
  sa Subdivision Research under
    Universities and colleges
    [geographic subdivision]
    e.g., Universities and
    colleges. Gt. Brit. Re-
    search.

Universities and colleges (Continued)
--Societies.
    sa Subdivision Societies under
        Universities and colleges
        [geographic subdivision]
        e.g., Universities and
        colleges. U.S. Societies.
--War work. See European war, 1914-1918.
    War work. Schools; World War, 1939-
    1945. War work. Schools.

University extension.
    sa Correspondence schools and
        courses.
        Education of adults.
    x Extension work in universities
        and colleges.
    xx Education.
        Education, Higher.
        Universities and colleges.
        Education of adults.

University libraries. See Libraries,
    University.

University of the United States. See
    National university for the U.S.

Unloading. See Loading and unloading.

Unox.
    xx Wetting agents.

Unterengadin. See Lower Engadine,
    Switzerland.

Unterwesterwaldkreis, Ger.
--Agriculture.
    sa Subdivision Germany. Unter-
        westerwaldkreis under:
        Agriculture. Economic
        aspects.

Upas.
    x Antaris toxicaria.

Upholstery.
    sa Inner-spring pillows.
        Drapery.
        Furniture.
        House decoration.
    xx Furniture.
        House decoration.
--Legislation.

Upland, Sweden. See Uppland, Sweden.

Upland cotton. See Cotton, Upland.

Upogebia.

Upper Adige. See South Tyrol.

Upper Austria. See Austria, Upper.

Upper Cimarron Valley.
    xx Cimarron Valley.

Upper Don Valley.
    xx Don Valley.

Upper Engadine, Switzerland.
    x Oberengadin.
    xx Engadine, Switzerland.
--Agriculture.
    sa Subdivision Switzerland. Upper
        Engadine under: Agriculture.
        Economic aspects.

Upper Freehold Township, Monmouth Co.,
    N.J.
--Social conditions.
    xx New Jersey. Social conditions.

Upper Grand River Basin, Mich. See
    Grand River Valley, Mich.

Upper Lusatia. See Lusatia.

Upper Michigan. See Michigan, Northern
    Peninsula.

Upper Mississippi Valley.
    sa Subdivision Upper Mississippi
        Valley under: Wild life.
        Conservation.
    xx Mississippi Valley.
--Agriculture.
    sa Subdivision Upper Mississippi
        Valley under: Farm manage-
        ment.
--Botany.
    sa Subdivision Upper Mississippi
        Valley under: Trees.
        Weeds.
        Fungi.
--Forestry.
    sa Subdivision Upper Mississippi
        Valley under: Trees.
        Wood-lots.

Uranium.
--Physiological effect.

Uranus (planet)
    xx Astronomy.

Uranyl chloride.

Urase. See Urease.

Urban-rural relationships. See Rural-
  urban relationships.

Urbanism. See City and town life.

Urbenville district, New South Wales.
--Forestry.

Urd bean.
    x Black gram.
      Blackgram.
      Gram, Black.
      Phaseolus mungo.
      Mungo bean.

Urdu language.
    sa Hindustani language.
    xx Hindustani language.
--Dictionaries.

Ure-ox. See Aurochs.

Urea.
    sa Urease.
      Thiourea.
    x Carbamide.
--Therapeutic use. See Urea in
  veterinary medicine.

Urea as feeding stuff.
--Abstracts.
--Research.

Urea as fertilizer.
    xx Fertilizer.
      Fertilizers, Nitrogenous.

Urea in plants.

Urea in veterinary medicine.
    x Urea. Therapeutic use.
    xx Veterinary materia medica
      and pharmacy.

Urease.

Urechis.
    xx Echiuridae.

Urechis caupo.

Uredinales. See Uredineae.

Uredineae.
    sa Puccinia.
      Calyptospora.
      Cedar rust.
      Amerosporae.
      Phragmosporae.
      Pucciniastrum.
      Ravenelia.
      Oat rust.
      Coleosporium.
      Gymnoconia.
      Caeoma.
      Apple rust.
      Wheat rust.
      Cereal rust.
      Carnation rust.
      Melampsoraceae.
      Flax rust.
      Coleopuccinia.
      Stem rust.
    x Uredinales.
      Rust fungi.

Uredineae, Effect of temperature on.
  See Temperature. Effect on rust.

Uredinopsis.
    xx Melampsoraceae.

Uredo aurantiaca.

Ureido-phenylacetylurea.

Urellia.

Uremia.
    xx Veterinary medicine.

Urena.
    xx Malvaceae.

Ureña, Venezuela.
--Goats.

Urena lobata.
     x Aramina fibre.
     Guaxima roxa.
     xx Fiber plants and vegetable
        fibers.

Ureters.
     xx Anatomy, Comparative.

Urethane.
     xx Anesthetics.

Urethra.
 --,Diseases.
     sa Urethrotomy.

Urethrotomy.
     xx Veterinary surgery.
     Urethra. Diseases.

Urginea maritima.
     x Squill, Red.
     Red squill.
     Scilla maritima.
 --Toxicity.
     xx Toxicology.

Uri (Canton)
 --Agriculture.
     xx Switzerland. Agriculture.
 --Forestry.
     xx Switzerland. Forestry.

Uric acid.

Uric acid as fertilizer.
 --Periodicals.

Uric acid in plants.

Urinary calculi. See Calculi, Urinary.

Urinary organs.
 --Calculi. See Calculi, Urinary.

Urine.
     sa Urea.
     Cynurenic acid.
     Hematuria.
 --Analysis and pathology.
     sa Diazo-reaction.
 --Bacteriology.
 --Fermentation.

Urine, Sugar in.

Urine of pregnant mares.
 --Tariff.

Urn burial.

Urns.

Urobilin.

Uroceridae.

Urochorda. See Tunicata.

Urocyon californicus sequoiensis.

Urocystis cepulae.

Urocystis tritici.

Urolithiasis. See Calculi, Urinary.

Uromyces.

Uromyces appendiculatus.

Uromyces phaseoli typica. See Bean
    rust.

Uromyces trifolii.

Uromycladium notabile.

Uronic acids.
     xx Acids.

Urophlyctis alfalfae.

Uroplatus.
     xx Lizards.

Uropoda.

Uropoda krameri.

Uropoda vegetans.

Uropodidae.
     sa Uropoda.

Uropygial gland.
     xx Ornithology, Physiological
        and structural.

Urothemis.
     xx Libellulidae.

Urotrema lasiurensis.

Ursidae.

Ursolic acid.
    x Urson.

Ursus.

Urtica.
    xx Urticaceae.

Urtica canadensis.

Urtica dioica.

Urtica nivea.   See Ramie.

Urtica sinensis.

Urticaceae.
    sa Artocarpus.
        Cecropia.
        Cannabis.
        Castilla elastica.
        Cudrania.
        Myriocarpa.
        Musanga.
        Humulus.
        Elatostema.
        Pilea.
        Urtica.

Urticales.

Urticaria.
    x Nettle-rash.

Uruguay.
    sa Minas, Uruguay.
--Agricultural experiment stations.
    sa Instituto fitotecnico y semil-
        lero nacional La Estanzuela.
--Agriculture.
    sa Uruguay. Domestic animals.
        Subdivision Agriculture under:
        Names of departments, etc.

Uruguay (Continued)
--Agriculture.
    sa Subdivision Uruguay under:
        Agricultural laborers.
        Agriculture. Economic
            aspects.
        Forage plants.
        Poultry.
        Sugar-beet.
        Cereals.
        Flax.
        Maize.
        Rice.
        Agricultural credit.
        Sugar-cane.
        Potatoes.
        Agriculture, Cooperative.
        Colonization, Agricultural.
        Agricultural policies and
            programs.
        Agricultural surveys.
        Agricultural administration.
        Agricultural outlook.
-- --Bibliography.
-- --Education.
-- --Statistics.
    xx Agriculture. Statistics.
--Apiculture.
    xx South America. Apiculture.
--Biography.
-- --Dictionaries.
--Botany.
    sa Subdivision Uruguay under:
        Trees.
        Mosses.
        Botany, Medical.
        Vegetable pathology.
        Subdivision Botany under:
        Montevideo.
--Cattle.
    xx Uruguay. Domestic animals.
--Cattle trade.
--Climate.
--Commerce.
    sa Subdivision Uruguay under:
        Farm produce. Marketing.
        Subdivision Commerce under:
        Names of cities, towns,
            etc.
 - --Brazil.
 - --Gt. Brit.
 - --U.S.
-- --Periodicals.
    xx Commerce. Periodicals.
-- --Statistics.

Uruguay (Continued)
--Commercial policy.
--Dairying.
--Domestic animals.
    sa Subdivision Uruguay under:
        Turkeys.
        Cattle.
        Swine.
    xx South America. Domestic ani-
        mals.
-- --Statistics.
--Economic conditions.
    sa Subdivision Uruguay under:
        History, Economic.
-- --Periodicals.
    xx Economic conditions. Periodi-
        cals.
--Economic policy.
    xx Economic policy.
--Entomology.
    sa Subdivision Uruguay under:
        Moths.
        Entomology, Economic.
-- --Periodicals.
--Forestry.
    sa Subdivision Uruguay under:
        Afforestation and reforesta-
          tion.
        Timber.
        Wood-using industries.
        Forest policy.
        Silviculture.
--History.
    sa Subdivision History under:
        History, Economic.
--Ichthyology.
--Industries and resources.
    sa Subdivision Uruguay under:
        Mines and mineral resources.
--Land.
    sa Subdivision Uruguay under:
        Land tenure.
        Land reform.
--Learned institutions and societies.
-- --Directories.
--Manufactures.
--Meteorology.
--Milk trade.
--Natural history.
--Ornithology.
--Politics and government.
--Pomology.
    xx South America. Pomology.

Uruguay (Continued)
--Roads.
    sa Subdivision Roads under:
        San Jose.
--Sericulture.
--Sheep.
--Social conditions.
    sa Subdivision Uruguay under:
        Cost and standard of
          living.
--Soils.
--Statistics.
    sa Subdivision Statistics under:
        Uruguay. Commerce.
        Montevideo.
--Swine.
    xx Uruguay. Domestic animals.
--Viticulture.

Uruguayan literature.
--Bibliography.

Uruguayan periodicals.
--Bibliography.

Urundi.
        Formerly a district of German
        East Africa; now part of
        Ruanda-Urundi trust territory
        of Belgium. All entries in
        this catalog are under Ruanda-
        Urundi.

Urus.
    x Aurochs.

Use tax. (DIRECT)
    xx Taxation.

Usechini.

Useful arts. See Technology.

Useful plants. See Botany, Economic.

Usneaceae.

Usnic acid.

Ussuri. See Usuri.

Ustilaga carbo.

Ustilaginaceae.
 sa Mycosyrinx.
  Ustilago.
  Tilletia.
  Cintractia.
  Sphacelotheca.
  Urocystis cepulae.
  Sorosporium.
 xx Ustilagineae.

Ustilaginales. See Ustilagineae.

Ustilagineae.
 sa Ustilaginaceae.
  Tilletiaceae.
 x Smut fungi.
  Ustilaginales.
 xx Fungi.
 --Bibliography.

Ustilago antherarum.

Ustilago avenae.
 sa Oat smut.

Ustilago crameri.

Ustilago hordei. See Barley smut.

Ustilago kolleri.
 x Ustilago levis.

Ustilago levis. See Ustilago kolleri.

Ustilago longissima.

Ustilago nuda.

Ustilago perennans.

Ustilago striaeformis.

Ustilago tritici.

Ustilago zeae.

Ustilina zonata.

Ustulina. See Ustilina.

Usuri Region.
 --Forestry.

Usury. See Interest and usury.

Usury laws. (DIRECT)
 xx Interest and usury.

Uta.
 xx Iguanidae.

Uta (Disease) See Leishmaniosis.

Uta stansburiana stansburiana.

Utah.
 sa Salt Lake Valley, Utah.
  Great Salt Lake.
  Tooele Valley, Utah//
 --Agricultural Experiment Station.
 -- --Bibliography.
  xx U.S. Agricultural experiment
   station. Bibliography.
   Agricultural experiment
    stations. Publications.
 --Agriculture.
  sa Subdivision Agriculture under:
   Utah Lake Valley.
   Cache Co., Utah//
   Subdivision Utah under:
    Agriculture. Economic
     aspects.
    Ranges.
    Sugar-beet.
    Agricultural outlook.
    Agricultural credit.
    Agricultural policies and
     programs.
    Wheat.
    Forage plants.
    Potatoes.
    Agricultural extension.
    Rehabilitation, Rural.
    Farms.
    Crops and climate.
 -- --Directories..
 -- --Education.
  sa Utah. Agricultural College,
   Logan.
   Subdivision Utah under:
    Agricultural extension.
 -- --Periodicals.
 --Altitudes.
  xx Altitudes.
 --Antiquities.
 --Botany.
  sa Subdivision Botany under:
   Uintah Mountains, Utah.
   Escalante Valley, Utah.
   Wild flowers.

Utah (Continued)
--Botany.
    xx Utah. Natural history.
--Cattle.
    xx U.S. Cattle.
--Climate.
    sa Subdivision Utah under:
      Crops and climate.
--Description and travel.
--Directories.
--Domestic animals.
    sa Subdivision Sheep under: Utah.
-- --Statistics.
--Economic conditions.
    sa Subdivision Economic conditions
      under: Washington Co., Utah.
-- --Bibliography.
    sa Subdivision Utah. Bibliography
      under: Agriculture. Economic
        aspects.
-- --Periodicals.
--Entomology.
    sa Subdivision Utah under:
      Hymenoptera.
      Entomology, Economic.
--Fisheries.
--Forest reservations.
    sa Wasatch National Forest.
      Fishlake National Forest,
        Utah.
      Ashley National Forest, Utah-
        Wyoming//
--Forestry.
--Gazetteers.
--Geology.
    sa Subdivision Geology under:
      Park City district.
      Henry Mountains.
      Wasatch Mountains, Utah//
      Subdivision Utah under:
      Water, Underground.
      Mines and mineral resources.
--Government salaries.
    xx U.S. Government salaries.
--History.
-- --Sources.
    sa Subdivision Utah under:
      Archives.
    xx U.S. History. Sources.
--Industries and resources.
    sa Subdivision Utah under:
      Conservation of natural
        resources.

Utah (Continued)
--Land.
    sa Subdivision Utah under:
      Land utilization.
      Land. Classification.
--Legislative manuals.
    sa Utah. Directories.
--Libraries.
    xx U.S. Libraries.
--Manufactures.
--Maps.
--Meteorology.
    sa Subdivision Utah under:
      Precipitation (Meteorology)
--Natural history.
    sa Utah. Botany.
      Utah. Zoology.
    xx U.S. Natural history.
--Ornithology.
--Paleontology.
--Parks.
    sa Cedar Breaks, Utah.
    xx U.S. Parks.
--Politics and government.
    xx U.S. Politics and government.
--Population.
    xx U.S. Population.
--Roads.
-- --Law.
    xx Roads. Legislation.
      U.S. Roads. Law.
--Sanitary affairs.
--Sheep.
    xx Utah. Domestic animals.
--Soils.
    sa Subdivision Soils under:
      Salt Lake Valley, Utah.
      Sevier Valley, Utah.
      Escalante Valley, Utah//
      Subdivision Utah under:
      Soil-surveys.
      Soil erosion.

Utah. State Planning Board.
--Bibliography.
    xx Economic planning. Bibliog-
      raphy.

Utah.
--Statistics.
    sa Utah. Industries and re-
      sources.
--Water-supply.
    sa Subdivision Water-supply un-
      der: Salt Lake City//

2279

Utah (Continued)
--Water-supply.
  sa Subdivision Utah under:
    Water, Underground.
    Water-rights.
    Water conservation.
--Zoology.
  sa Subdivision Zoology under:
    Beaver Co., Utah.
    Uinta Mountains, Utah.
    Subdivision Utah under:
    Myriapoda.
    Mammalia.
    Batrachia.
    Reptilia.
    Game.
  xx Utah. Natural history.

Utah Co., Utah.
  xx Utah.
--Social conditions.
  sa Subdivision Utah. Utah Co.
    under: Community life.
--Statistics.

Utah juniper. See Juniperus utahensis.

Utah Lake Drainage System.

Utah Lake Valley.
--Agriculture.
  sa Subdivision Utah Lake Valley
    under: Agriculture. Economic
    aspects. Utah.

Ute Indians.
  xx Indians, North American.

Utensils. See Implements, utensils, etc.

Uterus.
  xx Cattle. Anatomy and physiology.
--Diseases.
  sa Pyometra.
    Metritis.
    Uterus. Displacements.
--Displacements.
  x Prolapse.
  xx Uterus. Diseases.

Utetheisa.

Utica, N.Y.
--Botany.

Utica, N.Y. (Continued)
--Commerce.
  sa Subdivision Utica, N.Y. under:
    Produce trade.
--Markets.

Utilization of farm produce. See Farm
  produce. Utilization.

Utilization of farm produce (Chemical)
  See Chemurgy.

Utilization of natural resources. See
  Natural resources. Utilization.

Utilization of waste. See Waste products.

Utopias.

Utowana (Yacht)

Utrasonic waves.
--Industrial applications.

Utrecht.
--Natural history.

Utricularia.
  xx Aquatic plants.

Utricularia vulgaris.

Uttar Pradesh.
  Before 1949 was named United
    Provinces of Agra and Oudh.
  x India. Uttar Pradesh.
--Agriculture.
  sa Subdivision Uttar Pradesh
    under: Agricultural poli-
    cies and programs.
    Rural surveys.
    Subdivision India. Uttar
    Pradesh under: Coloniza-
    tion, Agricultural.
    Rehabilitation, Rural.
-- --Periodicals.
-- --Statistics.
--Cattle.
--Commerce.
--Domestic animals.
--Economic conditions.
  sa Subdivision Uttar Pradesh
    under: Rural surveys.

Uttar Pradesh (Continued)
--Forestry.
-- --Research.
--Land.
    sa Subdivision Uttar Pradesh
        under: Land reform.
--Research.
-- --Periodicals.
--Social conditions.
    sa Subdivision Uttar Pradesh
        under: Rural surveys.
--Soils.
    sa Subdivision Uttar Pradesh
        under: Soil conservation.
        Soil-surveys.

Uva ursi.

Uvalde Co., Tex.
    xx Texas.

Uzbekistan.
--Agricultural experiment stations.
--Agriculture.
    sa Subdivision Uzbekistan under:
        Sugar-beet.
        Agricultural policies and
        programs.
        Mechanized farming.
        Farm management.
- --History.
-- --Periodicals.
-- --Statistics.
--Bibliography.
-- --Periodicals.
--Botany.
    sa Subdivision Uzbekistan under:
        Plants, Cultivated.
        Trees.
        Shrubs.
-- --Research.
--Cattle.
    xx Uzbekistan. Domestic animals.
--Climate.
--Domestic· animals.
    sa Uzbekistan. Goats.
        Uzbekistan. Cattle.
-- --Research.
--Economic conditions.
-- --Periodicals.
--Economic policy.
--Entomology.
    sa Subdivision Entomology under:
        Turkestan.

Uzbekistan (Continued)
--Entomology.
    sa Subdivision Uzbekistan under:
        Entomology, Economic.
--Forestry.
    sa Subdivision Uzbekistan under:
        Trees.
        Shrubs.
-- --Research.
--Goats.
    xx Uzbekistan. Domestic animals.
--Industries.
--Land.
    sa Subdivision Uzbekistan under:
        Land utilization.
--Meteorology.
--Ornithology.
--Pomology.
    xx U.S. S. R. Pomology.
-- --Research.
--Research.
--Sheep.
--Soils.
--Statistics.
--Viticulture.
--Zoology.
-- --Research.

Vaal River.

Vacant lot cultivation.
    xx Gardens.
        Community gardens.

Vacations.
    sa Holidays.
        Farm vacations.
    xx Holidays.
        Recreation.

Vacations, Employee.
    x Company vacations.
        Employee vacations.
        Employees' vacations.
        Holidays with pay.
        Leave with pay.
        Paid vacations.
        Vacations with pay.
    xx Hours of labor.
        Labor and laboring classes.
        Labor laws and legislation.
        Non-wage payments.

Vacations with pay.   See Vacations,
    Employee.

Vaccination.
    sa Inoculation.
    xx Serumtherapy.
       Inoculation.
--Societies.

Vaccine.
    sa Bruschettini's hog cholera
       vaccine.
       Crystal violet hog cholera
       vaccine.
       Brucella abortus vaccines.
       Pigeon-pox virus vaccine.
       Hog cholera vaccine.
       Spray vaccine.

Vaccine, Bacterial.   See Bacterins.

Vaccine.
--Research.

Vaccine lymph.
    sa Viruses.

Vaccinia.

Vaccinium.

Vaccinium caespitosum.

Vaccinium virgatum.
    x Rabbit eye blueberry.

Vaccinium vitis idaea.

Vacuum.
--Periodicals.

Vacuum cleaner, Electric.   See Electric
  vacuum cleaner.

Vacuum dryer.
    xx Drying apparatus.

Vacuum for insect control.
    xx Entomology, Economic.
       Insecticides.

Vacuum-gages.
    xx Gages.

Vacuum-pumps.

Vacuum-tube circuits.
    x Electronic circuits.
       Thermionic valve circuits.
    xx Electric circuits.
       Vacuum-tubes.

Vacuum-tubes.
    sa Cathode ray tubes.
       Amplifiers, Vacuum-tube.
       Geiger-Müller counters.
       Vacuum-tube circuits.
    x Klystrons.
       Triodes.
       Electron tubes.
       Thermionic tubes.
       Diodes.

Vagina.
--Diseases.
    sa Vagina. Displacements.
--Displacements.
    x Prolapse.
    xx Vagina. Diseases.

Vagina tendinis.

Vaginitis infectiosa.
    x Contagious granular vaginitis
       of cattle.
       Granular vaginitis of cattle.
       Granular vaginitis of sheep.

Vagrancy.

Vakhsh Valley.
--Pomology.
-- --Research.
--Viticulture.

Val Bregaglia, Switzerland.
    xx Bergell.
--Forestry.

Valais (Canton)
--Agriculture.
--Botany.
--Cattle.
--Domestic animals.
    xx Switzerland. Domestic animals.
--Entomology.
    sa Subdivision Switzerland.
       Valais (Canton) under:
       Coleoptera.
       Lepidoptera.
--Pomology.

Valais (Canton) (Continued)
--Viticulture.

Valdivia (Ship)

Valdivia.
--Forestry.

Valdostana cattle.

Valdres Valley, Norway.
--Social life and customs.

Valdrôme sheep.   See Préalpes du Sud
sheep.

Vale irrigation project, Or.
x Vale-Owyhee project, Or.
xx Irrigation projects.

Vale-Owyhee project, Or.   See Owyhee
irrigation project, Or.; Vale irrigation project, Or.

Valence (Theoretical chemistry)

Valencia, Lake.   See Lake Valencia.

Valencia, Spain (Province)
--Agriculture.
sa Subdivision Spain. Valencia
(Province) under: Poultry.
Irrigation.
- --History.
-- --Statistics.
--Commerce.
-- --History.
--Economic conditions.
sa Subdivision Spain. Valencia
under: History, Economic.
--Geology.
--History.
sa Subdivision Spain. Valencia
under: History, Economic.
--Natural history.

Valencia Co., N.M.
xx New Mexico.
--Zoology.
sa Subdivision New Mexico.
Valencia Co. under:
Mammalia.

Valencia orange.   See Orange, Valencia.

Valency.
sa Valence (Theoretical chemistry)

Valeriana officinalis.

Valerianaceae.

Valgus hemipterus L.

Valhalla (Yacht)

Valier Valley, Mont.
--Agriculture.
sa Subdivision Valier Valley
under: Wheat.

Valine.
--Metabolism.

Valladolid, Spain (Province)
--Botany.
sa Subdivision Spain. Valladolid
(Province) under: Vegetable
pathology.
--Domestic animals.
sa Valladolid, Spain (Province) ⌐\
Horse.
--Entomology.
sa Subdivision Spain Valladolid
(Province) under: Ento- ˙ ˙
mology, Economic.
--Horse.
sa Subdivision Spain. Valladolid
(Province) under: Horses.
Breeding.
xx Valladolid, Spain (Province)
Domestic animals.
--Statistics.

Valle de Cuyamel, Honduras.
--Economic conditions.

Valle del Cauca, Departamento del.   See
Colombia. Departamento del Valle del
Cauca.

Vallesia glabra.

Valley Co., Neb.
--Soils.
sa Subdivision Nebraska. Valley
Co. under: Soil-surveys.

Valley Forge Park.

Valley of Ten Thousand Smokes.

Valley View Farm, New Boston, N.H.

Valleys.
--Temperature.

Vallisneria spiralis.

Vallisnerieae.
    sa Vallisneria.
    xx Aquatic plants.

Vallombrosa.
--Botany.

Vallombrosa, Istituto forestale di.

Valonia.
    xx Valoniaceae.

Valoniaceae.
    sa Microdictyon.
    Valonia.

Valorization of coffee.   See Coffee.
    Valorization.

Valouyskaya, Russia.
--Experiment Station.

Valsa.

Valsa japonica.

Valsa leucostoma.

Valsaceae.
    sa Valsa.
    Diaporthe.

Valsonectria parasitica.   See Diaporthe
    parasitica.

Valuation.
    Here are entered only the most
    general works. For valuation
    for taxing purposes, See As-
    sessment. For valuation of spe-
    cial classes of property for
    purposes other than taxation,
    See Subdivision Valuation, e.g.,
    Agriculture. Implements and
    machinery. Valuation; Farm
    produce. Valuation.

Valuation (Continued)
    sa Farm valuation.
    Real estate business.
    Mine valuation.

Valuation of land.   See Farm valua-
    tion.

Value.
    Here are entered works on the
    theory of value in economics;
    works on moral and esthetic
    values, etc., are entered
    under Worth.
    sa Index numbers (Economics)

Valutin.
    xx Drugs.

Valvatae.

Valves.
    xx Mechanical engineering.

Vampirops lineatus.
--Parasites.

Vampyrella lateritia.

Van Buren Co., Iowa.
--Soils.
    sa Subdivision Iowa. Van Buren
        Co. under: Soil-surveys.

Van Wyk's Estate, Cape of Good Hope.

Van Zandt Co., Tex.
--Soils.
    sa Subdivision Texas. Van Zandt
        Co. under: Soil-surveys.

Vanadium.
--Effect on plants.
    x Plants, Effect of vanadium on.

Vanaspati.
    x Banaspati.
    xx Fats and oils.
    Shortening.

Vancouver Island.
--Agriculture.
    sa Subdivision British Columbia.
       Vancouver Island under:
       Agriculture. Economic
         aspects.
       Part-time farming.
--Botany.
--Forestry.
--Geology.
--Natural history.
--Ornithology.
--Paleobotany.
--Paleontology.
--Zoology.

Vanderburgh Co., Ind.
    xx Indiana.
--Agriculture.
-- --Periodicals.
--Soils.
    sa Subdivision Indiana.
       Vanderburgh Co. under:
       Soil-surveys.

Van Dieman's Land.　See Tasmania.

Vanellus cristatus.

Vanessa.

Vanessa californica.

Vanessa urticae.

Vang, Norway (Hedmark)
--Public lands.

Vanilla.
    sa Spices.
       Vanillin.
--Bibliography.
--Chemistry.
    xx Chemistry, Vegetable.
--Curing.
    xx Curing.
--Diseases.
    sa Root-rot of vanilla.
--Fertilization.
--Research.
--Statistics.

Vanillin.
    sa Soil, Vanillin in.

Vanillosmopsis.
    xx Asteraceae.

Vanillosmopsis erythropappa.

Van't Hoff's law.

Vanua Levu.

Vapor absorption.　See Vapors. Ab-
    sorption and adsorption.

Vapor-liquid equilibrium.
    xx Liquids.
    Vapors.

Vapor pressure.
    sa Vaporization, Heats of.
--Bibliography.

Vaporization, Heats of.
    x Heats of vaporization.
    xx Specific heat.
    Vapor pressure.

Vaporized insecticides.　See Insecti-
    cidal vapors.

Vapors.
    sa Insecticidal vapors.
       Vapor-liquid equilibrium.
--Absorption and adsorption.
    x Vapor absorption.
       Sorption.
    xx Adsorption.
--Bibliography.

Vapourer moth.　See Notolophus antiqua.

Var.　See France. Département du Var.

Varese (Province)
--Agriculture.
--Economic conditions.
-- --Periodicals.
--Land.

Variable oak leaf caterpillar.　See
    Heterocampa manteo.

Variation (Biology)
    sa Adaptation (Biology)
       Botany. Variation.
       Evolution.
       Mendel's law.

Variation (Biology) (Continued)
    sa Color of animals [birds,
        flowers, insects, leaves,
        plants].
        Natural selection.
        Species, Origin of.
        Variegation.
        Zoology. Variation.
        Color variation (Biology)
--Statistics. See Biometry.

Variation, Climatic. See Climatic varia-
    tion.

Variegated cut worm. See Perodroma
    saucia.

Variegation.

Variety testing.

Variola. See Smallpox.

Variola ovina. See Sheep-pox.

Varitypers.
    xx Type-writers.

Varnish and varnishing.
    xx Protective coatings.
       Finishes and finishing.
--Bibliography.
-- --Periodicals.
--Dictionaries.
--Directories.
--Legislation.
--Periodicals.
    sa Varnish and varnishing. Bib-
        liography. Periodicals.
--Prices.
--Research.
--Societies.
--Statistics.
--Testing.
    xx Testing.
--Year-books.

Varsuga.
--Botany.

Vas deferens.

Vasates quadripedes.
    x Maple bladder-gall mite.
    xx Maple. Pests.

Vascular cryptogams. See Pteridophyta.

Vascular plants. See Botany.

Vascular system.
    sa Blood. Circulation.
       Blood vessels.
    x Circulatory system.
    xx Blood vessels.
--Diseases.
--Research.

Vasectomy.

Västerbotten, Sweden. See Vesterbotten,
    Sweden.

Västernorrland, Sweden. See Vester-
    norrland, Sweden.

Västervik, Sweden.
--Botany.

Västmanland, Sweden. See Vestmanland,
    Sweden.

Vaucheria.

Vaucheria geminata.

Vaucheriaceae.
    xx Algae.

Vaud (Canton)
    sa Drainage. Switzerland. Vaud
        (Canton)
--Agriculture.
    sa Vaud (Canton) Domestic ani-
        mals.
    Subdivision Switzerland. Vaud
        (Canton) under: Agri-
        cultural administration.
--Botany.
--Cattle.
    xx Vaud (Canton) Domestic ani-
        mals.
--Dairying.
--Domestic animals.
    sa Vaud (Canton) Cattle.
    xx Vaud (Canton) Agriculture.
--Viticulture.
-- --History.

Vaudreuil Co., Que.
--Soils.
        sa Subdivision Quebec (Province)
          Vaudreuil Co. under: Soil-
            surveys.

Vaux de Nevers, France.
--Agriculture.

Vavaea.

Veal.
        xx Digestion.
--Composition.
--Digestibility.
--Grading and standardization.
--Prices.
        xx Meat. Prices.
--Statistics.
        xx Meat. Statistics.

Vealers. See Calves.

Vector analysis.
        sa Calculus of tensors.
          Linear programming.

Vectors. See Animals as carriers of
contagion; Insects as carriers of contagion; Insects and plant diseases.

Vedalia. See Rodolia.

Vedas.

Vega (Ship)

Vegetable allocations. See Vegetables.
Allocations.

Vegetable auctions. See Auctions.

Vegetable breeding. See Vegetables.
Breeding.

Vegetable charcoal.
        xx Charcoal.

Vegetable containers. See Food containers.

Vegetable cooperatives. See Vegetable
growers' cooperative associations.

Vegetable culture. See Vegetable
gardening.

Vegetable dealers associations.
--Directories. See Produce trade.
Directories.

Vegetable dehydration. See Drying of
fruits and vegetables.

Vegetable dehydration plants. See
Dehydration plants.

Vegetable dehydrators. See Drying
apparatus. Food.

Vegetable drying. See Drying of fruits
and vegetables.

Vegetable embryology.
        x Botany. Embryology.
          Embryology, Vegetable.
          Plant embryology.
          Embryogenesis.
        xx Embryology.
--Bibliography.

Vegetable estimating. See Vegetables.
Estimating of crop.

Vegetable fibers. See Fiber plants and
vegetable fibers.

Vegetable gardening.   (INDIRECT)
        sa Vegetables.
          Market gardening.
        x Truck gardening.
          Vegetable culture.
          Kitchen-gardens.
        xx Gardening.
          Vegetables.
          Market gardening.
--Abstracts.
--Bibliography.
        sa Vegetable gardening [geo-
           graphic subdivision] Bib-
           liography, e.g., Vegetable
           gardening. U.S. Bibliog-
           raphy.
        xx Gardening. Bibliography.
--Calendars.
        xx Calendars.
--Congresses.

Vegetable gardening (Continued)
--Dictionaries.
    x Vegetable gardening. En-
       cyclopaedias.
--Economic aspects.
--Encyclopaedias. See Vegetable
    gardening. Dictionaries.
--Handbooks, manuals, etc.
--Implements and machinery.
    xx Agriculture. Implements and
      machinery.
    Gardening. Implements and
      machinery.
--Juvenile literature.
    xx Gardening. Juvenile literature.
--Periodicals.
--Societies. See Vegetables. Societies.
--Study and teaching.
--Text-books.

Vegetable growers' associations. See
    Vegetables. Societies.

Vegetable growers' cooperative associa-
    tions.
    sa Subdivision Societies, Coopera-
      tive under: Potatoes.
    x Vegetable cooperatives.
    xx Cooperation. Societies.
    Vegetables. Societies.
    Agriculture, Cooperative.
    Societies.

Vegetable histology. See Histology,
    Vegetable.

Vegetable-ivory.
    sa Phytelephas.
    xx Phytelephas.
--Grading and standardiztion.

Vegetable juices.
    sa Vitamins in vegetable juices.

Vegetable lamb.

Vegetable leaf meals.
    x Leaf meals, Vegetable.
    xx Leaves.
    Vegetables. By-products.

Vegetable marrow. See Squash.

Vegetable milk.
    sa Canarium seed as food.
    Soy-bean milk.

Vegetable mold. See Humus.

Vegetable oils. See Fats and oils;
    Essences and essential oils.

Vegetable organography. See Botany.
    Morphology.

Vegetable oyster. See Salsify.

Vegetable pathology. (INDIRECT)
    sa Names of plant diseases, e.g.,
      Anthracnose; Black rot;
      Peach yellows.
    Subdivision Diseases under:
      Names of plants, e.g.,
      Apricot. Diseases; Wheat.
      Diseases.
    Subdivision Effect on plants
      under: Poison.
    Copper sulphate.
    Sulphurous acid.
    Winds.
    Subdivision Effect on plant
      diseases under: Moisture.
    Weather.
    Soil temperature.
    Soil moisture.
    Light.
    Antibiotics.
    Fungi.
    Fungicides.
    Mildew.
    Decomposition.
    Spraying.
    Insecticides.
    Noxious vapors.
    Root knots.
    Farm pests.
    Fruit diseases.
    Smoke.
    Seed sterilization.
    Tobacco wilt.
    Bermuda lily disease.
    Disease resistant plants.
    Bacteria and plant diseases.
    Injecting solutions in plants.
    Ringspot of crucifers.
    Plant protection.
    Virus diseases of solanaceous
      plants.

Vegetable pathology (Continued)
  sa Soil reaction diseases.
     Diseased plants. Physiological.
     Diseased plants. Chemical re-
        actions.
     Diseased plants. Cytology.
     Insects and plant diseases.
     Deficiency diseases in plants.
     Physiological diseases of
        plants.
     Plant quarantine.
     Plant disease transmission.
     Cancer in plants.
     Seed. Disinfection.
     Plant disease organisms.
     Nematode diseases of plants.
     Fungus diseases of plants.
--Abstracts.
-- --Periodicals.
--Addresses, essays, lectures.
--Bibliography.
  sa Subdivision Bibliography under:
     Mottle leaf.
     Mosaic disease.
     Vegetable pathology. Peri-
        odicals//
     Subdivision Diseases. Bibliog-
        raphy under: Apple.
     Chestnut.
     Cereals//
     Disease resistance in plants.
        Bibliography//
     Vegetable pathology. Gt. Brit.
        Bibliography.
     Vegetable pathology. Japan.
        Bibliography//
-- --Periodicals.
--Charts.
--Collection and preservation of speci-
     mens.
  xx Pathological specimens. Col-
     lection and preservation.
--Congresses.
  sa Subdivision Congresses under:
     Blister rust.
     Plant quarantine.
     Spraying apparatus//
--Diagnosis.
  sa Subdivision Diagnosis under:
     Virus diseases of plants.
     Virus diseases of potatoes.
  xx Diagnosis.
--Dictionaries.

Vegetable pathology (Continued) ·
--Environmental factors.
-- --Bibliography.
  xx Vegetable pathology. Bibliog-
     raphy.
--Experimental stations.
--Extension work. See Plant pathology
     extension work.
--Forecasting.
  xx Agricultural forecasting.
--Handbooks, manuals, etc.
--History.
--Laboratory methods.
  xx Laboratory methods.
--Legislation.
  sa Plant quarantine.
     Subdivision Legislation under:
        Barberry eradication//
  x Plant quarantine. Legislation.
-- --Bibliography.
  xx Vegetable pathology. Bibliog-
     raphy.
--Maps.
  x Maps of plant diseases.
  xx Maps.
--Names.
  sa Subdivision Names under:
     Virus diseases of plants.
--Outlines, syllabi, etc.
--Periodicals.
  sa Subdivision Periodicals under
     Vegetable pathology ₍geo-
        graphic subdivision₎ e.g.,
     Vegetable pathology.
        France. Periodicals.
-- --Bibliography.
--Pictorial works.
--Research.
  sa Subdivision Research under
     Vegetable pathology ₍geo-
        graphic subdivision₎ e.g.,
     Vegetable pathology.
        Russia. Research.
-- --Directories.
-- --Societies.
--Societies.
-- --Directories.
--Study and teaching.
--Terminology.
--Text-books.
--Weather influences. See Weather.
     Effect on plant diseases.

Vegetable pathology as an occupation.

Vegetable policies and programs. (DI-
RECT)
    xx Agricultural policies and
        programs.

Vegetable processing plants. See Food
    processing plants.

Vegetable products.

Vegetable products, Fatty acids in.
    xx Acids, Fatty.

Vegetable seeds. See Vegetables. Seed.

Vegetable soils.
    xx Soil.
        Soil and crops.

Vegetable supply.

Vegetable teratology.

Vegetable tops. See Greens.

Vegetable toxicology. See Toxicology.

Vegetable trade. See Produce trade.

Vegetable wastes. See Vegetables. By-
    products.

Vegetable waxes. See Waxes.

Vegetable workers.
    xx Agricultural laborers.

Vegetable yields.
    xx Crop yields.

Vegetables. (INDIRECT)
    sa Cookery (Vegetables)
       Canning crops.
       Food, Raw.
       Market gardening.
       Greens.
       Root-crops.
       Vegetable gardening.
       Vegetarianism.
       Names of vegetables, e.g.,
         Celery; Peas; Potatoes.
       Subdivision Vegetables under:
         Rotation of crops.
    x Truck (Vegetables)
    xx Vegetable gardening.

Vegetables (Continued)
    --Acreage.
    --Advertising.
       sa Subdivision Advertising under:
         Potatoes.
       xx Farm produce. Advertising.
    --Allocations.
       x Vegetable allocations.
    --Bacteriology.
    --Bibliography.
       sa Subdivision Bibliography
         under: Peas.
         Vegetables, Canned.
         Vegetables. Cost of
           production.
         Potatoes.
         Onions.
         Vegetables [geographic sub-
           division] e.g., Vege-
           tables. Tropics. Bib-
           liography.
    --Biochemistry.
       xx Chemistry, Vegetable.
    --Breeding.
       sa Subdivision Breeding under:
         Tomatoes.
         Pepper.
         Egg-plant.
         Cucurbitaceae.
         Onions.
         Peas.
         Beans.
         Brassica.
         Salad plants.
         Cucumbers.
         Rutabaga.
         Turnips.
         Root-crops.
       x Vegetable breeding.
    --By-products.
       sa Subdivision By-products
         under: Asparagus.
         Potatoes.
         Sweet potatoes.
         Tomatoes.
         Vegetable leaf meals.
       x Vegetable wastes.
       xx Waste products.

Vegetables, Canned.
    sa Beans, Canned.
       Peas, Canned.
       Greens, Canned.
       Maize, Canned.
       Potatoes, Canned.

Vegetables, Canned (Continued)
  x Canned vegetables.
--Bibliography.
  xx Vegetables. Bibliography.
     Canned goods. Bibliography.
--Cost of production.
  sa Subdivision Cost of pro-
     duction under: Peas,
     Canned.
--Grading and standardization.
  sa Subdivision Grading and
     standardization under:
     Asparagus, Canned.
     Beet, Canned.
     Carrots, Canned.
     Beans, Canned.
     Maize, Canned.
     Peas, Canned.
     Tomatoes, Canned.
     Spinach, Canned.
     Succotash, Canned.
     Pumpkin, Canned.
     Squash, Canned.
     Maize, Sweet, Canned.
     Sweet potatoes, Canned.
     Beans, Lima, Canned.
     Potatoes, Canned.
     Onions, Canned.
     Okra, Canned.
     Sauerkraut, Canned.
     Greens, Canned.
  xx Canned goods. Grading and
     standardization.
     Vegetables, Grading and
     standardization.
--Legislation.
--Marketing.
  xx Canned goods. Industry and
     trade.
     Vegetables. Marketing.
--Prices.
  sa Subdivision Prices under:
     Peas, Canned.
     Tomatoes, Canned.
  xx Vegetables. Prices.
     Canned goods. Prices.
-- --Subsidies.
  xx Price subsidies.
--Statistics.
  sa Subdivision Statistics under:
     Maize, Canned.
     Peas, Canned.
     Tomatoes, Canned.
     Beans, Canned.
     Beet, Canned.

Vegetables, Canned (Continued)
--Transportation.
  sa Railroads. Rates. Vegetables,
     Canned.
  xx Vegetables. Transportation.

Vegetables.
--Canning.
  sa Subdivision Canning under:
     Beet.
     Maize.
     Peas//
  xx Canning and preserving.
-- --Congresses.
 . --Costs.
  xx Canned goods. Industry and
     trade. Costs.
     Canning and preserving. Costs.

Vegetables, Carbohydrates in.
  xx Carbohydrates.

Vegetables, Carotin in.
  sa Lettuce, Carotin in.
  xx Carotin.

Vegetables.
--Coloring.
  x Coloring vegetables.
--Composition.
  sa Subdivision Composition
     under: Tomatoes.
     Soy-bean.
     Rhubarb.
     Egg-plant.
     Rutabaga.
     Turnips.
     Dried vegetables.
-- --Bibliography.
  xx Food. Analysis. Bibliography.
--Consumption.   (INDIRECT)
  sa Subdivision Consumption
     under: Sweet potatoes.
  x Consumption of vegetables.
  xx Food consumption.
-- --Statistics.
-- -- --Bibliography.
--Containers. See Food containers.
--Control of production.
  xx Farm produce. Control of
     production.
--Cookery. See Cookery (Vegetables)
--Cost of marketing. See Vegetables.
     Marketing. Costs.

Vegetables (Continued)
--Cost of production.
    sa Subdivision Cost of production
       under: Beans.
       Potatoes.
       Asparagus.
       Cabbage.
       Melons.
       Onions.
       Tomatoes.
       Peas.
       Broccoli.
       Beans.
-- --Bibliography.
    sa Subdivision Cost of production.
       Bibliography under: Peas.
    xx Vegetables. Bibliography.
--Crop reports.
    xx Crop reports.
-- --Bibliography.
--Cytology.
    xx Plant cells and tissues.
--Dictionaries.
--Directories. See Nurseries (Horti-
    culture) Directories.
--Disease resistant varieties.
    sa Subdivision Disease resistant
       varieties under: Beans.
       Brussels sprouts.
       Cabbage.
       Cowpeas.
       Kohl-rabi.
       Onions.
       Peas.
       Potatoes.
       Sweet potatoes.
       Tomatoes.
--Diseases.
    sa Subdivision Diseases under
       names of vegetables, e.g.,
       Beans. Diseases.
       Storage and transportation
       diseases and injuries.
-- --Bibliography.

Vegetables, Dried. See Dried vegetables.

Vegetables.
--Drying. See Drying of fruits and
    vegetables.
--Economic aspects.
    xx Agriculture. Economic aspects.
--Effect of climate.

Vegetables, Effect of temperature on.
    See Temperature. Effect on vegetables.

Vegetables.
--Estimating of crop.
    x Vegetable estimating.
    xx Crop estimating.
--Evaporation. See Drying of fruits
    and vegetables.
--Exhibitions.
    xx Agriculture. Fairs and ex-
       positions.
--Fermentation.
--Fertilization.
--Fertilizers. See Fertilizers for
    vegetables.
--Flavors and odors.
--Freezing and frost injury.
    xx Freezing of plants.
    Temperature. Effect on vege-
       tables.

Vegetables, Frozen. (INDIRECT)
    sa Peas, Frozen.
    Pumpkin, Frozen.
    Squash, Frozen.
    Cauliflower, Frozen.
    x Frozen vegetables.
    xx Food. Freezing.
    Vegetables. Preservation.
--Bibliography.
--Consumption.
--Cookery. See Cookery (Frozen vege-
    tables)
--Directories.
--Grading and standardization.
    sa Subdivision Grading and
       standardization under:
       Beans, Frozen.
       Cauliflower, Frozen.
       Asparagus, Frozen//
    xx Vegetables, Grading and
       standardization.
--Statistics.
--Transportation.
    xx Vegetables. Transportation.

Vegetables.
--Fumigation.
    xx Fumigation.
--Grading and standardization.
    sa Subdivision Grading and stand-
       ardization under: Tomatoes.
       Cabbage.
       Cauliflower//

Vegetables (Continued)
--Grading and standardization.
-- --Bibliography.
-- --Congresses.
    xx Standardization. Congresses.
--Hardiness.
    sa Subdivision Hardiness under:
      Tomatoes.
    xx Hardiness.
--Harvesting.
    sa Subdivision Harvesting under:
      Beans.
      Field pea.
      Onions//
    xx Harvesting.
- --Costs.
    sa Subdivision Harvesting. Costs
      under: Tomatoes.
      Potatoes.
    xx Harvesting. Costs.
--Harvesting time.
--History.
    sa Subdivision History under:
      Potato.
      Beet.
--Identification.
--Injuries.
    sa Subdivision Injuries under:
      Beans.
      Potatoes.
      Tomatoes.
--Inspection.
    sa Subdivision Inspection under:
      Potatoes.
      Soy-bean.
      Beans//
    xx Inspection.
      Farm produce. Inspection.
      Food. Adulteration and in-
        spection.
-- --Congresses.
-- --Directories.
    sa Subdivision Inspection. Direc-
      tories under: Beans.
      Peas.
-- --Fees and fee-bills.
-- --Handbooks, manuals, etc.
-- -- --Bibliography.
-- --Periodicals.
-- --Statistics.

Vegetables, Iodine in.
    xx Iodine.

Vegetables.
--Irrigation.
    sa Subdivision Vegetables under:
      Watering.
    xx Irrigation.
      Garden irrigation.
--Juvenile literature.
--Legislation.
    sa Subdivision Legislation under:
      Asparagus.
    xx Farm produce. Legislation.
--Loading and unloading equipment.
    xx Loading and unloading equip-
      ment.
--Marketing.   (INDIRECT)
    sa Subdivision Marketing under:
      Onions.
      Spinach.
      Cabbage//
      Storage and transportation
        diseases.
      Vegetables. Inspection.
      Vegetables. Grading and
        standardization.
-- --Bibliography.
    sa Subdivision Marketing. Bib-
      liography under: Tomatoes.
-- --Congresses.
    xx Farm produce. Marketing.
      Congresses.
-- --Control.
    sa Subdivision Marketing. Control
      under: Asparagus.
    xx Marketing. Control.
--Marketing, Cooperative.
    sa Subdivision Marketing, Co-
      operative under:
      Sweet potatoes.
    xx Marketing, Cooperative.
-- --Congresses.
-- --Societies.
--Marketing.
-- --Costs.
    sa Subdivision Marketing. Costs
      under: Potatoes.
      Beans, Dried.
    x Vegetables. Cost of marketing.
-- --Directories.
    xx Farm produce. Marketing.
      Directories.
· --Law.
-- --Periodicals.
- --Research.

Vegetables (Continued)
--Marketing.
-- --Spoilage and waste.
    xx Farm produce. Marketing.
       Spoilage and waste.
-- -- --Statistics.
-- --Study and teaching.
--Marketing agreements.
    sa Subdivision Marketing agree-
       ments under: Asparagus.
       Beans, Dried.
       Potatoes.
       Tomatoes.
       Celery.
       Dried peas.
       Peas.
    xx Marketing agreements.
--Mineral elements.
    xx Plants. Mineral elements.
--Names.
--Nomenclature.
    xx Botany. Nomenclature.
--Nutritive value. See Vegetables as
  food.

Vegetables, Packaged. See Vegetables.
  Packaging.

Vegetables.
--Packaging.
    x Vegetables. Prepackaging.
      Vegetables, Packaged.
-- --Congresses.
-- --Statistics.
--Packing.

Vegetables, Pectin in.
    xx Pectin.

Vegetables.
--Peeling. See Peeling (Vegetables)
--Periodicals.
    sa Vegetables [geographic sub-
       division] Periodicals, e.g.,
       Vegetables. Israel. Peri-
       odicals.

Vegetables (Continued)
--Pests.
    sa Subdivision Pests under:
       Peas.
       Asparagus.
       Celery.
       Parsley.
       Parsnip.
       Tomatoes.
       Sweet potato.
       Cauliflower.
       Vegetables.
-- --Bibliography.
--Physiology and morphology.
    sa Subdivision Physiology and
       morphology under:
       Cauliflower.
       Celery.
       Lettuce.
       Onions.
       Red pepper.
       Cabbage.
       Potatoes.
       Soy-bean.
    xx Botany. Physiology.
--Planting time.
    sa Subdivision Planting time
       under: Potatoes.
       Sweet potatoes.
    xx Planting time.
--Precooling.
    sa Subdivision Precooling under:
       Celery.
       Lettuce.
    xx Precooling.
--Prepackaging. See Vegetables.
  Packaging.
--Preservation.
    sa Subdivision Preservation
       under: Potatoes.
       Asparagus.
       Cabbage.
       Tomatoes.
       Brined vegetables.
       Drying of fruits and vege-
         tables.
       Pickling.
       Vegetables. Canning.
       Vegetables, Frozen.
    xx Food. Preservation.
       Farm produce. Preservation.
-- --Apparatus and supplies.

Vegetables (Continued)
--Prices.
      sa Subdivision Prices under:
         Cucumbers.
         Sweet potatoes.
         Potatoes.
         Tomatoes.
         Lettuce.
         Peas.
         Cabbage.
         Onions.
         Celery.
         Spinach.
         Vegetables, Canned.
-- --Bibliography.
- --Fixing.
      sa Subdivision Prices. Fixing
         under: Beans, Dried.
         Beans, Lima, Dried.
      xx Prices. Fixing.
--Processing.
      sa Drying of fruits and vege-
         tables.
         Vegetables, Canned.
         Vegetables, Frozen.
         Food processing plants.
      xx Food. Processing.
-- --Grading and standardization.
      xx Vegetables. Grading and
         standardization.
-- --Inspection.
      xx Food. Processing. Inspection.
-- --Laboratories.
      xx Food laboratories.
-- --Research.
--Quality.
      sa Subdivision Quality under:
         Potatoes.
         Dried vegetables.
      xx Farm produce. Quality.
--Research.
      sa Subdivision Research under:
         Canning crops//
         Vegetables [geographic sub-
         division] Research, e.g.,
         Vegetables. Israel. Re-
         search.
      xx Horticultural research.
--Respiration.
      xx Respiration.
--Ripening.
--Seed.
      xx Vegetable seeds.

Vegetables (Continued)
--Seed.
-- --Disinfection.
      sa Subdivision Disinfection under:
         Potatoes. Seed.
         Sweet potatoes. Seed.
         Tomatoes. Seed.
         Peas. Seed.
      xx Seeds. Disinfection.
-- --Harvesting.
-- --Labels.
      xx Seeds. Labels.
· --Sowing.
      xx Sowing.
-- --Statistics.
      xx Vegetables. Statistics.
-- --Storage.
      xx Seeds. Storage.
--Seedlings.
      xx Seedlings.
--Societies.
      sa Vegetable growers' cooperative
         associations.
      x Vegetable gardening. Socie-
         ties.
--Spacing.
      xx Plant spacing.
--Spraying. See Spraying. Vegetables.
--Sprouting.
--Statistics.
      sa Subdivision Statistics under:
         Potatoes.
         Vegetables, Canned.
         Vegetables. Transporta-
         tion//
         Vegetables [geographic sub-
         division] Statistics, e.g.,
         Vegetables. U.S. Sta-
         tistics.
      xx Agriculture. Statistics.
         Seeds. Statistics.
-- --Bibliography.
      sa Subdivision Statistics. Bib-
         liography under: Beans.

Vegetation maps. See Botany. Geography.
Maps.

Vegetative control. See Cover crops;
Soil-binding plants.

Vehicles.
 sa Carriages.
  Cars.
  Coaching.
  Transportation.
  Tires.
  Wagons.
 --Lighting. See Automobiles. Lighting.
 --Periodicals.
 --Statistics.
  sa Automobiles. Industry and
    statistics.
 --Taxation.
  sa Automobiles. Taxation.
  xx Taxation.

Veile amt, Denmark.
 --Agriculture.

Vein spot of pecan.

Veins.
 sa Blood vessels.
 xx Blood vessels.

Veld.
 x Grasslands.

Veld conservation act. See Forest and
veld conservation act.

Velebit Mountains.
 --Botany.
  xx Yugoslavia. Botany.

Veliidae.
 sa Rhagovelia.

Velikaia region.
 --Botany.

Vellinge, Sweden.
 --Botany.

Velloziaceae.

Veliko-Anadol.
 --Forestry.

Velocity of chemical reaction. See
Chemical reaction. Velocity.

Velsicol 104. See Heptachlor.

Velsicol 1068. See Chlordane.

Veltheim, Switzerland.
 --Statistics.

Veluwe region.
 --Natural history.
  xx Netherlands. Natural history.
 --Soils.
 --Water-supply.
  xx Netherlands. Water-supply.
 --Zoology.

Velva fruit.
 xx Ice cream.
  Fruit, Frozen.

Velvet bean as feeding stuff.
 xx Feeding stuffs.

Velvetbean caterpillar. See Anticarsia
gemmatilis.

Velvet-beans.
 sa Vitamins in velvet-beans.
 --Statistics.
  xx Beans. Statistics.

Velvet mesquite. See Mesquite.

Velvet-roll separator.
  xx Seeds. Cleaning. Implements
   and machinery.

Vena cava.

Venation.

Vending machines.
 sa Milk vending machines.
 x Slot-machines.
 xx Machinery, Automatic.

Veneer. See Veneers and veneering.

Veneers and veneering.
 x Veneer.
 --Drying.
  x Drying of veneers.
 --Periodicals.

Veneers and veneering (Continued)
--Specific gravity.
  xx Specific gravity.
--Specifications.
--Statistics.
--Waste.
  xx Factory and trade waste.

Venereal diseases.
  sa Syphilis.
--Periodicals.
  sa Subdivision Periodicals under:
    Syphilis.

Venetia.   See Veneto.

Venetian sumac.   See Cotinus coggygria.

Veneto.
  Modern region of Italy, comprising
    the provinces of Belluno,
    Padova, Rovigo, Treviso,
    Venezia, Verona, Vicenza. These
    provinces form three modern
    compartimenti known collec-
    tively as the Tre Venezie,
    i.e., the Three Venetias:
    (1) Venezia (2) Venezia Tri-
    dentina (3) Venezia Giulia.
  x Tre Venezie.
    Venetia.
--Agriculture.
  sa Subdivision Veneto under:
    Maize.
    Reclamation of land.
    Agriculture. Economic
      aspects.
  xx Italy. Agriculture.
-- --Statistics.
--Botany.
  xx Italy. Botany.
--Cattle.
  xx Italy. Cattle.
--Economic conditions.
--Industries.
--Natural history.
  xx Italy. Natural history.
--Viticulture.
--Water-supply.
-- --Bibliography.
--Zoology.
  xx Italy. Zoology.

Venezia (Province)   See Venice (Province)

Venezia Giulia.
  After 2d World War this region
    united with the Friuli Region
    to become Friuli-Venezia
    Giulia.
  sa Trieste (Free Territory)
--Economic conditions.
--Entomology.
  sa Subdivision Venezia Giulia
    under: Coleoptera.
--Statistics.

Venezia Tridentina.
--Entomology.
  sa Subdivision Venezia Tridentina
    under: Entomology, Economic.

Venezuela.
  sa Caura River//
--Agricultural experiment stations.
  sa Caracas. Estación experimental
    de agricultura y selvi-
    cultura.
    El Valle, Distrito federal,
    Venezuela. Estacion ex-
    perimental de agricultura
    y zootecnia.
--Agriculture.
  sa Subdivision Venezuela under:
    Coffee.
    Agriculture, Cooperative.
    Tobacco.
    Agriculture. Economic
      aspects.
    Cotton.
    Maize.
    Colonization, Agricultural.
    Agricultural credit.
    Wheat.
    Potatoes.
    Ranges.
    Agricultural policies and
      programs.
    Sugar-cane.
    Rice.
    Field crops.
    Flax.
    Agricultural administration.
    Agricultural extension.
    Cacao.
    Forage plants.
    Agricultural industries.
    Farm produce.
    Subdivision Land under regions,
      etc.

Venezuela (Continued)
--Agriculture.
-- --Bibliography.
-- --Education.
    sa Subdivision Venezuela under:
      Agricultural extension.
- --Maps.
-- --Periodicals.
-- --Statistics.
    xx Venezuela. Statistics.
--Bibliography.
--Botany.
    sa Subdivision Botany under:
      La Guaira.
      Coche Island.
      Margarita Island//
      Subdivision Venezuela under:
      Trees.
      Fungi.
      Mosses.
      Botany, Medical.
      Botany, Economic.
      Palmae.
      Vegetable pathology.
      Oleaginous plants.
--Boundaries.
--Cattle.
    sa Subdivision Cattle under
    names of states, etc.,
    e.g., Zulia, Venezuela.
    Cattle.
-- --Bibliography.
-- --Statistics.
--Cattle trade.
--Census.
--Climate.
--Commerce.
    sa Subdivision Venezuela under:
    Cocoa trade.
    Coffee trade.
    Fruit trade.
- --Brazil.
-- --Directories.
-- --Periodicals.
    xx Commerce. Periodicals.
-- --Statistics.
--Commercial policy.
--Dairying.
    sa Subdivision Venezuela under:
    Dairy industry and trade.
    xx South America. Dairying.
--Description and travel.
--Domestic animals.
    sa Subdivision Goats under:
    Venezuela.

Venezuela (Continued)
--Domestic animals.
-- --Research.
-- --Statistics.
    xx Venezuela. Statistics.
--Economic conditions.
    sa Subdivision Venezuela under:
    Geography, Economic.
    History, Economic.
    Economic surveys.
-- --Periodicals.
    xx Economic conditions. Peri-
      odicals.
--Economic policy.
    xx South America. Economic
      policy.
--Emigration and immigration.
--Entomology.
    sa Subdivision Entomology under:
    Mount Roraima, Venezuela.
    Aragua, Venezuela.
    Subdivision Venezuela under:
    Moths.
    Entomology, Economic.
    Diptera.
-- --Periodicals.

Venezuela. Exposicion nacional en 1883.

Venezuela.
--Fisheries.
-- --Statistics.
--Foreign population.
--Foreign relations.
--Forestry.
    sa Subdivision Venezuela under:
    Forest products.
    Forest policy.
    Timber.
    Subdivision Forestry under
    names of states, etc.,
    e.g., Trujuillo, Venezuela
    (State) Forestry.
-- --Research.
--Gazetteers.
--Geography.
    sa Subdivision Venezuela under:
    Geography, Economic.
    Anthropo-geography.
--Geology.
--Goats.
    xx Venezuela. Domestic animals.
--History.
    sa Subdivision Venezuela under:
    History, Economic.

Venezuela (Continued)
--Horse.
    sa Subdivision Venezuela under:
      Horses. Breeding.
--Industries.
    sa Subdivision Venezuela under:
      Agricultural industries.
-- --Directories.
--Land.
    sa Subdivision Venezuela under:
      Land reform.
      Soil erosion.
      Land utilization.
      Land tenure.
      Subdivision Land under names
      of regions, etc.
--Learned institutions and societies.
-- --Directories.
--Literature. See Venezuelan litera-
  ture.
--Manufactures.
--Milk supply.
--Milk trade.
    xx South America. Milk trade.
--Natural history.
--Ornithology.
    sa Subdivision Ornithology under:
      Orinoco region.
--Paleobotany.
--Periodicals. See Venezuelan peri-
  odicals.
--Politics and government.
    sa Subdivision Venezuela under:
      Administrative and political
      divisions.
--Pomology.
--Population.
--Public lands.
--Sericulture.
--Sheep.
--Social conditions.
    sa Subdivision Venezuela under:
      Cost and standard of living.
    xx South America. Social condi-
      tions.
--Social life and customs.
--Soils.
    sa Subdivision Venezuela under:
      Soil conservation.
      Soil erosion.
      Soil erosion. Prevention
      and control.
      Soil-surveys.

Venezuela (Continued)
--Statistics.
    sa Subdivision Statistics under:
      Venezuela. Agriculture.
      Venezuela. Commerce.
      Venezuela. Domestic animals.
--Swine.
-- --Statistics.
--Transportation.
--Viticulture.
--Water-supply.
--Zoology.
    sa Subdivision Venezuela under:
      Mammalia.
      Batrachia.
      Reptilia.
      Araneida.

Venezuelan literature.
  x Venezuela. Literature.
--Bibliography.

Venezuelan periodicals.
  x Venezuela. Periodicals.
--Bibliography.

Vengai. See Pterocarpus marsupium.

Venice (City)
--Orto botanico.

Venice (Province)
  x Venezia (Province)
--Agriculture.
    sa Subdivision Venice (Province)
      under: Agriculture. Eco-
      nomic aspects. Italy.
      Rehabilitation, Rural.
      Italy.
      Farms. Italy.
--Botany.
--Cattle.
--Commerce.
-- --Congresses.
--Economic conditions.
--Land.
    sa Subdivision Venice (Province)
      under: Land reform. Italy.

Venice (Republic)
--Agriculture.
-- --History.

Venison.
    sa Cookery (Venison)
    x Elk meat.
      Deer meat.
    xx Meat.

Venom.
    sa Poisonous animals.
    xx Poisonous animals.
--Bibliography.
--Physiological effect.
    x Venomous bites.
--Therapeutic use.
    x Bee venom therapy.
    xx Venom. Physiological effect.

Venomous bites. See Venom. Physiological effect.

Ventilating fans. See Fans, Electric.

Ventilation.
    sa Air conditioning.
      Chimneys.
      Flues//
      Subdivision Ventilation under:
      Barns and stables.
      Textile factories.
      Tunnels.
      Poultry houses.
      Kitchens.
      Farm houses.
      Swine houses and equipment.
      Beehives.
      Subdivision Heating and ventilation under: Greenhouses.
      Farm buildings.
--Exhausts. See Exhaust systems.
--Periodicals.
--Societies.
--Specifications.
--Tables, calculations, etc.

Ventrase.

Ventura Co., Calif.
--Agriculture.
    sa Subdivision California.
    Ventura Co. under:
    Field crops.
    xx California. Agriculture.
--Botany.
    sa Subdivision California.
    Ventura Co. under:
    Vegetable pathology.

Ventura Co., Calif. (Continued)
--Entomology.
    sa Subdivision California.
    Ventura Co. under:
    Entomology, Economic.
--Land.
    sa Subdivision California.
    Ventura Co. under: Land
    utilization.
--Water-supply.
    xx California. Water-supply.

Ventura River reclamation project, Calif.

Venturia inaequalis.
    xx Sphaeriaceae.

Venturia pirina.

Vera Cruz (City) Mexico.

Vera Cruz, Mexico (State)
--Agriculture.
    sa Subdivision Mexico. Vera Cruz
    (State) under: Coffee.
    Agriculture. Economic
    aspects.
--Forestry.
    sa Subdivision Mexico. Vera Cruz
    (State) under: Afforesta-
    tion and reforestation.

Vera de Bidasoa, Spain.
--Social life and customs.

Veraguas, Panama (Province)
--Agriculture.
-- --Statistics.
--Domestic animals.
-- --Statistics.

Verapaz, Alta (Dept.)
--Botany.
    sa Subdivision Guatemala.
    Verapaz, Alta (Dept.)
    under: Botany, Medical.

Veratrine. See Veratrum.

Veratrum.
    x Veratrine.

Veratrum album.

Veratrum viride.

Verband der erwerbs-und wirtschafts-
genossenschaften der provinzen
Posen und Westpreussen.

Verband für die wissenschaftliche erfor-
schung der deutschen kalisalzlager-
stätten.

Verbascum.

Verbena bud moth.   See Olethreutes
hebesana.

Verbenaceae.
     sa Clerdendron.
        Citharexylum.
        Tectona.
        Gmelina arborea.
        Lantana.
        Avicennia.

Vercelli, Italy (Province)
--Agriculture.
--Botany.
     xx Italy. Botany.
--Commerce.
-- --Periodicals.
--Economic conditions.
-- --Periodicals.

Verde River district, Ariz.
--Water-supply.

El Vergel (Farm)

Vergotinine.

Vermandois region, France.
--Agriculture.

Vermes.   See Worms.

Vermicelli.   See Macaroni.

Vermicularia zingibereae.

Vermiculite.

Vermifuge.   See Anthelmintics.

Vermilion Co., Ill.
        xx Illinois.

Vermilion District, Colo.

Vermilion Parish, La.
--Industries.

Vermilion River region, Ill.
--Entomology.

Vermillion Co., Ind.
--Soils.
        sa Subdivision Indiana. Vermil-
           lion Co. under: Soil-
           surveys.

Vermillion River.

Vermin.   See Household pests; Pests.

Verminous bronchitis.
        x Strongylose pulmonaire.
          Lungworm disease of cattle.
       xx Cattle, Diseases.
          Dictyocaulus viviparus.

Verminous conjunctivitis.   See Eye.
        Worms.

Verminous dermatitis.   See Dermatitis,
        Verminous.

Vermipsylla alacurt.

Vermipsylla dorcadia.

Vermivora.
        xx Compsothlypidae.

Vermland, Sweden.
--Agriculture.
--Botany.
--Forestry.
        sa Subdivision Vermland under:
           Lumbering.
--Natural history.

Vermont.
        sa Ascutney Mountain, Vt.
           Passumpsic River.
           West River, Vt.
           Addison Co.

Vermont (Continued)
--Agriculture.
    sa Subdivision Vermont under:
      Farms.
      Rural surveys.
      Agricultural policies and
        programs.
      Agriculture. Economic
        aspects.
      Agricultural laborers.
      Agricultural surveys.
      Mechanized farming.
      Agricultural extension.
      Agricultural credit.
      Subdivision Agriculture under:
        Washington Co., Vt.//
-- --Education.
    sa Vermont. State School of
      Agriculture, Randolph.
      Vermont. State schools of
        agriculture.
      Agricultural extension.
      Vermont.
-- --Periodicals.
-- --Statistics.
    xx U.S. Agriculture. Statistics.
--Altitudes.
    xx Altitudes.
--Bibliography.
--Botany.
    sa Subdivision Botany under:
      Willoughby.
      Burlington//
      Subdivision Vermont under:
      Trees.
      Shrubs.
      Fungi.
--Census.
--Climate.
--Dairying.
    sa Subdivision Vermont under:
      Dairy industry and trade.
-- --Statistics.
--Description and travel.
--Domestic animals.
-- --Statistics.
    xx U.S. Domestic animals. Sta-
      tistics.
--Economic conditions.
    sa Subdivision Vermont under:
      History, Economic.
      Rural surveys.
      Subdivision Economic conditions
        under: Addison Co., Vt.
-- --Bibliography.

Vermont (Continued)
--Education.
--Entomology.
    sa Subdivision Vermont under:
      Entomology, Economic.
--Forest reservations.
    sa Green Mountain National
      Forest, Vt.
    xx Forest reservations.
--Forestry.
    sa Subdivision Vermont under:
      Forest fires.
      Forest policy.
      Afforestation and
        reforestation.
-- --Statistics.
--Geology.
    sa Subdivision Vermont under:
      Mines and mineral re-
        sources.
--Government publications.
-- --Bibliography.
--History.
    sa Subdivision Vermont under:
      History, Economic.
    xx U.S. History.
· --Sources.
    sa Subdivision Vermont under:
      Archives.
    xx U.S. History. Sources.
--Industries and resources.
    sa Subdivision Vermont under:
      Industrial surveys.
      Conservation of natural
        resources.
--Land.
    sa Subdivision Vermont under:
      Land utilization.
      Land grants.
-- --Prices.
--Legislative manuals.
    xx Legislative manuals.
--Milk supply.
    xx New England. Milk supply.
--Milk trade.
    x U.S. Milk trade.
--Natural history.
--Paleobotany.
--Paleontology.
--Politics and government.
    sa Subdivision Vermont under:
      Local government.

Vermont (Continued)
--Pomology.
    sa Subdivision Pomology under:
        Grand Isle Co., Vt.
        Addison Co., Vt.
--Population.
    sa Subdivision Vermont under:
        Rural population.
    xx U.S. Population.
--Railroads.
--Roads.
-- --Law.
    xx Roads. Legislation.
       U.S. Roads. Law.
--Social conditions.
    sa Subdivision Social conditions
        under: Addison Co., Vt.
--Soils.
    sa Subdivision Vermont under:
        Soil-surveys.
        Soil conservation.
        Soil conservation surveys.
        Soil erosion.
--Transportation.
    xx U.S. Transportation.

Vermont. University and State Agricultural
   College.

Vermont.
--Water-supply.

Vernacular plant names.   See Plant
   names.

Vernalization.   See Yarovization
   (Botany)

Vernin.
    sa Maize seedlings, Vernin in.

Vernon, Tex.
--Water-supply.

Vernon Co., Wis.
    xx Wisconsin.
--Agriculture.
    sa Subdivision Wisconsin. Vernon
        Co. under: Farm management
        surveys.
    xx Wisconsin. Agriculture.

Vernon Co., Wis. (Continued)
--Soils.
    sa Subdivision Wisconsin. Vernon
        Co. under: Soil conserva-
        tion.
        Soil-surveys.
    xx Wisconsin. Soils.

Vernonia fysoni.

Vernonieae.

Verona.
--Ornithology.

Verona (Province)
--Agriculture.
    sa Subdivision Italy. Verona
        (Province) under: Wheat.
        Agriculture. Economic
        aspects.
        Reclamation of land.
        Irrigation.
-- --Statistics.
--Botany.
--Meteorology.
--Pomology.

Veronica.

Veronicella.

Verrucariaceae.

Verruga.

Versailles.
--Parks.

Versailles, Treaty of, June 29, 1919.
    xx Treaties.

Vertebrae.
    sa Intervertebral disk.

Vertebrate anatomy.   See Vertebrates.
   Anatomy.

Vertebrate embryology.   See Embryology.
   Vertebrates.

Vertebrates.   (INDIRECT)
    sa Tetrapoda.

Vertebrates (Continued)
--Anatomy.
    sa Subdivision Vertebrates under:
      Embryology.
    x Vertebrate anatomy.
-- --Terminology.
-- --Text-books.
--Congresses.
--Effect of insecticides. See Insecti-
  cides. Effect on vertebrates.

Vertebrates, Fossil.
    x Fossil vertebrates.
    xx Paleontology.

Vertebrates.
--Parasites.
    sa Nematoda. Parasitic in verte-
      brates.

Vertical farm diversification. See
  Farming, Diversified (Vertical)

Vertical integration.
    x Integration, Vertical.
    xx Integration (Economics)
      Agriculture and business.
      Contracts, Agricultural.
--Bibliography.

Verticillium alboatrum.

Verticillium dahliae.

Verticillium disease of mushrooms.
    x Brown spot of mushrooms.
    xx Mushrooms. Diseases.

Verticillium hadromycosis.

Vesicular diseases in animals.
    sa Vesicular exanthema of swine.
    Vesicular stomatitis.
    Foot-and-mouth disease.
    xx Veterinary medicine.

Vesicular exanthema of swine.
    xx Swine. Diseases.
    Vesicular diseases in animals.

Vesicular stomatitis.
    xx Vesicular diseases in animals.
    Swine. Diseases.

Veslud, France.
    sa Subdivision France. Veslud
      under: History, Economic.

Vespa.
    xx Wasps.

Vespa crabro.

Vespa de Uganda. See Prorops nasuta.

Vespa maculata.

Vespa vulagris.

Vespamima sequoia.

Vespertilio longicrus.

Vespertilionidae.

Vespidae. See Wasps.

Vespoidea.
    xx Wasps.

Vessels (Ships) See Ships.

Vessels (Utensils) See Implements,
  utensils, etc.

Vesterbotten, Sweden.
    x Västerbotten, Sweden.
--Agriculture.
--Botany.
--Forestry.

Vesternorrland, Sweden.
    x Västernorrland, Sweden.
--Agriculture.

Vestervik, Sweden. See Västervik,
  Sweden.

Vestfold, Norway.

Vestland cattle.
    x Sør-og vestlandsfe.

Vestmanland, Sweden.
    x Västmanland, Sweden.
--Agriculture.
--Botany.

Vesuvius.
--Botany.
    xx Italy. Botany.

Vetch.
    sa Vicia.
--Breeding.
    xx Plant-breeding.
--Digestibility.
--Fertilizers.   See Fertilizers for
    vetch.

Vetch, Hairy.
    x Hairy vetch.
      Vicia villosa.
--Seed.
-- --Adulteration.

Vetch, Hungarian.
    x Hungarian vetch.
      Vicia pannonica.

Vetch, Kidney.
    x Anthyllis vulneraria.

Vetch, Monantha.

Vetch, Nitrogen in.

Vetch.
--Pest resistant varieties.
    xx Pest resistant plants.
--Pests.
--Pictorial works.
--Seed.
-- --Fumigation.
    xx Seeds. Fumigation.
--Tariff.
    xx Tariff.
--Varieties.

Veterans.   (DIRECT)
    sa Bounties, Military.
      Disabled. Rehabilitation, etc.
      Pensions, Military.
      Soldiers.
      Farms for veterans.
    x Soldiers, Discharged.
      Ex-service men.
    xx Soldiers.
--Adjustment problems.
    x Veterans. Readjustment problems.
-- --Bibliography.

Veterans (Continued)
--Education.
    sa Veterans ₍geographic subdivi-
      sion₎ Education, e.g.,
      Veterans. Illinois. Educa-
      tion.
    x Education of veterans.
-- --Directories.
--Employment.   (INDIRECT)
    x Employment of veterans.
      Seamen. Civil employment.
      Soldiers. Civil employment.
    xx Labor and laboring classes.
      Reconstruction (1914-1939)
      Reconstruction (1939-)
-- --Bibliography.
-- --Congresses.
-- --Directories.
    sa Veterans. Employment ₍country
      subdivision₎ Directories,
      e.g., Veterans. Employment.
      Connecticut. Directories.
--Housing.
    xx Housing.
--Laws and legislation.
    sa Servicemen's readjustment act
      of 1944.
--Periodicals.
--Readjustment problems.   See Veterans.
    Adjustment problems.
--Societies.

Veterinarians.   (DIRECT)
    Used for biographical and literary
      works.
    sa Veterinary medicine. Bio-
      bibliography.
    x Veterinary medicine. Biography.
--Correspondence, reminiscences, etc.
--Directories.
    Used for official and business
      directories.
    sa Subdivision Directories under:
      Veterinary medicine exten-
      sion specialists.
      Veterinarians ₍geographic
      subdivision₎ e.g., Vet-
      erinarians. Sweden. Di-
      rectories.
    x Veterinary medicine. Direc-
      tories.
--Portraits.

Veterinary anatomy.   See Domestic ani-
    mals. Anatomy and physiology.

Veterinary anesthesia.   See Anesthesia
  in veterinary medicine.

Veterinary bacteriology.
    xx Veterinary microbiology.
  --Laboratory manuals.

Veterinary botany.   See Botany, Medical.

Veterinary colleges.   See Veterinary
  medicine. Schools.

Veterinary dentistry.

Veterinary dermatology.
    xx Dermatology.
  --Congresses.

Veterinary diagnosis.   See Veterinary
  medicine. Diagnosis.

Veterinary embryology.
    x⸴ Embryology, Veterinary.

Veterinary endocrinology.
    xx Endocrinology.

Veterinary gynaecology.
    xx Gynaecology.

Veterinary histology.
    x Histology, Veterinary.

Veterinary hospitals.   See Hospitals,
  Veterinary.

Veterinary hygiene.
    sa Stock inspection.
    xx Stock inspection.
  --Congresses.
  --Legislation.
  --Periodicals.
  --Research.
  --Societies.

Veterinary inspectors.
  --Directories.

Veterinary instruments and apparatus.

Veterinary jurisprudence.   See Veterinary medicine. Legislation.

Veterinary laboratories.⸴   See Veterinary
  medicine. Laboratories.

Veterinary laws and legislation.   See
  Veterinary medicine. Legislation.

Veterinary materia medica and pharmacy.
    sa Cornhusker (Veterinary medica-
        ment)
      Urea in veterinary medicine.
      Quinox powder//
    x Veterinary medicine.
      Veterinary medicine. Drugs.
      Veterinary pharmacology.
    xx Pharmacology.
      Materia medica.
  --Periodicals.
  --Prices.
  --Substitutes.
    xx Substitute products.

Veterinary medicine.   (INDIRECT)
    sa Bloodletting.
      Deficiency diseases in ani-
        mals.
      Diseases. Transmission from
        animal to man.
      Domestic animals. Parasites.
      Epizoötic diseases.
      First aid for animals.
      Infectious diseases in ani-
        mals.
      Nosology, Veterinary.
      Quarantine, Veterinary.
      Soil and disease (animal,
        other than human)
      Stock inspection.
      Weather. Effect on animals.
      Pyotherapy.
      Tissue therapy.
      Vesicular diseases in animals.
      Names of particular diseases,
        e.g., Anthrax; Foot-and-
        mouth disease.
      Headings beginning with the
        word Veterinary.
      Subdivision Diseases under:
        Classes of animals, e.g.,
        Cattle. Diseases; Horses.
        Diseases.
      Disease resistant animals.
      Phrase headings; ⸤Various
        drugs, Minerals, etc.⸥ in
        Veterinary medicine.

Veterinary medicine (Continued)
    x Diseases.
      Livestock diseases.
      Animals. Diseases.
      Diseases of animals.
      Domestic animals. Diseases.
      Farriery.
  --Abstracts.
  -- --Periodicals.
  --Addresses, essays, lectures.
  --Bibliography.
    sa Subdivision Bibliography under:
      Tropical veterinary medi-
        cine.
      Anthrax.
      Encephalomyelitis. Horses//
  -- --Periodicals.
  --Bio-bibliography.
    xx Bio-bibliography.
      Veterinarians.

Veterinary medicine, Biochemic.

Veterinary medicine.
  --Biography.   See Veterinarians.
  --Calendars.
  --Congresses.
    sa Subdivision Congresses under:
      Foot-and-mouth disease.
      Abortion.
  --Correspondence schools and courses.
  --Diagnosis.
    sa Subdivision Diagnosis under:
      Tuberculosis.
      Blackleg.
      Anemia, Infectious//
    x Diagnosis, Veterinary.
      Veterinary diagnosis.
    xx Diagnosis.
  --Diagnosis, Radioscopic.
  --Dictionaries.
  --Directories.   See Veterinarians. Di-
    rectories.
  --Drugs.   See Veterinary materia medica
    and pharmacy.
  --Education.   See Veterinary medicine.
    Schools.
  --Examinations, questions, etc.
  --Exhibitions.
  --Experimentation.   See Veterinary medi-
    cine. Research.
  --Fees and fee-bills.
    sa Subdivision Fees and fee-bills
      under: Stock inspection.
  --Formulae, receipts, prescriptions.

Veterinary medicine (Continued)
  --Handbooks, manuals, etc.
  --History.
    sa South African War, 1889-1902.
      Veterinary history.
      European War, 1914-1918.
      Veterinary service.
      Horses. Diseases. History.
      Veterinary medicine. Peri-
        odicals. History.
      Veterinary medicine ₍geo-
        graphic subdivision₎ His-
        tory, e.g., Veterinary
        medicine. U.S. History.

Veterinary medicine, Homeopathic.

Veterinary medicine.
  --Instruments and apparatus.   See
    Veterinary instruments and appara-
    tus.
  --Laboratories.
    x Veterinary laboratories.
    xx Laboratories.
  --Laboratory methods.
    xx Laboratory methods.
  --Laboratory records.
  --Legislation.   (DIRECT)
    sa Quarantine, Veterinary.
      Stock inspection.
      Tuberculosis in cattle.
      Legislation.
    x Veterinary laws and legis-
      lation.
    _ Infectious diseases in ani-
      mals. Legislation.
      Veterinary jurisprudence.
    xx Agriculture. Law.
      Domestic animals. Legislation.
  -- --Dictionaries.
  --Nomenclature.
  --Outlines, syllabi, etc.
  --Periodicals.
    sa Subdivision Periodicals
      under: Tropical veterinary
      medicine.
      Veterinary medicine ₍geo-
        graphic subdivision₎ Peri-
        odicals, e.g., Veterinary
        medicine. Czechoslovak Re-
        public. Periodicals.
  -- --Bibliography.
  -- --History.
    xx Veterinary medicine. History.
      Periodicals. History.

Veterinary medicine (Continued)
--Public health aspects.
    x Veterinary medicine and public
      health service.
    Public health service and vet-
      erinary medicine.
-- --Congresses.
--Research.
    sa Veterinary medicine ₍geographic
      subdivision₎ Research, e.g.,
      Veterinary medicine. Gt.
      Brit. Research.
    x Veterinary medicine. Experi-
      mentation.
    Veterinary research.
    xx Research.
-- --Directories.
    xx Research. Societies. Direc-
      tories.
--Schools.
    sa Names of schools.
    x Veterinary medicine. Education.
    Veterinary colleges.
    Veterinary schools.
--Societies.
    sa Subdivision Societies under:
      Tropical veterinary medicine.
--Statistics.
    sa Horse. Diseases. Statistics.
    Subdivision Statistics under
      Veterinary medicine ₍geo-
      graphic subdivision₎ e.g.,
      Veterinary medicine. Loui-
      siana. Statistics.
--Study and teaching.
--Technique.
--Text-books.

Veterinary medicine, Tropical. See
  Tropical veterinary medicine.

Veterinary medicine and public health
  service. See Veterinary medicine.
  Public health aspects.

Veterinary medicine as an occupation.

Veterinary medicine extension.

Veterinary medicine extension specialists.
--Directories.
    xx Veterinarians. Directories.

Veterinary medicines. See Veterinary
  materia medica and pharmacy.

Veterinary microbiology.
    sa Veterinary bacteriology.
    x Animal disease organisms.
    Microbiology, Veterinary.
    xx Micro-organisms.
--Text-books.

Veterinary necropsy. See Autopsy.

Veterinary obstetrics.
    sa Still-birth.
    Cesarian section.
    xx Obstetrics.

Veterinary ophthalmology.
    xx Ophthalmology.

Veterinary parasitology. See Domestic
  animals. Parasites.

Veterinary pathology. See Veterinary
  medicine.

Veterinary pharmacology. See Veterinary
  materia medica and pharmacy.

Veterinary pharmacy. See Veterinary
  materia medica and pharmacy.

Veterinary physical therapy.
    xx Physical therapy.

Veterinary physiology. See Domestic
  animals. Anatomy and physiology;
  Physiology, Comparative.

Veterinary research. See Veterinary
  medicine. Research.

Veterinary schools. See Veterinary
  medicine. Schools.
--Legislation.

Veterinary science. See Veterinary
  medicine.
    xx Cattle.

Veterinary service, Military. (INDI-
  RECT)
    x Military veterinary service.

Veterinary surgeons act, 1948.

Veterinary surgery.
    sa Urethrotomy.
       Nephrectomy.
       Castration.
       Spaying.
       Narcosis.
       First aid for animals.
       Foreign bodies (Surgery)
       Rumenotomy.
       Cesarian section.
       Orthopedia.
    x Farriery.
--Congresses.
--Study and teaching.

Veterol.

Vetiveria.
    xx Oleaginous plants.

Veveno Pibor diversion scheme.

Vevey, Switzerland.
--Natural history.
--Soils.

Viability of seeds.   See Germination.

Viaducts.
    sa Bridges.
    xx Bridges.

Viani, Colombia.
--Land.
    sa Subdivision Colombia. Viani
       under: Land. Classification.
--Soils.
    sa Subdivision Colombia. Viani
       under: Soil conservation.

Viannaia bursobscura.

Viborg, Denmark (Province)
--Agriculture.
-- --History.

Vibration.
    sa Ultrasonics.
       Sound-waves.
       Oscillations.
    xx Sound. Velocity.
       Sound.

Vibration, Traffic.

Vibrio.
    xx Cholera.

Vibrio coli of swine.   See Vibrio coli
    suis.

Vibrio coli suis.
    x Vibrio coli of swine.

Vibrio tritici.   See Tylenchus.

Vibrionic dysentery.
    xx Swine dysentery.

Vibriosis, Cattle.
    x Cattle vibriosis.
       Bovine genital vibriosis.
    xx Cattle. Diseases.

Viburnum.

Viburnum nudum.

Viburnum prunifolium.

Vicenza (Province)
--Agriculture.
    sa Subdivision Vicenza (Province)
       under: Agricultural poli-
       cies and programs.
--Cattle.
--Commerce.
-- --Periodicals.
--Economic conditions.
-- --Periodicals.
--Economic policy.
--Entomology.
--Industries.
--Statistics.

Vichy water.

Vicia.
    xx Vetch.

Vicia faba.   See Broad bean.

Vicia grandiflora.

Vicia monantha.   See Vetch, Monantha.

Vicia obscura.

Vicia pannonica.   See Vetch, Hungarian.

Vicia sativa L.   See Vetch.

Vicia villosa.   See Vetch, Hairy.

Victoria, Australia.
    sa Port Phillip region.
       Rivers. Victoria.
--Agricultural colleges.
--Agricultural experiment stations.
    sa Dookie Agricultural College
       and Experimental Farm.
       Werribee. Central Research
       Farm.
       Rutherglen Experiment Farm.
    xx Australia. Agricultural ex-
       periment stations.
--Agriculture.
    sa Subdivision Victoria under:
       Wheat.
       Forage plants.
       Agriculture. Economic
          aspects.
       Colonization, Agricultural.
       Farm buildings.
       Sugar-beet.
       Farm produce. Cost of pro-
          duction.
       Subdivision Victoria, Aus-
          tralia under: Agricultural
          policies and programs.
       Agricultural extension.
-- --Education.
    sa Richmond, Victoria. School of
       Horticulture.
    xx Australia. Agriculture. Edu-
       cation.
-- --Statistics.
--Apiculture.
--Botany.
    sa Subdivision Victoria under:
       Weeds.
       Trees.
       Botany, Economic.
       Ferns.
       Subdivision Botany under:
          Geelong, Victoria.
       Subdivision Victoria, Aus-
          tralia under: Honey-bearing
          plants.
       Wild flowers.
       Fungi.
--Census.

Victoria, Australia (Continued)
--Climate.
    sa Subdivision Victoria, Aus-
       tralia under: Crops and
       climate.
--Commerce.
    xx Australia. Commerce.
-- --Directories.
    xx Australia. Commerce. Direc-
       tories.
-- --Statistics.
    xx Victoria. Statistics.
--Dairying.
--Description and travel.
--Domestic animals.
    sa Subdivision Sheep under:
       Victoria, Australia.
    xx Domestic animals.
--Economic conditions.
-- --Periodicals.
    xx Australia. Economic condi-
       tions. Periodicals.
--Education.
    sa Subdivision Education under:
       Victoria. Agriculture.
       Subdivision Victoria, Aus-
          tralia under: Agricultural
          extension.
--Entomology.
    sa Subdivision Victoria under:
       Entomology, Economic.
--Fisheries.
--Forestry.
    sa Subdivision Victoria, Aus-
       tralia under: Wood-lots.
       Forest fires.
       Forest products.
       Lumber trade.
       War and forestry (1939-
          1945)
       Community forests.
       Lumbering.
       Tree planting.
       Lumber.
       Forest management.
       Forest industries.
    xx Australia. Forestry.
--Geology.
-- --Bibliography.
--Hygiene.
    sa Subdivision Victoria, Aus-
       tralia under: Hygiene,
       Public.
--Ichthyology.
--Industries and resources.

Victoria, Australia (Continued)
--Land.
    sa Subdivision Victoria, Australia
        under: Land utilization.
        Land. Classification.
--Law.
--Maps.
--Natural history.
--Paleobotany.
--Politics and government.
    sa Subdivision Victoria, Australia
        under: Local government.
--Pomology.
    xx Australia. Pomology.
--Roads.
--Sheep.
    xx Victoria, Australia. Domestic
        animals.
--Social conditions.
    sa Subdivision Australia. Victoria
        under: Social surveys.
--Soils.
    sa Subdivision Victoria, Australia
        under: Soil-surveys.
        Soil erosion. Prevention
          and control.
        Soil erosion surveys.
        Soil conservation.
        Soil erosion.
        Soil drifting.
        Wind erosion. Prevention
          and control.
        Wind erosion.
        Soil drifting. Prevention
          and control.
      Subdivision Soils under:
        Swan Hill irrigation dis-
          trict, Victoria, Aus-
          tralia.
        Merbein irrigation district,
          Victoria, Australia//
--Statistics.
    sa Subdivision Statistics under:
        Victoria, Australia. Agri-
          culture.
        Victoria, Australia. Com-
          merce.
--Transportation.
    xx Transportation.
        Australia. Transportation.
--Viticulture.
--Water-supply.
--Zoology.
    xx Australia. Zoology.

Victoria, Lake.   See Victoria Nyanza.

Victoria blight.
    x Victorian blight.
      Blight disease of oats.
      Helminthosporium blight.
    xx Oats. Diseases.

Victoria Co., Ont.
--Botany.
    xx Ontario. Botany.

Victoria Co., Tex.
--Soils.
    sa Subdivision Texas. Victoria
        Co. under: Soil-surveys.

Victoria lyre bird.   See Menura
    Victoriae.

Victoria Nyanza.
    x Lake Victoria Nyanza.
      Victoria, Lake.
--Botany.
    xx Africa. Botany.

Victoria regia.

Victorian blight.   See Victoria blight.

Victory farm volunteers.
    xx U.S. Crop corps.
      World War, 1939-1945. Girls'
        work.
      Agricultural laborers.
      World War, 1939-1945. Boys'
        work.
--Periodicals.

Victory garden program.   See Food for
    freedom program.

Vicuña.
    xx Textile industry and fabrics.

Vienna.
    sa Wienerwald.
--Agriculture.
--Botanic garden.
--Botany.
--Congress, 1814-1815.
    x Congress of Vienna, 1814-1815.
--Dairying.
    xx Austria. Dairying.
--Description and travel.

Vienna (Continued)
--Entomology.
    sa Subdivision Austria. Vienna
       under: Butterflies.
--Paleobotany.
    xx Austria. Paleobotany.
--Parks.
    sa Vienna. Türkenschanzpark.
--Statistics.

Vienna. Türkenschanzpark.
--Botany.

Vienne, France (Dept.)   See France.
  Département de la Vienne.

Vierlande, Ger.
--Agriculture.
    sa Subdivision Germany. Vierlande
      under: Agriculture. Economic
      aspects.
    xx Germany. Agriculture.

Vietnam.
--Agriculture.
    sa Subdivision Vietnam under:
      Agriculture and business.
      Agriculture, Cooperative.
      Agricultural administration.
      Agricultural credit.
      Agricultural policies and
      programs.
-- --Periodicals.
-- --Statistics.
--Botany.
--Description and travel.
--Domestic animals.
--Economic conditions.
--Economic policy.
--Forestry.
    sa Subdivision Vietnam under:
      Forest policy.
--Industries.
--Land.
    sa Subdivision Vietnam under:
      Land reform.
--Politics and government.
--Soil.
--Statistics.

Vigna catjang.   See Black-eye peas.

Vigna sinensis.   See Cow-peas.

Vigo Co., Ind.
--Agriculture.
-- --Periodicals.
--Botany.
    sa Subdivision Indiana. Vigo Co.
      under: Ferns.

Vilas Co., Wis.
--Land.
    sa Subdivision Wisconsin. Vilas
      Co. under: Land. Classifi-
      cation.
    xx Wisconsin. Land.

Villach, Austria.
--Botany.

Village communities.   (INDIRECT)
    sa Commons.
    xx Society, Primitive.
    Communism.
    Peasantry.
    Political science.
    Land tenure.
    Commons.

Village industries.   See Home labor.

Villages.   (INDIRECT)
--Sanitation.
--Water-supply.
    xx Water-supply.

Villard-de-Lans cattle.

Villard-d'Héry, France.
    sa Subdivision France. Villard-
      d'Héry under: Sociology,
      Rural.

Villefranche-de-Rouerge, France.
--Agriculture.

Villoresi canal.
    xx Canals. Italy.

Vilna, Russia.   See Wilna, Russia.

Viñales, Cuba.
--Paleontology.

Vinca rosea.

Vincennes. Exposition internationale
    hippique.   See Paris. Exposition
    internationale hippique.

Vincetoxicum officinale.   See Cynanchum
    vincetoxicum.

Vine.   See Viticulture; Grapes.

Vine-mesquite.   See Panicum obtusum.

Vinegar.
    sa Oxymel.
        Peach vinegar.
        Fermentation, Acetic.
        Grape vinegar.
--Analysis.
--Periodicals.
--Statistics.
        xx Food. Statistics.
            Food. Preservatives. Sta-
                tistics.
--Transportation.
        sa Subdivision Vinegar under:
            Railroads. Rates.

Vinegar eel.   See Anguillula aceti.

Vinegar fly.   See Drosophila ampelophila.

Vines.   See Climbing plants.

Vineyards.   See Grapes; Viticulture.

Viniculture.   See Viticulture.

Vinnitsa Region.
--Agriculture.
--Cattle.
--Swine.

Vinton Co., Ohio.
--Soils.
        sa Subdivision Ohio. Vinton Co.
            under: Soil-surveys.

Vinyl alcohol.
        sa Trimesitylvinyl alcohol.
            Polyvinyl alcohol.
        x Alcohol, Vinyl.
        xx Alcohol.

Vinyl plastics.   See Vinyl polymers.

Vinyl polymers.
        sa Plastic materials in horti-
            culture.
        x Vinyl plastics.
        xx Plastic materials.
            Polymers and polymerization.

Vinyl resin.
        xx Gums and resins, Artificial.

Vinylite.
        xx Gums and resins, Artificial.
            Plastic materials.

Vinyllithium compounds.

Vinyltoluene.
        xx Paint materials.
            Styrene.
            Thinner (paint mixing)

Viola ipecacuanha.   See Ionidium
    ipecacuanha.

Viola tricolor.

Violaceae.
        sa Hymenanthera.
            Rinorea.

Violet, African.   See Saintpaulia.

Violet rove-beetle.   See Apocellus
    sphaericollis.

Violets.
        sa Saintpaulia ionantha.
--Pests.
        sa Diplosis violicola.
--Diseases.

Violin.

Viorna.

Virachola livia.   See Deudorix livia.

Virales.
        xx Viruses.

Vireo olivacea.

Vireonidae.
        sa Vireo.

Vireos.
--Food.
.xx Birds. Food.

Virgin forests.
x Primeval forests.
Forests, Virgin.
Forests, Primeval.

Virgin Islands (British)
sa Tortola Island.
x British Virgin Islands.
--Agriculture.
sa Subdivision Virgin Islands
(British) under: Agri-
cultural policies and
programs.
--Census.

Virgin Islands of the United States.
sa Santa Cruz.
--Agriculture.
sa Subdivision Virgin Islands
of the United States under:
Agricultural credit.
Agricultural policies and
programs.
Agriculture. Economic
aspects.
-- --Statistics.
xx U.S. Agriculture. Statistics.
--Bibliography.
--Botany.
sa Subdivision Virgin Islands of
the United States under:
Algae.
Lichens.
Mosses.
Poisonous plants.
--Census, 1917.
--Commerce.
sa Subdivision Virgin Islands of
the United States under:
Sugar trade.
-- --Statistics.
--Description and travel.
xx West Indies. Description and
travel.
--Economic conditions.
--Entomology.
sa Subdivision Virgin Islands of
the United States under:
Lepidoptera.
Moths.
Heteroptera.

Virgin Islands of the United States
(Continued)
--Geographic names.
--Industries.
--Labor. See Labor and laboring
classes. Virgin Islands.
--Meteorology.
--Natural history.
--Ornithology.
--Politics and government.
xx U.S. Politics and government.
--Soils.
sa Subdivision Virgin Islands of
the United States under:
Soil-surveys.
Soil conservation.
--Statistics.
sa Virgin Islands of the United
States. Census, 1917.
--Zoology.
sa Subdivision Virgin Islands of
the United States under:
Araneida.

Virginia.
sa Norfolk, Va.
Richmond.
Charlotte Co., Va.//
--Agriculture.
sa Subdivision Agriculture under:
Culpeper Co.
Rappahannock Valley.
Southampton Co.//
Subdivision Virginia under:
Cereals.
Farm produce.
Farms.
Poultry.
Sugar-beet.
Agricultural policies and
programs.
Agricultural outlook.
Farm organization.
Farm management surveys.
Rural surveys.
Agricultural laborers.
Potatoes.
Agricultural credit.
Crops and climate.
Maize.
-- --Bibliography.
--Education.
sa Appomattox (Va.) Agricultural
High School, Appomattox.
. --History.

Virginia (Continued)
--Agriculture.
-- --Periodicals.
-- --Statistics.
    sa Subdivision Statistics under:
      Farm produce. Virginia.
--Altitudes.
    xx Altitudes.
--Bibliography.
    sa Subdivision Bibliography under:
      Virginia. State publica-
      tions.
--Biography.
    xx U.S. Biography.
--Botany.
    sa Subdivision Virginia under:
      Trees.
      Vegetable pathology.
      Weeds.
      Ferns.
      Subdivision Botany under:
      Dismal Swamp.
      Wythe Co.
      Richmond//
--Boundaries.
--Cattle.
    sa Subdivision Russell Co., Va.
      under: Cattle.
    xx U.S. Cattle.
--Cattle trade.
    xx U.S. Cattle trade.
--Census.
--Climate.
    sa Subdivision Climate under names
      of counties, cities, etc.
      Subdivision Virginia under:
      Crops and climate.
--Commerce.
    sa Subdivision Virginia under:
      Farm produce. Marketing.
      Tobacco manufacture and
        trade.
      Fruit trade.
      Subdivision Commerce under
      names of cities, etc.
--Dairying.
    sa Subdivision Dairying under:
      Norfolk.
-- --Bibliography.
    sa Subdivision Bibliography under:
      Dairy industry and trade.
      Virginia.
    xx U.S. Dairying. Bibliography.
-- --Societies.

Virginia (Continued)
--Description and travel.
    sa Subdivision Description and
      travel under: Prince
      William Co., Va.
-- --Guide-books.
--Economic conditions.
    sa Subdivision Economic conditions
      under: Albemarle Co., Va.
      Rockingham Co., Va.
      Fairfax Co., Va.//
      Subdivision Virginia under:
      History, Economic.
      Rural surveys.
-- --Periodicals.
    xx Economic conditions. Peri-
      odicals.
--Economic policy.
--Education.
    sa Subdivision Education under:
      Winchester, Va.
      Student cooperative associa-
      tions.
--Emigration and immigration.
--Entomology.
    sa Subdivision Virginia under:
      Entomology, Economic.
      Wasps.
      Orthoptera.
--Farmers' institutes.
--Fisheries.
--Forest reservations.
    sa George Washington National
      Forest.
--Forestry.
    sa Subdivision Forestry under:
      Tazewell Co.
      Buchanan Co.
      Dickenson Co.//
      Subdivision Virginia under:
      Timber.
      Forest surveys.
      Lumber.
      Wood-using industries.
      Forest industries.
      Wood-lots.
      Forest fires.
      Forest fires. Prevention.
      Afforestation and reforest-
      ation.
      Tree planting.
      Forest policy.
      Lumbering.
-- --Periodicals.
-- --Statistics.

Virginia (Continued)
--Gazetteers.
--Geology.
    sa Subdivision Geology under:
      Dickenson Co., Va.
      Russell Co., Va.
      Lee Co., Va.
      Subdivision Virginia under:
      Water, Underground.
      Mines and mineral resources.
--Historic houses, etc.
--History.
    sa Subdivision History under:
      Carolina Co., Va.
      Southampton Co., Va.
      Rockbridge Co., Va.//
      Subdivision Virginia under:
      History, Economic.
-- --Bibliography.
-- --Colonial period.
    sa Bacon's Rebellion, 1676.
    xx U.S. History. Colonial period.
-- --Revolution.
    xx U.S. History. Revolution.
 --Sources.
    sa Subdivision Virginia under:
      Archives.
    xx U.S. History. Sources.
--Horse.
    sa Subdivision Virginia under:
      Horses. Breeding.
--Ichthyology.
--Immigration. See Virginia. Emigration
    and immigration.
--Industries.
    sa Industrial surveys. Virginia.
-- --Directories.
--Land.
    sa Subdivision Virginia under:
      Land utilization.
      Land grants.
      Land tenure.
      Floyd Co., Va. Land//
--Libraries.
    xx U.S. Libraries.
--Manufactures, useful arts, etc.
--Maps.
    sa Subdivision Maps under:
      Richmond, Va.
      Mount Vernon, Va.
-- --Bibliography.
--Markets.
    sa Subdivision Markets under:
      Roanoke.
--Meteorology.

Virginia (Continued)
--Milk trade.
--Natural history.
    sa Subdivision Natural history
      under: Staunton.
--Officials and employees.
    xx U.S. Officials and employees.
--Ornithology.
    sa Subdivision Virginia under:
      Game-birds.
    xx U.S. Ornithology.
--Paleobotany.
--Parks.
    sa Seashore State Park, Cape
      Henry, Va.
      Subdivision Parks under names
      of counties, cities,
      towns, etc.
    xx U.S. Parks.
--Politics and government.
    sa Subdivision Virginia under:
      County government.
      Suffrage.
      Subdivision Politics and
      government under:
      Albemarle Co.
--Pomology.
    sa Subdivision Pomology under:
      Frederick Co., Va.
-- --Bibliography.
    xx Pomology. Bibliography.
-- --History.
--Population.
    sa Subdivision Virginia under:
      Rural population.
    xx U.S. Population.
--Public works.
    xx U.S. Public works.
--Railroads.
--Roads.
    sa Mt. Vernon Memorial Highway.
 --History.
 --Law.
    xx Roads. Legislation.
    U.S. Roads. Law.
--Social conditions.
    sa Subdivision Social conditions
      under: Albemarle Co., Va.
      Fairfax Co., Va.
      Rockingham Co., Va.//
      Subdivision Virginia under:
      Social surveys.
-- --Bibliography.
--Social life and customs.
    xx U.S. Social life and customs.

Virginia (Continued)
--Soils.
    sa Subdivision Soils under:
        Albemarle area, Va.//
        Subdivision Virginia under:
        Soil-surveys.
        Soil conservation.
        Soil erosion. Prevention and
            control.
        Soil erosion.
--State publications.
-- --Bibliography.
--Statistics.
    sa Subdivision Statistics under:
        Virginia. Agriculture.
--Swine.
    sa Nansemond Co., Va. Swine.
--Water-supply.
    sa Subdivision Virginia under:
        Water, Underground.
        Water-rights.
-- --Bibliography.
--Zoology.
    sa Subdivision Virginia under:
        Wild life.
        Mammalia.
    xx U.S. Zoology.

Virginia City, Nev.
    xx Nevada.

Virginia pine.   See Pinus virginiana.

Virginia Seashore State Park.   See Sea-
    shore State Park, Cape Henry, Va.

Virola surinamensis.
    x Ucuhuba.
    xx Myristicaceae.
        Feeding stuffs.

Virus diseases.
    xx Virus research.
--Maps.
--Periodicals.

Virus diseases of beans.
    x Black root.
    xx Beans. Diseases.
        Virus diseases of plants.

Virus diseases of beets.

Virus diseases of blueberries.
    x Blueberry stunt disease.
    xx Blueberries. Diseases.

Virus diseases of cabbage.
    xx Virus diseases of plants.

Virus diseases of cacao.
    x Swollen shoot disease of
        cocoa.
    xx Cacao. Diseases.

Virus diseases of carnations.
    xx Carnations. Diseases.

Virus diseases of cherries.
    sa Mottle-leaf of cherry.
        Western X little cherry.
        Western X disease.
    xx Virus diseases of plants.
        Cherry. Diseases.

Virus diseases of citrus.
    xx Citrus. Diseases.

Virus diseases of cow-peas.
    xx Cow-peas. Diseases.

Virus diseases of fruit.
    xx Fruit diseases.
        Virus diseases of plants.

Virus diseases of grapes.
--Transmission.

Virus diseases of hops.
    xx Hops. Diseases.

Virus diseases of legumes.

Virus diseases of peaches.
    sa Western X disease.
    xx Peach. Diseases.

Virus diseases of plants.
    sa Mosaic disease.
        Virus diseases of potatoes.
        Virus diseases of raspberries.
        Virus diseases of solanaceous
            plants.
        Virus diseases of tomatoes.
        Virus diseases of legumes.
        Virus diseases of tobacco.
        Virus diseases of sugar-beets.
        Virus diseases of cabbage.

Virus diseases of plants (Continued)
    sa Virus diseases of cherries.
       Virus diseases of beans.
       Phloem necrosis of elms.
       Virus diseases of fruit.
--Bibliography.
--Catalogs and collections.
--Congresses.
--Diagnosis.
    xx Vegetable pathology. Diagnosis.
--Names.
    xx Vegetable pathology. Names.
--Transmission.
    sa Subdivision Transmission under:
       Virus diseases of grapes
       [and other plants]

Virus diseases of potatoes.
    xx Potatoes. Diseases.
--Diagnosis.
    xx Vegetable pathology. Diagnosis.
--Transmission.

Virus diseases of raspberries.
    sa Mosaic disease of raspberries.
    xx Raspberries. Diseases.

Virus diseases of rice.
    sa Hoja blanca.
    xx Rice. Diseases.

Virus diseases of solanaceous plants.
    xx Vegetable pathology.
       Solanaceae. Diseases.

Virus diseases of strawberries.
    xx Strawberries. Diseases.

Virus diseases of sugar-beets.
    sa Yellows.

Virus diseases of sugar-cane.
    sa Names of specific diseases,
       e.g., Ratoon stunting
       disease of sugar-cane.
    xx Sugar-cane. Diseases.

Virus diseases of tobacco.
    sa Mosaic disease of tobacco.
       Rattle disease of tobacco.
    xx Tobacco. Diseases.
       Virus diseases of plants.

Virus diseases of tomatoes.
    sa Mosaic disease of tomato.
       Tomato yellows.
       Spotted wilt of tomatoes.

Virus names. See Viruses. Names.

Virus research.
    x Viruses. Research.
    xx Virus diseases.
       Viruses.
--Periodicals.
--Societies.

Viruses.
    sa Subdivision Viruses under:
       National industrial re-
       covery act, 1933. Codes.
       Neurotropic viruses.
       Rabbit plague virus.
       Foot-and-mouth disease virus.
       Virus research.
       Vaccine lymph.
       Virales.
       Newcastle disease virus.
    xx Bacteria.
       Vaccine lymph.
--Catalogs and collections.
--Names.
    x Virus names.
--Nomenclature.
--Periodicals.
--Research. See Virus research.

Viscera.
    x Organs.
       Splanchnology.
    xx Anatomy.
--Analysis.
    xx Food. Analysis.
--Pests.

Viscera, Rudimentary.

Visceral gout in poultry.
    xx Poultry. Diseases.
       Gout.

Visceral leishmaniosis. See Kála-azár.

Viscometer. See Viscosimeter.

Viscopast.

Viscose.

Viscose rayon. See Rayon.

Viscose silk. See Rayon.

Viscosimeter.
 x Viscometer.

Viscosity.
 sa Viscosimeter.
  Rheology.
 xx Rheology.
--Bibliography.
--Tables, etc.

Viscous organic liquids.

Viscum.

Viscum album.

Visibility.

Vision. See Color-sense; Eye; Sight.

Visiting housekeepers.
 x Homemaker service.
  Housekeepers, Visiting.
  Housekeeping service (Social
   work)
 xx Social service.

Visiting nurses. See Nurses and nursing.

Visitors, International. See International visits.

Visits, International. See International visits.

Vistra. See Rayon.

Vistula Valley.
--Agriculture.
 sa Subdivision Germany. Vistula
  Valley under: Agriculture.
  Economic aspects.
 xx Germany. Agriculture.
--Botany.

Visual aids. See Visual instruction.

Visual education. See Visual instruction.

Visual instruction.
 sa Moving-pictures in education.
  Audio-visual instruction.
  Television in education.
  Radio in education.
 x Visual aids.
 xx Communication and traffic.
  Audio-visual instruction.
  Teaching. Aids and devices.
--Bibliography.
--Catalogs.
--Congresses.
--Directories.

Visual methods. See Statistics. Graphic methods.

Vitaceae.
 sa Vitis.
 x Ampllideae.

Vitaglass. See Ultra-violet rays.

Vital force. See Bioenergetics.

Vital statistics.
 sa Death. Causes.
  Mortality.
  Subdivision Statistics, Vital
   under names of countries,
   cities, etc.

Vitaliana.
 xx Aquatic plants.

Vitamin B complex. See Vitamins (B)

Vitamin deficiency. See Deficiency diseases.

Vitamin enrichment of food. See Food, Enriched.

Vitamin fortification of food. See Food, Enriched.

Vitamin therapy.
 x Vitamins. Therapeutic use.
 xx Vitamins.
--Periodicals.

Vitaminized bread. See Bread, Enriched.

Vitaminized flour. See Flour, Enriched.

Vitaminized food.   See Food, Enriched.

Vitamins.
    sa Food, Enriched.
       Deficiency diseases.
       Lactobacillus casei factor.
       Vitamin therapy.
       Antivitamins.
    xx Catalysts.
       Deficiency diseases.

Vitamins (A)
    sa Carotin.

Vitamins (B)
    x Vitamin B complex.

Vitamins (B_1)
    x Aneurin.
      Thiamine.
      Thiamine hydrochloride.
      Thiamin chloride.
      Antineuritic vitamin.

Vitamins (B_2)   See Vitamins (G)

Vitamins (B_6)
    x Pyridoxine.
      Adermin.

Vitamins (B_{12})
    sa Animal protein factor.
--Bibliography.

Vitamins (B_c)   See Lactobacillus casei
  factor.

Vitamins (B_T)

Vitamins (C)
    sa Dehydroascorbic acid.
    x Antiscorbutic vitamin.
      Ascorbic acid.

Vitamins (D)

Vitamins (D_2)

Vitamins (E)
    x Tocopherol.
--Bibliography.

Vitamins (G)
    x Riboflavin.
      Vitamins (B_2)
      Lactoflavin.

Vitamins (H)
    x Biotin.

Vitamins (K)
    x Methyl-naphthoquinone.

Vitamins (K_1)
--Bibliography.

Vitamins (M)   See Lactobacillus casei
  factor.

Vitamins (P)
    x Rutin.
      Quercetin.
--Bibliography.

Vitamins (P) in buckwheat.
    x Buckwheat, Vitamins (P) in.

Vitamins (T)

Vitamins.
--Abstracts.
--Allocation agreements.
    xx Allocation agreements.
--Analysis.
--Bibliography.
--Charts.
--Directories.
--Grading and standardization.
    xx Biological products. Grading
       and standardization.
--Periodicals.
    sa Subdivision Periodicals under:
       Vitamins in animal nutri-
       tion.
--Research.

Vitamins, Synthetic.
    x Concentrated vitamins.
    xx Synthetic products.

Vitamins.
--Therapeutic use.   See Vitamin therapy.

Vitamins in alfalfa.
    xx Alfalfa.

Vitamins in algae.
  x Algae, Vitamins in.

Vitamins in animal nutrition.
  xx Animal nutrition.
--Bibliography.
--Grading and standardization.
--Periodicals.
  xx Animal nutrition. Periodicals.
  Vitamins. Periodicals.

Vitamins in apple.

Vitamins in apricots.

Vitamins in asparagus.

Vitamins in barley.

Vitamins in beef.
  xx Beef.

Vitamins in bread.
  sa Bread, Enriched.
  xx Bread.
  Bread, Enriched.

Vitamins in broccoli.

Vitamins in butter.
  x Butter. Vitamin content.

Vitamins in canned fish.
  xx Fishery products. Preservation.

Vitamins in canned goods.
  x Canned goods, Vitamins in.

Vitamins in carrots.

Vitamins in citrus juices.
  xx Citrus juices.

Vitamins in colostrum.
  xx Colostrum.

Vitamins in cow-peas.
  x Cow-peas, Vitamins in.

Vitamins in dairy products.

Vitamins in eggs.
  xx Eggs.

Vitamins in feeding stuffs.
  xx Feeding stuffs.
  Animal nutrition.

Vitamins in fish-oil.
  xx Fish-oil.

Vitamins in flour.
  sa Flour, Enriched.
  xx Flour.
  Flour, Enriched.

Vitamins in food.
  x Food, Vitamins in.
  xx Food. Analysis.
--Bibliography.

Vitamins in fruit.
  x Fruit, Vitamins in.

Vitamins in grape juice.

Vitamins in grapes.

Vitamins in grasses.

Vitamins in hay.

Vitamins in hegari.
  xx Hegari.

Vitamins in lettuce.

Vitamins in maize.
  xx Maize.

Vitamins in maize products.

Vitamins in mangoes.

Vitamins in meat.
  x Meat, Vitamins in.

Vitamins in meat extracts.
  xx Meat extracts.

Vitamins in milk.

Vitamins in milo.
  xx Milo.

Vitamins in peanuts.

Vitamins in pears.
  xx Pear.

Viticulture (Continued)
--Implements and machinery.
    xx Agriculture. Implements and
        machinery.
--Legislation.
--Periodicals.
    sa Subdivision Viticulture. Peri-
        odicals under names of coun-
        tries, etc., e.g., Tunis.
        Viticulture. Periodicals.
--Pests.   See Grapes. Pests.
--Pictorial works.
--Research.
--Societies.
--Statistics.
    sa Viticulture. Statistics under
        names of countries, etc.,
        e.g., U.S. Viticulture. Sta-
        tistics.
    xx Agriculture. Statistics.
--Terminology.
--Text-books.
--Yearbooks.

Vitis.
    sa Vitis Berlandieri.

Vitis Berlandieri.

Vitis vinifera.
    x Grapes, Vinifera.

Vitis vulpina.

Vitória, Brazil.
--Commerce.
    sa Subdivision Vitória, Brazil
        under: Coffee trade.

Vitreous humor.

Vitrinellidae.

Vittaria.

Vittarieae.
    sa Vittaria.

Vivariums.

Viverridae.
    sa Genetta.

Vivianite.

Vivipara.
    A genus of fresh water snails.

Vivisection.
    xx Animal experimentation.
--Periodicals.

Vizcaya, Spain (Province)
    x Biscay, Spain (Province)
--Botany.
--Commerce.
-- --Statistics.
--Entomology.
    sa Subdivision Spain, Vizcaya
        (Province) under: Ento-
        mology, Economic.

Vizeu, Portugal.
--Agriculture.

Vladimir, Russia (Province)
--Botany.

Vladimir (Government)
--Agriculture.
    sa Subdivision Vladimir (Govern-
        ment) under: Reclamation
        of land.

Vladimir Draft horse.

Vladimir Il'ich Collective Farm.
    xx Collective farms.

Vladimir Region.
--Swine.

Vladivostok region.
--Sericulture.

Vlieland (Island)
--Botany.

Voandzeia subterranea.

Vocabulary.   See English language.
    Vocabulary; Russian language.
    Vocabulary; English language.
    Glossaries, vocabularies,
    etc.

Vocation, Choice of.   See Vocational
    guidance.

Vocational agricultural education.   See
Agriculture. Education; Agriculture.
Study and teaching.

Vocational agriculture.   See Agriculture.
Education; Agriculure. Study and
teaching.

Vocational counselors.
sa Vocational guidance.
xx Vocational guidance.

Vocational counseling. ` See Vocational
guidance.

Vocational education.   (INDIRECT)
sa Technical education.
Cooperation in education.
Education and national de-
fense.
Vocational guidance.
Agriculture. Education.
Engineering. Education.
Forestry. Education.
Library schools and training.
Manual training.
Professional education.
Textile schools.
Disabled. Rehabilitation, etc.
Personnel training.
x Education, Vocational.
xx Part-time education.
Vocational guidance.
--Bibliography.
sa Subdivision Bibliography under:
Cooperation in education.
--Congresses.
xx Education. Congresses.
--Directories.
sa Vocational education [geo-
graphic subdivision] Direc-
tories, e.g., Vocational
education. U.S. Directories.
--Government aid.
xx Education. Government aid.
--History.
xx Education. History.
--Legislation.
--Periodicals.
--Societies.

Vocational guidance.
sa Occupations.
Personnel service in education.
Employee counseling.

Vocational guidance (Continued)
sa Professions.
Vocational education.
Vocational counselors.
Counseling.
x Choice of profession.
Guidance, Vocational.
Counseling, Vocational.
Vocational counseling.
Occupation, Choice of.
Profession, Choice of.
Vocation, Choice of.
xx Counseling.
Occupations.
Personnel service in educa-
tion.
Professions.
Vocational education.
--Bibliography.
--Periodicals.
--Societies.
-- --Directories.

Vocational rehabilitation.   See Disabled. Rehabilitation, etc.

Vocational training.   See Vocational
education.

Vochysiaceae.

Vodka.
xx Liquors.

Vogelsberg cattle.
xx Cattle.

Vogtland.
--Paleobotany.
--Paleontology.

Voice.

Voice culture.   See Singing and voice
culture.

Voight Creek Experimental Forest, Wash.

Voivodina Region.
--Agriculture.
-- --Periodicals.
--Botany.
sa Subdivision Voivodina Region
under: Botany, Medical.
--Soils.

Volatile acids.
--Determination.

Volatile oil plants.
sa Cymbopogon coloratus.

Volatile oils.   See Essences and essential oils.

Volatile products.

Volcanic ash, tuff, etc.
x Tuff.
xx Rocks, Igneous.
Ashes.
Pumicite.

Volcanic soil.   See Soil, Volcanic.

Volcanoes.
sa Lava.
Vesuvius.
Stromboli, Eruption of, 1912.

Volclay.
xx Bentonite.

Vole acid-fast bacillus.
x Vole bacilli.
xx Bacteria, Acid-fast.
Tuberculosis. Bacilli.

Vole bacilli.   See Vole acid-fast
bacillus.

Voles.
sa Microtinae.
Arvicola.
--Diseases.
sa Tuberculosis in voles.

Volga Region.
x Zavolz'e.
--Agriculture.
sa Subdivision Volga Region under:
Agriculture. Economic aspects.
Wheat.
Farm management.
Types of farming.
Field crops.
Potatoes.
-- --Periodicals.

Volga Region (Continued)
--Botany.
sa Subdivision Volga Region
under: Trees.
Shrubs.
--Entomology.
sa Subdivision Volga Region
under: Entomology, Economic.
xx Russia. Entomology.
--Forestry.
sa Subdivision Volga Region
under: Tree planting.
Afforestation and reforestation.
Trees.
Shrubs.
--Maps.
--Natural history.
--Ornithology.
--Paleobotany.
--Physical geography.
--Soils.
--Zoology.

Volga River.

Volhynia.
--Agriculture.
sa Subdivision Volhynia under:
Agriculture. Economic
aspects.
--Pomology.

Volkhof Valley.
--Botany.
--Soils.

Volkhov.   See Volkhof.

Vologda.
--Dairying.

Vologda Region.
--Agriculture.
sa Subdivision Vologda Region
under: Agricultural policies and programs.
--Swine.

Volstead law.   See Prohibition. U.S.

Voltage regulators.
x Regulators, Voltage.

Volterra.
--Agriculture.
    sa Subdivision Italy. Volterra
        under: Reclamation of land.
        Agriculture. Economic as-
          pects.

Volucella.

Volume and yield tables.
    sa Wood. Utilization tables.
    x Stand tables.
      Yield tables.
    xx Forest mensuration.
      Forest accretion and yield.
--Bibliography.

Volume-weight. See Soil. Volume-weight.

Volumetric analysis.
    x Titration.
      Chemistry. Volumetric analysis.
    xx Chemistry, Analytic. Quantita-
      tive.

Voluntary domestic allotment plan. See
  Domestic allotment plan.

Volusia Co., Fla.
--Water-supply.

Volusia loam.

Volusia silt loam.

Volutidae.

Volvocaeeae.
    sa Volvox.

Volvocineae.
    sa Pleodorina illinoisensis.

Volvox.

Volvox globator.
    xx Volvocaeeae.

Vorarlberg.
    sa Tyrol.
--Agriculture.
--Botany.
    xx Austria. Botany.
--Domestic animals.

Vorarlberg (Continued)
--Land.
    sa Subdivision Austria. Vorarlberg
        under: Land utilization.
--Maps.
--Natural history.
--Soils.
    sa Subdivision Austria. Vorarl-
        berg under: Peat.
    xx Austria. Soils.
--Zoology.
-- --Bibliography.

Vorarlberg brown cattle. See Montafon
  cattle.

Vorgebirg. See Cape Verde Islands.

Vormela negans.

Voronezh Region.
--Agriculture.
--Domestic animals.
--Natural history.
    xx Natural history.
--Paleobotany.
--Zoology.

Vosges cattle.

Vosges Mountains.
    sa Subdivision Vosges Mountains
        under: Irrigation. France.
--Botany.
--Forestry.
    sa Subdivision Vosges Mountains
        under: Afforestation and
          reforestation.
--Irrigation.

Vouraikos Valley.

Vouvray, France.
--Viticulture.

Voyages and travels.
    sa Scientific expeditions.
      Subdivision Description and
        travel under names of
        countries, etc.
--Periodicals.

Vpered Collective Farm.
    xx Collective farms.

Vsesoiuznoe sotsialisticheskoe sorevno-
  vanie.
      xx Competition, Socialist.

Vucine. See Isoctylhydrocuprein.

Vulcanization.

Vulpes.
      sa Fox.

Vultures. See Vulturidae.

Vulturidae.
      sa Gypaëtus.

Vulturidae, Fossil.

Vulva.

Vyatka. See Viatka.

Vyzunonis (Forest) See Vyzuonio miskas.

Vyzuonio miskas.
  --Botany.
      xx Lithuania. Botany.

W.A.R.F.-42. See Warfarrin.

Wabash clay.

Wabash Co., Ill.
  --Soils.
      xx Illinois. Soils.

Wabash Co., Ind.
  --Botany.
  --Geology.

Wabash River.
      sa Flood control. Wabash River.

Wabash silt loam.

Wabash Valley.
  --Botany.
      sa Subdivision Wabash Valley
          under: Trees.
  --Forestry.

Wabasha Co., Minn.
      xx Minnesota.

Wachusett, Mount. See Mount Wachusett.

Waco, Tex.
  --Markets.

Waco area.
  --Water-supply.
      sa Subdivision Texas. Waco area
          under: Water, Underground.

Wad Dra. See Dra River.

Wadden Zee. See Waddenzee.

Waddenzee.
      sa Griend Island, Waddenzee.

Wadena Co., Minn.
  --Soils.
      sa Subdivision Minnesota. Wadena
          Co. under: Soil-surveys.

Wadi Tumilat.

Wady Rayan.

Waffle irons.
      sa Electric waffle irons.

Waffles.
      xx Cookery.
          Food.

Wage and hour law. See Fair labor
      standards act.

Wage control. See Wages. Regulation.

Wage-hour law. See Fair labor standards
      act.

Wage regulation. See Wages. Regulation.

Wage stabilization. See Wages. Regula-
      tion.

Wages. (DIRECT)
      sa Cost and standard of living.
          Labor contract.
          Piece-work.
          Prices.
          Profit-sharing.
          Bonus system.
          Family allowances.
          Non-wage payments.
          Wages, Forestry.
          Wages, Textile.

Wages (Continued)
    sa Wages, Building.
       Salaries.
       Wages, Food industry.
    x Labor and laboring classes.
       Wages.
       Pay.

Wages, Agricultural.   (INDIRECT)
    x Farm wages.
       Agricultural wages.
       Labor and wages, Agricultural.
    xx Agricultural laborers.
--Law.
--Tables and ready-reckoners.

Wages.
--Annual wage.
    xx Unemployment, Seasonal.

Wages, Building.
    xx Wages.

Wages.
--Control. See Wages. Regulation.
--Family allowances. See Family
   allowances.

Wages, Food industry.
    x Food industry and trade. Wages.
    xx Wages.

Wages, Forestry.
    xx Wages.
       Forestry. Labor.

Wages.
--History.
    sa Wages [geographic subdivision]
       History, e.g., Wages. U.S.
       History.
    xx Labor and laboring classes.
       History.
--Legislation.
    sa Fair labor standards act.
    xx Law.
--Minimum wage.   (DIRECT)
--Regulation.
    x Wage control.
       Wages. Control.
       Wages. Stabilization.
       Wage regulation.
       Wage stabilization.
-- --Congresses.
--Stabilization. See Wages. Regulation.

Wages (Continued)
--Statistics. See Wages.

Wages, Textile.
    xx Textile workers.
       Wages.

Wages.
--Women.
    x Woman. Wages.
-- --Bibliography.

Wages in kind.

Wagner-Ellender-Taft general housing
   bill. See General housing act of
   1945.

Wagner housing bill. See United States
   housing act of 1936.

Wagon tires.

Wagon tongue.

Wagons.
    x Farm wagons.

Wagtails. See Motacillidae.

Wahehe.
    xx Bantus.

Wai Taluka, India.
    sa Subdivision India. Wai Taluka
       under: Farm management sur-
       veys.

Waikeri irrigation area, South Australia.
--Soils.
    sa Subdivision Waikeri irrigation
       area under: Soil-surveys.
       South Australia.
    xx South Australia. Soils.

Waimea Co., N.Z.
--Agriculture.
    sa Subdivision Waimea Co. under:
       Agriculture. Economic as-
       pects. New Zealand.
--Soils.

Waipoua Kauri Forest.

Waiters.
    sa Stewards.

Waiting-line theory. See Operations
    research.

Waitresses. See Waiters.

Wakayama-Ken, Japan.
--Agriculture.
-- --Periodicals.
--Industries.

Wakefield, Mass.

Walchandnagar, India.
--Agriculture.
    sa Subdivision Walchandnagar,
        India under: Agriculture
        and business.

Walcheren Island.
--Agriculture.
    sa Subdivision Netherlands.
        Walcheren Island under:
        Reclamation of land.

Waldeck.
--Agriculture.
-- --History.
--Botany.
    xx Germany. Botany.

Waldecker cattle.
    xx Cattle.

Waldemar, Prince of Prussia, 1817-1849.

Waldenburg, Silesia.
--Agriculture.
    xx Silesia. Agriculture.

Waldo Co., Me.
--Agriculture.
    sa Subdivision Maine. Waldo Co.
        under: War and agriculture
        (1939-1945)
    xx Maine. Agriculture.
--Land.
    sa Subdivision Maine. Waldo Co.
        under: Land utilization.
--Soils.
    sa Subdivision Maine. Waldo Co.
        under: Soil conservation.
        Soil surveys.

Waldo Co., Me. (Continued)
--Water-supply.
    sa Subdivision Maine. Waldo Co.
        under: Water. Conservation.

Wales.
--Agriculture.
    sa Subdivision Agriculture under:
        Brecknockshire, Wales.
        Cardiganshire, Wales.
        Carmarthenshire, Wales//
    Subdivision Wales under:
        Agricultural laborers.
        Agriculture. Economic
          aspects.
        War and agriculture (1939-
          1945)
        Tenant farming.
        Farm management surveys.
        Types of farming.
        Farm management.
        Agriculture, Cooperative.
        Farm produce. Cost of
          production.
        Agricultural clubs.
        Farms.
        Agricultural policies and
          programs.
        Potatoes.
        Mechanized farming.
        Agricultural surveys.
        Borgoed farm, Lyncelyn, Wales.
-- --Bibliography.
-- --Education.
    sa University College of South
        Wales and Monmouthshire.
        University College of Wales,
        Aberystwyth. Agricultural
        Dept.
-- --History.
    sa Subdivision Agriculture. His-
        tory under: Cardiganshire,
        Wales.
-- --Statistics.
--Antiquities.
--Apiculture.
    xx Gt. Brit. Apiculture.
-- --Periodicals.
--Botany.
    sa Subdivision Botany under:
        Anglesey.
        Glamorganshire//

Wales (Continued)
--Botany.
    sa Subdivision Wales under:
      Vegetable pathology.
      Ferns.
      Grasses.
      Fungi.
      Weeds.
      Wild flowers.
--Cattle.
    sa Subdivision Cattle under names
      of counties, etc.
    xx Wales. Domestic animals.
--Cattle trade.
--Census.
--Dairying.
    sa Subdivision Dairying under
      names of counties, etc.
-- --Statistics.
--Description and travel.
--Domestic animals.
    sa Subdivision Wales under:
      Cattle.
--Economic conditions.
    sa Subdivision Wales under:
      Geography, Economic.
      History, Economic.
      Wales, South. Economic condi-
        tions.
--Economic policy.
    xx Gt. Brit. Economic policy.
--Education.
--Entomology.
    sa Subdivision Entomology under:
      Swansea.
    Subdivision Wales under:
      Lepidoptera.
--Forest reservations.
    sa Snowdonia National Forest Park.
      Rheola Forest, Wales.
      Coed y Brenin Forest, Wales.
    xx Gt. Brit. Forest reservations.
--Forestry.
    sa Snowdonia National Forest Park.
--Geography.
    sa Subdivision Wales under:
      Geography, Economic.
    xx Gt. Brit. Geography.
--Harbors.
    xx Harbors.
--History.
    sa Subdivision Wales under:
      History, Economic.

Wales (Continued)
--Industries.
    sa Subdivision Wales under:
      Industrial surveys.
      Rural industries.
--Land.
    sa Subdivision Land under names
      of shires, etc.
    xx Gt. Brit. Land.
--Maps.
--Milk supply.
    xx Gt. Brit. Milk supply.
--Milk trade.
--Natural history.
    sa Swansea, Wales. Natural
      history//
--Politics and government.
    sa Subdivision Wales under:
      Local government.
--Sheep.
--Social conditions.
    sa Subdivision Wales under:
      Community life.
--Social life and customs.
    xx England. Social life and
      customs.
--Soils.
    sa Subdivision Wales under:
      Soil-surveys.
    xx Gt. Brit. Soils.
--Statistics.
--Swine.

Wales, South.
--Economic conditions.

Walhalla gold field.

Walk-about disease. See Kimberley
  horse disease.

Walker Co., Ala.
--Economic conditions.
--Industries and resources.
    sa Industrial surveys. Alabama.
      Walker Co.

Walker River irrigation district.
    xx Irrigation projects.

Walking.

Walkingstick. See Diapheromera
  femorata.

Walks.
    x Paths.

Wall board.
    x Wallboard.
      Building boards.
    xx Building materials.
      Insulation (Heat)
  --Statistics.

Wall-paper.
    x Wallpaper.
  --Periodicals.

Wall Street, New York City.

Walla Walla River.

Walla Walla River Watershed, Oregon and
    Washington.

Wallachia.

Wallboard. See Wall board.

Walled Lake, Mich.

Waller Co., Tex.
  --Social conditions.
    sa Subdivision Waller Co., Tex.
        under: Cost and standard of
          living.
        Negroes.
  --Water-supply.

Wallis and Futuna Islands (Protectorate)
    x Futuna Island (Protectorate)
  --Entomology.
    sa Subdivision Wallis and Futuna
        Islands (Protectorate)
        under: Entomology, Economic.

Walloon dialect.
  --Dictionaries.

Walloon Lake region, Mich.
  --Botany.

Wallowa Co., Or.
  --Agriculture.
    sa Subdivision Oregon. Wallowa Co.
        under: Agricultural poli-
          cies and programs.

Wallowa Mountains, Or.
  --Natural history.
    xx Oregon. Natural history.

Wallowa National Forest, Or.

Wallpaper. See Wall-paper.

Wallrothiella arceuthobii.

Walls.
    sa Clay as a building material.
      Foundations.
      Masonry.
      Retaining walls.

Walls, Concrete.
  --Testing.

Walls.
  --Fire resistance.
  -- --Testing.
    xx Fire tests.
  --Fireproofing.
    xx Fireproofing.

Walnut.
      · This heading used for works about
      the English walnut tree. For
      works about the nuts see Wal-
      nuts; for works about the wood
      see Walnut wood.
    x Circassian walnut.
      English walnut.
      Persian walnut.
      California walnut.
  --Bibliography.

Walnut, Black. See Black walnut.

Walnut.
  --Congresses.
    xx Nuts. Congresses.
  --Cost of production.
    xx Nuts. Cost of production.
  --Diseases.
    sa Bacterium juglandis.
    xx Juglans. Diseases.
  --Grafting.
  --Periodicals.
  --Pests.
    sa Rhagoletis suavis.
      Myelois venipars.
    xx Juglans. Pests.
  --Prices.

Walnut (Continued)
--Societies.

Walnut-blight.

Walnut cake.

Walnut husk-maggot.   See Rhagoletis
suavis.

Walnut Lake, Mich.
--Botany.

Walnut span-worm.   See Conoides plumi-
geraria.

Walnut wood.
    xx Cabinet woods.
       Wood.

Walnuts.
    This heading used for works about
    nuts of the English walnut
    tree. For works about the tree
    see Walnut; for works about the
    wood see Walnut wood.
    sa Ethylene. Effect on walnuts.
    xx Nuts.
--Drying.
--Fertilization.
    xx Nuts. Fertilization.
--Grading and standardization.
    xx Nuts. Grading and standardiza-
       tion.
--Grafting.
--Marketing.
--Marketing, Cooperative.
    xx Nuts. Marketing, Cooperative.
-- --Societies.
--Marketing agreements.
--Periodicals.
--Prices.
    xx Prices.
--Statistics.
    xx Nuts. Statistics.
       Statistics.
-- --Bibliography.
    xx Nuts. Statistics. Bibliography.
--Tariff.
    xx Nuts. Tariff.
--Testing.
--Varieties.
    xx Nuts. Varieties.

Walpole grant.
    xx Land grants.

Walrus.
--Parasites.

Walsh-Healey act.   See Public contracts
act.

Waltham, Mass.
--Botany.

Walton Co., Fla.
--Land.
    sa Subdivision Florida. Walton
       Co. under: Land utiliza-
       tion.
    xx Florida. Land.

Walton Co., Ga.
--Land.
    sa Subdivision Georgia. Walton
       Co. under: Land utiliza-
       tion.
       Subdivision Walton Co., Ga.
       under: Land tenure.

Walworth Co., S.D.
--Soils.
    sa Subdivision South Dakota.
       Walworth Co. under:
       Soil-surveys.

Walworth Co., Wis.
--Agriculture.
    sa Subdivision Wisconsin. Wal-
       worth Co. under: Agri-
       culture. Economic as-
       pects.
--Social conditions.
    sa Subdivision Wisconsin. Wal-
       worth Co. under: Social
       surveys.
--Soils.
    sa Subdivision Wisconsin. Wal-
       worth Co. under: Soil-
       surveys.

Wapato Indian irrigation project.
    xx Irrigation projects.

Wapinitia Federal reclamation project,
Or.

Wapinitia project.

Wappapello Reservoir, Mo.

War.
        sa European war, 1914-1918.
        U.S. History. Civil War.
        U.S. History. Revolution.
        World War, 1939-1945.
        Bombardment.
        Soldiers.

War, Animals in.   See Animals in war.

War.
--Bibliography.
        sa Subdivision Bibliography under:
            War and agriculture (1939-
                1945)
            War. Economic aspects.
            U.S. Defenses.
            World War, 1939-1945. Eco-
                nomic aspects.

War, Cost of.
        sa European war, 1914-1918. Fi-
            nance.
        World War, 1939-1945. Finance.
        x War finance.

War, Declaration of.

War.
--Economic aspects.
        Under this heading are entered
        works dealing with the economic
        causes of war, and with the ef-
        fect of war and preparation for
        war on industrial and com-
        mercial activity.
        sa Competition, International.
        Excess profits tax.
        Munitions.
        War, Cost of.
        European war, 1914-1918. Fi-
            nance.
        World War, 1939-1945. Finance.
        Postwar planning (1939-   )
        European war, 1914-1918. Man-
            power.
        World War, 1939-1945. Manpower.
        War contracts.
        Priorities, Industrial.
        Blacklists, Commercial.

War (Continued)
--Economic aspects.
        sa Subdivision Economic aspects
            under: European war, 1914-
                1918.
            World War, 1939-1945.
        x War and business.
        Economic warfare.
        Economics of war.
-- --Bibliography.
        sa Subdivision Economic aspects.
            Bibliography ,under:
            World War, 1939-1945.
            European war, 1914-1918.
        xx War. Bibliography.
        Economic conditions. Bibliog-
            raphy.
-- -- --Periodicals.
        xx Bibliography. Periodicals.

War, Outlawry of.

War.
--Prisoners.   See Prisoners of war.

War, Psychology of.
        x Psychology of war.
        Military psychology.
        Psychology, Military.
        Psychological warfare.
--Bibliography.
        xx Psychology. Bibliography.

War against insects.
        x Insects vs. man.
        xx Entomology, Economic.

War agricultural executive committees
  (Gt. Brit.)
        sa County agricultural committees
            (Gt. Brit.)
        xx County agricultural committees
            (Gt. Brit.)

War and agriculture.
        Under this heading are entered
        general works. For works on
        the European war (1914-1918)
        and agriculture, see European
        war (1914-1918) Economic as-
        pects; for works on the World
        War, 1939-1945 and agriculture
        see War and agriculture (1939-
        1945)
--Periodicals.

War and agriculture (1939-1945)   (INDI-
  RECT)
        When subdivided geographically,
          indicate see also ref. from
          name of place with subdivision
          Agriculture.
        sa Food for freedom program.
         x Agriculture and war.
          Impacts of war on agriculture.
        xx World War, 1939-1945.
          Agriculture and defense.
          Defenses.
          War and food supply.
          Agriculture. Economic aspects.
          Agricultural policies and
          programs.
  --Bibliography.
        sa Subdivision Bibliography under
          War and agriculture (1939-
          1945) [geographic subdivi-
          sion] e.g., War and agri-
          culture (1939-1945) U.S.
          Bibliography.
        xx War. Bibliography.
  --Congresses.
        xx Agriculture. Congresses.
  --Periodicals.
        sa Subdivision Periodicals under
          War and agriculture (1939-
          1945) [geographic subdivi-
          sion] e.g., War and agri-
          culture (1939-1945) U.S.
          Periodicals.

War and animals.   See Animals in war.

War and business.   See War. Economic
  aspects.

War and clothing.   See Clothing and
  dress, Wartime.

War and education.
        sa Education and national defense.
          European war, 1914-1918. War
          work. Schools.
          World War, 1939-1945. War work.
          Schools.

War and food supply.
        sa War and agriculture (1939-1945)
          Nutrition in defense.
          European war, 1914-1918. Food
          question.
          World War, 1939-1945. Food
          question.
         x Food and war.
        xx Food supply.
  --Congresses.
        sa Subdivision Congresses under:
          Nutrition in defense.
  --Government control.   See Food control
          (Economic measures)
  --Periodicals.

War and forestry.   (INDIRECT)
         x Forests and war.
          Forestry and war.
        xx Forestry.

War and forestry (1914-1918)   (DIRECT)

War and forestry (1939-1945)   (DIRECT)
        When subdivided geographically,
          indicate see also ref. from
          name of geographic area with
          subdivision Forestry.
        xx World War, 1939-1945.
  --Bibliography.

War and health.
        sa European war, 1914-1918. Medi-
          cal and sanitary affairs.
          World War, 1939-1945. Medical
          and sanitary affairs.
        xx Hygiene, Public.
  --Bibliography.
        xx Hygiene, Public. Bibliography.

War and industry.   See War. Economic
  aspects.

War and libraries.   See Libraries and
  war.

War and literature.
        sa World War, 1939-1945. Litera-
          ture and the war.
         x Literature and war.

War and medicine.   See Medicine, Military.

War and nutrition.
    sa Nutrition in defense.

War and science.
    sa European war, 1914-1918.
       Science.
       World War, 1939-1945. Science.
    x Science and war.

War and transportation.
    sa Subdivision Transportation
       under: European war, 1914-
       1918.
       World War, 1939-1945.
    x Transportation and war.
      Transportation, War.
    xx Transportation.

War bonds.
    sa Defense savings program.
      Savings bonds.
    x Defense savings bonds.
      Defense savings stamps.
      Defense stamps.
      Defense bonds.
      War savings bonds.
    xx Bonds.
      Defense savings program.
      Savings bonds.

War claims. See Claims and adjustments.

War claims act of 1928. See Settlement
of war claims act of 1928.

War claims act of 1948.

War contracts. (DIRECT)
    x Contracts, War.
    xx Public contracts.
      Contracts.
      War. Economic aspects.
 --U.S.
 -- --Bibliography.
 --Renegotiation.
 -- --U.S.
    x Renegotiation of war contracts.
 -- -- --Bibliography.
 --Termination.
    x Cancellation of war contracts.
      Termination of war contracts.

War damage acts, 1941.

War damage compensation. See Insurance,
War risks.

War economics. See War. Economic aspects.

War finance. See War, Cost of.

War finance corporation. See U.S. War
Finance Corporation.

War gases. See Gases, Asphyxiating and
poisonous. War use.

War legislation. See European war,
1914-1918. Law and legislation; World
War, 1939-1945. Law and legislation.

War medicine. See Medicine, Military.

War powers act, 1941.

War powers act, 1942.
    x Second war powers act, 1942.
    xx World War, 1939-1945. Law and
      legislation. U.S.

War prisoners. See Prisoners of war.

War production drives. See Incentives
in industry.

War profits tax. See Excess profits
tax.

War risk insurance. See Insurance.
War risks.

War savings bonds. See War bonds.

War surpluses. See Surplus war property.

Waratah. See Telopea speciosissima.

Warble-flies. See Hypoderma.

Warblers. See Mniotiltidae; Sylviidae;
Timeliidae; Dendroica; Geothlypis;
Helminthophila; Granatellus; Basi-
leuterus; Locustella; Compsothlypidae;
Phylloscopus; Acrocephalus.

Ward Co., N.D.
    sa Subdivision North Dakota.
        Ward Co. under: County
          surveys.
        Social surveys.
    xx North Dakota.
--Agriculture.
    sa Subdivision North Dakota.
        Ward Co. under: Agriculture.
        Economic aspects.
        Farm management surveys.
--Education.
    sa Subdivision North Dakota.
        Ward Co. under: Rural
        ` schools.
    xx North Dakota. Education.
--Land.
    sa Subdivision North Dakota.
     · Ward Co. under: Land utili-
        zation.

Ward Co., Tex.
--Water-supply.
    sa Subdivision Texas. Ward Co.
        under: Water, Underground.

Wardian cases.

Ware collection of Blaschka glass models
  of flowers. See Harvard University.
  Botanical Museum. Ware Collection of
  Blaschka glass models of flowers.

Warehouse act.
    x United States Warehouse act.
    xx Warehouses. Legislation.

Warehouses.
    sa Subdivision Storage under:
        Cotton.
        Sugar.
        Cereals//
    x Storage warehouses.
--Bibliography.
--Construction.
--Cost of operation.
--Designs and plans.
--Directories.
--Fires and fire prevention.
    xx Fire prevention.
--Fumigation.
    xx Fumigation.

Warehouses (Continued)
--Legislation.
    sa Warehouse act.
        Pamphlet collection; Vertical
          file.
--Machinery.
    xx Machinery.
--Periodicals.
--Pests. See Stored products. Pests.
--Sealing.
    xx Sealing of warehouses.
--Societies.
--Statistics.

Warfare gases. See Chemical warfare.

Warfarin.
    x W.A.R.F.-42.

Warm Springs Reservation, Or.

Warner-Bratzler shear.
    xx Dynamometer.

Warping.
    xx Weaving.

Warrants, Agricultural.

Warren, Ohio.
--Water-supply.

Warren Co., Ill.
--Soils.
    xx Illinois. Soils.

Warren Co., Ind.
--Agriculture.
-- --Periodicals.
--Soils.
    sa Subdivision Indiana. Warren
        Co. under: Soil-surveys.

Warren Co., Iowa.
    xx Iowa. Maps.
--Soils.
    sa Subdivision Iowa. Warren Co.
        under: Soil-surveys.

Warren Co., N.Y.
    sa Subdivision New York. Warren
        Co. under: County surveys.
    xx New York.
--Agriculture.

Warren Co., N.Y. (Continued)
--Forestry.
   sa Subdivision New York (State)
      Warren Co. under: Forest
         management.
--Geology.

Warren Co., N.C.
--Soils.
   sa Subdivision North Carolina.
      Warren Co. under: Soil-
         surveys.

Warren Co., Pa.
--Botany.

Warrensburg, N.Y.
--Charles Lathrop Pack Demonstration
   Forest.   See Charles Lathrop Pack
   Demonstration Forest, Warrensburg,N.Y.

Warrick Co., Ind.
   xx Indiana.
--Agriculture.
-- --Periodicals.

Warrington, Eng.
--Botany.

Warrior River.
   xx Alabama.
      Mississippi.

Warsaw.
--Agricultural experiment stations.
   sa leczyca. leczyckiej stacyi
      doswiadezalnej.
--Maps.

Wart disease of potato.   See Potato wart.

Wartheland.
--Agriculture.
   sa Subdivision Germany. Wartheland
      under: Colonization, Agri-
         cultural.
--Physical geography.

Wartime clothing.   See Clothing and
   dress, Wartime.

Wartime dress.   See Clothing and dress,
   Wartime.

Warts.

Warwickshire, Eng.
--Agriculture.

Wasabi.

Wasatch Co., Utah.
--Agriculture.
   sa Subdivision Utah. Wasatch Co.
      under: Ranges.

Wasatch Mountains, Utah.
--Geology.

Wasatch National Forest, Utah.

Wasco Co., Or.
   xx Oregon.
--Water-supply.

Washabaugh Co., S.D.
   xx South Dakota.

Washburn Co., Wis.
   xx Wisconsin.
--Land.
   sa Subdivision Wisconsin. Washburn
      Co. under: Land. Classifi-
         cation.
   xx Wisconsin. Land.

Washing.   See Laundry.

Washing machines.   See Laundry machinery.

Washing solutions.

Washington, D.C.
   sa United States.
      Capitol.
      District of Columbia.
      Rock Creek, Washington, D.C.
--Biography.
-- --Dictionaries.
--Botanical Gardens.
--Botany.   See District of Columbia.
   Botany.
--Bridges.
   sa Arlington Memorial Bridge.
--Center Market.
-- --Legislation.
--Dairying.
   sa Subdivision Washington, D.C.
      under: Dairy industry and
         trade.
   xx U.S. Dairying.

Washington, D.C. (Continued)
--Description.
-- --Guide-books.
--Directories.
--East Potomac Park.
--Entomology.
    sa Subdivision Washington, D.C.
        under: Trees. Pests.
--Harbor.
    xx Harbors.
--History.
-- --Colonial period.
    xx U.S. History. Colonial period.
--Lafayette Park.
--Land.
    sa Subdivision Washington, D.C.
        Land grants.
    xx U.S. Land.
--Learned institutions and societies.
-- --Directories.
--Libraries.
    xx U.S. Libraries.
--Mall.
--Maps. See District of Columbia.
    Maps.
--Markets.
    sa Special markets, e.g.,
        Washington, D.C. Center
        Market.
--Meteorology.
--Milk depots.
--Milk supply.
    xx U.S. Milk supply.
--Milk trade.
    xx U.S. Milk trade.
    Dairy industry and trade.
    Washington, D.C.
--Monuments.
--Parks.
    sa Washington, D.C. National
        Zoological Park.
    Washington, D.C. Rock Creek
        Park.
    Washington, D.C. East Potomac
        Park//
--Politics and government. See District
    of Columbia. Politics and govern-
    ment.
--Public buildings.
    xx U.S. Public buildings.
--Roads.
--Rock Creek Park.
--Sewerage.
--Social conditions.
-- --Bibliography.

Washington, D.C. (Continued)
--Social life and customs.
    xx U.S. Social life and customs.
--Soils. See District of Columbia.
    Soils.
--Statistics.
    sa District of Columbia. Sta-
        tistics.
--Water-supply.

Washington (State)
    sa Yakima Valley, Wash.
    Touchet Valley, Wash.
    Seattle, Wash.//
--Agriculture.
    sa Subdivision Agriculture under:
        Snohomish Co., Wash.
        Yakima Valley, Wash.//
    Subdivision Washington (State)
        under: Grasses.
    Agriculture. Economic as-
        pects.
    Cereals.
    Agricultural laborers.
    Poultry.
    Rural surveys.
    Farm management.
    Agricultural credit.
    War and agriculture (1939-
        1945)
    Agricultural conservation
        program.
    Agricultural credit.
    Agricultural administration.
    Agricultural extension.
-- --Education.
    sa Subdivision Washington (State)
        under: Agricultural exten-
        sion.
- --History.
-- --Periodicals.
-- --Statistics.
    xx Washington (State) Statistics.
    U.S. Agriculture. Statistics.
--Altitudes.
    xx Altitudes.
--Apiculture.
    xx U.S. Apiculture.
--Bibliography.
    sa Subdivision Bibliography
        under: Washington (State)
        State publications.

Washington (State) (Continued)
--Botany.
    sa Subdivision Botany under:
        Mount Rainier National
          Park.
        Kaniksu National Forest.
        Olympic Peninsula Whatcom
          Co.
        Subdivision Washington (State)
          under: Trees.
        Ethnobotany.
        Botany, Medical.
        Lichens.
        Shrubs.
--Boundaries.
--Census.
--Commerce.
    sa Subdivision Washington (State)
        under: Farm produce. Mar-
          keting.
        Fruit trade.
        Wholesale trade.
--Constitution.
--Dairying.
    sa Subdivision Washington (State)
        under: Dairy industry and
          trade.
--Description and travel.
    sa Yakima Co., Washington.
--Domestic animals.
--Economic conditions.
    sa Subdivision Economic conditions
        under: Seattle.
        Subdivision Washington (State)
          under: Rural surveys.
        Economic surveys.
--Education.
    sa Washington (State) Normal
        School, Cheney.
        Washington (State) Public
        schools.
--Engineering Experiment Station. See
    Washington (State) State College.
    Engineering Experiment Station.
--Entomology.
    sa Subdivision Washington (State)
        under: Coleoptera.
        Entomology, Economic.
        Trees. Pests.
        Plecoptera.
--Fisheries.
    xx U.S. Fisheries.

Washington (State)
--Forest reservations.
    sa Mount Baker National Forest.
        Washington National Forest.
        Wind River Experimental
          Forest, Wash.//
--Forestry.
    sa Subdivision Forestry under:
        Mount Rainier National
          Park.
        Olympic Peninsula.
        Grays Harbor area//
        Subdivision Washington (State)
          under: Trees.
        Timber.
        Forest surveys.
        Wood-using industries.
        Forest products.
        Forest fires.
        Forest ownership.
        Wood-lots.
        Afforestation and re-
          forestation.
        Forest policy.
        Forest industries.
-- --Statistics.
--Gazetteers.
--Geology.
    sa Subdivision Geology under:
        Yakima Co., Wash.
        Pierce Co., Wash.
        Ellensburg.
        Stevens Co., Wash.
        Subdivision Washington (State)
          under: Water, Underground.
        Mines and mineral re-
          sources.
-- --Bibliography.
--Government publications.
-- --Bibliography.
    xx Washington (State) Bibliog-
        raphy.
--History.
-- --Sources.
    sa Subdivision Washington (State)
        under: Archives.
    xx U.S. History. Sources.
--Industries.
--Land.
    sa Subdivision Washington (State)
        under: Waste lands.
        Land. Classification.
        Farm valuation.
        Land utilization.

Washington (State) (Continued)
--Land.
   sa Subdivision Land under:
     Grays Harbor Co.
     Snohomish Co.
--Legislative manuals.
--Libraries.
   xx U.S. Libraries.
--Maps.
--Markets.
   xx U.S. Markets.
--Meteorology.
   sa Subdivision Washington (State)
     under: Precipitation.
   xx U.S. Meteorology.
--Ornithology.
   sa Subdivision Ornithology under:
     Mt. Rainier National Park.
--Paleobotany.
--Paleontology.
--Parks.
   sa Subdivision Parks under:
     Tacoma.
   xx U.S. Parks.
--Politics and government.
   xx U.S. Politics and government.
--Pomology.
   sa Subdivision Pomology under:
     Yakima Valley, Wash.
-- --Statistics.
--Population.
   sa Subdivision Population under:
     Seattle.
     Subdivision Washington (State)
     under: Rural population.
--Public lands.
--Public schools.
   xx Washington (State) Education.
--Public works.
   xx U.S. Public works.
--Railroads.
--Roads.
   sa King Co., Wash. Roads.
- --Law.
   xx Roads. Legislation.
     U.S. Roads. Law.
--Sheep.
--Social conditions.
   sa Subdivision Social conditions
     under: Pend Oreille Co.,
     Wash.
     Seattle, Wash.
     Subdivision Washington (State)
     under: Social surveys.

Washington (State) (Continued)
--Soils.
   sa Subdivision Soils under:
     Quincy Valley.
     Yakima Valley//
     Subdivision Washington (State)
     under: Soil-surveys.
     Soil erosion.
     Soil erosion surveys.
     Soil erosion. Prevention
     and control.
     Soil conservation.
     Soil conservation surveys.
--Statistics.
   sa Subdivision Agriculture. Sta-
     tistics under: Washington
     (State)
--Viticulture.
   sa Subdivision Viticulture under:
     Lewiston - Clarkston Valley.
--Water-supply.
   sa Subdivision Washington (State)
     under: Water, Underground.
     Water-rights.
     Subdivision Water-supply under:
     Seattle.
-- --Bibliography.
   xx U.S. Water-supply. Bibliog-
     raphy.
--Zoology.
   sa Subdivision Zoology under:
     Olympic Mountains, Wash.
     Mt. Rainier National Park.
     Subdivision Washington (State)
     under: Araneida.
     Worms.
     Vertebrates.
     Wildlife.

Washington Botanical Society.

Washington Bridge, Providence, R.I.

Washington Co., Ark.
--Agriculture.
   sa Subdivision Arkansas.
     Washington Co. under:
     Agricultural policies and
     programs.

Washington Co., Ind.
--Agriculture.
-- --Periodicals.

Washington Co., Ind. (Continued)
--Soils.
    sa Subdivision Indiana. Washington
       Co. under: Soil-surveys.

Washington Co., Iowa.
--Soils.
    sa Subdivision Iowa. Washington
       Co. under: Soil-surveys.

Washington Co., Md.
    xx Maryland.

Washington Co., Minn.
    xx Minnesota.
--Land.
    sa Subdivision Minnesota. Washing-
       ton Co. under: Land utili-
       zation.
--Soils.
    sa Subdivision Minnesota. Washing-
       ton Co. under: Soil conser-
       vation surveys.

Washington Co., Miss.
    sa Subdivision Mississippi.
       Washington Co. under:
       Drainage.
--Soils.
    sa Subdivision Mississippi.
       Washington Co. under: Soil-
       surveys.

Washington Co., N.Y.
--Geology.
--History.

Washington Co., N.C.
--Soils.
    sa Subdivision North Carolina.
       Washington Co. under:
       Soil-surveys.

Washington Co., Ohio.
--Agriculture.
    sa Subdivision Ohio. Washington
       Co. under: Farm management
       surveys.
--Soils.
    sa Subdivision Ohio. Washington
       Co. under: Soil-surveys.

Washington Co., Or.
    xx Oregon.

Washington Co., Or. (Continued)
--Agriculture.
    sa Subdivision-Oregon. Washington
       Co. under; Agricultural
       policies and programs.
--Soils.
    sa Subdivision Oregon. Washington
       Co. under: Soil conserva-
       tion.

Washington Co., Penn.
--Geology.

Washington Co., R.I.
--Ornithology.

Washington Co., Tenn.
--Politics and government.

Washington Co., Utah.
    sa Subdivision Washington Co.,
       Utah under: Planning,
       County.
--Economic conditions.
    xx Utah. Economic conditions.
--Water-supply.

Washington Co., Vt.
--Agriculture.
    sa Subdivision Vermont. Washing-
       ton Co. under: Agricultural
       policies and programs.
    xx Vermont. Agriculture.

Washington Co., Va.
    sa Subdivision Washington Co.
       under: County surveys.
       Virginia.
    xx Virginia.
--Economic conditions.
    sa Subdivision Virginia. Washing-
       ton Co. under: Economic
       surveys.
--Industries and resources.
    sa Industrial surveys. Virginia.
       Washington Co.
--Soils.
    sa Subdivision Virginia. Washing-
       ton Co. under: Soil-
       surveys.

Washington Co., Wis.
--Soils.

Washington forestry reserve.

Washington Parish, La.
--Agriculture.
    sa Subdivision Louisiana.
        Washington Parish under:
        Agriculture. Economic
          aspects.
        Farm management surveys.
        Types of farming.
        Agriculture, Cooperative.
    xx Louisiana. Agriculture.

Washington University, St. Louis.
--Henry Shaw School of Botany.

Washington's headquarters at Newburgh,
  N.Y.

Washita Co., Okla.
--Soils.
    sa Subdivision Oklahoma. Washita
        Co. under: Soil-surveys.

Washita River Basin.   See Washita River
  Valley.

Washita River Valley.
--Water-supply.

Washoe Co., Nev.
  xx Nevada.
--Social conditions.
    sa Subdivision Washoe Co., Nev.
        under: Cost and standard of
          living.
    xx Nevada. Social conditions.

Washoe reclamation project.

Washouts.

Washtenaw Co., Mich.
--Botany.
    xx Michigan. Botany.
--Roads.
    xx Michigan. Roads.
--Soils.
    sa Subdivision Michigan. Washtenaw
        Co. under: Soil-surveys.

Wasps.   (INDIRECT)
    sa Larridae.
    Odynerus.
    Sphegidae.
    Polistes.
    Vespa.

Wasps (Continued)
    sa Sphegoidea.
    Bembecidae.
    Eumenidae.
    Masaridae.
    Habrobracon.
    Microbracon.
    Podalonia.
    Tiphia.
    Ichneumonidae.
    Solitary wasps.
    Vespoidea.
    Catolaccus group.
    x Hornets.
    xx Insect societies.

Wasps, Fossil.

Wasps, Fossorial. See Sphecoidea.

Wasps.
--Nests. See Nests of insects.
--Parasites.

Wassermann test.

Waste (Economics)
    sa Waste products.
    Factory and trade waste.
    Efficiency, Industrial.

Waste lands.   (INDIRECT)
    sa Bogs.
    Clearing of land.
    Drainage.
    Fens.
    Irrigation.
    Marshes.
    Moors and heaths.
    Reclamation of land.
    Sand-dunes.
    xx Public lands.

Waste materials. See Waste products!

Waste paper.
    x Paper scrap.
--Bibliography.
--Periodicals.
--Statistics.

Waste products.
    sa Animal products.
       Cotton waste.
       Factory and trade waste.
       Refuse and refuse disposal.
       Waste paper.
       Waste (Economics)
       Cotton-seed products.
       Waste water.
       Pineapple trash.
       Salvage (Waste, etc.)
       Packing-house products.
       Food waste.
       Rubber, Scrap.
       Sulphite liquor.
       Wood waste.
       Wool-fat.
       Radioactive waste.
       Refuse as fertilizer.
       Wood. Chemical utilization.
       Subdivision By-products under:
         Brewing.
         Citrus.
         Dairy.
         Gas manufacture and works.
         Tanning.
         Sugar.
         Peanuts.
         Blast-furnaces.
         Cacao.
         Agriculture.
         Fisheries.
         Coke.
         Cotton gins.
         Creameries.
         Tobacco.
         Wood.
         Sawmills.
         Wheat.
         Distilling industries.
         Hemp.
         Vegetables.
         Alcohol.
         Sugar-cane.
         Banana.
         Apple.
         Coal.
         Salmon, Canned.
   x Waste materials.
  xx Waste products. Utilization.
       Utilization of waste.
       Commercial products. Sta-
         tistics.
--Bibliography.
--Periodicals.

Waste products (Continued)
--Statistics.
    xx Statistics.
--Utilization. See Waste products.

Waste rubber. See Rubber, Scrap.

Waste sulphite liquor. See Sulphite
  liquor.

Waste water.
--Abstracts.
--Bibliography.

Waste water disposal. See Sewage disposal.

Waste wood. See Wood waste.

Wasteful lumbering. See Lumbering,
  Wasteful.

Watauga Co., N.C.
--Soils.
    sa Subdivision North Carolina.
       Watauga Co. under: Soil-
        surveys.

Watch-dogs.
    xx Dogs.

Watches. See Clocks and watches.

Water.
    sa Color of water.
       Dew.
       Evaporation.
       Bottled waters.
       Feed-water.
       Floods.
       Fog.
       Frost.
       Geysers.
       Glaciers.
       Hail.
       Hydraulic engineering.
       Hydrotherapy.
       Ice.
       Lakes.
       Mineral waters.
       Moisture.
       Precipitation (Meteorology)
       Ocean.
       Rivers.

Water (Continued)
    sa Sea-water.
       Snow.
       Soil erosion.
       Springs.
       Steam.
       Waterspouts.
       Wells.
       Headings beginning with the
         word Water.
--Acid content.
--Analysis.
    sa Water. Bacteriology.
       Irrigation water. Analysis.
    x Water assay.
-- --Laboratory manuals.
--Bacteria.   See Water. Bacteriology.
--Bacteriology.
    xx Bacteriology.

Water, Carbon dioxide in.   See Carbon
   dioxide in water.

Water.
--Composition.
    x Hydro-chemistry.
--Conservation.   (INDIRECT)
    sa Water. Utilization.
       Water conservation extension
         work.
    x Conservation of water re-
       sources.
       Water-supply. Conservation.
    xx Water policies and programs.
-- --Abstracts.
-- --Bibliography.
    sa Water. Conservation [geographic
       subdivision] Bibliography,
       e.g., Water. Conservation.
       Oklahoma. Bibliography.
-- --Congresses.
    sa Water. Conservation [geographic
       subdivision] Congresses,
       e.g., Water. Conservation.
       U.S. Congresses.
-- --Law.   See Water. Law.
-- --Periodicals.
    sa Water. Conservation [geographic
       subdivision] Periodicals,
       e.g., Water. Conservation.
       U.S. Periodicals.
-- --Pictorial works.

Water (Continued)
--Conservation.
-- --Research.
    sa Water. Conservation [geographic
       subdivision] Research, e.g.,
       Water. Conservation. U.S.
       Research.
-- --Study and teaching.
    sa Moving-pictures in water
       conservation.
    xx Conservation of natural re-
       sources. Study and teaching.
-- --Terminology.
--Cooling.
    x Water coolers.
       Water cooling.
    xx Cooling.
--Costs.   See Water-supply. Costs.
    xx Cost.
--Distilled.
-- --Effect on plants.
--Distribution.
    sa Aqueducts.
       Hydraulics.
       Water-pipes.
       Water-supply engineering.
    xx Hydraulics.
       Water-supply engineering.
--Effect on concrete.   See Concrete,
    Effect of water on.
--Effect on metabolism.   See Meta-
    bolism, Effect of water on.
--Effect on plants.
    sa Soil moisture. Effect on
       plants.
       Water, Distilled. Effect on
       plants.

Water, Ground.   See Water, Underground.

Water, Heavy.
    x Heavy water.

Water, Iodine in.

Water, Iron in.   See Iron in water.

Water.
  --Law.   (DIRECT)
    x Water. Conservation. Law.
-- --Abstracts.

Water (Continued)
--Law.
-- --Bibliography.
    sa Subdivision Bibliography under
       Water. Law [geographic sub-
       division] e.g., Water. Law.
       U.S. Bibliography.
--Lime in.   See Lime in water.

Water, Mineral.   See Mineral waters.

Water.
--Nitric acid in.
--Physiological effect.
--Policies and programs.   See Water
   policies and programs.
--Pollution.
    sa Water. Purification.
       Factory and trade waste.
       Refuse and refuse disposal.
       Sewage disposal.
       Water. Analysis.
       Water. Law.
       Water-supply.
    x River pollution.
       Water pollution.
       Stream pollution.
       Pollution of water.
       Rivers. Pollution.
-- --Bibliography.
-- --Congresses.
-- --Legislation.
-- --Research.
--Purification.
    sa Water. Pollution.
       Filters and filtration.
       Water-supply engineering.
       Feed-water purification.
    x River purification.
       Rivers. Purification.
-- --Ammonia-chlorine treatment.   See
   Water. Purification. Chlorina-
   tion.
-- --Bibliography.
-- --Chlorination.
    sa Subdivision Purification.
       Chlorination under: Sea-
       water.
    x Chlorination of water.
       Chloramine treatment of water.
-- -- --Bibliography.
    xx Chloramines. Bibliography.
-- --Congresses.
--Research.

Water, Saline.   See Saline waters.

Water.
--Sanitation.
    x Water sanitation.
--Softening.
    sa Feed-water purification.
       Water softeners.
--Storage.   See Water-storage.

Water, Subsoil.   See Water, Underground.

Water.
--Terminology.
--Therapeutic use.   See Hydrotherapy.

Water, Underground.   (INDIRECT)
    When subdivided geographically,
       indicate see also ref. from
       name of place with subdivision
       Water-supply.
    sa Soil moisture.
       Soil. Water capacity.
       Observation wells.
--Artificial recharge.
--Bibliography.
    sa Water, Underground [geographic
       subdivision] Bibliography,
       e.g., Water, Underground.
       U.S. Bibliography.
--Effect on cotton.
--Effect on plants.
    x Plants. Effect of underground
       water on.
--Research.

Water.
--Utilization.
    sa Water. Conservation.
       Water-supply.
    x Water utilization.
    xx Water policies and programs.
       Water. Conservation.
       Water-supply.
-- --Abstracts.
-- --Bibliography.
-- --Congresses.
-- --Legislation.
-- --Terminology.

Water act, 1912-1946 (New Zealand)

Water and soils.   See Soil moisture;
   Water, Underground; Soil. Water
   capacity.

Water animals.　See Aquatic animals;
　Fresh-water fauna; Marine fauna;
　Plankton.

Water area.　See Water supply.

Water as a spray.

Water as an insecticide.

Water assay.　See Water. Analysis.

Water beetles.　See Hydradephaga.

Water-birds.　See Water-fowl.

Water buffalo.
　　　sa Blood. Water buffalo.
　--Parasites.

Water bugs.　See Hydrocorisae.

Water bugs, Giant.　See Belostomatidae.

Water caltrops.　See Trapa natans.

Water chestnut.　See Trapa natans.

Water chestnut, Chinese.　See Eleocharis
　dulcis.

Water chinquapin.　See Nelumbo penta-
　petala.

Water-closets.
　　　sa Turf-closets.

Water-color painting.
　　　xx Art.

Water-colors.

Water companies, Mutual.　See Mutual
　water companies.

Water conservation.　See Water. Con-
　servation.

Water conservation extension work.
　　　　　x Extension work in water con-
　　　　　　　servation.
　　　　　xx Water. Conservation.

Water content of plants.
　　　sa Subdivision Water content
　　　　　under: Barley.
　　　　　Leaves.
　　　　　Trees.
　　　x Plants. Water content.

Water content of trees.　See Trees.
　Water content.

Water coolers.　See Water. Cooling.

Water-core.
　　　xx Apple. Diseases.

Water-cress.
　　　x Watercress.
　--Periodicals.

Water-cress leaf-beetle.　See Phaedon
　aeruginosus.

Water-cress sowburg.　See Mancasellus
　brachyurus.

Water culture.
　　　This subject is used for publi-
　　　　　cations issued before 1931.
　　　　　For publications issued after
　　　　　1931 see Hydroponics.
　　　sa Hydroponics.
　　　x Growing plants without soil.
　　　　　Chemiculture.
　　　　　Culture solutions.
　　　　　Dirtless farming.
　　　　　Plant chemiculture.
　　　xx Chemicals. Effect on plants.
　　　　　Plant growth.

Water engineering.　See Water-supply
　engineering.

Water facilities act.

Water finding.

Water flow.　See Hydraulics.

Water for butter making.

Water for livestock.　See Water-supply
　for stock.

Water-fowl.
    sa Ducks.
       Geese.
       Swans.
    x Water-birds.
      Wild-fowl.
      Wildfowl.
--Anatomy and physiology.
--Bibliography.
--Diseases.
    sa Subdivision Diseases under:
       Ducks.
       Grebes.
--Feeding.
--Food.
    sa Food plants for water-fowl.
    xx Birds. Food.
      Wild life. Food.
--Outlines, syllabi, etc.

Water gardens.
    x Marsh gardens.
      Bog gardens.
      Swamp gardens.
    xx Gardening.
      Aquariums.
--Bibliography.
    xx Horticulture. Bibliography.

Water gates. See Gates, Hydraulic.

Water-glass. See Soluble glass.

Water hammer.
    x Surge pressure.
    xx Hydraulics.
      Water-pipes.

Water heaters.
    sa Electric water heaters.

Water hemlock. See Cicuta.

Water holes. See Ponds.

Water-hyacinth.
    x Eichhornia crassipes.

Water in animal physiology.
    xx Physiology.

Water in food. See Food, Water in.

Water in the body.
    xx Physiological chemistry.
      Physiology.

Water laws. See Water. Law.

Water level fluctuations. (DIRECT)

Water level recorders.
    xx Hydraulic engineering. Im-
      plements.

Water-lilies.
    Used for cultural books. For
      botanical books see Nymph-
      aeaceae, Nymphaea, and names
      of other genera.
    sa Aquatic plants.
      Nymphaeaceae.
    x Pond lilies.
--Diseases.
    xx Vegetable pathology.

Water-marks.
    xx Trade-marks.

Water measurement. See Stream measurements.

Water-meters.
    sa Weirs.
      Flumes.
      Flow meters.

Water-mites. See Hydracarina.

Water-pipes.
    sa Water hammer.
    xx Water. Distribution.

Water plants. See Aquatic plants.

Water policies and programs. (INDI-
  RECT)
    sa Water. Conservation.
      Water. Utilization.
      Water-supply.
    x Water. Policies and programs.
      Water-supply. Policies and
       programs.
      Water resources policies.
--Bibliography.
--Congresses.

Water pollution.   See Water. Pollution.

Water pollution control act.   See Federal
  water pollution control act.

Water-power.   (DIRECT)
     sa Hydraulic engineering.
        Dams.
        Flumes.
        Stream measurements.
        Subdivision Power utilization
           under: Columbia River.
           St. Lawrence River.
           Snake River.
      x Hydro-electric power.
        Hydroelectric power.
  --Bibliography.
     sa Subdivision Bibliography under
        Water-power [geographic sub-
        division] e.g., Water-power.
        U.S. Bibliography.
  --Congresses.
  --Periodicals.

Water-power electric plants. . (DIRECT)
     sa Names of specific project, /
        e.g., McKenzie River Hydro-
        electric Project.
      x Hydro-electric plants.
        Hydroelectric plants.
  --Bibliography.
  --Law.
  --Statistics.
  --Taxation.
     xx Taxation.

Water proofing.   See Waterproofing.

Water purification.   See Water. Purification.

Water requirements of animals.
     sa Subdivision Watering under:
        Swine.
     xx Animal nutrition.
        Watering of animals.

Water requirements of crops.
     sa Subdivision Water requirements
        under: Barley.
        Maize.
      ⅃ Sorghum//
      x Moisture requirements of crops.
     xx Plant nutrition.

Water requirements of crops (Continued) ⅃,
  --Bibliography.
     sa Subdivision Bibliography
        under: Trees. Water re-
        quirements. '

Water requirements of trees.   See Trees.
  Water requirements.

Water resources.   See Water-supply.

Water resources policies.   See Water
  policies and programs. '

Water rice.   See Rice.

Water-rights.   (INDIRECT)
     sa Subdivision Law under:
        Irrigation.
        Water.
        Riparian rights.
  --Bibliography.
  --Congresses.

Water-rights settlement act.

Water sanitation.   See Water. Sanitation.

Water secretion in plants.   See Plant
  transpiration.

Water sheds.   See Watersheds.

Water softeners.
     xx Water. Softening.

Water soluble extractives.   See Extractives, Water soluble.

Water-soluble fertilizers.   See Fertilizers, Liquid.

Water-spiders.   See Argyroneta aquatica.

Water spreading.
      x Waterspreading.
     xx Water-storage.
  --Congresses.

Water-storage.
     sa Water spreading.
        Dams.
        Irrigation.
        Rain and rainfall.

ater-storage (Continued)
    sa Reservoirs.
      Water-supply.
      Weirs.
      Cisterns, Concrete.
--Congresses.

'ater-supply.
    Here are entered works on surveys
    of the water resources of a
    region, both superficial and
    underground, primarily with
    reference to the supply of
    water for domestic and manu-
    facturing purposes, or for
    agriculture. For works on the
    water-supply of a particular
    city see subdivision Water-
    supply under the name of the
    city.
    sa Subdivision Water-supply under:
      Australia.
      Europe.
      United States//
      Arid regions.
      Ships.
      Railroads.
      Fire extinction.
      Deserts.
      Villages.
      Filtration.
      Reservoirs.
      Canals.
      Irrigation.
      Hydraulic engineering.
      Artesian wells.
      Water finding.
      Observation wells.
      Ponds.
      Water. Utilization.
      Springs.
      Wells.
      Snow surveys.
    x Water area.
    xx Weather control.
      Water policies and programs.
--Abstracts.
--Bibliography.
    sa Subdivision Bibliography under:
      Water-supply, Rural.
      U.S. Water-supply//
--Congresses.
    sa Subdivision Congresses under:
      Hydrology.
      Water. Conservation.

Water-supply (Continued)
--Congresses.
    sa Water-supply. Congresses
      under names of countries,
      etc., e.g., U.S. Water-
      supply. Congresses.
--Conservation. See Water. Conserva-
    tion.
--Costs.
    x Water. Costs.
      Irrigation water. Costs.
--Forecasts.
    x Water-supply forecasts.
    xx Forecasting.
--History.
--Periodicals.
--Policies and programs. See Water
    policies and programs.

Water-supply, Rural.
    x Rural water-supply.
--Bibliography.
--Government aid.
    xx Government aid.
--Handbooks, manuals, etc.

Water-supply.
--Societies.
--Terminology.

Water-supply and forests.
    sa Protection forests.
    x Forestry. Hydrology.
      Forest hydrology.
    xx Forest influences.
--Bibliography.
--Congresses.

Water-supply engineering.
    sa Water. Distribution.
    xx Water. Distribution.
--Apparatus and supplies.
-- --Statistics.
--Bibliography.
--Handbooks, manuals, etc.
--History.
--Periodicals.
    xx Engineering. Periodicals.
--Tables, calculations, etc.

Water-supply for stock.
    x Water for livestock.
    xx Watering of animals.

Water-supply forecasts. See Water-
supply. Forecasts.

Water transportation. See Transportation, Water.

Water-tube boilers. See Steam-boilers,
Water-tube.

Water utilization. See Water. Utilization.

Water vapor.
    x Aqueous vapor.
      Atmospheric moisture.
--Determination.
--Effect on textile fabrics.
    x Textile industry and fabrics.
      Effect of water vapor.

Water weeds.
    x Weeds, Water.
      Channel weeds.
    xx Weeds.
--Eradication.
    xx Weeds. Eradication.
-- --Periodicals.

Water-ways. See Waterways.

Water-wheels.
    xx Turbines.

Water willow. See Dianthera.

Waterberg, South Africa.

Waterbugs. See Hydrocorisae.

Waterbury, Conn.
--Botany.

Watercress. See Water-cress.

Waterford, Ire. (County)
--Agriculture.
-- --Periodicals.

Waterfowl. See Water-fowl.
      Entries under Waterfowl are filed
      with same entries spelled as
      two words.

Waterfowl food plants. See Food plants
for water-fowl.

Watergates. See Gates, Hydraulic.

Waterholes. See Ponds.

Watering of animals.
      sa Subdivision Watering under:
        Poultry.
        Cattle, Dairy.
        Swine.
      Water supply for stock.
      Water requirements of animals.
      Electric stock waterer.
      Electric stock tank de-icer.
      Watering-trough.
    x Domestic animals. Watering.

Watering of fields. See Spray irrigation.

Watering of gardens. See Gardens.
    Watering.

Watering of vegetables. See Vegetables.
    Watering.

Watering-trough.
      sa Electric stock waterer.
        Electric stock tank de-icer.
    xx Watering of animals.

Waterlogged soil. See Soil, Waterlogged.

Waterlogging.

Waterloo, Ont.
--Economic conditions.
      sa Subdivision Ontario. Waterloo
          under: Economic surveys.

Watermelon.
    xx Melons.
--Breeding.
    xx Plant breeding.
--Diseases.
      sa Watermelon wilt.
        Anthracnose of watermelons.
--Grading and standardization.
    xx Agricultural products. Grading
        and standardization.
--Inspection.
--Marketing.
    xx Fruit harvesting and marketing.
-- --Societies.
--Prices.

Watermelon (Continued)
--Societies.
 xx Horticulture. Societies.
--Statistics.
--Storage.
--Transportation.
 sa Subdivision Watermelon under:
  Railroads. Rates.

Watermelon as feeding stuff.

Watermelon wilt.
 xx Watermelon. Diseases.

Waterproofing.
 sa Corrosion and anti-corrosives.
  Dampness in buildings.
 x Water proofing.

Waterproofing of fabrics.
 x Textile industry and fabrics.
  Waterproofing.
 xx Textile industry and fabrics.
  Textile industry and fabrics.
  Protective treatments.

Waterproofing of soils.
 x Soil. Waterproofing.
  Soil waterproofing.

Waters, Saline. See Saline waters.

Watershed protection and flood prevention
 act.

Watersheds.
 sa Names of individual watersheds,
  e.g., Gypsum Creek Water-
  shed, Colo.
 x Water sheds.
--Abstracts.
--Bibliography.
--Congresses.
--Economic aspects.
--Exhibitions.
--Maps.
--Periodicals.
--Policies and programs.
--Societies.
--Statistics.

Waterspouts.

Waterspreading. See Water spreading.

Waterton-Glacier International Peace
 Park. See Glacier National Park.

Waterton Lakes Park, Alberta.

Watertown, Mass.
--Water-supply.

Watertown, N.Y.
--Milk trade.

Waterville, N.Y.

Waterways.
 sa Inland navigation.
--Bibliography.

Waterways, Grassed. See Grassed waterways.

Waterways, Inland. See Inland navigation.

Waterways.
--Periodicals.

Watery soft rot.
 x White mold.
 xx Beans. Diseases.

Watkins Glen, N.Y.

Watling Estate, Eng.
--Social conditions.
 sa Subdivision Watling Estate.
  England under: Social
  surveys.

Watobius.

Watson, Ark.
--Social conditions.

Watsonius.

Watt-hour meter.
 x Watthour meter.
 xx Electric meters.

Wattensas farmers' club. See Agricultural wheel (Agricultural society)

Watthour meter. See Watt-hour meter.

Wattle (Tree)
    xx Acacia.
        Arboriculture.
        Trees.
--Bark.
    sa Wattle tannin.
--Pests.

Wattle bagworm.   See Acanthopsyche
   junodi.

Wattle leaf-tier.   See Polychrosis in-
   cultena.

Wattle tannin.
    xx Tannins.
        Wattle (Tree) Bark.

Waukesha Co., Wis.
--Agriculture.
    sa Subdivision Wisconsin. Waukesha
        Co. under: Agriculture. Eco-
        nomic aspects.
    xx Wisconsin. Agriculture.
--Directories.
--Maps.
--Soils.
    sa Subdivision Wisconsin. Waukesha
        Co. under: Soil-surveys.

Waupaca Co., Wis.
--Soils.
    sa Subdivision Wisconsin. Waupaca
        Co. under: Soil-surveys.

Wauseon, Ohio.
--Climate.

Waushara Co., Wis.
    xx Wisconsin.
--Agriculture.
    sa Subdivision Wisconsin. Waushara
        Co. under: Farm management
        surveys.
--Soils.
    sa Subdivision Wisconsin. Waushara
        Co. under: Soil-surveys.

Wave mechanics.

Wavellite.

Waves.
    sa Sound-waves.
    xx Hydrodynamics.

Wax.   See Waxes.

Wax fruit.   See Fruit, Artificial.

Wax glands.   See Glands, Wax.

Wax-modeling.

Wax moth.   See Galleria mellonella;
   Achroia grisella.

Wax-palm of Brazil.   See Copernicia
   cerifera.

Wax-palms.
    sa Cocos coronata.
        Copernicia cerifera.
        Palm-wax.
    xx Palmae.

Waxahachie, Tex.
--Water-supply.

Waxahachie Creek Watershed, Tex.

Waxes.
    sa Sugar-cane wax.
        Ambergris.
        Spermaceti.
        Vine, Wax in.
        Palm-wax.
        Wool wax alcohols.
        Wool-fat.
        Candelilla wax.
    x Wax.
        Vegetable waxes.
--Analysis.
--Bibliography.
--Periodicals.

Waxes, Synthetic.
    sa Acrawax C.
    xx Synthetic products.

Waxing of fruit.   See Fruit. Waxing.

Waxwing.   See Ampelidae.

Wayne Co., Ga.
--Soils.
    sa Subdivision Georgia. Wayne Co.
        under: Soil-surveys.

Wayne Co., Ill.
--Soils.

Wayne Co., Ind.
--Agriculture.
-- --Periodicals.
--Soils.
    sa Subdivision Indiana. Wayne Co.
        under: Soil-surveys.

Wayne Co., Mich.
--Education.
--Geology.
--Libraries.
    xx Libraries, County.
--Parks.
--Politics and government.
    xx County government.
--Roads.

Wayne Co., N.Y.

Wayne Co., Ohio.
--Agriculture.
    xx Ohio. Agriculture.
--Geology.
--Ornithology.

Wayne Co., Pa.
    xx Pennsylvania.
--Agriculture.
--Forestry.
    sa Subdivision Pennsylvania. Wayne
        Co. under: Forest surveys.
--Soils.
    sa Subdivision Pennsylvania. Wayne
        Co. under: Soil-surveys.

Waynesville watershed, N.C.

Wayside stands.   See Refreshment stands.

Weald.

Weald, Eng.
--Agriculture.

Wealth.
    sa Gross national product.
--Bibliography.

Wealth, Distribution of.   See Economics;
   Wealth.

Weasels.

Weather.
    sa Meteorology.
       Climate.
       Hot waves.
       Crops and climate.
       Evaporation.
       Weather control.
--Bibliography.

Weather, Effect of moon on.   See Moon.
   Effect on weather.

Weather, Effect of planets on.   See
   Planets. Effect on weather.

Weather.
--Effect of solar disturbances.
--Effect on aeronautics.   See Aero-
    nautics, Effect of weather on.
--Effect on animal diseases.
    xx Veterinary-medicine.
--Effect on barley.   See Barley.
    Weather influences.
--Effect on beans.   See Beans. Weather
    influences.
--Effect on canning crops.   See Canning
    crops. Weather influences.
--Effect on cotton yarn.   See Cotton
    yarn. Weather influences.
--Effect on field crops.   See Field
    crops. Weather influences.
--Effect on fires.
--Effect on forage plants.   See Forage
    plants. Weather influences.
--Effect on forest fires.
    sa Subdivision Effect on forest
        fires under: Winds.
       Forest fires. Causes. Light-
        ning.
       Forest fire danger rating.
    x Forest fires and weather.
       Forest fires. Weather factors.
    xx Forest fires. Forecasting.
--Effect on fruit trees.
    sa Fruit. Freezing and frost in-
        juries.
--Effect on grass.
    x Grasses. Effect of weather.
       Grasses. Weather influences.
    xx Crops and climate.
--Effect on insects.   See Insects and
    the weather.
    x Insects. Effect of weather.
--Effect on materials.
    x Materials. Effect of weather.

Weather (Continued)
--Effect on milk production.
    x Milk. Production. Effect of
        weather.
--Effect on naval stores yield.
--Effect on oranges.
    x Orange. Effect of weather.
--Effect on plant diseases.
    x Vegetable pathology. Weather
        influences.
    xx Vegetable pathology.
--Effect on plants.
    x Plants, Effect of weather on.
    xx Crops and climate.
--Effect on potatoes.   See Potato.
    Weather influences.
--Effect on rye.   See Rye. Weather in-
    fluences.
--Effect on sugar-cane.   See Sugar-cane.
    Effect of weather on.
--Effect on tree diseases.
    xx Trees. Diseases.
--Effect on trees.   See Trees. Weather
    influences.
--Effect on viticulture.
--Effect on wheat.   See Wheat. Weather
    influences.
--Forecasting.   See Weather forecasting.

Weather, Influence of the moon on.
    x Moon. Effect on weather.

Weather.
--Influence on insects.   See Insects
    and the weather.
--Mental and physiological effects.
--Terminology.

Weather and crops.   See Crops and
    climate.

Weather and prices.

Weather charts.

Weather code.

Weather control.
    sa Meteorology, Aeronautical.
        Rain-making.
        Water-supply.
    x Artificial weather control.
        Cloud modification.
        Weather modification.

Weather control (Continued)
    xx Clouds.
        Meteorology.
        Weather.
--Research.

Weather folk-lore.   See Weather-lore.

Weather forecasting.
    sa Flood forecasts.
        Precipitation (Meteorology)
        Forecasting.
    x Weather. Forecasting.

Weather forecasting, Long range.

Weather forecasts.
--Distribution.

Weather influences.   See Crops and
    climate; Weather. Mental and physio-
    logical effects.

Weather lore.

Weather map.

Weather modification.   See Weather
    control.

Weather resistant plants.

Weather service.   (DIRECT)

Weather service and the press.

Weather signals.
    sa Storm signals.
        Wind signals.

Weather signs.

Weather telegraphy.

Weather types.

Weatherproofing.

Weaver-bird.   See Ploceidae.

Weavers.   (DIRECT)

Weaving.   (DIRECT)
    sa Basket making.
       Lace and lace making.
       Looms.
       Silk manufacture and trade.
       Textile fibers.
       Textile industry and fabrics.
       Woolen and worsted manufacture.
       Braid.
       Warping.
       Cotton weaving.
       Indians, North American.
         Textile industry and
         fabrics.
    xx Arts and crafts movement.
--Bibliography.
--History.
--Periodicals.
--Pictorial works.

Webb Co., Tex.
--Geology.
    xx Texas. Geology.

Webster Co., Iowa.
--Botany.

Webster Co., Ky.
--Soils.
    sa Subdivision Kentucky. Webster
       Co. under: Soil-surveys.

Webster Co., Neb.
    xx Nebraska.
--Soils.
    sa Subdivision Nebraska. Webster
       Co. under: Soil-surveys.

Webster Parish, La.

Webworms.   See Crambus; Homadaula.

Weed control.   See Weeds. Eradication.

Weed destroying fungi.

Weed destroying insects.   See Insects in
    weed control.

Weed eradication.   See Weeds. Eradica-
    tion.

Weed killers.   See Herbicides.

Weed seedlings.   See Weeds. Seedlings.

Weeding by air.   See Airplanes in weed
    eradication.

Weedkillers.   See Herbicides.

Weedone.   See Dichlorophenoxyacetic
    acid, 2,4-.

Weeds.   (INDIRECT)
    sa Botany, Economic.
       Farm pests.
       Forest weeds.
       Weed destroying fungi.
       Water weeds.
       Orobanche minor.
       Galium.
       Artemisia tridentata//
    x Ditchbank weeds.
      Forbs.
    xx Agriculture.
--Abstracts.
--Bibliography.
--Chemical control.   See Weeds. Eradi-
    cation (Chemical)
--Control.   See Weeds. Eradication.
--Ecology.
    xx Botany. Ecology.
--Eradication.
    sa Airplanes in weed eradication.
       Insects in weed control.
       Herbicides.
       Subdivision Eradication under
         names of weeds, e.g.,
         Chicory. Eradication;
         Thistles. Eradication;
         Water weeds. Eradication.
       Subdivision Weed control under
         names of crops, e.g.,
         Cereals. Weed control;
         Flax. Weed control.
    x Control of weeds.
      Weed control.
      Weed eradication.
      Weeds. Control.
-- --Bibliography.
-- --Congresses.
-- --Implements and machinery.
    xx Agriculture. Implements and
       machinery.
-- --Periodicals.
- --Research.
    xx Weeds. Research.
-- -- --Directories.

Weeds (Continued)
--Eradication (Chemical)
    sa Herbicides.
        Subdivision Eradication
        (Chemical) under names of
        weeds, e.g., Chondrilla
        juncea. Eradication
        (Chemical)
    x Chemical control of weeds.
      Chemical weed control.
      Weeds. Chemical control.
--Identification.
--Legislation.
--Physiology.
--Pictorial works.
    xx Botany. Pictorial works.
--Research.
    sa Weeds ₍geographic subdivision₎
      Research. e.g., Weeds.
      Belgium. Research.
--Seed.
    sa Buckhorn seed.
      Cuscuta. Seed.
    xx Seeds. Legislation.
--Seedlings.
    x Weed seedlings.
    xx Seedlings.
--Spraying. See Spraying. Weeds.

Weeds, Water. See Water weeds.

Weeds and plant diseases.
    xx Plant disease transmission.

Weeks law.
    xx Forestry. Law.

Weeping lovegrass. See Eragrostis
survula.

Weeping spruce. See Picea breweriana.

Weeping Water, Neb.
--Social conditions.
    sa Subdivision Nebraska. Weeping
      Water under: Community life.
      Social surveys.

Weevers.

Weevils. See Rhynchophora; Listroderes;
Sitophilus granarius.

Wei River, China.
    sa Subdivision China. Wei River
      under: Irrigation.

Weighing-machines.
    sa Scales.
      Weights and measures.

Weighing of animals.

Weight of wood. See Wood. Weight.

Weights and measures. (INDIRECT)
    sa Subdivision Weights and
      measures under: Cereals.
      Milling products.
      Food.
      Seeds.
      Vegetables.
      Dairy products.
      Subdivision Weight under:
      Butter.
      Bread.
      Automobiles.
      Cotton.
      Wool.
      Wood.
      Time measurement.
      Forestry. Mensuration.
      Measurements.
      Domestic animals. Weight and
      measurement.
      Steelyards.
      Bushel measure.
      Scales.
      Barrel.
      Apple. Grading.
      Fruit trade.
      Decimal system.
      Measuring tape.
      Metric system.
      Scales (Weighing instru-
      ments)
      Standards of length.
    x Metrology.
    xx Units.
--Bibliography.
--Catalogs.
--Congresses.
--Inspection.
--Legislation.
--Periodicals.
--Tables, etc.
    sa Metric system. Conversion
      tables.

Weihaiwei, China.

Weil's disease. See Leptospirosis.

Weimar, Ger.
--Botany.

Weimaraner (Dogs)

Weirs.
    sa Flumes.
       Water-meters.
    x Stream measurements.

Weiser National Forest, Idaho.
    xx Idaho. Forest reservations.

Weiserianum.
    xx Staphylinidae.

Weissenstein bei Cassel, Germany.

Weisskirchen, Austria. Höhere forstlehran-
stalt und waldbauschule.

Welcome Chemical Research Laboratories.

Weld Co., Colo.
--Land.
    sa Subdivision Colorado. Weld Co.
        under: Land utilization.
--Libraries.
    xx Libraries, County.
       Colorado. Libraries.

Welding.
    sa Electric welding.
       Solder and soldering.
       Oxyacetylene welding and
          cutting.
       Glass-metal sealing.

Welding, Arc. See Electric welding.

Welding, Electric. See Electric welding.

Welding, Oxyacetylene. See Oxyacetylene
  welding.

Welding.
--Periodicals.
--Specifications.
--Testing.

Welfare associations. See Charitable
  societies.

Welfare federations. See Federations,
  Financial (Social service)

Welfare institutions for laborers.
    xx Charitable societies.

Welfare services. See Public welfare.

Welfare work. See Public welfare.

Welfare work in industry.
    sa Agricultural laborers.
       Medical care.
       Counseling.
    x Industrial welfare work.
    xx Non-wage payments.
       Counseling.
       Social service.
       Labor and laboring classes.

Welikaja. See Velikaia.

Welland Valley, Eng.
--Agriculture.
    sa Subdivision Welland Valley
        under: Farm management.

Wellesley, Mass.
--Ornithology.

Wellfleet, Mass.

Wellington, N.Z.
--Milk supply.
    xx New Zealand. Milk supply.

Wells.
    xx Water-supply.

Wells, Irrigation. See Irrigation
  wells.

Wells, Observation. See Observation
  wells.

Wells Co., Ind.
    xx Indiana.
--Agriculture.
-- --Periodicals.

Wells Co., Ind. (Continued)
--Soils.
  sa Subdivision Indiana. Wells Co.
   under: Soil-surveys.
  xx Indiana. Soils.

Welsbach mantles. See Incandescent
 mantles.

Welsh black cattle.
  xx Cattle.

Welsh mountain sheep.

Weltrichia.

Welwitschia.

Welwitschia mirabilis.

Welwyn, Eng.

Wenaha National Forest.

Wenatchee National Forest, Wash.

Wenatchee reclamation district.
  xx Reclamation projects.

Wenderothia. See Canavalia.

Werder, Ger.
--Soils.

Werneria poposa.

Wernigerode.
--Agriculture.
--Forestry.
-- --History.
  xx Saxony. Forestry. History.
--Natural history.

Wertheim, Ger.
--Botany.

Wescoatt plow.
  xx Plow, Motor.

Weser Mountain region.
--Botany.
  sa Subdivision Weser Mountain
   region under: Fungi.
   Lichens.

Weser River Valley, Ger.
--Botany.
  sa Subdivision Germany. Weser
   River Valley under: Fungi.

Weslaco Camp. See Camp Weslaco, Tex.

Wessex saddleback pig.

West, The. See Western States.

West Africa. See Africa, West.

West Bengal.
  x Bengal, West.
--Agriculture.
  sa Subdivision India. West Bengal
   under: Agricultural poli-
   cies and programs.
   Farms.
  Subdivision West Bengal under:
   Agricultural extension.
   Agriculture. Economic
   aspects.
   Rural surveys.
-- --Education.
  sa Subdivision West Bengal under:
   Agricultural extension.
-- --Statistics.
--Economic conditions.
  sa Subdivision West Bengal under:
   Rural surveys.
-- --Statistics.
--Emigration and immigration.
--Forestry.
  xx India. Forestry.
--Industries.
-- --Statistics.
--Land.
  sa Subdivision India. West Bengal
   under: Land utilization.
--Social conditions.
  sa Subdivision West Bengal under:
   Rural surveys.
--Soils.
  sa Subdivision West Bengal under:
   Soil-surveys.
--Statistics.

West Branch Valley, Pa.
--Botany.
  sa Subdivision Pennsylvania.
   West Branch Valley under:
   Trees.

West Branch Valley, Pa. (Continued)
--Forestry.
    sa Subdivision Pennsylvania. West
      Branch Valley under: Trees.

West coast hemlock. See Tsuga heterophylla.

West coast hemlock wood. See Tsuga
heterophylla (Wood)

West Flanders. See Flanders, West.

West Frankfort Reservoir, Ill.
    xx Reservoirs.

West Friesian cattle. See Dutch-Friesian
cattle.

West Griqualand. See Griqualand, West.

West Highland white terriers.
    xx Terriers.

West Indian Cotton Growers' Association.
See West Indian Sea Island Cotton
Association.

West Indian fruit flies. See Fruit
flies.

West Indies.
    sa Cuba.
      Puerto Rico.
      Leeward Islands.
      West Indies (British)
      West Indies (Danish)
      West Indies (Dutch)
      West Indies (French)
      Antigua.
    x Middle America.
      Greater Antilles.
      Antilles, Greater.
--Agricultural experiment stations.
    sa Montserret.
      Tortola Island.
      St. Augustine.
--Agriculture.
    sa Subdivision Agriculture under:
      Caribbees.
      Santa Cruz.
      Virgin Islands of the United
        States.
      West Indies (British)
      Bahama Islands.

West Indies (Continued)
--Agriculture.
    sa Subdivision West Indies under:
      Tobacco.
      Sugar-cane.
      Maize.
      Coffee.
      Poultry.
      Agriculture. Economic
        aspects.
    xx Agriculture, Tropical.
-- --History.
    sa Subdivision Agriculture. His-
      tory under: West Indies
      (British)
    xx Agriculture. History.
--Apiculture.
    sa Subdivision Apiculture under:
      Cuba.
      Puerto Rico.
    xx Apiculture.
--Bibliography.
    sa Subdivision Bibliography
      under: West Indies (British)
      West Indies (Dutch)
      West Indies (French)
--Botany.
    sa Jamaica.
      Virgin Islands.
      Caribbees//
      Subdivision West Indies under:
      Fungi.
      Vegetable pathology.
      Mosses.
      Algae.
      Ethnobotany.
      Botany, Economic.
      Botany, Medical.
-- --Bibliography.
--Civilization.
    sa Subdivision Civilization
      under: Cuba.
    xx Civilization.
--Climate.
--Commerce.
    sa Subdivision Commerce under:
      West Indies, British.
      Haiti.
      Dominican Republic//
-- --Directories.
-- --Statistics.
    sa Subdivision Commerce. Sta-
      tistics under: Haiti.
      Dominican Republic.
      Grenada.

West Indies (Continued)
--Commercial treaties.
    sa Subdivision Commercial treaties
       under: Haiti.
    xx Commercial treaties.
--Description and travel.
    sa Subdivision Description and
       travel under: Cuba.
       Dominican Republic.
       Puerto Rico.
       Virgin Islands of the United
        States.
       West Indies (French)
--Domestic animals.
    sa Subdivision Domestic animals
       under: Cuba.
       Trinidad.
       Puerto Rico//
    xx Domestic animals.
-- --Statistics.
    sa Subdivision Domestic animals.
       Statistics under: Puerto
       Rico.
--Economic conditions.
    sa Subdivision Economic conditions
       under: Cuba.
       Haiti.
       Dominican Republic//
       Subdivision West Indies under:
       Geography, Economic.
-- --Periodicals.
--Economic policy.
    sa Subdivision Economic policy
       under: Puerto Rico.
--Entomology.
    sa Subdivision Entomology under:
       Bahama Islands.
       Cuba.
       Dominica.
       Grenada.
       Jamaica.
       Leeward Islands.
       Subdivision West Indies under:
       Entomology, Economic.
       Lepidoptera.
       Hymenoptera.
       Orthoptera.
       Diptera.
       Hemiptera.
       Coleoptera.
       Moths.
--Entomology, Economic.
    sa Subdivision Antigua under:
       Entomology, Economic.

West Indies (Continued)
--Finance.
    sa Subdivision Finance under:
       Dominican Republic.
       Haiti.
    xx Finance.
--Fisheries.
    sa Subdivision Fisheries under:
       Cuba.
    xx Fisheries.
--Foreign relations.
    sa Subdivision Foreign relations
       under: Cuba.
    xx Foreign relations.
--Forestry.
    sa Subdivision West Indies under:
       Forest fires.
       Timber.
       Forest policy.
--Geographic names.
--Geography.
    sa Subdivision West Indies under:
       Geography, Economic.
--Geology.
    sa Subdivision Geology under: '
       Bahama Islands.
       Cuba.
       Grenada//
-- --Bibliography.
    xx Geology. Bibliography.
--History.
--Horticulture.
    sa Subdivision Horticulture under:
       Haiti.
--Industries and resources.
    sa Subdivision Industries and re-
       sources under: West Indies
       (Dutch)//
--Land.
    sa Subdivision West Indies under:
       Land utilization.
--Maps.
--Meteorology.
--Natural history.
    sa Subdivision Natural history
       under: Puerto Rico.
       Virgin Islands of the United
        States.
       Antigua.
       Barbados.
       Trinidad.

West Indies (Continued)
--Ornithology.
    sa Subdivision Ornithology under:
      Dominica.
      Grenada.
      Trinidad.
      Costa Rica.
      Jamaica.
      Leeward Islands.
      Puerto Rico.
      Antigua.
      Barbuda.
      Saint Lucia.
--Paleobotany.
    sa Subdivision Paleobotany under:
      Trinidad.
--Paleontology.
    sa Subdivision Paleontology under:
      Jamaica.
      Trinidad.
      Puerto Rico.
--Pomology.
    sa Subdivision Pomology under:
      Puerto Rico.
      Haiti.
      Dominica.
--Population.
    sa Subdivision Population under:
      Dominican Republic.
      Cuba.
    xx Population.
--Roads.
--Social conditions.
    sa Subdivision Social conditions
      under: Puerto Rico.
      Jamaica.
-- --Periodicals.
--Social life and customs.
    sa Subdivision Social life and
      customs under: Cuba.
--Soils.
    sa Subdivision Soils under: Cuba.
      West Indies (British)
--Zoology.
    sa Subdivision Zoology under:
      Mona Island.
      Subdivision West Indies under:
      Arachnida.
      Araneida.
      Myriapoda.
      Batrachia.
      Reptilia.
      Echinodermata.

West Indies (British)
    sa Antigua.
      Bahama Islands.
      Barbados//
--Agriculture.
    sa Subdivision Agriculture under:
      Windward Islands.
      Barbuda.
      St. Kitts//
      Subdivision West Indies
      (British) under: Cotton.
      Sugar-cane.
      Maize.
      Agriculture. Economic
      aspects.
      Agricultural policies and
      programs.
-- --History.
    xx West Indies. Agriculture.
      History.
--Bibliography.
    sa Subdivision Bibliography
      under: West Indies
      (British) Economic con-
      ditions.
--Botany.
    sa Subdivision Botany under:
      Tobago.
      Dominica.
      Subdivision West Indies
      (British) under: Vegetable
      pathology.
--Cattle.
    sa Subdivision Cattle under:
      Jamaica.
      Trinidad.
--Commerce.
    sa Subdivision West Indies
      (British) under: Farm
      produce. Marketing.
-- --Statistics.
    sa Subdivision Commerce. Sta-
      tistics under: Dominica.
--Domestic animals.
    sa Subdivision Domestic animals
      under: Saint Lucia.
--Economic conditions.
    sa Subdivision Economic condi-
      tions under: Jamaica.
-- --Bibliography.
    xx West Indies (British) Bibliog-
      raphy.

West Indies (British) (Continued)
--Economic policy.
    sa Subdivision Economic policy
        under names of islands in
        British West Indies.
    xx Gt. Brit. Economic policy.
--Entomology.
    sa Subdivision Entomology under:
        St. Vincent.
    xx Gt. Brit. Entomology.
--Fisheries.
    sa Subdivision Fisheries under
        names of various islands,
        e.g., Trinidad. Fisheries.
--Geology.
    sa Subdivision Geology under:
        Grenada.
--History.
    sa Subdivision West Indies
        (British) under: History,
        Economic.
-- --Bibliography.
--Industries and resources.
--Ornithology.
    sa Subdivision Ornithology under:
        Dominica.
        Grenada.
        Trinidad.
        Costa Rica.
        St. Vincent.
--Periodicals.
--Physical geography.
    sa Subdivision Physical geography
        under: Tobago.
        Trinidad.
    xx Physical geography.
--Politics and government.
--Pomology.
    sa Subdivision Pomology under:
        St. Lucia//
--Sericulture.
--Social conditions.
    xx Gt. Brit. Social conditions.
--Soils.
    sa Subdivision Soils under:
        St. Lucia.
        Trinidad.
        Bahama Islands.
        Dominica.
--Statistics.
    sa West Indies (British) Commerce.
        Statistics.

West Indies (Danish)   See Virgin Islands
    of the United States, for publications
    issued after Mar. 31, 1917.

West Indies (Dutch)
    sa Curacao.
    x Dutch West Indies.
      Netherlands Antilles.
      Nederlandse Antilles.
      Netherlands West Indies.
      Antilles, Dutch.
--Agriculture.
    sa Subdivision West Indies
        (Dutch) under: Agriculture.
        Economic aspects.
--Bibliography.
--Biography.
--Botany.
--Commerce.
-- --Statistics.
--Description and travel.
--Economic conditions.
    xx West Indies. Economic condi-
        tions.
--History.
--Industries and resources.
--Natural history.
--Statistics.

West Indies (Federation)
--Agriculture.
-- --Statistics.
--Commerce.
-- --Statistics.
--Economic conditions.
-- --Periodicals.

West Indies (French)
    sa Guadeloupe.
        Martinique.
--Agriculture.
    sa Guadeloupe.
--Bibliography.
    sa Subdivision Bibliography under:
        Martinique.
    xx West Indies. Bibliography.
--Botany.
    sa Subdivision Botany under:
        Martinique.
        Guadeloupe.
--Commerce.
--Description and travel.
--Industries and resources.
--Pomology.
--Soils.

West Lothian, Scot.   See Linlithgowshire, Scot.

West Midland Province, Eng.
--Agriculture.
   sa Subdivision West Midland
      Province under: Agriculture.
      Economic aspects. Gt.
      Brit.

West Pakistan.
--Forestry.
--Soils.
--Water-supply.

West Punjab.
   xx Punjab.
--Agriculture.
-- --Statistics.
--Economic conditions.
--Social conditions.
--Statistics.

West River, Vt.
   xx Vermont.

West Roxbury Park.   See Franklin Park, Boston.

West Turkestan.   See Turkestan, West.

West Virginia.
   sa Randolph Co.
      Harrison Co.
   xx United States.
--Agriculture.
   sa Subdivision West Virginia
      under: Maize.
      Farms.
      Farm management.
      Agricultural policies and
        programs.
      Agriculture. Economic
        aspects.
      Subdivision Agriculture under:
        Barbour Co., W.Va.
        Preston Co.
-- --Education.
   sa West Virginia. State College.
--Altitudes.
--Biography.
   xx U.S. Biography.
--Botany.
   sa Subdivision Botany under:
      Braxton Co.

West Virginia (Continued)
--Botany.
   sa Subdivision West Virginia
      under: Ferns.
      Trees.
      Shrubs.
      Botany, Medical.
-- --Bibliography.
--Census.
--Description and travel.
-- --Guide-books.
--Directories.
--Economic conditions.
   sa Subdivision Economic condi-
      tions under: Lewis Co.,
      W.Va.
-- --Periodicals.
   xx U.S. Economic conditions.
      Periodicals.
--Education.
--Entomology.
   sa Subdivision West Virginia
      under: Entomology, Eco-
      nomic.
--Farmers' institutes.
--Forest reservations.
   sa George Washington National
      Forest.
      Monongahela National Forest.
--Forestry.
   sa Subdivision West Virginia
      under: Timber.
      Trees.
      Lumber.
      Forest fires. Prevention.
      Forest fires.
      Forest policy.
      Wood-lots.
-- --Statistics.
--Gazetteers.
--Geology.
   sa Subdivision Geology under:
      Fayette Co., W.Va.
      Monongalia Co., W.Va.
      Pocahontas Co., W.Va.//
-- --Bibliography.
--History.
   sa Subdivision History under:
      Jefferson Co., W.Va.//
   xx U.S. History.
 · --Sources.
   sa Subdivision West Virginia
      under: Archives.
   xx U.S. History. Sources.
--Industries and resources.

West Virginia (Continued)
--Land.
    sa Subdivision West Virginia
        under: Land utilization.
        Land. Classification.
--Legislative manuals.
    x Legislative manuals.
--Maps.
--Milk trade.
--Ornithology.
--Paleobotany.
--Paleontology.
    xx U.S. Paleontology.
--Parks.
    sa Oglebay Park, Wheeling, W.Va.
--Politics and government.
    sa Subdivision West Virginia
        under: Local government.
        County government.
    xx U.S. Politics and government.
--Pomology.
    sa Subdivision West Virginia under:
        Berries.
-- --Directories.
--Population.
    sa Subdivision West Virginia under:
        Rural population.
--Public works.
    xx U.S. Public works.
--Railroads.
--Roads.
-- --Law.
    xx Roads. Legislation.
        U.S. Roads. Law.
--Sheep.
--Social conditions.
    sa Subdivision Social conditions
        under: Monongahela Valley,
        W.Va.
        Logan Co.//
--Soils.
    sa Subdivision West Virginia under:
        Soil-surveys.
        Soil erosion. Prevention and
          control.
        Soil conservation.
        Subdivision Soils under names
          of counties, etc.
--Statistics.
--Water-supply.
-- --Bibliography.
--Zoology.
    xx U.S. Zoology.

Westallgäu. Alpen-versuchs-stationen.
    See Allgäu. Alpen-versuchs-stationen.

Westchester Co., N.Y.
    sa Subdivision Westchester Co.,
        N.Y. under: Hygiene, Public.
        World War, 1939-1945.
--Agriculture.
    xx New York (State) Agriculture.
--Botany.
    sa Subdivision New York (State)
        Westchester Co. under:
        Trees.
        Shrubs.
--Forestry.
    sa Subdivision New York (State)
        Westchester Co. under:
        Trees.
--Politics and government.
    xx County government. New York
        (State)
--Transportation.

Western Australia.
    xx Australia.
--Agriculture.
    sa Subdivision Western Australia
        under: Agriculture. Economic
          aspects.
        Colonization, Agricultural.
        Agriculture, Cooperative.
        Farms.
        Forage plants.
        Grasses.
        Crops and climate.
-- --Education.
-- --History.
-- --Periodicals.
-- --Statistics.
    xx Western Australia. Statistics.
--Botany.
    sa Subdivision Botany under:
        Sharks'Bay, Western
          Australia.
        Swan River Colony.
        Subdivision Western Australia
          under: Wild flowers.
    xx Australia. Botany.
--Climate.
    sa Subdivision Western Australia
        under: Crops and climate.
--Commerce.
-- --Statistics.
--Dairying.
-- --Societies.

Western Australia (Continued)
--Description and travel.
--Domestic animals.
-- --Statistics.
--Economic conditions.
 sa Subdivision Western Australia
  under: Economic surveys.
 xx Australia. Economic conditions.
--Entomology.
--Forestry.
 sa Subdivision Western Australia
  under: Timber.
  Forest policy.
 xx Australia. Forestry.
--Industries and resources.
--Meteorology.
 sa Subdivision Western Australia
  under: Precipitation
  (Meteorology)
--Milk supply.
 xx Australia. Milk supply.
--Paleobotany.
--Paleontology.
--Pomology.
--Public lands.
 xx Australia. Public lands.
--Sheep.
--Soils.
 sa Subdivision Western Australia
  under: Soil-surveys.
--Statistics.
 sa Western Australia. Agriculture.
  Statistics.
--Water-supply.

Western cabbage flea-beetle. See
 Phyllotreat pusilla.

Western cedar pole borer. See
 Trachykele blondeli.

Western dwarfmistletoe. See Arceuthobium
 campylopodum.

Western Europe. See Europe, Western.

Western gall rust. See Peridermium
 harknessii.

Western grass-stem sawfly. See Cephus
 occidentalis.

Western Gulf States. See Gulf States.

Western hemisphere. See America.

Western hemlock. See Tsuga heterophylla.

Western horn sheep. See Wiltshire
 sheep.

Western Islands. See Hebrides.

Western Jumna Canal. See Jumna Canal,
 Western.

Western larch. See Larix occidentalis.

Western New York Fruit Growers' Cooperative Packing Association.
 xx Cooperation. Societies.

Western Pacific Islands. See Islands
 of the Pacific.

Western peach borer. See Sanninoidea
 opalescens.

Western pine bark-beetle. See Dendroctonus brevicomis; Dendroctonus
 jeffreyi.

Western pine beetle. See Dendroctonus
 brevicomis; Dendroctonus jeffreyi.

Western red cedar. See Thuya plicata.

Western red cedar wood. See Thuya
 plicata (Wood)

Western red rot. See Red rot.

Western Reserve University. Experimental
 Drug Garden.
 xx Drug plant gardens.

Western Samoa (New Zealand)
--Agriculture.
--Commerce.
-- --Statistics.
 xx New Zealand. Commerce. Statistics.
--Economic conditions.
 xx New Zealand. Economic conditions.

Western States.
 sa Subdivision Western States
  under: Wild life management.

Western States (Continued)
--Agriculture.
    sa Subdivision Western States
        under: Irrigation.
        Agriculture. Economic
          aspects.
        Wheat.
        Forage plants.
        Ranges.
        Farm buildings.
        Poultry.
        Agricultural policies and
          programs.
        War and agriculture (1939-
          1945)
        Cotton.
        Labor and laboring classes.
        Agricultural laborers.
        Sugar-beet.
        Farms.
        Potatoes.
        Agricultural conservation
          program.
        Agricultural surveys.
        Irrigation farming.
        Western States. Domestic ani-
          mals.
        Subdivision Agriculture under
          names of Western States.
-- --Bibliography.
    xx U.S. Agriculture. Bibliography.
 · --History.
-- --Statistics.
    xx U.S. Agriculture. Statistics.
--Bibliography.
    sa Subdivision Bibliography
        under: Western States. His-
          tory.
--Biography.
--Botany.
    sa Subdivision Western States
        under: Trees.
        Fungi.
        Algae.
        Lichens.
        Weeds.
        Shrubs.
--Cattle.
    xx Cattle.
--Cattle trade.
-- --History.
-- -- --Bibliography.
--Church history.

Western States (Continued)
--Climate.
    sa Subdivision Climate under:
        Northwest, Pacific.
-- --Bibliography.
--Commerce.
    sa Subdivision Western States
        under: Farm produce. Mar-
          keting.
        Fruit trade.
        Subdivision Commerce.under:
          Northwest, Pacific.
-- --Statistics.
    sa Subdivision Commerce. Sta-
        tistics under: Northwestern
        States.
        Northwest, Pacific.
    xx U.S. Commerce. Statistics.
--Dairying.
-- --Statistics.
    xx Dairying. Statistics.
        Western States. Statistics.
--Description and travel.
    sa Subdivision Western States
        under: Hunting.
-- --Guide-books.
--Domestic animals.
    sa Subdivision Western States
        under: Cattle.
        Ranges.
        Live stock reports.
-- --Bibliography.
-- --Legislation.
-- --Periodicals.
--Statistics.
    xx U.S. Domestic animals. Sta-
        tistics.
--Economic conditions.
    sa Subdivision Western States
        under: Geography, Economic.
    xx U.S. Economic conditions.
-- --Periodicals.
    xx U.S. Economic conditions.
        Periodicals.

Western States (Continued)
--Entomology.
    sa Subdivision Western States
        under: Orthoptera.
        Coleoptera.
        Butterflies.
        Hymenoptera.
        Diptera.
        Neuroptera.
        Hemiptera.
        Pseudoneuroptera.
        Moths.
        Trees. Pests.
        Entomology, Economic.
--Forestry.
    sa Subdivision Forestry under:
        Platte River region.
        Northwest, Pacific.
        Subdivision Western States
        under: Forest fire. Pre-
        vention.
        Timber.
        Forest policy.
        Afforestation and reforesta-
        tion.
        Wood-using industries.
        Forest management.
        War and forestry (1939-1945)
-- --History.
    xx U.S. Forestry. History.
--Geography.
    sa Subdivision Western States
        under: Geography, Economic.
--Geology.
    sa Subdivision Western States
        under: Water, Underground.
        Mines and mineral resources.
--History.
    sa Western States. Church history.
        Subdivision History under:
        Northwest, Pacific.
        Ranges.
-- --Bibliography.
    xx Western States. Bibliography.
--Horse.
--Industries.
--Land.
    sa Subdivision Western States
        under: Land tenure.
        Land. Classification.
-- --Prices.
--Maps.
-- --Bibliography.

Western States (Continued)
--Meteorology.
    sa Precipitation (Meteorology)
        Western States.
--Natural history.
--Ornithology.
    sa Subdivision Ornithology under:
        Colorado Valley//
--Paleobotany.
--Paleontology.
    sa Subdivision Paleontology
        under: Great Basin.
--Physical geography.
    xx U.S. Physical geography.
--Politics and government.
-- --Bibliography.
    xx U.S. Politics and government.
        Bibliography.
--Pomology.
    xx U.S. Pomology.
--Population.
    sa Subdivision Western States
        under: Rural population.
    xx U.S. Population.
--Public lands.
-- --Statistics.
--Railroads.
    xx U.S. Railroads.
--Roads.
--Sheep.
--Social conditions.
    sa Subdivision Western States
        under: Social surveys.
--Social life and customs.
--Soils.
    sa Subdivision Western States
        under: Soil conservation.
        Soil erosion. Prevention
        and control.
    xx U.S. Soils.
--Statistics.
    sa Subdivision Statistics under:
        Western States. Dairying.
--Swine.
--Water-supply.
    sa Subdivision Water-supply under:
        Arizona.
        California.
        Colorado//
        Subdivision Western States
        under: Water, Underground.
        Water-rights.
-- --Bibliography.
    xx U.S. Water-supply. Bibliog-
        raphy.

Western States (Continued)
--Zoology.
    sa Subdivision Zoology under:
        Colorado Valley.
        Sierra Nevada Mountains,
          Calif.
        Subdivision Western States
          under: Mammalia.
        Batrachia.
        Reptilia.
        Wild life.

Western tussock-moth.   See Hemerocampa
    vetusta.

Western wheat aphis.   See Brachycolus
    tritici.

Western wheat grass.   See Wheat grass,
    Western.

Western white pine.   See Pinus monticola.

Western X disease.
    xx Virus diseases of cherries.
    Virus diseases of peaches.

Western X little cherry.
    xx Virus diseases of cherries.

Western yellow pine.   See Pinus pon-
    derosa.

Westfield River.

Westmorland, Eng.
--Agriculture.
-- --History.
    xx England. Agriculture. History.
--Botany.

Westmoreland Co., Pa.
    x Ligonier Valley, Westmoreland
      Co., Pa.
--Agriculture.
    sa Subdivision Pennsylvania. West-
      moreland Co. under: Agri-
      culture. Economic as-
      pects.
--Soils.
    sa Subdivision Pennsylvania. West-
      moreland Co. under: Soil
      conservation.

Westmoreland Co., Va.
--Economic conditions.
    xx Virginia. Economic conditions.
--Social conditions.
    sa Subdivision Virginia. West-
      moreland Co. under: Social
      surveys.

Weston-super-Mare, Eng.
--Botany.

Westonbirt Arboretum.

Westphalia.
    sa Subdivision Westphalia under:
      Cooperation.
      Labor and laboring classes.
    xx Germany.
--Agriculture.
    sa Subdivision Westphalia under:
      Agriculture. Economic as-
      pects.
      Agricultural laborers.
      Colonization, Agricultural.
      Agricultural industries.
    xx Germany. Agriculture.
-- --Periodicals.
--Botany.
    sa Subdivision Westphalia under:
      Vegetable pathology.
--Cattle.
    sa Subdivision Cattle under:
      Minden, Ger.
--Dairying.
--Entomology.
    sa Subdivision Westphalia under:
      Lepidoptera.
--Forestry.
-- --History.
    xx Germany. Forestry. History.
--Horse.
    sa Subdivision Westphalia under:
      Horses. Breeding.
--Industries.
    sa Subdivision Westphalia under:
      Agricultural industries.
--Land.
    xx Germany. Land.
--Milk supply.
    xx Germany. Milk supply.
--Sheep.

Wetter Valley.
--Botany.
    sa Subdivision Wetter Valley under:
        Botany, Economic.

Wetting agents.
    sa Unox.
       Santomerse.
    xx Santomerse.

Wexford, Ireland (County)
--Agriculture.

Whale fisheries.   See Whaling.

Whale meat.
    xx Meat.

Whale-oil.
    xx Fats and oils.

Whales.
    sa Cetacea.

Whaling.
--Bibliography.
--Periodicals.

Wharton Co., Tex.
--Water-supply.

Wharves.
    sa Subdivision Wharves under:
        New Orleans.

Whatcom Co., Wash.
--Agriculture.
    sa Subdivision Washington. Whatcom
        Co. under: Agricultural
        industries.
--Botany.
    xx Washington (State) Botany.
--Industries.
    sa Subdivision Washington, Whatcom
        Co. under: Agricultural
        industries.
--Soils.
    sa Subdivision Washington (State)
        Whatcom Co. under: Soil-
        surveys.

Wheat.   (INDIRECT)
    sa Flour testing.
       Gluten.
       Fertilizers for wheat.

Wheat (Continued)
    sa Spelt.
       Flour.
       Bran.
       Emmer.
       Einkorn.
       Wheat kernels.
       Subdivision Wheat under:
          Rotation of crops.
    x Spring wheat.
      Winter wheat.
    xx Cereals.
--Abstracts.

Wheat, Acidity in.

Wheat.
--Acreage adjustments.
    x Wheat acreage allotment.
-- --Periodicals.
--Ash analysis.
    xx Ash analysis.
--Baking qualities. See Wheat. Milling
    and baking qualities.
--Bibliography.
    sa Subdivision Bibliography
       under: Wheat. Harvesting.
       Wheat. Cost of production.
       Wheat, Durum.
       Wheat. Breeding.
       Wheat. Milling and baking
        qualities.
       Wheat. Prices.
       Wheat as feeding stuff.
--Biochemistry.
--Breeding.
-- --Bibliography.
--Bulk handling.
    xx Grain. Bulk handling.
       Wheat transportation.
--By-products.
    xx Waste products.
-- --Prices.
    xx Wheat. Prices.
--Chemistry. See Wheat. Composition.
--Cleaning.
-- --Bibliography.

Wheat, Club.
    x Club wheat.
    xx Wheat. Varieties.

Wheat.
--Competitions. See Wheat com-
    petitions.

Wheat (Continued)
--Composition.
    x Wheat. Chemistry.
    xx Chemistry, Vegetable.
--Congresses.
    sa Subdivision Congresses under:
      Wheat trade.
      Wheat smut.
--Control of production. See Wheat.
    Acreage adjustments.
--Cost of production.
-- --Bibliography.
    xx Wheat. Bibliography.
      Cereals. Cost of production.
      Bibliography.
--Crop insurance.
    x Wheat crop insurance.
    xx Crop insurance.
--Crop reports. See Wheat crop reports.
--Cytology.
    xx Plant cells and tissues.
--Disease resistance.
--Disease resistant varieties.
    xx Wheat. Varieties.
      Disease resistant plants.
--Diseases.
    sa Tylenchus tritici.
      Wheat mildew.
      Puccinia.
      Wheat rust.
      Tilletia tritici.
      Flag smut.
      Take-all of wheat.
      Mosaic disease of wheat.
      Loose smut.
      Yellow berry of wheat.
      Wheat smut.
      Root-rot of wheat.
      Downy mildew of wheat.
      Wheat-scab.
      Black-point of wheat.
      Black chaff disease of wheat.
      Foot rot of wheat.
      Browning root-rot of wheat.
      Speckled leaf blotch of wheat.
-- --Bibliography.
    sa Subdivision Bibliography under:
      Tilletia tritici.
--Diseases, Physiological.
    sa Subdivision Lodging under:
      Wheat.
    xx Physiological diseases of
      plants.
--Disinfection. See Wheat. Seed. Dis-
    infection.

Wheat (Continued)
--Dockage.
    xx Dockage.
--Drying.
    xx Cereals. Drying.

Wheat, Dural.
    x Dural wheat.
    xx Wheat. Varieties.

Wheat, Durum.
    sa Wheat, Kubanka.
    xx Wheat. Varieties.
--Acreage adjustments.
-- --Legislation.
--Statistics.
    xx Wheat. Statistics.
--Testing.
    xx Wheat. Testing.

Wheat.
--Economic aspects.
    xx Agriculture. Economic aspects.
      Cereals. Economic aspects.
-- --Statistics.

Wheat, Effect of climate on. See
    Wheat. Weather influences.
    x Climate. Effect on wheat.

Wheat, Effect of drought on.
    xx Droughts. Effect on plants.

Wheat.
--Effect of environment.

Wheat, Effect of freezing on. See
    Wheat. Freezing and frost injury.

Wheat, Effect of heat on. See Heat.
    Effect on wheat.

Wheat, Effect of light on. See Light.
    Effect on wheat.

Wheat, Effect of moisture on.
    xx Moisture. Effect on plants.

Wheat, Effect of nitrogen on. See
    Nitrogen. Effect on wheat.

Wheat, Effect of snow on.
    x Wheat. Winter killing.

Wheat.
--Effect of sulphur dioxide.
    xx Sulphur dioxide.

Wheat, Effect of temperature on.   See
Temperature. Effect on wheat.

Wheat.
--Effect of weather.   See Wheat. Weather
   influences.
--Estimating of crop.
    xx Cereals. Estimating of crop.
--Fat content.
    xx Fats and oils.
--Fertilizers.   See Fertilizers for
   Wheat.
--Financing.
    xx Farm produce. Financing.
--Freezing and frost injury.
    x Wheat. Winter killing.
--Fumigation.

Wheat, Garlic in.

Wheat.
--Genetics.
--Germination.
    sa Wheat. Sprouting.

Wheat, Gluten in.

Wheat.
--Grading and standardization.
    sa Flour. Nomenclature.
      Wheat. Inspection.
    x Wheat grading.
--Growth.

Wheat, H-44.

Wheat, Hard red spring.
    xx Wheat. Varieties.

Wheat, Hard red winter.
    xx Wheat. Varieties.

Wheat.
--Hardiness.
    xx Cereals. Hardiness.
--Harvesting.
-- --Bibliography.
--History.
    sa Subdivision History under:
      Bread.
      Wheat trade.

Wheat, Hope.

Wheat.
--Hybrids.
    sa Wheat-rye hybrids.
      Wheat-Haynaldia hybrids.
      Wheat agropyron hybrids.
--Implements and machinery.
    x Wheat. Machinery.
    xx Cereals. Implements and
      machinery.
-- --History.
--Injuries.
    xx Cereals. Injuries.
--Inspection.
--Introduction.
--Irrigation.
--Juvenile literature.
    xx Cereals. Juvenile literature.

Wheat, Kanred.
    xx Wheat. Varieties.

Wheat, Kota.
    x Kota wheat.
    xx Wheat. Varieties.

Wheat, Kubanka.
    x Kubanka wheat.
    xx Wheat, Durum.
      Wheat. Varieties.

Wheat.
--Laws and legislation.
    sa Wheat. Marketing. Law.
--Lodging.
    xx Lodging of grain.
      Wheat. Diseases, Physiological.

Wheat, Macaroni.

Wheat.
--Machinery.   See Wheat. Implements
   and machinery.
--Marketing.
    sa Wheat. Dockage.
-- --Bibliography.
--Marketing, Cooperative.
    sa Wheat pooling.

Wheat (Continued)
--Marketing, Cooperative.
-- --Periodicals.
-- --Societies.
--Marketing.
-- --Costs.
    xx Cereals. Marketing. Costs.
-- --Holding for higher price.
    xx Cereals. Marketing. Holding for
        higher price.
. --Law.
    xx Wheat. Laws and legislation.
--Marketing agreements.
    xx Cereals. Marketing agreements.
--Marketing quotas.
    x Wheat marketing quotas.
-- --Bibliography.
--Milling. See Flour-mills.
--Milling and baking qualities.
    x Flour. Milling and baking tests.
    xx Wheat. Quality.
-- --Bibliography.
    xx Wheat. Bibliography.

Wheat, Moisture content.

Wheat.
--Morphology and physiology. See Wheat.
    Physiology and morphology.

Wheat, Newturk.
    xx Wheat. Varieties.

Wheat, Nitrogen in.

Wheat.
--Nutritive value. See Wheat as food.
--Periodicals.
--Pest resistant varieties.
    xx Wheat. Varieties.
        Pest resistant plants.
--Pests.
    sa Prosopothrips cognatus.
       Harmolita grandis.
       Harmolita tritici.
       Meromyza americana.
       Cephus tabidus.
       Cephus pygmaeus.
       Eurygaster.
       Aelia.
--Physiology and morphology.
    sa Wheat. Hardiness.
       Wheat. Germination.
    xx Wheat. Morphology and
       physiology.

Wheat, Polish.
    x Polish wheat.
      Triticum polonicum.
    xx Wheat. Varieties.

Wheat, Poulard.
    x Poulard wheat.
    xx Wheat. Varieties.

Wheat.
--Pooling. See Wheat pooling.
--Price policy.
    x Wheat pricing.
--Prices.
    sa Subdivision Prices under: --
      Wheat. By-products.
-- --Bibliography.
    xx Prices. Bibliography.
      Wheat. Bibliography.
-- --Fixing.
    xx Prices. Fixing.
-- --Subsidies.
    x Wheat price supports.
    xx Farm produce. Prices. Sub-
        sidies.
--Processing.
-- --Bibliography.
--Processing tax.
    xx Processing tax.
--Production, Control of. See Wheat.
    Acreage adjustments.

Wheat, Proteins in.
    x Wheat proteins.
    xx Proteins.
--Bibliography.

Wheat.
--Quality.
    sa Subdivision Quality under:
      Cereals.
      Wheat. Milling and baking
        qualities.
    xx Cereals. Quality.
      Farm produce. Quality.
--Research.
    sa Wheat [geographic subdivision]
      Research, e.g., Wheat.
      Japan. Research.
--Ripening.

Wheat, Sandomir.
    xx Wheat. Varieties.

Wheat, Sargolla.
    xx Wheat. Varieties.

Wheat.
--Seed.
    x Wheat seed.
    xx Cereals. Seed.
-- --Disinfection.
    x Wheat. Disinfection.
    xx Cereals. Seed. Disinfection.
--Seed beds.
    x Wheat seed beds.
    xx Seed beds.
--Seedlings. See Wheat seedlings.
--Societies.
    sa Subdivision Societies under
       Wheat [geographic subdi-
       vision] e.g., Wheat.
       Australia. Societies.
    xx Cereals. Societies.

Wheat, Soft.

Wheat.
--Spacing.
    xx Plant spacing.
--Speculation.
    sa Wheat trade. Futures.

Wheat, Spelt. See Spelt.

Wheat.
--Sprouting.
    xx Sprouting.
     Wheat. Germination.
--Standards. See Wheat. Grading and
    standardization.
--Statistics.
    sa Wheat supply.
       Wheat yields.
       Wheat cycles.
       Subdivision Statistics under:
       Wheat, Durum.
       Wheat [geographic subdivision]
       Statistics, e.g., Wheat. U.S.
       Statistics.
-- --Bibliography.

Wheat, Stoner.
    xx Wheat. Varieties.

Wheat.
--Stooling.

Wheat (Continued)
--Storage.
    sa Grain elevators.
       Wheat. Bulk handling.
--Surplus.
    xx Wheat supply.
       Agricultural surpluses.
--Tariff.
    sa Wheat products. Tariff.
--Testing.
    xx Cereals. Testing.
--Therapeutic use.
    sa Subdivision Therapeutic use
       under: Wheat germ.
    xx Materia medica and thera-
       peutics.
--Toxicity.
    xx Toxicity.
--Transportation.
    sa Railroads. Rates. Wheat.
       Wheat. Bulk handling.
--Varieties.
    sa Wheat, Club.
       Wheat, Durum.
       Wheat, Hard red spring//
--Water requirements.
    xx Water requirements of crops.
--Weather influences.
    sa Subdivision Effect on wheat
       under: Heat.
       Temperature.
       Cold.
       Wheat. Effect of drought.
       Wheat. Freezing and frost
       injury.
       Wheat. Effect of moisture.
       Wheat. Effect of snow.
    x Wheat. Effect of weather.
       Weather. Effect on wheat.
--Weights and measures.
--Winter killing. See Wheat. Freezing
    and frost injury; Wheat, Effect of
    snow on.

Wheat acreage allotment. See Wheat.
    Acreage adjustments.

Wheat-Agropyron hybrids.
    xx Hybridization.

Wheat as feeding stuff.
    xx Cereals as feeding stuff.
--Bibliography.
    xx Wheat. Bibliography.
       Feeding stuffs. Bibliography.

Wheat as feeding stuff (Continued)
--Prices.
  xx Feeding stuff. Prices.
--Statistics.

Wheat as food.
  x Wheat. Nutritive value.
  xx Cereals as food.
--Congresses.

Wheat bran.
--Digestibility.

Wheat bunt. See Tilletia tritici; Stinking smut of wheat.

Wheat competitions.
  x Wheat. Competitions.
  xx Agriculture. Competitions.

Wheat crop insurance. See Wheat. Crop insurance.

Wheat crop reports.
  x Wheat. Crop reports.

Wheat cycles.
  x Cycles.
  xx Crop cycles.
    Wheat. Statistics.

Wheat eel-worm. See Tylenchus tritici.

Wheat flour substitutes. See Wheat substitutes.

Wheat futures. See Wheat trade. Futures.

Wheat germ.
  xx Cereal germ.
--Therapeutic use.
  xx Wheat. Therapeutic use.

Wheat germ as food.
  xx Nutrition.

Wheat germ oil.
  x Wheat oil.
  xx Cereal germ oil.

Wheat grading. See Wheat. Grading and standardization.

Wheat grass.
  x Agropyron.
  xx Grasses and forage plants.

Wheat grass, Bluestem. See Wheat grass, Western.

Wheat grass, Crested.
  x Crested wheat grass.
    Agropyron cristatum.
--Seed.

Wheat grass.
--Seed.

Wheat grass, Western.
  x Western wheat grass.
    Bluestem wheat grass.
    Wheat grass, Bluestem.

Wheat grass as feeding stuff.
  xx Grasses as feeding stuff.

Wheat hay.
  xx Hay.

Wheat-Haynaldia hybrids.

Wheat jointworm. See Harmolita tritici.

Wheat kernels.
  xx Wheat.
    Kernels.

Wheat leaf miner. See Agromyza parvicornis.

Wheat marketing quotas. See Wheat. Marketing quotas.

Wheat meal.
  sa Whole wheat meal.
  xx Meal.
    Whole wheat meal.

Wheat midge. See Sitodiplosis mosellana.

Wheat mildew.
  sa Wheat rust.

Wheat oil. See Wheat germ oil.

Wheat plans. See Wheat policies and programs.

Wheat policies and programs.   (INDIRECT)
    sa Wheat purchase program.
    x Wheat plans.
    Wheat programs.
    xx Agricultural policies and
        programs.
--Bibliography.
--Congresses.

Wheat pooling.   (DIRECT)
    x Wheat. Pooling.
    xx Wheat trade.
    Grain pooling.
--Legislation.
    xx Grain trade. Law.

Wheat price supports.   See Wheat. Prices.
  Subsidies.

Wheat pricing.   See Wheat. Price policy.

Wheat products.
    sa Flour.
--Statistics.
--Tariff.

Wheat programs.   See Wheat policies and
  programs.

Wheat proteins.   See Wheat, Proteins in.

Wheat purchase program.
    xx Purchase programs (Government)
    Wheat policies and programs.

Wheat research act, 1957 (Australia)

Wheat rosette.   See Mosaic disease of
  wheat.

Wheat rust.
    sa Puccinia.
--Congresses.

Wheat scab.

Wheat seed.   See Wheat. Seed.

Wheat seed beds.   See Wheat. Seed beds.

Wheat seedlings.

Wheat-sheaf miner.   See Cerodonta
  femoralis.

Wheat smut.
    sa Stinking smut of wheat.
    Loose smut of wheat.
--Control.
    sa Subdivision Control under:
    Loose smut of wheat.
    Stinking smut of wheat.
    xx Smut. Control.

Wheat soils.
    xx Wheat. Soils.
    Cereal soils.

Wheat speculation.   See Wheat. Speculation.

Wheat stacking.

Wheat starch.

Wheat stem maggot.   See Meromyza.

Wheat stem sawfly.   See Cephus cinctus.

Wheat storage.   See Wheat. Storage.

Wheat straw.

Wheat strawworm.   See Harmolita grandis.

Wheat substitutes.
    xx Flour substitutes.
    Substitute products.
--Composition.

Wheat supply.
    sa Wheat. Statistics.
    Wheat. Surplus.

Wheat surplus.   See Wheat. Surplus.

Wheat trade.   (DIRECT)
    sa Grain elevators.
    Wheat. Bulk handling.
    Wheat pooling.
--Abstracts.
--Accounting.
--Bibliography.
--Congresses.
    xx Wheat. Congresses.
--Futures.
    sa Wheat. Speculation.
-- --Directories.
--History.
    xx Wheat. History.

Wheat trade (Continued)
--Periodicals.
    sa Subdivision Periodicals under
        Wheat trade ₍geographic sub-
        division₎ e.g., Wheat trade.
        Canada. Periodicals.
--Statistics.
    sa Subdivision Statistics under
        Wheat trade ₍geographic sub-
        division₎ e.g., Wheat trade.
        U.S. Statistics.
--Tables and ready-reckoners.

Wheat weevil. See Anisoplia austriaca.

Wheat worm. See Tylenchus tritici.

Wheat yields.
    xx Crop yields.
        Wheat. Statistics.

Wheatgrass. See Wheat grass.

Wheatland, N.Y.
--Statistics.
    xx Monroe Co., N.Y. Statistics.

Wheel (Agricultural society) See Agricultural wheel (Agricultural society)

Wheelbarrows.

Wheeler-Case act, 1940.
    x Great plains act.

Wheeler-Lea act.
    xx Cosmetics. Legislation.
        Drugs. Legislation.
        Food. Legislation.

Wheeler Co., Neb.
--Soils.
    sa Subdivision Nebraska. Wheeler
        Co. under: Soil-surveys.

Wheeler Co., Tex.
--Soils.
    sa Subdivision Texas. Wheeler Co.
        under: Soil-surveys.

Wheeler Dam.
    xx Dams.

Wheels.
    sa Automobiles. Wheels.

Whey.
    sa Lactochrome.
        Cookery (Whey)
    x Milk serum.
--Composition.
--Grading and standardization.

Whey, Proteins in.
    x Whey proteins.
    xx Proteins.

Whey.
--Statistics.

Whey as feeding stuff.

Whey products.
--Bibliography.

Whey proteins. See Whey, Proteins in.

Whey-separators.

Whip-scorpions. See Pedipalpida.

Whippets.

Whippoorwills.

Whirligig beetles. See Gyrinidae.

Whiskey Insurrection, 1794.
    xx Pennsylvania. History.

Whisky.
    xx Alcoholic liquors.

White, Gilbert, 1720-1793.
--Bibliography.

White ants. See Termites.

White ash. See Fraxinus americana.

White ash land.

White-bark pine. See Pinus albicaulis.

White birch, Australian. See
    Schizomeria ovata.

White cattle.

White clover. See Clover, White.

White coffee borer. See Xylotrechus
quadripes.

White collar workers. See Clerks.

White Co., Ark.
--Agriculture.
     sa Subdivision White Co., Ark.
        under: Farm mangement.

White Co., Ind.
--Agriculture.
-- --Periodicals.
--Soils.
     sa Subdivision Indiana. White Co.
        under: Soil-surveys.
     xx Indiana. Soils.

White cypress pine. See Callitris
glauca.

White diarrhea. See Pullorum disease.

White Earth Indian Reservation, Minn.

White elm. See Ulmus americanus.

White fir. See Abies concolor.

White fir, Lowland. See Abies grandis.

White fir wood. See Abies amabilis
(Wood); Abies concolor (Wood); Abies
grandis (Wood); Abies magnifica (Wood)

White flies. See Aleurodidae.

White fly. See Aleurodes citri.

White fly, Mulberry (China) See
Aleurolobus marlatti.

White fox. See Arctic fox.

White-fringed beetles.
     Used for publications describing
     several species and for those
     where species is not specified.
     For publications describing a
     specific species, e.g., leu-
     coloma see Pantomorus leucoloma,
     or whatever specific name is.
     x Pantomorus (Graphognathus)
     Graphognathus.

White German goat.
     x White goat.
     German goat.
     xx Goats.

White goat. See Rocky Mountain goat;
White German goat.

White-grub.
     sa Phyllophaga.
     xx Phyllophaga.

White Hollow Watershed, Tenn.

White lead.

White lop-eared pig.

White-marked tussock moth. See Hemerocampa leucostigma.

White marlin.
     xx Marlin.

White mice. See Mice, White.

White mold. See Watery soft rot.

White Mountain butterfly. See Oeneis
semidea.

White Mountain National Forest.

White Mountains.
     sa Mt. Washington.
--Bibliography.
--Botany.
     sa Subdivision Botany under:
        Mt. Washington.
--Entomology.
--Ornithology.

White Mountains Forest Reserve. See
White Mountain National Forest.

White oak. See Quercus alba.

White oak wood. See Quercus alba
(Wood)

White pepper.
Here are entered publications on
white pepper as a spice. For
works on its cultivations, see
Black pepper. For botanical
studies, See Piper.

White pepper, Carbohydrates in.

White pine. See Pine; Pinus strobus;
Pinus monticola; Pinus lambertiana.

White-pine blister rust.
sa Cronartium ribicola.
xx Pinus monticola. Diseases.
--Congresses.
--Legislation.
--Quarantine.
xx Plant quarantine.
--Research.
--Weather influences.
xx Crops and climate.
Weather.

White pine weevil.
sa Cylindrocopturus eatoni.
x Pissodes strobi.
--Bibliography.
--Parasites.

White pitch.

White Plains Road, N.Y.

White River, Ark.

White River, Ind.
sa Subdivision White River, Ind.
under: Flood control.

White River, Mo.

White River, Or.

White River, S.D.

White River National Forest, Colo.
xx Colorado. Forest reservations.

White River Valley, Ark.
sa Arkansas-White-Red River
Valleys.

White Russia.
--Agriculture.
sa Subdivision Agriculture under:
Polesia.
Subdivision White Russia under:
Agriculture. Economic
aspects.
Flax.
Farm management.
Cereals.
Agricultural policies and
programs.
Cropping systems.
Agriculture, Cooperative.
Sugar-beet.
Mechanized farming.
Field crops.
Agricultural laborers.
Drug plants.
Soy-bean.
Grasses.
-- --Education.
- --History.
-- --Periodicals.
-- --Statistics.
--Bibliography.
--Botany.
sa Subdivision White Russia
under: Lichens.
Vegetable pathology.
Food plants.
Trees.
Shrubs.
--Cattle.
--Census.
--Climate.
--Domestic animals.
sa White Russia. Swine.
White Russia. Horse.
-- --Statistics.
sa Subdivision Domestic animals.
Statistics under: Minsk
(Government)
--Economic policy.
--Entomology.
sa Subdivision White Russia
under: Trees. Pests.
--Forestry.
sa Subdivision White Russia
under: Lumbering.
Afforestation and re-
forestation.
Wood-lots.
Forest management.
Trees.

White Russia (Continued)
--Forestry.
-- --Statistics.
--Horse.
    xx White Russia. Domestic animals.
--Ichthyology.
--Industries and resources.
    sa Subdivision White Russia under:
        Mines and mineral resources.
--Land.
    sa Subdivision White Russia under:
        Land tenure.
        Land utilization.
        Land laws.
--Language.
-- --Dictionaries.
--Maps.
--Meteorology.
--Natural history.
--Politics and government.
    sa Subdivision White Russia under:
        Administrative and political
          divisions.
--Pomology.
    sa Subdivision White Russia under:
        Berries.
-- --Research.
--Research.
--Soils.
    sa Subdivision Soils under:
        Briansk (Government)//
        Subdivision White Russia under:
        Peat.
--Statistics.
--Swine.
    xx White Russia. Domestic animals.
--Veterinary service.
--Viticulture.
--Water-supply.
--Zoology.

White Russian literature.
--Bibliógraphy.
-- --Periodicals.

White scale.   See Icerya purchasi.

White scour.
    sa Broncho-pneumonia, Septic.

White snakeroot.   See Eupatorium urticaefolium.

White-spotted sawyer.   See Monochamus
scutellatus.

White spruce.   See Picea canadensis.

White-tailed deer.
    xx Deer.

White willow.   See Salix alba.

White woolly aphis.   See Oregma lanigera.

Whitefish.

Whiteheaded Kazakh cattle.
    x Kazakh whiteheaded cattle.

Whiteside Co., Ill.
--Agriculture.

Whitewater River.
    sa Subdivision Whitewater River
        under: Flood control.

Whitewood.   See Liriodendron.

Whitfield Example Farm.

Whiting.

Whitley Co., Ind.
--Agriculture.
--Soils.
    sa Subdivision Indiana. Whitley
        Co. under: Soil-surveys.

Whitley Co., Ky.
--Geology.

Whitlow.
    x Panaris.

Whitman National Forest, Or.
    xx Oregon. Forest reservations.

Whittlesea (Shire) Australia.
--Agriculture.

Whole wheat flour.   See Graham flour.

Whole wheat meal.
    sa Cookery (Whole wheat meal)
        Wheat meal.
    xx Meal.
        Wheat meal.

Wholesale dealers.
--Directories.   See Wholesale trade.
   Directories.

Wholesale trade.   (DIRECT)
   When subdivided geographically,
   indicate see also ref. from
   name of place with subdivision
   Commerce.
   x Food distribution.
   Food. Distribution.
--Bibliography.
--Congresses.
--Directories.
   sa Subdivision Directories under:
      Wholesale trade. U.S.
      Wholesale trade. Minnesota.
   x Wholesale dealers. Directories.
--Periodicals.

Whorled milkweed.   See Asclepias gali-
   cides; Asclepias pumila; Asclepias
   verticillata.

Whortleberry wine.

Wiatka.   See Viatka.

Wibaux Co., Mont.
--Soils.
   sa Subdivision Montana. Wibaux Co.
      under: Soil-surveys.

Wiborgh phosphate.

Wichita Buffalo Range.   See Wichita
   National Forest and Game Preserve,
   Okla.

Wichita Co., Tex.
--Soils.
   sa Subdivision Texas. Wichita Co.
      under: Soil-surveys.

Wichita Game Reserve.   See Wichita
   National Forest and Game Preserve,
   Okla.

Wichita Indians.
--Legends.
--Religion and mythology.

Wichita National Forest and Game Preserve,
   Okla.
      x Wichita Buffalo Range.
      Wichita Game Reserve.
   xx Forest reservations.
      Game-preserves.

Wicken fen, Eng.
--Natural history.
   xx Natural history.
      England. Natural history.

Wicklow, Ireland (County)
--Botany.

Wicomico Co., Md.
   sa Subdivision Wicomico Co., Md.
      under: Planning, County.
   xx Maryland.
--Agriculture.
   sa Subdivision Maryland. Wicomico
      Co. under: Farm management
      surveys.
--Land.
   sa Subdivision Maryland. Wicomico
      Co. under: Land utilization.

Wiedenbrück, Prussia.
--Agriculture.

Wielkopolski Park Narodowy, Poland.

Wien.   See Vienna.

Wienerwald.

Wieringermeer.
--Social conditions.
   sa Subdivision Wieringermeer
      under: Cost and standard
      of living.

Wiesbaden.
--Agriculture.

Wiesbaden, Chemisches laboratorium
   Fresenius.

Wiesbaden.
--Cost and standard of living.   See
   Cost and standard of living.
   Wiesbaden.
--Description and travel.
   sa Subdivision Wiesbaden under:
      Hunting.

Wiesbaden (Continued)
--Entomology.
    sa Subdivision Wiesbaden under:
        Hemiptera.
    xx Germany. Entomology.
--Forestry.

Wight, Isle of.　See Isle of Wight.

Wilbarger Co., Tex.
--Soils.
    sa Subdivision Texas. Wilbarger
        Co. under: Soil-surveys.
--Water-supply.
    sa Subdivision Texas. Wilbarger
        Co. under: Water, Under-
        ground.

Wilcox Co., Ala.
--Soils.
    sa Subdivision Alabama. Wilcox Co.
        under: Soil-surveys.

Wild animals.
--Diseases.　See Game. Diseases.

Wild boar.　See Wild swine.

Wild carrot.　See Daucus carota.

Wild cat.　See Felis catus.

Wild dog.　See Canis dingo.

Wild figs.　See Caprifig.

Wild flower cultivation.　See Native
  plants for cultivation.

Wild flower gardening.　See Native plants
  for cultivation.

Wild flowers.　(INDIRECT)
    Beginning Mar. 1953 omit x-ref.
      from place with subdivision
      Botany.
    sa Native plants for cultivation.
    xx Botany.
        Flowers.
--Identification.
    x Identification of wild flowers.
--Names.
    xx Plant names.
--Pictorial works.
    xx Flowers. Pictorial works.

Wild flowers, Protection of.　See Plant
  conservation.

Wild-fowl.　See Game-birds; Water-fowl.

Wild fruits as food.　See Food plants.

Wild gardens of Acadia, Bar Harbor, Me.
    sa Acadia National Park.

Wild garlic.　See Garlic.

Wild life.　(INDIRECT)
    sa Game.
        Subdivision Wild life under:
          Marshes, Tide.
          Marshes.
    x Wildlife.
        Animal life.
--Bibliography.
--Conservation.　(INDIRECT)
    sa Birds, Protection of.
        Forest preservation.
        Forest reservations.
        Game-laws.
        Game protection.
        National parks and reserves.
        Natural monuments.
        Natural resources.
        Game-preserves.
        Pittman-Robertson program.
    x Wild life, Protection of.
        Wild life protection.
        Game conservation.
        Game. Conservation.
    xx Conservation of natural re-
        sources.
-- --Bibliography.
    sa Subdivision Bibliography
        under: U.S. Fish and Wild-
        life Service.
    xx Conservation of natural re-
        sources. Bibliography.
-- --Congresses.
    sa Game protection. Congresses.
-- --Government aid.
-- --Outlines, syllabi, etc.
-- --Periodicals.
    sa Game protection. Periodicals.
- --Research.
-- --Societies.
    sa Game protection. Societies.
    xx Game protection. Societies.

Wild life, Effect of pesticides on.　See
　Pesticides. Effect on wild life.

Wild life.
　--Food.
　　　　sa Food plants for birds.
　　　　Game-fowl. Food.
　　　　Food plants for wild life.
　　　　xx Game. Food.
　　　　Birds. Food.
　--Forestry relations.　See Forestry.
　　　Wild life relations.
　--Legislation.
　　　　sa Federal aid to wildlife resto-
　　　　　ration act, 1937.
　　　　National wilderness preserva-
　　　　　tion act.
　--Management.　(INDIRECT)
　　　　sa Wild life management as an
　　　　　occupation.
　　　　Forestry. Wild life relations.
　-- --Abstracts.
　-- -- --Periodicals.
　-- --Bibliography.
　-- -- --Periodicals.
　-- --Outlines, syllabi, etc.
　-- --Study and teaching.
　--Periodicals.
　--Pictorial works.

Wild life, Protection of.　See Wild life.
　Conservation.

Wild life.
　--Research.
　　　xx Research.
　-- --Bibliography.

Wild life and forestry relations.　See
　Forestry. Wild life relations.

Wild life as farm pests.　See Farm pests.

Wild life conservation.　See Wild life.
　Conservation.

Wild life extension work.
　　　x Extension work in wildlife
　　　　conservation and restora-
　　　　tion.

Wild life management.　See Wild life.
　Management.

Wild life management as an occupation.

Wild life preservation.　See Wild life.
　Conservation.

Wild life preserves.　See Game-preserves.

Wild life protection.　See Wild life.
　Conservation.

Wild mustard.　See Charlock.

Wild oats.　See Oats, Black.

Wild onion.　See Garlic.

Wild parsnip.　See Cicuta.

Wild plant cultivation.　See Native
　plants for cultivation.

Wild plants, Edible.　See Food plants.

Wild plants as food.　See Food plants.

Wild radish.　See Raphanus raphanistrum.

Wild rice.　See Indian rice.

Wild roses.
　　　x Roses, Wild.
　　　xx Roses.

Wild sage.　See Artemisia frigida.

Wild swine.
　　　x Sus scrofa.
　　　Swine.
　　　Boar hunting.
　　　Wild boar.
　　　Swine, Wild.
　--Anatomy and physiology.
　--Parasites.

Wild turkeys.　See Turkeys, Wild.

Wild winter pea.　See Lathyrus hirsutus.

Wilder Dam.

Wilderness areas.　(INDIRECT)
　　　xx National parks and reserves.
　　　Forest reservations.
　--Periodicals.

Wildfire.　See Tobacco wildfire.

Wildfowl. See Game-birds; Water-fowl.

Wildlife. See Wild life.

Wildlife refuges. See Game-preserves.

Wildpark bei Potsdam. K.gärtner lehranstalt.

Wildwood, Camp, Me.

Wilenska. See Wilna.

Wilkes Exploring Expedition.

Will Co., Ill.
--Agriculture.
     sa Subdivision Illinois. Will Co.
          under: Farm management surveys.
--Soils.
     sa Subdivision Illinois. Will Co.
          under: Soil-surveys.

Will-Varrentrapp method of nitrogen determination.

Willacy Co., Tex.
--Soils.
     sa Subdivision Texas. Willacy Co.
          under: Soil-surveys.

Willamette National Forest, Or.

Willamette River.
     sa Subdivision Willamette River
          under: Flood control.

Willamette Valley, Or.
     sa Subdivision Willamette Valley,
          Or. under: Planning, Regional.
          Willamette Valley, Or. Agriculture.
--Agriculture.
     sa Subdivision Oregon. Willamette
          Valley under: Agriculture.
          Economic aspects.
          Colonization, Agricultural.
          Agricultural laborers.
--Economic conditions.
--Soils.
     sa Subdivision Willamette Valley,
          Or. under: Soil erosion.
     xx Oregon. Soils.

Willcox Basin, Ariz.
--Geology.
--Water-supply.
     sa Subdivision Arizona. Willcox
          Basin under: Water, Underground.

William A. Jump Memorial Award.
     xx Jump, William Ashby, 1891-1949.
     U.S. Dept. of Agriculture.
          Officials and employees.
     Rewards (Prizes, etc.)

William Howard Taft Memorial Highway.
     See Taft Memorial Highway.

Williams Co., N.D.
     xx North Dakota.
--Agriculture.
     sa Subdivision North Dakota.
          Williams Co. under: Agricultural credit.
--Entomology.
--Land.
     sa Subdivision North Dakota.
          Williams Co. under:
          Land. Classification.

Williamsburg, Va.
     xx Virginia.

Williamsburg Co., S.C.
--Soils.
     sa Subdivision South Carolina.
          Williamsburg Co. under:
          Soil-surveys.

Williamson Co., Tex.
--Soils.
     sa Subdivision Texas. Williamson
          Co. under: Soil-surveys.
--Water-supply.

Williamsport, Penn.
--Milk trade.
     xx Pennsylvania. Milk trade.

Williston irrigation project.

Willistoniella.

Willow borer. See Phryneta spinator;
     Cryptorhynchus lapathi.

Willow leaf beetle. See Plagiodera
    versicolora.

Willow-warblers. See Phylloscopus.

Willows. See Salix; Basket-willow.

Wills.

Wilmington, N.C.
--Botany.
--Economic conditions.
    sa Subdivision Wilmington under:
        Economic surveys. North
        Carolina.
    xx North Carolina. Economic con-
        ditions.
--Social conditions.
    sa Subdivision North Carolina.
        Wilmington under: Social
        surveys.

Wilna, Russia.
--Botany.
--Directories.
--Streets.

Wilson chamber. See Cloud chamber.

Wilson cloud chamber. See Cloud chamber.

Wilson Co., Kan.
--Land.
    sa Subdivision Kansas. Wilson Co.
        under: Land utilization.
--Soils.
    sa Subdivision Kansas. Wilson Co.
        under: Soil-surveys.
        Soil conservation surveys.

Wilson Co., N.C.
--Soils.
    sa Subdivision North Carolina.
        Wilson Co. under: Soil-
        surveys.

Wilson Co., Tex.
    xx Texas.

Wilson Dam.

Wilstermarsch cattle.

Wilt disease (Gipsy moth)   See Gipsy
    moth. Diseases.

Wilt diseases.
    sa Bacillus tracheiphilus.
        Fusarium tracheiphilum.
        Neocosmospora vasinfecta.
        Potato wilt.
        Cotton wilt.
        Cow-pea wilt.
        Tomato wilt.
        Banana wilt.
        Bacterial wilt of lespedeza.
        Fusarium perniciosum.
        Elm wilt.
        Oak wilt.
        Sugar-cane wilt.

Wilting of plants.

Wiltshire, Eng.
--Agriculture.
    sa Agriculture. Economic aspects.
        Gt. Brit. Wiltshire.
--Botany.
--Economic conditions.
    sa Subdivision England. Wiltshire
        under: Geography, Economic.
--Geography.
    sa Subdivision England. Wiltshire
        under: Geography, Economic.
--Land.
    sa Subdivision England. Wiltshire
        under: Land. Classifica-
        tion.
--Social conditions.

Wiltshire sheep.

Wimmera rye grass. See Swiss rye grass.

Winchester, Mass.
--Forestry.

Wind. See Winds.

Wind and soil. See Soil drifting; Dust
    storms.

Wind-bent-grass.

Wind-breaks.
    sa Trees, Shelter.
    x Wind screens.
    xx Plant protection from weather.
        Trees, Shelter.
--Bibliography.
--Statistics.

Wind Cave National Park.

Wind damage to trees.   See Trees. Wind
  injury.

Wind erosion.   (INDIRECT)
      When subdivided geographically,
      indicate see also ref. from
      name of place with subdivision
      Soils.
      sa Dust storms.
         Soil drifting.
       x Soil drifting.
         Soil blowing.
         Soil and wind.
      xx Soil erosion.
         Winds.
  --Prevention and control.   (INDIRECT)
      When subdivided geographically,
      indicate see also ref. from
      name of place with subdivision
      Soils.
  -- --Congresses.

Wind motors.   See Windmills.

Wind power.
      sa Air-turbines.
      xx Power resources.

Wind pressure.

Wind River Arboretum.

Wind River Experimental Forest, Wash.
      xx Washington (State) Forest
                reservations.
  --Climate.

Wind River Valley, Wyo.
  --Economic conditions.

Wind screens.   See Wind-breaks.

Wind signals.

Wind turbines.   See Air-turbines.

Wind velocity.

Windbreaks.   See Wind-breaks.

Windemere, Lake.   See Lake Windemere.

Windgalls.

Windmills.
      sa Air-turbines.
  --Statistics.

Window curtains.   See Drapery.

Window drapery.   See Drapery.

Window-dressing.   See Show-windows.

Window-gardening.
      xx House plants.

Windows.
      sa Skylights.
         Barns and stables. Windows.
      xx Building.
  --Standards.
      xx Standardization.

Winds.
      sa Monsoons.
         Hurricanes.
         Tornadoes.
         Cyclones.
         Anemometer.
         Chinook wind.
         Anemometry.
         Soil and wind.
         Typhoons.
         Sea breeze.
         Föhn.
         Northers.
         Insects and wind.
         Birds and wind.
         Wind erosion.
         Dry winds.
       x Atmospheric circulation.
  --Bibliography.
      sa Wind velocity. Bibliography.
  --Effect on forest fires.
       x Forest fires, Effect of winds
           on.
         Forest fires and winds.
         Winds and forest fires.
      xx Weather. Effect on forest
           fires.
  --Effects on plants.
  --Effect on trees.
      sa Trees. Wind injury.
       x Trees. Effect of wind.
  --Variation with altitude.

Winds and forest fires.   See Winds.
      Effect on forest fires.

Windsor bean.   See Broad bean.

Windsor, Conn.
--Commerce.

Windsor Co., Vt.
--Agriculture.
    sa Subdivision Vermont. Windsor
        Co. under: Agricultural
        surveys.
        Agriculture, Cooperative.
-- --Statistics.

Windsor Forest.
    xx England. Forest reservations.
--Entomology.
    sa Subdivision England. Windsor
        Forest under: Coleoptera.
    xx England. Entomology.

Windstorm insurance.   See Insurance,
    Tornado.

Windward Islands.
--Agriculture.
    sa Subdivision Windward Islands
        under: Agriculture. Eco-
        nomic aspects.
--Forestry.

Wine.   See Wine and wine making.
    x Enology.
--Adulteration.
    sa Wine, Arsenic in.
    xx Adulterations.
--Alcohol content.

Wine, Aluminum in.
    x Aluminum in wine.

Wine, Ammonia in.
    x Ammonia in wines.

Wine.
--Analysis.
    x Wine and wine making. Analysis.

Wine, Arsenic in.
    xx Arsenic.
    Wine. Adulterations.

Wine.
--Bibliography.

Wine, Color of.   See Color of wine.

Wine.
--Composition.
--Diseases.
--Dry matter determination.

Wine, Effect of temperature on.   See
    Temperature, Effect on wines.

Wine.
--Extractives.

Wine, Fat in.

Wine.
--Flavor.
-- --Testing.
    xx Food. Flavor. Testing.

Wine, Glycerin in.

Wine.
--Judging.
    xx Judging.
--Legislation.   See Wine and wine
    making. Legislation.
--Liming.
--Marketing.
--Pasteurization.
    xx Sterilization.
--Physiological effect.
--Prices.

Wine, Racking.

Wine.
--Statistics.
--Therapeutic use.
-- --Congresses.
    xx Wine and wine making. Con-
        gresses.
--Unfermented.

Wine and wine making.   (DIRECT)
    sa Bordeaux wines.
    Whortleberry wine.
    Tokay wine.
    Champagne (Wine)
    Madeira wine.
    Port wine.
    Cookery (Wine)
    Viticulture.
    Grapes.
    Fruit wines.
    Brandy.
    Fermentation.

Wine and wine making (Continued)
    sa Sherry.
       Chianti wine.
       Berry wines.
       Orange wine.
       Sauterne.
       Currant wine.
       Marsala wine.
       Côtes-de-Provence wines.
    x Wine.
      Wine industry.
    xx Alcoholic liquors.
--Accounting.
    xx Cost. Accounting.
--Analysis. See Wine. Analysis.
--Bibliography.
    sa Wine and wine making ₍geo-
       graphic subdivision₎ Bib-
       liography, e.g., Wine and
       Wine making. Africa, South.
       Bibliography.
--Biochemistry.
--By-products.
    sa Subdivision By-products under:
       Grapes.
    xx Grapes. By-products.
--Congresses.
    sa Subdivision Congresses under:
       Wine. Therapeutic use.
       Subdivision Congresses under
       Wine and wine making ₍geo-
       graphic subdivision₎ e.g.,
       Wine and wine making. Italy.
       Congresses.

Wine and wine making, Cooperative.
  (DIRECT)
    xx Agriculture, Cooperative.
--Periodicals.
--Societies.

Wine and wine making.
--Dictionaries.
--Directories.
    sa Wine and wine making ₍geo-
       graphic subdivision₎ Di-
       rectories, e.g., Wine and
       wine making. Spain. Direc-
       tories.
--Equipment.
--Expositions.
--Handbooks, manuals, etc.
--History.
--Implements and machinery.
    xx Machinery.

Wine and wine making (Continued)
--Legislation.
--Marketing agreements.
    xx Marketing agreements.
--Microbiology.
--Periodicals.
    sa Wine and wine making ₍geo-
       graphic subdivision₎ Peri-
       odicals, e.g., Wine and
       wine making. Germany. Peri-
       odicals.
--Research.
-- --Periodicals.
--Residues.
--Societies.
--Statistics.
--Study and teaching.
--Taxation.
    xx Taxation.
--Trade and industry. See Wine and
    wine making.
--Year-books.
    xx Yearbooks.

Wine-casks.

Wine consumption.

Wine industry. See Wine and wine
  making.

Wine making. See Wine and wine making.

Wine marc.

Wine trade. See Wine and wine making.

Wingendorf, Saxony.
--Soils.

Wings.
    sa Venation.
       Subdivision Wings under:
       Airplanes.
--Birds.
--Insects.
    x Insect wings.
    xx Flight. Insects.

Wings (Aeroplane) See Airplanes. Wings.

Winkler Co., Tex.
--Water-supply.
    sa Subdivision Texas. Winkler Co.
       under: Water, Underground.

Winnebago Co., Ill.
--Botany.
　　xx Illinois. Botany.
--Education.

Winnebago Co., Wis.
--Soils.
　　sa Subdivision Wisconsin. Winne-
　　　　bago Co. under: Soil-
　　　　surveys.

Winneshiek Co., Iowa.
--Botany.

Winnipeg.
--Charities.
--History.
--Milk supply.

Winnowing machines.　See Grain cleaning
　machines.

Winona, Minn.
--Harbor.
　　xx Harbors.

Winona Co., Minn.
--Agriculture.
　　xx Minnesota. Agriculture.
--Land.
　　sa Subdivision Minnesota. Winona
　　　　Co. under: Land utilization.
--Soils.
　　sa Subdivision Minnesota. Winona
　　　　Co. under: Soil conservation
　　　　surveys.

Winona Lake, Ind.
--Entomology.

Winooski River, Vt.
　　sa Subdivision Winooski River, Vt.
　　　　under: Flood control.

Winschoten.
--Economic conditions.

Winston Co., Ala.
--Soils.
　　sa Subdivision Alabama. Winston
　　　　Co. under: Soil-surveys.

Winston Co., Miss.
--Agriculture.
　　sa Subdivision Mississippi.
　　　　Winston Co. under: Agri-
　　　　cultural credit.
　　　　Agricultural indebtedness.

Winston-Salem.
--Markets.

Winter.

Winter-killing of cereals.　See Cereals.
　Freezing and frost injury.

Winter-killing of fruit trees.　See.
　Fruit. Freezing and frost injury.

Winter moth.　See Ophteroptera brumata.

Winter sports.
　　sa Skis and ski-running.
　　　Ice fishing.
　　xx Sports.

Winter wheat.　See Wheat.

Wintering of plants.

Wintering of stock.

Winters Farm, Tioga Co., N.Y.

Winterthur, Switzerland.
--Statistics.

Winthemia quadripustulata.

Wire.
　　sa Fence-wire.
　　　Electric wire.
　　　Welded wire fabric.
--Bibliography.
　　xx Iron and steel. Bibliography.
--Congresses.
--Deterioration.
　　sa Fungus deterioration of wire.
　　xx Deterioration.

Wire clearance from trees.　See Trees:
　Wire clearance.

Wire-grass.　See Quitch-grass.

Wire-haired pinschers.

Wire-haired terrier.

Wire rope.

Wire screens.
    x Insect screens.
    xx Screens.

Wire tapping.
    xx Telephone. Laws and regulations.

Wire-worm. See Elateridae.

Wire-worm, Sand. See Horistonatus
uhlerii.

Wire-worm, Twisted. See Haemonchus
contortus.

Wirebound containers. See Containers,
Wirebound.

Wireless telegraph. See Telegraph, Wireless.

Wireless telephone. See Telephone, Wireless.

Wireworms. See Elateridae.

Wiring. See Electric wiring.

Wisbech, Eng.
 --Pomology.
    xx England. Pomology.
 --Soils.
    xx England. Soils.

Wisconsin.
    sa Rock Co.
    Madison.
    Lake Mendota//
    Subdivision Wisconsin under:
      Planning, Regional.
 --Agriculture.
    sa Subdivision Agriculture under:
    Dane Co.
    Racine Co.
    Marinette Co.//

Wisconsin (Continued)
 --Agriculture.
    sa Subdivision Wisconsin under:
    Agriculture. Economic as-
      pects.
    Maize.
    Poultry.
    Sugar-beet.
    Agriculture, Cooperative.
    Rural surveys.
    Agricultural outlook.
    War and agriculture (1939-
      1945)
    Farm management surveys.
    Farm produce. Cost of pro-
      duction.
    Agricultural policies and
      programs.
    Potatoes.
    Agricultural surveys.
    Farm ownership.
    Grassland farming.
    Grasses.
 -- --History.
 -- --Periodicals.
 -- --Statistics.
    sa Agriculture. Statistics.
 --Altitudes.
    xx Altitudes.
 --Antiquities.
 --Blue books. See Wisconsin. Legisla-
    tive manuals.
 --Botany.
    sa Subdivision Botany under:
    Madison.
    Dalles, Wis.
    Kenosha Co., Wis.//
    Subdivision Wisconsin under:
    Trees.
    Fungi.
    Algae.
    Wild flowers.
 --Cattle.
 --Census.
 --Climate.
 --Commerce.
    sa Subdivision Wisconsin under:
    Farm produce. Marketing.
 --Dairying.
    sa Subdivision Dairying under:
    Green Co., Wis.
    Subdivision Wisconsin under:
    Dairy industry and trade.
 -- --History.
 --Description and travel.

Wisconsin (Continued)
--Domestic animals.
 xx Domestic animals.
  U.S. Domestic animals.
--Economic conditions.
 sa Subdivision Economic conditions
  under: Milwaukee.
  Subdivision Wisconsin under:
  History, Economic.
  Rural surveys.
--Education.
 sa Subdivision Education under:
  Kenosha, Wis.
  Trempealeau Co., Wis.
  Subdivision Wisconsin under:
  Rural schools.
--Entomology.
 sa Subdivision Entomology under:
  Racine Co., Wis.
  Milwaukee Co.
  Subdivision Wisconsin under:
  Hymenoptera.
  Trichoptera.
  Lepidoptera.
  Trees. Pests.
--Forest reservations.
 sa Chequamegon National Forest,
  Wis.
  Nicolet National Forest, Wis.
 xx Forest reservations.
--Forestry.
 sa Subdivision Wisconsin under:
  Timber.
  Lumber.
  Wood-lots.
  Afforestation and reforesta-
  tion.
  Forest fires.
  Tree planting.
  Forest policy.
  Forest management.
  Subdivision Forestry under
  names of counties, etc.
 xx U.S. Forestry.
  Wisconsin. Forestry.
-- --Research.
--Geology.
 sa Subdivision Geology under:
  Fox River Valley, Wis.
  Subdivision Wisconsin under:
  Water, Underground.
  Mines and mineral resources.
--History.
 sa Subdivision Wisconsin under:
  History, Economic.

Wisconsin (Continued)
--History.
 sa Subdivision History under
  names of cities, towns,
  etc.
-- --Sources.
 sa Subdivision Wisconsin under:
  Archives.
 xx U.S. History. Sources.
--Horse.
 sa Subdivision Wisconsin under:
  Horses. Breeding.
--Ichthyology.
--Industries.
--Land.
 sa Subdivision Wisconsin under:
  Land utilization.
  Land tenure.
  Subdivision Land under:
  Ashland Co.
  Bayfield Co.
  Vilas Co.//
--Legislative manuals.
 x Legislative manuals.
--Libraries.
--Manufactures.
--Maps.
 sa Subdivision Maps under names
  of counties, etc., e.g.,
  Waukesha Co., Wis. Maps.
--Markets.
--Meteorology.
--Milk supply.
 sa Subdivision Milk supply
  under: Milwaukee.
  Barron Co., Wis.
  Dodge Co., Wis.
 xx U.S. Milk supply.
--Milk trade.
 sa Subdivision Milk trade under:
  Milwaukee.
  Barron Co., Wis.
  Dodge Co., Wis.
--Natural history.
--Ornithology.
 sa Subdivision Ornithology under:
  Outagamie Co., Wis.
  Door Peninsula, Wis.
--Parks.
 sa Subdivision Parks under:
  La Crosse.
  Milwaukee.

Wisconsin (Continued)
--Parks.
    sa Devil's Lake State Park.
    Northern Forest State Park.
    Cushing Memorial Park.
    xx U.S. Parks.
--Pharmacy.
--Physical geography.
    xx U.S. Physical geography.
--Politics and government.
--Population.
    sa Subdivision Wisconsin under:
    Rural population.
    xx U.S. Population.
--Public lands.
    xx U.S. Public lands.
--Public works.
    xx U.S. Public works.
--Railroads.
--Roads.
--Sheep.
--Social conditions.
    sa Subdivision Social conditions
    under: Walworth Co.
    Subdivision Wisconsin under:
    Social surveys.
    Community life.
--Soils.
    sa Subdivision Soils under:
    Marinette Co., Wis.
    La Crosse Co., Wis.
    Iowa Co., Wis.//
    Subdivision Wisconsin under:
    Soil-surveys.
    Peat.
    Soil erosion. Prevention
    and control.
    Soil conservation.
    Soil erosion.
    Soil conservation. Economic
    aspects.
--Statistics.
    sa Subdivision Statistics under:
    Wisconsin. Agriculture.
--Viticulture.
--Water-supply.
    sa Subdivision Wisconsin under:
    Water, Underground.
--Zoology.
    sa Subdivision Zoology under:
    Lake Mendota.
    Racine Co., Wis.
    Subdivision Wisconsin under:
    Mammalia.

Wisconsin River.

Wise Co., Tex.
--Water-supply.
    sa Subdivision Texas. Wise Co.
    under: Water, Underground.

Wise Co., Va.
    sa Subdivision Virginia. Wise Co.
    under: County surveys.
    Social surveys.
    xx Virginia.
--Economic conditions.
    xx Virginia. Economic conditions.
--Industries and resources.
    sa Industrial surveys. Virginia.
    Wise Co.
--Social conditions.
    sa Subdivision Virginia. Wise Co.
    under: Social surveys.
--Soils.
    sa Subdivision Virginia. Wise Co.
    under: Soil-surveys.

Wisley Gardens, Eng.

Wissadula.

Wissenschaftliche anstalten für brauin-
    dustrie in Prag. See Bohemia. Ver-
    suchaanstalt für brauindustrie in
    Böhmen.

Wistar Institute of Anatomy and Biology,
    Philadelphia.
--Bibliography.

Wister Reservoir, Okla.

Wit and humor.
    sa American wit and humor.
    x Jokes.
    Humor.
    xx Caricature.

Witch-hazel. See Hamamelis virginiana.

Witchcraft.

Witches broom.
    xx Vegetable pathology.

Witches' broom disease of alfalfa.
    xx Alfalfa. Diseases.

Witches' broom disease of cacao.
    xx Cacao. Diseases.

Witches broom disease of jack pine.
    x Mistletoe broom disease of
       jack pine.
      Jack pine mistletoe.
    xx Pinus banksiana. Diseases.

Witches' broom disease of potato.
    xx Potatoes. Diseases.

Witches' broom disease of tomato.
    xx Tomatoes. Diseases.

Witchgrass. See Quitch-grass.

Witch's broom. See Witches' broom.

Witchweed. See Striga asiatica.

Witham River, Eng.

Wither-tip.

Witloof.
    sa Cookery (Witloof)
    x Endive, French.
      French endive.
      Chicory, Belgian.
    xx Chicory.

Wittrockiella. See Chaetophoraceae.

Witwatersrand, Transvaal.
  --Botany.
  --Water-supply.

Woad.

Woburn Abbey.

Wohanka and Co.

Wohlfahrtia magnifica.

Wojnowicia graminis.

Wokas. See Water lilies.

Wolf. See Wolves.

Wolf-spider. See Tarentula.

Wolfram. See Wolframite.

Wolframite.
    sa Tungsten.
    x Wolfram.

Wolman salts. See Tanalith; Triolith.

Wolves.
  --Extermination.

Wolves, Prairie. See Coyote.

Woman.
    sa Girls.
    x Women.
  --Bibliography.
    sa Subdivision Bibliography
       under: European war, 1914-
        1918. Women's work.
       Woman. Biography.
  --Biography.
  -- --Bibliography.
    xx Woman. Bibliography.
       Biography. Bibliography.
  -- --Dictionaries.
  --Body measurements.
    xx Body measurements.
  --Clothing.
    xx Clothing and dress.
  -- --Statistics.
  --Congresses.
    sa Subdivision Congresses under:
       Women in agriculture.
  --Education.
    sa Swanley, Kent, Eng. Horti-
       cultural College.
      Lowthorpe School of Landscape
       Architecture, Gardening,
       and Horticulture for Women.
      Pennsylvania School of Horti-
       culture for Women//
    x Education for women.
  -- --Periodicals.
  --Employment. (DIRECT)
    sa Women in agriculture.
      European war, 1914-1918.
       Women's work.
      Women in forestry.
      Women as scientists.
      Girls. Employment.

Woman (Continued)
--Employment.
    sa World War, 1939-1945. Women's
       work.
      Labor supply.
      Home economics as an occupation.
      Women in food processing plants.
    xx World War, 1939-1945. Women's
       work. Gt. Brit.
-- --Bibliography.
    sa Subdivision Bibliography under:
      Girls. Employment.
      World War, 1939-1945. Women's
       work.
--Health and hygiene.
    x Health of women.
--Nutrition.
--Periodicals.
--Social and moral questions.
--Societies and clubs.
    sa Associated Country Women of the
      World.
      Women's institutes.
      International Cooperative
       Women's Guild.
      American Farm Bureau Federa-
       tion. Associated Women.
    xx Clubs.
-- --Directories.
-- --Periodicals.
    sa Woman. Year-books.
--Wages.   See Wages. Women.
--Year-books.

Woman power.   See Labor supply.

Womanpower.   See Labor supply.

Womb.   See Uterus.

Women.   See Woman.

Women and the World War.   See World War,
   1939-1945. Women's work.

Women as butchers.
    xx Butchers.

Women as farmers.   See Women in agriculture.

Women as scientists.

Women in agriculture.
    sa Women in horticulture.
      Gt. Brit. Women's land army.
      U.S. Women's land army.
      Women in dairy farming.
      Women in poultry farming.
    xx Woman. Employment.
--Congresses.
    xx Woman. Congresses.
--Periodicals.
    xx Agriculture. Periodicals.
--Societies.

Women in dairy farming.
    xx Women in agriculture.

Women in defense.   See World War,
   1939-1945. Women's work.

Women in domestic economy.   See Home
   economics as an occupation.

Women in food processing plants.
    xx Woman. Employment.

Women in forestry.

Women in home economics.   See Home
   economics as an occupation.

Women in horticulture.
    sa Women in agriculture.

Women in industry.   See Woman. Employment.

Women in poultry farming.
    xx Women in agriculture.

Women in rural communities.
    sa Women's institutes.
      Country life.
      Children in rural communities.
--Bibliography.
    xx Woman. Bibliography.

Women in the Southern States.

Women in urban communities.
    xx Cities and towns.

Women in war.   See World War, 1939-1945.
   Women's work.

Women's clubs.   See Woman. Societies and
    clubs.

Women's Co-operative Guild.

Women's institutes.
        sa Country life.
           Women in rural communities.
           Woman. Societies and clubs.

Women's land army.   See Gt. Brit. Women's
    land army; U.S. Women's land army.

Wood.
        sa Lumber.
           Timber.
           Timber physics//
           Specific subjects, e.g., Pinus
           echinata (Wood); Thuya
           plicata (Wood)

Wood, Acetylated.   See Acetylated wood.

Wood.
    --Analysis.
        sa Wood. Chemistry.
    --Anatomy.   See Wood structure.
    --Bibliography.
        sa Subdivision Bibliography under:
           Plywood.
           Balsa.
           Wood-using industries.
           Wood. By-products.
           Wood preservation.
           Wood. Seasoning.
           Wood. Diseases.
           Wood. Chemistry.
           Wood. Properties and uses.
    --Bleaching.
         x Wood bleaching.
        xx Bleaching.
    --Bleeding.
         x Bleeding of wood.
           Wood bleeding.
    --By-products.
        sa Sulphite liquor.
           Wood flour.
           Excelsior.
           Shavings.
           Sawdust.
           Subdivision By-products under:
           Sawmills.

Wood (Continued)
    --By-products.
         x Forest by-products.
           Forestry. By-products.
           Forest industries. By-products.
           Wood. Utilization.
        xx Forestry. Utilization.
           Wood-using industries.
           Waste products.
           Wood waste.
           Wood sugar.
           Sawmills. By-products.
    -- --Bibliography.
        xx Wood. Bibliography.
    -- --Dictionaries.
        xx Wood. Dictionaries.

Wood, Carbohydrates in.
        xx Carbohydrates.

Wood.
    --Chemical treatments.
    --Chemical utilization.
        sa Wood waste. Chemical utiliza-
           tion.
           Compressed wood.
           Plastic materials, Laminated.
           Heat-stabilized wood.
         x Chemical utilization of wood.
        xx Wood waste. Chemical utiliza-
           tion.
           Waste products.
    --Chemistry.
        sa Forest chemistry.
           Wood distillation.
           Wood saccharification.
           Lignin.
           Delignification.
         x Wood. Analysis.
        xx Wood technology.
    -- --Bibliography.
    --Cleaning.
         x Wood cleaning.
    --Color.   See Color of wood.
    --Combustibility.

Wood, Compressed.   See Compressed wood.

Wood.
    --Decay.   See Wood decay.

Wood (Continued)
--Identification.
    sa Trees. Identification.
    x Identification of timber.
    Timber. Identification.

Wood, Improved. See Wood, Modified.

Wood.
--Injuries.
    sa Wood. Defects.
    x Wood. Defects.
    ·Wood injuries.
    xx Trees. Injuries.

Wood, Laminated. See Laminated wood.

Wood.
--Marketing. See Forest products.
    Marketing.
--Mechanical properties. See Wood.
    Properties and uses.
--Microbiology.

Wood, Modified.
    sa Compressed wood.
    Laminated wood.
    Plywood.
    x Composite wood.
    Improved wood.
    Wood, Improved.
--Periodicals.

Wood.
--Moisture content.
    x Lumber. Moisture content.
    xx Moisture.
--Nomenclature.
    sa Subdivision Nomenclature under:
    Tropical woods.
    xx Nomenclature.
--Painting.
    xx Painting, Industrial.
--Penetration of liquids. See Wood.
    Permeability.
--Periodicals.
    sa Subdivision Periodicals under:
    Wood. Chemistry.
    Wood technology//
--Permeability.
    xx Wood preservation.
    Permeability.

Wood (Continued)
--Pests.
    sa Hellgrammite.
    Wood. Fungi.
    Powder-post beetle.
    Polyporus gilvus.
    Cerambycidae.
    Wood-boring insects.
    Subdivision Pests under:
    Mesquite.
    Trees.
    Chestnut wood.
    x Wood destroying insects.
--Physical properties. See Wood.
    Properties and uses.
--Physics. See Timber physics.
--Plasticity.
    xx Plasticity.
--Preservation. See Wood preservation.
--Prices. See Lumber. Prices.
--Properties and uses.
    sa Wood. Weight.
    Wood as building material.
    Subdivision Properties and
    uses under: Tropical
    woods.
    x Wood. Mechanical properties.
    Wood. Physical properties.--
    Wood properties.
    Wood utilization.
    xx Strength of materials.
    Forestry. Utilization.
    Wood technology.
-- --Bibliography.
    xx Wood. Bibliography.
-- --Congresses.
-- --History.
-- --Periodicals.
-- --Research.

Wood, Pulverized. See Wood flour.

Wood.
--Research. See Forest products.
    Research.
--Saccharification. See Wood
    saccharification.
--Seasoning. See Lumber. Drying.
--Shrinkage.
    sa Collapse of timber.
    Checking in wood.
    Balsa. Shrinkage.
    x Shrinkage of wood.
    Wood shrinkage.
    xx Wood. Seasoning.

Wood, Soft.   See Soft woods.

Wood.
--Specific gravity.
--Stabilization.
    sa Acetylated wood.
       Heat-stabilized wood.
    x Wood stabilization.
--Storage.
    sa Lumber sheds.
       Lumber. Piling.
--Structure.   See Wood structure.
--Substitutes.
    sa Subdivision Substitutes under:
        Chamaecyparis lawsoniana.
    x Wood substitutes.
--Technology.   See Wood technology.
--Terminology.
--Testing.
    sa Subdivision Testing under:
        Bamboo.
        Liquidambar styraciflua.
        Yellow birch//
        Timber physics.
--Utilization.   See Forestry. Utiliza-
    tion; Wood. Properties and uses;
    Wood. By-products; Lumber. Utiliza-
    tion.
--Utilization tables.
    sa Subdivision Utilization tables
        under: Spruce.
        Pine.
        Oak.
        Maple.
        Ash (Wood)
        Fir.
        Cypress.
        Cedar.
    x Assortment tables.
    xx Volume and yield tables.
       Forest mensuration.
       Logs. Grading and standardiza-
         tion.
       Lumber. Grading and standardi-
         zation.
--Waste.   See Wood waste.
--Weight.
    x Lumber. Weight.
       Lumber weight.
       Wood weight.
    xx Weights and measures.
--Yearbooks.

Wood alcohol.
    sa Wood distillation.
    x Alcohol, Wood.
       Alcohol, Methyl.
       Methanol.
    xx Alcohol.

Wood-apple.   See Feronia limonia.

Wood as a substitute material.
    xx Substitute products.

Wood as airplane material.
    x Aircraft lumber.
       Aircraft wood.
       Airplane wood.
       Timbers for airplanes.
       Wood for airplanes.
       Wood in airplane construction.
       Airplane lumber.
       Aircraft timber.
       Airplane timber.
    xx Wood as building material.
       Airplanes. Materials.
--Bibliography.

Wood as building material.
    sa Wood as airplane material.
       Roofing, Wooden.
       Pile timbers.
       Lumber, Reinforced.
    x Girders, Wooden.
       Timber as building material.
       Lumber as engineering ma-
        terial.
       Structural timbers.
       Wood as engineering material.
       Building timbers.
       Building woods.
       Timber, Building.
       Lumber as building material.
    xx Building materials.
       Wood. Properties and uses.
       Building, Wooden.
--Bibliography.
--Periodicals.

Wood as engineering material.   See
    Wood as building material.

Wood as feeding stuff.
    xx Feeding stuffs.

Wood as fuel.
    sa Wood gas as motor fuel.
    x Forest fuels.
      Wood for fuel.
--Congresses.
--Marketing.
    x Timber, Marketing.
--Prices.
    xx Prices.
--Statistics.

Wood as raw material. See Forest
   products. Utilization.

Wood-ash stones, Fused.
    x Fused wood-ash stones.

Wood ashes.
    xx Ashes.
      Potash.

Wood bending.
    xx Woodwork.

Wood bleaching. See Wood. Bleaching.

Wood bleeding. See Wood. Bleeding.

Wood boats. See Ships, Wooden.

Wood-boring insects.
    sa Anobium.
      Hylotrupes.
      Glycobius speciosus.
      Podosesia.
      Monochamus scutellatus.
    xx Wood. Pests.

Wood-carving.
    sa Marquetry.
    xx Carving (Art industries)
      Decoration and ornament.
      Manual training.
      Woodwork.
      Arts and crafts movement.

Wood chemistry. See Wood. Chemistry.

Wood chips.

Wood cleaning. See Wood. Cleaning.

Wood conservation. See Wood preservation.

Wood container industry.

Wood containers.
    sa Barrels.
      Boxes.
      Crates.
    x Wooden containers.
      Wood in packaging.
    xx Crates.
      Containers.

Wood converting machinery.

Wood Co., Ohio.
--Agriculture.
-- --Periodicals.

Wood Co., Wis.
--Soils.
    sa Subdivision Wisconsin. Wood
      Co. under: Soil-surveys.

Wood-creosote oil.

Wood cutting. See Timber. Felling.

Wood decay.
    sa Wood. Fungi.
      Wood. Decay resistance.
      Trees. Decay.
    x Fungus deterioration of
      wood.
      Decay of wood.
      Wood. Decay.
    xx Wood. Deterioration.
      Trees. Decay.

Wood-decaying fungi. See Wood. Fungi.

Wood defects. See Wood. Defects.

Wood destroying fungi. See Wood. Fungi.

Wood destroying insects. See Wood.
   Pests.

Wood deterioration. See Wood. Deterioration.

Wood distillation.
    sa Wood. Chemistry.
    x Hardwood distillation.
    xx Distillation.
--Bibliography.

Wood distillation (Continued)
--Periodicals.
      sa Subdivision Periodicals under:
        Wood. Chemistry.

Wood drying. See Lumber. Drying.

Wood-duck.

Wood durability. See Wood. Durability.

Wood engraving.

Wood feeding roach. See Cryptocercus
punctulatus.

Wood fiber.
    xx Fibers.

Wood finishing.
    x Finishing of wood.
      Furniture refinishing.
    xx Painting, Industrial.
      Stains and staining.
      Finishes and finishing.

Wood flour.
    x Woodflour.
      Wood, Pulverized.
      Pulverized wood.
    xx Wood. By-products.

Wood for airplanes. See Wood as airplane material.

Wood for fuel. See Wood as fuel.

Wood fungi. See Wood. Fungi.

Wood gas as motor fuel.
    xx Producer gas.
      Wood as fuel.
      Motor fuels.

Wood grain. See Grain in wood.

Wood-grouse. See Tetrao urogallus.

Wood in airplane construction. See Wood
as airplane material.

Wood in packaging. See Wood containers.

Wood industries. See Wood-using industries.

Wood injuries. See Wood. Injuries.

Wood-lice. See Oniscidae; Armadilli-
dium.

Wood-lots. (INDIRECT)
    x Farm woodlands.
      Farm wood-lots.
      Woodlots.
      Farm trees.
      Farm forestry.
    xx Forestry.
      Forest management.
      Farm management.
--Bibliography.
--Periodicals.
    xx Forestry. Periodicals.

Wood-louse. See Oniscidae.

Wood molasses. See Wood sugar molasses.

Wood oil.
    sa Linden oil.
      Tung oil and tung oil tree.
    xx Fats and oils.
--Bibliography.
    xx Fats and oils. Bibliography.

Wood oil, Chinese. See Tung oil and
tung oil tree.

Wood oil tree, Chinese. See Tung oil
and tung oil tree.

Wood paving. See Pavements, Wooden.

Wood physics. See Timber physics.

Wood preservation.
    sa Wood. Seasoning.
      Wood. Pests.
      Creosoted timber.
      Wood. Permeability.
      Wood preservatives.
    x Wood conservation.
      Poles. Preservation.
      Timber. Preservation.
      Treated wood.
    xx Wood preservatives.
--Bibliography.
    xx Wood. Bibliography.
--Congresses.
--Implements and machinery.
--Periodicals.

Wood preservation (Continued)
--Research.
--Societies.
--Statistics.
--Study and teaching.

Wood preservatives.
      sa Wood preservation.
      Carbolineum.
      Permatol.
      Pentachlorophenol solutions.
      Naphthenic acids.
      Benzene hexachloride.
      xx Wood preservation.
--Bibliography.
--Directories.
--Periodicals.
--Testing.

Wood product industries.   See Wood-using
   industries.

Wood products.   See Forest products;
   Wood technology.

Wood properties.   See Wood. Properties
   and uses.

Wood-pulp.
      This subject to be used for
      mechanically ground or chemi-
      cally digested wood used in the
      manufacture of paper and allied
      products.
      sa Pulp board.
      Bamboo pulp.
      Pulpwood.
      x Pulp, Wood.
      xx Forest products.
      Paper making and trade.
      Pulpwood.
      Cellulose.
--Analysis.
--Bibliography.
-- --Periodicals.
--Bleaching.
      xx Bleaching.
--Congresses.
--Cost of production.
      xx Cost of production.
--Directories.
--Evaluation.
      xx Wood-pulp. Testing.
--Moisture content.
      xx Moisture content.

Wood-pulp (Continued)
--Periodicals.
--Prices.
--Research.
--Societies.
--Statistics.
--Testing.
      sa Wood-pulp. Evaluation.

Wood-pulp industry.
--Research.

Wood-rats.   See Neotoma.

Wood research.   See Forest products.
   Research.

Wood residues.   See Wood waste.

Wood River Valley, Idaho.
      sa Subdivision Idaho. Wood River
         Valley under: Irrigation.

Wood-rotting fungi.   See Wood. Fungi.

Wood saccharification.
      sa Wood sugar.
      x Wood. Saccharification.
      xx Wood. Chemistry.
      Saccharification.

Wood seasoning.   See Lumber. Drying.

Wood sections.
      xx Wood structure.

Wood shrinkage.   See Wood. Shrinkage.

Wood stabilization.   See Wood. Stabilization.

Wood staining fungi.
      sa Stain in lumber.
      Ceratostomellae.
      xx Stain in lumber.

Wood stoves.   See Stoves, Wood.

Wood structure.
      sa Wood sections.
      Wood. Defects.
      x Wood. Anatomy.
      Wood. Structure.
      xx Wood technology.

Wood structure (Building)   See Building, Wooden.

Wood substitutes.   See Wood. Substitutes.

Wood sugar.
  sa Wood. By-products.
  xx Wood saccharification.
--Analysis and testing.
  xx Sugar. Analysis and testing.
--Fermentation.
  xx Fermentation.

Wood sugar molasses.
  x Wood molasses.
  xx Molasses.

Wood sugar molasses as feeding stuff.

Wood sugar yeast.
  xx Yeast.

Wood supply.
  sa Lumber supply.
  xx Lumber supply.

Wood tanks.   See Tanks, Wood.

Wood-tar.
  sa Naval stores.

Wood technology.
  sa Timber physics.
    Wood. Chemistry.
    Wood. Properties and uses.
    Wood structure.
  x Wood products.
--Bibliography.
-- --Periodicals.
--Congresses.
--Periodicals.
  xx Wood. Periodicals.
--Research.
--Terminology.
--Year-books.

Wood-testing.   See Wood. Testing.

Wood tick.   See Dermacentor occidentalis.

Wood turning.   See Turning.

Wood turpentine.

Wood-using industries.   (DIRECT)
  sa Turning.
    Wood distillation.
    Woodwork.
    Wood. By-products.
  x Milling (of wood)
    Wood industries.
    Wood product industries.
  xx Lumbering.
    Forest industries.
--Abstracts.
--Accidents.
--Accounting.
  xx Accounting.
--Bibliography.
  sa Wood-using industries [geo-
    graphic subdivision] Bib-
    liography, e.g., Wood-
    using industries. U.S. Bib-
    liography.
  xx Wood. Bibliography.
--Congresses.
--Dictionaries.
--Directories.
  sa Subdivision Directories under
    Wood-using industries [geo-
    graphic subdivision] e.g.,
    Wood-using industries.
    Austria. Directories.
--Diseases and hygiene.
  xx Occupations. Diseases and
    hygiene.
--Legislation.
  sa Subdivision Legislation under
    Wood-using industries [geo-
    graphic subdivision] e.g.,
    Wood-using industries.
    Germany. Legislation.
--Periodicals.
--Research.
--Safety measures.
--Statistics.
  sa Wood-using industries [geo-
    graphic subdivision] Sta-
    tistics, e.g., Wood-using
    industries. Tennessee
    Valley. Statistics.
--Work management.
  xx Work management.
--Year-books.

Wood utilization.   See Forestry. Utili-
    zation; Wood-using industries; Wood.
    Properties and uses.

Wood waste.
        sa Wood. By-products.
        x Wood residues.
          Woody residues.
          Wood. Waste.
          Woodwaste.
          Forest waste.
          Lumber waste.
          Waste wood.
        xx Waste products.
  --Chemical utilization.
        sa Subdivision Chemical utiliza-
            tion under: Wood.
        xx Wood. Chemical utilization.
  --Congresses.

Wood waste mulches.
        sa Sawdust mulches.
        xx Mulch and mulches.
  --Research.

Wood weight. See Wood. Weight.

Wood wool.
        sa Excelsior.

Wood work. See Woodwork.

Wood working. See Woodwork.

Woodbine farm.

Woodbury Co., Iowa.
        xx Iowa.

Woodchuck.
        sa Marmota.

Woodcock.
        x Philohela minor.

Wooden beams. See Girders.

Wooden boats. See Ships, Wooden.

Wooden cases. See Crates.

Wooden containers. See Wood containers.

Wooden pavements. See Pavements, Wooden.

Wooden roofing. See Roofing, Wooden.

Wooden ships. See Ships, Wooden.

Wooden stair building. See Stair
  building.

Wooden vessels. See Ships, Wooden.

Woodflour. See Wood flour.

Woodford, Eng.
  --Botany.

Woodland management. See Forest
  management; Wood-lots.

Woodlark Island.
  --Zoology.

Woodlot. See Wood-lots.

Woodpeckers.
        sa Dryobates.
          Centurus.
          California woodpecker.
          Ivory billed woodpecker.

Woods Co., Okla.
  --Soils.
        sa Subdivision Oklahoma. Woods
            Co. under: Soil-surveys.

Woods Hole, Mass.
  --Zoology.

Woodson Co., Kan.
  --Land.
        sa Subdivision Kansas. Woodson
            Co. under: Land utiliza-
            tion.
  --Soils.
        sa Subdivision Kansas. Woodson
            Co. under: Soil-surveys.
          Soil conservation surveys.

Woodward Co., Okla.
  --Soils.
        sa Subdivision Oklahoma.
            Woodward Co. under:
            Soil-surveys.

Woodwardia radicans.

Woodwaste. See Wood waste.

Woodwork.
      sa Lathes.
         Turning.
         Cabinet-work.
         Carpentry.
         Wood-carving.
         Joinery.
         Aircraft woodwork.
         Wood bending.
         Marquetry.
      xx Carpentry.
         Wood-using industries.
--Bibliography.
--Directories.
--Handbooks, manuals, etc.

Woodwork, Interior.   See Interior
   woodwork.

Woodwork.
--Periodicals.
      xx Wood. Periodicals.

Woodwork (Manual training)
      xx Manual training.

Woodworkers.

Woodworking machinery.
      sa Planing-machines.
         Sanding-machines.
      x Woodworking tools.
--Directories.
--Periodicals.
--Terminology.

Woodworking tools.   See Woodworking
   machinery.

Woodworthia.
      xx Araucarinae.

Woodworthia arizonica.

Woody plants.   See Climbing plants;
   Shrubs; Trees.

Woody residues.   See Wood waste.

Wool.
      sa Angora rabbit wool.
         Wool trade and industry.
         Woolen and worsted manufacture.
         Woolen fabrics.
         Yarn.

Wool (Continued)
      x Wool fibers.
         Wool. Fibers.
      xx Arts, Useful.
         Animal products. Prices.
--Analysis.

Wool, Artificial.
      x Artificial wool.
      xx Textile fibers, Synthetic.
         Textile industry and fabrics,
         Synthetic.
         Textile industry and fabrics.
         Synthetic products.

Wool.
--Baling.   See Wool baling.
--Bibliography.
      sa Subdivision Bibliography
         under: Wool trade and
         industry.
         Wool. Grading and
         standardization.
         Wool. Marketing.
         Wool. Prices.
--By-products.
      sa Wool-fat.
--Chemistry.
--Bibliography.
--Classification.   See Wool. Grading
   and standardization.
--Cleaning.   See Wool scouring.
--Color.
      x Color of wool.
      xx Color.
--Combing.   See Wool-combing.
--Competitive commodities.
--Cost of production.
      sa Woolen and worsted manu-
         facture. Costs.
--Dictionaries.
--Disinfection.
--Dyeing.
      x Dyes and dyeing. Wool.

Wool, Effect of alkalies on.   See
   Alkalies. Effect on wool.

Wool.
--Effect of humidity.   See Humidity.
   Effect on wool.
--Effect of sulphur.   See Sulphur.
   Effect on wool.
--Fibers.   See Wool.

Wool (Continued)
--Financing.
    xx Wool financing.
--Futures. See Wool trade and industry.
    Futures.
--Grading and standardization.
    x Wool. Classification.
      Wool classing.
-- --Bibliography.
    xx Wool. Bibliography.
--Legislation.
    sa Agricultural adjustment act,
       1933. Licenses (Wool)
--Lubrication.
    x Wool oiling.
--Manufacture. See Woolen and worsted
    manufacture.
--Marketing.
    xx Farm produce. Marketing.
-- --Bibliography.
    xx Marketing. Bibliography.
      Wool. Bibliography.
-- --Congresses.
    xx Marketing of farm produce.
      Congresses.
--Marketing, Cooperative.
-- --Periodicals.
    xx Marketing, Cooperative.
      Periodicals.
      Wool. Periodicals.
      Wool trade and industry.
      Periodicals.
-- --Societies.
--Marketing.
-- --Legislation.
    sa British wool marketing scheme,
      1950.
-- --Periodicals.
-- --Research.
-- --Statistics.
-- --Study and teaching. See Wool trade
    and industry. Study and teaching.
--Measuring.
    xx Fibers. Measuring.
--Packing.
    sa Wool baling.
    xx Packing for shipment.
--Periodicals.
    sa Subdivision Periodicals under:
      Yarn.
      Wool. Marketing, Coopera-
        tive.
--Pests.
--Physics.
--Pictorial works.

Wool (Continued)
--Prices.
-- --Bibliography.
    xx Wool. Bibliography.
      Prices. Bibliography.
-- --Fixing.
    xx Prices. Fixing.
-- --Subsidies.
    sa National wool act, 1954.
    xx Price subsidies.'

Wool, Proteins in.
    x Wool protein.
    xx Proteins.

Wool.
--Quality.
    xx Farm produce. Quality.

Wool, Reclaimed.
    x Recovered wool.
      Reclaimed wool.
      Wool, Recovered.
      Shoddy.
      Mungo.
    xx Fibers, Reclaimed.

Wool, Recovered. See Wool, Reclaimed.

Wool.
--Research.
    x Wool research.
-- --Bibliography.
-- --Congresses.
-- --Societies.
--Samples. See Wool samples.
--Scouring. See Wool scouring.
--Shrinkage.
    sa Woolen fabrics, Shrink-
      resistant.
    x Wool shrinkage.
    xx Shrinkage.
--Societies.
    x Wool trade and industry.
      Societies.
-- --Directories.
--Spinning. See Wool spinning.
--Statistics.
    sa Subdivision Statistics under:
      Wool trade and industry.
    xx Animal products. Statistics.
      Fibers. Statistics.
      Wool trade and industry.
      Statistics.
--Storage.

Wool (Continued)
--Tables, etc.
--Tariff.
    sa Subdivision Tariff under:
        Woolen fabrics.
    xx Woolen fabrics. Tariff.
--Technology. See Wool technology.
--Terminology.
--Testing.
    sa Subdivision Testing under:
        Angora rabbit wool.
--Trade and industry. See Wool trade
    and industry.
--Transportation.
    sa Railroads. Rates. Wool.
--Weight.
    xx Weights and measures.

Wool, Wood. See Wood wool.

Wool alcohols. See Wool wax alcohols.

Wool auctions. See Auctions.

Wool baling.
    x Wool. Baling.
    xx Wool. Packing.

Wool classing. See Wool. Grading and
standardization.

Wool cleaning. See Wool scouring.

Wool-combing.

Wool fabrics. See Woolen fabrics.

Wool-fat.
    sa Wool wax alcohols.
    x Wool wax.
      Wool oil.
      Wool grease.
      Lanolin.
      Lanoline.
    xx Waxes.
      Wool. By-products.
      Fats and oil.
      Waste products.

Wool felt. See Felt.

Wool fibers. See Wool.

Wool financing.
    sa Wool. Financing.

Wool futures. See Wool trade and
industry. Futures.

Wool grease. See Wool fat.

Wool industry and trade. See Wool
trade and industry.

Wool maggot. See Phormia regina.

Wool oil. See Wool-fat.

Wool oiling. See Wool. Lubrication.

Wool products labeling act, 1939.

Wool protein. See Wool, Proteins in.

Wool purchase program.
    xx Purchase programs (Government)

Wool research. See Wool. Research.

Wool samples.
    x Wool. Samples.

Wool scouring.
    x Wool. Scouring.
      Wool. Cleaning.
      Wool cleaning.

Wool shrinkage. See Wool. Shrinkage.

Wool spinning.
    x Wool. Spinning.
    xx Spinning.
--History.

Wool standards. See Wool. Grading and
standardization.

Wool substitutes.
    xx Substitute products.

Wool technology.
    x Wool. Technology.
    xx Technology.

Wool top futures. See Wool trade and
industry. Futures.

Wool trade and industry. (DIRECT)
    x Sheep industry.
      Sheep trade.
--Accounting.

Wool trade and industry (Continued)
--Bibliography.
    sa Wool trade and industry ₍geo-
       graphic subdivision₎ Bib-
       liography., e.g., Wool trade
       and industry. Africa, South.
       Bibliography.
--Congresses.
--Directories.
    sa Wool trade and industry ₍geo-
       grapic subdivision₎ Direc-
       tories, e.g., Wool trade
       and industry. U.S. Direc-
       tories.
--Futures.
    xx Future trading.
-- --Periodicals.
    xx Wool trade and industry.
       Periodicals.
       Future trading. Periodicals.
--History.
--Laboratory manuals.
    x Wool technology. Laboratory
       manuals.
--Periodicals.
    sa Subdivision Periodicals under:
       Wool trade and industry.
       Futures.
       Wool. Marketing, Coopera-
       tive.
--Research.
--Societies. See Wool. Societies.
--Statistics.
    sa Subdivision Statistics under:
       Wool.
       Subdivision Statistics under
       Wool trade and industry
       ₍geographic subdivision₎
       e.g., Wool trade and in-
       dustry. Africa, South.
       Statistics.
    xx Wool. Statistics.
--Study and teaching.
--Waste.

Wool wax. See Wool-fat.

Wool wax alcohols.
    x Wool alcohols.
    xx Alcohols.
       Wool fat.
       Waxes.

Wool yarn.
    sa Worsted.
    x Woolen yarn.
--Prices.

Woolen and worsted fabrics. See
    Woolen fabrics; Worsted.

Woolen and worsted manufacture. (DI-
    RECT)
    sa Wool trade and industry.
       Woolen and worsted spinning.
    x Shoddy manufacture.
       Mungo manufacture.
--Accounting.
--Bibliography.
--Costs.
--Employees.
    xx Textile workers.
       Labor and laboring classes.
--Periodicals.
--Statistics.
    xx Textile industry and fabrics.
       Statistics.

Woolen and worsted spinning.

Woolen fabrics.
    sa Woolen and worsted manu-
       facture.
       Felt.
       Worsted.
    x Flannel.
--Dictionaries.
--Labels.
    xx Textile industry and fabrics.
       Labels.
--Periodicals.
--Prices.
    sa Subdivision Prices under:
       Mohair.
    xx Prices.
--Research.

Woolen fabrics, Shrink-resistant.
    x Shrink-resistant woolen
       fabrics.
    xx Textile industry and fabrics,
       Shrink-resistant.
       Wool. Shrinkage.

Woolen fabrics.
--Statistics.
    sa Subdivision Statistics under:
       Mohair.

Woolen fabrics (Continued)
--Tariff.
    sa Subdivision Tariff under:
        Wool.
    xx Wool. Tariff.
--Testing.

Woolen yarn.   See Wool yarn.

Woolly aphis.   See Eriosoma lanigerum.

Woolly-bear caterpillars.   See Arctiidae.

Woolly fingergrass.   See Panicum eriantha
   stolonifera.

Woolly maple-leaf scale.   See Phena-
   coccus acericola.

Woolly pear aphis.   See Eriosoma
   pyricola.

Woolly-pod mildweed.   See Asclepias
   eriocarpa.

Woolly white fly.   See Aleurothrixus
   howardi.

Worcester, Mass.
--Altitudes.
--Botany.
--Milk trade.
   xx Massachusetts. Milk trade.
--Ornithology.
--Parks.
--Water-supply.
   xx Massachusetts. Water-supply.

Worcester Co., Md.
   sa Subdivision Maryland. Worcester
       Co. under: County surveys.
       Land utilization.
--Agriculture.
   sa Subdivision Maryland. Worcester
       Co. under: Farm management
       surveys.
       Land utilization.
   xx Maryland. Agriculture.
--Botany.
--Land.
   sa Subdivision Maryland. Worcester
       Co. under: Land utilization.

Worcester Co., Md. (Continued)
--Soils.
   sa Subdivision Maryland. Worcester
       Co. under: Soil-surveys.

Worcester Co., Mass.
   sa Subdivision Worcester Co.,
       Mass. under: Planning,
       County.
--Agriculture.
   sa Subdivision Massachusetts.
       Worcester Co. under:
       War and agriculture
       (1939-1945)
--Botany.

Worcesteria grata.

Worcestershire, Eng.
--Agriculture.
-- --History.
   xx England. Agriculture. History.
--Botany.
   sa Subdivision England.
       Worcestershire under:
       Algae.
--Ornithology.
--Pomology.

Word division.   See Syllabication.

Work, Therapeutic effect of.   See
   Occupational therapy.

Work camps.
   sa Civilian Conservation Corps.

Work horses.   See Horses, Draft; Horses
   in agriculture; Horses in lumbering.

Work management.
   sa Subdivision Work management
       under: Lumbering.
       Threshing.
       Bakers and bakeries.
       Traction-engines. Main-
       tenance and repair.
       Sawmills.
       Wood-using industries.
       Meat industry and trade.
   xx Labor and laboring classes.
       Efficiency, Industrial.
--Congresses.

Work measurement.
--Bibliography.

Work standards.
    sa Standards of performance.
      Efficiency rating.
    xx Efficiency in farming.
      Efficiency, Industrial.
      Employment management.
--Tables and ready-reckoners.

Working force.   See Labor supply.

Working-men's gardens.
    sa Gardens, Employees'.
    xx Community gardens.

Working-men's insurance.   See Insurance,
   Social.

Workingmen's livestock associations.
    x Employees' livestock associa-
      tions.
      Live stock associations.

Working plans (Forestry)   See Forestry.
   Working plans.

Workmen's compensation.   See Employers'
   liability.

Works financing act of 1939.
    xx U.S. Public works.

Workshop receipts.   See Receipts.

Workshops, Educational.   See Educational
   workshops.

Workshops, Farm.   See Farm workshops.

World affairs.   See World politics.

World agricultural census, 1930.

World agricultural census, 1940.

World agricultural census, 1950.

World agricultural census, 1960.

World census of agriculture.   See World
   agricultural census.

World court.   See Hague. Permanent
   court of international justice.

World Economic Conference, Geneva, 1927.
   See International Economic Conference,
   Geneva, 1927.

World federation.   See International
   organization.

World Health Day.

World organization.   See International
   organization.

World planning.   See Planning, World.

World politics.
    Here are entered historical
    accounts of international
    intercourse. Theoretical
    works are entered under
    International relations.
    Works dealing with foreign
    relations from the point of
    view of an individual country
    are entered under the name of
    the country with the subdi-
    vision Foreign relations.
    sa Geopolitics.
      United Nations.
      European war, 1914-1918.
      World War, 1939-1945.
      International organization.
    x World affairs.
    xx International organization.
      International relations.
--Bibliography.
--Periodicals.

World textile conference, Washington,
   D.C., 1937.   See Tripartite
   technical textile conference,
   Washington, D.C., 1937.

World War, 1914-1918.   See European
   war, 1914-1918.

World War, 1939-1945.   (INDIRECT)
    sa European war, 1914-1918.
      War and agriculture (1939-
      1945)
      Defenses.

World War, 1939-1945 (Continued)
   sa United Nations.
     War and forestry (1939-1945)
     Subdivision World War, 1939-
      1945 under: Subject head-
      ings.
   x European war, 1939-1945.
     World War, Second.
   xx Libraries and war.
     War.
     European war, 1914-1918.
--Addresses, sermons, etc.
--Atrocities.
   xx Atrocities.
--Bibliography.
   sa Subdivision Bibliography under:
     World War, 1939-1945. Food
      question.
     World War, 1939-1945.
      Children.
     World War, 1939-1945.
      Finance.
     Subdivision Bibliography under
     World War, 1939-1945 ₍geo-
     graphic subdivision₎ e.g.,
     World War, 1939-1945. U.S.
     Bibliography.
--Blockades.
--Boys' work.
   sa Victory farm volunteers.
   xx Boys in agriculture.
--Causes.
--Censorship.   (INDIRECT)
   xx Censorship.
--Chemistry.
--Children.
   x Children and the war.
     School children in war.
   xx Children.
     Children in war.
-- --Bibliography.
   xx Children. Bibliography.
     World War, 1939-1945. Bib-
     liography.
--Chronology.
--Civilian relief.   (INDIRECT)
   sa Reconstruction (1939-)
     Reconstruction (1939- ·)
     Food relief.
     World War, 1939-1945. Medical
     and sanitary affairs.
     World War, 1939-1945. Refugees.
   x Civilian relief.
     World War, 1939-1945. Relief
     work.

World War, 1939-1945 (Continued)
   xx Reconstruction (1939-)
     World War, 1939-1945. Food
     question.
     World War, 1939-1945. Medi-
     cal and sanitary affairs.
     World War, 1939-1945.
     Refugees.
     Economic assistance.
-- --Bibliography.
--Civilian.service.
   sa Civilian defense.
   xx Civilian defense.
--Commerce.   See World War, 1939-1945.
   Economic aspects.
--Confiscations and contributions.
   (INDIRECT)
--Congresses, conferences, etc.
--Damage to property.   See World War,
   1939-1945. Destruction and
   pillage.
--Destruction and pillage.   (IN-
   DIRECT)
   x World War, 1939-1945. Damage
     to property.
     World War,·1939-1945. Pillage.
--Diplomatic history.
--Displaced persons.
   x Displaced persons (World
     War, 1939-1945)
   xx Repatriation.
     World War, 1939-1945.
     Refugees.
     Population transfers.
--Documents, etc., sources.·
   x World War, 1939-1945.
     Sources.
--Economic aspects.   (INDIRECT)
   When subdivided geographically,
   indicate see also ref. from
   name of place with subdivision: Economic conditions.
   sa Subdivision Economic aspects
     under: European war,
     . 1914-1918.
     World War, .1939-1945.
     Manpower. .·
     Rationing, Consumer..
     Reconstruction (1939-)
     Industrial reconversion. ·
-- --Bibliography.
   xx War. Bibliography.
     War. Economic aspects.
     Bibliography.

World War, 1939-1945 (Continued)
--Evacuation of civilians.
    x Civilian defense.
     Civilian evacuation.
     Evacuation of civilians.
--Fiction.
    xx Fiction.
--Fighting French.
    x Free French.
     Fighting French.
     De Gaulle movement.
     French volunteer force, 1940.
     World War, 1939-1945. French
      volunteer force.
--Finance.   (INDIRECT)
    sa Lend-lease operations (1941-
)
    xx War, Cost of.
     Debts, Public.
-- --Bibliography.
    xx Finance. Bibliography.
     World War, 1939-1945. Bib-
      liography.
--Food question.   (INDIRECT)
    sa Subdivision Food question
     under: European war, 1914-
     1918.
     Food for freedom program.
     Rationing. Food.
     Food. Protection from poison
      gas.
     World War, 1939-1945. Civilian
      relief.
    x Food production goals.
    xx War and food supply.
     Food supply.
     Food.
-- --Bibliography.
    xx Food. Bibliography.
     World War, 1939-1945. Bib-
      liography.
--French volunteer force. See World
    War, 1939-1945. Fighting French.
--Girls' work.
    sa Victory farm volunteers.
    xx Girls in agriculture.
--Hospitals, charities, etc.
    xx Charities.
     Hospitals.
--Influence and results.
--Jews.
    xx Jews.
--Labor. See World War, 1939-1945.
    Manpower.

World War, 1939-1945 (Continued)
--Law and legislation.
    x War legislation.
--Lend-lease shipments. See Lend-lease
    operations (1941-)
--Libraries.
--Literature and the war.
    xx War and literature.
--Manpower.   (DIRECT)
    Under this heading are entered
    works on both the military
    and economic aspects of man-
    power.
    x Man power.
     Manpower.
     World War, 1939-1945. Labor.
-- --Bibliography.
--Maps.
--Medical and sanitary affairs.
    sa World War, 1939-1945. Civilian
     relief.
    xx Entomology and war.
--Negroes.
    xx Negroes.
--Neutrality of Portugal. See Portugal.
    Neutrality.
--Occupied territories.
    For works dealing with enemy
    occupied territories collec-
    tively. For works on the
    occupation of a single country
    see under the name of the
    country, e.g., France. History.
    German occupation, 1940-
    xx Military occupation.
     World War, 1939-1945. Terri-
     torial questions.
--Peace.
    sa Reconstruction (1939-)
     Atlantic Declaration, Aug. 14,
     1941.
    xx Peace.
     Reconstruction (1939-)
--Periodicals.
--Personal narratives.
--Personal narratives, American.
    x Personal narratives.
--Personal narratives, English.
--Petroleum supply.
    xx Petroleum industry and trade.
--Pictorial works.
    xx Pictures.
--Pillage. See World War, 1939-1945.
    Destruction and pillage.

World War, 1939-1945 (Continued)
--Prisoners and prisons.
　　xx Prisoners of war.
--Propaganda.
　　sa Propaganda, German.
　　　　Propaganda, Italian.
　　xx Propaganda.
-- --Bibliography.
　　sa Subdivision Bibliography under:
　　　　Propaganda, German.
　　xx Propaganda. Bibliography.
--Public opinion.　　(INDIRECT)
　　xx Public opinion.
--Rationing.　　See Priorities, Industrial;
　　Rationing, Consumer.
--Reconstruction.　　See Reconstruction
　　(1939-　　)
--Recruiting, enlistment, etc.　　See U.S.
　　Army. Recruiting, enlistment, etc.
　　World War, 1939-1945.
--Refugees.
　　sa World War, 1939-1945. Civilian
　　　　relief.
　　　　World War, 1939-1945. Displaced
　　　　persons.
　　xx Refugees, Political.
--Relief work.　　See World War, 1939-1945.
　　Civilian relief.
--Reparations.
　　x Reparations.
--Sabotage.　　See Sabotage.
--Science.　　(INDIRECT)
　　xx War and science.
--Shipping.
　　xx Shipping.
--Sources.　　See World War, 1939-1945.
　　Documents, etc., sources.
--Supplies.
　　sa Lend-lease operations (1941-
　　　　1945)
　　　　Surplus war property.
--Territorial questions.　　(INDIRECT)
　　sa World War, 1939-1945. Occupied
　　　　territories.
　　　　Mandates.
--Transportation.　　(INDIRECT)
　　When subdivided geographically,
　　　indicate see also ref. from
　　　name of place with subdivision
　　　Transportation.
　　xx War and transportation.
　　　　Transportation.
--Transportation, Farm.
　　xx Farm produce. Transportation.

World War, 1939-1945 (Continued)
--War work.
-- --Red cross.　　See Red Cross. U.S.
　　American National Red Cross.
· --Schools.
　　x Universities and colleges. War
　　　　work.
　　xx Schools.
　　　　Schools in war.
　　　　War and education.
--Women's work.　　(INDIRECT)
　　sa Gt. Brit. Women's land army.
　　　　U.S. Women's land army.
　　　　U.S. Women's Army Auxiliary
　　　　Corps.
　　x Women and the World War.
　　　　Women in defense.
　　　　Women in war.
　　xx Woman. Employment.
　　　　Women in agriculture.
-- --Bibliography.
　　xx Woman. Employment. Bib-
　　　　liography.

World War, First.　　See European war,
　　1914-1918.

World War, Second.　　See World War, 1939-
　　1945.

World's Columbian Exposition, Chicago,
　　1893.　　See Chicago. World's Columbian
　　Exposition, 1893.

World's Fair.　　See Chicago. World's
　　Columbian Exposition, 1893; New York
　　(City) World's Fair, 1939-1940.

Worm-lions.　　See Rhagionidae.

Worms.　　(INDIRECT)
　　sa Annelida.
　　　　Cestoidea.
　　　　Echinorhynchidae.
　　　　Nematoidea.
　　　　Nemertea.
　　　　Rotifera.
　　　　Trematoda.
　　　　Turbellaria.
　　　　Chaetognatha.
　　　　Gephyrea.
　　　　Dero.
　　　　Polychaeta.
　　　　Dendrocoela.
　　　　Entozoa.

Worms (Continued)
    sa Parasites.
      Amphineura.
      Pentastomida.
      Heterakis.
      Trichosomum.
      Phagocata gracilis.
      Simondsia paradoxa.
      Alciopidae.
      Tomopteridae.
      Sipunculidae.
      Aphroditidae.
      Amphinomidae.
      Leodicidae.
      Diplocardia.
      Dipleuchlanis.
      Epomidiostomum.
      Earthworms.
      Subdivision Worms under:
        Eye.
        Embryology.
        Nervous system.
  --Bibliography.

Worms, Effect of ammonium compounds on.
  See Ammonium compounds. Effect on
  worms.

Worms, Effect of electricity on.   See
  Electricity. Effect on worms.

Worms, Fossil.

Worms, Free-living.

Worms, Intestinal and parasitic.
    sa Ichthyobdellidae.
      Ascaridae.
      Nematoidea.
      Echinostomata.
      Brachycoelium.
      Taenia.
      Brachiocephalus.
      Coenurus cerebralis.
      Trematoda.
      Trichina.
      Cestoda.
      Pentastoma.
      Lamblia duodenalis.
    x Endoparasites.
      Entozoa.
  --Bibliography.
    xx Parasites. Bibliography.
  --Dictionaries.
  --Parasites.

Worms, Intestinal and parasitic (Con.)
  --Periodicals.
  --Research.
  --Societies.

Worms.
  --Nomenclature.
  --Parasites.
    sa Nematoda. Parasitic in worms.

Worms as carriers of contagion.

Worms Island.
  --Botany.

Wormseed oil.   See Chenopodium oil.

Wormsö Island.   See Worms Island.

Wormwood.
    x Flores cinae.
      Artemisia absinthium.
    xx Drugs.

Worry.
    xx Conduct on life.
      Mental physiology and hygiene.
      Nervous system. Diseases.

Worsted.
    sa Yarn.
      Woolen and worsted manu-
        facture.
      Woolen and worsted spinning.
      Wool yarn.
    xx Wool yarn.

Worth.
    Here are entered works on moral
      and esthetic values, etc. Eco-
      nomic works on the theory of
      value are entered under Value.
    xx Esthetics.
      Ethics.

Worth Co., Ga.
  --Agriculture.
    sa Subdivision Worth Co., Ga.
      under: Farm management.
  --Soils.
    sa Subdivision Georgia. Worth Co.
      under: Soil-surveys.

Wounds.

Wounds in plants.
    sa Tree wounds.
        Sweet potatoes. Wounds.
        Potatoes. Wounds.
    x Plant wounds.
       Pruning wounds.

Wrapping materials.

Wrecks.

Wren-tits.   See Chamaea.

Wrens.
    sa Troglodytes.
       Thryomanes.

Wright Co., Iowa.
  --Maps.
       xx Iowa. Maps.

Wright Co., Minn.
       xx Minnesota.

Wrightia tinctoria.
       xx Apocynaceae.

Writing.
  --Identification.
       x Identification of handwriting.

Writing (Authorship) See Authorship.

Writing materials.

Writing of letters. See Letter-writing.

Wrocław (City) See Breslau.

Wuchereria.
       xx Filariidae.

Würrttemberg.
  --Agriculture.
    sa Subdivision Württemberg under:
       Agricultural laborers.
       Agriculture. Economic
         aspects.
       Farm management.
       Agriculture, Cooperative.
       Farm produce. Cost of pro-
         duction.
       Sugar-beet.
       Types of farming.

Württemberg (Continued)
  --Agriculture.
    sa Subdivision Württemberg-
       Hohenzollern under: Agri-
         culture. Economic as-
         pects.
  -- --Education.
  --Botany.
    sa Subdivision Württemberg under:
       Mushrooms.
       Trees.
       Mosses.
  --Cattle.
  --Domestic animals.
  --Education.
  --Entomology.
       xx Germany. Entomology.
  --Forestry.
    sa Subdivision Württemberg under:
       Lumber.
  --Geology.
  --Horse.
    sa Subdivision Württemberg under:
       Horses. Breeding.
  --Meteorology.
  --Milk supply.
       xx Germany. Milk supply.
  --Natural history.
  --Paleobotany.
    sa Subdivision Paleobotany under:
       Stuttgart, Württemberg.
  --Paleontology.
  --Pomology.
  --Social conditions.
    sa Subdivision Württemberg under:
       Social surveys.
  --Soils.
    sa Subdivision Württemberg under:
       Peat.
       Soil-surveys.
  --Statistics.
  --Viticulture.
  --Zoology.

Würzburg.
  --Botany.

Wyandot Co., Ohio.
  --Botany.
  --Social conditions.
    sa Subdivision Ohio. Wyandot Co.
       under: Community life.

Wyandottes.
  --Periodicals.

Wych elm.   See Ulmus glabra var.

Wychwood, Lake Geneva, Wis.

Wye River.

Wye Valley.

Wyethia.

Wyethia amplexicaulis.
    x Mule ears.

Wyoming.
    sa Jackson Hole, Wyo.
       Goshen Co., Wyo.
  --Agriculture.
    sa Subdivision Wyoming under:
       Agricultural outlook.
       Rural surveys.
       War and agriculture (1939-
         1945)
       Agricultural policies and
         programs.
       Agriculture. Economic
         aspects.
       Ranges.
       Agricultural conservation
         program.
       Range conservation program.
  -- --Statistics.
    xx U.S. Agriculture. Statistics.
  --Altitudes.
  --Bibliography.
    xx U.S. Bibliography.
  --Botany.
    sa Subdivision Wyoming under:
       Forage plants.
       Trees.
  --Cattle trade.
  -- --History.
  --Census.
  --Description and travel.
  --Domestic animals.
    sa Wyoming. Horse.
  -- --Legislation.
  --Economic conditions.
    sa Subdivision Wyoming under:
       Rural surveys.
  --Education.
  --Entomology.
    sa Subdivision Wyoming under:
       Entomology, Economic.
       Grasshoppers.

Wyoming (Continued)
  --Forest reservations.
    sa Wyoming National Forest.
       Bighorn National Forest, Wyo.
       Shoshone National Forest,
         Wyo.//
  --Forestry.
  --Geology.
    sa Subdivision Geology under:
       Fremont Co.
       Bighorn Co.
       Jackson Hole//
       Subdivision Wyoming under:
       Water, Underground.
       Mines and mineral resources.
  -- --Bibliography.
  --History.
    sa Subdivision History under:
       Cattle trade.
  -- --Sources.
    sa Subdivision Wyoming under:
       Archives.
    xx U.S. History. Sources.
  --Horse.
    xx Wyoming. Domestic animals.
  --Industries.
  --Industries and resources.
  --Land.
    sa Subdivision Wyoming under:
       Land utilization.
    xx U.S. Land.
  --Legislative manuals.
  --Libraries.
  --Manufactures.
  --Maps.
  --Ornithology.
  --Paleobotany.
  --Paleontology.
  --Politics and government.
    sa Subdivision Wyoming under:
       County government.
    xx U.S. Politics and government.
  --Pomology.
  --Public lands.
  --Roads.
  --Soils.
    sa Subdivision Wyoming under:
       Soil-surveys.
       Soil erosion.
       Soil conservation.
       Subdivision Soils under names
         of counties, etc.
    xx U.S. Soils.
  --Statistics.

Wyoming (Continued)
--Water-supply.
    sa Subdivision Water-supply under:
        Bighorn Co., Wyo.
      Subdivision Wyoming under:
        Water, Underground.
        Irrigation.
        Water-rights.
--Zoology.

Wyoming Co., N.Y.
--Agriculture.
    sa Subdivision New York (State)
        Wyoming Co. under: Farms.
--Soils.
    sa Subdivision New York (State)
        Wyoming Co. under: Soil-
         surveys.

Wyoming Co., Pa.
--Agriculture.
--Forestry.
    sa Subdivision Pennsylvania.
        Wyoming Co. under: Forest
         surveys.
--Soils.
    sa Subdivision Pennsylvania.
        Wyoming Co. under: Soil-
         surveys.

Wyoming Development Co.

Wyoming National Forest.
    xx Forest reservations.
      Wyoming. Forest reservations.

Wythe Co., Va.
    sa Subdivision Wythe Co. under:
        County surveys. Virginia.
    xx Virginia.
--Botany.
--Economic conditions.
    sa Subdivision Wythe Co. under:
        Economic surveys. Virginia.
    xx Virginia. Economic conditions.
--Industries and resources.
    sa Industrial surveys. Virginia.
        Wythe Co.

Wytheville, Va.
--Economic conditions.
    sa Subdivision Wytheville under:
        Economic surveys. Virginia.

Wytheville, Va. (Continued)
--Industries and resources.
    sa Industrial surveys. Virginia.
        Wytheville.

X disease in cattle.
    x Hyperkeratosis in cattle.
      Proliferative stomatitis.
      Stomatitis, Proliferative.
      Bovine hyperkeratosis.
--Congresses.

XIT Ranch, Tex.

X-ray crystallography.   See Crystallog-
    raphy, X-ray.

X-ray microscope.
    x Microscope, X-ray.
    xx Microscope and microscopy.
      X-rays.

X-ray nitrocellulose films.
    x Nitrocellulose films.

X-ray photography.   See Radiography.

X-rays.
    sa Cathode rays.
      Radiography.
      Radiotherapy.
      Radiology.
      Vacuum-tubes.
      Diagnosis, Radioscopic.
      Gamma rays.
      Pyelography.
      X-ray microscope.
    x Roentgenology.
      Roentgen rays.
    xx Radiant heating.
--Bibliography.
--Diffraction.
    xx Diffraction.
--Effect on bacteria.
-- --Bibliography.
--Effect on plants.
    x Plants, Effect of X-rays on.
--Effect on seeds.
    x Seeds, Effect of X-rays on.
--Industrial applications.
    x X-rays in industry.
    xx Metallography.
      Radiography.
      Testing.
--Periodicals.

X-rays (Continued)
--Physiological effect.
--Therapeutic use.
      sa Radiotherapy.
      xx Physical therapy.

X-rays for control of insects.
      xx Entomology, Economic.

X-rays for control of plant diseases.

X-rays in industry. See X-rays. Industrial applications.

Xalapa, Mexico.
--Botany.

Xanthgramma.

Xanthium.
--Seed.
-- --Germination.

Xanthium spinosum.

Xanthodes.
      xx Noctuidae.

Xanthodes graellsi.

Xanthomonas albilineans. See Leaf scald of sugar-cane.

Xanthomonas malvacearum.
      x Pseudomonas malvacearum.
      Bacterium malvacearum.
      Phytomonas malvacearum.

Xanthomonas solanacearum. See Bacterium solanacearum.

Xanthone as an insecticide.
      xx Insecticides.

Xanthophyll.

Xanthopimpla.

Xanthoptera Ridingsii.

Xanthorrhoea and insects.

Xanthorrhoea resin. See Acaroid gum.

Xanthosoma sagittifolium. See Yautia.

Xanthostemon.
      xx Myrtaceae.

Xanthostemon verdugonianus.

Xanthozyleae.

Xenia.

Xenopsylla cheopis.
      x Oriental rat flea.
      Indian rat flea.

Xenopus laevis.
      x South African frog.
      South African clawed frog.
      xx Frogs.
--Bibliography.

Xerophilous plants. See Xerophytes.

Xerophytes.
      sa Desert flora.
      Drought-resistant plants.
      x Xerophilous plants.

Xerotherms. See Drought-resistant plants.

Xiphidium.
      xx Acridiidae.

Xiphidium fuscum.

Xiphocolaptes.

Xiphosura.

Xochinacaztli.

Xorididae.

Xoridini.

Xyela.

Xyelidae.
      sa Kaliosyphinga.
      Xyela.

Xylan.

Xylaria.

Xylariaceae.
    sa Xylaria.

Xyleborus.
    xx Scolytoidae.

Xyleborus affinis.

Xyleborus coffeae.

Xyleborus dispar.
    x Anisandrus dispar.

Xyleborus fornicatus.
    x Shot-hole borer [India]

Xyleborus morstatti.

Xyleborus perforans.

Xylene.
    sa Xylol.

Xylia dolabriformis.

Xylococcus betulae.

Xylocopa.
    xx Apidae.

Xylocopidae.

Xylol.
    sa Meta-xylol.

Xylol as a fungicide.
    xx Fungicides.

Xylomiges.

Xylophagidae.

Xylophilidae.
    sa Aderidae.
    xx Aderidae.

Xyloporosis of citrus.
    xx Citrus. Diseases.

Xyloryctidae.
    xx Moths.

Xylose.

Xyloterus lineatus.
    xx Ipidae.

Xylotini.
    xx Syrphidae.

Xylotrechus quadripes.
    xx Cerambycidae.

Xyridaceae.
    sa Xyris.
    Abolboda.

Xyridales.   See Farinosae.

Xyris.

Xyris americana.

YMW clubs.
    xx Youth in rural communities.
    Societies.

Yadkin Co., N.C.
  --Soils.
    sa Subdivision North Carolina.
    Yadkin Co. under: Soil-
    surveys.

Yak.
  --Breeding.
    xx Cattle. Breeding.

Yakima Co., Wash.
    xx Washington (State)
  --Agriculture.
    sa Subdivision Washington (State)
    Yakima Co. under: Part-time
    farming.
  --Description and travel.·
  --Soils.
    sa Subdivision Washington. Yakima
    Co. under: Soil-surveys.
  --Water-supply.

Yakima Indian Reservation, Wash.

Yakima irrigation project.

Yakima Valley, Wash.
  --Agriculture.
    sa Yakima Valley, Wash. Domestic
    animals.

Yakima Valley, Wash. (Continued)
--Agriculture.
    sa Subdivision Washington (State)
        Yakima Valley under: Agri-
        cultural laborers.
        Agriculture. Economic as-
        pects.
    xx Washington (State) Agriculture.
--Domestic animals.
    xx Yakima Valley, Wash. Agri-
        culture.
--Industries.
--Pomology.
--Soils.
    xx Soil.

Yakushima Island, Japan.
--Botany.
    xx Japan. Botany.

Yakut (Province)
--Agriculture.
    sa Subdivision Yakut (Province)
        under: Cereals. Siberia.

Yakut Republic.
--Agriculture.
    sa Subdivision Yakut Republic
        under: Agriculture. Economic
        aspects.
        Agricultural laborers.
        Cereals.
        Potatoes.
-- --Congresses.
--Bibliography.
--Botany.
--Cattle.
--Climate.
--Forestry.
--Horse.
--Natural history.
--Research.
--Soils.

Yakutat Bay region, Alaska.
--Geology.
    xx Alaska. Geology.

Yale University.
--Forest School.
-- --Biography.
--School of Forestry.
    sa Keene Forest, N.H.

Yalta. See Ialta.

Yam bean. See Pachyrrhizus.

Yama-mai.
    x Oak silkworm.
    Antheraea yama-mai.

Yamagata-ken, Japan.
--Agriculture.
-- --Periodicals.
--Botany.
--Geology.
--Maps.
--Statistics.

Yamaguchi-ken, Japan.
--Fisheries.
--Forestry.

Yaman. See Yemen.

Yamanashi.
    xx Japan. Agricultural experiment
        stations.

Yamato River.

Yambean. See Pachyrrhizus.

Yamhill Co., Or.
--Agriculture.
    sa Subdivision Oregon. Yamhill
        Co. under: Agricultural
        policies and programs.
--Forestry.
    sa Subdivision Oregon. Yamhill
        Co. under: Forest surveys.
-- --Statistics.

Yampa River Watershed, Colo.

Yams.
    sa Cookery (Yams)
    x Kandala.
    x Kiriala.
    xx Food plants.

Yancey Co., N.C.
--Soils.
    sa Subdivision North Carolina.
        Yancey Co. under:
        Soil-surveys.

Yangtze River and Valley.
--Agriculture.
    sa Subdivision China. Yangtze
        Valley under: Agriculture.
        Economic aspects.
--Botany.
--Description and travel.
--Ornithology.
    xx China. Ornithology.

Yankee Doodle.

Yapygidae. See Iapygidae.

Yaqui Indians.
    xx Indians of Mexico.

Yaqui Valley (Mexico) Experiment Station.

Yaqui Valley, Sonora, Mexico.
--Agriculture.
    sa Subdivision Mexico. Sonora.
        Yaqui Valley under: Agri-
        culture, Cooperative.
        Agriculture. Economic
        aspects.

Yaquina, Or.
--Harbor.

Yaracuy, Venezuela.
--Agriculture.
    sa Subdivision Venezuela. Yaracuy
        under: Irrigation.
--Botany.
--Land.
    sa Subdivision Venezuela. Yaracuy
        under: Land utilization.
--Soils.
    sa Subdivision Venezuela. Yaracuy
        under: Soil-surveys.

Yarkand Mission.

Yarmouth, Great, Eng.
--Description and travel.
--Natural history.

Yarn.
    sa Cotton yarn.
        Rayon yarn.
        Worsted.
--Periodicals.
    xx Wool. Periodicals.

Yarn (Continued)
--Tables, calculations, etc.
    xx Textile industry and fabrics.
        Tables, calculations, etc.
--Testing.

Yarn strength.

Yaroslavl cattle.

Yarovization (Botany)
    x Vernalization.
    xx Seeds. Stimulation.
--Periodicals.
    xx Botany. Periodicals.

Yates Co., N.Y.
--Agriculture.
    xx New York (State) Agriculture.
--Domestic animals.
    sa Yates Co., N.Y. Sheep.
--Sheep.
    xx Yates Co., N.Y. Domestic ani-
        mals.
        New York (State) Sheep.
--Soils.
    sa Subdivision New York (State)
        Yates Co. under: Soil-
        surveys.

Yatren.

Yaupon. See Ilex cassine.

Yautia.
    xx Food plants.

Yavapai Co., Ariz.
--Water-supply.
    sa Subdivision Arizona. Yavapai
        Co. under: Water, Under-
        ground.

Yaws. See Framboesia.

Yazoo Delta, Miss.
    sa Subdivision Mississippi.
        Yazoo Delta under:
        Drainage.
--Agriculture.
    sa Subdivision Yazoo Delta, Miss.
        under: Mechanized farming.
        Farm produce. Cost of pro-
        duction.

Yazoo Delta, Miss. (Continued)
--Agriculture.
  sa Subdivision Mississippi.
    Yazoo Delta under: Agri-
     culture. Economic
     aspects.
    Agricultural policies and
     programs.
  xx Mississippi. Agriculture.
--Economic conditions.
--Forestry.
  xx Mississippi. Forestry.
--Industries and resources.
  sa Subdivision Industries and
    resources under: Yazoo
    Delta, Miss.
--Land.
  sa Subdivision Mississippi.
    Yazoo Delta under: Land
     utilization.
--Soils.
  xx Mississippi. Soils.

Yazoo River.
  sa Subdivision Yazoo River under:
    Flood control.
  xx Mississippi.

Year-books.
  sa Subdivision Year-books under:
    League of Nations.
    Commerce.
    Woman//
--Bibliography.

Yeast.
  sa Beer.
    Fermentation.
    Saccharomyces.
    Zygosaccharomyces.
    Cookery (Brewer's yeast)
    Food yeast.
    Brewers' yeast.
    Vitamins in yeast.
    Wood sugar yeast.
    Cookery (Yeast)
--Bibliography.
--Classification.
--Effect of heat. See Heat. Effect on
 yeast.
--Effect on digestion. See Digestion.
 Effect of yeast.
--Genetics.
  xx Plant genetics.
--Nutritive value. See Yeast as food.

Yeast (Continued)
--Periodicals.
--Research.
--Statistics.
  xx Food. Statistics.

Yeast as feeding stuff.
  sa Brewers' yeast as feeding
    stuff.
    Subdivision Effect of yeast
     under: Digestion.

Yeast as food.
  sa Brewers' yeast as food.
    Food yeast.
  x Yeast. Nutritive value.
  xx Nutrition.

Yeast cultures.
--Catalogs and collections.

Yeast extracts.
  sa Marmite.

Yeast therapy.
  sa Antigourmine.
    La zyma.

Yellow.
  xx Color.

Yellow-bear caterpillar. See Diacrisia
 virginica.

Yellow berry in wheat.
  xx Wheat. Diseases.

Yellow birch.
--Testing.
  xx Wood. Testing.

Yellow birch (Wood)

Yellow cedar. See Chamaecyparis
 nootkatensis.

Yellow chapote. See Sargentia greggi.

Yellow clover aphis. See Callipterus
 trifolii.

Yellow cupricide. See Cupricide.

Yellow currant fly. See Epochra
 canadensis.

Yellow dock. See Rumex crispus.

Yellow-dwarf of potato.
    xx Potatoes. Diseases.

Yellow fat of minks.
    x Nonsuppurative panniculitis of
      minks.
    xx Minks. Diseases.

Yellow fever.
--Bibliography.
--History.
--Periodicals.
--Prevention.
--Societies.

Yellow-fever mosquito. See Aedes aegypti.

Yellow Franconian cattle.
    x Maintaler cattle.
    Frank breed of cattle.

Yellow-headed spruce sawfly. See
  Pikonema alaskensis.

Yellow lupine. See Lupinus luteus.

Yellow mealworm. See Tenebrio molitor.

Yellow Medicine Co., Minn.
    xx Minnesota.

Yellow mottle decline of coconuts. See
  Kadang-kadang.

Yellow-necked apple-tree worm. See
  Datana ministra.

Yellow-necked flea beetle. See Disonycha
  mellicollis.

Yellow oak. See Quercus muhlenbergii.

Yellow pine.
    sa Pinus schinata.
       Pinus palustris.
       Pinus taeda.
       Pinus ponderosa.
--Diseases.

Yellow pine flax. See Linum neomexicanum.

Yellow poplar. See Liriodendron tulipifera.

Yellow River and Valley.
--Botany.

Yellow scale. See Aonidiella citrinus.

Yellow Springs, Ohio.
--Industries.

Yellow stripe disease. See Mosaic
  disease of sugar-cane.

Yellows.
    xx Virus diseases of sugar-
      beets.

Yellowstone Co., Mont.
    sa Subdivision Montana. Yellow-
      stone Co. under: County
      surveys.
    xx Montana.

Yellowstone National Park.
--Botany.
    sa Subdivision Yellowstone
      National Park under:
      Trees.
      Shrubs.
--Forestry.
    sa Subdivision Yellowstone
      National Park under:
      Trees.
--Maps.
--Paleobotany.
--Roads.
--Zoology.

Yellowstone Park irrigation project.

Yellowstone River.

Yellowstone Valley.
--Agriculture.
--Geology.
--Paleobotany.
--Soils.

Yellowtail Dam, Mont.

Yemen.
    x Yaman.
--Botany.
--Description and travel.
    xx Arabia. Description and
      travel.
--History.

Yemen (Continued)
--Natural history.
    xx Arabia. Natural history.

Yerba camagüeyana. See Andropogon
  pertusus.

Yerba loca.

Yerba maté. See Maté.

Yerli cotton. See Gossypium herbaceum.

Yermak (Ship)

Yew.
    sa Taxaceae.
    xx Taxus baccata.

Yezo, Japan.
--Botany.
    sa Subdivision Japan. Yezo under:
      Botany, Economic.

Yiddish language.
    sa Hebrew language.

Yield tables. See Volume and yield
  tables.

Yields (in agriculture) See Crop yields.

Ylang-ylang. See Cananga odorata.

Yoghurt. See Yogurt.

Yogurt.
    x Yoghurt.
      Yohourt.
    xx Milk, Fermented.

Yohimbine.
    xx Alkaloids.

Yoho Park, Canada.
--Botany.

Yohourt. See Yogurt.

Yokohama.
--Agriculture.
-- --Periodicals.
--Commerce.
-- --Statistics.
--Soils.

Yolo Co., Calif.
--Agriculture.
-- --Statistics.
--Soils.

Yonne. See France. Département de
  l'Yonne.

York, Eng.
--Milk supply.
    xx England. Milk supply.
--Poor.
    xx Gt. Brit. Poor.
--Social conditions.
    xx England. Social conditions.

York, Pa.
--Economic conditions.
    sa Subdivision Pennsylvania.
      York under: Geography,
      Economic.

York Co., Me.
--Soils.
    sa Subdivision Maine. York Co.
      under: Soil-surveys.

York Co., Neb.
--Soils.
    sa Subdivision Nebraska. York
      Co. under: Soil-surveys.

York Co., Pa.
--Antiquities.

York Co., S.C.
--Agriculture.
-- --Statistics.

Yorkshire, Eng.
    sa Hooton Pagnell, Eng.
--Agriculture.
    sa Subdivision Gt. Brit.
      Yorkshire under: Agri-
      culture. Economic
      aspects.
    xx England. Agriculture.
· --History.
    sa Subdivision Agriculture.
      History under: East
      Riding, Yorkshire,
      Eng.
      Hooton Pagnell, Eng.
--Apiculture.

Yorkshire, Eng. (Continued)
--Botany.
    sa Subdivision England. Yorkshire
      under: Fungi.
      Algae.
--Entomology.
    sa Subdivision England. Yorkshire
      under: Coleoptera.
      Lepidoptera.
--Geography.
    sa Subdivision Yorkshire, Eng.
      under: Geography, Economic.
    xx Gt. Brit. Geography.
--History.
--Industries and resources.
--Land.
    sa Subdivision England. Yorkshire
      under: Land. Classification.
--Natural history.
--Ornithology.
--Paleobotany.
--Zoology.

Yorkshire swine. See Small Yorkshire
swine; Middle Yorkshire swine; Large
Yorkshire swine.

Yorktown Battle Ground Park.

Yoruba language.

Yosemite National Park.
--Bibliography.
--Forestry.
--Maps.

Yosemite Valley.
--Description and travel.
--Zoology.

Yoshii River.

Yoshino, Japan.
--Forestry.

Yoshino River.

Youghiogheny River.
    sa Subdivision Youghiogheny
      River under: Flood control.

Young farmers' clubs.
    xx Youth in rural communities.
    Societies.
    Agricultural clubs.

Young farmers' clubs (Continued)
--Year-books.

Youngberries.
    xx Berries.

Youngia.
    sa Crepis.
    xx Crepis.

Youngstown, Ohio.
--Economic conditions.
--Industries.
--Parks.

Youth.   (DIRECT)
    sa Youth in rural communities.
    Youth movement.
    Boys.
    Girls.

Youth, Communist.
    x Komsomol.
--Bibliography.

Youth.
--Education.
    xx Education.
--Employment.
--Nutrition.

Youth in rural communities.
    x Farm youth.
    xx Boys.
    Girls.
    Youth.
    Social surveys.
--Periodicals.
--Societies.
    sa 4-H clubs.
    Young farmers' clubs.
    YMW clubs.

Youth movement.
--Periodicals.
--Societies.
-- --Directories.

Yponomeuta.

Yponomeuta malinellus.
--Parasites.

Yponomeuta padellus.

Yponomeutidae.
    sa Trichostibas.

Ypsolophus ligulellus.   See Dichomeris
    ligulella.

Ypthima.

Ystad, Sweden.
  --Botany.

Ytterbium.

Yuba Co., Calif.
    sa Subdivision Yuba Co., Calif.
        under: Planning, County.
    xx California.
  --History.
  --Land.
    sa Subdivision California. Yuba
        Co. under: Land utilization.
    xx California. Land.
  --Population.

Yuba River, Calif.

Yucatan.
  --Agriculture.
    sa Subdivision Mexico. Yucatan
        under: Agriculture. Eco-
          nomic aspects.
        Maize.
        Grasses.
        Forage plants.
  --Apiculture.
  --Botany.
    sa Subdivision Yucatan under:
        Ethnobotany.
        Botany, Medical.
    Subdivision Mexico. Yucatan
        under: Honey-bearing plants.
  --Cattle.
  --Civilization.
    xx Mexico. Civilization.
  --Description and travel.
  --Economic conditions.
    xx Mexico. Economic conditions.
  -- --Periodicals.
  --Ichthyology.
    xx Yucatan. Zoology.
        Central America. Ichthyology.

Yucatan (Continued)
  --Ornithology.
    sa Subdivision Ornithology under:
        Cozumel Island.
  --Social conditions.
  --Social life and customs.
    xx Mexico. Social life and
        customs.
  --Soils.
  --Water-supply.
  --Zoology.
    sa Subdivision Yucatan under:
        Mammalia.
    Yucatan. Ichthyology.

Yucca.
    x Izote.
      Isote.
      Ixote.
  --Fertilization.
  --Statistics.

Yucca angustifolia.

Yucca moth.

Yucceae.

Yugoslav literature.
  --Bibliography.

Yugoslavia.
    sa Bosnia and Herzegovina.
      Carniola.
      Croatia//
  --Agriculture.
    sa Subdivision Yugoslavia under:
        Agriculture. Economic
          aspects.
        Agriculture, Cooperative.
        Tobacco.
        Agricultural policies and
          programs.
        Land utilization.
        Forage plants.
        Farm management.
        Agricultural credit.
        Colonization, Agricultural.
        Cropping systems.
  -- --Bibliography.
  -- --Education.
  -- --Periodicals.
  -- --Statistics.

Yugoslavia (Continued)
--Apiculture.
    sa Subdivision Apiculture under:
        Banat.
-- --Periodicals.
--Bibliography.
--Botany.
    sa Subdivision Yugoslavia under:
        Algae.
        Weeds.
        Botany, Medical.
        Trees.
        Subdivision Botany under:
        Velebit Mountains.
--Cattle.
--Census.
--Climate.
--Commerce.
-- --Periodicals.
-- --Statistics.
-- --Commercial policy.
    xx Europe. Commercial policy.
--Dairying.
--Description and travel.
-- --Guide-books.
--Domestic animals.
-- --Statistics.
    xx Domestic animals. Statistics.
--Economic conditions.
    xx Economic conditions.
-- --Periodicals.
--Economic policy.
    xx Europe. Economic policy.
--Education.
--Entomology.
    sa Subdivision Yugoslavia under:
        Entomology, Economic.
-- --Societies.
--Foreign relations.
-- --U.S.
--Forestry.
    sa Subdivision Yugoslavia under:
        Afforestation and reforest-
         ation.
        Forest industries.
        Wood-using industries.
        Forest management.
        Trees.
        Forest policy.
    xx Europe. Forestry.
-- --Bibliography.
-- --Periodicals.
 - --Research.
-- --Statistics.
--Geographic names.

Yugoslavia (Continued)
--Geology.
--Horse.
--Industries.
--Land.
    sa Subdivision Yugoslavia under:
        Land reform.
    xx Europe. Land.
--Learned institutions and societies.
--Maps.
--Natural history.
-- --Periodicals.
--Politics and government.
--Pomology.
    sa Subdivision Yugoslavia under:
        Apple.
--Population.
--Research.
--Sericulture.
--Sheep.
--Social conditions.
--Soils.
    sa Subdivision Soils under:
        Drin region.
        Sava region.
        Morava region.
        Subdivision Yugoslavia under:
        Soil erosion. Prevention
         and control.
-- --Bibliography.
--Statistics.
--Statistics, Vital.
--Swine.
--Tariff.
--Transportation.
    xx Europe. Transportation.
--Viticulture.
--Water-supply.
--Zoology.
    sa Subdivision Yugoslavia under:
        Game.

Yugoslavian abbreviations. See
    Abbreviations, Croatian; Abbrevia-
    tions, Servian.

Yugoslavian literature.
--Bibliography.
-- --Periodicals.

Yugoslavian newspapers.
--Bibliography.

Yugoslavian periodicals.
    xx Periodicals.
--Bibliography.
--Indexes.

Yu-ju oil.   See Camphor oil.

Yukon.
--Bibliography.
--Botany.
--Description and travel.
    sa Subdivision Yukon under:
        Hunting.
--Entomology.
    sa Subdivision Yukon under:
        Diptera.
--Explorations.
--Forestry.
    sa Subdivision Yukon under:
        Lumber trade.
--Geology.
--Industries and resources.
--Zoology.
    sa Subdivision Yukon under: Game.

Yukon gold fields.
--Maps.

Yukon River.
--Description and travel.

Yukon-Tanana region, Alaska.
--Geology.
    xx Alaska. Geology.

Yukon Territory.   See Yukon.

Yukon Valley.
--Agriculture.
    xx Alaska. Agriculture.
--Botany.
    sa Subdivision Yukon Valley under:
        Fungi.
--Zoology.

Yuma, Ariz.
--Irrigation.
    xx Arizona. Irrigation.

Yuma Co., Ariz.
--Agriculture.
    sa Subdivision Arizona. Yuma Co.
        under: Agricultural surveys.
--Geology.

Yuma Co., Ariz. (Continued)
--Water-supply.
    sa Subdivision Arizona. Yuma Co.
        under: Water, Underground.

Yuma Co., Colo.
    xx Colorado.
--Land.
    sa Subdivision Colorado. Yuma
        Co. under: Land utiliza-
        tion.

Yuma Field Station, Bard, Calif.
    x U.S. Yuma Field Station,
        Bard, Calif.
    Bard, Calif. Yuma Field
        Station.
    xx Yuma irrigation project.

Yuma irrigation project.
    sa Yuma Field Station, Bard,
        Calif.

Yuma Valley, Calif.
--Agriculture.

Yuman Indians.
    sa Mohave Indians.
    xx Indians, North American.
        Indians of the Southwestern
        States.
--Agriculture.

Yungas, Bolivia.
--Pomology.
    xx Bolivia. Pomology.

Yungting River, China.

Yunnan (Province) China.
--Agriculture.
    sa Subdivision China. Yunnan
        (Province) under: Agri-
        culture. Economic
        aspects.
--Botany.
    sa Subdivision China. Yunnan
        (Province) under: Fungi.
--Description and travel.
--Land.
    sa Subdivision Yunnan (Province)
        China under: Land tenure.
--Ornithology.
--Social conditions.
--Zoology.

Yurok Redwood Experimental Forest, Calif.

Z-78. See Dithane Z-78.

Zabrotes.
    xx Bruchidae.

Zabrotes subfasciatus.

Zabrus gibbus.
    xx Carabidae.

Zabrus tenebrioides.

Zacate gordura. See Molasses grass.

Zacatecas, Mexico (State)
--Agriculture.
    sa Subdivision Mexico. Zacatecas
        (State) under: Colonization,
        Agricultural.
        Agriculture. Economic
        aspects.
--Paleontology.

Zacaton.

Zaculeu, Guatemala.
    xx Guatemala. Antiquities.

Zaglossus.
    x Acanthaceae.

Zaisansk, Siberia.
--Soils.

Zakynthos. See Zante (Province)

Zambesi River, Africa.

Zambesi River region.
--Botany.
    xx Africa. Botany.

Zambesia.
    xx Africa, Central.
--Cattle.
    xx Mozambique. Cattle.
--Description and travel.

Zamia.

Zamia muricata.

Zamora, Spain (Province)
--Domestic animals.

Zanesville, Ohio.
    sa Subdivision Zanesville, Ohio
        under: Cost and standard
        of living.
    xx Ohio.
--Statistics.
    xx Ohio. Statistics.

Zannichellia.
    xx Aquatic plants.

Zante (Province) Greece.
--Agriculture.
--Description and travel.
--Maps.
    xx Greece. Maps.

Zante currant. See Grape, Zante.

Zanzibar.
--Agriculture.
    sa Subdivision Zanzibar under:
        Agricultural policies and
        programs.
        Agriculture. Economic
        aspects.
    xx Africa. Agriculture.
--Botany.
    xx Africa. Botany.
--Census.
--Commerce.
    sa Subdivision Zanzibar under:
        Produce trade.
    xx Africa, East. Commerce.
-- --Statistics.
--Economic conditions.
--Economic policy.
--Entomology.
--Industries and resources.
--Land.
--Politics and government.
--Surveys.
--Zoology.
    sa Subdivision Zanzibar under:
        Myriapoda.

Zapotec Indians.
    xx Indians of Mexico.

Zapotec language.
    xx Indians of Mexico. Languages.

Zaporozh'e.
--Agriculture.

Zapodidae.
 sa Zapus.

Zapotec Indians.
--Religion and mythology.

Zapotec language.
--Etymology.

Zapupe.
 xx Agave.

Zapus.

Zaragoza. See Saragossa.

Zarhachis flagellator.

Zarhipis riversi.

Zarhynchus wagleri.

Zaria Province, Nigeria.
--Land.
 xx Nigeria. Land.

Zavala Co., Tex.
--Soils.
 sa Subdivision Texas. Zavala Co.
  under: Soil-surveys.
--Water-supply.
 sa Subdivision Texas. Zavala Co.
  under: Water, Underground.

Zavety Il'icha Collective Farm.
 xx Collective farms.

Zavety Lenina Collective Farm.
 xx Collective farms.

Zavolz'e. See Volga region.

Zea mays.
 sa Maize.

Zea ramosa.

Zea rostrata. See Pop corn.

Zea tunicata.

Zealand, Denmark.
--Agriculture.
--Botany.
 sa Subdivision Zealand under:
  Weeds.
--Domestic animals.
--Natural history.
--Roads.
 xx Denmark. Roads.
--Water-supply.
 sa Subdivision Denmark. Zealand
  under: Water, Underground.

Zealand, Netherlands.
--Agriculture.
-- --History.
 xx Netherlands. Agriculture.
  History.
--Botany.
--Dairying.
 sa Subdivision Zealand, Nether-
  lands under: Dairy in-
  dustry and trade.

Zealand belgian draft horse.

Zebra.

Zebra-wood. See Diospyros kurzii.

Zebus. See Brahman cattle.

Zeeland. See Zealand.

Zeeman effect. See Magneto-optics.

Zein.
 xx Maize products.

Zelia vertebrata.

Zelleria haimbachi.
 x Pine needle-sheath miner.

Zelotypia.

Zeolites.

Zeotokol. See Dolerite meal.

Zephronia.

Zeravshan region.
--Agriculture.
     sa Subdivision Zeravshan region
          under: Agriculture. Eco-
          nomic aspects.
          Mechanized farming.
-- --Statistics.
--Botany.
--Statistics.

Zerbst, Ger.
--Cattle.

Zero milestone.

Zetorchestidae.

Zeuglodon.

Zeugophora abnormis.

Zeugophora scutellaris.

Zeuzera aesculi.

Zeuzera pyrina.

Zewaphosphat.

Zexmenia.

Zeyen, Netherlands.
--Agriculture.

Zhashkov District.
--Domestic animals.

Zhdanov Collective Farm.
     xx Collective farms.

Zicrona coerulea.

Ziebach Co., S.D.
     sa Subdivision South Dakota.
          Ziebach Co. under: County
          surveys.
     xx South Dakota.

Zigadenus.   See Zygadenus.

Zinc.
     sa Soil. Effects of zinc fumes.
--Bibliography.

Zinc, Chloride of.
     x Chloride of zinc.
          Chromated zinc chloride.

Zinc.
--Effect on plants.
     sa Subdivision Effect on tobacco
          under: Zinc.
     x Plants, Effect of zinc on.
--Effect on tobacco.
     xx Zinc. Effect on plants.
--Physiological effect.

Zinc arsenite.

Zinc fumes.
     sa Soil. Effect of zinc fumes.

Zinc in plants.

Zinc organometallic compounds.

Zinc oxide.

Zinc oxide as a fungicide.
     xx Fungicides.

Zinc oxide as a soil disinfectant.
     xx Soil sterilization.

Zinc perhydrol.

Zinc poisoning.

Zinc salts.
--Effect on plants.

Zinc sulphate.
     xx Herbicides.
--Effect on plants.

Zinc sulphide.
     xx Sulphides.

Zincum peroxygenatum.

Zingiberaceae.
     sa Turmeric.

Zinnias.
     xx Floriculture.

Zinsen.   See Inchon.

Zion National Monument, Utah.　See Zion
　　National Park, Utah.

Zion National Park, Utah.
　--Natural history.
　　　xx U.S. Natural history.

Zionism.
　　　xx Jews in Palestine.
　　　　　Jewish question.
　--Bibliography.

Zirconium.

Zizania aquatica.　See Indian rice.

Zizia arenicola.

Zizyphus joazeiro.
　　　x Juazeiro.

Zizyphus jujuba.
　　　x Chinese date.
　　　　Chinese jujube.
　　　　Tsao.
　--Mineral elements.
　　　xx Plants. Mineral elements.

Zodiacal light.

Zodion.

Zollingeria.
　　　sa Rhynchospermum.

Zomba, Africa.
　--Botanic Station.
　--Botanical garden.

Zoning.　See Cities and towns. Planning.
　　Zone system; Planning, County. Zone
　　system; Roads. Planning. Zone system.

Zoning, Rural.　See Planning, County.
　　Zone system.

Zonitidae.

Zonitoides arboreus.

Zonocerus elegans.
　　　x Elegant grasshopper.

Zoobotryon verticillatum.
　　　xx Polyzoa.

Zoocecidia.　See Galls.

Zoogeography.　See Zoology. Geography.

Zoological collection.　See Zoological
　　specimens. Collection and preserva-
　　tion.

Zoological gardens.
　　　sa Washington, D.C. National
　　　　　Zoological Park.
　　　　　Berlin. Zoologischer garten.
　　　　　London. Zoological gardens//
　--Directories.
　--History.

Zoological illustrations.　See Zoology.
　　Pictorial works.

Zoological museums.
　　　sa Zoology. Catalogs and collec-
　　　　　tions.
　　　x Zoology. Museums.

Zoological specimens.
　--Collection and preservation.
　　　sa Subdivision Collecting under:
　　　　　Entomology.
　　　　　Ornithology.
　　　　　Subdivision Collection and
　　　　　preservation under:
　　　　　Mammalia.
　　　　　Anatomical specimens.
　　　　　Pathological specimens.
　　　　　Insects.
　　　　　Taxidermy.
　　　　　Zoology. Catalogs and
　　　　　collections.
　　　xx Collectors and collecting.
　　　　　Specimens. Preservation.

Zoological taxonomy.　See Zoology.
　　Classification.

Zoologists.
　　　sa Entomologists.
　　　　　Naturalists.
　　　x Zoology. Biography.
　--Bio-bibliography.
　--Correspondence, reminiscences, etc.

Zoology.
   sa Natural history.
      Mammalia.
      Taxidermy.
      Game.
      Physical geography.
      Science.
      Animal products.
      Animal painting and illustra-
        tion.
      Zoology, Economic.
      Animal psychology.
      Zoological gardens.
      Zoology. Laboratories.
      Animals of prey.
      Zoonomy.
      Invertebrates.
      Desert fauna.
      Chordata.
      Anatomy, Comparative.
      Physiology, Comparative.
      Poisonous animals.
      Sand fauna.
      Animal babies.
      Evolution.
      Ethnozoology.
      Animals, Legends and stories of.
      Subdivision Zoology under:
        Arctic regions.
        South America.
        Brazil//
        Forestry.
        Moors and heaths.
        Springs.
        Meadows.
        Soil.
   x Fauna.
 --Addresses, essays, lectures.

Zoology, Agricultural.   See Farm pests;
   Zoology, Economic.

Zoology.
 --Bibliography.
      sa Subdivision Zoology. Bibliog-
        raphy under: Austria.
        Canada.
        Denmark//
        Zoology, Medical. Bibliography.

Zoology (Continued)
 --Bibliography.
 -- --Periodicals.
 --Biography. See Zoologists.
 --Catalogs and collections.
      sa Subdivision Catalogs and
        collections under:
        Mammalia.
        Entomology.
        Subdivision Collection and
        preservation under:
        Zoological specimens.

Zoology, Classical.

Zoology.
 --Classification.
      sa Entomology, Systematic.
      Genus.
      Type species.
      Subdivision Classification
        under: Ornithology.
        Mammalia.
   x Zoology. Taxonomy.
      Zoology, Systematic.
      Zoological taxonomy.
 -- --Periodicals.
 --Collecting. See Zoological speci-
    mens. Collection and preserva-
    tion.
 --Congresses.
 --Dictionaries.
 --Directories.
 --Ecology.
      sa Life zones.
      Acclimatization.
      Phenology.
      Subdivision Ecology under:
        Entomology.
        Fresh-water fauna.
        Marine fauna.
        Plankton.
        Parasites.
        Mammalia.
        Ornithology.
        Arthropoda.
   x Animal ecology.
      Ecology of animals.
 -- --Periodicals.

Zoology, Economic.
    Here are entered general and com-
    prehensive works on animals
    injurious and beneficial to man
    in agriculture, the industrial
    arts, etc., and works on the
    extermination of wild animals,
    venomous snakes, etc. Works
    entirely on animals injurious
    in agriculture are entered
    under the subject Farm pests.
    sa Domestic animals.
        Entomology, Economic.
        Farm pests.
        Fur-bearing animals.
        Pests.
        Household pests.
        Ornithology, Economic.
        Poisoning of animals.
        Animals of prey.
        Birds of prey.
        Biological control of pests.
    x Zoology, Agricultural.
        Animals, Injurious and benefi-
            cial.
        Pest control.
--Bibliography.
--History.
--Periodicals.
--Research.

Zoology.
--Geography.
    sa Subdivision Geography under:
        Entomology.
        Ornithology.
-- --Periodicals.
--Geology.
    sa Zoology. Ecology.
--History.
    sa Subdivision History under:
        Protozoa.
        Embryology.
--Juvenile literature.
    sa Subdivision Juvenile literature
        under: Mammalia.
--Laboratories.
--Laboratory manuals.

Zoology, Marine.   See Marine fauna.

Zoology, Medical.
    sa Parasites.
        Animals as carriers of con-
            tagion.
        Materia medica, Animal.
--Bibliography.
--Periodicals.

Zoology.
--Morphology.   See Morphology (Animals);
    Entomology. Morphology; Anatomy,
    Comparative.
--Museums.   See Zoological museums.
--Nomenclators.
    Here are entered indexes of
    scientific names. For dis-
    cussions of the principles
    involved in the application
    of zoological names see
    Zoology. Nomenclature.
    sa Zoology. Nomenclature.
        Animal names.
    xx Nomenclators.
--Nomenclature.
    Here are entered works on the
    principles involved in the
    application of zoological
    names. For indexes of
    scientific names see Zoology.
    Nomenclators.
    sa Parasites. Nomenclature.
        Animal names.
        Zoology. Nomenclators.
    xx Nomenclature.
--Outlines, syllabi, etc.
--Periodicals.
    sa Subdivision Periodicals under:
        Natural history.
        Mammalia.
        Zoology. Ecology.
        Zoology. Geography.
        Zoology, Economic.
        Hybridization.
        Morphology (Animals)
        Animals, Treatment of.
-- --Bibliography.
 . --Indexes.

Zoology (Continued)
--Pictorial works.
      sa Subdivision Pictorial works
          under: Entomology.
          Domestic animals.
          Game.
          Ichthyology.
          Entomology, Economic.
    x Zoological illustrations.
--Research.
      sa Subdivision Zoology. Research
          under geographic names,
          e.g., U.S.S.R. Zoology.
          Research.
-- --Periodicals.
--Societies.
      sa Subdivision Societies under:
          Bison.
--Study and teaching.

Zoology, Systematic. See Zoology.
  Classification.

Zoology.
--Taxonomy. See Zoology. Classifica-
  tion.
--Text-books.
--Variation.
      sa Evolution.
      xx Variation (Biology)

Zoology as an occupation.
      xx Occupations.

Zoonomy.

Zoönosis.
      sa Diseases. Transmission from
          animal to man.
--Congresses.

Zoophytes.

Zootechny. See Domestic animals. Breeding.

Zootermopsis.

Zootermopsis angusticollis.

Zootomy. See Anatomy, Comparative.

Zophium.

Zophodia convolutella.
      xx Gooseberries. Pests.

Zor Hills, Arabia.
--Botany.

Zostera.
      xx Aquatic plants.

Zostera marina.

Zostera oceanica. See Posidonia
  caulini.

Zosteropidae.
      xx Ornithology.

Zoysia.
      x Meyer zoysia.
      xx Grasses.

Zoysia matrella. See Manila grass.

Zug (Canton)
--Agriculture.
-- --History.

Zugersee. See Lake of Zug.

Zuider Zee. See Zuyder Zee.

Zulia, Venezuela.
--Agriculture.
-- --Statistics.
--Cattle.
--Soils.

Zululand.
--Botany.
      sa Subdivision Zululand under:
          Shrubs.
          Trees.
--Entomology.
--Forestry.

Zulus.
      xx Bantus.
--Medicine.

Zuni Plateau, N.M.
--Agriculture.
    sa Subdivision New Mexico. Zuni
        Plateau under: Agriculture.
        Economic aspects.
        Farm management surveys.
    xx New Mexico. Agriculture.

Zürich.
--Agriculture.
--Botanic gardens.

Zurich (Canton)
--Agriculture.
    sa Subdivision Zurich (Canton)
        under: Agriculture. Eco-
        nomic aspects. Switzer-
        land.
--Dairying.
--Entomology.
    sa Subdivision Switzerland.
        Zürich (Canton) under:
        Coleoptera.
--Forestry.

Zürich, Lake of.

Zuyder Zee.
    x Zuider Zee.
--Botany.
--Soils.
    xx Netherlands. Soils.
--Zoology.

Zwartbont Fries-Holland cattle.   See
    Dutch-Friesian cattle.

Zygadenus.
    x Zigadenus.

Zygaenidae.
    sa Procris.
        Heterusia.
        Brachartona catoxantha.
        Hamps.
        Levuana.
        Therisimina.

Zygaenidae (Continued)
--Parasites.

Zygnemaceae.

Zygobothria nidicola.
    xx Tachinidae.

Zygocotyle lunata.

Zygocystis cometa.

Zygonyx.

Zygophyllaceae.
    sa Larrea.

Zygopides.
    x Zygopini.

Zygopini.   See Zygopides.

Zygoptera.
    sa Rhinocypha.

Zygosaccharomyces pini.
    xx Saccharomycetaceae.
        Yeast.

Zygosoma globosum.

Zygospores.

Zygothrica.

Zymase.

Zymology.   See Fermentation.